Frommer's

California
day BY day

1st Edition

by Mark Hiss & Garth Mueller

WILEY

John Wiley and Sons, Inc.

> The Venice Skatepark is just one
of many hotspots for grabbing air
and perfecting one's street moves
in Southern California.

Contents

PAGE 140

PAGE 173

PAGE 235

PAGE 302

PAGE 334

PAGE 369

PUBLISHED BY
Wiley Publishing, Inc.
111 River St., Hoboken, NJ 07030-5774

ISBN 978-0-470-57115-6; ISBN 978-1-118-02340-2 (EBK);
ISBN 978-1-118-02341-9 (EBK) ; ISBN 978-1-118-02342-6 (EBK)

Frommer's®

Editorial by Frommer's

EDITOR
Naomi P. Kraus

PHOTO EDITOR
Cherie Cincilla

CARTOGRAPHER
Andrew Dolan

CAPTIONS
Harriot Manley

COVER PHOTO EDITOR
Richard Fox

COVER DESIGN
Paul Dinovo

Produced by Sideshow Media

PUBLISHER
Dan Tucker

MANAGING EDITOR
Megan McFarland

PROJECT EDITOR
Abigail Wilentz

PHOTO EDITOR
John Martin

PHOTO RESEARCHER
Jennifer Senator

DESIGN
Kevin Smith, And Smith LLC

SPOTLIGHT FEATURE DESIGN
Em Dash Design LLC

For information on our other products and services or to obtain technical support,
please contact our Customer Care Department within the U.S. at 800/762-2974,
outside the U.S. at 317/572-3993 or fax 317/572-4002.

Wiley also publishes its books in a variety of electronic formats. Some content that
appears in print may not be available in electronic formats.

MANUFACTURED IN CHINA

5   4   3   2   1

How to Use This Guide

The Day by Day guides present a series of itineraries that take you from place to place. The itineraries are organized by time (The Best of Los Angeles in 1 Day), by region (The Northern Coast), by town (Ojai), and by special interest (Monterey & Big Sur for Culture Lovers). You can follow these itineraries to the letter, or customize your own based on the information we provide. Within the tours, we suggest cafes, bars, or restaurants where you can take a break. Each of these stops is marked with a coffee-cup icon ☕. In each chapter, we provide detailed hotel and restaurant reviews so you can select the places that are right for you.

The hotels, restaurants, and attractions listed in this guide have been ranked for quality, value, service, amenities, and special features using a **star-rating system.** Hotels, restaurants, attractions, shopping, and nightlife are rated on a scale of zero stars (recommended) to three stars (exceptional). In addition to the star-rating system, we also use a kids icon **kids** to point out the best bets for families.

The following **abbreviations** are used for credit cards:

AE American Express	**MC** MasterCard
DC Diners Club	**V** Visa
DISC Discover	

A Note on Prices

Frommer's lists exact prices in local currency. Currency conversions fluctuate, so before departing consult a currency exchange website such as **www.oanda.com/currency/converter** to check up-to-the-minute conversion rates.

How to Contact Us

In researching this book, we discovered many wonderful places—hotels, restaurants, shops, and more. We're sure you'll find others. Please tell us about them, so we can share the information with your fellow travelers in upcoming editions. If you were disappointed with a recommendation, we'd love to know that, too. Please email us at frommersfeedback@wiley.com or write to:

Frommer's California Day by Day, 1st Edition
Wiley Publishing, Inc.
111 River Street
Hoboken, NJ 07030-5774

Travel Resources at Frommers.com

Frommer's travel resources don't end with this guide. **Frommers.com** has travel information on more than 4,000 destinations. We update features regularly, giving you access to the most current trip-planning information and the best airfare, lodging, and car-rental bargains. You can also listen to podcasts, connect with other Frommers.com members through our active reader forums, share your travel photos, read blogs from guidebook editors and fellow travelers, and much more.

An Additional Note

Please be advised that travel information is subject to change at any time—and this is especially true of prices. We suggest that you write or call ahead for confirmation when making your travel plans. The authors, editors, and publisher cannot be held responsible for the experiences of readers while traveling. Your safety is important to us, so we encourage you to stay alert and be aware of your surroundings.

About the Authors

Mark Hiss has been traversing California's byways since he was 10 years old, when his traveling salesman father took him along on sales calls to such exotic locales as Hanford and Bakersfield. A third-generation Angeleno, Mark resided for many years in San Diego where he was founding editor of both the visitor guide *Where San Diego* and *Performances*—the playbill magazine for the city's leading performing arts groups. He is also author of *Frommer's San Diego* and *Frommer's San Diego Day by Day*, and is a contributor to *Frommer's California*. In a previous life he was a publicist who worked for several of San Diego's leading theater companies. Accomplishing a Golden State hat trick, he currently resides in San Francisco.

Garth Mueller is a writer who lives in Los Angeles. He was born in California's Central Valley in Modesto, and among his earliest memories are camping trips to nearby Yosemite National Park. Garth's crackerjack road crew and research staff, aka his loving family, includes his wife Barb and their young sons Miles and Benjamin. He is the author of *Frommer's Los Angeles Day by Day*.

Acknowledgments

Mark: Thanks to Stacey and Naomi for their patience. And thanks for the road trips, dad.

Garth: Special thanks to my editor, the gracious Naomi Kraus, for the opportunity to rediscover my home state, and for continually steering me in the right direction.

About the Photographers

Award-winning photographer **Brian Baer** has been a photographer for newspapers and photo services including UPI, the *St. Petersburg Times* (FL), and the *Sacramento Bee* for more than 25 years. Based in California, Baer currently runs a successful freelance business as well as working as a photographer with the State of California, Department of Parks and Recreation, covering all of its 278 state parks.

Ken Cedeno is a Washington, D.C. photojournalist who has covered politics and breaking news in Congress and the White House for over 20 years. His clients include major wire services such as the Associated Press, Agence France-Presse, Reuters, UPI, and Bloomberg, as well as news outlets like the *New York Times, London Sunday Times, Time, Newsweek,* and other publications worldwide. He has traveled to many countries on assignment, including Costa Rica, Cuba, Croatia, Iceland, Italy, Spain, and Turkey.

Photographer **Sean DuFrene** is currently working on an art project documenting his father's quirky daily routine in a series titled *Jack*. Check it out at www.seandufrene.com.

Born and raised in California, **Christopher Kern** is a commercial advertising and editorial photographer specializing in fashion and portraiture. On the road, his camera in hand, Kern found this to be an ideal project, a chance to explore the familiar and unfamiliar alike.

Based in Southern California, award-winning freelance photojournalist **Eric Parsons** (www.ericparsonsphoto.com) regularly shoots for the *Los Angeles Times* and the Associated Press, as well as a variety of corporate clients. Having worked at six different newspapers across the country, Eric's eye-catching photos have been published in virtually every major newspaper in the U.S. including the *New York Times, Washington Post,* and *U.S.A. Today.* Eric's work is divided evenly between editorial photography and documentary wedding photography.

Los Angeles-based photographer **Ian White** has shot more than 60 national magazine covers and been published in over 30 countries. White's client list includes such nationally recognized names in the media as *Wired, People, Newsweek,* ESPN, Bravo, Nickelodeon, and Comedy Central.

1

The Best of California

Our Favorite Moments

> *PREVIOUS PAGE A Monterey cypress claims a rocky perch along the scenic 17-Mile Drive. THIS PAGE Moonrise over Yosemite Valley, carved by glaciers 2 to 3 million years ago.*

Go to Prison on Alcatraz Island. At this infamous, long-abandoned maximum-security penitentiary, listen to the excellent self-guided audio tour while peeking in the tiny, bleak cells that held some of the most hardened criminals of the day. Getting creeped out is part of the fun. See p. 58, ❶.

Crossing the Golden Gate Bridge. Get the blood flowing with a windy walk or bike ride across one of California's greatest landmarks. You'll be surrounded by magnificent views—the lush Marin Headlands to the north, eerie Alcatraz Island to the east, and the San Francisco cityscape to the south. See p. 62, ❷.

Dinner at Chez Panisse. Established in 1971, Alice Waters' restaurant is considered the birthplace of California Cuisine, which emphasizes fresh, local, seasonal, and organic ingredients—a popular enough notion nowadays, but revolutionary decades ago. The single, five-course, prix fixe menu changes daily and continues to dazzle diners. See p. 104.

Whale-Watching from Point Reyes Lighthouse. In the late winter and spring, California gray whales undergo one the longest migrations of any mammal, over 10,000 miles, from Alaska to Baja California and back. The lighthouse atop the headlands of Point Reyes National Seashore is the best place to see the 50-foot-long creatures surfacing and spouting while they pass along the California coastline. See p. 217, ❸.

Meeting the Monoliths of Yosemite National Park. Even if you've pored over all of Ansel Adams' famous photographs of the park, you still won't be prepared for the grandeur of the park's mighty granite monoliths—El Capitan and Half Dome—that soar 3,000 and 4,800 feet above the valley floor. See p. 276.

Walking through the Ghost Town of Bodie State Historic Park. Like so many mining towns across the state about a century ago, Bodie went belly-up when its resource—in this case, gold—ran dry. Today it's a genuine Wild West ghost town, and a National Historic Landmark to boot, with 150 abandoned buildings kept in a state of "arrested decay." Peek inside the weather-beaten structures and you can see dusty shelves still stocked with goods. See p. 268, ⑫ .

Watching the Sea Otters at the Monterey Bay Aquarium. At this world-class aquarium with 35,000 plants and animals and over 600 different species, it's hard to pick a favorite among the marvels—the mysterious giant octopus, the twig-like sea horses, the poor hammerhead shark that looks like a punch line, the diaphanous jellyfish, the demanding penguins. The rascally sea otters always draw crowds with their playful antics. See p. 316, ② .

Pay Your Respects at the Mission San Carlos Borroméo de Carmelo. The second of 21 Spanish missions in California served as headquarters for the entire chain and is the final resting place of its founder Father Junipero Serra. If you only have the chance to see one mission, make it this beauty, a National Historic Landmark. See p. 342, ① .

Drive Highway 1 in Big Sur. This National Scenic Byway, the 72-mile stretch from San Simeon to Carmel, is perhaps the best way to explore the breathtaking Big Sur coastline, preferably in a convertible with the top down. Take your time, and take advantage of the many scenic vistas along the way. *Photo tip*: For the best photo of the highway's iconic Bixby Bridge, pull off just north of the bridge onto Old Coast Road and follow it inland until you get the perfect panorama. See p. 313, ⑤ .

Catch a Show at the Hollywood Bowl. The most magical musical venue in the entire state, the Bowl has got it all: a rich history dating back to the 1920s, a lovely setting in a lush canyon, and a diverse schedule of great music—the L.A. Philharmonic led by the passionate Gustavo Dudamel, jazz concerts curated by Herbie Hancock, and such touring acts as Paul McCartney and Radiohead. See p. 412, ⑩ .

Meeting Mickey at Disneyland. Few things are more Californian—or more American— than Walt Disney's original park, which opened in 1955 with the quaint notion that families should have fun together. Sure, it gets crowded, and maybe it costs more than you'd like, but when you see a child's face light up during a ride or while meeting his or her favorite character, it just may feel like the Happiest Place on Earth. See p. 506.

Lounging Poolside in Palm Springs. The desert is hot. The pool is cool. Sinatra croons in the background. Palm trees sway in the breeze. Dilemma: take a nap now, or order another cocktail? See p. 554.

Spending the Day at Balboa Park. The biggest urban cultural park in America, Balboa contains beautiful gardens and Spanish architecture, the famous San Diego Zoo, the Old Globe Theatre, and 15 of the city's best museums. See p. 582.

> *The 1-million-gallon Outer Bay exhibit at the Monterey Bay Aquarium, where hammerhead sharks circle just inches away from visitors.*

Our Favorite Small Towns

> *Savor to-die-for apple pie in Julian, a favorite escape in Southern California during October's harvest.*

Mendocino. This lumber community turned artists colony sits atop foggy headlands along an isolated stretch of Northern Californian coast. Listed on the National Register of Historic Places, the idyllic coastal village features Cape Cod-style architecture, art galleries, and organic restaurants, and is surrounded by state parks with redwood forests and the relatively undiscovered Alexander Valley wine region. On summer weekends, Bay Area residents rush up here to slow down. See p. 244.

Pacific Grove. Living in the shadow of high-profile neighbors Monterey, Pebble Beach, and Carmel is just fine with this quiet seaside town, which likes to call itself America's Last Hometown. Situated on the tip of the Monterey Peninsula, it boasts a picturesque coastline with a historic lighthouse, a sanctuary for migrating monarch butterflies and several hundred century-old Victorian homes, many of which have been turned into charming B&B's. See p. 340.

Ojai. Frank Capra chose this verdant valley tucked between Santa Barbara and Ventura to stand in for the utopian village of Shangri-La in the 1936 movie *Lost Horizon*, but it's the air of tranquillity that settles over the town like the "Pink Moment," the locals' term for the way the sun warms the face of the surrounding Topa Topa mountains at the end of each day. No wonder the setting is so popular with artists, New Age spiritualists, and burnt-out Angelenos seeking peace and quiet and a spa treatment. See p. 398.

Julian. If apple pie is an enduring symbol of America, then this historic gold-mining town in the Cuyamaca Mountains outside San Diego may be the most patriotic town in the country. From October, harvesting season, through Thanksgiving and the holidays, tourists, especially Southern Californians, tumble in by the bushels to stock up on apple pie and cider made from the fruit of the local orchards, which thrive in the cold mountain air. Mosey up the quaint, cinnamon-scented Main Street, which has several to-die-for pie shops—including Julian Pie Company and Mom's Pie House—within walking distance of one another. See p. 632.

The Best Food & Wine Experiences

Ferry Building Marketplace, San Francisco. A paradise for foodies, the Ferry Building Marketplace houses the city's best fish and meat mongers, chocolatiers, coffee roasters, tea shop, cheese shop, bakery, and specialty items like olive oil, mushrooms, and herbs. Year-round on Tuesdays and Saturdays, a farmers market fills outdoor stalls with the fresh, organic bounty of Northern California's small farms and draws thousands of appreciative locals. See p. 59, ❷.

Oxbow Public Market, Napa Valley. Before a long day of tastings at Napa Valley's many wineries, stock up on supplies at this foodie destination, which has been called a more intimate version of Ferry Building Marketplace. You can enjoy a sit-down meal—gourmet burgers at Gott's Roadside, or innovative tacos like spiced lamb and mint and goat cheese from C Casa—or pick up picnic fixings from one of the many artisanal vendors such as the Fatted Calf Charcuterie or Anette's Chocolate Factory. See p. 134, ❷.

Point Reyes Oysters. Drakes Bay Oyster Farm cultivates some of the world's best oysters in the pristine waters of Drake's Estero, a nutrient-rich saltwater lagoon in the heart of Point Reyes National Seashore. Oysters are harvested daily and can be purchased whole, shucked, or on the half-shell, so pack a cooler and picnic down the beach. See p. 217, ❸.

Paso Robles Wine Festival. Napa Valley doesn't have a monopoly on outstanding wine in California. Every year on a long weekend in late May, Paso Robles revels in its status as the fastest-growing wine country in the state with wine-tasting events that take place under the large oak trees of the old-fashioned town square. A $55 ticket buys you entry to the Grand Tasting, which features 90 wineries pouring hundreds of different wines, and Artisan Alley, a buffet of tasty treats from restaurants that emphasize locally grown, sustainably farmed food. See p. 390, ❶.

> Al fresco in Frisco—in-the-know foodies graze at Ferry Building Marketplace, overflowing with artisan foods.

Coachella Valley's Dates. Dates, considered the world's oldest cultivated fruit, thrive in the blistering hot Coachella Valley, which produces 95% of the nation's date supply. The National Date Festival takes place in February, but year-round you can sample a variety of dates—from the popular Deglet Noor to the "King of Dates," the Medjool—from the local date farms. A cold date crystal shake from **Shields Date Garden** is the perfect way to beat the desert heat. See p. 556.

The Best Architectural Landmarks

> *For the best photos of the "Painted Ladies," come in late afternoon when they're lit by a warm sunset glow.*

Golden Gate Bridge. The iconic bridge is a masterly and audacious feat of engineering. At the time of its completion in 1937, the suspension bridge was the longest (4,200 ft. between the towers, and 8,981 ft. in total) and tallest (746 ft.) of its kind in the world, and required steel cables with the tensile strength of 200 million pounds. A husband-and-wife team, Irving and Gertrude Morrow, gave the bridge its Art Deco look, lighting, and color (called International Orange). See p. 62, ❷.

"Painted Ladies," San Francisco. These colorful Victorian homes in San Francisco were built towards the end of the 19th century. "Postcard Row" refers to the city's most famous, certainly the most photographed, examples—six ornate, pastel-painted Queen Anne beauties near Alamo Square. See p. 65, ❽.

California State Capitol, Sacramento. Evoking the image of its national counterpart in Washington D.C., this gleaming white, Neo-classical-style building (completed in 1874) has porticos with Corinthian columns and decorative pediments, and a majestic rotunda crowned with a gold ball (a nod to the state's Gold Rush days). See p. 172, ❷.

Hearst Castle, San Simeon. Newspaper baron William Randolph Hearst and architect Julia Morgan labored nearly three decades to create this 165-room estate stuffed with Renaissance oil paintings, Flemish tapestries, Spanish carved-wood ceilings, Italian choir stalls, Egyptian sarcophagi, and whatever else Hearst could gobble up at New York's finest auction houses. The hilltop complex includes terraced gardens, three lavishly furnished guesthouses, a movie theater, and two swimming pools, one ringed by a Roman marble colonnade, and the other shimmering in glass and gold leaf tiles. See p. 354, ❶.

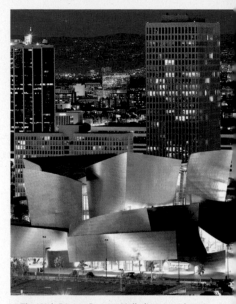

Gamble House, Pasadena. If you love American Arts and Crafts architecture, then this 1908 masterpiece of the style is a must see. Charles and Henry Greene's design fuses a traditional Japanese sense of proportion with an inviting California aesthetic. The interiors are a rich display of meticulously handcrafted woodwork—staircases, cabinetry, structural beams, and furniture. Informative tours are run by the University of Southern California School of Architecture. See p. 436, ❶.

Walt Disney Concert Hall, Los Angeles. Since its debut in 2003, Frank Gehry's audacious architectural masterpiece has quickly become the shining beacon of downtown Los Angeles. Sculpted and shaped with curvilinear panels of stainless steel, the building has been compared to billowing ship sails or blooming petals of a flower. It's a structure that reveals itself through repeated viewings, from different angles, at different distances, at different times of day. See p. 438, ❹.

> The Walt Disney Concert Hall glistens with stainless steel wings; inside, it's clad in Douglas fir.

The Hollyhock House, Los Angeles. For his first building in Los Angeles, Frank Lloyd Wright took advantage of the hilltop location and mild climate to blend indoor and outdoor (private and public) space with a central courtyard, split levels, terraced rooftops, and colonnaded walkways. A geometric abstraction of a hollyhock flower is a recurring motif that decorates the roofline, columns, and interior walls. See p. 438, ❼.

Mission San Luis Rey de Francia, Oceanside. The "King of the Missions" was the 18th of the 21 Spanish missions in California and one of the largest and most prosperous. The mission complex includes a church with a rare cruciform layout, a large quadrangle, arched corridors, sunken gardens, and an open-air laundry area fed by an irrigation system through open-mouthed stone gargoyles. The mission's architecture is considered significant for its graceful combination of Spanish, Moorish, and Mexican elements. See p. 580.

Building a Mystery

California's weirdest architectural marvel is likely **Winchester Mystery House**, 525 S. Winchester Blvd., San Jose (☎ 408/247-2101; www.winchestermysteryhouse.com), a monument to one woman's paranoia. After the death of her husband, rifle magnate William Winchester, Sara Winchester (1839–1922) was convinced by a seer that she was cursed by the spirits of those who'd died by a Winchester rifle and that said spirits could only be appeased by perpetual construction on her home. The widow used much of her $20-million inheritance to finance the construction on this National Historic Landmark, which started in 1884 and went on 24 hours a day, 7 days a week, 365 days a year, for 38 years. With 160 rooms, the Victorian home sprawls across a half-dozen acres and is full of disturbing features: a staircase leading nowhere, a Tiffany window with a spiderweb design, and doors that open onto blank walls. You can visit the home on one of several guided tours ($25–$33 adults; $22–$30 kids 5–12; check website for current hours); it's about an hour's drive from San Francisco.

The Best Drives

> Feel Lilliputian while driving between trunks of century-old giants at Sequoia National Park.

Avenue of the Giants. The altar of the church of California's coast redwoods, this 31-mile-long two-laner runs roughly parallel to U.S. 101 and follows the Eel River through the Humboldt Redwoods State Park, with 53,000 acres of ancient redwood forest, including some trees more than 2,000 years old. Their immensity will humble you and completely skew your sense of scale. Plan on taking time to explore kitschy roadside attractions like the Shrine Drive-Thru Tree, or to wander short trails on foot. See p. 221, **6**.

17-Mile Drive. This private toll road between Pebble Beach and Pacific Grove is a famously scenic drive along a stunning coastline marked by crashing waves and windswept cypress trees rising from rocky perches. You'll also see pockets of white-sand beaches, birds and seals, and some of the state's swankiest real estate, complete with immaculate golf courses and gated mansions. See p. 312, **3**.

Highway 1, Big Sur. Without a doubt, this 72-mile stretch of road is California's most iconic drive. If you've ever seen a slick commercial featuring a sports car expertly navigating a windy road high above some waves crashing against a rocky shore, chances are good that you've seen Highway 1. Finally completed in 1937 after an arduous 18-year effort (which took New Deal dollars and prison labor), the two-lane highway is the only way to traverse the spectacular Big Sur coastline. See p. 416, **4**.

Sunset Boulevard, Los Angeles. It's not always scenic and you can count on thick, stop-and-go traffic, but fabled Sunset Boulevard, more than any other road in Los Angeles, links so much of the city's history and its diverse communities—the good, the bad, the ugly. It begins near the city's first settlement, El Pueblo de los Angeles, and winds west 25 miles to the Pacific Ocean. See p. 411, **7**.

Mojave Road. The other drives listed here are about the sights you see from the road, but this route is noteworthy for what you don't see much of—signs of civilization. The 138-mile trail was originally blazed by Indians walking from waterhole to waterhole, and later brought American pioneers in covered wagons. Today the road remains unpaved, and is dangerous in parts, requiring four-wheel drive, determination, and a few days to complete. But a quick couple-mile side trip can take you back to a vision of California centuries ago. See p. 537, **8**.

The Best Beaches

> *The stunning beaches of La Jolla work just as well for a romantic stroll as they do for sunning and swimming.*

Natural Bridges State Beach, Santa Cruz. The best beach in a great beach town, Santa Cruz's Natural Bridges State Beach is defined by its striking natural bridge rock formation that stands amidst the crashing blue waves and white sea foam. Tide pools north of the bridge host star fish, crabs, and sea anemones, while the coastal scrub meadows overlooking the beach brighten with yellow wildflowers in the spring and orange monarch butterflies from October to February. See p. 333, **6**.

Pismo Beach. Pismo Beach offers 23 miles of sandy shoreline and a wide array of beach activities, especially surfing. Once known for its bountiful clam hunting, Pismo is the only place on the California coast with land set aside (1,500 acres) for dune buggies and all-terrain vehicles to bound wildly among the sand dunes. The rest of the majestic coastal dune complex that runs south from Pismo is protected and wonderful to explore on foot. See p. 364, **7**.

Zuma Beach, Malibu. Malibu's biggest beach draws monster crowds with its wide swath of golden sand, clean water, good surfing, and a

long list of amenities—huge parking lot (for a fee), showers, children's playground, volleyball courts, lifeguards, and snack bars. If there's too much action for you, drift south towards quieter Westwards Beach near Point Dume. See p. 417, **7**.

Crystal Cove State Park, Newport Beach. Tucked into the rugged coastal bluffs between Laguna Beach and Newport Beach is this jewel of a state park with sandy coves and rocky tide pools. Part of its rustic charm is the presence of the historic beach cottages from the 1930s that are available for rent (and insanely popular, so book way ahead). See p. 512.

La Jolla Beaches, San Diego. Just north of San Diego, La Jolla offers a series of gorgeous beaches that have something for everyone: surfers ride the waves at Windansea; harbor seals lounge at the Children's Pool; family-friendly La Jolla Shores is best for swimming and sunbathing; La Jolla Cove has clear waters perfect for snorkeling among the bright orange Garibaldi fish; while kayakers love to explore the caves in the sandstone cliffs between La Jolla Shores and La Jolla Cove. See p. 594.

The Best Outdoor Adventures

> *Traditional champagne toasts await balloon passengers once they touch down in Napa Valley.*

Hot-Air Balloon Ride over Napa Valley. Of all the ways to travel through California's famous wine region, a hot-air balloon is undoubtedly the most glorious. Popular too—Napa Valley is one of the world's busiest "flight corridors" for hot-air balloons. At an altitude of 3,500 feet, drift peacefully over lush valleys and fertile rolling hills lined with rows of grapevines. See p. 151.

Hiking the Lost Coast Trail. Experience a sense of isolation on this rugged, 35-mile-long trek through some of the most remote and pristine coastline in the United States. It's a true test of your hiking (and survival) skills—you'll need to avoid black bears, cross creeks, scale small boulders, and time the tides to pass along black-sand beaches. See p. 231, ❽.

Scaling Mount Shasta. Mighty Mount Shasta, a 14,162-foot-high dormant volcano with 17-mile-diameter base, stands solo, unconnected to any mountain range, and dominates the surrounding landscape. Poet Joaquin Miller referred to the striking image of Shasta as "lone as God, and white as the winter moon." Topping the snowcapped summit of this beast is no easy feat, requiring the uses of crampons and ice axes, and only one out of three who attempts it actually succeeds. See p. 234, ❹.

Snow Skiing, Lake Tahoe. The sparkling blue waters of Lake Tahoe, the largest alpine lake on the continent, are surrounded by beautiful mountains and some of the best ski resorts in the country, including Squaw Valley, the site of the 1960 Olympic Winter Games. See p. 292.

Kayaking the Channel Islands. Like the Chumash tribe in their sewn-plank canoes centuries earlier, navigate the wild, clear waters surrounding the string of virtually untouched islands 20 or so miles off the mainland. Paddle through the striking Arch Rock on Anacapa Island, find hidden coves brimming with resting seals and sea lions, or explore the largest known sea cave in the world—Santa Cruz Island's Painted Cave, whose walls are coated with colorful lichen and algae. See p. 378, ❾.

Rock Climbing, Joshua Tree National Park. The park, especially Hidden Valley, offers hundreds of formations and thousands of routes, making it a major destination for rock climbers of all skill levels. Sheer faces of rock challenge seasoned pros, while novice climbers can improve their skills with lessons. Most visitors prefer the simplicity of "bouldering"—scrambling on, over, and around the piles of rounded boulders. See p. 548.

Our Favorite Scenic Wonders

> *Riotous wildflower displays like these magenta monkey flowers paint Anza-Borrego Desert State Park with color.*

Giant Trees of Redwood National and State Parks. Awesome, in the truest sense of the word. Found only in northwestern California and the southwestern corner of Oregon, coastal redwoods are the tallest species of trees on Earth, with some specimens reaching a height of 370 feet. A walk through a misty redwoods grove with the trees soaring above you—even the ferns are 10 feet tall—will make all your worries seem a little less mighty. See p. 231, **9**.

Tufa Towers of Mono Lake. Weird, knobby spires rise—some up to 30 feet high—from the mirrored surface of the lake's silvery waters. Originally formed by underwater chemical reactions, these calcium-carbonate deposits were exposed when the lake level fell, revealing surreal-looking formations more fitting to a sci-fi film than the popular perception of California geography. See p. 269, **13**.

McWay Falls of Big Sur. If you had a single snapshot to capture the dramatic beauty of Big Sur's 90 miles of rugged coastline, this is it. From a steep, tree-lined granite cliff of the Santa Lucia mountains, an 80-foot waterfall rains down onto a sandy beach cove, or when it's high tide, directly into the aquamarine waters of the Pacific Ocean. Soak it up—this is one of the few "tidefalls" in the world. See p. 348, **8**.

The Racetrack at Death Valley National Park. These mysterious moving rocks on a dry lakebed in Death Valley are a scenic marvel that will truly make you wonder. A small boulder sits alone on a vast desert landscape, with a long trail in the dirt tracing a path across the parched ground—but how did it move? Some scientists speculate that a combination of wind and rain is the answer, yet no one has ever witnessed the rocks in motion. See p. 545, **10**.

Wildflowers of Anza-Borrego Desert State Park. For a few weeks every spring, California's largest, and often overlooked, state park comes alive as colorful blankets of wildflowers drape the normally barren desert landscape. Experienced wildflower spotters will find dune evening primrose, sand verbena, phacelia, chicory, monkey flowers, and brittlebrush, while the rest of us simply see beautiful waves of yellows, golds, whites, pinks, and purples. See p. 552.

AUTO OBSESSION

California's long love affair with the car

BY LINDA BARTH

BEACHES, MOUNTAINS, MOVIE STARS. Visitors to California are treated to a wide range of fabulous sights, but two of the most memorable may come as a surprise: miles of asphalt and millions of automobiles. There is no arguing with the fact that Californians are in love with their cars. Car culture is featured in California-based movies from *Rebel Without a Cause* to *Grease* to *The Fast and the Furious*. California musicians have scored big with songs about cars (the Beach Boys "Little Deuce Coup," War's "Low Rider," and Janis Joplin's "Mercedes Benz" to name a few). And because the state is home to more cars—and more car buyers—than any other, Californians essentially drive the American car market. California has had a huge impact on auto manufacturing, particularly when it comes to design.

Crosstown Traffic

In California, the car is king—and traffic is constant. Cities boomed fast in the state, and they grew out, not up, and that suburban sprawl means all kinds of highway headaches. To put things in some perspective, consider that 6 of the 18 most traffic congested communities in the U.S. are in California. A 2-mile section of Highway 5 in San Diego is the world's widest roadway, coming in at a whopping 22 lanes. There are 32 million registered cars in the state—roughly equal to the number in Great Britain—and nearly 24 million licensed drivers. It's little wonder that Californians are so crazy about their cars—L.A. residents, for example, average 4 full days of any given year sitting in one.

Hot Rods & Lowriders

When you spend a lot of time stuck in a car, you want to look good. Southern California is the birthplace of custom car culture, and of its various offshoots. Harley Earl (1893–1969), the General Motors design genius responsible for the Corvette, tailfins, and wraparound windshields, got his start customizing cars in L.A. Before heading off to Detroit in the 1930s, Earl spent his youth building cars to race on the then relatively quiet streets of Southern California. In the 1920s, the burgeoning movie business brought big money—and big egos—to the city. Cars were status symbols, and Earl Automotive Works churned out eye-catching rides for Hollywood's top stars. Inspired, a generation of young Californians began tinkering with cars, often beat-up older models, and by the 1930s, they were meeting at dry lake beds northeast of L.A. to race the so-called "hot rods" they'd souped up themselves. After World War II, GIs returning to California and craving an adrenaline rush used the skills they'd learned in the army to create ever more outlandish (and fast) hot rods. But hot rodders weren't the only ones customizing cars. An influx of Mexican workers in the 1930s infused California's car culture with a new style: low-riders. These cars, adapted so that the front, rear, or both ends ride just above the ground, became a symbol of Mexican-American pride, and they still are. Today, lowriders are often elaborate creations, fat-wheeled, colorful, and equipped with hydraulic systems that allow the cars to raise high above their wheels before dropping down, nearly to the ground.

California Cruising

Crusing, the practice of loading up a car with friends and checking out everyone else's carload of friends, has been a source of American teenage entertainment for generations. Need proof? Watch *American Graffiti*, George Lucas's sweet ode to the 1950s and 1960s cruising culture of his hometown, Modesto. The practice was born—where else?—in Southern California, and some historians link it to *paseo*, the Mexican tradition of allowing young singles to walk around the village square, men in one direction, women in another. In a conservative society, it allowed for a little flirtation. The same can be said for cruising, which was (and is—cruising strips can be found all over the U.S.) often as much about meeting someone cute as about showing off one's ride.

The Best Museums

> *Terraced gardens, stellar architecture, astounding art—hard to believe admission to the Getty Center is free.*

de Young Museum, San Francisco. The city's oldest museum dates back to 1895 and reinvented itself in 2005 with an audacious architectural makeover—the facade sparkles with nearly a million pounds of textured copper, and a 144-foot tower rises above the surrounding gardens of Golden Gate Park and offers a spectacular 360-degree panorama of the entire Bay Area. Oh, and the art: the museum boasts a stunning collection of American paintings (Edward Hopper, Georgia O'Keeffe, Wayne Thiebaud), as well as art from Africa, Oceania, and the Americas. Visiting exhibitions have included Impressionist and Post-Impressionist masterpieces on loan from the Musée d'Orsay. See p. 64, **4**.

California State Railroad Museum, Sacramento. You can't truly understand the history of California and the West without knowing the impact of the railroads. This 225,000-square-foot complex in Old Sacramento may be the largest and most popular railroad museum in America, displaying over 20 immaculately restored locomotives from the 1860s and exhibits of dining, sleeper, and refrigerator cars. During the summer you can hop aboard a steam locomotive for a 40-minute round-trip along the Sacramento River. See p. 173, **4**.

Getty Center, Los Angeles. With its Italian travertine marble blocks gleaming in the California sun, this modern hilltop complex designed by Richard Meier is one of L.A.'s most striking landmarks. The permanent collection includes works by major Impressionists like Monet, Cézanne, Renoir, Manet, and van Gogh (whose *Irises* the museum acquired for $54 million), and photography by Edward Weston, Walker Evans, and Man Ray. After soaking up all the art, take a stroll through the Central Garden, a lush landscape that is ever evolving. See p. 411, **8**.

Petersen Automotive Museum, Los Angeles. Angelenos have an awful habit of defining themselves by the kinds of cars they drive, so it's no wonder that the city pays homage to the art of the automobile at this four-story, 300,000-square-foot museum, which displays more than 150 cars and motorcycles with such rotating exhibits as French Curves, Misfits of Motordom (like the Edsel), La Vida Lowrider, Alternative Power, Muscle Cars, Microcars, Ferraris, and Hot Wheels Hall of Fame, full-scale versions of the classic toys. See p. 426, **7**.

The Best Shopping Experiences

Haight-Ashbury, San Francisco. Ground zero of the hippie culture in the psychedelic '60s, the Haight still kicks a pretty groovy street scene with throngs of fashionistas, punks, street musicians, and tourists trying to make sense of it all—all of which makes shopping along here feel like a spectator sport. Vintage clothing boutiques, head shops, music stores (with plenty of vinyl), and kooky bookstores draw a straight line to the Haight's heyday, but there are also trendy gift shops and high-end fashion boutiques. See p. 65, ⑥.

Telegraph Avenue, Berkeley. The great thing about shopping along these 4 blocks near Cal Berkeley isn't the merchandise or the stores per se, but rather the academic (read: laid back) attitude of the locals. A trip to the bookstore, for example, might take all day. Peruse funky shops with vintage clothing, hats, homeopathic herbs and teas, or get lost in the massive selection at the original Amoeba Music. See p. 127, ⑤.

Rodeo Drive, Beverly Hills. The words Rodeo Drive are synonymous with luxury retail, 3 blocks of chi-chi boutiques with such big names as Armani, Prada, Hermès, Chanel, Tiffany, Harry Winston, etc. Think twice before cracking open your wallet here or you'll have a financial hangover in the morning. Window shopping is perfectly acceptable (as is celebrity gawking). Walk up the pedestrian-only cobblestone street of Via Rodeo, then descend the "Spanish Steps" on Wilshire Boulevard to feel like a star. See p. 417, ⑧.

Abbot Kinney Boulevard, Venice. Forget tired stereotypes about shopping in Los Angeles—it's not just valley girls in malls or society women on Rodeo Drive. Some of the city's best shopping is on pedestrian-friendly stretches like Abbot Kinney, which offers an eclectic and unpredictable mix of independent boutiques where you can browse boho-chic home decor, men and women's fashion, supercool bicycles, hard-to-find books, and art. See p. 447, ⑪.

> *Treasure hunting is easy on Palm Canyon Drive in Palm Springs, a mecca for midcentury modernist collectors.*

Palm Canyon Drive, Palm Springs. Palm Springs is known as a mecca of midcentury modernist architecture and design, and Palm Canyon Drive is where all the hip interior decorators go to buy, sell, and trade home furnishings such as Eames lounge chairs, Saarinen tables, and '60s-era ceramic lamps. On Thursday evenings the street closes for the Villagefest street fair, with over 200 vendors peddling antiques, handcrafted trinkets, and fresh produce. See p. 561.

The Best Luxury Hotels

> *The ultimate perch for spotting migrating whales—the infinity pool at Big Sur's Post Ranch Inn.*

The Mandarin Oriental, San Francisco. You can practically tour San Francisco's sights— Golden Gate Bridge, Transamerica Pyramid, Coit Tower, the Bay—without leaving the comfy luxury of your room, which sits on an upper floor of one of city's tallest buildings. In fact, binoculars are provided. Now add warm and elegant Asian decor, an array of high-end amenities, and impeccable service, and you've got yourself a stay to remember. See p. 114.

Calistoga Ranch, Calistoga. Set in a secluded canyon, this upscale Napa Valley property blows away the competition, with individual luxury cabins stocked with every imaginable luxury. Other pluses include a fabulous pool, spa, gym, and guest-only restaurant overlooking a lake. See p. 154.

Post Ranch Inn, Big Sur. Few hotels in the world can compete with the stunning views from this property, perched 1,200 feet over the Pacific Ocean on the dramatic cliffs of the Big Sur coast. Nestled among 100 acres of redwood trees are 40 eco-friendly cottages. Slip into one of two hot-water infinity pools and contemplate the edge of the continent—or the person you're with. See p. 349.

San Ysidro Ranch, Santa Barbara. White country cottages and suites are nestled among terraced lawns, orange trees, lavender shrubs, and trellises of bougainvillea in the sun-drenched Santa Ynez mountains. If you're looking to splurge on one of California's most romantic and luxurious accommodations, book the Kennedy Cottage, where John and Jackie honeymooned in 1953. See p. 386.

Peninsula Beverly Hills, Los Angeles. To the old maxim "location, location, location," let's add "service, service, service." Sophisticated travelers with a taste for European-style luxury come here for around-the-clock pampering, which could include High Tea, a spa treatment, or a complimentary spin in a Rolls Royce Phantom. See p. 486.

Montage Resort & Spa, Laguna Beach. The Orange Coast has no shortage of seriously swanky hotels, but this one takes the cake— lovely Arts and Crafts architecture, lavishly appointed rooms, a mosaic-tiled infinity pool, an oceanfront spa, perhaps the best restaurant in town. All that and you get easy access to secluded, gorgeous cove beaches. See p. 519.

The Best Moderately Priced Hotels & Inns

> Madonna Inn's kitschy themed rooms wrap you in everything from rock walls to fake fairways.

The Hotel Bohème, San Francisco. Located among the sidewalk cafes of Columbus Avenue in bohemian North Beach, this small, Beat-inspired hotel is the perfect place to stay if you're chasing the ghosts of Kerouac and Ginsberg. Rooms are simple (free Wi-Fi, no TV), but exude a romantic, Old World charm. See p. 112.

St. Orres, Gualala. This real eye-catcher on the North Coast has a stunning Russian-style design, complete with two Kremlinesque, onion-domed towers. The cottages offer more privacy than the rooms in the main house, but staying in either is a truly unique experience. See p. 243.

Olallieberry Inn, Cambria. Run by friendly owners and named for a locally grown fruit—a hybrid of a blackberry, raspberry, and dewberry—this charming B&B occupies an 1873 Greek Revival home on the Santa Rosa Creek, and is an easy stroll into the village. If you like the food here, cooking classes ($20 for guests) are offered once a month. See p. 389.

Madonna Inn, San Luis Obispo. Bed down in a bona fide piece of pop culture—Italian novelist Umberto Eco famously likened this to an LSD trip, and even *The Simpsons* parodied the place. This 50-year-old roadside landmark halfway between Los Angeles and San Francisco is famous for its garish assortment of over-the-top, individually decorated rooms, many with rock walls and cascading waterfall showers. See p. 395.

Farmer's Daughter, Los Angeles. This boutique hotel wins you over with its reasonable (for L.A.) rates, bright and kitschy barnyard decor, sunny courtyard with pool, and cozy restaurant. But best of all is its very central location. See p. 484.

Ace Hotel & Swim Club, Palm Springs. A has-been Howard Johnson's motel has morphed into a stylish and happening hipster hangout. The rooms go for a summer camp vibe (think canvas window treatments and tree stump bedside tables), while the dark and cozy Amigo Room serves up fresh cocktails. See p. 559.

Horton Grand, San Diego. You get vintage charm at this winning property—Wyatt Earp called one of its buildings home, and you'll find genteel furnishings and fine fixtures in the rooms. Staying in the suites in the new wing means opting for modern convenience over character...and you might miss out on Roger, the resident ghost. See p. 616.

The Most Memorable Dining Experiences

> What's cookin' at Berkeley's Chez Panisse? Since 1971, some of the best farm-to-table cuisine in the country.

Chez Panisse, Berkeley. Alice Waters is called "the queen of California cuisine," and a meal at the Berkeley restaurant she founded in 1971 should be on every gourmand's must-do list. The Mediterranean-inspired menu changes daily and relies on fresh, local, and sustainably sourced ingredients that reflect the season. If you're not a food connoisseur, don't sweat it—simply surrender to the prix-fixe menu, and prepare to be educated and delighted. See p. 104.

Restaurant Gary Danko, San Francisco. Elegant but unstuffy, intimate yet theatrical—this restaurant has stood among the elite of the ultra-competitive San Francisco dining scene for over a decade with its contemporary French cuisine bolstered by a phenomenal cheese cart (bring on the Brillat-Savarin!) and an endless wine list. Can't score a res? A 10-stool bar is first-come, first-served, and you can order a la carte. See p. 106.

La Super-Rica Taqueria, Santa Barbara. The sight of a long line of tourists spilling out of this tiny Mexican restaurant (shack may be a better word) may scream "tourist trap," but rest assured, it's not. The word has long been out on this legendary joint, but that doesn't make their tacos any less amazing. Try the *adobado* (marinated pork) tacos or the spicy *chilaquiles*, and wash it down with a sweet cold *horchata*. See p. 387.

Lucques, Los Angeles. James Beard Award–winning chef and titan of the Los Angeles culinary scene, Suzanne Goin dazzles with her simple but sophisticated Cal-Med menu in a warm, intimate atmosphere—the small brick building was once the carriage house of silent-comedian Harold Lloyd. Sunday Supper offers a three-course prix-fixe dinner and is a bargain at $45. A mint gimlet from the bar is the perfect way to whet your appetite. See p. 477.

Pizzeria Mozza, Los Angeles. Take Mario Batali's expertise in Italian cooking and toss in La Brea Bakery founder Nancy Silverton's bread skills, and you get one seriously gourmet pizzeria that took Los Angeles by storm when it opened in 2006. The best choice for pizza is the bacon, salami, fennel sausage, *guanciale* (cured pork cheek), and the daily pasta specials such as the *lasagna al forno* never disappoint. Save room for dessert—made-from-scratch gelato or butterscotch pudding with sea salt. See p. 478.

Our Favorite Festivals & Special Events

> *Gorillas, human centipedes, and even serious runners take on the annual Bay to Breakers race.*

Bay to Breakers, San Francisco. This 12K race includes world-class runners, but the true spirit of the race, and the city, is seen in the participants who make the trek from the city's bay side at the Embarcadero to the breakers of Ocean Beach in full costume—*Star Wars* storm troopers, giant M&Ms, Santa Clauses, and a gang of Richard Simmonses. See p. 672.

Monterey Jazz Festival. Since 1958 this beloved festival has presented all varieties of jazz with performers like Billie Holiday, Dizzie Gillespie, Herbie Hancock, and Diane Krall. See p. 673.

Old Spanish Days, Santa Barbara. A cultural tradition dating back 85 years, Santa Barbara proudly celebrates its Spanish heritage each August with several days of parades, arts and crafts displays, authentic eats, Flamenco music, colorful dancing, horse shows, and rodeos. See p. 673.

Tournament of Roses Parade, Pasadena. Before college football's oldest bowl game, the Rose Bowl, is played on the afternoon of New Year's Day, the nationally televised Rose Parade streams down Colorado Boulevard with fabulous floats, beauty queens, energetic marching bands, and orderly equestrian units. See p. 670.

U.S. Open of Surfing, Huntington Beach. Every summer Surf City, U.S.A, otherwise known as Huntington Beach, hosts this week-long surfing competition, which pulls in hundreds of thousands of people for a week-long party on the beach. See p. 673.

Festival of Arts & Pageant of the Masters, Laguna Beach. Founded as an art colony a century ago, Laguna Beach celebrates its rich history with exhibitions, workshops, crafts sales, and best of all, a performance-art event, which recreates famous works of art using people instead of paint. See p. 673.

Coachella Music Festival, Indio. One of the biggest and best musical events in the country, this 3-day festival presents rock, alternative, and hip-hop acts on multiple stages in a desert oasis, the vast green lawn of the Empire Polo Grounds. See p. 671.

Comic-Con, San Diego. Comic books are the main draw at this four-day-long pop-culture juggernaut, but there's also animation, sci-fi film and television, fantasy literature, video games, and licensed toys, in a non-stop blitz of panel discussions, sneak previews, auctions, and autograph sessions. See p. 673.

2
The Best All-California Itineraries

The Best of California in 1 Week

California is simply too vast and too diverse a place to capture all its charms in a week. We'll stick mostly to the coast, with San Francisco and Los Angeles acting as tent poles, tacking on Napa Valley in the north, and San Diego in the south. Connect it all with a dash along the Central Coast, including picture-perfect Carmel, sublime Big Sur, and the mighty Hearst Castle.

> PREVIOUS PAGE *Skiers take flight at Heavenly Resort, the highest ski area (topping off at 10,000 ft.) in the Lake Tahoe basin.* THIS PAGE *Since 1873, San Francisco's cable cars have taken riders for a spin.*

START **Fly into San Francisco International Airport or Oakland International Airport; you won't need a car for the first 2 days of this tour.** TRIP LENGTH **about 670 miles.**

1 San Francisco. Spend 2 full days exploring one of America's most exciting cities. Hop aboard the nation's only moving National Historic Landmark, the San Francisco **cable cars** (p. 55, **2**), and enjoy the views on the way to **Fisherman's Wharf** (p. 56, **4**). Ferry out to the infamous **Alcatraz Island** (p. 58, **1**) and take the fascinating tour. Explore the **North Beach** (p.82) neighborhood, then get lost in the maze of **Chinatown**'s (p. 78) trinket shops and restaurants. For dinner, the **Ferry Building**

Marketplace (p. 59, **2**) is a foodie paradise, where you can sample a wide array of local gourmet foods.

Start Day 2 with an invigorating stroll (pack a camera and a jacket) across the iconic **Golden Gate Bridge** (p. 62, **2**) and back. The city loves its **Golden Gate Park** (p. 72), and you will, too, with highlights like **Stow Lake**, the **Conservatory of Flowers**, and the big and bold **de Young Museum** (p. 64, **4**). At the hippie hotbed of **Haight-Ashbury** (p. 65, **6**), take a stroll through the funky vintage shops and Summer of Love hangers-on. End the day at one of San Francisco's many world-class restaurants, such as **Restaurant Gary Danko** (p. 106). ☺ 2 days.

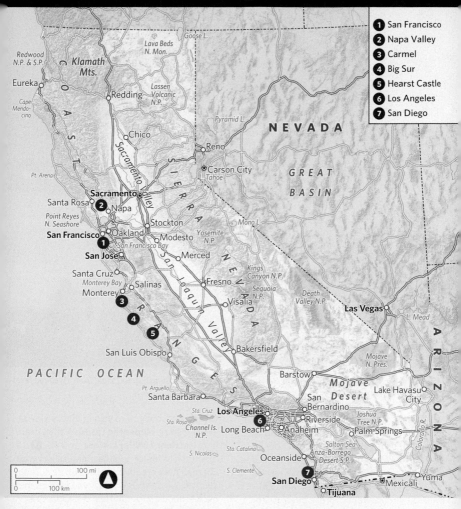

On Day 3, rent a car and head north on U.S. 101 for 22 miles. At Hwy. 37 take a right and go 7 miles. At Hwy. 121 take a left and follow for 18 miles. Continue on Hwy. 29 heading north. Trip time: about 1½ hr.

2 Napa Valley. Day 3 is all about the wine and food of one of the world's most renowned wine regions, Napa Valley. Start by stocking up on supplies—cheese, sandwiches—at the **Oxbow Public Market** (p. 134, **2**), then hit several wineries for tastings. Favorites include **Artesa Vineyards & Winery** (p. 142), **The Hess Collection Winery** (p. 145), **Rubicon Estate** (p. 146), and the old-world-style **Schramsberg** (p.146). Note that some wineries

require advance reservations; for more information on Napa's best wineries, see p. 142. Enjoy a brilliant meal at Thomas Keller's legendary **French Laundry** (p. 162), if you can swing a reservation. ⏱ 1 day.

Start as early as possible on Day 4. Head south on Hwy. 29 to Hwy. 12/Jameson Canyon Rd., take a left, and go 6 miles. Merge briefly with I-80 east, then take I-680 south exit. Head south on I-680 for 70 miles, then take the U.S. 101 exit. Take U.S. 101 south for 49 miles. Merge onto Hwy. 156 west and go 6 miles to Hwy. 1. Continue south on Hwy. 1 for 23 miles. Trip time: about 3 hr.

> *Look for the footprints of Johnny Depp (boots), Marilyn Monroe (pumps), and Donald Duck (webbed feet) in the courtyard at Grauman's Chinese Theatre.*

❸ Carmel. Drive through the cutesy village of tidy English-style cottages, high-end boutiques, and art galleries. Spend an hour at the **Carmel Mission** (p. 342, ❶), the second Spanish mission in California. Take a brief stroll on **Carmel City Beach** (p. 344, ❺) ringed by windswept cypress trees. ⏲ 2 hr.

Head south on Hwy. 1 for 27 miles. Trip time: 45 min.

❹ Big Sur. The Big Sur stretch of **Highway 1**, roughly Carmel to Cambria, contains some of California's most iconic scenery and is a drive that should be savored. Pull off for photos of **Bixby Bridge** (p. 346, ❶) and the **Point Sur Lighthouse** (p. 346, ❷). You won't have too much time, but stop off at idyllic **Pfeiffer Beach** (p. 348, ❺) for an up-close look at the dramatic coastline. Pull off at **Julia Pfeiffer Burns State Park** (p. 348, ❽), and scamper along the short trail to the overlook for **McWay Falls**, an 80-foot waterfall cascading onto the pristine beach below. Stop for a snack

(overpriced, but you're paying for the views) at the historic **Nepenthe** (p. 349), then drop in to the **Henry Miller Library** (p. 348, ❼), a memorial to Miller and the many artists who charged their creativity at Big Sur. Be sure to keep an eye on your watch if you plan on making a scheduled tour at Hearst Castle. ⏲ At least 3 hr.

Head south on Hwy. 1 for 63 miles. Trip time: 1½ hr.

❺ Hearst Castle. Reserve tickets ahead of time for a tour of the jaw-dropping, sprawling hilltop home of William Randolph Hearst. The last guided tours of the day begin around 3:20pm; self-guided tours are available and begin in the late afternoon. As you stroll among the sprawling gardens and 165 rooms dripping with European antiquities, imagine persnickety Mr. Hearst presiding over a glittering party with Hollywood guests like Charlie Chaplin, Cary Grant, and the Marx Brothers. ⏲ 2½ hr. See p. 354, ❶.

Head south on Hwy. 1 to Cambria for the night. On Day 5, head east on the scenic Hwy. 46 to Paso Robles. At U.S. 101, head south. In Oxnard, take exit 62B and follow the signs for Hwy. 1. Continue south on Hwy. 1 for about 20 miles to Malibu. Trip time: 4½ hr.

6 Los Angeles. Bask in the sun at one of several **Malibu Beaches** (p. 417, **7**). Zuma Beach is your best bet for a wide variety of activities; the photogenic pocket beaches of El Matador, La Piedra, and El Pescador are gorgeous, although less user-friendly. Cruise down the **Pacific Coast Highway** (p. 416, **4**) for a classic Los Angeles experience. Visit oceanfront **Getty Villa** (p. 416, **5**) to view the fine collection of Greek, Roman, and Etruscan artifacts. Continue south to Venice and take in the wild parade of people along the **Venice Boardwalk** (p. 445, **5**), which snags my vote for best people-watching on the planet. Take a spin down Beverly Hills' famed **Rodeo Drive** (p. 417, **8**), and across the street, eat at Wolfgang Puck's steakhouse **CUT** (p. 483).

On Day 6, start at the stunning **Getty Center** (p. 411, **8**) with a world-class art collection that includes works by van Gogh and Monet. Drive all the way to Hollywood on **Sunset Boulevard** (p. 411, **7**) and look for the legendary music clubs and sceney hotels along the **Sunset Strip** (p. 406, **7**). Park at **Hollywood & Highland** complex (p. 409, **2**), and walk the Walk of Fame in front of **Grauman's Chinese Theatre** (p. 409, **4**). Take Hollywood's best movie tour at **Warner Brothers** (p. 408, **1**) around the corner in Burbank. In the evening catch a show at the landmark **Hollywood Bowl** (p. 412, **10**) and enjoy music beneath the stars. Grab a nightcap at **Musso & Frank's** or the **Formosa Cafe**, two historic Hollywood watering holes (pp. 412 and 432). ☉ 2 days.

Get on the road early on Day 7 if you want to avoid rush hour. Head south on I-5 for about 116 miles. Trip time: 2½ hr.

7 San Diego. Spend Day 7 enjoying what may be California's most family-friendly city. With kids in tow, you have to go to the celebrated **San Diego Zoo** (p. 578, **1**) located in Balboa Park. Even if you skip the zoo, spend a couple hours at **Balboa Park** (p. 582), a huge cultural playground with a terrific selection of museums. Venture out to **Cabrillo National**

> *Balboa Park's Botanical Building, in San Diego, is one of the world's largest lath buildings.*

Monument (p. 574, **1**) at Point Loma where Juan Rodriquez Cabrillo first arrived in 1542. Zip across the **San Diego-Coronado Bay Bridge** and enjoy a walk along **Coronado Beach** (p. 617) near the historic **Hotel del Coronado** (p. 617). Enjoy a lively last night in the **Gaslamp Quarter**. (p. 590). ☉ 1 day.

Fly home from San Diego International Airport.

Highlights of California in 2 Weeks

Consider this 2-week itinerary a California sampler
platter that aims to give you a little bit of everything—from the wine country to the gold country, from *Baywatch* beaches to snowcapped peaks, from the happy-go-lucky chaos of Disneyland to the stark silence of Joshua Tree...and as much as we can pack in between.

> *The striking profile of Half Dome hints at Yosemite's glacial past.*

START Fly into San Francisco International Airport or Oakland International Aiport; you won't need a car for the first 2 days of this tour. TRIP LENGTH about 1,385 miles.

1 San Francisco. ⊕ 2 days. See p. 22, **1**.

2 Napa Valley. ⊕ 1 day. See p. 23, **2**.

Stay the night in Napa. Get on the road early on Day 4. Head east on I-80 for 42 miles. Continue east on U.S. 50 for 103 miles. Trip time: about 3½ hr.

3 Lake Tahoe. Mark Twain called Lake Tahoe, with its clear blue waters and ring of pine-covered mountains, the "fairest picture the whole earth affords." You just might agree, especially if you're taking the cable car up the freshly powdered slopes at **Squaw Valley USA** (p. 304). In summer, there's boating and sailing tours, mountain biking, or you can simply circle the lake and enjoy the views. ⊕ 1 day.

Stay the night. On Day 5, head west on U.S. 50 for 57 miles to Placerville. Trip time: about 1½ hr.

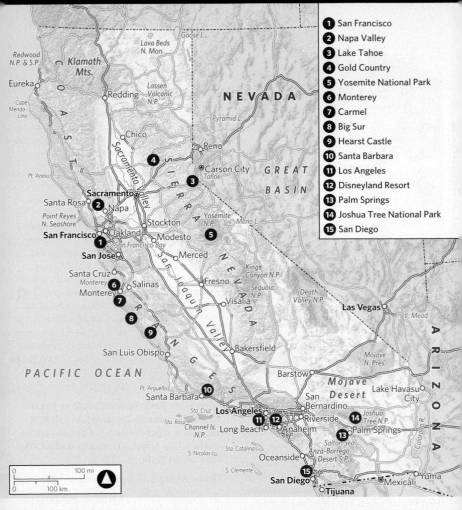

1. San Francisco
2. Napa Valley
3. Lake Tahoe
4. Gold Country
5. Yosemite National Park
6. Monterey
7. Carmel
8. Big Sur
9. Hearst Castle
10. Santa Barbara
11. Los Angeles
12. Disneyland Resort
13. Palm Springs
14. Joshua Tree National Park
15. San Diego

④ Gold Country. Highway 49 is a fascinating stretch that connects a slew of old Gold Rush towns like Sutter Creek and Jackson. Head north to Grass Valley to see the **Empire Mine State Historic Park** (p. 184, ❸), the site of California's biggest mine. In Coloma the **Marshall Gold Discovery State Historic Park** (p. 188, ❶) marks the discovery of gold in America and includes a Gold Discovery Museum and a replica of Sutter's Mill. Further south is the **Columbia State Historic Park** (p. 181, ⑳), maybe a bit hokey and over-the-top, but a hoot for kids interested in panning for gold. ⏱ half-day.

From Columbia, head south on Hwy. 49. Veer left onto Hwy. 120 and go east for 45 miles. Trip time: 2 hr.

❺ Yosemite National Park. This park is an onslaught of granite cliffs and cascading waterfalls. Gaze upon **El Capitan** (p. 280, ⑫), the world's largest granite monolith. Stand in the mist at the foot of **Bridalveil Fall** (p. 266, ❹) and **Lower Yosemite Falls**. Have your camera ready for **Tunnel View** (p. 266, ❸), which frames Yosemite Valley, El Capitan, and Half Dome. Drive up to **Glacier Point** (p. 272, ❹) to end the day with the best viewpoint in the park—Yosemite Valley, Half Dome, and three waterfalls.

> *A temple to William Randolph Hearst's passion for opulence, the Neptune Pool makes a splash at Hearst Castle.*

Start Day 6 with a gentle morning hike to **Mirror Lake** (p. 270, **②**) for amazing views of the magnificent **Half Dome** (p. 280, **⑪**). Consider a **white-water raft trip** (p. 303) on the Merced River. Check out **Tuolumne Meadows** (p. 268, **⑪**) in the park's stunning high country. ⏱ 1½ days. See p. 276.

On Day 7, head west on Hwy. 140 (78 miles), then South on Hwy. 59 (14 miles), then west on Hwy. 152 (52 miles), and then southwest on Hwy. 156 (34 miles). Continue south on Hwy. 1 for 13 miles. Trip time: about 4½ hr.

⑥ Monterey. Next to **Cannery Row** (p. 336, **③**), a gritty sardine-packing area turned tacky tourist haunt, is the **Monterey Bay Aquarium** (p. 316, **②**), one of the world's most impressive aquariums.

Monterey was the capital of Alta California during the Spanish and Mexican colonial era and is where California ratified its first state constitution in 1849. Take the self-guided Path of History tour through **Monterey State Historic Park** (p. 338, **⑦**).

Cruise **17-Mile Drive** (p. 312, **③**), a scenic drive by the cypress-covered coastline, including the Lone Cypress, a spectacular specimen of cypress alone on a rocky outcropping. ⏱ 5 hr.

Stay the night on the Monterey Peninsula. Start Day 8 in Carmel.

⑦ Carmel. ⏱ 2 hr. See p. 24, **③**.

⑧ Big Sur. ⏱ At least 3 hr. See p. 24, **④**.

⑨ Hearst Castle. ⏱ 2½ hr. See p. 24, **⑤**.

Head south on Hwy. 1 to Cambria for the night. On Day 9, head east on the scenic Hwy. 46 to Paso Robles. At U.S. 101, head south 132 miles to Santa Barbara. Trip time: about 3½ hr.

⑩ Santa Barbara. Enjoy your day at California's prettiest beach town. Spend an hour at the "Queen of the Missions," the **Santa Barbara Mission** (p. 380, **①**), then venture uphill to the natural beauty of the **Santa Barbara Botanic Garden** (p. 380, **②**). Head downtown where you can take the Red Tile Tour, a self-guided walking tour of the town's Spanish Mission-Revival architecture, which includes the lovely **Santa Barbara County Courthouse** (p. 382, **④**) as well as the last Spanish military outpost in California, **El Presidio de Santa Barbara** (p. 383, **⑧**). Take a drive, or better yet, a bike ride along the Cabrillo beachfront path, and then relax on Santa Barbara's most popular beach, **East Beach** (p. 385). For dinner, enjoy fresh seafood at **Brophy Brothers** (p. 387) on the harbor. ⏱ 1 day.

From Santa Barbara, head south on the U.S. 101 for 34 miles. In Oxnard, take exit 62B and follow signs for Hwy. 1. Continue south on Hwy. 1 for about 20 miles to Malibu. Trip time: about 1½ hr.

⑪ Los Angeles. ⏱ 2 days. See p. 25, **⑥**.

On the night of Day 11, from downtown Los Angeles, head south on I-5 for 25 miles to Anaheim. Follow signs to the Theme Parks. Trip time: about 1 hr. 45 min.

⑫ Disneyland Resort. Welcome to the Happiest Place on Earth. A Park Hopper pass admits you to both the original **Disneyland Park** and **Disney's California Adventure**. Purchase tickets ahead of time and prioritize which rides and attractions you want to see, because you won't have enough time—or energy—to do it all. Also, try to stay in or close to the parks to maximize your jam-packed day. ⏱ 1 day. See p. 506.

On Day 13, head north on Hwy. 57 for 20 miles. Head east on I-10 for 70 miles. Take Hwy. 111 east for 10 miles. Trip time: about 2 hr.

> *Seven familiar dwarves doing their part to create the "happiest place on Earth."*

⑬ **Palm Springs.** Take a ride on the **Palm Springs Aerial Tramway** (p. 554, ❷), a cable ride that climbs to Mount Jacinto's alpine forest, about 30 to 40 degrees cooler than the Coachella Valley spread out below. Stop by the **Palm Springs Visitor Center** (p. 554, ❶) to pick up a guide to midcentury modernist architecture that gives the town a sheen of retro glamour. Swing by the vintage shops along **Palm Canyon Drive** (p. 561), a mecca for midcentury furniture and design. Be sure to choose a hotel that suits you because poolside cocktails are a Palm Springs institution, owing to its long tradition as a Hollywood getaway. ⏲ half-day.

Head north on Indian Canyon Dr. At Hwy. 62 turn right and go 35 miles to the Oasis Visitor Center (trip time: about 45 min.) on the north side of

⑭ **Joshua Tree National Park.** The well-paved road **Park Boulevard,** which links the north and west entrances, may be the quickest and easiest way to capture some of the park's most essential high-desert scenery. From the well-stocked **Oasis Visitor Center** (p. 458, ❶), follow Palm Boulevard south and bear

right at the fork toward **Jumbo Rocks,** where you'll probably be tempted to hop out of the car and onto the boulders. See the much-photographed **Skull Rock,** a giant rock that appears to have eye sockets. After passing by the trail heads for **Ryan Mountain** (a vigorous hike with great views) and **Cap Rock** (an easy walk to a striking rock formation), continue on Keys Point Road to the spectacular **Keys View** (p. 549, ❼), the park's highest point reachable by car. Back on Palm Boulevard heading north, you'll skirt more highlights like the aptly named **Wonderland of Rocks, Barker Dam,** and old cattle-rustlers' **Hidden Valley** (p. 537, ❻). ⏲ At least 3 hr.

Head back to Palm Springs for the night. On Day 14, head west on I-10 to Hwy. 60 and continue west for 17 miles. Take I-215 south for 31 miles. Continue south on I-15 for 50 miles. Veer right onto Hwy. 162 and continue south for 11 miles. Trip time: about 2 hr. 45 min.

⑮ **San Diego.** ⏲ 1 day. See p. 25, ❼.

Fly home from San Diego International Airport.

California for Families

Southern California is one of the premier family destinations in the country thanks to its warm beaches and multitude of theme parks, including the one that seems to capture every child's imagination, Disneyland. On this 8-day jaunt en route to the classic kiddie attractions of San Francisco, you'll stop by the mesmerizing Monterey Bay Aquarium, Santa Cruz's beachside boardwalk, and hop a train through the redwoods.

> Lunchtime for giant pandas at the San Diego Zoo means bamboo, carrots, and yams.

START Fly into San Diego International Airport. TRIP LENGTH about 675 miles.

1 San Diego. Your first stop is the world-famous **San Diego Zoo** (p. 578, **1**), best visited in the morning before the crowds arrive. Founded in 1916, the zoo currently houses 4,000 animals from 800 species, including rare species like giant pandas and African lowland gorillas. Double-decker bus tours roll by the various habitats, especially useful if you have small children.

Spend some time wandering through **Balboa Park** (p. 582) and its many museums. Especially good options for kids include the Reuben H. Fleet Science Center, the Air & Space Museum, the Model Railroad Museum, the Natural History Museum, and the Miniature Railroad and Carousel.

Dolphins, otters, sea lions, and seals perform at **SeaWorld** (p. 600, **9**), but the rock star is Shamu, the jumping and splashing killer whale. You'll also find sharks, manatees, and

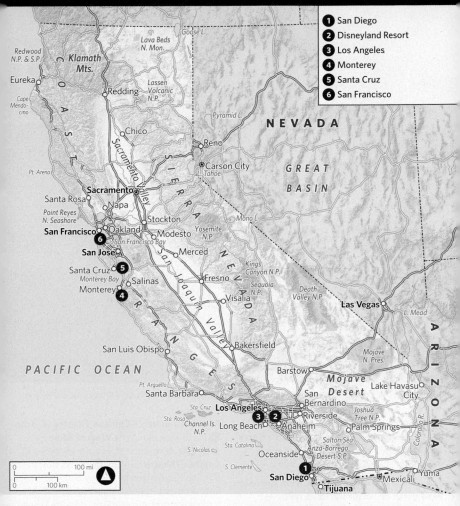

1	San Diego
2	Disneyland Resort
3	Los Angeles
4	Monterey
5	Santa Cruz
6	San Francisco

a variety of penguins, as well as rides with Sesame Street characters.

Thirty-four miles north of town, you can slip away to the wild savannahs of Africa at the 1,800-acre **San Diego Zoo Safari Park** (p. 628, **8**), where 3,500 animals—lions, zebras, elephants, cheetahs, and rhinos—roam "freely" within vast natural landscapes.

LEGOLAND California (p. 630), in Carlsbad, is an absolute must for kids obsessed with LEGO blocks—and even for those kids that aren't—with over 50 interactive exhibits, shows, and great role-playing rides where kids become knights, firefighters, skippers, and aviators. Even jaded adults will marvel at the intricate models of American cities. ☉ 2 days.

On Day 3, from San Diego, head north on I-5 for 80 miles to Anaheim. Trip time: 2 hr.

2 Disneyland Resort. Some die-hard Disney fans could happily spend a whole week here, but we'll budget a day for each of the two parks. Opened in 1955, the original **Disneyland** is the result of Walt Disney's personal vision and still works its magic on children as well as nostalgic adults with classic characters and impossible-to-forget rides like "it's a small world." The newer **California Adventure** showcases the glory of California, thematically anyway, with roller coasters and virtual reality rides.

> *Welcome to Krustyland at Universal Studios Hollywood, but beware: the walkway is Krusty's squishy tongue.*

If your kids are tweens or teens, you could swap the day at Disneyland for **Knott's Berry Farm** (p. 503), which is smaller, but offers more thrill rides. ⊕ 2 days. See p. 506.

Early in the morning on Day 5, from Anaheim, head north on I-5 for about 25 miles—typically quite congested—to Los Angeles. Trip time: about 1 hr. 45 min.

❸ Los Angeles. Start the day early at **Universal Studios Hollywood** (p. 427). The slick one-hour tour may be a bit hokey (compared to say, the in-depth Warner Bros. or Paramount studio tours), but kids will enjoy passing through the "sets" of *War of the Worlds*, *King Kong*, and *The Fast and the Furious*. The best rides are *The Simpsons* virtual roller coaster, the *Jurassic Park* jungle boat ride, and *Shrek 4-D*, a multi-sensory film using 3-D animation.

Head to Hollywood to gawk at the super-heroes and crazy costumed characters in front of **Grauman's Chinese Theatre** (p. 409, ❹), and walk along the **Walk of Fame** (p. 409, ❺). Across the street, the gorgeous **El Capitan Theatre** (p. 426, ❹) plays the latest blockbuster movies by Disney and Pixar. If you have a chance, catch a show; the pre-show hoopla features organ music, dancing Disney characters, and a rain of confetti—kids go bonkers before the curtains even part. Afterwards, indulge in a sundae or banana split at the **Disney Soda Fountain** (p. 426, ❺), an old-fashioned ice cream parlor.

At the **La Brea Tar Pits** (p. 418, ❶), the oozing black asphalt and skeletons of wooly mammoths and saber-toothed tigers never fail to excite kids, although you may have to explain why there aren't any dinosaurs (for dinosaurs, take a detour downtown to the **Natural History Museum**; p. 424, ❷).

End the day at the **Santa Monica Pier** (p. 416, ❸), an amusement park with a century of tradition. Take a spin on the solar-powered Ferris

Wheel, which takes you high over the Pacific Ocean. Ride the colorful, hand-carved horses on the 1922-built carousel in the Loof Hippodrome, a National Historic Landmark. ☉ 1 day.

Hit the road early on Day 6. Head north on U.S. 101 for 325 miles. Exit Hwy. 68 west, also called Monterey Salinas Hwy., and head west for 13 miles. Turn right at Hwy. 218 (Canyon Del Rey Blvd.) and go 2.6 miles. Turn left at Del Monte Ave. and follow until it turns into Lighthouse Ave. Turn right at David Ave. Trip time: about 6 hr.

❹ Monterey. Arrive in Monterey by early afternoon to have ample time at the **Monterey Bay Aquarium** (p. 316, ❷), quite simply one of the world's best and largest public aquariums, and a must-see for families. The **Outer Bay** features a 1.2 million-gallon tank where kids can "ooh" and "aah" in front of dolphin-fish, and hammerhead and Galapagos sharks. The sea otters and penguins are also popular personalities. ☉ At least 3 hr. See p. 336.

On Day 7, head north on Hwy. 1 for 40 miles. Trip time: about 1 hr.

❺ Santa Cruz. Santa Cruz's biggest family attraction is the **Beach Boardwalk** (p. 332, ❶), originally built in 1907 when seaside amusement parks were all the rage. There are plenty of new thrill rides, but the boardwalk's considerable charm comes from its throwback vibe, with two of its vintage rides—a 1924 wooden roller coaster called the **Giant Dipper** and a 1911 **Looff Carousel**—designated as national landmarks.

Afterwards, visit the towering trees at **Henry Cowell Redwoods State Park**. The **Roaring Camp Railroads** (p. 334, ❿) use century-old, authentically preserved steam locomotives to truck you through groves of old-growth redwoods, some nearly 1,800 years old and nearly 300 feet tall. ☉ half-day.

Head north on Hwy. 1 for 72 miles and stay the night in San Francisco. Trip time: about 2½ hr.

❻ San Francisco. For the quintessential San Francisco experience, hop a **cable car** (p. 55, ❷) at the turnaround at Market and Powell and enjoy the crisp air and thrilling views of the city on the way towards **Fisherman's Wharf** (p. 56, ❹).

> *Ride your trusty steed and grab a brass ring on the Looff Carousel in Santa Cruz.*

Unless you're with very young or easily frightened children, take a tour of **Alcatraz** (p. 58, ❶), the infamous island prison. The ferry ride to the island provides a perfect view of the **Golden Gate Bridge** (p. 62, ❷).

Frolic in the city's beloved **Golden Gate Park** (p. 72), where a million trees fill a thousand acres. Highlights include the Conservatory of Flowers; Stow's Lake, where you can rent boats; the Japanese Tea Garden; the Bison Paddock; and the Children's Playground, which is home to a 1912 carousel. Curious minds enjoy the excellent **California Academy of Sciences** (p. 64, ❺), which is a combination aquarium, planetarium, and natural history museum.

Another great science museum, called the best in the world by *Scientific American* magazine, is the hands-on, aptly named **Exploratorium** (p. 69), located at the gorgeous **Palace of Fine Arts** from 1915.

Little Leaguers should finish the day with a **San Francisco Giants** game at AT&T Park (p. 123), one of the premier stadiums in the Major Leagues. ☉ 1 day.

Fly home from San Francisco International Airport.

An Epicurean's Tour of California

Take the leading food and agricultural state in the country with easy access to fresh, local ingredients; sprinkle with the ethnic flavors of a diverse population; blend it all with a creative spirit that pushes to the forefront of culinary movements (organic, locavore, slow food)—and *voila*! You get this 1-week tour of California, an embarrassment of riches for foodies.

> *A mini masterpiece on china, a dish at Gary Danko looks as good as it tastes.*

START Fly into San Francisco International Airport or Oakland International Airport; check into your hotel for 4 nights. You won't need a car for the first 2 days of this tour. **TRIP LENGTH** about 620 miles.

❶ San Francisco. Start your day in the Embarcadero at the landmark **Ferry Building Marketplace** (p. 59, **❷**). Once the city's main point of access (before the completion of the Golden Gate and Bay Bridges in the 1930s), today it's a gateway to some of the finest artisanal food producers in Northern California: fresh loaves from Acme Bread, local cheeses from Cowgirl Creamery, the city's best java at Blue Bottle, and locally harvested oysters at the **Hog Island Oyster Co** (p. 60, **❸**). Time your visit for a Tuesday, Thursday, or Saturday morning to sample the seasonal bounty at the bustling **farmers market** (p. 60), which places an emphasis on sustainable agriculture and connecting consumers to their food sources. For fine dining, book a table ahead of time for **the Slanted Door** (p. 106), acclaimed for its modern take on Vietnamese cuisine.

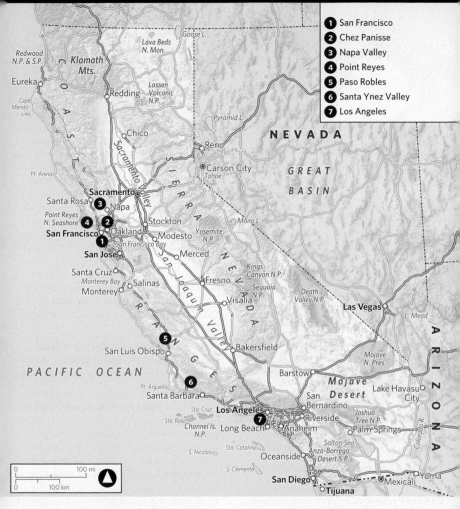

1. San Francisco
2. Chez Panisse
3. Napa Valley
4. Point Reyes
5. Paso Robles
6. Santa Ynez Valley
7. Los Angeles

Explore the vibrant sights, sounds, smells, and especially the tastes of **Chinatown** (p. 78), one of the oldest and largest Chinese communities on the continent. It's free to stop by the **Golden Gate Fortune Cookies Co.** (p. 80, ❼), where you can watch fortune cookies being made by hand, as they've been since 1962. Brave the lines of the no-frills **House of Nanking** (p. 105) for excellent Shanghai-style dishes. For a guided walking tour of Chinatown, consider Shirley Fong-Torres's popular **Wok Wiz Tours** (www.wokwiz.com; $25–$45).

For dinner, choose from an amazing selection of world-class restaurants, perhaps **Restaurant Gary Danko** (p. 106) or **Michael Mina** (p. 105).

Looking for something a little homier? Warm your hands around a delicious cup of clam chowder at **Swan Oyster Depot** (p. 106), a city mainstay since 1912.

Begin Day 2 with coffee and insanely delicious pastries at the always-mobbed **Tartine Bakery & Café** (p. 101). Poke around the shops of the Mission and work up an appetite for lunch. Prepare to be amazed at the quality of the street food, now that the city has become infiltrated by upscale food trucks (p. 107). **Spencer on the Go!**, for example, offers highfalutin French fare like escargot and foie gras. For dessert, head to **Humphry Slocombe** (p. 88, ❺) for some seriously gourmet ice cream. ⏱1½ days.

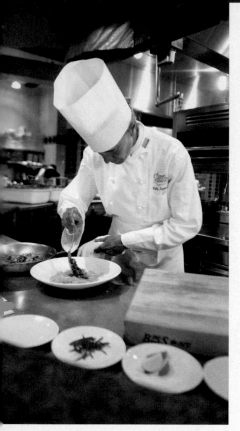

> *Dining, demos, cooking classes—the Culinary Institute of America at Greystone does it all.*

Take the BART to Downtown Berkeley. Trip time: 1 hr.

❷ Chez Panisse. Alice Waters' legendary **Chez Panisse** (p. 104) restaurant is considered both the physical and philosophical ground zero for the California food movement, which focuses on fresh, seasonal, organic ingredients of the highest quality. Dinner here is an absolute must, so book well in advance.

Return to San Francisco for a nightcap, perhaps an expertly concocted cocktail at the speakeasy-esque **Bourbon & Branch** (p. 121).

On Day 3, you're off on a day excursion from San Francisco. Head north on U.S. 101 for 22 miles. At Hwy. 37 take a right and go 7 miles. At Hwy. 121 take a left and follow for 18 miles. Continue on Hwy. 29 heading north. Trip time: about 1½ hr.

❸ Napa Valley. Before you go, check out the hands-on cooking classes for "food enthusiasts" offered at the renowned **Culinary Institute of America at Greystone** (p. 151, **❻**), where you can spend anywhere from a couple hours to 5 days learning about topics ranging from knife skills to artisan bread making to how to prepare Spanish tapas. The easiest (and cheapest) option is the live one-hour cooking demonstrations ($15) held on weekends, which you can combine with a tour ($10) of the historic Greystone property.

Pick up gourmet picnic supplies at **Dean & Deluca** (p. 138, **②**), then spend the rest of the afternoon snacking and sipping your way through the many **wineries** (p. 142).

Book far in advance for a table at Thomas Keller's **French Laundry** (p. 162), a Michelin 3-star winner and widely recognized as one of the finest restaurants in the world. It's a major splurge, but the experience is unforgettable. Otherwise, settle into **Bouchon** (p. 162), Keller's more casual but still excellent French brasserie. ☺1 day.

Return to San Francisco. On Day 4, head north on Hwy. 101 for about 10 miles. At Hwy. 1 veer left and head north for about 30 miles.

❹ Point Reyes. North of San Francisco in West Marin, **Point Reyes National Seashore** (p. 217, **❸**) is a beloved natural retreat for city folks and makes a great stop for food lovers who might enjoy burning off a few calories with hiking, biking, kayaking, or bird-watching. In a restored barn, the **Cowgirl Cantina** (p. 219, **④**) offers tours and tastings (reserve a spot online at www.cowgirlcreamery.com) of their artisanal cheeses—try the triple-cream Red Hawk made from organic cow's milk from the Strauss Family Dairy just up the road.

Stop by **Drakes Bay Oyster Farm** (p. 230, **④**) for fresh-as-can-be oysters straight from Drake's Estero, an amazingly pristine saltwater lagoon. The best way to enjoy them is to plop down at a picnic table and shuck them yourself. For more fresh seafood, or to try other oysters farmed in the area, stop by the local standout, **Nick's Cove Restaurant** (p. 242). ☺1 day.

Return to San Francisco. On Day 5, check out of your hotel and head south on Hwy. 101 for about 205 miles to Paso Robles. Trip time: 3 hr. 45 min.

> *Tiny olives grow to be big producers of exquisite oil at Pasolivo.*

⑤ Paso Robles. Spend the day exploring the wineries (p. 366) of Paso Robles, the fastest growing wine region in the state. Try the acclaimed Rhones of **Tablas Creek** (p. 367, ❸), or bordeaux-style blends at **Justin Winery** (p. 368, ❹). Stop by **Pasolivo** (p. 362, ❺) to sample their estate-grown olive oils—a perfect palate cleanser.

For dinner head to **the Range in Santa Margarita** (p. 363) for sophisticated comfort food made with locally-sourced ingredients—try a hearty, peppery steak from local Hearst Ranch grass-fed cattle and a glass of zinfandel from nearby Pozo Valley.

If you wanted to extend your Central Coast leg, consider a stay (☎ 805/438-5667; www.rinconadadairy.com; $150 a night, two-night minimum) at the **Rinconada Dairy**, a sheep's milk dairy where you can learn about cheese-making and perform light farm chores such as berry-picking or feeding the sheep and goats. ⊙ 1 day. See p. 390.

On the morning of Day 6, head south for 85 miles on Hwy. 101 (trip time: 1½ hr.) to the

⑥ Santa Ynez Valley. Start your morning off with some laid-back wine tasting in a location that had a star turn in the movie *Sideways*.

Take lunch at the **Hitching Post II** (p. 359), for a taste of Santa Maria-style barbecue. ⊙ half-day.

From Santa Ynez, head south on Hwy. 101 for about 120 miles. Trip time: 2 hr. 15 min.

⑦ Los Angeles. Challenging San Francisco for the best restaurants in California, Los Angeles offers a number of bold endeavors from such celebrity chefs as Wolfgang Puck, Suzanne Goin, and Nancy Silverton, as well as a dazzling array of international cuisines. For a traditional fine dining experience, you cannot go wrong at Puck's **Spago** (p. 479) or **CUT** (p. 483), Goin's **Lucques** (p. 477), or Silverton's **Pizzeria Mozza** (p. 478) restaurants.

More adventurous eaters should follow the path of Pulitzer Prize–winning food critic of the *Los Angeles Weekly* (www.laweekly.com), Jonathan Gold, who tirelessly mines strip malls and mom-and-pop shops for buried treasures like the super spicy Southern Thai dishes at **Jitlada** (p. 477).

However you decide to mix and match your meals, kick off your last day with brunch at Mark Peel's **Campanile** (p. 475). ⊙ 1½ days.

Fly out of Los Angeles International Airport.

The Great Outdoors

Two weeks is a good chunk of time, but you'll have to stay in motion to sample California's best natural attractions—towering redwoods and giant sequoias, the majestic granite monoliths of Yosemite Valley, the haunting desert landscapes of Death Valley and Joshua Tree national parks, as well as classic golden-sand beaches. When it comes to the great outdoors, timing is everything. This tour is best in the fall or early spring, when mountain roads are still passable, and when the desert has yet to soar to its highest temperatures.

> *Flying Sierra-style, a snowboarder gets big air on a Squaw Valley slope.*

START Fly into San Francisco International Airport. From San Francisco, head north on CA-1 for about 35 miles to Point Reyes. TRIP LENGTH about 2,260 miles.

❶ Point Reyes National Seashore. This pristine coastline and wetlands is perhaps best known for incredible **bird-watching**, with nearly 500 identified species. During the spring, **Point Reyes Lighthouse** is one of the best spots in the state to observe migrating California gray whales. Explore the San Andreas Fault Zone on the half-mile interpretive **Earthquake Trail,** accessible from the Bear Valley Visitor Center. If you have time,

the calm waters of Tomales Bay are perfect for **kayaking** (p. 239). Before hitting the road, take a moment to relax at **Drake's Beach,** a popular beach surrounded by white sandstone cliffs. English explorer Sir Francis Drake came ashore near this spot in 1579. ☺ 3 hr. See p. 217, ❸.

For a scenic route to your next stop, head north on Hwy. 1 for 180 miles. Merge with U.S. 101 and head north for about 33 miles to Philipsville. The faster route is to take U.S. 101 north the entire way. Trip time (quick route): 3½ hr.

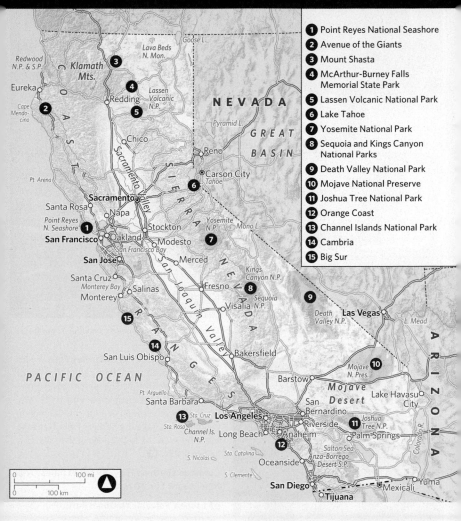

1. Point Reyes National Seashore
2. Avenue of the Giants
3. Mount Shasta
4. McArthur-Burney Falls Memorial State Park
5. Lassen Volcanic National Park
6. Lake Tahoe
7. Yosemite National Park
8. Sequoia and Kings Canyon National Parks
9. Death Valley National Park
10. Mojave National Preserve
11. Joshua Tree National Park
12. Orange Coast
13. Channel Islands National Park
14. Cambria
15. Big Sur

2 Avenue of the Giants. After you pass Garberville, follow signs for Avenue of the Giants, a spectacular road that parallels U.S. 101 and leads through **Humboldt Redwoods State Park's** awe-inspiring redwood trees. The park's Rockefeller Forest contains the world's largest continuous old-growth redwoods, with some specimens soaring to over 370 feet high. In Founders Grove, you can walk beside the fallen Dyerville Giant, formerly the world's tallest tree. Pick up maps at the visitor center in Weott, and hike into the heart of the hushed forest. ⏲ 2 hr. See p. 221, **6**.

Head 50 miles north on U.S. 101 to Arcata for the night. On Day 2 head east on Hwy. 299 for 140 miles. At I-5 head north for 60 miles. Trip time: 5½ hr.

3 Mount Shasta. If you're an avid climber and determined to conquer the 14,162-foot-high dormant volcano, spend the entire day here, and forgo the rest of the day's stops. Otherwise, drive up Everitt Memorial Highway to Old Ski Bowl Vista to enjoy a panorama of Panther Meadow, Castle Crags, Trinity Mountains, and Mount Shasta's legendary snow-capped peak. ⏲ 1 hr. See p. 234, **4**.

> *With over 750 miles of trails leading to waterfalls, alpine meadows, and up granite monoliths, Yosemite is a hiker's paradise.*

> *You have to hike to see gorgeous Alamere Falls tumbling 50 feet into the sea on Pt. Reyes.*

On Hwy. 89, head east then south for 50 miles. Trip time: about 1 hr. 20 min.

❹ McArthur-Burney Falls Memorial State Park. See the thundering (and picture-perfect) 129-foot **Burney Falls**, which Teddy Roosevelt (probably) called "the eighth wonder of the world." The water comes from underground springs upstream from the falls, which flow year-round at a rate of 100 million gallons a day. Take the popular Falls Trail hike from the overlook to the base of the falls. ⏲1 hr. See p. 235, ❻.

Continue south on Hwy. 89 for 41 miles. Trip time: about 1 hr. 10 min.

❺ Lassen Volcanic National Park. The volcano last blew its top in 1915, but the surreal landscape still percolates with geothermal activity, all of which is best experienced from the **Bumpass Hell Trail**. ⏲2 hr. See p. 224, ❺.

Continue south on Hwy. 89 for 141 miles to Truckee for the night. On the morning of Day 3, continue south on Hwy. 89 to Squaw Valley. Trip time: about 4 hr.

❻ Lake Tahoe. Lake Tahoe's crystal clear waters are surrounded by mountains, which offer some of best skiing in the West. During snow season, head to **Squaw Valley USA** (p. 304), site of the 1960 Winter Olympics, for a day of downhill skiing or snowboarding. Year-round

> *Even well into summer, 14,162-foot Mt. Shasta usually wears white.*

the Squaw Valley Cable Car climbs 2,000 feet to High Camp, which offers panoramic views, an ice-skating rink, hiking, and a pool and hot tub. In the summertime, rent a boat or take a **sailing** tour, go mountain biking, or relax on the shore. Make sure to get a photo from the **Emerald Bay Lookout**. ⊙ 1 day. See p. 292.

On Day 4, from South Lake Tahoe, head south on Hwy. 89 for about 50 miles. At U.S. 395 head south for 66 miles. Turn right at Hwy. 120/Tioga Pass Rd. and follow for 58 miles to the Big Oak Flat entrance. During the winter Hwy. 120 will be closed. Alternate route: Head south, then west on U.S. 50 for 60 miles. At Hwy. 49 head south for 75 miles. Turn left at Hwy. 120 and go almost 50 miles. Trip time: about 5 hr.

❼ Yosemite National Park. Spend Days 4 and 5 exploring the breathtaking beauty of one of America's most popular national parks. The glacier-sculpted park contains superlative natural scenery—three of the world's tallest waterfalls, the world's largest granite monolith (**El Capitan**; p.280, ⓬), one of the world's largest trees, and some of California's most iconic imagery like **Half Dome** (p. 280, ⓫) and **Tunnel View** (p. 266, ❸). Hike the **Mist Trail** (p. 267, ❻) to the top of Vernal Fall. Consider a **whitewater raft trip** (p. 303) on the Merced River.

Check out **Tuolumne Meadows** (p. 268, ⓫) in the park's stunning high country. Even if you're not Ansel Adams, pack a camera—it'll get quite a workout. ⊙ 2 days. See p. 276.

On the morning of Day 6, head south on Hwy. 41 for 86 miles. Turn left on Hwy. 180 and head east for about 55 miles. Trip time: about 4 hr.

❽ Sequoia and Kings Canyon National Parks. Admire giant sequoias, the world's largest tree species, on an easy stroll through **General Grant Grove** (p. 286, ❶). Take the scenic Generals Highway to the Giant Forest, home to the world's largest living tree, the 2,000-year-old **General Sherman Tree** (p. 287, ❷). Hike to the top of **Moro Rock** (p. 287, ❸), a granite dome with views of the Great Western Divide. If you have time, take a tour of the limestone wonderland of **Crystal Cave** (p. 288, ❹). ⊙ half-day. See p. 286.

On the morning of Day 7, head east on Hwy. 198 for about 40 miles. At Hwy. 99 turn left and head south for about 75 miles to Bakersfield. Head east on Hwy. 58 for 59 miles. At Hwy. 14 take a left and head north for 42 miles. At Hwy. 178 take a right and head west, then north for 85 miles to the park. Trip time: about 7 hr. Spend the rest of Day 7 and all of Day 8 in Death Valley.

> Rock stars love the challenging pitches at Joshua Tree National Park.

9 Death Valley National Park. Scramble atop the **Panamint Dunes** (p. 544, **7**) or hike through the intricate rock patterns of water-polished **Mosaic Canyon** (p. 538, **9**). If your vehicle has high clearance, rumble along the backcountry road of **Titus Canyon** (p. 538, **10**).

Catch the sunrise on the striking badlands at **Zabriskie Point** (p. 543, **2**). Make a quick stop at the endless salt flats of **Badwater Basin** (p. 543, **4**), the lowest point on the continent, then check out the salty spires of **Devil's Golf Course** (p. 544, **5**). See the stunning **Dante's View** (p. 543, **3**), which encompasses the lowest and highest points in the contiguous 48 states. Take the scenic **Artist's Drive** (p. 544, **6**) through multi-colored hills, and stop at **Artist's Palette** (p. 544, **6**). ⊕ 1½ days. See p. 542.

On the morning of Day 9, head southeast on Hwy. 190 from Furnace Creek for 30 miles. Take a right on Hwy. 127 and head south for 83 miles to Baker. Trip time: about 2½ hr.

10 Mojave National Preserve. After passing the volcanic cinder cones and lava beds along Kelbaker Road, stop at the **Kelso Depot** (p. 540, **1**) to learn about the natural history of the preserve. Hike the "singing sands" of **Kelso Dunes** (p. 540, **2**), one of the largest complexes of dunes in the country. ⊕ At least 3 hr. See p. 540.

From Kelso, head south on Kelbaker Rd. for 33 miles to National Trails Hwy. Go 6.5 miles, then take a left at Amboy Rd. Follow it 46 miles to Utah Trail (total Trip time: about 2 hr.). Head south 2 miles into

11 Joshua Tree National Park. Take the mile-long loop through **Hidden Valley** (p. 537, **6**), enclosed by massive boulder piles. At sunset drive to **Keys View** (p.549, **7**), which offers a panorama of the Coachella Valley, the San Gorgonio Mountain, the San Andreas Fault, and the Salton Sea. At night enjoy stellar **star-gazing** (p. 533) in the clear desert sky.

On the morning of Day 10, test your rock-climbing skills at the **Wonderland of Rocks** (p. 549, **4**; pick up a climbing guide from the visitor center, or plan ahead if you'd like to take a class). Hike the popular **Fortynine Palms Oasis** (p. 548, **2**) to a lovely oasis surrounded by California fan palms. You need to get on the road by late afternoon, but take a minute to stroll through the funky **Cholla Cactus Garden** (p. 550, **10**). ⊕ At least 4 hr. See p. 548.

From the Cottonwood entrance at I-10, head west on I-10 for 100 miles. Take I-215 south to Hwy. 91 west, then go 32 miles. At Hwy. 55 head south for 18 miles to Hwy. 1. Trip time: about 3 hr.

12 Orange Coast. Day 11 is literally a day at the beach, or beaches, depending on how you play it. You'll want to hit the waves at **Huntington Beach** (p. 514) if you're a serious surfer, or even if you're not—take surf lessons at **Corky Caroll's Surf School** (p. 514, **2**). Or head to the pretty cove beaches at **Laguna Beach** (p. 518) for great tidepooling. ⊕ 1 day.

From Huntington Beach, take Hwy. 1 north for 13 miles to I-405. Head north on I-405 for 36 miles to U.S. 101 and head north for 50 miles to Ventura. Trip time 1 hr. 15 min.

13 Channel Islands National Park. Plan ahead with **Island Packers** to visit one of these practically untouched islands, a chain of five separated from the California mainland by a mere 25 miles. Take a half-day tour of **Anacapa** to see the iconic **Arch Rock**. Better yet, take the full-day tour of **Santa Cruz** island,

> *An easy trail in Julia Pfeiffer Burns State Park leads to lyrical McWay Falls.*

which includes kayaking into beautiful **Painted Cave**. The journey to the islands is an adventure in itself—you may see whales or dolphins breaching alongside your speeding catamaran. ⏱1 day. See p. 378, **9**.

On the evening of Day 12, make the 150-mile trip up U.S. 101 to Paso Robles for the night. Trip time: 2½ hr. On the morning of Day 13, head west for 29 miles on pretty Hwy. 46 through rolling hills to the coast. Trip time: about 1 hr.

14 **Cambria.** Stretch your legs with a walk beneath the windswept Cypress trees along the moody, driftwood-strewn **Moonstone Beach** (p. 389, **4**). ⏱45 min.

Take Hwy. 1 north for about 70 miles.

15 **Big Sur.** The **scenic drive** to Big Sur is a classic California experience, so take it slow and pull off to as many vista points as you

like. Stop at **Julia Pfeiffer Burns State Park** (p. 348, **8**), and see the sublime McWay Falls. Look for the Sycamore Canyon turnoff just north of the post office area, and head down the road to **Pfeiffer Beach** (p. 348, **5**), one of the few places in Big Sur to access the shoreline. It's too cold to swim, but the crashing waves and dramatic rock formations make it one of my favorite retreats. Continue on to **Pfeiffer Big Sur State Park** (p. 347, **4**) and take a hike along the Big Sur River through coastal redwoods to the Pfeiffer Falls. ⏱1 day. See p. 346.

Stay the night in Big Sur. On the morning of Day 14, take Hwy. 1 north for 70 miles to Santa Cruz. Take Hwy. 17 north 22 miles. At Hwy. 85 head north for 13 miles. Take U.S. 101 north 23 miles to San Francisco International Airport. Trip time: about 3½ hr.

Undiscovered California

This 1-week tour shows off geologic oddities, such as Devil's Postpile National Monument; the world's oldest living trees; and California's best ghost town. You'll also mine Gold Country, one of California's most underrated destinations. After swinging through Sonoma, you'll discover the Lost Coast, then meander north to see the majestic redwoods.

> *Hitting it into the rough takes on new meaning in the ancient eroded salt floor of Devil's Golf Course.*

START **Fly into McCarron International Airport in Las Vegas, Nevada** on the night before your tour begins. Get up early and drive 120 miles (about 2 hr.) southeast to Death Valley. TRIP LENGTH about 1,015 miles.

❶ **Death Valley National Park.** One of the hottest and driest places on the planet, Death Valley rewards the intrepid traveler with its stark natural beauty, its sense of isolation, and its silence.

If possible, start Day 1 at dawn at **Zabriskie Point** (p. 543, ❷) to watch the sun break onto the badlands. See the salt flats of **Badwater Basin** (p. 543, ❹) and the salt spires of **Devil's Golf Course** (p. 544, ❺). Drive up to **Dante's View** (p. 543, ❸) with views of the lowest and highest points in the contiguous 48 states. Take the scenic **Artist's Drive** (p. 544, ❻) through vividly colored hills.

Tour **Scotty's Castle** (p. 545, ❽), then visit the half-mile-wide **Ubehebe Crater** (p. 545, ❾). For a truly offbeat adventure, in the evening head to Death Valley Junction to catch the one-woman show at the **Amargosa Opera House** (p. 544). ☺ 1 day.

1. Death Valley National Park
2. Ancient Bristlecone Pine Forest
3. Mammoth Lakes
4. Devils Postpile National Monument
5. Mono Lake Tufa State Natural Reserve
6. Bodie State Historic Park
7. Highway 49
8. Columbia State Historic Park
9. Marshall Gold Discovery State Historic Park
10. Empire Mine State Historic Park
11. Sonoma Valley
12. The Lost Coast
13. Ferndale
14. Redwood National and State Parks

On Day 2, from the park's east entrance, head west on Hwy. 190 for 33 miles. Continue right onto Hwy. 136 for 18 miles. Head north on U.S. 395 for 45 miles. Turn right at Hwy. 168 and go 13 miles. Turn right on White Mountain Rd. and go 8 miles. Trip time: about 3½ hr.

2 Ancient Bristlecone Pine Forest. Meet the oldest living creatures on earth. These ancient bristlecone pines can survive for over 4,000 years. The twisted trunks and gnarled roots of the trees—blasted by wind, sun, and frigid temperatures—cling to the 10,000-foot-high slopes of the White Mountains. ⊙ 1 hr. See p. 275, ❷⓪.

Retrace the route back to U.S. 395, then head north for 55 miles. Trip time: about 1½ hr.

3 Mammoth Lakes. Bypass the Tahoe crowds, and hit **Mammoth Mountain Ski Area** (p. 284, ❾), which many skiers and snowboarders swear is the best ski resort in the state. In summer, the mountain transforms into a circus of mountain biking with a variety of adrenaline-pumping trails. Whatever the season take the **Scenic Gondola** (p. 274, ⓯) to the top of the mountain for a sublime vista of the Eastern Sierras. In the Mammoth Lakes Basin, there's **trout fishing** (p. 301) galore. ⊙ The bulk of the day. See p. 282.

> The Bridgeport Covered Bridge is just one of many historic sites you'll see as you drive along Highway 49 through Gold Country.

Stay the night near the Mammoth Lakes. On Day 3, head west on Minaret Rd. (Hwy. 203) for 10 miles. Trip time: 30 min.

④ Devils Postpile National Monument. This fascinating geologic formation is one of the world's most impressive displays of basalt columns. Hike to the 101-foot **Rainbow Falls** (p. 275, **⑰**), which kicks up mist that traps little rainbows in the midday sunlight. ⊙ 2 hr. See p. 275, **⑯**.

Retrace your route back east on Minaret Rd. (Hwy. 203). At Mammoth Scenic Loop take a left and follow for 3 miles. At U.S. 395 head north for 19 miles. Trip time: 45 min.

⑤ Mono Lake Tufa State Natural Reserve. This salty and highly alkaline lake is known for its spectacular display of tufa towers—the bizarre-looking, calcium-carbonate spires that rise from the silver-blue water. A migratory stop for some 300 species of birds, the lake also offers excellent bird-watching. ⊙ 2 hr. See p. 269, **⑬**.

Continue north on U.S. 395 for 19 miles. Take a right on Bodie Rd. (Hwy. 270) and go 12 miles. Trip time: 45 min.

⑥ Bodie State Historic Park. The boom and bust gold-mining town of Bodie is one of the most authentic and best-preserved ghost towns in the West without any cheesy theme-park hoopla. Take the self-guided tour through the 150 or so abandoned buildings in a state of "arrested decay." ⊙ 1½ hr. See p. 268, **⑫**.

Retrace your route back to U.S. 395 and head north for 46 miles. Take a left onto Hwy. 89 and follow for 45 miles. At U.S. 50 head west 52 miles to Placerville, and spend the night here or in one of the surrounding towns like Sutter Creek or Coloma. Trip time: 3 hr. 45 min. On Day 4, hit

⑦ Highway 49. The best way to delve into the history of the California Gold Rush is a journey along this historic road, passing through a string of little towns—**Nevada City** (p. 179, **⑦**), **Sutter Creek** (p. 191, **⑧**), and **Jackson** (p. 191, **⑨**). Veer off to see a few gems on Highway 4, just off Highway 49, such as **Angels Camp** (p. 174, **⑨**) and **Murphys** (p. 175, **⑪**). You can even slip away on Shenandoah Road to check out the up-and-coming **Amador Wine Country** (p. 174, **⑧**), known for big zins.

⑧ Columbia State Historic Park. This is basically a theme-park version of a Gold Rush town, but kids love the lively atmosphere, the stagecoach rides, and panning for gold. ⊙ 1½ hr. See p. 181, **⑳**.

⑨ Marshall Gold Discovery State Historic Park. See the spot where James Marshall first discovered gold at John Sutter's sawmill. Check out the historic buildings (post office, church, blacksmith shop), the replica of Sutter's Mill, and the Gold Discovery Museum. ⊙ At least 2 hr. See p. 188, **❶**.

> *An impressive cliff of basalt columns rises into the sky at Devils Postpile National Monument.*

⑩ Empire Mine State Historic Park. This is the site of California's oldest, largest, and richest gold mine. Today you can walk around the mine buildings, massive machinery, and deep mine shafts. ⊕ 1½ hr. See p. 184, **❸**.

From Placerville, head west on U.S. 50 for 47 miles. Merge onto I-80 west for 42 miles. Turn right at Hwy. 12, follow to Sonoma and stay the night. Trip time: 2 hr. 15 min.

⑪ Sonoma Valley. Spend the bulk of Day 5 eating and drinking your way through the Sonoma Valley. Although it lives in the shadow of nearby Napa Valley, Sonoma is quieter, less crowded, and has a loose, down-home vibe, and delicious vino to boot. Visit the charming and historic **Sonoma Plaza** (p. 141, **⑪**) and the **Jack London State Historic Park** (p. 150, **❹**). For restaurant options, see p. 160; for winery recommendations, see p. 142. ⊕ At least 4 hr.

Get on the road while there's still a couple hours of daylight. From Healdsburg, head north on U.S. 101 for 19 miles. At Hwy. 128 head northwest 55 miles, through the charming towns of Boonville and Philo. At Hwy. 1 head north for 10 miles to idyllic Mendocino and stay the night. Trip time: about 2½ hr.

On Day 6 head north on Hwy. 1 for 53 miles to U.S. 101. Continue north for 23 miles, then take the Redway/Garberville exit. Head west on Briceland-Shelter Cove Rd. for 23 miles to Shelter Cove. Trip time: about 2¾ hr.

⑫ The Lost Coast. Discover the most secluded and most pristine stretch of coastline in California. Hike a few miles along the Lost Coast Trail near Black Sands Beach. ⊕ At least 4 hr. See p. 231, **❽**.

As you head back up Briceland Rd., make a left on Wilder Ridge Rd. Go left on Mattole Rd. and continue along the scenic Mattole-Ferndale-Petrolia Rd. for 75 miles to Ferndale. Trip time: about 2¾ hr.

⑬ Ferndale. Step back in time to the Victorian era. The entire town, with its tidy collection of ornately crafted Victorian homes, is a National Historic Landmark. ⊕ 2 hr. See p. 221, **❼**.

On Day 7 take Hwy. 211 to U.S 101 north. Go 57 miles to Orick. Trip time: about 1½ hr.

⑭ Redwood National and State Parks. These parks, which preserve the coast redwood ecosystem, are a World Heritage Site and an International Biosphere Reserve. ⊕ At least 4 hr. See p. 231, **❾**.

The closest airport is Arcata/Eureka Airport.

3
San Francisco

Our Favorite San Francisco Moments

Simply stated, San Francisco is one of the world's great cities. Surrounded by water on three sides and dominated by fine Victorian architecture, it's a place of striking physical beauty and colorful historical character. With a fiercely independent and iconoclastic populace, it's also breathtakingly artistic—walking through its vibrantly distinct neighborhoods you're likely to see some random act of circus or an amazing piece of street art. This compact and cosmopolitan city is also home to a collection of world-class restaurants, museums, and performing arts groups that help position it as one of California's must-see destinations.

> PREVIOUS PAGE *Whether you ride a boat under it or cross its span, you'll never forget the Golden Gate Bridge.* THIS PAGE *Savvy visitors know fall brings fog-free views of the Golden Gate.*

❶ Crossing the Golden Gate Bridge. However you choose to do it—on foot, by bike, or even just driving across—experiencing this marvelous piece of architecture and engineering is a thrilling experience. Completed in 1937, this Art Deco–style bridge was at the time the longest (1.7 mile) and tallest (746 ft.) suspension structure in the world. It was a marvel then and it's a marvel now. See p. 62, ❷.

❷ Tripping through the Haight. Once the perceived center of the hippie counterculture universe in the 1960s, Haight-Ashbury is now a monument to consumerism. With 6 blocks of wall-to-wall clothing boutiques, gift shops, vintage-clothing outposts, and music stores, this neighborhood offers some of the city's most eclectic shopping. Tune in, turn on, charge up. See p. 65, ❻.

❸ Diving into cocktail culture. San Francisco's cocktail culture is now on an equal footing with the Bay Area's renowned food scene. That means rock-star bartenders creating fabulous, seasonally inspired concoctions, brimming with organic products and primed with alcohol from boutique distilleries. And if

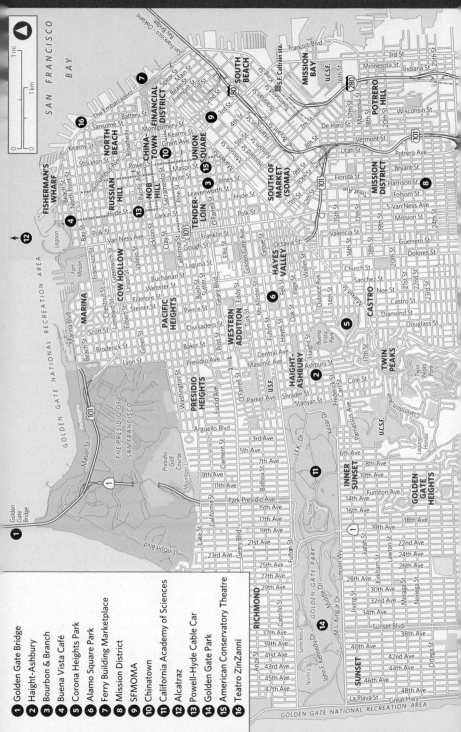

1 Golden Gate Bridge
2 Haight-Ashbury
3 Bourbon & Branch
4 Buena Vista Café
5 Corona Heights Park
6 Alamo Square Park
7 Ferry Building Marketplace
8 Mission District
9 SFMOMA
10 Chinatown
11 California Academy of Sciences
12 Alcatraz
13 Powell-Hyde Cable Car
14 Golden Gate Park
15 American Conservatory Theatre
16 Teatro ZinZanni

> *Calder's mobiles, Pollock's splotches, Warhol's soup cans—see them and more at spectacular SFMOMA.*

you just happen to be drinking your blackberry and cabernet caipirinha with muddled limes in a speakeasy setting like Bourbon & Branch, so much the better. See p. 121.

4 Having some whiskey with your coffee. Not to keep harping on the alcohol angle, but settling in for an Irish coffee at The Buena Vista is pretty much something you have to do in San Francisco. The American version of the Irish coffee was created here in 1952 and the protagonists showed all the tenacity and dedication in perfecting the recipe as the current crop of mixologists show in their new libations. Just watching the messy assembly-line production— the bar can serve up to 2,000 of these babies a day—is a treat. See p. 121.

5 Climbing the Rock. No, not Alcatraz (p. 58, **1**); this rock is at Corona Heights Park above the Castro district. You'll get a thigh-burning workout, but you'll be rewarded with one of the most incredible vistas in San Francisco—a 360-degree view of the city, laid out before you in all its glory. See p. 89.

6 Taking a can't-miss photo. One of the city's most reliable photo ops is available on a daily basis at Alamo Square Park. Here's where you'll find the Seven Sisters, a group of seven restored Victorian homes that you've seen in any number of photos, films, and TV shows. Though certainly not the city's most

beautiful Victorian Painted Ladies, they serve as the picture-perfect foreground to a classic cityscape beyond. See p. 65, **8**.

7 Browsing through the Ferry Building Marketplace. One of the city's great success stories, this renovated Embarcadero structure (originally opened in 1898) reemerged in 2003 as a mixed-use marketplace. Featuring gourmet products, eateries, and shops, this place should be high on the list of all foodies. See p. 59, **2**.

8 Going on a Mission artwalk. San Francisco's bustling Mission District is home to Latin American immigrants and arty hipsters, and there's an unbelievable collection of murals throughout the neighborhood. Take a self-guided tour for a colorful dose of culture. See p. 86.

9 Expanding your mind at SFMOMA. It doesn't matter what the current show might be, there's always something interesting to see at the San Francisco Museum of Modern Art. With more than 26,000 pieces (and counting) in its holdings, SFMOMA displays both cutting-edge new works and masterworks of modern and contemporary art. It has an especially strong photography collection. See p. 60, **4**.

10 Taking an international trip without leaving town. San Francisco's Chinatown is the largest Chinese neighborhood outside of Asia, and it hums with energy and activity. It's a place that never fails to entertain and fascinate with its ornate architecture, rich cultural heritage, and shopping and dining delights. See p. 78.

11 Spending quality time with Claude the albino alligator. There is so much to see and do at the California Academy of Sciences—it's a planetarium, an aquarium, and a natural history museum all rolled into one. It's also one very cool building with an undulating rooftop garden. Whatever you choose to do, though, don't forget to say "hi" to Claude. See p. 64, **5**.

12 Touring the Rock. Yes, Alcatraz Island, the infamous rock of an island that sits in the middle of San Francisco Bay. From 1934 to 1963 it was a maximum-security prison that held the likes of Al Capone and Machine Gun Kelly; now it's a national park that offers fascinating walking tours (including a really cool evening one). See p. 58, **1**.

13 Rumbling along on the Powell-Hyde cable car. San Francisco's innovative cable-car system dates back to 1873, promoted by Andrew Smith Hallidie after he witnessed a horrifying accident with a team of horses. Of course it probably didn't hurt that Smith Hallidie was also a cable

manufacturer. San Francisco is the only place in the world where you can still ride one of these vehicles, so hop on and savor the view as you hit the crest of Russian Hill. See p. 55, **2**.

14 Biking in Golden Gate Park. There are just so many fun things to see and do in Golden Gate Park, and the best way to get from one to the other is by bike. From the stoner drum circles at Hippie Hill to the Bloody Marys at the Beach Chalet and from the museums to the Japanese Tea Garden to where the buffalo roam—an entertaining day is assured. See p. 72.

15 Taking in an evening at the theater. Whether it's a world-premiere play at the American Conservatory Theatre, a rousing symphony, or a classic production from a world-class opera or ballet company, an evening spent in one of San Francisco's cultural palaces will be an evening well spent. See p. 122.

16 Taking in an evening at the Teatro. Though it's a Seattle import, Teatro ZinZanni is a perfect fit for San Francisco—it's a mash-up of Cirque du Soleil–style circus performance and European cabaret, with a five-course dinner thrown in for good measure. See p. 123.

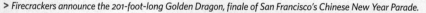

> *Firecrackers announce the 201-foot-long Golden Dragon, finale of San Francisco's Chinese New Year Parade.*

The Best of San Francisco in 1 Day

San Francisco is very small geographically (just 7 sq. miles), making it easy to fit plenty in on just 1 day. This itinerary connects some of the city's most iconic sights and neighborhoods, from Fisherman's Wharf to Chinatown. Put on your walking shoes, dress in layers (if you don't like the weather in San Francisco, don't worry; it will change in 10 min.), and get ready to explore.

> With curves like this, who cares if Lombard Street isn't technically "the crookedest street in the world"?

START **Union Square. Take the BART to Powell St. or Montgomery St., or use the one of numerous downtown bus routes, such as the 5, 6, 7, 9, or 38.**

1 Union Square. This square is a great spot to take in the ebb and flow of downtown's commercial heart. From its elevated position, surrounded by department stores, high-end retailers, hotels, and offices, you can watch the throngs go about their business while enjoying a cup of coffee.

The 97-foot column rising from the center of the square commemorates victory in the Spanish-American War, and was dedicated by Theodore Roosevelt in 1903. ⏱ 30 min. Located btw. Post, Geary, Stockton & Powell sts. Bus: 5, 6, 7, 9, or 38. Cable car: Powell lines.

Adjacent to Union Square on Powell St., catch the Powell-Hyde cable car; look for the red POWELL AND MARKET/HYDE AND BEACH sign on the car (there are two lines that travel on Powell St.).

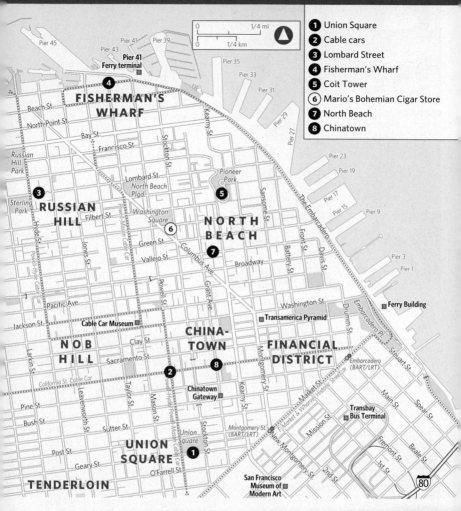

1 Union Square
2 Cable cars
3 Lombard Street
4 Fisherman's Wharf
5 Coit Tower
6 Mario's Bohemian Cigar Store
7 North Beach
8 Chinatown

2 ★★★ **Cable cars.** This is a truly one-of-a-kind San Francisco treat; you won't find a conveyance like this anywhere else in the world. Entirely motorless and pulled along by a cable beneath the street, the cable cars were originally promoted in 1873 by English immigrant Andrew Smith Hallidie, who had previously built bridges and systems for moving ore cars in mines. He was motivated to replace the city's horse-drawn trolleys after witnessing a trolley accident that led to the death of a team of horses. Initially dubbed "Hallidie's Folly," the cable cars eventually gained acceptance, but following the 1906 earthquake began to be replaced by electric streetcars and buses.

On the verge of extinction several times, these beloved vehicles are now designated as historical landmarks and are clearly here for the long haul. ⊕ 30 min.; long midday waits to board are common in summer. ☎ 311. www.sfmta.com/cablecar or www.sfcablecar.com. Rides $5. Daily 6–1am.

Hop off the cable car at Lombard St.

3 ★ **Lombard Street.** Known as "the crookedest street in the world," Lombard snakes its way down a precipitous 27-degree grade. The street was deemed too steep for cars to safely navigate in the 1920s, so zigzag hairpin turns were added as a safety measure.

> *Bypass the tacky and go straight for the fresh Dungeness crab along San Francisco's Fisherman's Wharf.*

Cars will line up to await a turn to drive down (it's a one-way street), but it's much nicer to take a walk down the stairs on either side; it's a beautifully landscaped stretch of road. ⏱ 20 min. Lombard St., btw. Hyde & Leavenworth sts. Cable car: Powell-Hyde line.

❹ Fisherman's Wharf. This lively destination is San Francisco's most relentlessly touristy area—don't look for too much authenticity—though there are pleasures to be discovered here, including street performers and sidewalk

SITE GUIDE PAGE 57

stalls selling boiled crab and clam chowder.

It's about a 10-block walk from PIER 39 to Coit Tower, and you're going to be gaining elevation. If you're a little low on energy at this point, take bus 39 from Stockton and Beach sts.

❺ ★★ Coit Tower. San Francisco is a city of wood, and fires have always been a frequent problem here, making it no surprise that firefighters have a lot of local fans. Lillie Hitchcock Coit was a *big* fan. Upon her death in 1929, she left a bequest of $125,000 to create a memorial to volunteer firefighters, and so in 1933

this phallic, 210-foot tower rose on Telegraph Hill. Inside are powerful murals celebrating the proletariat in the style of Diego Rivera (some of the artists actually trained under Rivera). Climb to the top of the tower for a spectacular 360-degree view of the city and the bay. ⏱ 30 min. 1 Telegraph Hill. ☎ 415/362-0808. Admission to top of tower $4.50. Daily 10am–6pm. Bus: 39.

❻ ★ Mario's Bohemian Cigar Store. Nothing conveys North Beach tradition like a meatball sandwich and a cup of coffee from this classic North Beach cafe, in business for more than a century. It has a great people-watching location in a slice-of-pie-shaped space across from Washington Square. And no, it's not a cigar bar. 566 Columbus Ave. ☎ 415/362-0536. Entrees $8–$10.

❼ ★★ North Beach. This was San Francisco's traditional Italian neighborhood, settled by fishing families from Sicily and Genoa, and where favorite son and baseball immortal Joe DiMaggio grew up. It's also where free-verse-spouting, bongo-playing Beats hung their berets in the 1950s; drop into the legendary **★★ City Lights Bookstore,** a literary landmark at 261 Columbus Ave. (☎ 415/362-8193; www.citylights.com). You can still hear the echoes of those long ago North Beach days, but mostly what you hear is the sound of a good time emanating from the numerous cafes and bars. Night or day, this place pulses with activity. ⏱ At least 1 hr. See p. 82.

❽ ★★ Chinatown. Chinatown is a busy, bustling microcosm unto itself; it's a riot of sight and sound, featuring fanciful Asian architecture, and vendors selling everything from cheap and tacky souvenirs to exquisite imported goods. This is the home of one of the country's largest Chinese communities, some 80,000 strong. At Washington Street make a right and then a quick left down **Waverly Place;** this colorful street is known as the "street of painted balconies," and it's where you'll find the **Tin How Temple,** a Buddhist sanctuary that's open to the public (daily 10am–4pm). ⏱ At least 1 hr. See p. 78.

SITE GUIDE

4 Fisherman's Wharf

Make a left on Beach Street, and you'll pass Ⓐ **Ghirardelli Square** (☎ 415/775-5500; www.ghirardellisq.com), a historic chocolate factory that's now a shopping center; at 900 Beach St. you'll find the ship-shaped Art Deco Ⓑ ★ **Maritime Museum** (☎ 415/561-7100; www.maritime.org)—be sure to pop in to check out the murals. The Maritime Museum also oversees a flotilla of historic ships nearby; you can get a closer look at them and the Golden Gate Bridge from the Ⓒ ★★ **Hyde Street Pier.** On Pier 45 you'll find the fascinating Ⓓ ★★ **Musée Mécanique** (☎ 415/346-2000; www.museemechanique.org), a privately owned collection of penny arcade machines. Ⓔ **PIER 39** (☎ 415/705-5500; www.pier39.com) is another shopping and entertainment complex. Its most interesting feature is a sea lion colony that hauls out to do a little catnapping on the docks. Up to 900 of these federally protected pinnipeds make their home here, although many depart for breeding grounds during the summer. ⊙ 2 hr. Beginning at Hyde and Beach sts. ☎ 415/674-7503. www.fishermanswharf.org.

Bus: 10, 30, 47, or 19. Cable car: Powell-Hyde line or Powell-Mason line.

The Best of San Francisco in 2 Days

Your second day in the city will focus on two things near and dear to San Franciscans: food and art. Throw in a little history out on Alcatraz Island, and you have yourself the makings of a memorable day.

> As if Alcatraz isn't eerie enough, take a twilight tour and get really creeped out.

START Alcatraz Landing at Pier 33. Take the F Market & Wharves streetcar to Bay St. station.

① ★★★ **Alcatraz Island.** Its name in Spanish refers to the shorebirds that nested here in the early 18th century, but most people know Alcatraz Island by its popular nickname, "the Rock." Sitting 1.5 miles offshore from San Francisco in the heart of the bay, the island functioned as a military installation from the mid-19th century (during the Civil War it was the largest fort west of the Mississippi) until 1934, when it came under civilian control and was transformed into the "prison within the prison system." This "escape-proof" location

was where the country's most dangerous and difficult prisoners were sent—among its notorious inmates were mobster Al Capone and bank robber and kidnapper George "Machine Gun" Kelly. In 1962, three jailbirds did, in fact, fly the coop (they were never found), and then the prison was shut down in 1963 for fiscal reasons. In 1969, Alcatraz was the site of further drama when Native American activists occupied the island for 18 months, reclaiming it as Indian land before they were expelled by the U.S. government. The island is now part of the Golden Gate National Recreation Area. ☉ 2½ hr. Alcatraz

1 Alcatraz Island
2 Ferry Building Marketplace
3 Hog Island Oyster Co.
4 San Francisco Museum of Modern Art (SFMOMA)
5 Yerba Buena Gardens
6 Contemporary Jewish Museum

Landing, Pier 33, Bay St. at the Embarcadero. ☎ 415/981-7625. www.alcatrazcruises.com or www.nps.gov/alcatraz. Admission (includes ferry) $26–$33 adults, $25–$31 seniors, $26–$32 kids 12–17, $16–$20 kids 5–11, free for kids 4 & under; family pack (2 adults & 2 kids 5–11) $79 for day tours only. Daily departures; check website for current ferry schedule. Arrive 20 min. prior to departure. Bus: 30. Cable car: Powell-Mason line. Streetcar: F.

❷ ★★★ **Ferry Building Marketplace.** Originally opened in 1898, the grand Beaux Arts Ferry Building was San Francisco's travel hub, the terminus for both trains and ferries. With its 245-foot clock tower, patterned after the

Alcatraz Essentials

There is only one concessionaire that operates ferries to Alcatraz, and during high season space may sell out more than a week in advance, so book early. For the purposes of this tour, try to get the first ferry and take the self-guided audio tour. Or invert the order and take the evening ferry (Thurs–Mon), which includes a guide and the pleasure of watching the sun setting behind the Golden Gate Bridge. *Note:* It can get cold and windy here any time of year, so dress appropriately; there are also steep hills on the island, so wear comfortable shoes.

> *Take your pick of über-fresh fruits, vegetables, and artisan foods at the Ferry Plaza Farmers Market.*

cathedral tower in Sevilla, Spain, it was also one of the city's proudest landmarks. Beautifully renovated and repurposed in 2003, the Ferry Building Marketplace features mosaic floors, terra-cotta arches, and a stunning 660-foot-long, sky-lit concourse laced with steel trusses.

What makes this project such a glowing success story, though, are the building's tenants—the ground floor of this mixed-use project is lined with gourmet food vendors, eateries, and foodie specialty stores. Graze your way from end to end or have a fabulous sit-down meal with bay views.

Every Tuesday, Thursday, and Saturday the ★★★ **Ferry Plaza Farmers Market** (☎ 415/291-3276; www.cuesa.org) sets up in the Ferry Building arcades and plaza, offering incredible bounty from all over the region; it's quite the scene, with literally thousands of people in attendance. There are free walking tours of the marketplace on Saturday and Tuesday at noon (www.sfcityguides.org). ☺ At least 1 hr. One Ferry Building. ☎ 415/983-8000. www. ferrybuildingmarketplace.com. Mon–Fri 10am–6pm; Sat 9am–6pm; Sun 11am–5pm. Restaurants

have later hours. Farmers Market Tues & Thurs 10am–2pm; Sat 8am–2pm. Bus: 30. Cable car: Powell-Mason line. Streetcar: F.

③ 🦪 ★★ **Hog Island Oyster Co.** They shuck 'em, you slurp 'em down at this stylishly contemporary oyster bar. It gets pretty crazy in here, especially at happy hour (Mon and Thurs 5–7pm), as folks happily consume fresh, locally farmed oysters and wash them down with champagne, beer, or wine. You'll also find salads, a great grilled cheese sandwich, and clam chowder on the menu. One Ferry Building. ☎ 415/391-7117. www.hogislandoysters. com. Half-dozen raw oysters $15–$17.

❹ ★★★ **San Francisco Museum of Modern Art (SFMOMA).** Founded in 1935, SFMOMA has resided in these imposing modern digs—highlighted by a massive cylindrical skylight—since 1995, and its collection includes more than 26,000 works of art, most of them created since 1900. The museum's roster of artists includes Constantin Brancusi, Henri Matisse, Olafur Eliasson, Frida Kahlo, Gordon

Matta-Clark, Jackson Pollock, and Andy Warhol; the museum also has one of Marcel Duchamp's seminal "fountains." An early flag bearer for the photography-as-art movement, SFMOMA has a very strong collection of photographic work; it also has film, sound, and computer-based pieces, video installations, furniture and graphic design, and installation architecture. Another plus: a rooftop sculpture garden with pieces by Alexander Calder and Louise Bourgeois. ⊙ At least 1 hr. 151 Third St. ☎ 415/357-4000. www.sfmoma.org. Admission $15 adults, $9 seniors and students, free for kids 12 & under with adult. Fri–Tues 11am–5:45pm; Thurs 11am–8:45pm (from 10am in summer). Bus: 14, 30, or 45. Streetcar: F, J, K, L, or M. BART: Montgomery.

➎ ★ **Yerba Buena Gardens.** The centerpiece of a redeveloped area of museums, galleries, and convention space, the Yerba Buena Gardens is a lovely oasis amid all the concrete. This landscaped 5½-acre park features a grassy meadow, butterfly-friendly gardens, and public art. There is a stirring monument to Dr. Martin Luther King, Jr., featuring 50-foot-high cascades of water, behind which is a walkway adorned with images and quotes from the civil rights leader. Another highlight is the androgynous robotic figure titled *Urge*. It is mounted atop a globe, and if you sit on the bench in front it—and weigh at least 130 pounds—the sculpture will sit, too; stand up and it follows suit. From May to October, nearly 100 free music, dance, theater, and children's productions are staged in the Esplanade (☎ 415/543-1718; www.ybgf.org). ⊙ 30 min. The gardens are bordered by Mission, Howard, Third & Fourth sts. ☎ 415/820-3550. www.yerbabuenagardens.com. Free admission. Daily 6am–10pm. Bus: 5, 9, 14, 30, or 45. Streetcar: F, J, K, L, or M. BART: Powell or Montgomery.

➏ ★★ **Contemporary Jewish Museum.** With Daniel Libeskind's incredible blue-steel formation grafted onto (and through) a classical revival brick building, originally built in 1881 as a power substation, the Contemporary Jewish Museum (CJM) is one of the city's top architectural wonders. Opened in 2008, the CJM space presents rotating exhibits exploring Jewish culture and history, and the structure itself is a work of art, a piece of abstract sculpture based upon the letters that make up the Hebrew expression "l'chaim" ("to life"). Even if the museum is closed, you can get detailed information on the building on a cellphone tour (no charge, except for your minutes), by calling ☎ 415/294-3605. ⊙ At least 15 min. 736 Mission St. ☎ 415/655-7800. www.thecjm.org. Admission $10 adults, $8 seniors and students, free for kids 18 & under; Thurs $5 after 5pm. Thurs 1–8:30pm; Fri–Tues 11am–5:30pm. Bus: 5, 9, 14, 30, or 45. Streetcar: F, J, K, L, or M. BART: Powell or Montgomery.

> *Walkways wind around fountains and pools at the expansive Yerba Buena Gardens.*

The Best of San Francisco in 3 Days

Day 3 gets you onto the amazing Golden Gate Bridge and into fabulous Golden Gate Park. From the park it's an easy walk into the Haight, where it's not so much about flashing back to the 1960s as it is flashing your credit card at one of its cool little boutiques. Finish your day at picture-perfect Alamo Square.

> *Still crazy after all these years, Haight-Ashbury hops with boutiques, bars, and head shops.*

START Palace of Fine Arts. Bus 28 to Richardson Ave. and Francisco St., walk a short distance to the north.

❶ ★★ **Palace of Fine Arts.** Start your day at one of the most serenely beautiful locations in San Francisco. Originally built for the Panama-Pacific International Exposition in 1915, this neoclassical rotunda was never intended to outlast the fair, but 33,000 signatures were gathered in support of saving the structure. With its Greco-Roman-inspired friezes,

towering columns, and reflective lagoon where swans and ducks glide by, you'll feel as if you're walking through a Maxfield Parrish painting. ⏲ 30 min. Bay and Lyon sts. Free admission. Daily 6am–10pm. Bus: 28 or 30.

❷ ★★★ **Golden Gate Bridge.** A study in graceful design, this iconic bridge was completed in 1937, at which point the *San Francisco Chronicle* described it as a "$35-million steel harp." With towers standing 746-feet high, it was the tallest structure west of New York's

1 Palace of Fine Arts
2 Golden Gate Bridge
3 Golden Gate Park
4 de Young Museum
5 California Academy of Sciences
6 Haight-Ashbury
7 Magnolia Gastropub & Brewery
8 Alamo Square

> *Bring bread to feed the swans swimming around the 1915 Palace of Fine Arts.*

Empire State Building, and the 4,200-foot main span of roadway is still one of the longest of any suspension bridge in the world. During its 4-year construction, 11 men were killed working on the project, 10 of them in one accident; 19 others were saved from a drop to the bay—which, depending on the tide, can be as much as 270 feet down—by a safety net strung from end to end below the bridge. Those survivors became known as the "Halfway to Hell Club."

The east sidewalk is open daily to pedestrians from 5am to 6pm (till 9pm in spring & summer); bicyclists have 24-hour access (they get buzzed in past the automatic gate). Even if you only walk to midspan, it's a spectacular sight, but be prepared for wind and cold. ⏱ At least 1 hr. Hwy. 101 N. ☎ 415/921-5858. www. goldengatebridge.org. $5 toll for southbound vehicles. Bus: 28.

❸ ★★★ Golden Gate Park. You could easily spend an entire day in this 1,017-acre playground, filled with museums, lakes, gardens, and sports facilities. Though it seems a slice of shady Northern California landscape, Golden Gate Park is actually man-made, created from an area comprised mostly of windswept sand dunes, a place locals ominously referred to as the "outside lands." By 1879, though, some 155,000 trees had been planted, and the park was embraced enthusiastically by the city. ⏱ At least 30 min. See p. 72. Administrative office: 501 Stanyan St. ☎ 415/831-2700. www. parks.sfgov.org. Mon–Fri 8am–5pm. Bus: 28.

❹ ★★★ de Young Museum. With its copper sheathing and twisting tower, this venerable museum's highly contemporary space resembles an abstract fort. You'll either be blown away by it or wonder when they're going to finish it. Founded in 1895 (the new building dates from 2005), the de Young has a vast collection of American paintings, as well as sculpture and decorative art, and evocative pieces from Africa, the Americas, and Oceania. It also hosts blockbuster exhibitions. Climb the 144-foot tower at the museum's northeast corner for a killer view; it's accessed from the lobby and is free. As you enter the museum, note Andy Goldsworthy's site-specific Drawn Stone, a continuous crack that runs through the stone courtyard. Also be sure to check out the de Young's adjacent sculpture garden. ⏱ 45 min. 50 Hagiwara Tea Garden Dr. ☎ 415/750-3600. www.famsf.org/deyoung. Admission $10 adults, $7 seniors, $6 students and kids 13–17, free for kids 12 & under (special exhibitions are extra). Tues–Sun 9:30am–5:15pm; Fri 9:30am–8:45pm (mid-Jan to Nov). Bus: 28.

❺ ★★★ California Academy of Sciences. This overachieving facility is a planetarium, aquarium, and natural history museum all in one, and its $500-million home, designed by architect Renzo Piano, is something special. The academy, which was established in 1853, opened its new space in 2008; it features a rainforest enclosure with 1,600 critters, including 600 free-flying birds and butterflies, a T-Rex skeleton, a colony of penguins, wildlife dioramas, a living coral reef, and an albino alligator. Topping it off, literally, is the building's amazing living roof, an undulating 2½-acre garden of native plants and flowers. ⏱ 2 hr.

55 Concourse Dr. ☎ 415/379-8000. www.cal academy.org. Admission $25 adults; $20 seniors, students, and kids 12–17; $15 kids 7–11; free for kids 6 & under. Mon–Sat 9:30am–5pm; Sun 11am–5pm. Bus: 28.

⑥ ★★ Haight-Ashbury. Simply referred to as the Haight, this neighborhood was put on the map in the 1960s by hippies and local bands like the Grateful Dead and Jefferson Airplane. It was the perceived heart of a counterculture revolution and the Summer of Love, but the times they went a-changin', and now it's a bustling commercial district where you'll find about 6 blocks worth of shopping, dining, and drinking. Oh, it's still a little bit funky, and there are plenty of places to buy a bong, but these days the Haight is more about fashion than revolution. ☺ At least 1 hr. Bus: 6, 7, 66, or 71.

---

⑦ 🍺 ★ Magnolia Gastropub & Brewery. Beware (or embrace) the Grateful Dead tunes you may hear on the sound system, but the upscale bar fare—along with the excellent brews created—deserves only your love. There are house-made sausages and charcuterie, a nice selection of cheeses, and munchies like Devils on Horseback (goat cheese–stuffed dates wrapped in bacon) and quail eggs with stone-ground mustard aioli. 1398 Haight St. ☎ 415/864-7468. www. magnoliapub.com. Entrees $11–$20.

⑧ ★ Alamo Square. If your timing is good, the setting sun will be casting the Seven Sisters in an oh-so-flattering glow. You're bound to recognize the scene here—seven Painted-Lady Victorian homes lined up in a row, anchoring a cityscape view that has been captured in countless photos, films, and TV shows. Take a walk around this small, hilltop park, popular with neighborhood folks and their pooches, and soak in the beauty of the Alamo Square Historic District. Be sure to look down Fulton Street on the park's north side for a great view of the gilded city hall. ☺ 30 min. Bordered by Scott, Fulton, Hayes, and Steiner sts. Bus: 21.

> *Duck for fish at the California Academy of Sciences, where you can walk beneath a rainforest river.*

San Francisco for Museum Lovers

While Golden Gate Park is home to two of the city's major museums, the California Academy of Sciences (p. 64, **5**) and the de Young (p. 64, **4**), it's actually the redeveloped SoMa (South of Market) area adjacent to downtown that has become San Francisco's cultural heart. For those who can't get enough of museums, SoMa's museum district makes it possible to indulge in a daylong binge of art, culture, and history—and it's all accessible on foot. *Note:* If you do plan on museum hopping, look into getting discount passes (p. 128).

> *Go down memory lane at San Francisco's Cartoon Art Museum, where you can try your hand at animation.*

START Cartoon Art Museum. Bus: 14, 30, or 45. Streetcar: F, J, K, L, or M. BART: Montgomery St. station.

① ★ **Cartoon Art Museum (CAM).** Boys and girls will want to make a beeline to this small museum that celebrates cartooning, illustration, digital animation, and video games. From Dr. Seuss and Charles Schulz to contemporary anime and manga, rotating exhibitions highlight the history, the creators, and the processes involved in producing these works of popular art. CAM also offers weekend workshops and drop-in classes in animation and illustration, as well as occasional guest-artist book signings and opening receptions. ⏱ 30 min. 655 Mission St. ☎ 415/227-8666. www.cartoonart.org. Tues–Sun 11am–5pm. Admission

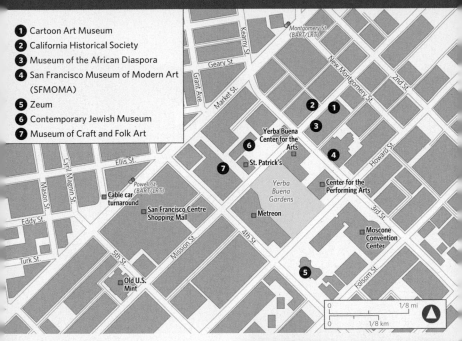

1. Cartoon Art Museum
2. California Historical Society
3. Museum of the African Diaspora
4. San Francisco Museum of Modern Art (SFMOMA)
5. Zeum
6. Contemporary Jewish Museum
7. Museum of Craft and Folk Art

$6 adults, $4 seniors and students, $2 kids 6–12, free for kids 5 & under. Bus: 14, 30, or 45. Streetcar: F, J, K, L, or M. BART: Montgomery.

② **California Historical Society.** This research library, gallery, and museum store presides over a vast collection of fine art, photography, books, posters, pamphlets, and other ephemera documenting California's rich history. Gallery exhibits rotate regularly and might focus on subjects from landscape painting to California presidential candidates; you are welcome to browse through the library as well. ⏱ **30 min.** 678 Mission St. ☎ 415/357-1848. www. californiahistoricalsociety.org. Admission $3 adults, $1 seniors and students, free for kids 5 & under. Galleries Wed–Sat noon–4:30pm; library Wed–Fri noon–5pm. Bus: 14, 30, or 45. Streetcar: F, J, K, L, or M. BART: Montgomery.

③ **Museum of the African Diaspora.** This gleaming modern museum with its three-story glass atrium focuses on the influence of African art, culture, and history around the globe, and particularly in the United States. Permanent, interactive exhibitions highlight culinary and musical traditions, as well as ceremonies and rituals; slave narratives and images of the African Diaspora are particularly moving.

> Add some Calder style to your home with a mobile from SFMOMA's gift store.

The museum also hosts traveling exhibitions, special events, workshops, and lectures. ⏱ 30 min. 685 Mission St. ☎ 415/358-7200. www. moadsf.org. Admission $10 adults, $5 seniors and students, free for kids 12 & under. Wed–Sat 11am–6pm. Bus: 14, 30, or 45. Streetcar: F, J, K, L, or M. BART: Montgomery.

④ ★★★ **San Francisco Museum of Modern Art (SFMOMA).** Housed in a modernist building designed by Swiss architect Mario Botta, this was the West Coast's first museum dedicated to artworks of the 20th century.

> *The abstract exterior of the Contemporary Jewish Museum is itself a work of art.*

SFMOMA's huge collection spans a myriad number of media, from painting and scupture to photography (a major highlight here) and design. There's also a great gift shop and a full roster of lectures, events, and films. Free self-guided audio tours and free docent tours are available and will do much to add to your enjoyment of the experience. ⊕ At least 1 hr. See p. 60, ④.

⑤ ★ kids **Zeum.** Unleash your child's creativity (or your own) at this interactive media arts and technology facility. Kids can make their own claymation short film, a music video, or produce a piece of digital art—and take it home with them. Small children will be most amused by the 1906 Charles Looff carousel. ⊕ 1 hr. 221 Fourth St. ☎ 415/820-3320. www. zeum.com. Admission $10 adults; $8 seniors, students, and ages 3–18, free for kids 2 & under. Carousel $3 for 2 rides. Museum Wed–Fri 1–5pm; Sat–Sun 11am–5pm. Carousel daily 11am–6pm. Bus: 8X, 12, 30, 45, or 76.

⑥ ★★ **Contemporary Jewish Museum.** Originally founded in 1984 (though its current $47.5-million building opened in 2008), this museum seeks to explore Jewish history, art, music, and culture. There's no permanent collection; rotating exhibitions here have focused on everything from writing a Torah to the works of Maurice Sendak. The gift shop has a decent selection of Judaica for sale. ⊕ 1 hr. See p. 61, ⑥.

⑦ ★ **Museum of Craft and Folk Art.** This tiny museum displays contemporary and traditional crafts from around the world— everything from origami to Shaker furniture. There's also a cool gift shop. ⊕ 30 min. 51 Yerba Buena Lane. ☎ 415/227-4888. www.mocfa. org. Admission $5 adults, $4 seniors, free for ages 18 & under. Thurs–Tues 11am–6pm; Sat–Sun 11am–5pm; first Tues of the month 11am–7:30pm. Bus: 5, 9, 14, 30, or 45. Streetcar: F, J, K, L, or M. BART: Powell.

More Museums

San Francisco's museum scene extends beyond SoMa and Golden Gate Park. If you have more than the day this tour takes to explore the local museum offerings, the following are some of the worthwhile institutions spread throughout the city.

Both kids and adults will be engaged by the ★★★ **Exploratorium,** 3601 Lyon St., Marina (☎ 415/397-5673 or 415/561-0360; www. exploratorium.edu). This innovative fun house puts principles of science, technology, and perception into clever, interactive action. *Note:* As of this writing, the Exploratorium is located at the Palace of Fine Arts, but it's expected to move to Pier 15/17 on the Embarcadero in 2012; call ahead for details.

The free ★ **Cable Car Museum** (pictured above), 1201 Mason St., Nob Hill (☎ 415/ 474-1887; www.cablecarmuseum.org), details the development of the city's singular form of transportation. It's also the working heart of the system, where you can observe the massive winches and pulleys in action.

The ★ **Asian Art Museum,** 200 Larkin St., Civic Center (☎ 415/581-3500; www.asian art.org), displays a collection that spans 6,000 years of Asian art and culture in a beautiful space that combines Beaux Arts and contemporary architecture.

The multisite ★ **San Francisco Maritime National Historical Park,** near Fisherman's Wharf (☎ 415/447-5000; www.nps.gov/ safr), features a flotilla of historic ships

along the Hyde Street Pier that you can board and tour (including the 19th-century square-rigger *Balclutha*). The Bathhouse building, 900 Beach St., shaped like an Art Deco ocean liner, is home to the park's **Maritime Museum;** the **Visitor Center** at 499 Jefferson St. also has exhibits relating the city's maritime history.

The ★ **Walt Disney Family Museum,** 104 Montgomery St., Presidio (☎ 415/345-6800; www.waltdisney.org), opened in 2009 and goes into thorough detail about the life, times, and genius of Walt Disney (1901–66). The museum also presents films, concerts, lectures, and animation workshops. *Note:* Though children probably won't feel the Disney magic here, the gift shop will likely get their attention.

The grand, neoclassical ★★ **Legion of Honor** (☎ 415/750-3600; www.famsf.org/ legion) has a spectacular Land's End setting in Lincoln Park (34th Ave. and Clement St.), and has a collection of European masterworks stretching from the 14th to the 20th century, as well as treasures from the ancient world.

Animal lovers may want to check out the **Aquarium of the Bay** at PIER 39 along the Embarcadero (☎ 888/732-3483 or 415/623-5300; www.aquariumofthebay.org) or the **San Francisco Zoo** (☎ 415/753-7080; www. sfzoo.org), located along the coast at Great Highway and Sloat Boulevard.

SHAKE RATTLE & ROLL

Why San Francisco really rocks in an earthquake

BY HARRIOT MANLEY

SAN FRANCISCO'S MOST JARRING BRAND OF ROCK AND ROLL? EARTHQUAKES. The city's catastrophic 1906 quake and fires killed over 1,000 people, and the 1989 Loma Prieta temblor cleaved the Bay Bridge in two. What makes the ground so lively here? Along the coast here, two tectonic plates—literally chunks of the earth's crust—meet at the San Andreas Fault. These plates usually shift in a benign process called "creep." But when plates get hung up, pressure builds, and boom—a devastating earthquake ensues. The key to predicting quakes would seem to lie in identifying pressure points and knowing when they'll jolt free, still a mystery to scientists. Some studies track time between quakes (fewer quakes could mean mounting pressure); other research looks for physical or chemical clues or other signals—even whether or not animals can detect earthquakes before humans.

Damage Control

Structural designs can help reduce destruction caused by a serious quake. To test new devices, scientists build scale models and jostle them on shake tables, which mimic earthquakes. Here are key designs that pass the shake test:

BASE ISOLATORS: These isolate the building from the earth's movement. Some isolators look like giant squishy hockey pucks that sit under the building. Others consist of giant friction-less plates, one attached to the building, one to the foundation, allowing the ground to lurch and slide beneath the building without jolting the structure.

ENERGY-DISSIPATING DEVICES: Think of these as shock absorbers for buildings, reducing damage by reducing shaking. Dissipators can use liquid pistons, springs, or other energy absorbing materials.

RETROFITS: On existing structures, engineers can install beefed-up supports and other devices to reduce damage. (The Golden Gate Bridge's multi-year seismic retrofit, now underway, is expected to top $500 million.)

SHEAR WALLS: One of the most common devices, these stiffened walls convert horizontal forces striking the building and transfer them to the structure's foundation.

Slip-Sliding Away

When two chunks of the earth's crust move past one another, that's an earthquake. Where they meet is called a fault line, and how the earth moves there can create different kinds of quakes.

STRIKE-SLIP FAULT Movement is lateral (sideways).

DIP-SLIP FAULT Also called normal or reverse fault; the movement here is vertical.

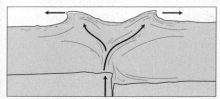

THRUST FAULT Movement is vertical, deep beneath the sea, leading to earthquake-induced tidal waves, or tsunamis.

Golden Gate Park

This verdant, beautifully landscaped greenbelt, the third-most-visited city park in the United States, stretches from the Haight to Ocean Beach. Its numerous museums, gardens, sports facilities, and attractions make it San Francisco's beloved backyard.

> Step into a magic world of head-high ferns, Venus flytraps, and orchids in the Conservatory of Flowers.

START **Fell and Stanyan sts. Bus 5 or 21.**

❶ McLaren Lodge and Park Headquarters. Pick up a park map and detailed park info at this lodge, built in 1896. The beautiful stone building was the home of John McLaren (1846–1943), the godfather of Golden Gate Park. A Scotsman who studied horticulture at the Edinburgh Royal Botanical Gardens, McLaren became park superintendent in 1887 and was so beloved he held the position for 53 years, until his death at age 96. Amazingly, McLaren was able to create this verdant, beautifully landscaped park out of a desolate, windswept area of sand dunes, which early residents of the city called the "outside lands." It's estimated McLaren planted some 2 million trees over his lifetime; he also vigorously opposed any deployment of "keep off the grass" signs. ⏱15 min. 501 Stanyan St. ☎ 415/831-2700. www.parks.sfgov.org. Mon–Fri 8am–5pm.

② ★ Hippie Hill. If you're looking for that Summer of Love vibe, you just might find it (or at least the millennial version of it) at this meadow and hillside near the park's eastern edge. Just about any afternoon, especially if the weather is nice, you'll find a drum circle in action, a hacky sack flying, and the scent of ganja wafting on the breeze. Hippie Hill does attract what you might politely refer to as "characters," but the crowd tends to be mellow and friendly; John McLaren would certainly approve of the lollygagging that goes on here. Look for the solitary tree along the path at the bottom of the hill; it's referred to as Janis Joplin's tree, and is supposedly a spot where the hard-living singer liked to hang out. ⊕ 30 min. Located south of John F. Kennedy Dr., just east of the tennis courts.

③ ★ kids Koret Children's Quarter and Carousel. This wonderful play area for kids is actually historic—it's considered the country's first public playground, opened in 1887. There's been a carousel here since the beginning, too, although the colorful merry-go-round in operation now dates from 1912 (and was originally steam powered). The other popular attraction is the concrete slide, where children can whoosh down on a piece of cardboard. **Note:** Adults need to be accompanied by children to play on the equipment. ⊕ 30 min. Kezar Dr. (at First Ave.). ☎ 415/831-2774. Carousel admission $2 adults, $1 kids 6–12, free for kids 5 & under with paying adult. Fri–Sun (daily in summer) 10am–4:30pm.

④ ★★ Conservatory of Flowers. Looking as intricate and proper as a lace doily, this stunning structure was shipped in crates piece by piece from Europe. This historic landmark was finally put together and opened to the public in 1879 and is the oldest wood and glass conservatory in North America. Battered by a series of storms from 1995 to 1996, the conservatory

> *While the elegant Japanese Tea Garden is always magnificent, spring brings an explosion of cherry blossoms and azaleas.*

was forced to shut down, but a $25-million restoration completed in 2003 got it back on its feet again. In its five galleries you can find a living museum of wondrous and exotic plants and flowers, including giant Amazon water lilies, delicate orchids, and carnivorous Venus flytraps. ⊕ 30 min. 100 John F. Kennedy Dr. ☎ 415/831-2090. www.conservatoryofflowers. org. Admission $7 adults, $5 seniors and kids 12–17, $2 kids 5–11. Tues–Sun 9am–5pm (last entry at 4:30pm).

Summer Shuttle

On summer weekends, a shuttle runs from the Ocean Beach parking lot along the Great Highway (look for the green sign) to stops throughout Golden Gate Park from 9am to 6pm. The cost is $2 for a round-trip ticket and shuttles come every 15 to 20 minutes.

Golden Gate Park

Balboa St.
48th Ave.
46th Ave.
44th Ave.
42nd Ave.
40th Ave.
38th Ave.
36th Ave.
34th Ave.
32nd Ave.
30th Ave.
28th Ave.
26th Ave.
24th Ave.
Fulton St.

Great Hwy.

11

North L.

Spreckels Lake

10

Golden Gate
Park Stables

Portals of
the Past

12

Golden Gate Park
Golf Course

Flycasting
Pools

Stadium/
Polo Grounds

Urban
Forestry
Center

Soccer
Fields

John F. Kennedy Dr.

Middle L.

Metson L.

no through traffic

Murphy
Windmill

Middle Dr. West

South L.

Martin Luther King Jr. Dr.

Mallard L.

Ocean Beach

La Playa St.
47th Ave.
45th Ave.
43rd Ave.
41st Ave.
39th Ave.
Sunset Blvd.
35th Ave.
33rd Ave.
31st Ave.
29th Ave.
27th Ave.
25th Ave.

Lincoln Wy.

Irving St.

Judah St.

Kirkham St.

0   1/2 mi
0   1/2 km

⑤ San Francisco Botanical Garden at Strybing Arboretum. Spread over 55 acres, there are more than 7,500 different species of plants growing here, representing habitats ranging from a coastal California redwood forest to a Southeast Asian cloud forest; you'll also find gardens featuring ancient plants, succulents, rhododendrons, and magnolias. The specimens are continually rotated in order to display plants and flowers as they reach their peak bloom. ⏱ 30 min. Ninth Ave. (at Lincoln Way). ☎ 415/661-1316. www.sfbotanicalgarden.org. Free admission. Mon–Fri 8am–4:30pm, Sat–Sun 10am–5pm. Free guided tours Mon,Tues & Thurs 1:30pm; Wed & Fri 1:30 and 2pm; Sat 10:30am & 1:30pm; Sun 10:30am, 1:30pm, & 2pm..

⑥ ★★ Japanese Tea Garden. One of the park's most popular sights, this beautifully contemplative and authentic attraction is the oldest public Japanese garden in the United States. It was created in 1894 for the California Midwinter International Exposition, designed by landscaper Makoto Hagiwara (d. 1925), who also lived here with his family (who were eventually

> *Portholes in the undulating roof of the California Academy of Sciences open to adjust temperatures for the towering rainforest within.*

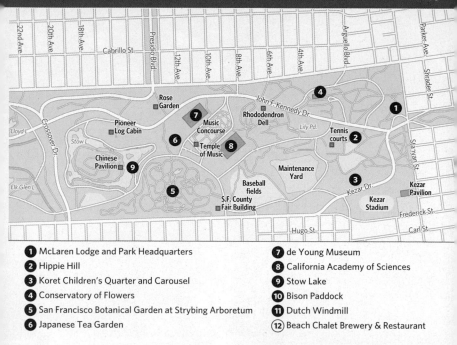

1 McLaren Lodge and Park Headquarters
2 Hippie Hill
3 Koret Children's Quarter and Carousel
4 Conservatory of Flowers
5 San Francisco Botanical Garden at Strybing Arboretum
6 Japanese Tea Garden
7 de Young Museum
8 California Academy of Sciences
9 Stow Lake
10 Bison Paddock
11 Dutch Windmill
12 Beach Chalet Brewery & Restaurant

interned with other Japanese Americans during World War II). Hagiwara's fame extends beyond this garden with its ponds, bridges, and pagodas—visitors to his home were treated to a novelty tea cake that, within its folds, had a slip of paper with a message written on it. Yup, the fortune cookie was born right here in a Japanese teahouse in Golden Gate Park. ⏱30 min. 7 Hagiwara Tea Garden Dr. ☎ 415/752-4227. www.japaneseteagardensf.com. Admission $5 adults, $3 seniors and kids 12–17, $1.50 kids 5–11. Free admission Mon, Wed & Fri before 10am. Daily 9am–4:45pm (summer till 6pm).

7 ★★★ de Young Museum. Another piece of distinctive architecture within the park, the de Young has one of the country's top caches of American painting. The collection features work dating from Colonial times right up to the present day; highlights include masterworks by John Singer Sargent, Thomas Eakins, Edward Hopper, and Georgia O'Keeffe. There's also an outstanding collection of totems, carvings, and masks from Papua New Guinea and New Zealand, as well as rotating exhibitions. ⏱1 hr. See p. 64, 4.

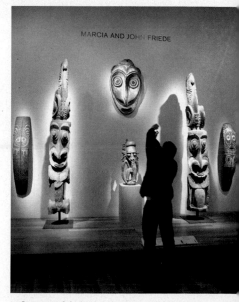

> Get an eyeful of art at the de Young Museum, known for everything from Old World masters to Maori masks.

> *Spend a lazy day on Stow Lake, where you can rent paddleboats and rowboats.*

8 ★★★ **California Academy of Sciences.** Nature lovers won't want to miss this amazing facility, which features a planetarium, aquarium, and natural history museum—all under one garden-growing roof. You'll also find a 3-D theater, a four-story rainforest enclosure, and a fine-dining restaurant open for lunch and dinner. ⏱ At least 1 hr. See p. 64, **5**.

9 **Stow Lake.** The largest body of water in the park surrounds Strawberry Hill, the park's highest point. You can circumnavigate the island in a rowboat or pedal boat, or cross the bridge and take a walk to the top of the 430-foot hill, which features a colorful Chinese pavilion along its shore. The rowboat is good fun, though it may be slightly humiliating when you can't figure out how to row straight. There's also a bike concessionaire in the park with a variety of two- and four-wheeled options; bikes are a great way to explore the park,

especially on Sunday when JFK Drive is closed to automobile traffic from Stanyan Street to Transverse Drive. From April to September, this road is also closed on Saturday from Tea Garden Drive to Transverse Drive. ⏱ 1 hr. Stow Lake Boathouse, 50 Stow Lake Dr. ☎ 415/752-0347. Rowboat $19 per hr.; pedal boat $24 per hr. Daily 10am–4pm. Wheel Fun Rentals ☎ 415/668-6699. www.wheelfunrentals.com. Cruiser and mountain bikes $8 per hr.; tandem $12 per hr. Mon–Fri 10am–5pm; Sat–Sun 9am–5pm.

10 **Bison Paddock.** Bison, North America's largest land mammal, were on the brink of extinction in the 19th century. In an effort to establish a breeding program, the park commission acquired a small herd in 1891, and the descendants of those original buffalo have been living in this paddock since 1899. ⏱ 15 min. On John F. Kennedy Dr.

> *The descendants of a 19th-century herd of American bison, originally assembled as a species conservation effort, graze in Bison Paddock.*

⑪ ★ Dutch Windmill. More than just a whimsical decoration, this windmill was built in 1903 and harnessed the ocean winds to pump irrigation water throughout the park. Once an electrical pump system was incorporated, though, it and the Murphy Windmill completed in 1908, became obsolete and decayed with neglect. The Dutch Windmill has been lovingly renovated (the Murphy still awaits its restoration), and is located next to the Queen Wilhelmina Tulip Garden, which bursts into colorful life in spring. ⏱ 15 min. At John F. Kennedy Dr. & Great Hwy.

⑫ 🍺 ★ Beach Chalet Brewery & Restaurant. A welcome oasis of house-crafted beer, cocktails, and modern American cuisine, the Beach Chalet features awesome ocean views. The back area, known as the Park Chalet, is a great spot to soak up some sun—or warm yourself by the fire. 1000 Great Hwy. ☎ 415/386-8439. www.beachchalet.com. Entrees $13–$29 Beach Chalet, $9–$15 Park Chalet.

> *Head to the Dutch windmill in spring, when it's flanked by beds of—naturally—tulips.*

Chinatown

You'll be forgiven if you think you have somehow been magically transported to Hong Kong the moment you step through the dragon archway leading into Chinatown. One of San Francisco's most enduring attractions, this is the largest Chinatown outside of Asia and the oldest in North America. Some estimates put the Chinese population in this area of the city as high as 200,000—the official U.S. Census count is half that, but there is no doubt this 16-block portion of the neighborhood bustles and buzzes with activity and frenetic energy.

> Like a mini–Hong Kong, Chinatown's Grant Avenue dazzles with bright lights, crowded sidewalks, and unidentifiable foods on the menus.

START **Bush St. and Grant Ave. Bus 30.**

❶ **Chinatown Gate.** Chinatown is essentially bordered by Broadway and Bush Street to the north and south, and Stockton and Kearny streets to the west and east, respectively. The neighborhood is formally accessed from the south on Grant Avenue, through a decorative ceremonial archway (aka the Dragon Gate), donated by the Taiwanese government in 1969. Guarded on either side by a pair of stone lions and crowned with golden dragons,

the gateway features a quote from Chinese nationalist hero Dr. Sun Yat-sen (1866–1925): "All under heaven is for the good of the people." **Bush St. & Grant Ave.**

❷ **Grant Avenue.** This is one of the oldest streets in Chinatown, originally named in 1845 as Calle de la Fundación (Foundation St.), and is the main tourist drag. You'll find shops filled with touristy schlock as well as imported treasures—there are places selling everything from kites to woks to Chinese herbs. And there are plenty of restaurants, too.

0 ___ 1/8 mi
0 ___ 1/8 km

1. Chinatown Gate
2. Grant Avenue
3. St. Mary's Square
4. Old St. Mary's Cathedral
5. Waverly Place
6. Tin How Temple
7. Golden Gate Fortune Cookie Co.
8. Stockton Street
9. Chinese Historical Society of America Museum
10. United Commercial Bank
11. Portsmouth Square
12. Chinese Culture Center
13. R&G Lounge

Make a right on Pine St.

3 St. Mary's Square. Towering in the square is a modernist sculpture of Dr. Sun Yat-sen, the beloved Chinese revolutionary leader who helped topple the last imperial dynasty. Looking serenely bulletproof, this stainless steel and red-granite statue was created by noted sculptor Beniamino Bufano in 1938. Pine St., at Quincy St.

Continue through the square to California St. and turn left.

4 ★ Old St. Mary's Cathedral. "Son, observe the time and fly from evil." So sayeth the inscription on the tower of California's first cathedral. This still-active Roman Catholic Church was dedicated in 1854 and was the city's most notable building at the time. It presided over a rough-and-tumble neighborhood that became so dangerous church fathers felt it necessary to relocate the cathedral to a less notorious spot. So in 1881, St. Mary's was demoted from cathedral to parish church, and a new cathedral was established elsewhere. Fly from evil, indeed. ⊙ 15 min. 660 California St. ☎ 415/288-3800. www.oldsaintmarys.org. Mass Mon–Fri 7:30am & noon; Sat noon & 5pm; Sun 8:30 & 11am. Classical concerts Tues 12:30pm ($10 suggested donation).

Go up Grant Ave., make a left on Sacramento St., and then a right down Waverly Place, on the north side of the street.

5 Waverly Place. This colorful and evocative side street, renovated by the city in 2006, is known as "the street of painted balconies." Most of the tenants here are family associations and temples, so the buildings are not open to the public, with one wonderful exception, the Tim How Temple.

6 ★ Tin How Temple. Through an inconspicuous doorway and up three flights of stairs you will find this Buddhist temple, which wholeheartedly welcomes visitors. Grateful immigrants who survived the long overseas journey to America dedicated this temple to the deity Mazu in 1852. Mazu, who is also referred to as Tin How (Heavenly Queen), is the protector of seafarers and is often depicted guiding ships to safety with a red lantern. If you are so inclined, you can shake out a divinity stick from a cup, a fortune-telling ritual that may reveal your lot in life. No photography is allowed; it's polite to leave a donation. ⊙ 30

> *What's your fortune? Find out in the city's last fortune cookie bakery, Golden Gate Fortune Cookies Co.*

min. 125 Waverly Place. Free admission; donation suggested. Daily 10am–4pm.

From Waverly Place, turn left on Washington St. and go right down Ross Alley, on the north side of the street.

7 ★ **Golden Gate Fortune Cookies Co.** Ross Alley was once the most disreputable street in Chinatown, filled with brothels and gambling dens. Now it features cookies. This is the last place in the city where fortune cookies are still made the old-fashioned way, and you can get an up-close look at the nimble handwork it

takes. You can also buy a bag of freshly made cookies to go. Check out the dignified, slice-of-life murals in the alley, as well. 56 Ross Alley. ☎ 415/781-3956. Daily 8am–8pm.

Return to Washington St., make a right and then a left down Stockton St.

8 **Stockton Street.** A stroll down Stockton Street will give you a taste of Chinatown's day-to-day, nontouristy side. This is where locals do their shopping for live frogs and eels and other exotic foodstuffs, medicinal herbs and roots, and all the other mundane necessities of life.

Go right on Clay St.

9 ★ Chinese Historical Society of America Museum. This small museum has a fascinating permanent exhibit detailing the Chinese immigrant experience through documents, photographs, and artifacts. The museum is housed in a beautiful building designed as a YWCA in 1932 by Julia Morgan (1872–1957), who's best known as the architect of Hearst Castle (p. 354, **1**). ⏱ 30 min. 965 Clay St. ☎ 415/391-1188. www.chsa.org. Admission $3 adults, $2 seniors and students, $1 kids 6–17, free for kids 5 & under; free first Thurs of the month. Tues–Fri noon–5pm.

Head back down Clay St. and go left on Grant Ave., then right on Washington St.

10 ★ United Commercial Bank. This, the oldest Asian-style building in Chinatown, dates from 1909 and was originally a telephone exchange. This part of San Francisco was completely destroyed in the 1906 earthquake, and as plans were drawn up for rebuilding, city officials intended to relocate the Chinese slum to the outskirts of the city. Chinatown businessmen moved fast, though, and began creating fantastical, idealized architecture—including colorful pagodas like this one—that would be sure to lure tourists and convince bureaucrats to let Chinatown remain where it was. And so from the rubble of a ghetto rose one of the city's most popular attractions. 743 Washington St.

Continue on Washington St. to Portsmouth Square.

11 Portsmouth Square. This is the heart of the neighborhood, a place for children to play and old men to gamble. On July 9, 1846, Capt. John Montgomery, commander of the USS *Portsmouth,* raised the American flag on this square, signaling that Yerba Buena (soon to be renamed San Francisco) was part of the United States. The square also features a tribute to *Treasure Island* author Robert Louis Stevenson, who was said to have whiled away his San Francisco hours here; and a bronze replica of the *Goddess of Democracy,* the inspirational sculpture erected by Chinese students at Tiananmen Square in 1989. **Bordered by Washington, Kearny & Clay sts. and Walter U. Lum Place.**

> *Nicknamed "the street of painted balconies," Waverly Place beckons with fluttering flags and the Tin How Temple.*

Go through the square and cross Kearny St. to the Hilton Hotel.

12 ★ Chinese Culture Center. This important community resource presents unique and surprisingly adventurous art and culture exhibits, as well as events, workshops, and classes. ⏱ 30 min. Inside the Hilton Hotel, 750 Kearny St., 3rd Floor. ☎ 415/986-1822. www.c-c-c.org. Free admission. Tues–Sat 10am–4pm.

Continue down Kearny St., past Clay St. to R&G Lounge.

13 🍴 ★ R&G Lounge. This popular spot is more upscale than most of the neighborhood joints. Anthony Bourdain devoured one of the signature deep-fried salt-and-pepper crabs on his TV show, but you can also content yourself with inexpensive rice-plate lunch specials ($6) or the flash-fried Special Beef dish, and a lychee martini. 631 Kearny St. ☎ 415/982-7877. www.rnglounge.com. Entrees $11–$60.

North Beach

Once the heart of San Francisco's immigrant Italian fishing community, North Beach later gained notoriety as the stomping grounds of Beat movement heroes such as Jack Kerouac and Allen Ginsberg. The neighborhood retains a strong independent streak and is popular with both locals and visitors for its lively cafes, bars, and clubs. And despite its name, you won't find a beach here—a finger of the bay did originally extend this far, but it was filled in long ago.

> Something old, something new: the copper-clad 1907 Columbus Tower, home to Coppola's American Zoetrope Studios, flanks the Transamerica Pyramid.

START Washington St. and Columbus Ave. Bus 1.

❶ ★ **Transamerica Pyramid.** With its needlelike spire, this is one of the city's most instantly recognizable landmarks. Completed in 1972, it's 48 stories tall and tops out at more than 850 feet. Check out the building's small Redwood Park and look for the commemorative plaque celebrating Bummer and Lazarus, two stray dogs who were the toast of the town in the 1860s for their prodigious rat-catching abilities. When Bummer passed away in 1865, even Mark Twain eulogized him in print: "The old vagrant 'Bummer' is really dead at last . . . he died full of years, and honor, and disease, and fleas." 600 block of Montgomery St.

Head straight down Columbus Ave., to Kearny St.

❷ ★ **Columbus Tower.** Originally known as the Sentinel building, this green-hued, copper-clad flatiron was completed in 1907. A corrupt political boss was the original top-floor tenant, but most of the building is occupied now by Francis Ford Coppola's American Zoetrope Studios. Coppola bought and renovated the building in 1972, the year *The Godfather* was released. The ground floor bistro, ★ **Cafe Zoetrope,** features wine from the director's ★★★ **Rubicon Estate** winery (p. 146). 916 Kearny St.

Continue on Columbus Ave., past Pacific Ave.; on the left-hand side of the street, at Jack Kerouac St., is Vesuvio.

❸ ★ **Vesuvio.** You are now entering the Beat movement's fertile crescent, starting with this

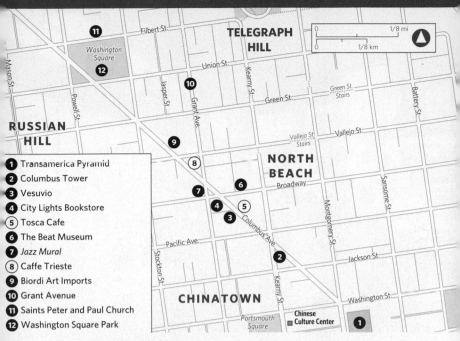

1. Transamerica Pyramid
2. Columbus Tower
3. Vesuvio
4. City Lights Bookstore
5. Tosca Cafe
6. The Beat Museum
7. *Jazz Mural*
8. Caffe Trieste
9. Biordi Art Imports
10. Grant Avenue
11. Saints Peter and Paul Church
12. Washington Square Park

saloon, first opened in 1948. In the mid-1950s it became the unofficial clubhouse for writers, poets, and bohemians like Jack Kerouac and Neal Cassady. Hey, the place opens at 6am, you're here—why not have a drink? What would Jack Kerouac do? 255 Columbus Ave. ☎ 415/362-3370. www.vesuvio.com. Daily 6–2am.

Cross the alley to City Lights.

❹ ★★ **City Lights Bookstore.** Lawrence Ferlinghetti and Peter D. Martin founded this bookstore in 1953; 2 years later they started up a publishing house. The bookstore became a salon for writers and creative types of all stripes; the publishing house sent their howl worldwide. ⏱ At least 30 min. 261 Columbus Ave. ☎ 415/362-8193. www.citylights.com. Daily 10am–midnight.

Cross to the other side of Columbus Ave.

❺ 🍷 ★ **Tosca Cafe.** If you're making this an evening stroll, take the chill off with a house cappuccino (actually a hot choco-late with brandy) at this charming, old-school bar, which has been operating here since 1919. 242 Columbus Ave. ☎ 415/986-9651. www.toscacafesf.com. Items $5–$10.

Continue on Columbus Ave., make a right on Broadway, and continue on the street's north side.

❻ **The Beat Museum.** If you are dying for a Jack Kerouac bobble head, this is the place to get one. This small museum has memorabilia from the Beat movement's key players, such as first-edition books, letters, and photos. If you're interested in learning more about the Beats or just want to do a little hero worship, you can watch a documentary while you're here. The museum gift shop also sells books, T-shirts, posters, and more. ⏱ 30 min. 540 Broadway. ☎ 800/537-6822. www.thebeat museum.org. Admission $5. Daily 10am–7pm.

Go west on Broadway until it intersects Grant Ave.

❼ ★ *Jazz Mural.* It's undergoing restoration, but Bill Weber and Tony Klaas' *Jazz Mural* is still impressive. Three stories high and wrap-ping 100 feet around 606 Broadway, this 1987 artwork features images from both the Chinese and Italian communities that merge at this intersection, as well as jazz musicians Teddy Wilson and Benny Goodman, and an

> *Ask for extra foam at Caffe Trieste, serving perfect cappuccinos in Little Italy since 1956.*

assortment of San Francisco mayors and characters. 606 Broadway. www.billwebermuralist.com.

Head north on Grant Ave. to reconnect with Columbus Ave. and make a left; turn right on Vallejo St.

⑧ ☕ ★ **Caffe Trieste.** Run by the same family since opening in 1956, this was another popular hangout for the Beats. It was also the first coffeehouse on the West Coast to serve espresso—leading one to wonder about the unsung role of caffeine in the be-bopping Beat movement. You can order tasty light fare such as pizza, gelato, pastries, and salads, as well as wine and beer. 601 Vallejo St. ☎ 415/392-6739. www.caffetrieste.com. Items less than $15 (cash only).

Go back to Columbus Ave. and make a right.

⑨ ★ **Biordi Art Imports.** A colorful dose of Italian style is on display here, featuring a gorgeous collection of hand-painted ceramics. Biordi has been dealing in majolica since 1946, and the goods in stock have a nearly museum-like quality; you just might need an endowment to buy something, too. 412 Columbus Ave. ☎ 415/392-8096. www.biordi.com. Tues–Fri 11am–5pm; Sat 9:30am–5pm.

Make a right on Green St., and then a left on Grant Ave.

⑩ **Grant Avenue.** This stretch of San Francisco's oldest street will give you a taste of the flavor that keeps North Beach not only popular with visitors, but also a vibrant, living and breathing neighborhood. You'll find boutiques, bakeries, galleries, and cafes along these blocks; be sure to stop in at the excellent ★ **Aria Antiques,** 1522 Grant Ave. (☎ 415/433-0219). Grant Ave., btw. Green & Filbert sts.

> Poet Lawrence Ferlinghetti created a hangout for Kerouac, Ginsberg, and other Beat Gen luminaries at City Lights Bookstore.

Make a left on Filbert St.

⓫ ★ **Saints Peter and Paul Church.** Ironically saddled with 666 as its street address, this gleaming Roman Catholic Church features distinctive twin spires that soar nearly 200 feet. Completed in 1924, there is also an intricately beautiful stained-glass rose window, 14 feet in diameter. In 1954, baseball great and North Beach native son Joe DiMaggio posed for wedding pictures on the steps of the church with his new bride, Marilyn Monroe—even though they had been unable to marry there. Because of Joltin' Joe's previous marriage and divorce, a church wedding was not permissible. ⏱ 15 min. 666 Filbert St. ☎ 415/421-0809. www.stspeterpaul. san-francisco.ca.us. Mass Mon–Fri 7:30am, 9am & 12:15pm; Sat 7:30am, 9am & 5pm; Sun 7:30am, 8:45am, 1pm & 5pm in English; 10:15am in Chinese; 11:45am in Italian. First Sun of the month 11:45am in Latin.

Across the street is Washington Square.

⓬ **Washington Square Park.** Beloved columnist Herb Caen (1916–97), who chronicled San Francisco for nearly 60 years, pointed out that this park is neither square nor on Washington Street., It also does not have a statue of George Washington. One of the city's oldest parks, dating from 1847, it does have a statue of Benjamin Franklin and a dramatic memorial to volunteer firefighters, courtesy of Coit Tower matriarch Lillie Hitchcock Coit. It's also a great spot to do some people-watching. Bordered by Columbus Ave. and Filbert, Stockton & Union sts.

Tattoo You

Lyle Tuttle was an instrumental figure in popularizing tattooing as an art form. He appeared on *The Tonight Show* with Johnny Carson, was photographed by Annie Leibovitz for *Rolling Stone*, and worked on the likes of Janis Joplin and Cher. Tuttle is semiretired now, but his namesake tattoo parlor lives on in North Beach at 841 Columbus Ave. (☎ 415/775-4991; www. lyletuttletattooing.com). It's open daily from noon to 8pm.

The Mission & the Castro

These two vibrant neighborhoods rub shoulders but have completely different feels. The Mission is home to a large population of Latin American immigrants but is liberally sprinkled with hipsters who fill the district's many bars, eateries, and eclectic shops; the Castro has long been known as the heart of queer San Francisco and has the bars, boutiques, and restaurants to prove it.

> Join a guided walking tour to learn the back story on the Mission District's vibrant murals, or follow a self-guided map.

START **Mission St. btw. 24th & 25th sts. BART to 24th St. Note: The Mission has one of the city's higher crime rates; exercise caution if you do this tour at night.**

① ★ Mission Cultural Center for Latino Arts. A hub of neighborhood activity since 1977, this cultural center presents a wide range of music, dance, visual arts, and literary events. There is a full schedule of drop-in classes and workshops, everything from capoeira to silk-screening, as well as cultural happenings such as *Día de los Muertos* (Day of the Dead), Carnaval, and mole-making competitions. ⏱ 30 min. 2868 Mission St. ☎ 415/643-5001. www.missionculturalcenter.org. Mon 5–10pm; Tues–Fri 10am–10pm; Sat 10am–5:30pm.

Walk back up to 24th St. and go right.

1. Mission Cultural Center for Latino Arts
2. 24th Street
3. Balmy Alley
4. Garfield Square
5. Humphry Slocombe
6. Precita Eyes Mural Arts and Visitors Center
7. Galería de la Raza
8. Taqueria Cancun
9. Mission Dolores Park
10. Mission Dolores
11. Harvey Milk Plaza
12. Castro Theatre
13. Harvey Milk Plaque

② **24th Street.** You may suddenly question your exact global whereabouts as you stroll past *tiendas* (shops), *panaderías* (bakeries), cantinas, and other businesses catering to the largely immigrant Latin American population. This tree-lined street will also give you a look at the Mission's justifiably renowned collection of murals. **24th St. btw. Mission & York sts.**

Make a right on Balmy Alley.

③ ★★ **Balmy Alley.** This block-long alleyway offers the city's most concentrated grouping of murals. Since 1971, artists have been adorning the fences and garages here with colorful

artworks that are moving, stridently political, and laugh-out-loud funny. **Balmy Alley btw. 24th & 25th sts.**

At the end of Balmy Alley is Garfield Square.

④ **Garfield Square.** Swing by this popular neighborhood park to view more murals along the walls of the swimming pool. From 1868 to 1884, this area was the site of California's first professional baseball park; today you're likely to find a soccer game in action. Garfield Square is also the gathering spot for the community's annual *Día de los Muertos* (Day of the Dead) celebration every November 2. **Bordered by 25th,**

> *The grounds of 1776 Mission Dolores include a serene cemetery with the grave of California's first Mexican governor, Luis Arguello.*

26th & Harrison sts., and Treat Ave.

Go up Harrison St. until just past 24th St.

⑤ 🍴 ★★ **Humphry Slocombe.** This gourmet ice cream parlor pushes the limits of what you thought possible with a frozen dairy treat. At any given time there will be 10 to 12 flavors available, such as pistachio bacon, honey thyme, pink grapefruit and tarragon, foie gras, or the classic Secret Breakfast with bourbon and cornflakes. 2790 Harrison St. ☎ 415/550-6971. www.humphryslocombe.com. Items $2–$6 (cash only).

Turn left on the south side of 24th St.

⑥ ★ **Precita Eyes Mural Arts and Visitors Center.** Since 1977, this community arts organization has been the driving force behind many of the Mission's mural projects. At the visitor center you can purchase a walking map, identifying dozens of the murals and their artists, or sign up for a weekend walking tour ($12–$15 adults, $8 seniors and students, $5 kids 12–16, $2 kids 11 & under). You can also find mural-related postcards, T-shirts, and books, as well as original artworks and art supplies. ⏱ 20 min. 2981 24th St. ☎ 415/285-2287. www.precitaeyes.org. Mon–Fri 10am–5pm; Sat 10am–4pm; Sun noon–4pm.

Continue east on 24th St.

⑦ ★ **Galería de la Raza.** Fight the power at this gallery that has been celebrating Latino and Chicano "art, thought, and activism" since 1970. There are visual-art exhibitions, many with a political bent, and an open-mic literary lounge held monthly on the night of the full moon. In the gift shop you can find cool and quirky gifts, from jewelry to Frida Kahlo messenger bags. ⏱ 30 min. 2857 24th St. ☎ 415/826-8009. www.galeriadelaraza.org. Tues 1–7pm; Wed–Sat noon–6pm.

Double back on 24th St. Make a right on Harrison St., a left on 23rd St., and then go right on Mission St.

⑧ 🍴 ★ **Taqueria Cancun.** A sure way to start a lively debate is to ask a group of locals to name the best *taquería* (taco shop) in the Mission. This place, with its ridiculously huge Super Burrito, is sure to be a frequent winner. 2288 Mission St. ☎ 415/252-9560. Items $5–$8 (cash only).

Go right on 19th St. to Mission Dolores Park.

⑨ **Mission Dolores Park.** San Francisco is a city of microclimates, and the Mission is one of the area's warmest, sunniest spots, so you'll often find folks soaking up a few rays in this pleasant park. For some great views, head to the park's highest point. Bordered by Dolores, Church, 18th & 20th sts.

Continue north on Dolores St., past 18th St., to Mission Dolores.

⑩ ★ **Mission Dolores.** Founded on June 29, 1776, this is the oldest structure in San Francisco and the oldest intact mission in California. Formally titled Mission San Francisco de Asís, over time the church came to be more commonly referred to as Mission Dolores, in reference to the Arroyo de los Dolores creek that once ran nearby. More than 5,000 people, many of them Native Americans who built the mission, are buried in the tranquil cemetery—one of only two within San Francisco's city limits. ⏱ 45 min. 3321 16th St. ☎ 415/621-8203. www.missiondolores.org. Admission $5 adults, $3 seniors and students. Daily May–Oct 9am–4:30pm, Nov–Apr 9am–4pm.

> The Castro Theatre, a 1,400-seat movie palace, shows foreign films, retrospectives, and the occasional Rocky Horror sing-along.

Turn left on 16th St. to where it intersects with Market St., and head left to Castro St.; turn left into the small plaza with the fluttering rainbow flag.

⑪ Harvey Milk Plaza. Harvey Milk (1930-78) was California's first openly gay elected public official, earning a spot on San Francisco's Board of Supervisors in 1977. The following year, he and San Francisco mayor George Moscone were assassinated in their city hall offices by a former supervisor, Dan White. Convicted of manslaughter, rather than murder, White received a lenient sentence that set off a wave of violence known as the White Night riots in 1979. Two years after serving a 5-year sentence, Dan White—known as the most-hated man in San Francisco history—committed suicide. **Castro & Market sts.**

⑫ ★★ Castro Theatre. Built in 1922, this regal movie palace has an exterior patterned after a Mexican cathedral and a lavish interior with mural-covered walls and an Art Deco chandelier. Hosting foreign films, special first-run presentations, rereleased classics, film festivals, and concerts, the Castro seats more than 1,400 and features a Wurlitzer organ that rises up from beneath the floor. **429 Castro St. ☎ 415/621-6120. www.castrotheatre.com.**

Tickets $10 adults, $7.50 seniors and kids 12 & under. Cash only at the box office; prices vary for film festivals and special events.

Continue down Castro St.

⑬ Harvey Milk Plaque. Here at 575 Castro St., Harvey Milk opened his camera store in 1973, living in the apartment above. Castro Camera would become his campaign headquarters in his quest for city office and a gathering spot for community activists; it was here that Milk would earn his nickname—the Mayor of Castro Street. **575 Castro St.**

King of the Hill

Perhaps San Francisco's best urban hike is the steep trek up to Corona Heights Park from the Castro. A former quarry, the park features a crownlike rock formation at its 540-foot peak, offering simply stunning, 360-degree views of the city. Be prepared: This is a walk that will get your heart pumping; bring some water and a jacket, as well—the wind can be merciless up here. From the Castro, head up Castro Street, make a left on 16th Street, and then a right on Flint Street.

Golden Gate National Recreation Area

Created in 1972, this is one of the largest urban parks in the world, encompassing nearly 60 miles of prime real estate in and around San Francisco. Not a contiguous park, but a patchwork of some of the Bay Area's most beautiful and biologically diverse land, it's home to many historic sites, museums, theaters, and restaurants. *Note:* This tour focuses only on the area within the San Francisco city limits.

> *Watch ferries, freighters, and Frisbee-chasing dogs along wide-open Crissy Field.*

START **Fort Mason** Bus 28, 30, 47, or 49.

❶ ★ **Fort Mason.** The Spanish first established a fort on this site in 1776, and from 1909 to 1962 several generations of American military personnel embarked overseas from the piers here. This 1,200-acre location now provides a home for the Golden Gate National Recreation Area (GGNRA) headquarters, a youth hostel, and the cultural arts complex known as **Fort Mason Center.** A variety of galleries, performing arts groups, museums, and educational facilities are part of Fort Mason

Center; highlights include **SFMOMA Artists Gallery** (☎ 415/441-4777; www.sfmoma. org), **Magic Theatre** (☎ 415/441-8822; www. magictheatre.org), and the **Long Now Museum & Store** (☎ 415/561-6582; www.long now.org). ⏱ At least 1 hr. Entrance at Franklin & Bay sts. or Marina & Laguna St. (pedestrians) or Buchanan St. (vehicles). GGNRA headquarters, Bldg. 201. ☎ 415/561-4700. www.nps.gov/goga. Mon–Fri 8:30am–4:30pm. Fort Mason Center ☎ 415/345-7500. www.fortmason.org. Free admission to grounds and galleries. Bus 28, 47, or 49.

② ♨ ★★ **Greens to Go.** Greens is the stylish, groundbreaking vegetarian restaurant that has been at Fort Mason since 1979; Greens to Go is the excellent takeout option where you can pick up some pastries, granola, veggie curry, or black bean chili for a picnic. In Fort Mason, Bldg. A. ☎ 415/ 771-6330. www.greensrestaurant.com. Items $8–$16.

❸ ★ **Crissy Field.** Some of San Francisco's most scenic—if windswept—walking, jogging, and biking take place along the Golden Gate Promenade in Crissy Field. Once a military airfield, the area was reclaimed beginning in 1999, and has been returned to a more original, marshlike state. There are flat trails, beaches, picnic areas, and great spots to watch kite boarders and windsurfers shred through the choppy waters of the bay. You'll also find the **Crissy Field Center,** offering programs for children and families and a cafe. ⏱ 30 min. Old Mason & Baker sts. Crissy Field Center ☎ 415/561-7690. www.crissyfield.org. Wed–Sun 9am–5pm. Bus 30.

❹ ★ **Fort Point.** This formidable fortress, "Guardian of the Golden Gate," was completed in 1861 and was originally intended to protect the flow of commerce generated by the Gold Rush. It eventually became obsolete and narrowly averted destruction to make way for the building of the Golden Gate Bridge. The fort now houses a museum that includes exhibits on the history of the African-American Buffalo Soldiers and the construction of the bridge. ⏱ 30 min. End of Marine Dr. ☎ 415/556-1693. www.nps.gov/fopo. Free admission. Fri–Sun 10am–5pm. Bus: 28.

> *"Hotshot furnaces" in 1861 Fort Point could heat iron cannonballs until red-hot and fire them at passing wooden ships.*

❺ **Presidio Visitor Information Center.** Located in the heart of this former military base—in continuous use for more than 200 years by Spanish, Mexican, and U.S. forces—the visitor center and bookstore can give you info and suggestions about park offerings, which include walking trails (such as the awesome Coastal Trail), historic buildings, a national cemetery, the **Walt Disney Family Museum** (p. 69), and a golf course. Fun fact: The Grateful Dead's Jerry Garcia was stationed here during his brief but colorful military career. In a span of 9 months he went AWOL eight times and was court-martialed twice. Bldg. 50 on Moraga Ave. near Arguello Blvd. ☎ 415/561-4323. www.nps.gov/ prsf. Free admission to Presidio grounds. Daily 9am–5pm. Bus: 28 or 43.

❻ ★★ **Baker Beach.** The currents (not to mention the frigid water) make this beach too dangerous for swimming, but the gorgeous views of the Golden Gate Bridge make this a

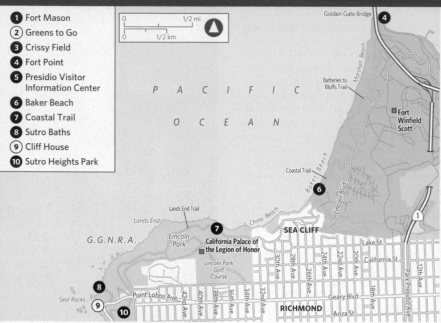

1 Fort Mason
2 Greens to Go
3 Crissy Field
4 Fort Point
5 Presidio Visitor Information Center
6 Baker Beach
7 Coastal Trail
8 Sutro Baths
9 Cliff House
10 Sutro Heights Park

memorable spot. Be prepared for chilly temps, and do note that the portion of the beach closest to the bridge is clothing optional. **Gibson Rd. below Bowery St.** ☎ 415/561-4323. www. nps.gov/prsf. Bus: 29.

7 ★★★ **Coastal Trail.** Incredible vistas of the wild, crashing ocean await those who make the easy hike to Lands End; you can follow the Coastal Trail to this aptly named location all the way from **Fort Point** (4). You can also combine

Biking the Bay

Despite San Francisco's justifiable reputation for being a hilly town, renting a bike and cruising through the Golden Gate National Recreation Area is a blast. A perfect itinerary is to pick up a set of wheels from **Blazing Saddles,** 2715 Hyde St., near Ghirardelli Square (☎ 415/202-8888; www.blazing saddles.com), and wind your way along an easy path all the way to the Golden Gate Bridge. Pedaling across the bridge is an experience you won't soon forget; then you can make your way into the charming town of Sausalito (p. 124) for a well-earned meal and drink and take a relaxing ferry ride back to near your starting point.

> *Cliffhanger gets a new meaning along the spectacular Coastal Trail, twisting above the Pacific from Fort Point to Lands End.*

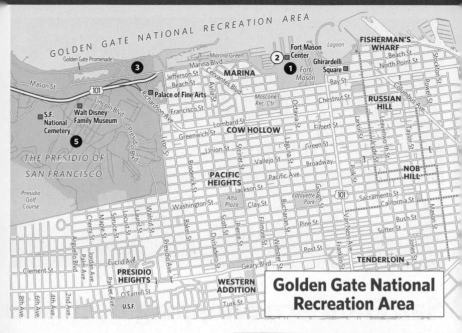

a visit here with a stop at the nearby **Legion of Honor** (p. 69). El Camino del Mar. www.parkcon servancy.org. Bus: 18.

8 Sutro Baths. Looking like the ruins of an ancient civilization, this is all that remains of a grand attraction—a collection of pools, promenades, and pavilions in an enormous glasshouse structure built in 1896 by Adolph Sutro (1830–98). A Prussian immigrant who made his fortune as a Gold-Rush mining engineer, Sutro also became mayor of San Francisco. At the time it was built, the complex was the largest of its kind in the world. Unfortunately, fire triumphed over water in 1966 when the building housing the complex burned and the site was ultimately abandoned. Off the Lands End Trail near Point Lobos Ave. www.sutrobaths.com. Bus: 38.

9 ★ Cliff House. A succession of Cliff Houses have stood sentinel here, overlooking Seal Rocks, since 1863, with the most recent renovation taking place in 2004. The main restaurant is pricey, but you can enjoy the same sweeping ocean views at the casual **Cliff House Bistro.** 1090 Point Lobos Ave. ☎ 415/386-3330. www.cliffhouse.com. $12–$29. Bus 38.

> On fog-free days, Baker Beach offers sweeping bridge views and sunbathing. Swimming? Forget about it—the water is frigid.

10 ★ Sutro Heights Park. Head up the trail located across the Great Highway from the **Cliff House** (9) to this park featuring magnificent overlooks of Ocean Beach. This was the location of Adolph Sutro's majestic estate, destroyed in 1939. ⏱ 30 min. Main entry at Point Lobos & Anza aves. ☎ 415/561-4323. www.parkconservancy.org. Bus: 38.

San Francisco Shopping Best Bets

Best Place for Outsider Art
Creativity Explored, 3245 16th St. (p. 95)

Best Place for CDs and DVDs
Amoeba Music, 1855 Haight St. (p. 99)

Best Gallery of Local Artists
Hang Art, 567 Sutter St. (p. 95)

Best Glassware
Gump's, 135 Post St. (p. 98)

Best Place for a Chinatown Souvenir
Canton Bazaar, 616 Grant Ave. (p. 99)

Best Place for Vintage Clothes Shopping
Haight Street (p. 99)

Best Museum Gift Shop
SFMOMA MuseumStore, 151 Third St. (p. 98)

Best Place to Max Out Your Credit Card
Maiden Lane (p. 99)

Best Hardware Store for Tourists
Cliff's Variety, 479 Castro St. (p. 98)

Best Place for Foodies
Ferry Building Marketplace, One Ferry Building (p. 98); and **Omnivore Books on Food,**
3885A Cesar Chavez St. (p. 98)

Best Place for Japanese Comic Books
Kinokuniya, 1581 Webster St. (p. 95)

Best Vintage Jewelry
Lang Antiques & Estate Jewelry, 323 Sutter St. (p. 95)

Best Place to Get Inspired
City Lights Bookstore, 261 Columbus Ave. (p. 95)

Best Place for San Francisco Style
RAG, 541 Octavia St. (p. 98)

Best Place to Drop a Bundle on a Suit
Wilkes Bashford, 375 Sutter St. (p. 98)

Best Place for Decorative Lanterns
Soko Hardware, 1698 Post St. (p. 98)

Best Spot for Boutiquing and Barhopping
Union Street (p. 99)

> *It's no surprise that the city's best place to find tunes is in its historic rock'n'roll heartland.*

San Francisco Shopping A to Z

Antiques

★ **Grand Central Station Antiques** SOMA
Three floors of quality, well-priced European and American antiques. 333 Ninth St. ☎ 415/252-8155. www.gcsantiques.com. DISC, MC, V. Bus: 12 or 19. Map p. 97.

★★ **Lang Antiques & Estate Jewelry** UNION SQUARE Since 1969 this has been a go-to spot for rings, watches, necklaces, and more, from all eras. 323 Sutter St. ☎ 415/982-2213. www. langantiques.com. AE, DC, DISC, MC, V. Bus: 2, 3, 30, or 45. Map p. 97.

Art

★★★ **Creativity Explored** THE MISSION
Artists with developmental disabilities create and sell amazing pieces of outsider art at this nonprofit center. 3245 16th St. ☎ 415/863-2108. www.creativityexplored.org. MC, V. Bus: 22. Streetcar: J. Map p. 96.

★★ **49 Geary** UNION SQUARE
Art lovers will love this five-story building of galleries; highlights include the contemporary work at the **Stephen Wirtz Gallery**

(☎ 415/433-6897; www.wirtzgallery.com) and photography at **Robert Koch Gallery** (☎ 415/421-0122; www.kochgallery.com). 49 Geary St. Bus: 38. Streetcar: F. BART: Montgomery Station. Map p. 97.

★★★ **Hang Art** UNION SQUARE
An ever-changing roster of talented Bay Area artists, and prices that won't break the bank. 567 Sutter St. ☎ 415/434-4264. www.hangart. com. AE, DC, DISC, MC, V. Bus: 2, 3, or 76. Cable car: Powell lines. Map p. 97.

Books

★★ **City Lights Bookstore** NORTH BEACH
This legendary bookstore and publishing house focuses on international literature, the arts, and progressive politics. 261 Columbus Ave. ☎ 415/362-8193. www.citylights.com. AE, DISC, MC, V. Bus: 30 or 41. Map p. 97.

★★★ **Kinokuniya** JAPANTOWN
This huge bookstore sells all manner of Japanese manga, DVDs, CDs, and more. 1581 Webster St. ☎ 415/567-7625. www.kinokuniya.com. AE, DISC, MC, V. Bus: 2, 3, or 38. Map p. 96.

> *Peruse paperbacks in City Lights Bookstore, once the hangout of Beat Gen writers like Ginsberg and Kerouac.*

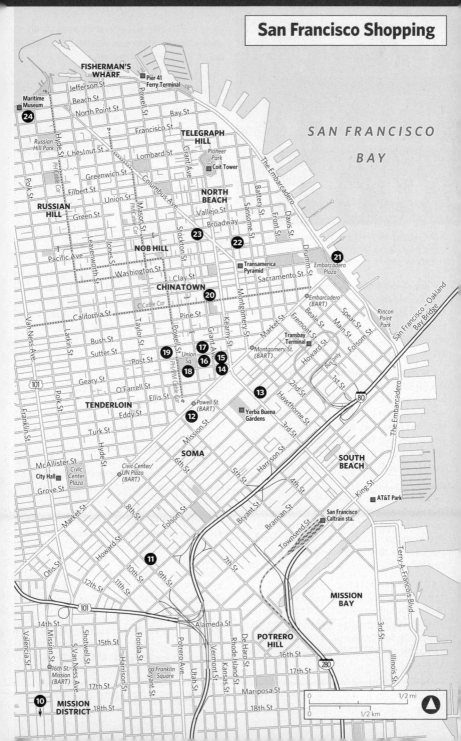

San Francisco Shopping

SAN FRANCISCO

BAY

FISHERMAN'S WHARF

Pier 41 Ferry Terminal

Jefferson St.

Beach St.

Maritime Museum

24

North Point St.

Bay St.

Francisco St.

Russian Hill Park

Chestnut St.

TELEGRAPH HILL

Pioneer Park

Coit Tower

Lombard St.

Greenwich St.

RUSSIAN HILL

Filbert St.

Union St.

NORTH BEACH

Green St.

Vallejo St.

23

Broadway

22

Pacific Ave.

NOB HILL

Washington St.

Transamerica Pyramid

21

Embarcadero Plaza

Clay St.

CHINATOWN

Sacramento St.

California St.

20

Embarcadero (BART)

Pine St.

Rincon Point Park

Bush St.

Market St.

Transbay Terminal

19

17

Union Sq.

16

15

Montgomery St. (BART)

Sutter St.

Post St.

18

14

Geary St.

O'Farrell St.

13

Ellis St.

TENDERLOIN

Powell St. (BART)

12

Yerba Buena Gardens

Eddy St.

SOMA

SOUTH BEACH

Turk St.

McAllister St.

Civic Center/ UN Plaza (BART)

City Hall

Civic Center Plaza

AT&T Park

Grove St.

San Francisco Caltrain sta.

11

MISSION BAY

Alameda St.

POTRERO HILL

16th St.

17th St.

10

MISSION DISTRICT

18th St.

16th St. Mission (BART)

0   1/2 mi

0   1/2 km

> Get wigged out in Haight-Ashbury, where wacky and weird seems the norm, even if it means a sapphire-blue bouffant.

★★ Omnivore Books on Food NOE VALLEY
This foodie haven sells vintage, and new cookbooks. It also hosts in-store events featuring chefs and authors. 3885A Cesar Chavez St. ☎ 415/282-4712. www.omnivorebooks.com. MC, V. Streetcar: J. Map p. 97.

★★ William Stout Architectural Books SOMA
Design buffs will lose themselves in this store's impressive collection of tomes on architecture, art, design, furniture, landscaping, and more. 804 Montgomery St. ☎ 415/391-6757. www.stoutbooks.com. Bus: 12, 30, or 41. Map p. 96. Another location at 678 Mission St. ☎ 415/357-1860. Bus: 14, 30, or 45. MC, V. Map p. 97.

Fashion
★★ Métier UNION SQUARE
This highly regarded women's boutique features lines that are bohemian and city chic. There's also an excellent selection of jewelry. 355 Sutter St. ☎ 415/989-5395. www.metiersf.com. AE, MC, V. Bus: 2, 3, 30, or 45. Map p. 97.

★ RAG HAYES VALLEY
Pick up some true San Francisco style at RAG (Residents Apparel Gallery), a clothing co-op where everything is created by local designers and artists. 541 Octavia St. ☎ 415/621-7718. www.ragsf.com. AE, DISC, MC, V. Bus: 21. Map p. 96.

★★ Wilkes Bashford UNION SQUARE
A luxury retailer for those who want to make a splash in the boardroom and on the society party circuit. 375 Sutter St. ☎ 415/986-4380. www.wilkesbashford.com. AE, DC, DISC, MC, V. Bus: 2, 3, 30, or 45. Map p. 97.

Gifts & Souvenirs
★ Canton Bazaar CHINATOWN
The best of Chinatown under one roof: tea sets, clothing, jewelry, jade and porcelain goods, furniture, antiques, and toys. 616 Grant Ave. ☎ 415/362-5750. www.cantonbazaar.com. AE, DISC, MC, V. Bus: 1, 30, or 45. Map p. 97.

★ Cliff's Variety CASTRO
A neighborhood institution since 1936, this hardware-cum-gift shop will put a smile on your face. 479 Castro St. ☎ 415/431-5365. www.cliffsvariety.com. AE, DC, DISC, MC, V. Bus: 24 or 33. Streetcar: F. Map p. 96.

★★ SFMOMA MuseumStore SOMA
Creative and cutting-edge jewelry, furniture, toys, and housewares. If that's not enough, there are also books, posters, and fashion accessories. 151 Third St. ☎ 888/357-0037. www.sfmoma.com. AE, DISC, MC, V. Bus: 14, 30, or 45. Map p. 97.

Housewares & Furnishings
★★ Gump's UNION SQUARE
Exquisite home decor, including china, stemware, linens, and furniture. 135 Post St. 415/982-1616. www.gumps.com. AE, DISC, MC, V. Bus: 2, 3, 30, or 45. Map p. 97.

★ Soko Hardware JAPANTOWN
All kinds of direct-from-Japan goods at good prices. You'll find everything from chopsticks to paper lanterns. 1698 Post St. ☎ 415/931-5510. MC, V. Bus: 2, 3, or 38. Map p. 96.

Shopping Centers & Districts
★★★ Ferry Building Marketplace EMBARCADERO This foodie emporium is a city treasure, featuring purveyors of specialty foods, cafes, and a farmers market. 1 Ferry Building. ☎ 415/983-8000. www.ferrybuildingmarketplace.com. Bus: 12. Streetcar: F. Map p. 97.

★★ Fillmore Street PACIFIC HEIGHTS
Nearly 10 blocks of stylish boutiques, with lots of eateries along the way. Highlights include knitwear at **★★ Margaret O'Leary,** 2400 Fillmore St. (☎ 415/771-9982; www.margaretoleary.com), and fabulous footwear at **★★ Gimme Shoes,** 2358 Fillmore St. (☎ 415/

441-3040; www.gimmeshoes.com). **Fillmore St.** btw. Geary & Jackson sts. www.sanfran ciscoshop.com. Bus: 1, 2, 3, 10, 22, 24, or 38. Map p. 96.

Ghirardelli Square FISHERMAN'S WHARF
This popular landmark is touristy, but if you have a sweet tooth head to the **Ghirardelli Ice Cream and Chocolate Shop** (☎ 415/474-3938; www.ghirardelli.com) or ★ **Kara's Cupcakes** (☎ 415/351-2253; www.karascupcakes. com). 900 N. Point St. ☎ 415/775-5500. www. ghirardellisq.com. Bus: 19, 30, or 47. Cable car: Powell-Hyde line. Map p. 97.

★ **Haight Street** THE HAIGHT
Hip boutiques, funky gift shops, and great vintage clothing stores stretch for 6 blocks. Don't miss mighty ★★★ **Amoeba Music,** 1855 Haight St. (☎ 415/831-1200; www.amoeba. com), or the sexy boots at ★★ **John Fluevog Shoes,** 1697 Haight St. (☎ 415/549-9784; www.fluevog.com). Haight St. btw. Central and Stanyan sts. Bus: 6, 33, 43, or 71. Map p. 96.

★ **Hayes Valley** HAYES VALLEY
There are several blocks worth of fashion-forward boutiques, modern home-furnishing stores, and neighborhood bars and bistros. Look for furniture and home accessories at ★★ **Propeller,** 555 Hayes St. (☎ 415/701-7767; www.propellermodern.com), and high-style footwear at ★★ **Bulo,** 418 Hayes St. (☎ 877/746-3790 or 415/255-4939; www. buloshoes.com). Hayes St. btw. Laguna & Franklin sts. Bus: 21. Map p. 96.

★★★ **Maiden Lane** UNION SQUARE
This chic pedestrian alley has European flair and brims with top designers like ★★ **Marc Jacobs** (☎ 415/362-6500; www.marcjacobs. com) and ★★ **Paul Smith** (☎ 415/352-3520; www.paulsmith.co.uk). Maiden Lane, btw. Geary & Post sts. and Stockton & Kearny sts. www.unionsquareshop.com. Bus: 30, 38, or 45. Map p. 97.

★★★ **Union Square** UNION SQUARE
The shopping mother lode—a concentration of department stores and high-profile retailers, including ★★ **Prada,** 201 Post St. (☎ 415/848-1900; www.prada.com); ★★ **Louis Vuitton,** 233 Geary St. (☎ 391-6200; www.louis vuitton.com); and ★★ **Kate Spade** 227 Grant

> *Fashion-forward boutiques fill the Fillmore Street shopping district, five blocks jammed with cute shops and appealing cafes.*

Ave. (☎ 415/216-0880; www.katespade. com). Union Square area btw. Market, Sutter, Kearny, & Mason sts. www.unionsquaresf.net. Bus: 2, 3, 30, 38, 45, or 76. Streetcar: F. Cable car: Powell lines. Map p. 97.

★★ **Union Street** COW HOLLOW
One of the city's best shopping and dining districts, where you can pick up beautiful jewelry at ★★ **Union Street Goldsmith,** 1909 Union St. (☎ 415/776-8048; www.unionstreetgold smith.com), or handmade sweaters at ★★ **Three Bags Full,** 2181 Union St. (☎ 415/567-5753; www.threebagsfull.com). Union St. btw. Steiner St. & Van Ness Ave. www. sanfranciscoshop.com. Bus: 41 or 45. Map p. 96.

★ **Westfield San Francisco Centre** SOMA
This huge indoor shopping center is anchored by Bloomingdale's and Nordstrom, plus more than 170 other shops and a movie theater. 865 Market St. ☎ 415/512-6776. www.westfield.com/ sanfrancisco. Bus: 27, 30, or 45. Streetcar: F. Cable car: Powell lines. Map p. 97.

San Francisco Restaurant Best Bets

Best Place for Dinner and a Movie
Foreign Cinema, 2534 Mission St. (p. 104)

Best Hotel Dining
Ame, 689 Mission St. (p. 101)

Best Place to Pretend You're a Parisian
Boulevardier
Boulevard, 1 Mission St. (p. 104)

Best Wine List
Michael Mina, 335 Powell St. (p. 105)

Best Dim Sum
Yank Sing, 101 Spear St. (p. 107)

Best Greek Food
Kokkari Estiatorio, 200 Jackson St. (p. 105)

Best Vegetarian Food
Greens Restaurant, Fort Mason Center
(p. 104)

Best Steakhouse
EPIC Roasthouse, 369 Embarcadero (p. 104)

Best Indian Food
Dosa, 1700 Fillmore St. and 995 Valencia St.
(p. 104)

Best Upscale Asian Food
The Slanted Door, 1 Ferry Plaza (p. 106)

Best Down-Home Chinese Food
House of Nanking, 919 Kearny St. (p. 105)

Best of the Best
Restaurant Gary Danko, 800 N. Point St.
(p. 106)

Best Hipster Brunch
Bar Tartine, 1199 Valencia St. (p. 101)

**Best Authentic North Beach Italian
Experience**
L'Osteria del Forno, 519 Columbus Ave.
(p. 105)

Best Classic Oyster Bar
Swan Oyster Depot, 1517 Polk St. (p. 106)

Best Place for Spätzle and Beer
Suppenküche, 525 Laguna St. (p. 106)

Best Tapas
Bocadillos, 710 Montgomery St. (p. 101)

Best Trattoria
A16, 2355 Chestnut St., (p. 101)

> From its classy curtains and mesquite flooring to its impeccable dishes, Ame aims to please—and succeeds.

San Francisco Restaurants A to Z

★★★ Ame SOMA *AMERICAN/JAPANESE*
This chic hotel restaurant fuses modern American cuisine with Asian touches like a sashimi bar. In the St. Regis Hotel, 689 Mission St. ☎ 415/284-4040. www.amerestaurant.com. Entrees $22-$38. AE, DC, DISC, MC, V. Dinner daily. Bus: 14, 14L, 30, or 45. Streetcar: F, J, K, L, or M. Map p. 103.

★★ A16 MARINA *ITALIAN*
Gourmet pizza, an outstanding wine list, and the rustic food of Southern Italy highlight this sleek, happening eatery. 2355 Chestnut St. ☎ 415/771-2216. www.a16sf.com. Entrees $8-$20. AE, DC, MC, V. Lunch Wed-Fri; dinner daily. Bus: 28, 30, 30X, 43, or 76. Map p. 102.

★★ Bar Tartine THE MISSION *AMERICAN*
Join the hipsters at this hard-to-spot favorite featuring a seasonal, contemporary American menu. A great place for breakfast and brunch, too, as is a nearby sister space, **★★ Tartine Bakery & Cafe,** 600 Guerrero St. (☎ 415/487-2600). 1199 Valencia St. ☎ 415/487-1600. www.bartartine.com. Entrees $14-$29, brunch $10-$16. AE, DISC, MC, V. Breakfast Wed-Fri; lunch Sat-Sun; dinner Tues-Sun. Bus: 14, 14L, 22, 33, or 49. BART: 16th St. Map p. 103.

★★ Beretta THE MISSION *ITALIAN*
A menu of seasonal antipasti and thin-crust pizzas designed for sharing; you'll want one of the creative cocktails all to yourself, though. 1199 Valencia St. ☎ 415/695-1199. www.beretta sf.com. Pizza $11-$15, antipasti $6-$15. AE, DISC, MC, V. Breakfast, lunch & dinner daily. Bus: 14, 48, or 49. BART: 24th St. Map p. 103.

Bistro Boudin at the Wharf FISHERMAN'S WHARF *DELI/AMERICAN* Grab some picnic fare to go or have a sit-down meal at this sourdough bread bakery, the city's oldest continuously operating business (since 1849). 160 Jefferson St., near Pier 43½. ☎ 415/928-1849. www.boudinbakery.com. Entrees $6-$33. AE, DC, DISC, MC, V. Lunch & dinner daily. Bus: 47. Streetcar: F. Map p. 103.

★★ Bocadillos FINANCIAL DISTRICT *SPANISH*
This casual and convivial tapas bar also serves breakfast, though getting a seat at the communal tables can be hard. 710 Montgomery St. ☎ 415/982-2622. www.bocasf.com. Entrees $2-$15. AE, DC, DISC, MC, V. Breakfast & lunch Mon-Fri; dinner Mon-Sat. Bus: 30X or 41. Map p. 103.

> *China's take on small plates, dim sum, served here at Yank Sing, means lots of ways to try weird stuff.*

San Francisco Restaurants

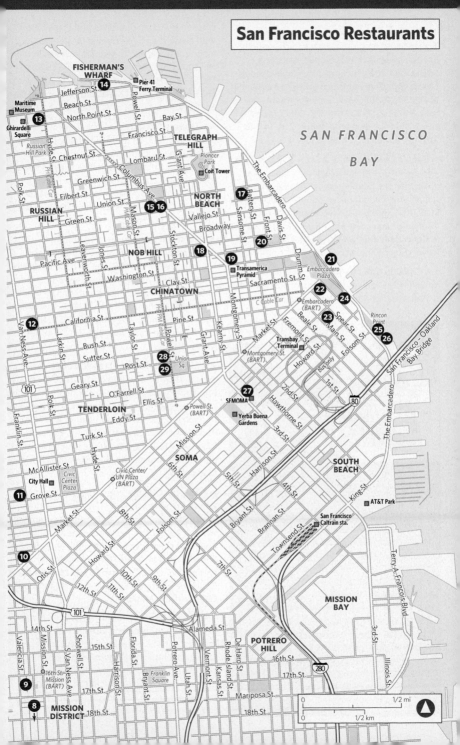

★★ **Boulevard** EMBARCADERO *AMERICAN*
This beloved restaurant oozes Parisian Belle
Epoque style. Is that Toulouse-Lautrec sitting in the corner tucking into a divine squab
breast with shaved black truffles? 1 Mission St.
☎ 415/543-6084. www.boulevardrestaurant.
com. Entrees $14–$39. AE, DC, DISC, MC, V.
Lunch Mon–Fri; dinner daily. Bus: 2, 6, 14, 14X,
21, or 31. Streetcar: F. Map p. 103.

★ **Capp's Corner** NORTH BEACH *ITALIAN*
The cheerful atmosphere here is more of a
draw than the heaping servings of standard
Italian fare, but character counts. 1600 Powell
St. ☎ 415/989-2589. www.cappscorner.com.
Complete dinner $15–$17. AE, DC, MC, V. Lunch
& dinner daily. Bus: 8X, 30, 41, or 45. Cable car:
Powell-Mason line. Map p. 103.

★★ **Cha Cha Cha** THE HAIGHT *CARIBBEAN*
You'll find a menu at this colorful and festive
restaurant that ranges from Jamaican jerk

Worth a Trek

For the serious diner, a pilgrimage to Chez
Panisse in nearby Berkeley (p. 126) is a
must. This is where the legendary Alice
Waters launched California cuisine in 1971,
and the ingredients on the Mediterranean-
inspired menu are still locally and organically
sourced. Housed in a lovely cottage, Chez
Panisse has two dining areas: an informal
cafe upstairs with an a la carte menu (entrees $12–$28) served at lunch and dinner
and the cozy downstairs restaurant, which
serves prix fixe gourmet dinners ($60–$95).
You can't go wrong with anything on either
menu. Chez Panisse is at 1517 Shattuck Ave.
(☎ 510/548-5525 main restaurant; 548-
5049 cafe; www.chezpanisse.com). Take the
BART to downtown Berkeley.

chicken to Cuban plantains and black beans,
with some sangria thrown in for geographical
incongruity. There's a second location in the
Mission at 2327 Mission St. (☎ 415/824-
1502). 1801 Haight St. ☎ 415/386-7670. www.
cha3.com. Entrees $12–$15. MC, V. Lunch & dinner daily. Bus: 33, 43, or 71. Map p. 102.

★★ **Delfina** THE MISSION *ITALIAN*
Star attractions on the daily-changing menu
at this busy neighborhood trattoria include
house-cured meats and fish, as well as house-
made pastas, sausages, and gelato. 3621
18th St. ☎ 415/552-4055. www.delfinasf.com.
Entrees $13–$22. MC, V. Dinner daily. Bus: 33.
Streetcar: J. Map p. 102.

★★ **Dosa** PACIFIC HEIGHTS *INDIAN*
Sexy and urban, Dosa serves up Southern
Indian specialties and spice-infused cocktails
to a hip crowd. A second location is located
in the Mission at 995 Valencia (☎ 415/642-
3672). 1700 Fillmore St. ☎ 415/441-3672. www.
dosasf.com. Entrees $7–$28. AE, DISC, MC, V.
Lunch & dinner daily. Bus: 2, 3, 22, 38, or 38L.
Map p. 102.

★★ **EPIC Roasthouse** EMBARCADERO *STEAK-
HOUSE* Stellar views and epic cuts of meat are
the main draws at this waterfront spot, which
has a huge exhibition kitchen and an upstairs
bar and lounge. 369 Embarcadero. ☎ 415/369-
9955. www.epicroasthousesf.com. Entrees
$27–$54. AE, DC, DISC, MC, V. Lunch Thurs–Fri,
dinner daily; brunch Sat–Sun. Streetcar: N Judah.
Map p. 103.

★★ **Foreign Cinema** THE MISSION *MEDITER-
RANEAN* The hearty food here lives up to the
unexpected, supercool outdoor dining space,
where classic movies are screened on a wall.
There's a chic indoor dining room as well.
2534 Mission St. ☎ 415/648-7600. www.
foreigncinema.com. Entrees $17–$26. AE, MC, V.
Dinner daily; brunch Sat–Sun. Bus: 14, 14L, or 49.
BART: 24th St. Map p. 103.

★★ **Greens Restaurant** MARINA *VEGETARIAN*
In 1979, groundbreaking Greens transformed
the concept of a vegetarian restaurant from
hippie cafe into a fine-dining experience with
big-city style (and bay views, to boot). Fort
Mason Center, Bldg. A (Buchanan and Marina
sts.). ☎ 415/771-6222. www.greensrestaurant.
com. Entrees $9.50–$20, brunch $8–$14. AE,

DISC, MC, V. Lunch Tues–Sat; dinner daily; brunch Sun. Bus: 28 or 30. Map p. 102.

★ **House of Nanking** CHINATOWN *CHINESE* Don't even look at the menu—just tell them how hungry you are and Nanking will take care of the rest. 919 Kearny St. ☎ 415/421-1429. Entrees $6–$12. MC, V. Lunch & dinner daily. Bus: 8X, 10, 12, or 41. Map p. 103.

★★ **Isa** COW HOLLOW *FRENCH* French tapas at reasonable prices. The beautifully prepared small plates include potato-wrapped sea bass, foie gras with apples and huckleberry, and baked goat cheese. Two- and three-course *prix-fixe* dinners are available Monday through Thursday. 3324 Steiner St. ☎ 415/567-9588. www.isarestaurant.com. Entrees $9–$16. MC, V. Dinner daily. Bus: 22, 28, 30, 30X, 43, or 76. Map p. 102.

★★ **Jardinière** HAYES VALLEY *CALIFORNIAN/ FRENCH* The domain of Traci Des Jardins, one of the city's top chefs, this snazzy, sophisticated spot is popular for a pre- or postsymphony meal and a bit of bubbly. 300 Grove St. ☎ 415/861-5555. www.jardiniere.com. Entrees $26–$38. AE, DC, DISC, MC, V. Dinner daily. Bus: 21, 47, or 49. Map p. 103.

★★ **Kokkari Estiatorio** FINANCIAL DISTRICT *GREEK/MEDITERRANEAN* Exposed wood beams and a roaring fireplace add to the rustic charm of this restaurant, which serves both classic and contemporary Greek recipes. 200 Jackson St. ☎ 415/981-0983. www.kokkari.com. Entrees $14–$39. AE, DC, DISC, MC, V. Lunch Mon–Fri; dinner Mon–Sat. Bus: 10, 12, or 41. Map p. 103.

★★ **L'Osteria del Forno** NORTH BEACH *ITALIAN* For the quintessential North Beach dining experience featuring authentic Italian food and an unfussy atmosphere, this is the place. The focaccia is fabulous. You might have to wait for a table because reservations aren't accepted. 519 Columbus Ave. ☎ 415/982-1124. www.losteriadelforno.com. Entrees $6–$18. Cash only. Lunch & dinner Wed–Mon. Bus: 8X, 30, 41, or 45. Map p. 103.

★★★ **Michael Mina** UNION SQUARE *AMERICAN* This elegant restaurant serves three- and six-course tasting menus and is one of the city's most lavish dining experiences. The wine list is

> *Art on a plate at Michael Mina, one of the finest in a city overflowing with extraordinary culinary experiences.*

mind-boggling. 335 Powell St. ☎ 415/397-9222. www.michaelmina.net. Tasting menu $98–$135. AE, DC, DISC, MC, V. Dinner daily. Bus: 2, 3, 30, 38, 45, or 76. Cable car: Powell-Mason and Powell-Hyde lines. Map p. 103.

★★ **One Market** EMBARCADERO *CALIFORNIAN* Going strong since 1993, this Michelin-starred restaurant delivers farm-to-table goodness, using local, organic products. 1 Market St. ☎ 415/777-5577. www.onemarket.com. Entrees $16–$33. AE, DC, DISC, MC, V. Lunch Mon–Fri; dinner Mon–Sat. Bus: 2, 6, 14, 14X, 21, or 31. Streetcar: F, J, K, L, or M. BART: Embarcadero. Cable car: California St. line. Map p. 103.

★★ **Piperade** NORTH BEACH *BASQUE* This comfortable eatery with exposed brick and woodwork serves "West Coast Basque cuisine." The menu might include such tasty offerings as peppers stuffed with goat cheese,

> *Slurp your way to oyster heaven along Fisherman's Wharf, where fresh seafood still reigns amongst the ticky-tack.*

or roasted salmon with broccolini and chorizo. 1015 Battery St. ☎ 415/391-2555. www. piperade.com. Entrees $17–$24. AE, DC, DISC, MC, V. Lunch Mon–Fri; dinner Mon–Sat. Bus: 82X. Streetcar: F. Map p. 103.

★★★ Restaurant Gary Danko FISHERMAN'S WHARF FRENCH The best restaurant in San Francisco? A meal at warmly stylish Gary Danko, where the cuisine and the service are duly impeccable, will make you a believer. 800 N. Point St. ☎ 415/749-2060. www.garydanko. com. Reservations required except at walk-in bar. 5-course prix-fixe menu $98. AE, DC, DISC, MC, V. Dinner daily. Bus: 30 or 47. Cable car: Powell-Hyde line. Map p. 103.

★ Sears Fine Foods UNION SQUARE AMERICAN People have been lining up at this local institution since 1938 for its famed Swedish silver-dollar pancakes (served all day!). The other classic diner fare isn't bad either. 439 Powell St. ☎ 415/986-0700. www. searsfinefood.com. Entrees $8–$29. AE, DC, MC, V. Breakfast, lunch & dinner daily. Bus: 2,

3, 38, or 76. Cable car: Powell-Mason and Powell-Hyde lines. Map p. 103.

★★ The Slanted Door EMBARCADERO VIETNAMESE This enormous and enormously popular spot offers zesty Asian fare, creative cocktails, and unique teas in a modern, bay-view setting at the Ferry Building Marketplace. 1 Ferry Plaza ☎ 415/861-8032. www.slanted-door.com. Entrees $6–$34. AE, MC, V. Lunch & dinner daily. Bus: 2, 6, 14, 14X, 21, or 31. Streetcar: F, J, K, L, or M. Map p. 103.

★★ Suppenküche HAYES VALLEY GERMAN This place kicks it old-country style—community tables, gigantic beers, and traditional Bavarian cooking. An *essen* good time. 525 Laguna St. ☎ 415/252-9289. www.suppenkuche. com. Entrees $10–$20. AE, DC, DISC, MC, V. Dinner daily; brunch Sun. Bus: 21. Map p. 102.

★★ Swan Oyster Depot NOB HILL SEAFOOD You'll probably have to wait in line to get into this speck of a place, opened in 1912, but after you have your oysters and clam chowder you'll

> *If you can't get a booth at still wildly popular The Slanted Door, sip a creative cocktail and watch the ferryboats go by.*

know it was worth it. 1517 Polk St. ☎ 415/673-1101. Seafood cocktails $7–$15, clams and oysters on the half shell $7.95 per half dozen. Cash only. Breakfast & lunch daily. Bus: 1, 19, 47, 49, or 76. Cable car: California St. line. Map p. 103.

★★ **Waterbar** EMBARCADERO *SEAFOOD* Sustainable seafood served in a striking location with a raw bar, towering floor-to-ceiling aquariums, and Bay Bridge views. If the weather's good, ask for a table on the outdoor patio. 399 Embarcadero. ☎ 415/284-9922. www.waterbarsf.com. Entrees $28–$36. AE, DISC, MC, V. Lunch & dinner daily. Streetcar: N Judah. Map p. 103.

★★ **Yank Sing** SOMA *CHINESE* One of the city's top choices for dim sum, where small plates of both familiar and exotic dishes are rolled through the large dining space on carts. 101 Spear St. (at Rincon Center). ☎ 415/957-9300. www.yanksing.com. Dim sum $3.65–$10 for 2–6 pieces. AE, DC, MC, V. Lunch daily. Bus: 2, 6, 14, 21, or 31. Streetcar: F, J, K, L, or M. BART: Embarcadero. Map p. 103.

★★ **Zuni Café** HAYES VALLEY *MEDITERRA-NEAN* Despite the Southwestern name, the seasonal fare at this longtime favorite riffs on Italian and French cooking. It's famous for its whole roasted chicken for two with a Tuscan-style bread salad. 1658 Market St. ☎ 415/552-2522. www.zunicafe.com. Entrees $10–$29. AE, MC, V. Lunch & dinner Tues–Sun. Bus: 6, 47, 49 or or 71. Streetcar: All Market St. streetcars. Map p. 102.

Meals on Wheels

By bike, pushcart, and tricked-out taco truck they come—creative, entrepreneurial chefs serving upscale street food at a corner near you. From **Boccalone's** artisan sandwiches to **Spencer on the Go!**'s French fare, San Francisco's dining scene has come to a real fork in the road. Legions of fans follow the action on Twitter, but you can get an overview of who's where at www.sfcartproject.com.

San Francisco Hotel Best Bets

Best for Families
Argonaut Hotel, 495 Jefferson St. (p. 109)

Best Place to Spot a Musician
The Phoenix Hotel, 601 Eddy St. (p. 114)

Best Green Hotel
The Orchard Garden Hotel, 466 Bush St.
(p. 114)

Best Place to Spot a Beefeater
Sir Francis Drake, 450 Powell St. (p. 115)

Best Pool
St. Regis Hotel, 125 Third St. (p. 115)

Best Luxury Hotel
Ritz-Carlton San Francisco, 600 Stockton St.
(p. 115)

Best Historic Hotel
 The Fairmont San Francisco, 950 Mason St.
(p. 109)

Best Place in the Haight
Stanyan Park Hotel, 750 Stanyan St. (p. 115)

Best Place in the Castro
The Parker Guest House, 520 Church St.
(p. 114)

Best Bargain
The Mosser, 54 Fourth St. (p. 114)

Best Place to Park Your Hybrid Car
The Good Hotel, 112 Seventh St. (p. 112)

Best Place for Bohemian Style
The Hotel Bohème, 444 Columbus Ave.
(p. 112)

Best Place for Nightlife
W San Francisco Hotel, 181 Third St. (p. 115)

Best Boutique Hotel
The Harbor Court, 165 Steuart St. (p. 112)

Best Modern Hotel
The InterContinental San Francisco, 888
Howard St. (p. 114)

Best Hotel for Art Lovers
Hotel des Arts, 447 Bush St. (p. 113)

> *Cheerful rooms, a friendly staff, and a great location near Fisherman's Wharf make the Argonaut Hotel tops
> for families.*

San Francisco Hotels A to Z

★★ **Argonaut Hotel** FISHERMAN'S WHARF
A favorite of families and lovers of maritime
history, this nautically themed hotel is located
in a restored 1907 building perfectly located
on the wharf. 495 Jefferson St. ☎ 866/415-
0704 or 415/563-0800. www.argonauthotel.
com. 252 units. Doubles $189–$389. AE, DC,
DISC, MC, V. Bus: 19, 30, or 47. Streetcar: F.
Cable car: Powell-Hyde line. Map p. 111.

★★ **Best Western Tuscan Inn at Fisherman's
Wharf** FISHERMAN'S WHARF This cozy hotel
features a rustic Italian motif, a great location
near many tourist attractions, well-decorated
rooms, and good bang for your hotel buck.
425 N. Point St. ☎ 800/648-4626 or 415/561-
1100. www.tuscaninn.com. 221 units. Doubles
$149–$269. AE, DC, DISC, MC, V. Bus: 8X or 47.
Streetcar: F. Cable car: Powell-Mason line. Map
p. 111.

★★ **Campton Place Hotel** UNION SQUARE
This European luxury charmer has an elegant,
residential feel; opulent decor; superior service; and an unbeatable Union Square locale.
340 Stockton St. ☎ 866/332-1670 or 415/781-
5555. www.camptonplace.com. 110 units.

Doubles $250–$685. AE, DC, MC, V. Bus: 2, 3,
8X, 30, 38, 45, or 76. Cable car: Powell lines.
BART: Powell St. Map p. 111.

★★★ **The Fairmont San Francisco** NOB HILL
Grandeur, elegance, and impeccable service
are the hallmarks of this historic landmark,
which occupies nearly an entire city block.
The Tower rooms have the best bathrooms;
the rooftop garden offers great city views. 950
Mason St. ☎ 866/540-4491 or 415/772-5000.
www.fairmont.com/sanfrancisco. 591 units.
Doubles $229–$469. AE, DC, DISC, MC, V. Bus:
1. Cable car: All lines. Map p. 111.

★★★ **Four Seasons Hotel San Francisco**
SOMA A luxe property featuring some of the
city's largest guest rooms, which offer stellar
views of downtown. Fine dining, a spa, a pool,
and top-notch service round out the high-end
experience. 757 Market St. ☎ 800/819-5053 or
415/633-3000. www.fourseasons.com/san
francisco. 277 units. Doubles $375–$855. AE,
DC, DISC, MC, V. Bus: All Market St. buses.
Streetcar: F and all underground streetcars.
BART: Montgomery or Powell St. Map p. 111.

> *Corinthian columns and gilded furniture are just some of the luxurious flourishes at The Fairmont San Francisco.*

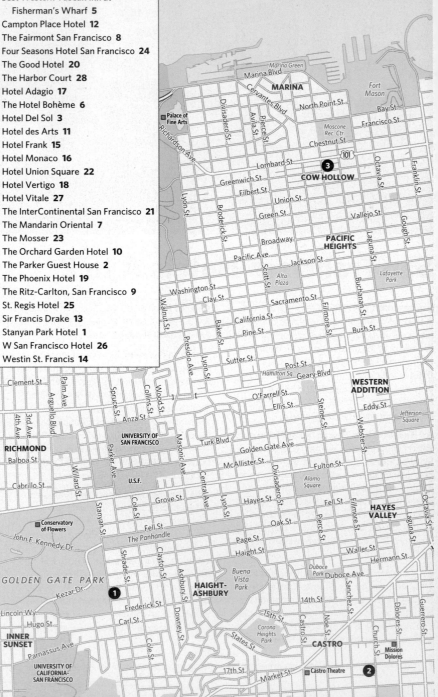

San Francisco Hotels

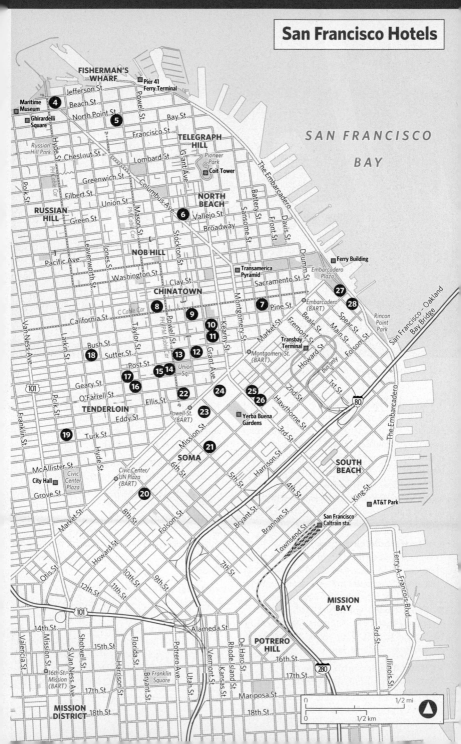

> *Like slipping into your own swanky pied à terre, a stay at the Four Seasons promises plenty of luxury.*

★ The Good Hotel SOMA

Eco-friendly good deeds are done daily at this clever hotel: Complimentary bikes are available, furniture is made from recycled materials, and you can park a hybrid vehicle overnight for free. 112 Seventh St. ☎ 800/738-7477 or 415/621-7001. www.jdvhotels.com/hotels/good. 117 units. Doubles $89–$139. AE, DC, DISC, MC, V. Bus: 6, 9, 9L, 14, 14L, 21, 19, or 71. BART: Civic Center. Map p. 111.

★★ The Harbor Court SOMA

This stylish waterfront boutique property is a great choice for its views of the Bay Bridge and Treasure Island, and for its proximity to the Ferry Building Marketplace. 165 Steuart St. ☎ 866/792-6283 or 415/882-1300. www.harborcourthotel.com. 131 units. Doubles $87–$295. AE, DC, DISC, MC, V. Bus: 2, 6, 14, 21, or 31. Streetcar: F. Map p. 111.

★★ Hotel Adagio UNION SQUARE

Hipness reigns at this stylish Spanish colonial revival hotel, featuring clean, contemporary interiors and sleek rooms with lots of upscale amenities. 550 Geary St. ☎ 800/228-8830 or 415/775-5000. www.thehoteladagio.com. 171 units. Doubles $159–$349. AE, DISC, MC, V. Bus: 2, 3, 27, 38, or 76. Map p. 111.

★★ The Hotel Bohème NORTH BEACH

An homage to the Beat era, these modest bohemian-style digs are stocked with art and literature from the late 1950s. Poetry readings take place on Sunday. 444 Columbus Ave. ☎ 415/433-9111. www.hotelboheme.com. 15 units. Doubles $174–$214. AE, DC, DISC, MC, V. Bus: 8X, 10, 12, 30, 41, or 45. Cable car: Powell-Mason line. Map p. 111.

★★ Hotel Del Sol MARINA DISTRICT

A colorful, beach-style motel that's great for families on a budget. An outdoor pool, palm trees, and hammocks aim to create a quintessential California experience. 3100 Webster St. ☎ 877/433-5765 or 415/921-5520. www.thehoteldelsol.com. 57 units. Doubles $139–$199 w/breakfast. AE, DC, DISC, MC, V. Bus: 22, 28, 41, 43, 45, or 76. Map p. 110.

> *Kermit meets Jagger in poolside sculpture at the hipster-wacky Phoenix Hotel.*

★★ **Hotel des Arts** UNION SQUARE
Artful, edgy, and a little eccentric, this small hotel near the gates of Chinatown offers rooms (only 26 have private bathrooms) painted floor-to-ceiling by local artists, a gallery, and an on-site brasserie. 447 Bush St. ☎ 800/956-4322 or 415/956-3232. www.sf hoteldesarts.com. 51 units. Doubles $59–$159 w/breakfast. AE, DC, MC, V. Bus: 2, 3, 8X, 30, 45, or 76. Cable car: Powell lines. Map p. 111.

★★ **Hotel Frank** UNION SQUARE
This chic boutique hotel is no shrinking violet—audacious design and upscale amenities make a big impression at this personality-laden gem. 386 Geary St. ☎ 800/553-1900 or 415/986-2000. www.hotelfranksf.com. 153 units. Doubles $169–$399. AE, DC, DISC, MC, V. Bus: 2, 3, 8X, 27, 30, 38, 45, or 76. Cable car: Powell lines. Map p. 111.

★★ **Hotel Monaco** UNION SQUARE
French-inspired architecture—from a giant fireplace to the frescoed lobby ceiling—highlights this delightful boutique hotel, where upscale amenities are plentiful. If only the rooms were a bit larger. 501 Geary St. ☎ 866/622-5284 or 415/292-0100. www.monaco-sf.com. 201 units. Doubles $139–$279. AE, DC, DISC, MC, V. Bus: 2, 3, 27, 38, or 76. Map p. 111.

★★ **Hotel Union Square** UNION SQUARE
Art Deco design and a sense of history permeate this comfy boutique hotel (San Francisco's first, opened in 1913); families should check out the wonderful children's suite. 114 Powell St. ☎ 800/553-1900 or 415/397-3000. www.hotelunionsquare.com. 131 units. Doubles $149–$349. AE, DC, DISC, MC, V. Bus: 8X, 27, 30, 38, or 45. Cable car: Powell lines. Streetcar: Powell St. BART: Powell St. Map p. 111.

★★ **Hotel Vertigo** NOB HILL
This playful boutique property starred in Hitchcock's classic *Vertigo* (catch the movie in your room) in a previous incarnation and provides cozy quarters in a location with slightly less bustle than Union Square, but still within easy reach of the theater district and

> An Italian Renaissance villa? Nope, it's the opulent hotel lobby, complete with antique chandeliers, at the Sir Francis Drake.

shopping. 940 Sutter St. ☎ 800/553-1900 or 415/885-6800. www.hotelvertigosf.com. 102 units. Doubles $169–$399. AE, DISC, MC, V. Bus: 2, 3, 27, or 76. Map p. 111.

★★ Hotel Vitale SOMA
Waterfront views, an on-site spa, and a farm-to-table Italian restaurant make this comfortable and stylish property an excellent option. 8 Mission St. ☎ 888/890-8868 or 415/278-3700. www.hotelvitale.com. 200 units. Doubles $269–$399. AE, DC, DISC, MC, V. Bus: 2, 6, 14, 21, or 31. Streetcar: F. Map p. 111.

★★ The InterContinental San Francisco
SOMA Sleek and contemporary, this 32-story luxury hotel opened in 2008 and boasts a great, central location and the usual amenities. You can often get a better deal here than at other comparable properties. 888 Howard St. ☎ 888/811-4273. www.intercontinentalsanfrancisco.com. 550 units. Doubles $139–$399. AE, DC, DISC, MC, V. Bus: 5, 8X, 12, 14, 14L, 27, 45, 71, or 76. BART: Powell St. Map p. 110.

★★★ The Mandarin Oriental FINANCIAL DISTRICT
The city's best combo of exceptional views and opulent accommodations. From the marble bathrooms in the contemporary Asian rooms to the regal service—this luxury leader is a winner. 222 Sansome St. ☎ 800/622-0404 or 415/276-9888. www.mandarinoriental.com. 158 units. Doubles $395–$640. AE, DC, DISC, MC, V. Bus: 2, 6, 10, 12, 21, or 31. Streetcar: F, J, K, L, or M. Cable car: California St. line. Map p. 111.

★ The Mosser SOMA
A great bargain, this hip budget hotel offers stylish and modern accommodations (some without a private bathroom), a convenient location, and an on-site bistro and bar; there's even a recording studio. 54 Fourth St. ☎ 800/227-3804 or 415/986-4400. www.themosser.com. 166 units. Doubles $47–$209. AE, DC, DISC, MC, V. Bus: 6, 8X, 21, 30, 31, or 45. Streetcar: F and all underground Muni. Cable car: Powell lines. BART: Powell St. Map p. 111.

★★ The Orchard Garden Hotel UNION SQUARE
California's first LEED-certified "green" hotel features tip-top tech amenities and luxurious comforts. 466 Bush St. ☎ 888/717-2881 or 415/399-9807. www.theorchardgardenhotel.com. 86 units. Doubles $169–$499. AE, DC, DISC, MC, V. Bus: 2, 3, 8X, 30, 45, or 76. Cable car: Powell lines. Map p. 111.

★★ The Parker Guest House THE CASTRO
This LGBT-friendly Edwardian B&B is quaint and relaxing, featuring a lovely garden and spacious guest rooms. 520 Church St. ☎ 888/520-7275 or 415/621-3222. www.parkerguesthouse.com. 21 units. Doubles $129–$199 w/breakfast. AE, DISC, MC, V. Bus: 22 or 33. Streetcar: F or J. Map p. 110.

★★ The Phoenix Hotel TENDERLOIN
A popular crash pad for touring musical acts, this retro-tropical spot has a sense of humor, a cool pool area, and a hipster-approved lounge. 601 Eddy St. ☎ 800/248-9466 or 415/776-1380. www.thephoenixhotel.com. 44 units. Doubles $119–$149 w/breakfast. AE, DC, DISC, MC, V. Bus: 19, 31, 38, 47, or 49. Map p. 111.

> *Slip into something comfortable at the St. Regis Hotel, where your room comes with a personal butler.*

★★★ The Ritz-Carlton San Francisco NOB HILL

Classic and contemporary luxuries abound at this regal 1909 landmark, the standard by which all other top-flight hotels in the city are measured. Pluses include an indoor pool, spa, stellar service, and very plush rooms. 600 Stockton St. ☎ 800/241-3333 or 415/296-7465. www.ritzcarlton.com. 336 units. Doubles $399–$579. AE, DC, DISC, MC, V. Bus: 1, 8X, 30, or 45. Cable car: All lines. Map p. 111.

★★★ St. Regis Hotel SOMA

Amenities at this 40-story ultraluxury hotel include an indoor lap pool, a spa, and personal butler service that promises to fulfill any request. The minimalist, high-tech guest rooms don't skimp on the lavish amenities. 125 Third St. ☎ 877/787-3447 or 415/284-4000. www.stregis.com/sanfrancisco. 260 units. Doubles $529–$679. AE, DC, DISC, MC, V. Bus: 8X, 14, 14L, 30, 45, or 76. Streetcar: F, J, K, L, or M. BART: Montgomery St. Map p. 111.

★★ Sir Francis Drake UNION SQUARE

Beefeater doormen add to the pomp and circumstance at this historic grande dame. The small rooms don't match the grandiose lobby, but have been modernized in bold fashion. The penthouse lounge is a classic. 450 Powell St. ☎ 800/795-7129 or 415/392-7755. www.sirfrancisdrake.com. 416 units. Doubles $134–$349. AE, DC, DISC, MC, V. Bus: 2, 3, 30, 45, or 76. Cable car: Powell lines. Map p. 111.

★★ Stanyan Park Hotel THE HAIGHT

Just steps from Golden Gate Park, this Victorian beauty is listed on the National Register of Historic Places. Soak up the period atmosphere in the antiques-filled rooms or at the hotel's afternoon tea. The six suites with full kitchens are great for families. 750 Stanyan St. ☎ 415/751-1000. www.stanyanpark.com. 36 units. Doubles $139–$225 w/breakfast. AE, DISC, MC, V. Bus: 33, 43, or 71. Streetcar: N. Map p. 110.

★★ W San Francisco Hotel SOMA

Hipsters and fashionistas are drawn to this way-cool haven, known for its sexy **XYZ** bar. Check out the panoramic views available from the fun and fabulous rooms (which come in a variety of styles). 181 Third St. ☎ 877/946-8357 or 415/777-5300. www.whotels.com/sanfrancisco. 410 units. Doubles from $359. AE, DC, DISC, MC, V. Bus: 8X, 14, 14L, 30, 45, or 76. Streetcar: F, J, K, L, or M. BART: Montgomery St. Map p. 111.

★★ Westin St. Francis UNION SQUARE

Choose from posh and ornate or decidedly modern accommodations at this majestic landmark hotel, where many a president has spent the night. 335 Powell St. ☎ 866/500-0038 or 415/397-7000. www.westinstfrancis.com. 1,195 units. Doubles $179–$559. AE, DC, DISC, MC, V. Bus: 2, 3, 30, 38, 45, or 76. Cable car: Powell lines. BART: Powell St. Map p. 111.

Nightlife & Entertainment Best Bets

Best Place to Dance Till Sunrise
The Endup, 401 Sixth St. (p. 117)

Best Jazz Club
Yoshi's Jazz Club and Japanese Restaurant,
1330 Fillmore St. (p. 123)

Best Blues Club
Biscuits and Blues, 401 Mason St. (p. 122)

Best Place for a Rock Show
Fillmore Auditorium, 1805 Geary Blvd. (p. 122)

Best Speakeasy
Bourbon & Branch, 501 Jones St. (p. 121)

Best Martini Menu
The Top of the Mark, 1 Nob Hill (p. 122)

Best Theater Company
American Conservatory Theatre, 415 Geary
St. (p. 122)

Best Agitprop Theater Company
San Francisco Mime Troupe, various locations
(p. 123)

Best Modern Dance Company
ODC Dance, 351 Shotwell St. (p. 123)

Best Classical Dance Company
San Francisco Ballet, 301 Van Ness Ave.
(p. 123)

Best Place for a Cocktail and a Movie
Sundance Kabuki Cinemas, 1881 Post St.
(p. 120)

Best Revue
Beach Blanket Babylon, 678 Green St. (p. 117)

Best Classical Music
San Francisco Symphony, 201 Van Ness
(p. 123)

Best Professional Sports Action
San Francisco Giants, AT&T Park, 24 Willie
Mays Plaza (p. 123)

Best Dinner Show
Teatro ZinZanni, Pier 29 at Battery St. (p. 123)

Best Retro Nightclub
Harry Denton's Starlight Lounge, 450 Powell
St. (p. 121)

Best Place for a Belly Laugh
Punch Line Comedy Club, 444 Battery St.
(p. 117)

> *Make it a point to see the San Francisco Ballet, one of the finest dance companies in the world.*

Nightlife & Entertainment
A to Z

Comedy & Cabaret

★ **Beach Blanket Babylon** NORTH BEACH
This cheeky revue, featuring amazing costumes, has been poking fun at pop culture since 1974. Club Fugazi, 678 Green St. ☎ 415/421-4222. www.beachblanketbabylon.com. Tickets $25–$80. Bus: 8X, 30, 41, or 45. Cable car: Powell-Mason line. Map p. 119.

★ **Punch Line Comedy Club** EMBARCADERO
The largest comedy club in San Francisco attracts local and national acts Tuesday through Sunday. You must be 18 to enter. 444 Battery St. ☎ 415/397-4337 or 415/397-7573. www.punchlinecomedyclub.com. Tickets $8–$20. Bus: 1, 10, 12, or 41. BART: Embarcadero. Map p. 119.

Dance Clubs

★ **The Endup** SOMA
You can literally dance the night away here, especially on Saturday when the music never stops (don't forget your sunglasses); you'll find beats of some kind every night of the week. 401 Sixth St. ☎ 415/646-0999. www.theendup.com. Cover free–$20. Bus: 8X, 12, 27, or 47. Map p.119.

Ruby Skye UNION SQUARE
A Victorian theater transformed into a huge dance palace with high-tech lighting and a thumping sound system. 420 Mason St. ☎ 415/693-0777. www.rubyskye.com. Cover free–$30. Bus: 2, 3, 38, or 76. Cable car: Powell lines. Map p. 119.

★ **1015 Folsom** SOMA
Sweaty good times are to be had in this enormous multilevel, multiroom warehouse, a longtime player on the club scene. Major DJ talent holds court in the main room. 1015 Folsom St. ☎ 415/431-1200. www.1015.com. Cover free–$25. Bus: 8X, 12, 27, or 47. Map p. 119.

Film

★★ **Castro Theatre** CASTRO
Foreign films, special engagements of first-run movies, and special events are screened at this beautiful landmark theater built in 1922. 429 Castro St. ☎ 415/621-6120. www.castrotheatre.com. Tickets $10 adults, $7.50 seniors and kids 12 & under. Prices vary for special events. Cash only at box office. Bus: 24 or 33. Muni: Castro Station. Streetcar: F. Map p. 118.

> *Raise the curtain at The Castro, a 1922 restored movie palace known for creative and sometimes outrageous films and festivals.*

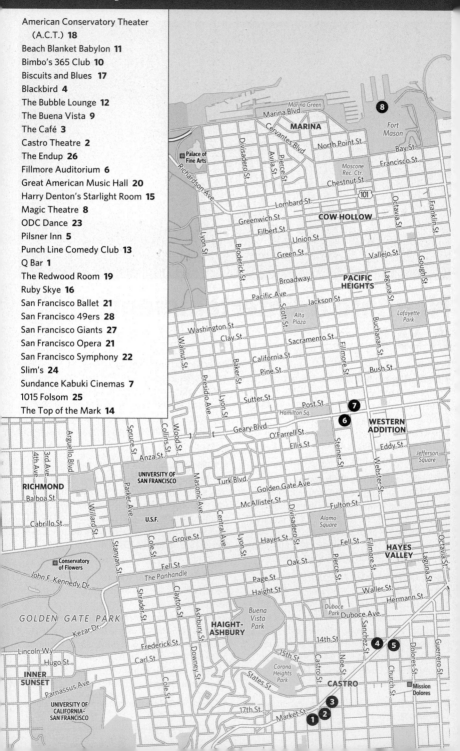

San Francisco Nightlife & Entertainment

> Get dolled up for Harry Denton's Starlight Lounge, with live music, smooth drinks, and even classy drag shows on Sundays.

★★ Sundance Kabuki Cinemas JAPANTOWN
The way moviegoing was meant to be, with reserved seating, cocktails, gourmet food (including a full-service restaurant), and chic surroundings. Eight screens show independent films; every April it's also the home base for the **★★ San Francisco International Film Festival** (☎ 415/561-5000; www.sffs.org). 1881 Post St. ☎ 415/326-3243. www.sundance cinemas.com. Tickets $9–$16 adults, $8–$13 kids. Bus: 2, 3, 22, or 38. Map p. 118.

Gay/Lesbian Bars & Clubs
★ Blackbird CASTRO
A cool and classy lounge where all are welcome, but men tend to dominate. There's a good selection of California wine and craft beer on tap. 2124 Market St. ☎ 415/503-0630. www.blackbirdbar.com. Bus: 22. Muni: Church St. Streetcar: F. Map p. 118.

The Café CASTRO
Remodeled in 2009, this bar and club features upgraded sound and lighting systems and draws a mixed gay, lesbian, and straight crowd. 2369 Market St. ☎ 415/861-3846. www.cafesf.com. Cover free–$5. Bus: 24 or 33. Muni: Castro Station. Streetcar: F. Map p. 118.

Pilsner Inn CASTRO
This longtime neighborhood bar attracts a mixed crowd and features lots of beers on tap, a pool table and darts, and a great garden patio. 225 Church St. ☎ 415/621-7058. www. pilsnerinn.com. Bus: 22. Muni: Church St. Streetcar: F. Map p. 118.

★ Q Bar CASTRO
Every night of the week has a different musical flavor, from indie to hip-hop to '80s; Tuesday night is specifically for women. 456 Castro St. ☎ 415/864-2877. www.qbarsf.com. Cover free–$3. Bus: 24 or 33. Muni: Castro Station. Streetcar: F. Map p. 118.

Discount Tickets
Tix Bay Area (☎ 415/433-7827; www. tixbayarea.org), Union Square, on Powell Street between Geary and Post streets, sells half-price, day-of tickets (beginning at 11am) to select performing arts shows. Full-price advance tickets are also available. It's open Tuesday to Friday 11am to 6pm, Saturday 10am to 6pm, and Sunday 10am to 3pm.

Lounges

★ **The Bubble Lounge** FINANCIAL DISTRICT More than 300 champagnes and sparkling wines are on hand at this posh two-story joint, a pick-up spot for the BMW crowd; there's dancing downstairs. 714 Montgomery St. ☎ 415/434-4204. www.bubblelounge.com. Bus: 1, 8X, 30, or 41. Map p. 119.

★ **The Buena Vista** FISHERMAN'S WHARF It's been a bar since 1916 and the Irish Coffee as we know it was conceived here in 1952. The messy, assembly-line production of the

Cocktail Culture

Cocktails are serious business in the city, with creative mixologists taking adult beverages to new heights, using seasonal, organic products and liquor from boutique distillers. Move over foodies, the drinkies are here. You'll need a password to access the 1920s-style Tenderloin speakeasy ★★★ **Bourbon & Branch,** 501 Jones St. (☎ 415/346-1735; www.bourbonandbranch.com); make a reservation by phone or online.

Other major players on the artisanal cocktail scene include ★★ **Absinthe Brasserie & Bar,** 398 Hayes St. (☎ 415/551-1590; www.absinthe.com); ★★ **Rickhouse,** 246 Kearny St. (☎ 415/398-2827; www.rickhousebar.com); ★★ **Elixir,** 3200 16th St. (☎ 415/552-1633; www.elixirsf.com); and ★★ the **Alembic,** 1725 Haight St. (☎ 415/666-0822; www.alembicbar.com). And don't forget an Irish coffee, a San Francisco tradition, at the Buena Vista Café, 2765 Hyde St. (☎ 415/474-5044; www.thebuenavista.com).

> *A high note in culture in the City by the Bay— the San Francisco Opera stages ten fabulous productions annually.*

drinks makes a great photo op. 2765 Hyde St. ☎ 415/474-5044. www.thebuenavista.com. No cover. Bus: 19, 30, or 47. Cable Car: Powell-Hyde. Map p 119.

★ **Harry Denton's Starlight Lounge** UNION SQUARE Dress to the nines for an evening of 1930s-style glamour, complete with awesome views and DJs and live bands playing everything from '80s hits to jazz. In the Sir Francis Drake Hotel, 450 Powell St. ☎ 415/395-8595. www.harrydenton.com. Cover Wed–Fri $10, Sat $15. Bus: 2, 3, 30, 38, 45, or 76. Cable car: Powell lines. Map p. 119.

★ **The Redwood Room** UNION SQUARE Drinks are pricey, but the expense-account crowd doesn't seem to mind. Do poke your head in to marvel at this fabulous wood-paneled room; note the living portraits on the wall—they move, like something out of

> *A splash hit by the bay, AT&T Park hosts the San Francisco Giants, the city's Major League Baseball team. Don't miss the garlic fries!*

Disneyland's Haunted Mansion. In the Clift Hotel, 495 Geary St. ☎ 415/929-2372. www.clifthotel.com. Bus: 2, 3, 27, 38, or 76. Map p. 119.

★ The Top of the Mark NOB HILL

With spectacular 360-degree city views and 100 martinis to choose from, this space is San Francisco at its romantic, nostalgic best. In the InterContinental Mark Hopkins Hotel, 1 Nob Hill. ☎ 415/616-6916. www.topofthemark.com. Cover $5–$10. Bus: 1. Cable car: All lines. Map p. 119.

Music Venues & Clubs

★★ Bimbo's 365 Club NORTH BEACH

Open since 1931 (and in this location since '51), this swanky club has seen performances by everyone from Rita Hayworth to the Raconteurs. 1025 Columbus Ave. ☎ 415/474-0365. www.bimbos365club.com. Tickets usually $20–$25; 2-drink minimum. Bus: 30. Cable car: Powell-Mason line. Map p. 119.

★ Biscuits and Blues UNION SQUARE

Blues legends and legends in the making play this intimate space featuring a great sound system and tasty Southern cuisine. 401 Mason St. ☎ 415/292-2583. www.biscuitsandblues.com. Cover $5–$25; 2-drink minimum if you're not dining. Bus: 2, 3, 4, 27, 38, or 76. Cable car: Powell lines. Map p. 119.

★★★ Fillmore Auditorium WESTERN ADDITION This legendary 1960s rock venue rolls on; check out the collection of vintage posters documenting the Fillmore's history. 1805 Geary Blvd.

☎ 415/346-6000. www.thefillmore.com. Tickets $20–$90. Bus: 2, 3, 22, or 38. Map p. 118.

★★ kids Great American Music Hall TENDERLOIN This all-ages venue is a gilded Edwardian music hall built in 1907—even if the band sucks, the building will still hold your attention. And you can get a full dinner with your show! 859 O'Farrell St. ☎ 415/885-0750. www.musichallsf.com. Tickets $10–$25. Bus: 19 or 38. Map p. 119.

★★ kids Slim's SOMA

Opened by musician Boz Scaggs in 1988, Slim's presents eclectic bands, from alternative to zydeco; dinner is available. 333 11th St. ☎ 415/255-0333. www.slims-sf.com. Cover free–$30. Bus: 9, 12, or 47. Map p. 119.

Performing Arts

★★★ American Conservatory Theatre (A.C.T.) UNION SQUARE

This Tony Award-winning theater company, one of the country's best, presents classics and new works from September to July in a historic theater. In the Geary Theater, 415 Geary St. ☎ 415/749-2228. www.act-sf.org. Tickets $14–$82. Bus: 2, 3, 27, 38, or 76. BART: Powell St. Cable car: Powell lines. Map p. 119.

★ Magic Theatre MARINA

Since 1967, this acclaimed theater has completely dedicated itself to developing new work and new voices; the season runs October to May. Fort Mason Center, Bldg. D, Marina Blvd. at Buchanan St. ☎ 415/441-8822. www.

magictheatre.org. Tickets $20–$55. Bus: 28. Map p. 118.

★★ ODC Dance THE MISSION

This innovative modern dance company is known for its athletic fusion of ballet and contemporary technique and for its collaborations with artists of various disciplines. In the ODC Theater, 351 Shotwell St. ☎ 415/863-6606. www.odcdance.org. Tickets $10–$90. Bus: 12, 14, 22, 33, or 49. BART: 16th St. Map p. 119.

★★★ San Francisco Ballet CIVIC CENTER

This is the oldest professional ballet company in the country, founded in 1933, and it's regarded as one of the best. The season generally runs February to May, with *The Nutcracker* staged in December. In the War Memorial Opera House, 301 Van Ness Ave. ☎ 415/865-2000. www.sfballet.org. Tickets $10–$205. Bus: 5, 21, 47, or 49. Streetcar: F. BART: Civic Center. Muni: Van Ness. Map p. 119.

★★★ San Francisco Opera CIVIC CENTER

North America's second-largest opera company, this has been one of the city's treasures since 1923. Ten operas are staged annually from September to July. In the War Memorial Opera House, 301 Van Ness Ave. ☎ 415/864-3330. www.sfopera.com. Tickets $24–$235. Bus: 5, 21, 47, or 49. Streetcar: F. BART: Civic Center. Muni: Van Ness. Map p. 119.

★★★ San Francisco Mime Troupe VARIOUS LOCATIONS

This Tony Award–winning guerilla theater company performs satirical, politically charged musical theater productions throughout the city at various parks. ☎ 415/285-1717. www.sfmt.org. Free.

★★★ San Francisco Symphony CIVIC CENTER

Another beloved cultural icon, the well-respected symphony was founded in 1911 and has earned 11 Grammy Awards for its recordings; since 1995 it has been under the direction of acclaimed conductor Michael Tilson Thomas. The season runs September to June, plus a summer festival. In Davies Symphony Hall, 201 Van Ness Ave. ☎ 415/864-6000. www.sfsymphony.org. Tickets $25–$114. Bus: 5, 21, 47, or 49. Streetcar: F. BART: Civic Center. Muni: Van Ness. Map p. 119.

Spectator Sports

San Francisco 49ers CANDLESTICK POINT

It's been a while since they've been to the Super Bowl, but tickets to San Francisco's National Football League team still sell out early. For public transportation info contact Silverado Stages (☎ 866/766-4937; www.49erbus.com). In Candlestick Park, Giants Dr. and Gilman Ave. ☎ 415/464-9377. www.sf49ers.com. Tickets $59–$113. Map p. 119.

★★ San Francisco Giants SOMA

The city's Major League Baseball team plays at one of the best and most modern ballparks in the country. Tickets are hard to come by. In AT&T Park, 24 Willie Mays Plaza, at King and Second sts. ☎ 415/972-2000. www.giants.mlb.com. Tickets $10–$120. Bus: 10, 30, 45, or 76. Streetcar: N or T. Map p. 119.

Dinner and a Show

For a pairing of a fine meal and a great night of entertainment you can't beat ★★ **Yoshi's Jazz Club and Japanese Restaurant,** 1330 Fillmore St. (☎ 415/655-5600; www.yoshis.com), or ★★★ **Teatro ZinZanni,** Pier 29 at Battery St. (☎ 415/438-2668; http://love.zinzanni.org). Yoshi's serves up its Japanese fare in a warmly modern dining room in front, then presents top-name jazz talent in a sweet 400-seat theater in back. Teatro ZinZanni is a cabaret-meets-cirque extravaganza that promises "love, chaos, and dinner."

Sausalito

Hillsides stacked with pricey homes drop down to a sparkling bay filled with yachts and houseboats, giving charming Sausalito the appearance of a seaside Mediterranean resort village. Located across the bay from San Francisco, this visitor-friendly town makes an excellent day trip destination thanks to its stupendous vistas, as well as a host of boutiques, galleries, and restaurants.

> Catch the sunset from a vantage point above Fort Baker and the north end of San Francisco Bay.

START SF Ferry Building downtown at the Embarcadero and Mission St. or Pier 41. Bus 30. Streetcar F. BART/Muni at the Embarcadero or Pier 41 (Fisherman's Wharf).

1 ★★ **Ferry across the bay.** Getting there really is part of the fun. There are two locations to hop on a ferry, either at the **Ferry Building** (p. 59, **2**) at the foot of Market Street or Pier 41 at **Fisherman's Wharf** (p. 56, **4**). It's about a 30-minute trip, but the ride is truly exhilarating, offering memorable views of the city skyline, Alcatraz, and the Golden Gate Bridge. The Society of American Travel Writers went so far as to rank it as one of the most exciting ferry rides in the

world. ⏱ 30 min. Golden Gate Ferry Service at the Ferry Building: ☎ 511 or 415/455-2000. www.goldengateferry.org. One-way tickets $8 adults, $4 seniors and kids 6–18, free for kids 5 & under. Departures Mon–Fri 7:30am–8pm, Sat–Sun 10:30am–6:30pm. Blue & Gold Fleet: ☎ 415/705-8200. www.blueandgoldfleet.com. One-way tickets $9.50 adults, $5.25 kids 5–11, free for kids under 5. Departures Mon–Fri vary seasonally ; Sat–Sun 10:30am–5:15pm. Call ahead for schedule.

2 ★ **Fort Baker.** Overlooking Horseshoe Cove and the Golden Gate Bridge, this former army base, established in 1866, is now home to the luxurious Cavallo Point Lodge and the Bay

Area Discovery Museum (**3**). Take a stroll around the lovely resort with its expansive grass parade grounds and beautifully restored 100-year-old structures; there's also a great bar and restaurant here. From the wharf at the cove's western edge you can practically touch the bridge. ⏱ 45 min. 601 Murray Circle. ☎ 888/651-2003 or 415/339-4700. www.cavallopoint.com.

3 ★ kids **Bay Area Discovery Museum.** Kids love this indoor/outdoor 7½-acre facility featuring lots of hands-on, interactive activities designed to spark young imaginations. There are programs featuring art, music, and science—as well as good old-fashioned play areas—aimed at children from age 6 months to 8 years old. Lookout Cove (with a scaled model of the Golden Gate Bridge and a "shipwreck") is a standout. ⏱ At least 1 hr. 557 McReynolds Rd.. ☎ 415/339-3900. www. baykidsmuseum.org. Admission $10 adults, $8 seniors and kids 1–17. Tues–Fri 9am–4pm; Sat-Sun 10am–5pm.

4 ★ **Bridgeway and Caledonia Streets.** Stroll along these two streets for boutique shopping, gallery hopping, wine tasting, and dining. ⏱ 1 hr.

5 ★ **Bay Model Visitor Center.** One of the region's quirkier attractions, this 1½-acre working hydraulic model of the San Francisco Bay was built in the 1950s by the U.S. Army Corps of Engineers to study environmental and other impacts on the bay. ⏱ 1 hr. 2100 Bridgeway. ☎ 415/332-3871. www.spn.usace.army.mil/bmvc. Free admission. Tues–Sat 9am–4pm.

6 ★★ **Venice Gourmet.** Gather all the fixings for an excellent waterfront picnic at this Mediterranean-style marketplace and deli, where you will find international treats, fine wines, and sweets. 625 Bridgeway. ☎ 415/332-3544. www. venicegourmet.com. Sandwiches $5.50–$7.50.

Visitor Information

For information on other things to do in Sausalito, contact the Chamber of Commerce (☎ 415/331-7262. www.sausalito.org).

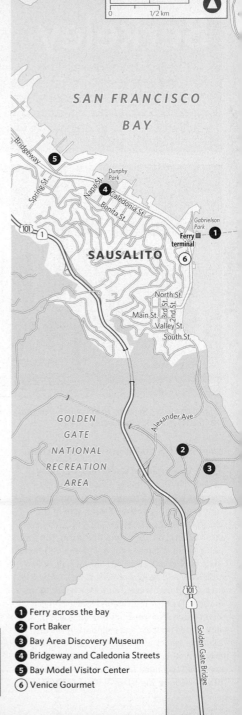

1 Ferry across the bay
2 Fort Baker
3 Bay Area Discovery Museum
4 Bridgeway and Caledonia Streets
5 Bay Model Visitor Center
6 Venice Gourmet

Berkeley

Across the bay from San Francisco is passionate and progressive Berkeley, birthplace of the 1960s free speech movement and home to the state's premier public university. It's not the hotbed of activism it once was, but it still retains its youthful zeal, as well as the intellectual and artistic curiosity that are the hallmarks of any great college town.

> Berkeley's major shopping thoroughfare, Telegraph Avenue, is a great place to soak up the alternative vibe of this eclectic and fun university town.

START BART to downtown Berkeley station.

❶ ★★ University of California, Berkeley.
Founded in 1868, this is a lovely, woodsy campus well worth exploring. An architectural highlight is **Sather Tower,** one of the world's tallest campaniles (307 ft.). You can stroll around on your own, but taking the free guided tour will make for a richer experience. ⏱ 1½ hr. Visitor Center, 101 Sproul Hall, at Bancroft Way and Telegraph Ave. ☎ 510/642-5215. http://visitors.berkeley.edu. Mon–Fri 8:30am–4:30pm. Free 90-min. guided tours Mon–Sat 10am & Sun 1pm (reservations suggested); self-guided podcast and cellphone tours also available (check website). Campanile: admission to observation platform $2 adults, $1 seniors and kids 17 & under. Mon–Fri 10am–3:45pm; Sat 10am–4:45pm; Sun 10am–1:30pm & 3–4:45pm.

❷ ★★ Berkeley Art Museum and Pacific Film Archive. Founded in 1935, the museum houses an impressive collection of works spanning the centuries (from Rubens to Rothko). The archive, founded in 1966, has an incredible holding of films and videos, most notably in the international genre. Film screenings take place daily. ⏱ At least 1 hr. 2626 Bancroft Way. ☎ 510/642-0808. www.bampfa.berkeley.edu. Admission $8 adults, $5 seniors and kids 13–17; films $9.50 adults, $6.50 seniors and kids 17 & under. Wed–Sun 11am–5pm.

Dining Tip

Food lovers can top off a visit to Berkeley with dinner at Chez Panisse (p. 104); just be sure to make a reservation well in advance.

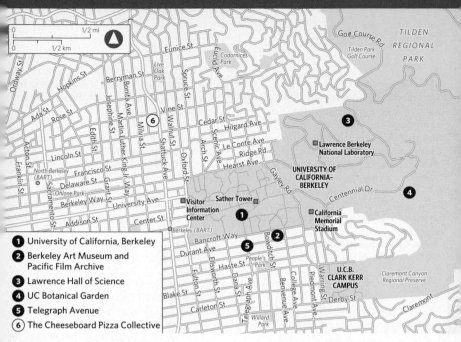

1. University of California, Berkeley
2. Berkeley Art Museum and Pacific Film Archive
3. Lawrence Hall of Science
4. UC Botanical Garden
5. Telegraph Avenue
6. The Cheeseboard Pizza Collective

3 ★★ kids Lawrence Hall of Science. Interactive science and nature exhibits appealing primarily to kids set atop a fabulous hilltop location. There's also a top-notch planetarium. ⏱ At least 1 hr. Centennial Dr. ☎ 510/642-5132. www.lhs.berkeley.edu. Admission $12 adults, $9 seniors and kids 7–18, $6 kids 3–6. Daily 10am–5pm. Bus: Hill shuttle (Mon–Fri) or 65.

4 ★★ UC Botanical Garden. A vast collection of some 13,000 species of plants and trees—from orchids to redwoods to cacti—can be found at this amazing 34-acre university facility. ⏱ 2 hr. 200 Centennial Dr. ☎ 510/643-2755. www.botanicalgarden.berkeley.edu. Admission $7 adults, $5 seniors and kids 13–17, $2 kids 5–12. Daily 9am–5pm. Bus: Hill shuttle (Mon–Fri).

5 Telegraph Avenue. This thoroughfare brims with local flavor (for better or worse), shops, street vendors, and eateries. Do stop in at ★★★ **Moe's Books,** 2476 Telegraph Ave. (☎ 510/849-2087; www.moesbooks.com), and ★★★ **Amoeba Music,** 2455 Telegraph Ave. (☎ 510/549-1125; www.amoeba.com). Telegraph Ave. btw. Bancroft Way & Dwight Way. www.telegraphave.org or www.telegraphshop.com.

6 ★★ The Cheeseboard Pizza Collective. Just one delicious gourmet, vegetarian pizza is offered every day. No choices? No problem. 1512 Shattuck Ave. ☎ 510/549-3055. www.cheeseboardcollective.coop. Full pizza $20. Cash only.

Berkeley Theaters

Catch a live performance at one of the city's arts and entertainment stalwarts—the ★★★ **Berkeley Repertory Theatre,** 2025 Addison St. (☎ 510/647-2949; www.berkeleyrep.org), or ★★ **Freight & Salvage Coffeehouse,** 2020 Addison St. (☎ 510/644-2020; www.thefreight.org). The Tony Award-winning Berkeley Rep is one of the country's most innovative and exciting theater companies (in 2009, it produced the world premiere of the rock opera *American Idiot* by local megaband Green Day). Freight & Salvage is an all-ages 1960s folkie holdover that presents traditional and world music, with an emphasis on American roots styles.

Fast Facts

Discount Passes

San Francisco CityPASS (☎ 888/330-5008; www.citypass.com) provides hefty savings on admission to five attractions (including the California Academy of Sciences and the Exploratorium), gives you unlimited access to all Muni transportation (including cable cars), and also features discount coupons for other activities. It's $59 for adults and $39 for kids 5 to 12, available at participating attractions or online, and valid for 9 days (Muni pass good for 7 days).

The **Go San Francisco Card** (☎ 800/887-9103; www.gosanfranciscocard.com) offers free or discounted admission to 50 attractions or tours, as well as deals on shopping and dining. You can purchase 1-, 2-, 3-, 5-, or 7-day cards; prices range from $55 for adults and $40 for kids 3 to 12 for a 1-day card to $160/$125 for a 7-day card. Go cards are available at the San Francisco Visitor Information Center (see "Visitor Information," below), Tix Bay Area at Union Square (☎ 415/433-7827), or online.

Emergencies

Dial ☎ **911** to report a fire, call the police, or get an ambulance. For nonurgent issues, call the **San Francisco Police Department,** Central Station, 766 Vallejo St. (☎ 415/553-0123; www.sf-police.org).

Saint Francis Memorial Hospital, 900 Hyde St. (☎ 415/353-6000; www.saint francismemorial.org) provides emergency service 24 hours a day; no appointment is necessary. The hospital also operates a **physician-referral service** (☎ 800/333-1355 or 415/353-6566).

Getting There

BY PLANE **San Francisco International Airport** (☎ 650/821-8211; www.flysfo.com), aka SFO, is 14 miles south of downtown San Francisco. To get into town from SFO, **Bay Area Rapid Transit,** better known as BART (☎ 415/989-2278; www.bart.gov), is quick and easy. The station is located adjacent to the International Terminal; the **AirTrain** shuttle can deliver you there from other terminals. The trip downtown takes about 35 minutes; the one-way fare to Powell Street (Union Square) is $8.10. Trains leave about every 15 minutes. **SuperShuttle** vans (☎ 800/258-3826 or 415/558-8500; www.supershuttle.com) will take you downtown for $17. A **cab** ride (20–40 min.) to town can be $35 to $40. Across the bay, **Oakland International Airport** (☎ 800/247-6255 or 510/563-3300; www.oaklandairport.com), or OAK, is often used by travelers making their way to San Francisco. It's farther away but is less crowded, is served by BART, and experiences less fog-related delays. From Oakland airport, take the **AirBART** shuttle bus ($3) to the Coliseum/Oakland Airport BART station, about a 15-minute ride. Buses run about every 10 minutes, Monday to Saturday 5am to midnight and Sunday 8am to midnight. BART fare to the Powell Street station (Union Square) is $3.80; trip time is about 45 minutes. **BayPorter Express** (☎ 877/467-1800 or 415/467-1800; www.bayporter.com) offers door-to-door service for $32 for adults ($15 for each additional adult in your party), and $10 for kids 11 & under. A **cab** ride to downtown San Francisco will run in excess of $50. BY TRAIN **Amtrak** (☎ 800/872-7245; www.amtrak.com) arrives and departs from the East Bay, with bus connections offered to several points in the city. **Caltrain** (☎ 800/660-4287; www.caltrain.com) operates train service between San Francisco and the towns of the peninsula. The station is at 700 Fourth St. BY CAR San Francisco is accessible from the north and south via U.S. 101 and Hwy. 1 and by I-80 and I-580 from the northeast and east, respectively. From Los Angeles, you can take either the scenic coastal route along Hwy. 1/U.S. 101 (437 miles), which takes about 11 hours, or the inland route along I-5 to I-580 (389 miles), which takes about 7 hours. The drive from Sacramento along I-80 is 88 miles and takes about 1½ hours.

Getting Around

BY BUS San Francisco has a good bus system run by the **San Francisco Municipal Transportation Agency,** better known as Muni (☎ 311 or 415/701-2311; www.sfmta.com), which also oversees the streetcars and cable cars. Bus fares are $2 (75¢ for seniors, disabled riders, and kids 5 to 17); transfers are good for 90 minutes. Bus stops are designated in a number of ways, including bus shelters, yellow bands painted on utility poles, and curb markings. Service generally runs from 6am to midnight, but there are several "owl" lines. **BY STREETCAR** There are seven streetcar lines, most of which run underground through downtown and then resurface to street level in the outer neighborhoods. The most popular and handy line for visitors is the F, made up of restored vintage streetcars from around the world. Fares are the same as buses; service runs from about 6am to 2am. **BY CABLE CAR** Due to their expense ($5 per ride) and limited coverage, these historic vehicles are more of a tourist attraction than a practical means of transportation. Service runs from 6am to 1am. **BY BART Bay Area Rapid Transit** (☎ 415/989-2278; www.bart.gov) is a high-speed rail network connecting San Francisco with the East Bay, including Berkeley and Oakland, as well as points south. It's also a convenient way to get to the Mission District from downtown. Fares range from $1.75 to $8.10; ticket vending machines accept up to a $20 bill, some machines accept credit and debit cards. Service is generally Monday to Friday 4am to midnight, Saturday 6am to midnight, and Sunday 8am to midnight. **BY FERRY** See p. 58, ❶. **BY TAXI** Try **De Soto Cab Company** (☎ 415/970-1300), **Yellow Cab** (☎ 415/333-3333), or **Luxor Cab Company** (☎ 415/282-4141). Expect competition for cabs on Friday and Saturday nights; call ahead for pickup. Taxis are $3.10 at the flag and 45¢ for each additional ⅕ mile. In compact San Francisco, cabs are definitely a useful mode of transportation. **BY CAR** San Francisco is not a car-friendly city, and I don't recommend driving. If you do have a vehicle, your best bet is to leave it parked at your hotel or in a garage (which can get expensive) and explore the city on foot and via public transportation.

Internet Access

One good option is **Quetzal Internet Cafe,** 1234 Polk St., Nob Hill (☎ 415/673-4181; www.quetzal.org). You can also find access at public libraries, including the main branch at the Civic Center, 100 Larkin St. (☎ 415/557-4400; www.sfpl.org), and copy/shipping stores such as **FedEx Office,** which has a 24-hour outlet in the Financial District, 100 California St. (☎ 415/(834-0240; www.fedex.com).

Pharmacies

You'll find pharmacies in drugstores and even in some grocery stores across the city. **Walgreens** (www.walgreens.com) has 24-hour pharmacies at their outlets in the Castro, 498 Castro St. (☎ 415/861-3136), and in the Marina, 3201 Divisidero St. (☎ 415/931-6417).

Safety

San Francisco is a relatively safe destination, but certain neighborhoods require you to exercise your best big-city vigilance. The Tenderloin, the Mission, Lower Haight, Golden Gate Park, and areas south of the Civic Center can be sketchy after dark. Petty theft is common throughout the city; if something's not locked down or kept out of sight, chances are someone might pinch it.

Taxes

A sales tax of 9.5% is added to almost all purchases. The hotel tax is 14%. Many restaurants pass along a "Healthy San Francisco" surcharge on the check (usually about 2%–4%).

Visitor Information

San Francisco Convention & Visitors Bureau Visitor Information Center, Hallidie Plaza, 900 Market St., at Powell Street (☎ 415/391-2000; www.onlyinsanfrancisco.com) is the best source of specialized information about the city.

4

Wine Country

The Best of Wine Country in 1 Day

The Napa and Sonoma valleys are two of the most famous wine-producing regions in the world—there are literally hundreds of wineries here, from cult boutique vintners to big-time heavy hitters. Wine Country's sophisticated charm, natural beauty, and renowned temples of gastronomy make it one California's must-do experiences. If you only have 1 day to explore, spend it in Napa Valley.

> PREVIOUS PAGE *Neatly trimmed grape vines (leaves are clipped back each winter) weave pretty patterns beneath broad oaks.* THIS PAGE *Taste a vintage from one of America's best-known filmmakers, Francis Ford Coppola, at Rubicon Estate.*

START Downtown Napa is 55 miles north of San Francisco; from San Francisco, head north on U.S. 101, turn east onto Hwy. 37 (Vallejo) and then north on Hwy. 29—the main road through Napa Valley. You will need a car to properly tour the region. TRIP LENGTH about 35 miles.

1 ★★ **Historic Napa Mill.** Highlighted by its 19th-century brickwork, tin silos, and river-front location, this complex offers shopping and dining pleasures, as well as lodgings.

These buildings are the remnants of a once-bustling embarcadero serviced by numerous wharves where schooners tied up to load and unload their goods. Today you'll find the ★ **Napa General Store,** 540 Main St. ☎ 707/259-0762; www.napageneralstore.com; Mon–Fri 8am–5pm, Sat–Sun 8am–6pm), selling artisan Wine Country products and furnishings (there's also a cafe serving break-fast and lunch); a bakery, ★ **Sweetie Pies,** 520

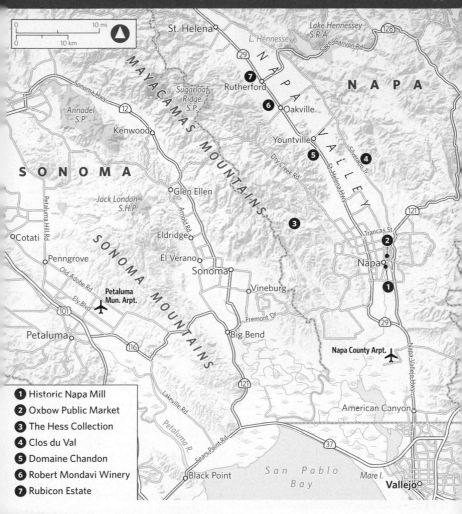

1 Historic Napa Mill
2 Oxbow Public Market
3 The Hess Collection
4 Clos du Val
5 Domaine Chandon
6 Robert Mondavi Winery
7 Rubicon Estate

Main St. (☎ 707/257-8817; www.sweetiepies.com; Sun–Wed 8am–8pm, Thurs–Sat 8am–10pm); and a confectionery, ★ **Vintage Sweet Shoppe,** 530 Main St. (☎ 707/224-2986; www.vintagesweetshoppe.com; Mon–Tues

Travel Tip

If you are doing this itinerary on a weekend in high season (late Aug to mid-Oct), you might want to reverse the order—hit the wineries early to avoid the crowds and return to Napa in the afternoon for shopping and browsing.

6:30am–6pm, Wed–Sat 6:30am–7pm, Sun 7am–5pm). If you return in the evening you can catch some live music at ★★ **Silo's Jazz Club,** 530 Main St. (☎ 707/251-5833; www.silosjazzclub.com; Wed–Thurs 5–10pm, Fri–Sat 5pm–midnight). Be sure to check out the colorful mosaic fountain that depicts the history (both good and bad), and flora and fauna of Napa Valley. ⏱ 1 hr. 500 Main St. www.historicnapamill.com.

Stroll down Main St. and take a right on First St. to Oxbow Public Market; about a ½-mile walk.

> Wine bars, move over. Now there are oyster bars in the Wine Country too. Hog Island shucks local bivalves at Oxbow Market.

❷ ★★ **Oxbow Public Market.** Food is a major recreational activity in Wine Country and this marketplace is one of its best playgrounds. Created by the folks who opened the ★★★ **Ferry Building Marketplace** in San Francisco (p. 59, **❷**), this cornucopia of purveyors and eateries offers the bounty of more than 150 local farms. Featuring everything from oysters to ice cream, this is the perfect place to pick up some gourmet picnic items for the road. There are also specialty boutiques selling culinary antiques, photography, books, and linens. ⏱ 1 hr. 610 First St. ☎ 707/226-6529. www.oxbowpublicmarket.com. Mon–Fri 9am–7pm; Sat–Sun 9am–6pm; restaurants close later. Tues and Fri often feature extended hours and special events.

Take Hwy. 29 north, exit at Trancas St., and go left on Redwood Rd.; about a 20-min. drive.

❸ ★★★ **The Hess Collection.** This site on Mount Veeder has hosted a winery since 1903, with Swiss entrepreneur Donald Hess first acquiring land here in 1978. Known for its cabernet sauvignon and chardonnay, this winery's "collection" also includes an amazing trove of contemporary art, featuring such artists as Francis Bacon, Robert Rauschenberg, and Andy Goldsworthy. Take a free self-guided iPod tour through the museum, then sample the winery's current offerings in the handsomely rustic tasting room ($10 per person). ⏱ 1 hr. 4411 Redwood Rd., Napa. ☎ 707/255-1144. www.hesscollection.com. See p. 145.

Head back down Redwood Rd. onto Trancas St., then turn left on Silverado Trail to Clos du Val. Trip time: about 20 min.

❹ ★ **Clos du Val.** In the Stags Leap District along the Silverado Trail, Napa Valley's road less traveled, is this ivy-covered winery. If you brought along some goodies from Oxbow (**❷**), the olive grove picnic area is a great place to break them out (*Note:* Many wineries do not allow you to eat any food not purchased on the premises; this place is an exception). You can play some lawn bowling, too—or *pétanque,* as the French say. To learn about sustainable viniculture, call ahead for a 30-minute tour of the demonstration vineyard; it's free with a paid tasting, but you need to make an appointment. Tastings are $10 per person; be sure to sample Ariadne, a Sémillon and sauvignon blanc blend. ⏱ 45 min. 5330 Silverado Trail, Napa. ☎ 800/993-9463 or 707/261-5200. www.closduval.com. See p. 144.

Double back on Silverado Trail to Oak Knoll Ave. and turn right, go left on Big Ranch Rd., then right again to return to Oak Knoll Ave. Make a right on Hwy. 29 N. Take the exit to Yountville and go left on California Dr. to Domaine Chandon. Trip time: 10 min.

❺ ★★ **Domaine Chandon.** Get your bubbly (don't call it champagne—only the stuff produced in France gets that privilege!) on at this contemporary, elegant spot. The Moët & Chandon folks have been producing sparkling wines for more than 250 years (and since 1973 at this location)—they know their business. And you can get to know their business

> *Inviting gardens and samplings of sparkling wines await at elegant Domaine Chandon.*

better at the visitor center and gift shop, which features a theater screening an informative winemaking video. The veranda is a great place to sample one of several flights of sparkling wine ($16–$22), and don't miss the whimsical patch of mushroom sculptures. ⏲ 45 min. 1 California Dr., Yountville. ☎ 888/242-6366. www.chandon.com. See p. 145.

Continue north on Hwy. 29 to Robert Mondavi Winery. Trip time: about 5 min.

❻ ★★ **Robert Mondavi Winery.** This Napa Valley icon opened in 1966 and features Cliff May's (1909–89) modernist mission architecture, sculptures, paintings, and winemaking antiques. A longtime leader in scheduling innovative programs and events, the winery offers a full roster of summertime concerts, culinary gatherings, and comprehensive tours. When most wineries are closing for the day, Mondavi offers a tour at 5pm Friday (1½ hr., $45); it's a great way to cap off the day. Tastings are $15 to $25 per person. ⏲ 45 min. 7801 St. Helena Hwy. (Hwy. 29), Oakville. ☎ 888/766-6328. www.robertmondaviwinery.com. See p. 146.

Keep heading north on Hwy. 29 to Rubicon Estate. Trip time: about 5 min.

❼ ★★★ **Rubicon Estate.** Exuding old-world grandeur, this château-style winery, built in 1882, has a natural flair for the dramatic—it's owned by director Francis Ford Coppola. The estate has a big-time wow factor, which isn't limited to the pricey $25 entrance fee (those under 21 enter free). A five-wine tasting flight, a 30-minute tour (11:30am, 1:30pm, and 3:30pm), and access to the château and museum (ever seen an Oscar before?) are, however, included. There are two tasting rooms, a traditional wine bar, and a retail area; kids can amuse themselves by sailing toy boats in the fountain. ⏲ 1½ hr. 1991 St. Helena Hwy., Rutherford. ☎ 800/782-4266 or 707/968-1100. www.rubiconestate.com. See p. 146.

Be Safe

Those little sips at each winery add up—be sure to have a designated driver when touring Wine Country.

The Best of Wine Country in 2 Days

If you have time to linger in Wine Country, you'll have a chance not only to explore more fabulous wineries with their gorgeous grounds and informative tours, but also to delve into the region's fascinating past. This cradle of California history is filled with sophisticated pleasures and natural wonders.

> *Walk into the inner sanctum of Sterling Vineyards, where motion-sensitive screens (very Dr. No) guide you through a self-guided tour.*

START The upscale enclave of St. Helena is 19 miles north of Napa on Hwy. 29. **TRIP LENGTH** about 40 miles.

Follow the itinerary in "The Best of Wine Country in 1 Day," above then start Day 2 in St. Helena.

❶ ★ St. Helena Main Street. This town, pronounced Saint Hel-*een*-uh, has a long history of pampering visitors, dating back to the founding of a nearby hot-springs resort in 1852. The combination of winemaking and a spa made the town a popular draw, especially among wealthy San Franciscans who built weekend retreats here, but the one-two punch of Prohibition and the Great Depression froze St. Helena in time. Its sophisticated rural pleasures were rediscovered in the 1970s, and today Main Street (principally btw. Pine & Pope sts.) is loaded with stylish and trendy shops. If the names Louboutin, Choo, and Blahnik make you go weak in the feet, check out **★★ Footcandy,** 1239 Main St. (☎ 707/963-2040; www.footcandyshoes.com; daily 11am–6pm). Other highlights include **★ I. Wolk Gallery,** 1354 Main St. (☎ 707/963-8800; www.

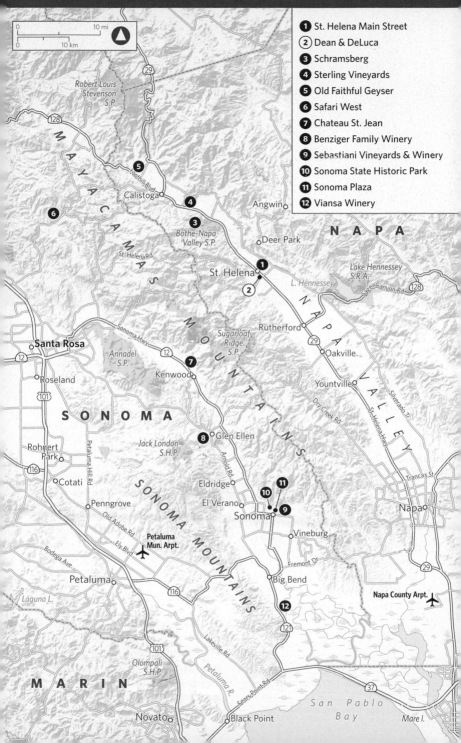

1 St. Helena Main Street
2 Dean & DeLuca
3 Schramsberg
4 Sterling Vineyards
5 Old Faithful Geyser
6 Safari West
7 Chateau St. Jean
8 Benziger Family Winery
9 Sebastiani Vineyards & Winery
10 Sonoma State Historic Park
11 Sonoma Plaza
12 Viansa Winery

0   10 mi
0   10 km

Robert Louis Stevenson S.P.

MAYACAMAS

NAPA

Calistoga

Angwin

Bothe-Napa Valley S.P.

St. Helena Rd.

Deer Park

St. Helena

Lake Hennessey S.R.A.

L. Hennessey

Sage Canyon Rd.

Rutherford

NAPA VALLEY

Santa Rosa

Sonoma Hwy.

Annadel S.P.

Sugarloaf Ridge S.P.

Oakville

Roseland

Kenwood

Yountville

Dry Creek Rd.

Silverado Tr.

St. Helena Hwy.

SONOMA

MOUNTAINS

Rohnert Park

Jack London S.H.P.

Glen Ellen

Cotati

Arnold Rd.

Eldridge

El Verano

Sonoma

Trancas St.

Penngrove

Old Adobe Rd.

Petaluma Hill Rd.

Ely Blvd.

SONOMA MOUNTAINS

Vineburg

Napa

Petaluma Mun. Arpt.

Bodega Ave.

Laguna L.

Petaluma

Fremont Dr.

Big Bend

Napa County Arpt.

Lakeville Rd.

Petaluma R.

Sears Point Rd.

San Pablo Bay

MARIN

Olompali S.H.P.

Novato

Black Point

Mare I.

> *Over two million bottles are stored in the extraordinary wine caves at Schramsberg Winery.*

iwolkgallery.com; daily 10am–5:30pm), one of several galleries featuring contemporary artwork from emerging and established artists; and ★ **On the Vine,** 1234 Main St. ☎ 800/992-4339 or 707/963-2209; www.onthevineonline.com; Mon–Sat 10am–5:30pm, Sun noon–5pm), carrying wearable art and clothing, including jewelry, scarves, and bags. ⏱ 1 hr. St. Helena Chamber of Commerce, 1010 Main St., Ste. A. ☎ 800/799-6456 or 707/963-4456. www.sthelena.com.

② 🍷 ★★ **Dean & DeLuca.** Gather the goods for a memorable picnic at this grocery store, which foodies just might mistake for heaven. It's part of a New York-based chain and there are lots of high-end (and pricey) international goodies to choose from, but the selection of local artisanal cheese, produce, and wine (1,400 different Californians in stock) is truly impressive. Pick up a few buttery baked goods, have a cappuccino at the espresso bar, and get some gazpacho to go from the gourmet takeout. 607 S. St. Helena Hwy. (Hwy. 29), St. Helena. ☎ 707/967-9980. www.deandeluca.com. Items $8–$20.

Go north on Hwy. 29/St. Helena Hwy., make a left on Peterson Dr., and a right on Schramsberg Rd. Trip time: about 10 min.

❸ ★★ **Schramsberg.** Robert Louis Stevenson (1850–94) was a fan. Visiting this wilderness winery outpost in 1880 he "tasted all . . . every variety and shade of Schramsberger." Here in Napa, he wrote, "Earth's cream was being skimmed and garnered." Schramsberg has gone through various owners and periods of abandonment since then, but the current operation, begun in 1965, would make Mr. Stevenson proud. A tour through the hand-dug sparkling wine caves, followed by a four-flight tasting, is by appointment only. Tours are at 10am, 11:30am, 12:30pm, 1:30pm, and 2:30pm; and cost $35 per person (you must be at least 21). Groups are small, so they can fill up quickly, but you get lots of face time with the knowledgeable staff. ⏱ 1¼ hr. 1400 Schramsberg Rd., Calistoga. ☎ 707/942-4558. www.schramsberg.com.

Head north on Hwy. 29/St. Helena Hwy., then go right on Dunaweal Lane to Sterling Vineyards. Trip time: 5 min.

④ ★★ **Sterling Vineyards.** Is the aerial tram approach to this winery (perched 300 ft. atop a rocky knoll) a gimmick? Who cares? It's an aerial tram—to a winery. The five tastings that come with your entrance fee ($25 adults, $10 ages 4–20) are uniquely spread throughout the winery grounds; it's a combination of progressive party and self-guided tour through the view-enhanced Greek-island-inspired property, with informative narration provided by a series of flatscreen TVs. ⏱ 1 hr. 1111 Dunaweal Lane, Calistoga. ☎ 800/726-6136 or 707/942-3345. www.sterlingvineyards.com. Mon–Fri 10:30–5pm; Sat–Sun 10am–5pm.

Continue north on St. Helena Hwy./Foothill Blvd. to Tubbs Lane and make a right. It's less than 10 min. to Old Faithful Geyser.

⑤ ★ kids **Old Faithful Geyser.** It's disputed whether this is an "actual" geyser or a man-made one, the result of a drilled well that tapped into a natural hydrothermal system around the turn of the 20th century. Whatever its provenance, it's still pretty cool (or hot, as the case may be)—about every 30 minutes Old Faithful blows steam and thousands of gallons of scalding water 60 to 100 feet in the air. The grounds also feature a gift shop filled with tchotchkes and a petting zoo with llamas and Tennessee fainting goats, which when startled stiffen up and tip over (seriously). ⏱ 30 min. 1299 Tubbs Lane, Calistoga. ☎ 707/942-6463. www.oldfaithfulgeyser.com. Admission $10 adults, $3 kids 6–12. Daily 9am–5pm (till 6pm in summer).

Turn left on Foothill Blvd./Hwy. 128, then turn right on Petrified Forest Rd., and right on Porter Creek Rd. Trip time: 15 min.

⑥ ★★ kids **Safari West.** A sip of chardonnay pairs nicely with a spot of cheetah, as they say at this wildlife facility in the heart of Wine Country. Not a zoo or a theme park, this wildlife preserve is involved in breeding and conservation programs and has some 500 animals in residence, including giraffes, gazelles, zebras, ostriches, and cheetahs. Many of the animals roam freely in large, natural enclosures, and there is also a walk-through aviary with exotic birds, like the African spoonbill and scarlet ibis. In order to pay the bills for this 400-acre private sanctuary—accredited

> *Yellowstone meets the Wine Country in Calistoga, where a West Coast version of Old Faithful blows every half hour.*

by the American Zoo and Aquarium Association—tours are offered daily *(reservations are a must!)*.

You'll explore the grounds both in an open-air safari vehicle and on foot; tours are a minimum of 2½ hours. There's also a cafe serving lunch and dinner (reservations required), a snack shop (limited winter hours), and luxury-tent lodgings (p. 159). ⏱ 3 hr. 3115 Porter Creek Rd., Santa Rosa. ☎ 800/616-2695 or 707/579-2551. www.safariwest.com. Admission $68 adults, $30 kids 3–12, $10 kids 1–2. Tours daily Apr–Oct 9am, 10am, 1pm, 2pm, & 4pm; Nov–Mar 10am & 2pm.

On Day 3, take Calistoga Rd. south from Porter Creek Rd. and turn left onto Sonoma Hwy./Hwy. 12. Trip time: 30 min. from Safari West.

> *Intensely manicured Chateau St. Jean includes lakes, terraced gardens, and intimate nooks perfect for gourmet picnics and wine tasting.*

7 ★ **Chateau St. Jean.** This beautifully manicured Mediterranean-style estate was originally built in 1920, with the winery itself dating from 1973. Included as part of the National Trust for Historic Preservation, the elegant gardens feature fishponds in the shape of Lake Michigan and Lake Huron, an homage created by the original owners who were Michigan natives. The winery produces chardonnay, cabernet sauvignon, merlot, and Gewürztraminer; tastings start at $10. Free terroir and garden tours are offered daily at 11am and 2pm. ⏱ 45 min. 8555 Sonoma Hwy. (Hwy. 12), Kenwood. ☎ 707/833-4134. www.chateaustjean.com. Daily 10am–5pm.

Continue south on Hwy. 12, go right on Arnold Dr., then veer right onto London Ranch Rd. Trip time: 10 min.

8 ★ **Benziger Family Winery.** This pastoral winery is on the leading edge of the green scene thanks to its holistic, biodynamic farming practices. Chemicals are out and natural harmony is in, with natural habitats created to sustain insects and wildlife that in turn act as pest control. Take the 45-minute tram tour ($15 including tastings; $5 for those under 21) and learn about this process from the ground up; tours are daily on the half-hour from 11am to 3:30pm (except noon). Be sure to try Benziger's signature bordeaux blend, Tribute. ⏱ 1 hr. 1883 London Ranch Rd., Glen Ellen. ☎ 888/490-2739. www.benziger.com. Daily 10am–5pm. Tastings start at $10.

Make a right on Arnold Dr., a left on W. Verano Ave., then a right onto Sonoma Hwy./Hwy. 12. Go left onto W. Napa St./Hwy. 12, and then left on Fourth St. E. Trip time: about 20 min.

9 ★★ **Sebastiani Vineyards & Winery.** Part of the vineyards at this winery dates back to 1824 and the mission era, when the padres planted grapes for sacramental wine. The Sebastiani winery has been here "only" since 1904, and was actually one of the few to remain open through Prohibition. In the tasting room $10 will get you seven pours (look for the Cherryblock cabernet sauvignon); there's also a marketplace and a variety of private and specialty tours, including a 1-hour wine and cheese seminar ($30). ⏱ 45 min. 389 Fourth St. E., Sonoma. ☎ 800/888-5532 or 707/933-3230. www.sebastiani.com. Daily 10am–5pm.

In high season parking can be difficult in town, so leave your car at the winery and walk a few blocks west along E. Spain St. to downtown's Sonoma State Historic Park.

10 ★★ **Sonoma State Historic Park.** Not a park per se, but a collection of six historic buildings that tell the story of early California. You'll find the last and most northerly of the state's missions, ★★ **Mission San Francisco Solano** (☎ 707/938-9560); as well as the ★ **Blue Wing Inn** (1840), the first inn built north of San Francisco; the ★★ **Sonoma Barracks** (☎ 707/939-9420), from which Mexico oversaw its northern frontier; and the **Toscano Hotel,** built in 1851. The mission and barracks both have displays and exhibits; there's also

> *It makes sense that Benziger looks brilliantly green in spring: the family-run winery practices eco-friendly biodynamic farming.*

a gift shop in the barracks. Free docent-led mission tours are offered Friday to Sunday on the hour from 11am to 2pm. ⏱ 1 hr. Start at E. Spain St. and First St. E. www.parks.ca.gov. Admission $3 adults, $2 kids 16 & under. Fri–Wed 10am–5pm.

Cross the street to:

⓫ ★★ **Sonoma Plaza.** The largest plaza in California, this 8-acre parcel was laid out in Mexican style in 1836, though the boutiques and eateries surrounding it nowadays are a far cry from the *tiendas* (shops) of yore. The plaza is anchored by the ruggedly handsome City Hall, made from basalt stone in 1908, and features a monument to the Bear Flag Republic. This sculpture marks the spot where in 1846 a rebel flag was defiantly hoisted by a group of immigrant settlers (Americans) pushing for independence from Mexico and the establishment of the California Republic. The flag was adorned with the image of a bear so badly drawn (and colored in with blackberry juice) it was mistaken for a pig. The flag would only fly briefly, but the writing was on the wall—California would not be Mexico's for much longer. ⏱ 20 min.

Get back on the road for a visit to one last winery. From Napa St. head south on Broadway, veer right onto Hwy. 121/Fremont Dr./Carneros Hwy., then go left on Hwy. 121/Arnold Dr./Carneros Hwy. Trip time: about 15 min.

⓬ ★★ **Viansa Winery.** Overlooking a 90-acre wetlands preserve, Viansa has a lovely, thoroughly convincing Tuscan style. Owned by members of the Sebastiani clan, the winery also features a marketplace and deli where you can fill up on gourmet pizza or focaccia sandwiches, and take-home olive oils (made from estate-grown olives), sauces and marinades, cookbooks, and wine-themed gifts. Viansa is known for its Italian varietals, including sangiovese and pinot grigio, as well as lesser-known grapes such as arneis and primitivo. Tastings cost $5 and tours run at 11am, 2pm, and 3pm. ⏱ 45 min. 25200 Arnold Dr. (Hwy. 121), Sonoma. ☎ 800/995-4740. www.viansa.com. Daily 10am–5pm.

Cool It

Wine does not age well in the trunk of your car, especially on a hot Wine Country afternoon. If you're going to be buying bottles of wine, invest in a cheap cooler and a bag of ice. Or check with the winery about shipping your purchases home, but be aware that the rules regarding shipping are byzantine.

The Best Wineries A to Z

★★ Artesa Vineyards & Winery NAPA

This architecturally dramatic (it has an artist in residence program) and contemporary winery is owned by Spain's Cordorníu Group, which has been making wine since 1551. Pinot noir and chardonnay are highlights. 1345 Henry Rd., Napa. ☎ 707/224-1668 or 707/254-2140. www.artesawinery.com. Daily 10am–5pm. Tastings $10–$15, last at 4:30pm. Tours $10, 11am & 2pm.

★★ Beaulieu Vineyard NAPA

Founded by Frenchman Georges de Latour in 1900, this renowned winery (its wines have been served by every U.S. president since FDR) is one of Napa's oldest. There are a variety of tasting experiences available; the $30 tasting features the highly prized vintage Private Reserve Cabernet Sauvignon. 1960 St. Helena Hwy., Rutherford. ☎ 800/264-6918. www.bvwines.com. Mon–Fri 10am–5pm (closed major holidays). Tastings $10–$30.

★★ Bella Vineyards & Wine Caves HEALDSBURG

Winemakers love caves and the folks here are no exception. Sample zinfandel and Syrah in this family-run winery's cave tasting room, or take cave and vineyard tours (1-week advance notice required—wholly worth the effort). 9711 W. Dry Creek Rd., Healdsburg. ☎ 866/572-3552 or 707/473-9171. www.bellawinery.com. Daily 11am–4:30pm. Tastings $5–$10.

★ Benziger Family Winery SONOMA

Learn about this winery's holistic biodynamic farming on tractor-pulled tram tours, followed by tastings in a German-style mansion (cabs, pinot noir, Petite Sirah, port); daily tours are every 30 minutes from 11am to 3:30pm, except noon ($15 adults, $5 under 21). A more exclusive vineyard tour followed by seated tastings is $40. 1883 London Ranch Rd., Glen Ellen. ☎ 888/490-2739. www.benziger.com. Daily 10am–5pm. Tastings $10–$15.

> *Sip and sniff the latest vintages at Bella Vineyards; reserve space in advance for wine-cave tours.*

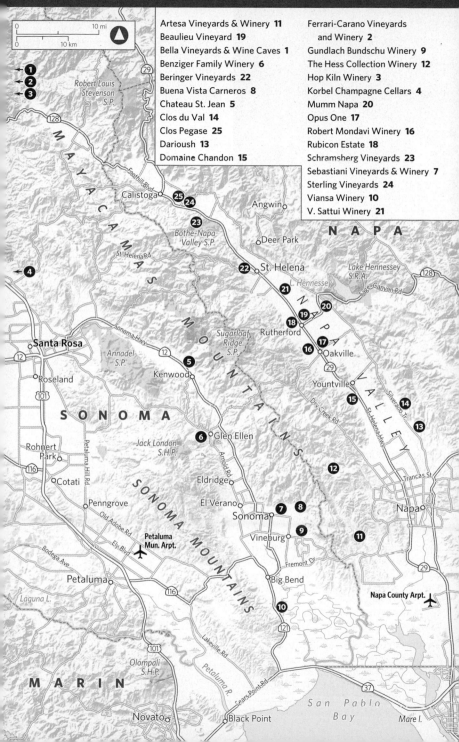

Artesa Vineyards & Winery 11
Beaulieu Vineyard 19
Bella Vineyards & Wine Caves 1
Benziger Family Winery 6
Beringer Vineyards 22
Buena Vista Carneros 8
Chateau St. Jean 5
Clos du Val 14
Clos Pegase 25
Darioush 13
Domaine Chandon 15

Ferrari-Carano Vineyards
   and Winery 2
Gundlach Bundschu Winery 9
The Hess Collection Winery 12
Hop Kiln Winery 3
Korbel Champagne Cellars 4
Mumm Napa 20
Opus One 17
Robert Mondavi Winery 16
Rubicon Estate 18
Schramsberg Vineyards 23
Sebastiani Vineyards & Winery 7
Sterling Vineyards 24
Viansa Winery 10
V. Sattui Winery 21

> *There's no escaping the noble history of Buena Vista Carneros, the oldest continuously operating winemaking facility in the state.*

★★ Beringer Vineyards NAPA

Established by a pair of German brothers in 1876, this landmark is Napa's oldest continuously operating winery (they got past Prohibition by making sacramental wine). Back in 1934 Beringer pioneered the concept of public tours, and it offers a menu of several from which to choose, including one of Frederick Beringer's spectacular Rhine House mansion, built in 1884. The Knights Valley Cabernet is a treat. 2000 Main St., St. Helena. ☎ 707/967-4412. www.beringer.com. Daily Nov–May 10am–5pm; Jun–Oct 10am–6pm. Tastings $10–$30. Tours $15–$40, 10:45am–3:45pm.

★★ Buena Vista Carneros SONOMA

California's wine industry began right here in 1857; this is also the oldest continuously operating winery in the country. The beautiful stone tasting room is a California Historical Landmark, but the actual winemaking

(chardonnay, pinot noir, merlot, Syrah) now takes place elsewhere; there's also a gift shop and cool picnic spots (outside food is okay). 18000 Old Winery Rd., Sonoma. ☎ 800/926-1266. www.buenavistacarneros.com. Daily 10am–5pm (closed major holidays). Tastings $10–$20. Tours $45–$65, reservations required.

★ Chateau St. Jean SONOMA

Highlights at this historic estate (it really looks like a French château), built in 1920, include a gourmet marketplace in the expansive tasting room and European-style gardens and landscaping. The cabernet sauvignon, merlot, and chardonnay are specialties. 8555 Sonoma Hwy. (Hwy. 12), Kenwood. ☎ 707/833-4134. www.chateaustjean.com. Daily 10am–5pm. Tastings $10–$15. Free tours, 11am & 2pm. Private tour and reserve tasting $25–$75, by appointment.

★ Clos du Val NAPA

This ivy-covered winery was one of the pioneers of Napa's overlooked Stags Leap District, opening in 1972; be sure to sample Ariadne, a Sémillon and sauvignon blanc blend. The winery's olive grove is a special place for a picnic, and staffers give tours of the demonstration vineyard where you can learn about sustainable farming. Tours are free with a paid tasting but must be scheduled in advance. 5330 Silverado Trail, Napa. ☎ 800/993-9463 or 707/261-5200. www.closduval.com. Daily 10am–5pm. Tastings $10 (waived with purchase); reserve tastings $20.

★★ Clos Pegase NAPA

Bacchus himself would approve of this striking facility—named for the mythical Pegasus—thanks to its Greek columns, art collection, and sculpture garden. It's a veritable "temple among the vines," where a room of towering oak-aging barrels makes for a dramatic art gallery. This estate winery's principal varieties are chardonnay, merlot, and cabernet sauvignon. 1060 Dunaweal Lane, Calistoga. ☎ 707/942-4981. www.clospegase.com. Daily 10:30am–5pm. Tastings $15. Free tours 11:30am & 2pm.

★★ Darioush NAPA

Founded in 1997 by Iranian Darioush Khaledi and evoking memories of the Seven Wonders of the Ancient World, this state-of-the-art winery channels ancient Persia and offers bordeaux-style estate wines. 4240 Silverado

Trail, Napa. ☎ 707/257-2345. www.darioush.
com. Daily 10:30am–5pm. Current-release
tastings $25. Private tasting and cheese pairing
tours $50, 2pm with reservation.

★ Domaine Chandon NAPA

Enjoy sparkling and still wines at this chic hot
spot, founded in 1973 by the French champagne house Moët & Chandon. There's also
a Michelin-rated restaurant. 1 California Dr.
(at Hwy. 29), Yountville. ☎ 707/944-2280.
www.chandon.com. Daily 10am–6pm. Tastings
$16–$22. Tours $12–$30.

★★ Ferrari-Carano Vineyards and Winery

SONOMA The colorful 5-acre gardens at this
Italian villa-style winery are as much of a
draw as the pinot grigio and fumé blanc; some
10,000 tulips bloom in early spring (call the
tulip hot line for updates; ☎ 707/433-5349).
8761 Dry Creek Rd., Healdsburg. ☎ 800/831-
0381 or 707/433-6700. www.ferrari-carano.
com. Daily 10am–5pm (closed major holidays).
Tastings $5–$15 (refundable with wine purchase). Private tastings $20–$35, reservations
required. Free tours Mon–Sat 10am, reservations
required.

★★ Gundlach Bundschu (GB) Winery SO-

NOMA The country's oldest family-owned
winery, founded in 1858, GB features pinot
noir, chardonnay, merlot, and more. Informative tours and tastings require a reservation
and itineraries change according to the season
(barrel caves in winter, harvest tour in summer).
2000 Denmark St., Sonoma. ☎ 707/938-5277 or
707/939-3015. www.gunbun.com. Tasting and
tour $20, Thurs–Mon 1:30pm. 2-hr vineyard tour
$40, May–Sept Fri–Sat 10am.

★★★ The Hess Collection Winery NAPA

A remote winery and gallery experience
where you can sample cabernet and chardonnay, as well as peruse holdings from a major
collection of contemporary art. Specialty tours
(reservations required) include a guided visit
to the galleries, followed by food and paired
wines ($35–$40). 4411 Redwood Rd., Napa.
☎ 707/255-1144. www.hesscollection.com.
Daily 10am–5:30pm (closed major holidays).
Tastings $10–$30. Free winery tours 10am &
3:30pm. Free self-guided art tours.

> The name sounds a bit like gesundheit, but Gund-
lach Bundschu, the oldest family-run winery in the
U.S., is nothing to sneeze at.

★★ Hop Kiln Winery SONOMA

This rustic, distinctive estate winery is a historical landmark, built in 1905. The gourmet
deli offers local bread, cheese, and charcuterie
to go along with your Rhone-inspired Rushin'
River Red or zinfandel-based Big Red; take a
stroll around the rose garden and duck pond.
6050 Westside Rd., Healdsburg. ☎ 707/433-
6491. www.hopkilnwinery.com. Daily 10am–
5pm. Free tastings.

★★ Korbel Champagne Cellars SONOMA

Begun in 1882 by a trio of Bohemian brothers (they were from what's now the Czech
Republic), this is the country's oldest méthode
champenoise (traditional winemaking) winery.
Tour the cellars and History Museum, or tour
the gardens filled with 250 rose varieties, and
then enjoy something from the excellent deli
on the redwood-shaded patio. 13250 River Rd.,
Guerneville. ☎ 707/824-7000. www.korbel.
com. Daily 10am–4:30pm. Free tastings & tours.
Cellar and museum tours 11am–3pm. Garden
tours Apr–Oct Thurs–Sun 1 & 3pm.

> *Using Chinese laborers who had been working mines in the Gold Country, Schramsberg Vineyards burrowed out wine caves in the 1800s.*

★★ Mumm Napa NAPA

Enjoy sparkling wines (the specialty here) with table service indoors or outside, as well as a photography collection featuring Ansel Adams and a rotating art collection by contemporary artists. The Oak Terrace Tasting is a 2-hour seating featuring special flights ($30, reservations required). 8445 Silverado Trail, Rutherford. ☎ 800/686-6272. www.mummnapa. com. Daily 10am–5pm. Tastings $6–$25. Free tours 10am–3pm.

★★ Opus One NAPA

A joint venture originally formed between Robert Mondavi (1913–2008) and Baron Philippe de Rothschild (1902–1988), this is a very cool operation, where contemporary form meets old-world style. And it's where mere mortals may sample the winery's one and only luxury (and pricey) libation. 7900 St. Helena Hwy., Oakville. ☎ 707/944-9442. www. opusonewinery.com. Daily 10am–4pm (closed major holidays). Tastings $30. Tours $35 (includes tasting), 10:30am. Reservations required for both tasting and tour.

★★ Robert Mondavi Winery NAPA

Thanks to its modernist mission design, art collection, and wide array of events (including summertime concerts by major acts), this is one of the Wine Country's major players. Tours and tastings range from simple 30-minute walk-abouts (daily 11am & 2pm, $15) to elaborate dinners paired with vintages from the reserve ($300). 7801 St. Helena Hwy. (Hwy. 29), Oakville. ☎ 888/766-6328. www.robertmondaviwinery. com. Daily 10am–5pm (closed major holidays). Tastings $15–$25. Check the website for a list of tours and programming.

★★★ Rubicon Estate NAPA

Formerly Niebaum-Coppola Estate Winery (founded in 1887 by Gustave Niebaum), Rubicon Estate, Francis Ford Coppola's operation, is utterly impressive and dramatic. A five-wine tasting flight (the Rubicon cabernet is the flagship vintage), a 30-minute tour, and access to the historic château and Centennial Museum (which honors film and wine) are included with admission; there are also several in-depth tours. 1991 St. Helena Hwy., Rutherford. ☎ 800/ 782-4266 or 707/968-1100. www.rubicon estate.com. Daily 10am–5pm. Admission $25 adults, free for ages 20 & under. Tours $20–$50. Check website for tour schedules.

★★ Schramsberg Vineyards NAPA

Adventure through the hand-dug sparkling wine caves (over 2 million bottles are stored here) of this historic winery, the second oldest in Napa, established in 1862. The relaxed, informative, and small tours conclude with a generous pouring of four wines; reservations are required and you must be 21 or older. 1400 Schramsberg Rd., Calistoga. ☎ 707/942-4558.

> *Santorini? Nope, it's the Greek-inspired Sterling Vineyards, perched 300 feet above the town of Calistoga.*

www.schramsberg.com. Tastings and tour $40, daily at 10am, 11:30am, 12:30pm, 1:30pm & 2:30pm.

★★ Sebastiani Vineyards & Winery SONOMA

The Cherryblock cabernet sauvignon is the calling card of this family winery established in 1904 (though the vineyards have been here since 1825). The winery, located within walking distance of historic downtown Sonoma, also offers seminars and private tours. 389 Fourth St. E., Sonoma. ☎ 800/888-5532 or 707/933-3230. www.sebastiani.com. Daily 10am–5pm. Tastings $10. Private tours $25–$35.

★★★ Sterling Vineyards SONOMA

Ride an aerial tram to a Greek island-inspired winery with amazing views; high-scoring reserve cabernet and chardonnay await. 1111 Dunaweal Lane, Calistoga. ☎ 800/726-6136 or 707/942-3345. www.sterlingvineyards.com. Admission and tastings $25 adults, $10 ages 4–20. Admission and upgraded tastings $30–$40 (ages 21 & above). Mon–Fri 10:30am–5pm; Sat–Sun 10am–5pm (closed major holidays).

★★ Viansa Winery SONOMA

Founded in 1989, this Tuscan-style villa and marketplace sits above a wetlands preserve; the Sangiovese and pinot grigio complete the Italian fantasy. 25200 Arnold Dr. (Hwy. 121), Sonoma. ☎ 800/995-4740. www.viansa.com. Daily 10am–5pm. Tastings $5–$10. Tours $5, 11am, 2pm, & 3:30pm.

★★ V. Sattui Winery NAPA

You'll find V. Sattui's vintages (cabs, chardonnays, ports, and more) nowhere else but at this family-owned winery, established in 1885. There's also a gourmet market and deli, as well as a barbecue and grill (closed in winter), and an oak-shaded picnic area. 1111 White Lane, St. Helena. ☎ 707/963-7774. www.vsattui.com. Daily Jan–Oct 9am–6pm; Nov–Feb 9am–5pm. Tastings $5–$10. Free self-guided tours.

Winery Reservations

Many wineries are fine with the casual drop-in; others require a reservation. If you're interested in a particular winery, call ahead to check on its policy.

The Best of Wine Country: Beyond the Wineries

There's more to Wine Country than just grapes. You'll find everything from world-class art collections to the Culinary Institute of America's foodie fortress, as well as places to pay homage to two uniquely American artists (both of whom had a fondness for canines).

> *Like a playground for grownups, Cornerstone Sonoma presents beautiful gardens, shops, and wine tasting.*

START di Rosa Preserve is **7 miles southwest of Napa. From Napa, head south on Hwy. 29 and then west on Hwy. 12/121. TRIP LENGTH 2 days, about 65 miles.**

❶ ★★★ **di Rosa Preserve.** Art and nature come together in stunning fashion at this 217-acre property where more than 2,000 works of art by more than 800 artists have been gathered. Collector Rene di Rosa and his late wife, Veronica, turned a 130-year-old winery into a campus of galleries, gardens, and meadows where you can get a primer on contemporary art in Northern California. You'll find everything from whimsical sculpture to cutting-edge conceptual pieces, and it's everywhere—even on the ceiling of the di Rosa's former home, now a salon-style museum. The ★★ **Gatehouse Gallery,** overlooking the 35-acre lake, is free but offers just a very small taste of what lies beyond; the main collection and grounds are accessible by tour only. Several tour options are available, the best being the 2½-hour **Art & Meadow** tour (Apr–Oct), which takes you through the main gallery and into the sculpture meadow. ⏲ 2½

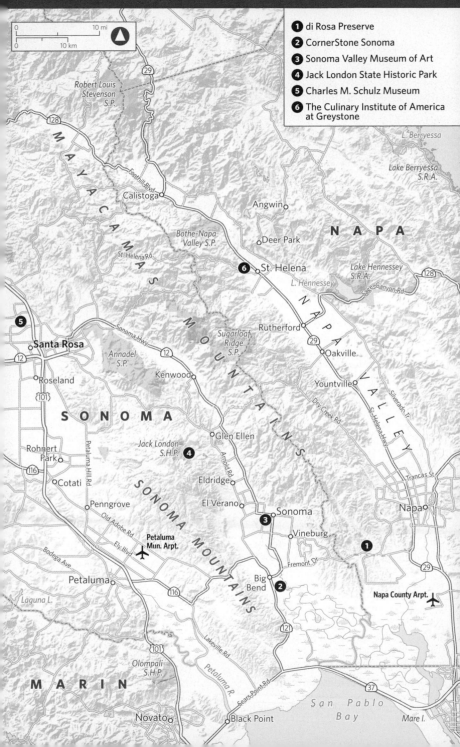

1 di Rosa Preserve
2 CornerStone Sonoma
3 Sonoma Valley Museum of Art
4 Jack London State Historic Park
5 Charles M. Schulz Museum
6 The Culinary Institute of America at Greystone

> *Gorgeous di Rosa Preserve presents over 2,000 works of art on over 200 acres. Be in the know and wear sturdy walking shoes.*

hr. 5200 Carneros Hwy. (Hwy. 12/121), Napa. ☎ 707/226-5991. www.dirosapreserve.org. Gatehouse Gallery: free admission; Wed–Fri 9:30am–3pm. Permanent collection and grounds by tour only. Tours $10–$15. Wed–Fri 10am, 11am, & 1pm; Sat 10am, 11am, & noon. Reservations recommended Wed–Fri, required Sat.

❷ ★★ **CornerStone Sonoma.** This complex features 9 acres of ever-changing garden installations designed to delight and inspire. There are some 20 parcels, each 1,800 square feet, that are turned over to landscape architects and artists, who then create walk-through gardens that range from the traditional to the conceptual. And if that weren't draw enough, CornerStone is also home to three wine-tasting rooms, home/garden shops and boutiques, a sculpture gallery, and a cafe serving local, organic food. You'll also find the **Sonoma Valley Visitor Center** (☎ 707/935-6715; www.sonomavalley.com; daily 10am–4pm). ⏱ 1 hr. 23570 Arnold Dr. (Hwy. 121), Sonoma. ☎ 707/933-3010. www.corner stonegardens.com. Free admission. Daily 10am–5pm. Gardens 10am–4pm (Sat–Sun gardens may close at 3pm for special events; call ahead).

❸ ★★ **Sonoma Valley Museum of Art (SVMA).** This gem of a museum features guest curators who bring in artwork from around the

> *The "other" CIA, the Culinary Institute of America, lets chefs learn new techniques—and the public can taste the results.*

world, anything from Rodin to Rauschenberg. But the primary emphasis for this space, located in an old furniture store, is primarily on Northern California artists. An array of styles and media are spotlighted, including painting, ceramics, design, and video; the LaHaye Sculpture Gallery also presents a rotating series of large-scale pieces. SVMA offers an ongoing schedule of events, lectures, and workshops, as well. ⏱ 30 min. 551 Broadway, Sonoma. ☎ 707/939-7862. www.svma.org. Admission Mon–Sat $5, $8 for families; free Sun. Wed–Sun 11am–5pm.

❹ ★★ **Jack London State Historic Park.** Author of The Call of the Wild and White Fang, Jack London (1876–1916) was an adventurer, journalist, novelist, and an avowed socialist who incongruously made a fortune. His pride and joy was Beauty Ranch, where he and his wife, Charmian, lived from 1905 until his death; Charmian spent the remainder of her days here, too, dying in 1955. Now a 1,400-acre park with a lake, trails, and a museum dedicated to London, these beautiful grounds also feature the remains of a spectacular mansion, Wolf House, that burned to the ground shortly before London and his wife were to move in; nearby are more remains—those of Jack and Charmian London. In summer you can rent horses here from **Triple Creek Horse Outfit** (☎ 707/887-8700; www.triplecreekhorseoutfit.com). ⏱ At least 1 hr. 2400 London Ranch Rd., Glen Ellen. ☎ 707/938-5216. www.parks.ca.gov or www.parks.sonoma.net. Admission $8 per vehicle, $7 with a senior . Sat–Wed 10am–5pm.

⑤ ★★ kids Charles M. Schulz Museum. Good ol' Charles Schulz (1922–2000) gets his due at this very nice museum that celebrates his career and his *Peanuts* comic-strip characters. Exhibits change several times a year, and there are original strips and memorabilia on display, as well as Schulz's re-created studio, a 100-seat theater, a research center and library, and (of course) a gift shop. International artists pay homage to Schulz, who lived in Santa Rosa most of his adult life, including Christo, who contributed his *Wrapped Snoopy House,* and Yoshiteru Otani, whose *Tile Mural* and *Morphing Snoopy* are museum highlights. The mural is composed of more than 3,500 comic-strip images on ceramic tiles; *Morphing Snoopy* is a massive wooden sculpture depicting the evolution of one of pop culture's favorite pooches. ⏱ At least 1 hr. 2301 Hardies Lane, Santa Rosa. ☎ 707/579-4452. www.schulzmuseum.org. Admission $10 adults, $5 seniors and kids 4–18, free for kids 3 & under. Mon–Fri 11am–5pm; Sat–Sun 10am–5pm; closed Tues Sept–May.

⑥ ★★★ The Culinary Institute of America at Greystone. Housed in a grand and solemn stone château, this culinary Hogwarts turns out new generations of kitchen wizards. Even if you're not interested in a cooking career, there is plenty here to experience. The ★★ **Wine Spectator Greystone Restaurant** (staffed by professionals along with a rotating cast of students) serves high-end Wine Country cuisine (☎ 707/967-1010, entrees $14–$28); the ★★ **Spice Island Marketplace** (☎ 888/424-2433) has more than 1,700 cookbook titles on hand and every imaginable kitchen tool and gadget you could ever want, as well as wine accessories, jewelry, and more. One-hour cooking demos are also held by CIA instructors (call ☎ 707/967-2320 for the schedule; $15). 2555 Main St. (Hwy. 29), St. Helena. www.ciachef.org. Spice Island Marketplace: daily 10am–6pm.

Wine Country Adventures

★★ **Napa Valley Bike Tours,** 6795 Washington St., Yountville (☎ 800/707-2453; www.napavalleybiketours.com), offers half-day guided winery tours ($115)—van support included (it can carry your purchases and you, if you get tired). ★★ **Sonoma Valley Bike Tours,** 520 Broadway, Sonoma (☎ 877/308-2453; www.sonomavalleybiketours.com), is the sister operation.

Napa Valley is perhaps the world's busiest ballooning spot, so see what all the excitement is about with ★★★ **Napa Valley Aloft** (☎ 800/627-2759 or 707/944-4400; www.nvaloft.com); the early-morning flights from Yountville start at $225 for adults and $190 for children.

★★ **River's Edge,** 13840 Healdsburg Ave., Healdsburg (☎ 707/433-7247; www.riversedgekayakandcanoe.com), can set you up for a memorable day of paddling down the Russian River. It will provide all the gear, shuttle pickup, and even a gourmet picnic lunch (picnic packages start at $110).

CULINARY CALIFORNIA

The ingredients for a foodie's paradise

BY JENNIFER SENATOR

EVER SINCE MEMBERS OF THE STATE'S first known commune, Fountain Grove, started their own dairy farm and vineyard in Santa Rosa in 1875, Californians have had utopian ideas about food. And why shouldn't they? Because of its temperate year-round climate, the state has long provided fruit, vegetables, dairy, and meat for the rest of the country. By the late 1970s, "California cuisine" had become a popular term for dishes that combine Mediterranean and Asian influences with California-grown ingredients like avocados and nuts; in the 1980s, California menu items like Chinese chicken salad began showing up nationwide. The Golden State continues to pioneer culinary trends such as the sustainable food movement and introducing gardening into public school curriculums—as Alice Waters has done with the "Edible Schoolyard."

Where to Buy the Best

THE FERRY BUILDING MARKETPLACE
San Francisco
The country's top chefs frequent this San Francisco market, housed in and around the historic Ferry Building. More than 85 farmers set up three days a week. See p. 59, **②**.

OXBOW PUBLIC MARKET
Napa Valley
Before a day of wine tasting, grab picnic essentials such as wine, cheese, and charcuterie from one of more than 20 artisan vendors at this specialty market. See p. 134, **②**.

SANTA MONICA FARMERS' MARKET
Santa Monica
While this see-and-be-seen market is also open on weekends, the Wednesday market draws the biggest crowds. See p. 407, **⑮**.

SPICE ISLAND MARKETPLACE
St. Helena
Located at the Culinary Institute of America at Greystone, this market offers hard-to-find culinary ingredients. Try avocado oil, rose petal jam, and Greystone chocolate, made on-site. See p. 151, **⑥**.

The Innovators

ALICE WATERS This onetime Montessori school teacher changed the way America eats with the opening of her Berkeley restaurant, Chez Panisse, in 1971. It remains a world-renowned foodie destination, and Waters continues to innovate, serving as vice president of Slow Food International and reforming school lunch menus.

MICHAEL MCCARTY McCarty was just 25 when he opened his eponymous restaurant, Michael's, in Santa Monica in 1979. By focusing on regional food and California wines, Michael's pioneered contemporary California cuisine in the southern part of the state.

WOLFGANG PUCK This Austrian native, often referred to as the first celebrity chef, spread the gospel of California cuisine with his nationwide chain of restaurants and fine dining spots, such as the flagship Spago in West Hollywood, a celebrity magnet and recipient of two Michelin stars.

BILL NIMAN When he opened Niman's Ranch, just north of San Francisco, in the 1970s, Niman was unique in offering meats produced from humanely raised, vegetarian-fed cattle, pigs, and lamb. His products gained the attention of Alice Waters, who featured them on the menu at Chez Panisse. Niman is innovating once again, offering organic goat meat in a new venture, BN Ranch.

The Ingredients

California produces almost half of all U.S.-grown fruits, nuts, and vegetables, and is the sole U.S. supplier of the following top 10 agricultural products, all of them stars of California cuisine:

Almonds	Grapes	Clingstone
Artichokes	Raisins	Peaches
Dates	Kiwifruit	Pistachios
Figs	Olives	

Wine Country Hotels A to Z

Napa Valley

★★★ **Bardessona** YOUNTVILLE

Hands down the coolest new place in the valley, this modernist, LEED-certified resort is a gorgeous amalgamation of wood, steel, and stone. The all-suite property, which opened in 2009, also has a farm-to-table restaurant that utilizes bounty from its own thriving garden. 6526 Yount St., ☎ 877/932-5333 or 707/204-6000. 62 units. Suites from $550 w/breakfast. AE, DISC, MC, V.

★★★ **Calistoga Ranch** CALISTOGA

This is the luxury resort that may spoil you for any other lodging (of course you'll pay for the pleasure). The chic, freestanding cottages are set on 157 acres of oak-studded hillsides and feature cedar decks with outdoor fireplaces and showers, and high-end furnishings; the

> *Like your own private wine-country hideaway, private cottages at Calistoga Ranch are a worth-it-splurge.*

fabulous indoor/outdoor spa has a natural thermal pool where you can "take the waters." You can also take a yoga class or a hike on the private trails; don't miss dinner at the guests-only, lodge-style restaurant. 580 Lommel Rd. ☎ 707/254-2800. www.calistogaranch.com. 48 units. Doubles $550–$4,000. AE, DC, DISC, MC, V.

★ **Calistoga Spa Hot Springs** CALISTOGA

This family-friendly (and family-owned) spot doesn't exactly have cutting-edge design, but it does have four naturally heated mineral pools, kitchenettes and barbecue grills, and a convenient location. You can take a mud bath in the spa. 1006 Washington St. (at Gerard St.). ☎ 866/822-5772 or 707/942-6269. www.calistogaspa.com. 57 units. Doubles $142–$202. MC, V.

★ **Chablis Inn** NAPA

Budget-conscious travelers should make a beeline for this simple, clean, and comfortable property. This is one of Wine Country's best

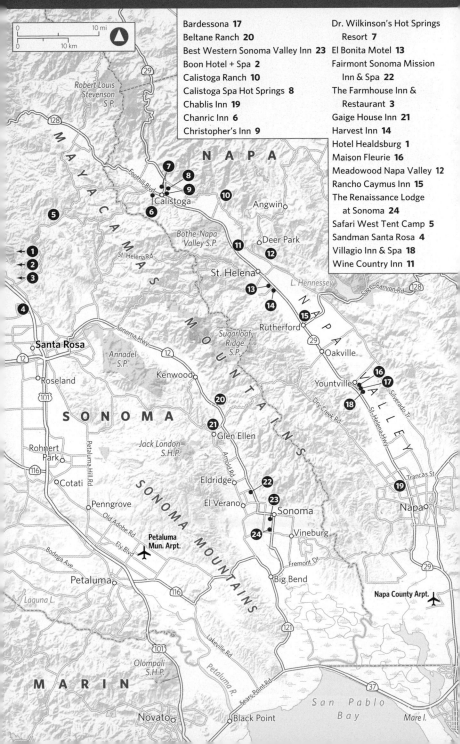

Bardessona 17
Beltane Ranch 20
Best Western Sonoma Valley Inn 23
Boon Hotel + Spa 2
Calistoga Ranch 10
Calistoga Spa Hot Springs 8
Chablis Inn 19
Chanric Inn 6
Christopher's Inn 9
Dr. Wilkinson's Hot Springs
   Resort 7
El Bonita Motel 13
Fairmont Sonoma Mission
   Inn & Spa 22
The Farmhouse Inn &
   Restaurant 3
Gaige House Inn 21
Harvest Inn 14
Hotel Healdsburg 1
Maison Fleurie 16
Meadowood Napa Valley 12
Rancho Caymus Inn 15
The Renaissance Lodge
   at Sonoma 24
Safari West Tent Camp 5
Sandman Santa Rosa 4
Villagio Inn & Spa 18
Wine Country Inn 11

> *Napa meets Provence in the French-country ruffles and luxury of Yountville's Maison Fleurie.*

deals, and it's pet friendly. **3360 Solano Ave.**
☎ 800/443-3490 or 707/257-1944. www.
chablisinn.com. 34 units. Doubles May to mid-
Nov $99–$250; mid-Nov to Apr $79–$150. AE,
DC, DISC, MC, V.

★★ Chanric Inn CALISTOGA

The sumptuous three-course breakfast is just
one of many highlights at this B&B. There's
no explosion of Victoriana here—the design
is contemporary and elegant; there's also a
view-enhanced pool and Jacuzzi area, along
with excellent service. **1805 Foothill Blvd.**
☎ 877/281-3671 or 707/942-4535. www.chanric
inn.com. 6 units. Doubles $189–$349 w/break-
fast. AE, MC, V.

★ Christopher's Inn CALISTOGA

Rooms at this homey place vary in size and the
amenities included; some have fireplaces, private patios, whirlpool tubs, and/or four-poster
beds—all rooms have feather mattresses. The
espresso machine in the lobby is a bonus. **1010
Foothill Blvd.** ☎ 866/876-5755 or 707/942-5755.
www.christophersinn.com. 24 units. Doubles
$165–$395 w/breakfast. AE, MC, V.

★ Dr. Wilkinson's Hot Springs Resort

CALISTOGA The retro neon sign out front is
no gimmick—this family-owned hotel and spa

has been around since 1952. There's a wide
range of accommodations, from bungalows
and rooms in a Victorian house to modern
lodgings in the 1960s-style motel. The mud
bath in the highly recommended spa is a must
do. **1507 Lincoln Ave. (Calif. 29, btw. Fairway
& Stevenson aves.).** ☎ 707/942-4102. www.
drwilkinson. com. 42 units. Doubles $149–$299;
cottages $164–$600. AE, MC, V.

★ El Bonita Motel ST. HELENA

The spotless rooms at this pleasant, shady,
1940s Art Deco location are motel basic but
sport balconies or patios, microwaves, and
fridges; some have whirlpool tubs. It's pet
friendly, too. **195 Main St. (at El Bonita Ave.).**
☎ 800/541-3284 or 707/963-3216. www.
elbonita.com. 41 units. Doubles $94–$289 w/
breakfast. AE, DC, DISC, MC, V.

★★ Harvest Inn ST. HELENA

Spread over 8 beautifully landscaped acres,
this Tudor-style country manor has cottages
and guest rooms close enough to the neighboring vineyard that you could probably filch
a few grapes. Some of the spacious rooms
feature fireplaces (gas or wood-burning) and
terraces or decks; the hotel is also pet friendly.
1 Main St. ☎ 800/950-8466 or 707/963-
9463. www.harvestinn.com. 74 units. Doubles

$359–$535; suites $645–$799. Rates include breakfast. AE, MC, V.

★★ Maison Fleurie YOUNTVILLE
This "flowering house" certainly lives up to its name with its colorful French country accents and garden, all set amid a trio of brick and stone buildings built in 1873. Some rooms have fireplaces, spa tubs, and private patios. 6529 Yount St. (btw. Washington St. &Yountville Cross Rd.). ☎ 800/788-0369 or 707/944-2056. www.maisonfleurienapa.com. 13 units. Doubles $135–$285 w/breakfast & afternoon hors d'oeuvres. AE, DC, DISC, MC, V.

★★★ Meadowood Napa Valley ST. HELENA
This exclusive resort—one of the finest in the region—started out as a private club in 1964 and now features cottages, suites, and lodges spread throughout its secluded 250-acre property. There's golf, tennis, croquet, hiking trails, and a Michelin two-star restaurant. This is where the good life gets great. 900 Meadowood Lane. ☎ 800/458-8080 or 707/963-3646. www.meadowood.com. 85 units. Doubles $475–$825; suites $775–$6,150. AE, DC, DISC, MC, V.

★ Rancho Caymus Inn RUTHERFORD
Though built in 1984, this character-filled property takes Napa's hacienda history to heart, with its Mexican courtyard, tile roofs, and wood and stucco accents. Rooms feature hand-carved walnut bed frames and wrought-iron fixtures; many have wood-burning fireplaces and balconies. 1140 Rutherford Rd. ☎ 800/845-1777 or 707/963-1777. www.ranchocaymus.com. 26 units. Doubles 17–$435; suites $215–$450. Rates include breakfast. AE, MC, V.

★★ Villagio Inn & Spa YOUNTVILLE
Right in the heart of town, this beautifully landscaped property has a residential feel that's given a Roman twist with frescoes, sculptures, fountains, and crumbling pillars. There's also a celebrity-chef restaurant (Michael Chiarello's **Bottega,** p. 162), a stylish marketplace, a luxurious spa, and a champagne breakfast that's not to be missed. 6481 Washington St. ☎ 800/351-1133 or 707/944-8877. www.villagio.com. 138 units. Doubles $330–$650 w/breakfast. AE, DC, DISC, MC, V.

★★ Wine Country Inn ST. HELENA
Surrounded by vineyards and mature landscaping, this attractive property has a distinctly European feel. The rooms and cottages feature individualized decor, and many have fireplaces, balconies, and spa tubs (but none have TVs). The family-owned inn also has a free shuttle that will take you to any one of a dozen area restaurants. 1152 Lodi Lane, St ☎ 888/465-4608 or 707/963-7077. www.winecountryinn.com. 29 units, 12 with shower only. Doubles $215–$405; cottages $535–$660. Rates include breakfast appetizers. MC, V.

> Meadowood Napa Valley caters to a chic crowd with a wealth of amenities and recreational activities.

> Now and zen at Gaige House, where the suites offer granite soaking tubs and private Japanese gardens.

Sonoma Valley

★★ Beltane Ranch GLEN ELLEN

This cheery and rustic two-story ranch house, set on a 102-acre estate, dates from 1892. All the individually decorated rooms have a private entrance and private bathrooms; the grounds are lush with vineyards, fruit trees, and produce (which will end up in your breakfast). Walking trails and tennis, too. 11775 Sonoma Hwy./Hwy. 12. ☎ 707/996-6501. www.beltaneranch.com. 5 units, 1 cottage. Doubles $150–$200; cottages $220. Rates include breakfast. No credit cards.

Best Western Sonoma Valley Inn SONOMA

This is a clean, reliable chain hotel, but is in Wine Country, meaning it has amenities like fireplaces, steam room, spa services, and continental breakfast delivered to your room. The location is also great—just a block from Sonoma's plaza. 550 Second St. W. ☎ 800/334-5784 or 707/938-9200. www.sonomavalleyinn.com. 80 units. Doubles $114–$369. AE, DC, DISC, MC, V.

★★ Boon Hotel + Spa GUERNVILLE

You can tell from the "+" this place is cool and modern, and so it is, with uncluttered contemporary rooms and an ecoconscious vibe. There's a salt-water pool, a fleet of loaner bikes, in-room fireplaces, a small-plates bistro, and a very helpful staff. Dogs are welcome. 14711 Armstrong Woods Rd. ☎ 707/869-2721. www.boonhotels.com. 14 units. Doubles $185–$250 w/breakfast. AE, MC, V.

★★★ Fairmont Sonoma Mission Inn & Spa

SONOMA Originally built in 1927, the main building does indeed mimic a California mission. Set on 12 pristine acres, it's a popular retreat for the moneyed and famous. Upscale amenities include wood-burning fireplaces (in many rooms), a nearby championship 18-hole golf course, hiking and biking outings, and a Michelin-rated restaurant. The world-class spa taps directly into the heated thermal waters below. 101 Boyes Blvd. (corner of Boyes Blvd. and Calif. 12). ☎ 800/441-1414 or 707/938-9000. www.fairmont.com/sonoma. 226 units. Doubles $259–$1,259 w/free wine tasting (4:30–5:30pm) and a complimentary bottle of wine. AE, DC, MC, V.

★★ The Farmhouse Inn & Restaurant

FORESTVILLE Luxury and pampering—with a friendly family touch (like evening gourmet s'mores around the fire pit)—are standard at this award-winning property, owned for four generations by the Bartolomei family. Pluses include a Michelin-rated restaurant with a master sommelier, a spa exclusively for guest use, a seriously attentive staff, and individually appointed guest rooms. 7871 River Rd. ☎ 800/464-6642 or 707/887-3300. www.farmhouseinn.com. 18 units. Doubles $295–$650. AE, DISC, MC, V.

★★ Gaige House Inn GLEN ELLEN

Though the main house on this 3-acre property was built in 1900 in the Queen Anne style, this creekside inn has been fashioned into an Asian-inspired retreat best suited to adults. The spa suites feature granite soaking tubs and private Japanese gardens; there are also indoor/outdoor spa services available. 13540 Arnold Dr. ☎ 800/935-0237 or 707/935-0237. www.gaige.com. 23 units. Doubles $365–$375 summer, $200–$325 winter; suites $395–$695 summer,

> *Slip into the naturally heated mineral waters at one of the Wine Country's grand dames, Fairmont Sonoma Mission Inn & Spa.*

$300–$595 winter. Rates include evening wine tasting. AE, DC, DISC, MC, V.

★★ Hotel Healdsburg HEALDSBURG

Those seeking a modern hotel with all the bells and whistles, look no further than this hotel, opened in 2001. Accommodations are classy and simple, with hardwood floors, Tibetan carpets, and feather beds, plus MP3 players and Wi-Fi. Acclaimed chef Charlie Palmer has his ★★ **Dry Creek Kitchen** here. 25 Matheson St. (at the square). ☎ 800/889-7188 or 707/431-2800. www.hotelhealdsburg.com. 55 units. Doubles $325–$510; suites $495–$820. Rates include breakfast. AE, MC, V.

★★ The Renaissance Lodge at Sonoma

SONOMA This is Sonoma's biggest hotel, but its contemporary take on old California style has charm. The accommodations are tasteful and spacious, and include an assortment of rooms, suites, and cottages; some rooms have fireplaces, balconies, and deep tubs. The on-site spa and bistro are both top-notch; the hotel has a great location, too. 1325 Broadway. ☎ 866/263-0758 or 707/935-6600. www.thelodgeatsonoma.com. 182 units. Doubles $249–$449. AE, MC, V.

★★ kids Safari West Tent Camp SANTA ROSA

Wine Country's most unique lodgings are on a wildlife preserve (p. 139, **6**) where more than 500 animals—including giraffes, gazelles, and zebras—roam in large enclosures. Luxury tents with hardwood floors, en suite bathrooms, and hot showers (essentially a hotel room with canvas walls and ceiling), sit on raised decks overlooking the preserve; for those who insist on hard walls, there's also a cottage. 3115 Porter Creek Rd. ☎ 800/616-2695 or 707/579-2551. www.safariwest.com. 32 units. Doubles $170–$295; cottages $350. Rates include breakfast. AE, MC, V.

kids Sandman Santa Rosa SANTA ROSA

A great option for families on a budget, this clean and comfortable motel has in-room fridges, microwaves, and Wi-Fi, as well as a large pool and Jacuzzi; it's also pet friendly. The location is generic, but it's right off the highway, providing easy access to Wine Country sights. 3421 Cleveland Ave. (at Piner Rd.). ☎ 707/293-2100. www.sandmansantarosa.com. 136 units. Doubles $82–$92; suites $140. Rates include breakfast. AE, DC, DISC, MC, V.

Wine Country Restaurants A to Z

Napa Valley

★★ **All Seasons** CALISTOGA *CALIFORNIAN*
For more than 25 years, this eatery has been serving creative, seasonally driven fare; much of the product used is sourced locally and is organic and chemical free. Look for stalwarts like the house-made gnocchi and the crispy skin chicken breast. 1400 Lincoln Ave. ☎ 707/ 942-9111. www.allseasonsnapavalley.net. Reservations recommended Sat–Sun. Entrees $10–$24. DISC, MC, V. Lunch Fri–Sun; dinner daily.

★★ **BarBersQ** NAPA *BARBECUE*
You can't really call this place a barbecue "joint" because it's pretty upscale, what with the tablecloths and all. But it does serve a mean Memphis-style barbecue, along with other "American heritage" fare like (natural-beef) meatloaf and (free-range) chicken

> *Relax in the Napa Valley Wine Train and wave as you pass the traffic that sometimes clogs Wine Country roads.*

potpie. It offers takeout and delivery service, as well. 3900 D Bel Aire Plaza. ☎ 707/ 224-6600. www.barbersq.com. Reservations recommended. Entrees $8–$30. AE, MC, V. Lunch & dinner daily.

★★ **Bistro Don Giovanni** NAPA *ITALIAN*
This busy, boisterous bistro specializes in thin-crust pizzas from a wood-burning oven; other favorites include grilled sea bass and duck Bolognese. There's also romantic outdoor seating, surrounded by gardens and mountain views, with ambience added by a flickering fireplace. 4110 Howard Lane. ☎ 707/224-3300. www.bistrodongiovanni.com. Reservations recommended. Entrees $12–$24. AE, DC, DISC, MC, V. Lunch & dinner daily.

★★ **Bistro Jeanty** YOUNTVILLE *FRENCH*
This Michelin-rated bistro serves France's greatest hits, from cassoulet to filet au poivre, as well as such fiendishly rich creations as house-cured pork belly with foie gras ragout. The tomato soup in puff pastry is not to be

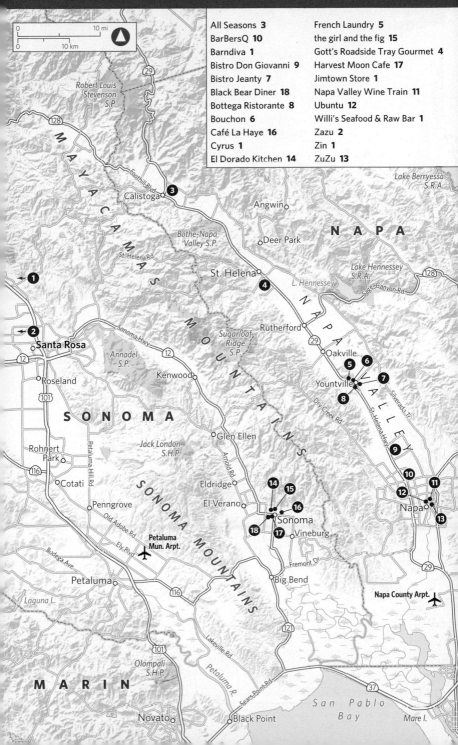

All Seasons **3**
BarBersQ **10**
Barndiva **1**
Bistro Don Giovanni **9**
Bistro Jeanty **7**
Black Bear Diner **18**
Bottega Ristorante **8**
Bouchon **6**
Café La Haye **16**
Cyrus **1**
El Dorado Kitchen **14**

French Laundry **5**
the girl and the fig **15**
Gott's Roadside Tray Gourmet **4**
Harvest Moon Cafe **17**
Jimtown Store **1**
Napa Valley Wine Train **11**
Ubuntu **12**
Willi's Seafood & Raw Bar **1**
Zazu **2**
Zin **1**
ZuZu **13**

> *Another sparkling star in the brilliance that is chef Thomas Keller, Bouchon dazzles with perfect bistro fare.*

missed. 6510 Washington St. ☎ 707/944-0103. www.bistrojeanty.com. Reservations recommended. Entrees $15–$38. AE, MC, V. Lunch & dinner daily.

★ **Bottega Ristorante** YOUNTVILLE *ITALIAN* This stylish hot spot was created by Emmy-winning Food Network personality and cookbook author Michael Chiarello, who can often be found working the room (or cool outdoor lounge). The menu has a pan-Italian approach, with influences coming from around the country, executed with local, artisanal, and house-made product—pastas, cured meats and olives, and cheeses are all made on the premises. 6525 Washington St. ☎ 707/945-1050. www.bottega napavalley.com. Reservations recommended. Entrees $15–$28. AE, DC, DISC, MC, V. Lunch Tues–Sun; dinner daily.

★★ **Bouchon** YOUNTVILLE *FRENCH* Couldn't get that reservation at ★★★ **French Laundry** (see below)? Never fear—Bouchon is here to ease your pain. You can still brag about the Thomas Keller meal you had at this Michelin-starred brasserie, French Laundry's little sister. And adjacent is the amazing ★★★ **Bouchon Bakery** (☎ 707/944-2253; www.bouchonbakery.com), where you can

pick up some Keller magic to go. 6534 Washington St. ☎ 707/944-8037. www.bouchon bistro.com. Reservations recommended. Mon–Fri, required Sat. Entrees $16–$30. AE, MC, V. Lunch & dinner daily.

★★★ **French Laundry** YOUNTVILLE *AMERICAN/ FRENCH* Yountville has more Michelin stars per capita than anyplace else on Earth, and French Laundry, considered one of the best restaurants in the *world,* accounts for three of them. Two tasting menus are created daily, one of them vegetarian. You'll get nine courses of food porn that will most likely end up being one of the most memorable meals of your life. If you're already in town and didn't make a reservation 2 months ago, you're out of luck; if you show up at the beginning of lunch or dinner service, though, there's a very slim chance you could snag a canceled reservation. Other than that, content yourself with ★★ **Bouchon** and ★★★ **Bouchon Bakery** (above). 6640 Washington St. ☎ 707/944-2380. www.frenchlaundry.com. Reservations required and can be made up to 2 months in advance. 9-course tasting menu $240. AE, MC, V. Lunch Fri–Sun; dinner daily. No jeans or tennis shoes; jackets required for men.

★ **kids** **Gott's Roadside Tray Gourmet**
ST. HELENA *DINER* Fast-food, Wine Country style, featuring grass-fed, hormone-free natural beef, a choice of fresh salads, sweet potato fries, and a pleasantly surprising wine and beer list. This walk-up spot, formerly known as Taylor's Automatic Refresher (and still owned by the same people), features grassy picnic-grounds-style seating, and often sports long lines. There's also a branch at the ★★ **Oxbow Public Market** (p. 134, **②**) in Napa. 933 Main St. ☎ 707/963-3486. www.gottsroadside.com. Entrees $4–$16. AE, MC, V. Lunch & dinner daily.

★ **Napa Valley Wine Train** NAPA *AMERICAN*
A unique wining and dining experience aboard lavishly restored vintage train cars, running from Napa to St. Helena and back again on a 3-hour excursion. Both lunch and dinner services are offered, as well as wine tasting, and ride-only fares ($50; daytime only, with the option to purchase a la carte items and wine if you like); there are also packages that allow you to disembark for a special winery tour along the way. The 1952 Vista Dome Pullman is the swankiest option. 1275 McKinstry St. ☎ 800/427-4124. www.winetrain.com. Lunch $94–$124; dinner $99–$129; winery tour package $119–$184. AE, DC, DISC, MC, V. Lunch & dinner daily.

★★ **Ubuntu** NAPA *VEGETARIAN*
Chic and urbane, with a touch of Asian industrial design (not to mention a yoga studio upstairs), this vegetable-driven restaurant uses local product, much of it from its own biodynamic garden. The vegetarian menu is hardly boring—the *New York Times* declared this one of the country's 10 best restaurants outside of New York City. Next door, **Ubuntu Annex** sells kitchen and tableware, foods, and gifts. 1140 Main St. ☎ 707/251-5656. www.ubuntunapa. com. Entrees $15–$20. Reservations recommended. AE, DC, DISC, MC, V. Lunch Mon–Fri; dinner daily.

★★ **ZuZu** NAPA *TAPAS*
This friendly and comfortable spot jumps with locals and visitors alike. You'll find traditional Spanish tapas, as well as small plates with a Californian and Latin American flair; ingredients are local, seasonal, and organic. 829 Main St. ☎ 707/224-8555. www.zuzunapa.com.

> *Magic is in the details (and the food) at the incomparable French Laundry. Can't get in? Try lunch reservations.*

Reservations not accepted. Tapas $3–$13. AE, MC, V. Lunch Mon–Fri; dinner daily.

Sonoma Valley

★★ **Barndiva** HEALDSBURG *CALIFORNIAN*
This hip and artsy space serves seasonal, sustainable, and local ingredients. It has a way-cool dog-friendly "backyard," perfect for Sunday brunch, but it does take some dings in the service department. Wednesday features prix-fixe meals ($35), and there's occasional live music. The creative cocktail list is a winner. 231 Center St. ☎ 707/431-0100. www.barndiva.com. Reservations recommended. Entrees $10–$29. AE, MC, V. Lunch & dinner Wed–Sun.

kids **Black Bear Diner** SONOMA *DINER*
A break from the gourmet grind. Dine on huge portions of classic (and cheap!) American food, served in a friendly and fun atmosphere. Drop some cash in the jukebox and chow down. 201 W. Napa St. (at Second St.). ☎ 707/935-6800. www.blackbeardiner.com. Entrees $5–$17. AE, DISC, MC, V. Breakfast, lunch & dinner daily.

> Gourmet fast food? The burgers and sweet potato fries at Gott's Roadside Tray Gourmet will make you a believer.

★★ Cafe La Haye SONOMA *CALIFORNIAN*
This intimate (small), bilevel restaurant is a longtime favorite, serving seasonally inspired dishes such as pan-seared quail and chipotle-glazed pork chops. The tasty desserts include a butterscotch pudding and a yuzu citrus cheesecake with blackberry-zinfandel sauce. 140 E. Napa St. ☎ 707/935-5994. www.cafelahaye.com. Reservations recommended. Entrees $17–$25. AE, MC, V. Dinner Tues–Sat.

★★★ Cyrus HEALDSBURG *CALIFORNIAN/FRENCH* Second perhaps only to **French Laundry** (p. 162) as Wine Country's high temple of gastronomy. Chef Douglas Keane (a James Beard award winner) presents beautiful and sophisticated five- and eight-course tasting menus. The caviar and champagne cart appears tableside to get your evening rolling. 29 North St. ☎ 707/433-3311. www.cyrusrestaurant.com. Reservations required. 5-course menu $108; 8-course menu $130. AE, MC, V. Dinner daily.

★★ El Dorado Kitchen SONOMA *CALIFORNIAN*
This stylish, hip space has as its centerpiece a 21-foot-long wooden communal table reclaimed from a bridge. You can watch from there as the open kitchen turns out a seasonal menu that might include pan-roasted trout or duck prepared three ways. Start off with the house-made charcuterie, artisanal cheeses, and the truffle fries. 405 First St. W. ☎ 707/996-3030. www.eldoradosonoma.com. Reservations recommended. Entrees $15–$29. AE, MC, V. Lunch & dinner daily.

★★ the girl and the fig SONOMA *FRENCH*
The girl and the fig are sure to live happily ever after once they've shared this local favorite's *fromage* (cheese) tower, featuring cheeses, cured meats and sausage, house-made charcuterie, and fruits and nuts. And figs do make a frequent appearance on the Provençal-style menu. 110 W. Spain St. ☎ 707/938-3634. www.thegirlandthefig.com. Reservations recommended. Entrees $13–$24. AE, DISC, MC, V. Lunch & dinner daily; Sun brunch. Late-night brasserie menu till 11pm Fri–Sat.

★★ Harvest Moon Cafe SONOMA *AMERICAN*
Shine on, Harvest Moon. It's hard to resist the pumpkin ravioli or the pork chop with creamy polenta and cherry sauce, but you never know what might show up on the nightly changing menu at this small bistro. 487 First St. W. ☎ 707/933-8160. www.harvestmooncafesonoma.com. Reservations recommended. Entrees $18–$25. AE, DISC, MC, V. Dinner daily; brunch Sun.

★★ Jimtown Store HEALDSBURG *DELI*
It's been a country store since 1895, but instead of nails and flour, it now sells gourmet treats (brie and chopped olive sandwiches, for instance), house-made condiments, vintage collectibles, toys, and folk art. Preordered takeout box lunches are perfect for winery picnics. 6706 State Hwy. 128. ☎ 707/433-1212. www.jimtown.com. Box lunches $12–$16. AE, MC, V. Breakfast & lunch daily.

★ Willi's Seafood & Raw Bar HEALDSBURG *SEAFOOD* This lively and colorful eatery has sidewalk dining and creative seasonal cocktails to go along with seafood that often flashes a Latin flare (such as the hamachi ceviche with chili, lime juice, and pepitas). The

> *It's easy to toast sheer elegance at exquisite Cyrus, where diners are greeted with a champagne and caviar cart.*

barbecued bacon-wrapped scallops, skewered and served with cilantro-pumpkinseed pesto, are a highlight. 403 Healdsburg Ave.☎ 707/433-9191. www.starkrestaurants.com/willis_seafood.html. Reservations recommended for parties of 8 or more. Small plates $7–$14. AE, DISC, MC, V. Lunch & dinner daily.

★★ **Zazu** SANTA ROSA *AMERICAN/ITALIAN*
It's not the most centrally located place, but a lot of people still beat a path to this friendly roadhouse. Rustic Northern Italian fare meets Americana comfort food on a menu that changes daily and features the freshest seasonal ingredients. On Pinot and Pizza Night (Wed, Thurs, & Sun), pizzas are paired with flights of pinot noir. 3535 Guerneville Rd. (about 5 miles west of Hwy. 101) ☎ 707/523-4814. www.zazurestaurant.com. Reservations recommended. Entrees $17–$28. AE, DISC, MC, V. Dinner Wed–Sun.

★★ **Zin** HEALDSBURG *AMERICAN*
Contemporary takes on American classics are coupled with a zealous use of house-made

> *Country store meets gourmet deli (and plenty of other cool stuff) at Carrie Brown's delightful Jimtown Store.*

ingredients; everything from bread, pasta, and cheeses to ice cream, sausages, and pickles are made on-site. The signature dish is coq au Zin—local chicken braised in zinfandel, with bacon and roasted mushrooms, served over celery root mashed potatoes. 344 Center St. ☎ 707/473-0946. www.zinrestaurant.com. Entrees $15–$26. AE, DISC, MC, V. Lunch Mon–Fri; dinner daily.

Don't Miss Out

Dining is serious business in Wine Country. Take the time to make reservations. And the sooner the better.

Fast Facts

American Express

American Express Travel Service, 455 Market St., San Francisco (☎ 415/536-2600; www.amextravelresources.com), is the closest office. It's open Monday to Friday 9am to 5:30pm and Saturday 10am to 2pm. Or call ☎ 800/221-7282.

Dentists & Doctors

For a dentist, call **1-800-DENTIST** (☎ 800/336-8422; www.1800dentist.com). For a doctor, see "Emergencies," below.

Emergencies

In an emergency dial ☎ 911.

To contact the police in nonemergency situations in Napa Valley, call the **Napa County Sheriff's Office,** 1535 Airport Blvd., Napa (☎ 707/253-4509; www.countyofnapa.org/sheriff). In Sonoma, call the **Sonoma County Sheriff's Office,** 2796 Ventura Ave., Santa Rosa (☎ 707/565-2511; www.sonomasheriff.org).

For medical emergencies, in Napa head to **Queen of the Valley Medical Center,** 1000 Trancas St., Napa (☎ 707/257-4038; www.thequeen.org). In Sonoma, go to **Sonoma Valley Hospital,** 347 Andrieux St., Sonoma (☎ 707/935-5000; www.svh.com).

Getting There

BY PLANE **Oakland International Airport** (☎ 800/247-6255 or 510/563-3300; www.oaklandairport.com) is a little over an hour's drive from downtown Napa; **San Francisco International Airport** (☎ 650/821-8211; www.flysfo.com) is about a 2-hour drive from Wine Country. Oakland (OAK) does not experience the fog-related delays that San Francisco International (SFO) does, but it also has fewer carriers. The best option to get into Wine Country from either airport is to rent a car; both airports have car-rental desks for the major agencies. If you do want to take a shuttle to a Napa hotel, **Evans Transportation** (☎ 707/255-1559; www.evanstransportation.com) runs nine daily shuttles from SFO and six from OAK ($29, cash only). **Sonoma County Airport Express** (☎ 800/327-2024 or 707/837-8700; www.airportexpressinc.com) will take you to Santa Rosa (the driver can call ahead to have a cab

meet you at the drop-off location). There are 19 daily shuttles from SFO and 9 from OAK ($32, cash or check). BY TRAIN **Amtrak** (☎ 800/872-7245; www.amtrak.com) has rail and bus service to Healdsburg, Napa, and Santa Rosa.

BY CAR To get to **Napa Valley** from San Francisco, cross the Golden Gate Bridge and go north on U.S. 101; turn east on Hwy. 37 (toward Vallejo), then north on Hwy. 29, the main road through Napa Valley. You can also take Hwy. 121/12 from Hwy. 37 and follow the signs. From Oakland, head east on I-80 toward Sacramento; a few miles past the Carquinez Bridge ($4 toll) and the city of Vallejo, exit on Hwy. 12 west, which intersects with Hwy. 29 and leads directly into Napa. To get to **Sonoma Valley** from San Francisco, cross the Golden Gate Bridge and stay on U.S. 101 north. Exit at Hwy. 37, then head north on Hwy. 121. After 10 miles, turn north onto Hwy. 12 (Broadway), which leads directly into the town of Sonoma. From Oakland, go east on I-80 toward Sacramento. Cross the Carquinez Bridge ($4 toll) and go past the city of Vallejo; take Hwy. 12, which intersects with Hwy. 29 at the south end of Napa Valley. Just before the town of Napa, you'll come to a major intersection where Hwy. 29 meets Hwy. 12/121. Turn left onto Hwy. 12/121, which leads directly into Sonoma Valley. To get to **northern Sonoma** from San Francisco, cross the Golden Gate Bridge and stay on U.S. 101 north. Exit anywhere from Santa Rosa to Healdsburg, depending on your final destination. From Oakland, head east on I-80 toward Sacramento. Cross the Carquinez Bridge ($4 toll) and go past Vallejo; take Hwy. 12, which intersects with Hwy. 29 at the south end of Napa Valley. Just before the town of Napa, you'll come to a major intersection where Hwy. 29 meets Hwy. 12/121. Turn left onto Hwy. 12/121, then right onto Hwy. 116/Arnold Drive. When the road forks, veer right onto Adobe Road. Turn left on East Washington Street, merge onto U.S. 101 north, and exit at your destination.

Getting Around

BY CAR This is hands down the best way to get around the region, and I strongly recommend you rent a car if you're not driving your own.

Wine Country's picturesque highways are well marked, but you may run into confusion with stretches that have multiple names or numbers. For instance, Hwy. 12 is also Hwy. 121, and it's also known as the Carneros Highway and the Sonoma-Napa Highway; a decent map will help sort things out. Be aware also that high-season (late-Aug to mid-Oct) weekends are notorious for traffic. BY LIMOUSINE **Beau Wine Tours and Limousine Service** (☎ 800/387-2328 or 707/938-8001; www.beauwinetours.com) has town cars, vans, and limos that serve both valleys; the cost is $60 to $90 per hour. **Celebrity Limousine** (☎ 707/552-7752; www.celeblimo.com) covers similar ground for $55 to $80 per hour. BY BUS In Napa Valley, **Napa County Transportation and Planning Agency** (☎ 800/696-6443 or 707/251-2800; www.nctpa.net) connects Napa, Yountville, Rutherford, and St. Helena via VINE route 10, which runs the length of the valley. Other routes cover the individual towns themselves. There are both basic fares and zone fares ($1.25–$3.50). Hours of service are Monday to Friday 5:30am to 9:30pm, Saturday 6:30am to 8:30pm, and Sunday 8:30am to 7pm. **Sonoma County Transit** (☎ 800/345-7433 or 707/576-7433; www.sctransit.com) has routes covering Sonoma, Healdsburg, Santa Rosa, and more; check the website for maps and schedules. Fares are based on a zone system and run $1.25 to $3.45. BY TAXI **Napa Valley Cab** (☎ 707/257-6444) and **Yellow Cab** (☎ 707/226-3731) offer service in Napa. In Sonoma, try **Vern's Taxi Service** (☎ 707/938-8885) or **Healdsburg Taxi Cab** (☎ 707/433-7099; www.healdsburgtaxicab.com). In towns, fares are usually metered (around $2.50 per mile); destinations beyond town limits are often a flat rate and very expensive (Napa to Calistoga is $65). Expect long waits for pickup.

Hospital
See "Emergencies," above.

Internet Access
Wi-Fi hotspots are plentiful; Internet cafes are not. Public libraries are a good alternative for those without a laptop: Napa's library is at 580 Coombs St. (☎ 707/253-4241; www.countyofnapa.org); Sonoma's is at 755 W. Napa St. (☎ 707/996-5217; www.sonomalibrary.org).

Pharmacies
Chain drugstores with pharmacies, like **CVS** (☎ 800/746-7287; www.cvs.com) and **Rite Aid,** (☎ 800/748-3243; www.riteaid.com), are found throughout Wine Country. **Walgreens** in Santa Rosa, 4610 Sonoma Hwy. (☎ 707/538-9275; www.walgreens.com), has a 24-hour pharmacy.

Post Office
The main post office in Napa is at 1625 Trancas St. (☎ 707/255-0190; Mon–Fri 9am–6pm). In Sonoma, it's at 617 Broadway (☎ 707/996-9311; Mon–Fri 8:30am–5pm). For other locations call ☎ 800/275-8777 or go to www.usps.com.

Safety
Wine Country is a very safe destination; the biggest concern is drunk driving. Always use a designated driver when touring wineries and keep an eye out for motorists who may be impaired.

Visitor Information
In the Napa Valley, the **Napa Valley Destination Council** is at 1310 Napa Town Center, Napa (☎ 707/226-5813; www.legendarynapavalley.com); the **Yountville Chamber of Commerce** is at 6484 Washington St., Ste. F, Yountville (☎ 707/944-0904; www.yountville.com); the **St. Helena Chamber of Commerce** is at 1010 Main St., Ste. A, St. Helena (☎ 800/799-6456 or 707/963-4456; www.sthelena.com); and the **Calistoga Chamber of Commerce** is at 1133 Washington St., Calistoga (☎ 866/306-5588 or 707/942-6333; www.calistogavisitors.com).

In the Sonoma Valley, try the **Sonoma Valley Visitors Bureau,** 453 First St. E. and 23570 Arnold Dr. (Hwy. 121), Sonoma (☎ 866/996-1090 or 707/996-1090; www.sonomavalley.com); the **Sonoma County Tourism Bureau,** 420 Aviation Blvd., Ste. 106, Santa Rosa (☎ 800/576-6662 or 707/522-5800; www.sonomacounty.com); the **Santa Rosa Convention & Visitors Bureau,** 9 Fourth St., Santa Rosa (☎ 800/404-7673 or 707/577-8674; www.visitsantarosa.com) or the **Healdsburg Chamber of Commerce & Visitors Bureau,** 217 Healdsburg Ave., Healdsburg (☎ 800/648-9992 or 707/433-6935; www.healdsburg.org).

5 Sacramento & the Gold Country

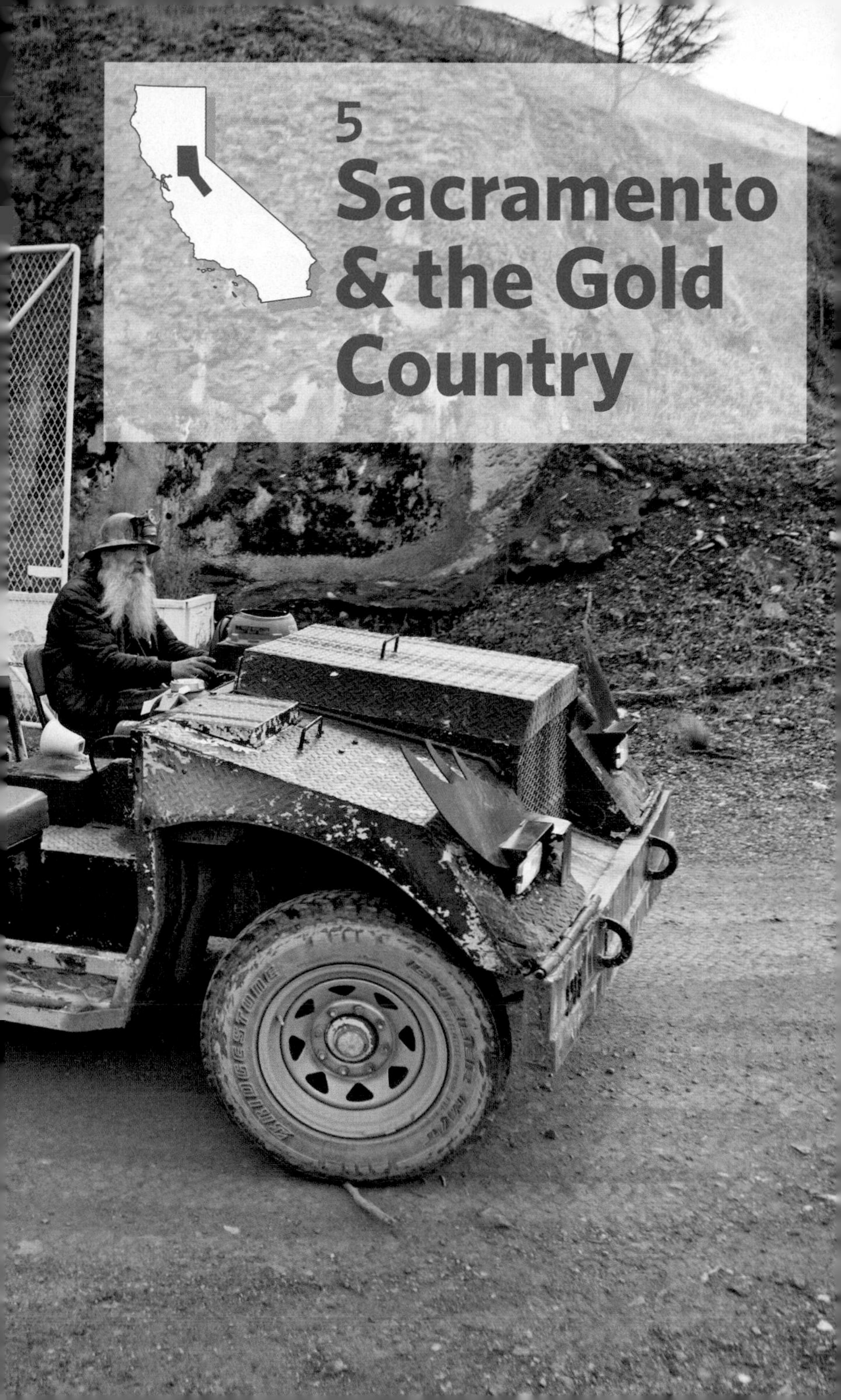

The Best of Gold Country in 3 Days

Cozying up to the western Sierra Nevada, California's Gold Country is a huge swath of land arcing from above Lake Tahoe (p. 292) to below Yosemite (p. 276). In just a few days, however, you can get a unique taste of California's past and present—from the region's historic boomtowns, which sprang to life after the discovery of gold in 1848, to the state's burgeoning capital, Sacramento.

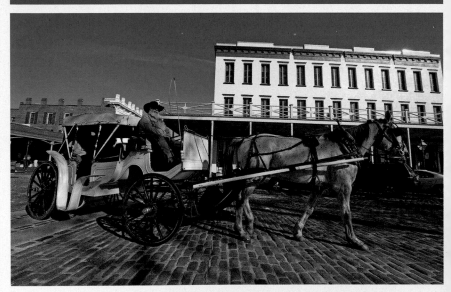

> PREVIOUS PAGE *Get the rough-and-tumble feel of a miner's life on Sutter Gold Mine tours.*
> THIS PAGE *Time travel in once rowdy but now tame Old Sacramento.*

START **Sutter's Fort State Historic Park, Sacramento. You'll be able to navigate the capital without a vehicle, but days 2 and 3 will require a car. TRIP LENGTH about 160 miles.**

❶ ★ **Sutter's Fort State Historic Park.** Johann Suter (1803–80), a Swiss immigrant who became known as John Sutter, established the first nonindigenous settlement in California's Central Valley here in 1839. His "fort" was an adobe outpost, the headquarters for an agricultural empire he hoped to cultivate from the Mexican land grants awarded to him. Reconstructed to its 1846 appearance, Sutter's Fort features a collection of pioneer and early California artifacts, including items from the ill-fated Donner Party. It was from Sutter's Fort that a relief expedition was dispatched to rescue those snowbound travelers in 1847. ⏱ 45 min. 2701 L St. ☎ 916/445-4422. www. parks.ca.gov./suttersfort. Admission $5 adults, $3 kids 6–16, free for kids 5 & under. Daily 10am–5pm.

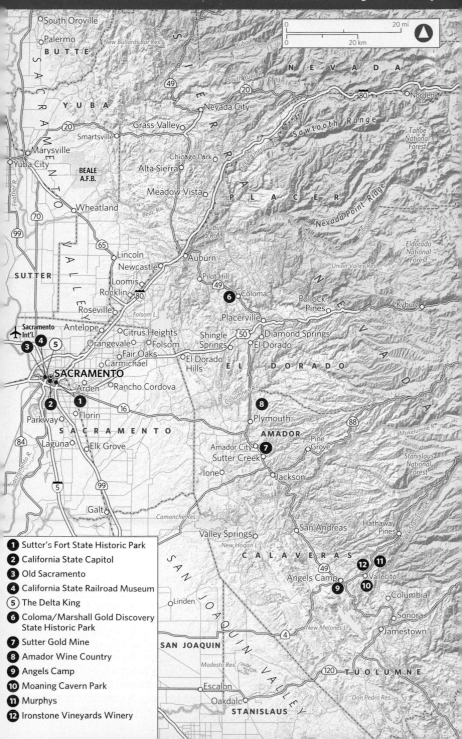

1 Sutter's Fort State Historic Park
2 California State Capitol
3 Old Sacramento
4 California State Railroad Museum
5 The Delta King
6 Coloma/Marshall Gold Discovery
   State Historic Park
7 Sutter Gold Mine
8 Amador Wine Country
9 Angels Camp
10 Moaning Cavern Park
11 Murphys
12 Ironstone Vineyards Winery

> *Get into the swing of pioneer life at Sutter's Fort, the first nonindigenous settlement in California's Central Valley established in 1839.*

Take bus 30 or 31 west on L St. to the State Capitol.

❷ ★★★ **California State Capitol.** The grandeur of this complex is truly impressive. A leafy park featuring beautiful gardens and memorials surrounds the magnificent capitol building, completed in 1874. The state also oversees a rich collection of art, including antique furnishings, murals tracing California history, and the requisite governor portraits (a quirky, modernist Jerry Brown; a predictably perky Ronald Reagan). The centerpiece of the awe-inspiring rotunda is a sculpture of Columbus and Queen Isabella. Why Columbus? At the dedication ceremony in 1883, it was declared: "California, more than any other state in the American union, fulfills (Columbus') vision of marvelous lands beyond the setting sun." ⏱ 1 hr. 10th St. (btw. N & L sts.). ☎ 916/324-0333. www.capitolmuseum.ca.gov. Free admission. Daily 9am–5pm. Tours every hour on the hour till 4pm.

Take downtown trolley 143 to Old Sacramento, or make the 20-minute walk.

❸ ★ **Old Sacramento.** The California dream was born on January 24, 1848, when gold was discovered along the American River, 40 miles to the east of here. Sacramento—and California—was changed forever by the tide of humanity that washed up onto the banks of the Sacramento River seeking fortune in the state's gold fields. The newly minted boomtown was prone to flood and fire, but this 28-acre National Historic Landmark District and State Historic Park preserve more than 50 structures, some dating back to 1849. There are restaurants, touristy shops, entertainment, and museums; you can pick up a walking-tour map at the visitor center. As you stroll through this slice of Wild West Americana, you can get a taste of what Old Sac was like back in the day—minus the mud and cholera outbreaks. ⏱ At least 1 hr. West of I-5 (btw. I & L sts.). Visitor center: 1002 Second St.; ☎ 916/442-7644; www.oldsacramento.com.

Park: ☎ 916/445-7387; www.parks.ca.gov. Free admission. Grounds daily 24 hr.; shops usually 11am–7pm; restaurants till 10 or 11pm.

Walk to the north end of the district to the

④ ★★★ kids California State Railroad Museum. More than 20 painstakingly restored railroad cars and locomotives are on display at this popular and engaging museum. The exhibits, along with a variety of special events scheduled throughout the year, explore and celebrate railroading and the impact it has had on our history, economy, and imaginations. From April to September, the museum operates a steam locomotive line that takes a short trip along the Sacramento River levee, departing from a station in Old Sacramento ($8 adults, $3 kids). ⏲ At least 1 hr. 125 I St. (at Second St.). ☎ 916/445-6645. www.csrmf.org. Admission $9 adults, $4 kids 6–17, free for kids 5 & under. Daily 10am–5pm.

⑤ 🍴 ★ The Delta King. Complete your Old Sacramento time warp with some vittles in the lounge of this restored sternwheeler riverboat. Commissioned in 1927, the *Delta King* worked the river between San Francisco and Sacramento; during World War II the U.S. Navy appropriated it for home-front duty. The menu is pretty standard bar-and-grill fare, but the surroundings are classic. 1000 Front St., Old Sacramento. ☎ 800/825-5464 or 916/444-5464. www.deltaking.com. Items $10–$20.

On Day 2, take U.S. 50 east to Hwy. 49 north and the town of Coloma, a 1 hr. drive.

⑥ ★ Coloma/Marshall Gold Discovery State Historic Park. It was here along the South Fork of the American River that James Marshall, a carpenter in the employ of John Sutter, discovered gold while building a lumber mill. There's a replica of the original sawmill, as well as more than 20 other historic buildings to explore; the **Gold Discovery Museum and Visitor Center** interprets the tumultuous events of 1848–49, and you can also pick up a walking map to guide you along the trails and through the pretty town, 70 percent of which is considered part of the park. You can also try your hand at panning for gold. **Note:**

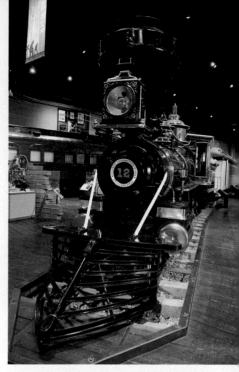

> *All aboard at the eye-popping California State Railroad Museum, with meticulously restored locomotives, cabooses, and rail cars.*

Be prepared in summer for the crowds that swarm into town in search of white-water rafting thrills (p. 179, ⑨). ⏲ At least 1 hr. 310 Back St., Coloma. ☎ 530/622-3470. www.parks.ca.gov or www.coloma.com. Admission $6 per person. Summer Thurs–Mon 8am–6pm; winter Tues–Sat 8am–4pm. Museum 10am–3pm.

Head south on Hwy. 49 and look for the turn-off to Amador City; it's about a 50-min. drive.

⑦ ★ kids Sutter Gold Mine. Gear up, tag in, and drop down into a real, modern gold mine. You'll get a lesson in mining and geology on a 1-hour tour; up top you can pan for gold or gemstones, or crack a geode—everyone is guaranteed to strike pay dirt. ⏲ 1½ hr. 13660 Hwy. 49 (about ½ mile south of Amador City, just north of Sutter Creek). ☎ 866/762-2837 or 209/736-2708. www.suttergold.com. Admission $18 adults, $12 kids 4–13 (tour not recommended for kids 3 & under). Summer daily 9am–5pm; winter Mon–Fri 10am–4pm, Sat–Sun 10am–5pm.

> *The red-brick Altaville School in historic Angels Camp was built in 1859 with funds from a dance.*

Head north on Hwy. 49, to the town of Plymouth and Shenandoah Plymouth Rd., turn right, then continue on Shenandoah Rd. to Amador County Wine Country.

8 ★ **Amador Wine Country.** Amador County boasts some 40 wineries, many of which are noted for their zinfandels; most wineries are clustered along or just off of Shenandoah Road. Winemaking in this area dates back to the early days of the Gold Rush when fortune hunters from Europe made their way to the Sierra foothills, bringing their vintner techniques with them. Top choices include **Shenandoah Vineyards,** 12300 Steiner Rd. (☎ 209/245-4455; www.shenandoahvineyards.com; tasting room daily 10am–5pm); **Sobon Estate,** 14430 Shenandoah Rd. (☎ 209/245-6554; www.sobonwine.com; tasting room daily 9:30am–5pm); and **Story Winery,** 10525 Bell Rd. (☎ 209/245-6208; www.zin.com; tasting room Mon–Fri noon–4pm, Sat–Sun 11am–5pm). Shenandoah Vineyards has a contemporary art gallery on-site; Sobon Estate houses the **Shenandoah Valley Museum,** which gives an overview of the area's agricultural and winemaking history; and Story Winery has one of the Wine Country's prettiest picnic grounds. ⏱ At least 2 hr. Amador Vintners Association, ☎ 888/655-8614. www.amadorwine.com.

On Day 3, follow Hwy. 49 south to Angels Camp, about 1 hr. from Amador City.

9 ★ **Angels Camp.** This friendly town is best known as the place where Mark Twain first heard the tall tale that became his story *The Celebrated Jumping Frog of Calaveras County.* There really is a frog-jumping competition, the **Jumping Frog Jubilee,** held the third weekend in May as part of the **Calaveras County Fair** (☎ 209/736-2561; www.frogtown.org)—and anyone can enter. The rest of the year you can browse antiques stores or check out the **Angels Camp Museum Carriage House,** 753 S. Main St. (☎ 209/736-2963; www.angelscamp.gov; Thurs–Mon 10am–4pm, Sat–Sun only Jan–Feb), with its 3-acres of historic artifacts, carriages, and mining equipment. ⏱ At least 1 hr. Calaveras Visitors Bureau, 1192 S. Main St. ☎ 800/225-3764 or 209/736-0049. www.gocalaveras.com.

Take Hwy. 4 east, make a right on Parrotts Ferry Rd., and a right on Moaning Cave Rd.; total trip is about 7 miles.

⑩ ★ Moaning Cavern Park. Take a tight spiral staircase 100 feet down into a huge cavern that's big enough to hold the Statue of Liberty. Or take the quick route down—a 165-foot rappel (no experience necessary). There are several activities available at this cave complex, which really does emit a mournful sound when the conditions are just right, including a 45-minute walking tour, a 3-hour adventure expedition (advance reservations required), and above-ground zip lines that will whisk you 1,500 feet at speeds up to 40 mph. ⏱ At least 1 hr. 5350 Moaning Cave Rd., Vallecito. ☎ 866/762-2837 or 209/736-2708. www.caverntours.com. Walking tours $14 adults, $7 kids 3–12; rappel $65; adventure tour $130; zip line $39. Minimum age to ride is 12 for rappel and adventure tour. Summer daily 9am–6pm; winter Mon–Fri 10am–5pm, Sat–Sun 9am–5pm.

Return to Hwy. 4 east for a 6-mile drive to

⑪ ★ Murphys. Known as the Queen of the Sierra, this genteel lady is a charming, shady Gold Rush town that is lined with Victorian structures housing galleries, boutiques, wine-tasting rooms, and restaurants. Be sure to visit **Murphys Historic Hotel,** 457 Main St. (☎ 800/532-7684 or 209/728-3444; www.murphyshotel.com)—particularly its popular saloon. This National Historic Landmark has been in continuous operation since 1856, and Ulysses S. Grant and John Wayne are among those who have laid their heads here. Another highlight is **Murphys Olde Timers Museum,** 470 Main St. (☎ 209/728-1160), which interprets the town's history. Free walking tours usually depart from in front of the museum on Saturday at 10am (call ☎ 209/728-3517 to confirm). ⏱ At least 1 hr. Calaveras Visitors Bureau, ☎ 800/225-3764 or 209/736-0049. www.gocalaveras.com or www.visitmurphys.com.

Take Big Trees Rd., which becomes Six Mile Rd., to Ironstone Vineyards, 1 mile south of Murphys.

⑫ ★ Ironstone Vineyards Winery. The wines may not blow you away, but you should still pay a call on these beautiful grounds, where a wide range of events and activities are scheduled. There are concerts and silent-movie nights (complete with restored pipe organ), cooking demonstrations, and gold panning. The **Heritage Museum** displays mining artifacts, with the star attraction being the remarkable 44-pound gold nugget discovered 15 miles away in 1992 (yes, there's still gold in them thar hills). There's also an upscale jewelry store, a tasting room and delicatessen with a massive limestone fireplace, and colorful gardens. ⏱ At least 1 hr. 1894 Six Mile Rd., Murphys. ☎ 209/728-1251. www.ironstonevineyards.com. Free admission; concerts & other special events prices vary. Winter Wed–Sun 10am–5pm; summer daily 10am–5pm. Free winery tours 1:30pm daily, also 11:30am Sat–Sun.

> *Wine pairings and cooking demos are just some of the calendar-full of events offered at the lushly landscaped Ironstone Vineyards Winery.*

The Best of Gold Country in 1 Week

In a full week you can delve more deeply into Gold Country's living history, as well as partake in the region's world-class outdoor offerings. Stroll through quaint-but-sophisticated Victorian towns, get your adrenaline flowing with some white-water rafting, wile away an afternoon with a leisurely wine tasting, or try your hand at panning for gold.

> Rolling down the river, kayakers take on the rapids of the American, filled with Sierra snowmelt.

START Sutter's Fort State Historic Park, Sacramento. You won't need a car while in Sacramento, but a vehicle is a must to explore the rest of Gold Country. TRIP LENGTH about 265 miles.

1 ★ Sutter's Fort State Historic Park. See p. 170, **1**.

2 ★★★ California State Capitol. See p. 172, **2**.

3 ★ Old Sacramento. See p. 172, **3**.

4 ★★★ kids California State Railroad Museum. See p. 173, **4**.

Start Day 2 at the Crocker Art Museum.

5 ★ Crocker Art Museum. The pride of Sacramento, the Crocker is the oldest public art museum in the West, founded in 1885. It celebrated its 125th anniversary with the opening in late 2010 of an expansion that

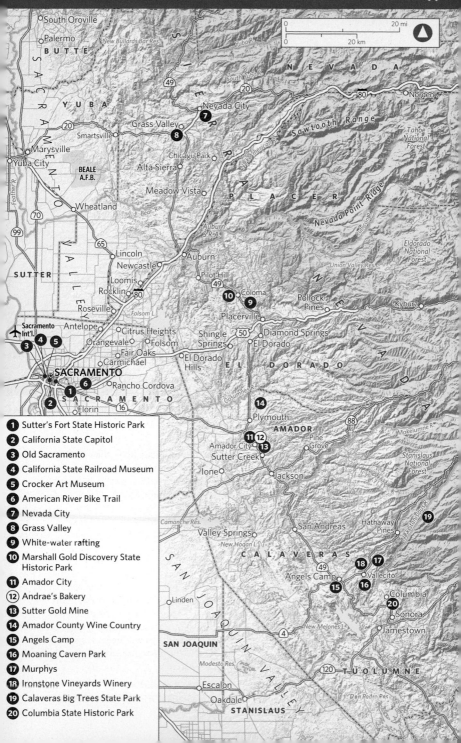

1. Sutter's Fort State Historic Park
2. California State Capitol
3. Old Sacramento
4. California State Railroad Museum
5. Crocker Art Museum
6. American River Bike Trail
7. Nevada City
8. Grass Valley
9. White-water rafting
10. Marshall Gold Discovery State Historic Park
11. Amador City
12. Andrae's Bakery
13. Sutter Gold Mine
14. Amador County Wine Country
15. Angels Camp
16. Moaning Cavern Park
17. Murphys
18. Ironstone Vineyards Winery
19. Calaveras Big Trees State Park
20. Columbia State Historic Park

> Life's a free ride on the lovely, 32-mile-long *Jedediah Smith Memorial Trail*, one of the longest bike paths in the country. Rent bikes in Sacramento or Folsom.

tripled the size of the museum. The Crocker holdings include everything from ancient Chinese sculpture to drawings by European masters (Rembrandt, for one); there is also an extensive ceramics collection as well as works by 20th-century California artists (Xavier Martinez and William Keith, for example). The new wing joins the museum's original building, a grand Victorian-Italianate structure first commissioned in 1869. ⊙ At least 1 hr. 216 O St. ☎ 916/808-7000. www.crockerartmuseum.org. Admission $6 adults, $3 kids 6–17 and students with ID, free for kids 6 & under, free Sun 10am–1pm. Tues–Sun 10am–5pm; 1st & 3rd Thurs of the month 10am–9pm.

Take bus 30, 31, 36, 62, or downtown trolley 143 along J St. to Mike's Bikes, 1411 I St., at 14th St. (☎ 916/446-2453; www.mikesbikes.com). They have rental bikes for $10 per hour or $40 per day; hours are daily 10am–6pm.

⑥ ★★ **American River Bike Trail.** Stretching 32 miles from Old Sacramento to Folsom Lake, this is one of the longest built-from-scratch bike paths in the country. The paved, mostly flat lanes follow the river along a riparian habitat favored by birds and even the occasional deer; along the path are mile markers, restrooms, water fountains, parks, picnic areas, and places to cool off in the river. You may completely forget you are in the middle of a metropolitan area. The trail, also known as the **Jedediah Smith Memorial Trail** (Smith, an early fur trapper, explored the area in the late 19th century), is well used, though, so watch out for pedestrians, joggers, and dogs. ⊙ At least 1½ hr. www.msa2.saccounty.net or www.saccycle.com.

On Day 3 go east on I-80 to Hwy. 49 north to Nevada City. Trip time: about 1¼ hr.

7 ★★ **Nevada City.** First settled in 1849, this is one of the state's best-preserved Victorian towns; its entire downtown is designated a National Historic Landmark. In the early years of the Gold Rush Nevada City's population swelled to 10,000 (it's currently around 2,800), and it trailed only Sacramento and San Francisco in size, if not importance—these hills were the state's richest gold fields. Pick up a walking-tour map at the **Nevada City Chamber of Commerce,** 132 Main St. (☎ 800/655-6569 or 530/265-2692; www.nevadacitychamber.com).

This lively and sophisticated place is also an official "Book Town" (one of only a handful in the U.S.) thanks to the number of bookstores both here and in nearby Grass Valley (**8**). Also be sure to check in with the ★ **Miners Foundry Cultural Center,** 325 Spring St. (☎ 530/265-5040; www.minersfoundry.org) for any special events. This rough-hewn facility opened as a blacksmith shop and foundry in 1855, and now hosts concerts, plays, film festivals, and workshops. It has a small museum, as well (Mon–Fri 10am–4pm). ⏱ At least 1 hr. Nevada City Chamber of Commerce, Mon–Fri 9am–5pm; Sat 11am–4pm; most Sun 11am–3pm.

It's less than a 10-min. drive down Hwy. 49 south to

8 **Grass Valley.** More commercial and less precious than its neighbor to the north, Grass Valley nonetheless makes for a rewarding visit. The **Grass Valley/Nevada County Chamber,** 248 Mill St. (☎ 800/655-4667 or 530/273-4667; www.grassvalleychamber.com; Mon–Fri 9am–5pm, Sat 10am–3pm), is in the rebuilt house of internationally scandalous and bohemian singer/dancer Lola Montez, who lived here in the 1850s; you can pick up a walking-tour map from the chamber. The **Grass Valley Museum** relates town history from Gold Rush days to the 1930s; it's located in the **St. Joseph's Cultural Center,** 410 S. Church St. (☎ 530/272-4725; www.saintjosephsculturalcenter.org). Originally a Sisters of Mercy convent and orphanage built in 1866, this complex features artists studios and a rose garden, where some of the bushes are more than 100 years old. Bibliophiles will want to stop by ★ **Ames Bookstore,** 309 Neal St. (☎ 530/273-9261; Tues–Sat 10am–6pm), with its seemingly endless inventory of used, rare, and out-of-print books. ⏱ At least 1 hr.

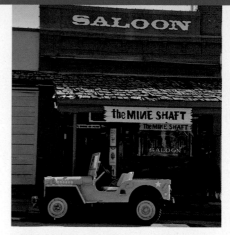

> *The honky-tonk cool of Nevada City makes a fun getaway, with charming B&Bs, shops, and yes, even kickback saloons.*

On Day 4, head south on Hwy. 49 to Coloma, about a 1 hr. drive.

9 ★★ **White-Water Rafting.** For eons, the spring run-off currents that cascaded down from the High Sierra brought gold tumbling down along with it, fueling the 19th-century Gold Rush. Nowadays these torrents of water are responsible for another kind rush—an adrenaline rush, induced by the thrill of navigating white-water rapids. Every year, from April to October, thousands of white-water rafters descend on local rivers, enjoying everything from lazy drifts to suicidal plunges. Coloma and the South Fork of the American River is the perfect place for something right in between. Sign up for a half-day trip with **Whitewater Connection** on these Class 3 rapids—which despite nicknames such as Meat Grinder and Troublemaker, are perfect for those with little or no experience. This may be the most popular river-rafting spot in California, so look into a weekday run for better prices and availability. ⏱ 3 hr. Whitewater Connection, 7170 Hwy. 49, Coloma. ☎ 800/336-7238 or 530/622-6446. www.whitewaterconnection.com. Half-day trips $94–$114 per person.

10 ★ **Marshall Gold Discovery State Historic Park.** Close to Whitewater Connection's home base is the actual site where gold was discovered in 1848, sparking the California Gold Rush. See p. 188, **1**.

> *How big is big? At Calaveras Big Trees State Park, giant sequoias measure up to 25 feet wide.*

On Day 5 continue south on Hwy. 49 to Amador City, about a 50-min. drive. *Note:* The highway bypasses Amador City and Sutter Creek, so look for the turnoff into town.

⑪ ★ Amador City. All of 1 block long, the smallest incorporated city in California is nevertheless very visitor friendly, with a number of antiques stores, galleries, and boutiques. The **Amador Whitney Museum,** 14170 Main St. (☎ 209/267-0928; Sat–Sun noon–4pm), on Main Street honors the female pioneers who helped tame these parts. Back when the nearby Keystone mine was producing millions of dollars worth of gold, the ★ **Imperial Hotel,**

14202 Main St. (☎ 209/267-9172; www.imperialamador.com), was the place to be— and it still is. Built in 1879, this red-brick hotel is still a classy retreat, with a great little bar serving lots of local wine; be sure to poke your head in. Behind the hotel is the **Amador City Cemetery,** where you'll find headstones dating back to the town's earliest Gold Rush days. ⏱ At least 1 hr. www.amador-city.com.

⑫ ☕ ★★ Andrae's Bakery. Andrae's alone is worth a detour into Amador City. It offers freshly baked goods (using organic, often local products), including breads, pastries, pizzas, and quiches; there are also some 50 different artisan cheeses in stock, as well as charcuterie. But Andrae's is best known for its Basque cake—a pound cake with pastry cream baked right into it. 14141 Main St., Amador City. ☎ 209/267-1352. www.andraesbakery.com. Items $3–$10.

⑬ ★ kids Sutter Gold Mine. You can get a taste of what it's really like to work underground at this modern hard-rock mine. See p. 173, ❼.

Backtrack on Hwy. 49 north, through the town of Plymouth to Old Sacramento Rd., turn right, then make a left on Shenandoah Rd. to Amador County Wine Country.

⑭ ★ Amador County Wine Country. There are about 40 wineries in Amador County, and many are found along or just off Shenandoah Road. They offer tastings, picnic facilities, and art galleries. See p. 174, ❽.

On Day 6, go south on Hwy. 49 to Angels Camp, about a 1-hr drive from Amador City.

⑮ ★ Angels Camp. This pretty town was named for two ex-soldier prospectors (surnamed Angel), who set up the trading post in the mid-1800s that eventually morphed into what you see today. See p. 174, ❾.

Take Hwy. 4 east, make a right on Parrotts Ferry Rd., and a right on Moaning Cave Rd.; total trip is about 7 miles.

⑯ ★ Moaning Cavern Park. This limestone cave is the largest public cavern in California, "discovered" (the natives had known about it for centuries) by gold miners in 1851. See p. 175, ❿.

Return to Hwy. 4 east for a 6-mile drive to

17 ★ **Murphys.** When you arrive in this charming town, do remember to ask a local what happened to the town's apostrophe. See p. 175, **11**.

Take Big Trees Rd., which becomes Six Mile Rd., 1 mile south to

18 ★ **Ironstone Vineyards Winery.** This winery has something for just about everyone, from movie nights to gold panning. Oh, yes, it also has wine. See p. 175, **12**.

On Day 7 take Hwy. 4 east from Murphys, about 15 miles to

19 ★★ **Calaveras Big Trees State Park.** In 1852, a hunter named Augustus Dowd was tracking a wounded grizzly bear when he came upon something few white men had ever reported seeing before: a giant sequoia tree. The specimen was called the **Discovery Tree,** and it was promptly cut down and put on display in New York. The public's imagination had been stoked, and although this grove didn't become a state park until 1931, this area is considered to be California's oldest continuously operating tourist facility. Though eventually eclipsed in popularity by groves in Yosemite (p. 276), and Sequoia and Kings Canyon (p. 286) national parks, these babies are no slouches—the tallest tree here, the ★ **Louis Agassiz Tree** (named for a 19th-century naturalist), is 250 feet tall with a 25-foot diameter. Avoid the summer crowds at the **North Grove** and head for the 5-mile loop trail at the ★★ **South Grove,** where you can say hi to Louis. Once you're in the park, go 9 miles down the Walter W. Smith Memorial Parkway to get to the trail head. The park is open year-round and has campsites but this road is closed by snow in winter (and is a great spot for cross-country skiing or snowshoeing). ⏱ 3–4 hr. ☎ 209/795-2334. www.parks.ca.gov. Visitor center ☎ 209/795-3840. Admission $8 per car, $7 with a senior. Daily Apr–Nov; Sat–Sun Dec–Mar; call for specific hours.

Head back toward Angels Camp on Hwy. 4, and make a left on Parrotts Ferry Rd. at Vallecito; it's about 28 miles total to

20 ★★ kids **Columbia State Historic Park.** Welcome to 1857. Once known as the "Gem of the Southern Mines," Columbia was for a

> *Making music at Columbia State Historic Park, where costumed docents, like this dulcimer player, shed light on bygone times.*

time California's second-largest city and came within two legislative votes of becoming the state capital. Unlike other boomtowns that faded away, Columbia persevered until 1945 when the town was made a state park and preserved as a colorful remnant of a bygone era. This is a real town with saloons, hotels, restaurants, and shops that will all gladly help you play along with the Wild West fantasy; there are stagecoach rides (no cars are allowed in the central area), a working blacksmith, and gold panning. Numerous Hollywood westerns have been filmed here, including *High Noon* and *Pale Rider.* ⏱ At least 1 hr. ☎ 209/588-9128. www.parks.ca.gov or www.columbiacalifornia.com. Free admission. Most businesses 10am–5pm; restaurants and bars open later.

Northern Gold Country

These hills were the site of California's biggest, richest gold mines—some of which are now state parks where you can bear witness to audacious mining projects spawned by gold fever; you can also hike miles of trails and find a river with a swimming hole in which you can take a dip. Gold Rush ambience and history are also on display in the evocative towns of Auburn, Grass Valley, and Nevada City.

> *Snake through the subterranean world of the extraordinary Empire Mine, one of California's deepest and longest mines with 367 miles of tunnels and shafts.*

START Auburn, 33 miles north of Sacramento.
TRIP LENGTH 2 days, about 75 miles.

❶ ★ Old Town Auburn. When gold was discovered here in 1848, the mining camp that subsequently sprang up went by various names until "Auburn" was settled upon in 1849. This was the end of the line for wagons from Sacramento—to reach the more remote Sierra gold fields from here required pack animals. Auburn's importance was solidified when it became the seat for Placer County in 1851, and the coming of the Central Pacific Railroad in 1865 ensured that the town would continue to thrive.

Auburn's Old Town, a registered National Historic District, is a 5-square-block area beginning at the intersection of Sacramento Street and Lincoln Way. It has more than 60 boutiques,

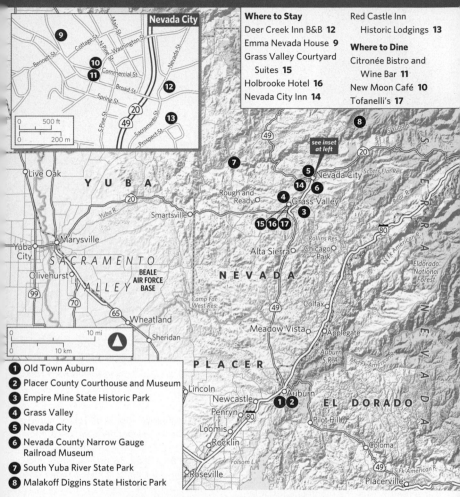

Nevada City

Where to Stay
Deer Creek Inn B&B **12**
Emma Nevada House **9**
Grass Valley Courtyard
  Suites **15**
Holbrooke Hotel **16**
Nevada City Inn **14**

Red Castle Inn
  Historic Lodgings **13**

Where to Dine
Citronée Bistro and
  Wine Bar **11**
New Moon Café **10**
Tofanelli's **17**

1 Old Town Auburn
2 Placer County Courthouse and Museum
3 Empire Mine State Historic Park
4 Grass Valley
5 Nevada City
6 Nevada County Narrow Gauge
  Railroad Museum
7 South Yuba River State Park
8 Malakoff Diggins State Historic Park

galleries, antiques stores, restaurants, and bars set in buildings dating back to the boomtown days; Commercial Street, with its brick buildings, is particularly evocative. Year-round there are special events held here, including a summertime blues festival and a fall wine festival; every Saturday there's a farmers market. A free, 1-hour walking tour of Old Town departs from the courthouse (**2**) every Saturday at 10am (☎ 530/889-6500; www.placer.ca.gov). ⊕ At least 1 hr. California Welcome Center: 13411 Lincoln Way; ☎ 866/752-2371 or 530/887-2111; www.visitcwc.com. Auburn Chamber of Commerce: 601 Lincoln Way; ☎ 530/885-5616; www.auburnchamber.net. Tues–Fri 10am–4pm.

2 ★ **Placer County Courthouse and Museum.** Sitting grandly over the town of Auburn, on a site that once hosted hangings and bull-and-bear fights, is this impressive seat of local government. A handsome classical revival-style building completed in 1898, it houses the **Placer County Museum** on the first floor (it used to be the jail). The museum offers an overview of Placer history and includes a re-creation of the old sheriff's office, Native American art, and a dazzling collection of local gold. ⊕ 30 min. 101 Maple St., Auburn. ☎ 530/889-6500. www.placer.ca.gov. Free admission. Daily 10am–4pm.

> *A former convent, orphanage, and school (not at the same time), the 1856 Grass Valley Museum houses Gold Rush memorabilia.*

Take Hwy. 49 north, about 25 miles, to

③ ★ Empire Mine State Historic Park. This is one of the oldest, deepest, longest, and richest mines in California history. From its opening in 1850 to when it shut operations down more than a century later, this mine complex, with its 367 miles of tunnels and shafts, produced 5.6 million ounces of gold. The 845-acre site features the owner's stone "cottage" (more like a manor house), complete with restored rose garden, as well as mine-yard buildings, and 8 miles of forested trails for hikers, bikers, and equestrians. There's also a souvenir shop selling minerals and fossils. ⊙ At least 45 min. 10791 E. Empire St., Grass Valley. ☎ 530/273-8522. www. parks.ca.gov or www.empiremine.org. Admission $5 adults, $3 kids 6–16. Guided cottage and mine-yard tours $2 per person. Summer daily 9am–6pm; winter Thurs–Mon 10am–3pm. Hours may vary, call to confirm.

It's about a 5 min. drive north on Hwy. 49 to

④ Grass Valley. This "Book Town," noted for the number of independent and used-bookstores in the area, is the commercial and retail center of the region. Be sure to mosey into the saloon at the historic ★ **Holbrooke Hotel** (p. 187) for a drink—it's been in continuous operation since 1852 and you'll be following in the footsteps of Mark Twain (1835–1910). See p. 179, ⑧.

On Day 2, drive north on Hwy. 49 for about 10 min. to

⑤ ★★ Nevada City. This town is one of Gold Country's best destinations, with a beautifully preserved downtown loaded with Victorian architecture. As you stroll through the historic district, imagine the town in its boomtown heyday, when its red-light district offered visitors and locals a rollicking good time. One of its former residents went on to create some history of his own: President Herbert Hoover (1874–1964) once worked here as a gold miner. See p. 179, ⑦.

6 ★ **Nevada County Narrow Gauge Railroad Museum.** Train buffs (and others) will love this museum dedicated to preserving local transportation history, in particular the narrow gauge rail line that ran in these parts from 1876 to 1942, hauling lumber, supplies, and passengers, as well as $200 million in gold. There's a museum, rail yard, and restoration shop where you can see wooden railcars and Engine No. 5, which saw duty here from 1899 to 1940. Thereafter, No. 5 went Hollywood, relocating to a Los Angeles studio back lot where it appeared in numerous films and TV shows until finally returning home in 1985. ⊕ 45 min. 5 Kidder Court, Nevada City. ☎ 530/470-0902. www.ncngrrmuseum. org. Free admission (donations appreciated). May–Oct Fri–Tues 10am–4pm; Nov–Apr Sat–Sun 10am–4pm.

North on Hwy. 49, go left on Pleasant Valley Rd.; it's about 20 miles to

7 ★ **South Yuba River State Park.** Encompassing 20 miles of the South Yuba River Canyon, this park offers summer swimming holes, hiking, gold panning, and spectacular blooms of spring wildflowers. It's most notable, though, for the ★ **Bridgeport Covered Bridge** and the ★ **Independence Trail.** The bridge, in use from 1862 to 1971, is armored in pine-shake roofing and siding, and at 229 feet is the longest single-span covered bridge still standing (and it straddles a nice stretch of river in which to frolic). The Independence Trail is the country's first wheelchair-accessible wilderness trail—and this shady path, with its beautiful vistas, is equally popular with ambulatory nature lovers. The trail began life as an aqueduct in 1859, bringing water to hydraulic mining operations, and was an impressive engineering feat in its time. ⊕ At least 1 hr. 17660 Pleasant Valley Rd., Penn Valley (accessible from either Hwy. 49 or 20). ☎ 530/432-2546. www.parks.ca.gov. Free admission. Sunrise–sunset (remote areas till 10pm); visitor center parking lot 10am–sunset.

Return to Hwy. 49 and go south about 1 mile, then turn left on Tyler Foote Rd. Continue on main paved road to Malakoff Diggins. *Note:* This road goes through several name changes. Total trip is about 23 miles.

> *This bucolic setting within Malakoff Diggins belies the environmental havoc wreaked here by hydraulic mining in the 1800s.*

8 ★ **Malakoff Diggins State Historic Park.** A wondrous geological formation carved out by the elements over the millennia? No. The half-mile-long, nearly 600-foot-high cliffs in this park are the result of an ecological horror story. With their soft pastel colors and broad striations, these cliffs resemble the painted canyons of Arizona and Utah, but this was a hydraulic mining pit where high-pressure water cannons were used to scrape away the mountain in search of gold. The ensuing environmental devastation that resulted, including flooding and silted rivers, was too much to bear even by Wild West standards and a permanent injunction was levied against the practice in 1884—a landmark victory in conservation history. This 3,000-acre park also has a museum and refurnished period buildings, hiking trails, and a campsite (closed in winter). ⊕ At least 1 hr. 23579 N. Bloomfield Rd. (this road is not recommended; take Tyler Foote Rd. from Hwy. 49). ☎ 530/265-2740. www. parks.ca.gov. Admission $8 per car, $7 with a senior. Museum: hours vary; call to confirm. Park: sunrise–sunset.

Where to Stay & Dine

> Step inside the 1862 Holbrooke Hotel and have a cool one in the oldest continuously running bar west of the Mississippi.

★★ Citronée Bistro and Wine Bar NEVADA CITY *AMERICAN/FRENCH* One of Gold Country's top dining experiences. The menu ranges from American comfort food to classic French cuisine, and the ingredients are seasonal, local, and sustainable. There's casual dining up front; dine in the back for a more romantic atmosphere of exposed brick and wood beams. 320 Broad St. ☎ 530/265-5697. www.citronee bistro.com. Entrees $16-$34. AE, MC, V. Lunch Wed-Sun; dinner Wed-Mon.

★ Deer Creek Inn Bed & Breakfast NEVADA CITY A three-story Victorian sitting above lovely gardens and bordered by two creeks, this homey inn is within walking distance of downtown Nevada City. If you can get one, snag one of the individually decorated rooms with a private veranda. Breakfast is a three-course gourmet affair, and the afternoon social hour features local wines. 116 Nevada St., Nevada City, CA 95959. ☎ 800/655-0363 or 530/265-0363. www.deercreekinn.com. 6 units. Doubles $160-$230 w/ breakfast. MC, V.

★★ Emma Nevada House NEVADA CITY The childhood home of Victorian opera star Emma Nevada (1859-1940) is now an elegant, tastefully appointed B&B. Guest rooms come in a variety of sizes and styles; the Empress Chamber is the most romantic. It's only a short walk to Nevada City's historic downtown. 528 E. Broad St., Nevada City, CA 95959. ☎ 800/916-3662 or 530/265-4415. www.emmanevadahouse.com. 6 units. Doubles $169-$249 w/breakfast. AE, DISC, MC, V.

Grass Valley Courtyard Suites GRASS VALLEY This pet-friendly property, just 1 block from the historic downtown, offers spacious and quiet rooms with lots of amenities. All rooms have a microwave and fridge, and some have fireplaces and a full kitchen. There's also a pool and self-service laundry facility. 210 N.

Auburn St., Grass Valley, CA 95945. ☎ 530/272-7696. www.gvcourtyardsuites.com. 33 units. Doubles $150–$180; suites $195–$325. Rates include breakfast. AE, DISC, V.

★ Holbrooke Hotel GRASS VALLEY

Since 1862, Gold Country wits, writers, miners, and highwaymen—as well as four U.S. presidents—have favored this Victorian-themed hotel. The restored property's ★ **Golden Gate Saloon** lays claim to being the oldest continuously operating bar west of the Mississippi (it predates the hotel by several years). The rooms still evoke that Gold Rush era (despite the Wi-Fi and TVs); some have balconies (worth the splurge) and fireplaces. 212 W. Main St., Grass Valley, CA 95945. ☎ 800/933-7077 or 530/273-1353. www.holbrooke.com. 28 units. Doubles $109–$239 w/breakfast. AE, DC, DISC, MC, V.

Nevada City Inn NEVADA CITY

This 1940s motor lodge has a parklike setting and amiable charm. It's nothing fancy but offers great value, including cottages with kitchens. It's about a mile from downtown Nevada City. 760 Zion St., Nevada City, CA 95959. ☎ 800/977-8884 or 530/265-2253. www.nevadacityinn.net. 20 units, 7 cottages. Doubles $69–$139; cottages $130–$189. Rates include breakfast. AE, DC, DISC, MC, V.

★★ New Moon Café NEVADA CITY *AMERICAN*

Casual but sophisticated, this eatery is another of the region's best restaurant contenders. New Moon serves creative and contemporary American fare utilizing seasonal, local, and organic products, and tops it off with a serious beer and wine list. 203 York St. ☎ 530/ 265-6399. www.thenewmooncafe.com. Entrees $15–$28. DC, MC, V. Lunch Tues–Fri; dinner Tues–Sun.

★ Red Castle Inn Historic Lodgings NEVADA CITY

This striking Gothic revival-style mansion, built in 1860, has been welcoming guests to its hillside retreat since 1960. Just a 3-minute walk from town, this refined inn offers a sumptuous six-course buffet breakfast

> *It's locavore love at Citronée Bistro and Wine Bar, known for exceptionally fresh, local, sustainably produced ingredients.*

and afternoon tea. Rooms do not have a TV or phone. 109 Prospect St., Nevada City, CA 95959. ☎ 800/761-4766 or 530/265-5135. www.redcastleinn.com. 7 units. Doubles $125–$200 w/breakfast. MC, V.

Tofanelli's GRASS VALLEY *AMERICAN/ITALIAN*

The menu features 101 omelets—count 'em—with ingredients ranging from apples to zucchini, plus more than a dozen burgers, entree salads, and Italian favorites. You're bound to find something you like at this local institution, which has been serving up food in one form or another since the 1890s. There's also a tree-shaded patio and a full bar. 302 W. Main St. ☎ 530/272-1468. www.tofanellis.com. Entrees $12–$26. AE, DISC, MC, V. Breakfast, lunch, & dinner daily.

Central Gold Country

Deep in the heart of the Gold Country you can still hear the echoes of '49 in the perfectly preserved Gold Rush towns and historic mines of the Sierra foothills. But how about some zinfandel and a little apple pie to go along with your visit? History is so much better on a full stomach.

> *Bark houses, the native Miwok Indians' take on teepees, have been recreated at Marshall Gold Discovery Park.*

START Coloma is 51 miles northeast of Sacramento. **TRIP LENGTH** 3 days, about 60 miles.

❶ ★ Marshall Gold Discovery State Historic Park. The course of United States history was forever altered in 1848 when gold was discovered here along the South Fork of the American River. Check out the re-created sawmill where James Marshall (1810–85) made his discovery (ironically, he never profited from the find), along with other historic buildings. The park is the centerpiece of the town of Coloma, itself a historic ghost town that boomed during the Gold Rush, but now numbers its inhabitants in the mere hundreds. ⏱ At least

1 hr. 310 Back St., Coloma. ☎ 530/622-3470. www.parks.ca.gov or www.coloma.com. Admission $6 per person. Park: summer Thurs–Mon 8am–6pm; winter Tues–Sat 8am–4pm. Museum: 10am–3pm.

Go south on Hwy. 49, then east on Hwy. 50 (about 9 miles total) to

❷ Placerville. This town was anything but placid back in its Gold Rush days when it was known as Hangtown, in honor of the locals' penchant for frontier justice. Things are considerably more congenial today, and strolling Placerville's **Historic Main Street** makes for a pleasant excursion. You can pick up maps and local info at

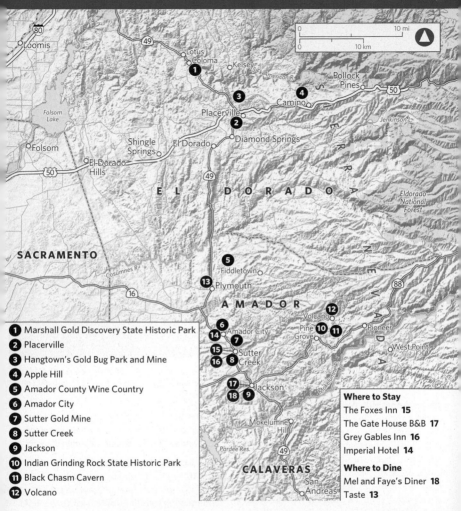

1 Marshall Gold Discovery State Historic Park

2 Placerville

3 Hangtown's Gold Bug Park and Mine

4 Apple Hill

5 Amador County Wine Country

6 Amador City

7 Sutter Gold Mine

8 Sutter Creek

9 Jackson

10 Indian Grinding Rock State Historic Park

11 Black Chasm Cavern

12 Volcano

Where to Stay

The Foxes Inn **15**

The Gate House B&B **17**

Grey Gables Inn **16**

Imperial Hotel **14**

Where to Dine

Mel and Faye's Diner **18**

Taste **13**

the El Dorado County Chamber of Commerce. ⏱ At least 1 hr. Chamber of Commerce: 542 Main St.; ☎ 530/621-5885; www.visit-eldorado.com; Mon–Fri 9am–5pm, limited hours Sat. Placerville Downtown Association: ☎ 530/672-3436; www.placerville-downtown.org.

From downtown, head north on Bedford Ave., about 1 mile to Gold Bug Lane, turn right to

3 ★ **Hangtown's Gold Bug Park and Mine.** You can go deep enough into this hard-rock gold mine to feel a little bit of panic or at least get a sense of what mining is really like. Self-guided audio tours, as well as guided tours, of Gold Bug (which closed in 1942) are available;

also on-site are a museum, a stamp mill and mineral display, a gift shop, gemstone panning, hiking trails, and picnic areas. This is a city park so there's no charge for hiking or picnicking; there are about 2 miles of trails. ⏱ At least 45 min. 2635 Gold Bug Lane (about 1 mile north of Placerville off Hwy. 50). ☎ 530/642-5207. www.goldbugpark.org. Admission $5 adults, $3 kids 10–17, $2 kids 3–9. Mine and museum: Apr–Oct daily 10am–4pm; Nov–Mar Sat–Sun noon–4pm.

Take Hwy. 50 east about 1 mile to the Schnell School Rd. exit, go left, then make a right on Carson Rd. to

> A sleepy still life on the sidewalks of Amador City, a deceivingly grand name for the state's smallest incorporated city.

> Try your hand at gold panning at Sutter Gold Mine, where you're guaranteed to net out with gold or gemstones.

❹ ★★ **Apple Hill.** A collection of nearly 60 farms, ranches, and wineries (plus a brewery) that combine to create all things apple: pies, cider, butter, doughnuts, milkshakes, wine, and beer. There are also arts and crafts, a corn maze, a fishing pond for the kids, and more. Perennial favorites include ★ **High Hill Ranch,** 2901 High Hill Rd. (☎ 530/644-1973); ★ **Larsen Apple Barn,** 2461 Larsen Dr. (☎ 530/644-1415); ★ **Boa Vista Orchards,** 2952 Carson Rd. (☎ 866/684-7696 or 530/622-5522; www.boavista.com); and ★ **Abel's Apple Acres,** 2345 Carson Rd. (☎ 530/626/0138; www.abelsappleacres.com). Apple Hill is an utter madhouse on fall weekends, so check the growers' association website for info on the shuttle buses, or consider a weekday visit. Most of the farms are open seasonally, but the wineries, brewery, and Boa Vista Orchards are open year-round. ◷ At least 1½ hr. Located btw. Placerville and Pollock Pines, north of Hwy. 50. Apple Hill Growers Association, ☎ 530/644-7692. www.applehill.com.

On Day 2, take Hwy. 50 west to Hwy. 49 south. At the town of Plymouth, go left on Plymouth Shenandoah Rd. It's about a 25-mile drive to

❺ ★ **Amador County Wine Country.** More than three-dozen wineries congregate in Amador County's Shenandoah Valley, where winemaking traditions date back to the Gold Rush and the European immigrants who came to work in the mines. The wineries, many specializing in zinfandels, offer tasting rooms, picnic grounds, museums, and galleries. See p. 174, ❽.

From Plymouth it's about 7 miles to Amador City down Hwy. 49. Keep an eye out for the Old Hwy. 49 exit to town (the main highway bypasses it).

❻ ★ **Amador City.** This block-long hamlet is the smallest incorporated city in California but it's very visitor friendly. Browse the antiques stores and boutiques, then enjoy a glass of local wine at the stylish **Oasis Bar** in the stately ★★ **Imperial Hotel** (p. 193). See p. 180, ⓫.

Go about a ½ mile south on Old Hwy. 49 to

7 ★ **kids** **Sutter Gold Mine.** Get your hardhat on and go deep into a hard-rock mine for a 1-hour tour; up top you can pan for gemstones. See p. 173, **7**.

About a mile farther south is

8 ★ **Sutter Creek.** A pretty town dipped in amber, preserved and refurbished to look as it did 150 years ago. The **J. Monteverde Store Museum,** 11A Randolph St. (☎ 209/267-0493), started out as a typical general store that opened in 1896 and didn't change much until the day in 1971 when the owner put up a sign that read, "This store will be closed for a few days." It never reopened and its shelves are stocked exactly as they were that day. It's usually open by appointment only. **Knight Foundry,** 81 Eureka St. (☎ 209/267-5647; www.knight foundry.org), listed on the National Register of Historic Places, began building mining machinery in 1872 and was uniquely powered by water cascading 400 feet down into a water wheel. As of this writing it is closed to visitors, but there is hope it will reopen as a tourist attraction and working foundry. Stop by the visitor center for a walking-tour map. ⏲ 1 hr. Sutter Creek Visitor Center, 71 Main St. ☎ 800/400-0305 or 209/267-1344. www.suttercreek.org.

Old Hwy. 49 rejoins Hwy. 49 south; it's about 5 miles to

9 ★ **Jackson.** This may not be the Jackson that Johnny Cash sang about, but no doubt plenty of people have danced on pony kegs in this town. The county seat of Amador, Jackson was known for its gambling houses and "girls' dormitories" well into the 1950s; it was the last place in California to outlaw prostitution. Downtown Jackson is on the National Register of Historic Places and features stores selling arts and crafts, vintage clothing, jewelry, books, and more. For a walking-tour map or info, contact the Historic Jackson Business Association, 10 Water St. (☎ 209/223-2327; www.hjba.homestead. com). Not far from town is the **Kennedy Mine** (☎ 209/223-9542; www.kennedygoldmine. com), one of the deepest mines in the world, which produced more than $34 million in gold before closing in 1942. Aboveground guided and self-guided tours are available on weekends

March through October ($10 adults, $6 kids 6–12). ⏲ At least 1 hr.

On Day 3, take Hwy. 88 east from Jackson, turn left on Pine Grove-Volcano Rd. (it's about 8 miles total drive) to

10 ★ **Indian Grinding Rock State Historic Park.** The idyllic meadows and stands of oaks and pines alone would be enough to recommend this park, but you'll also get immersed in Native American culture as well. The on-site ★ **Chaw'se Regional Indian Museum** is an attractive facility housing a collection of baskets, tools, jewelry, clothing, and more from several regional tribes. More than 1,100 grinding holes, used to crush acorns into flour, pock the park's limestone rock; there is also a re-created Miwok village, including tepeelike bark houses and a large ceremonial roundhouse. Local tribes use the roundhouse on special occasions, including an acorn-gathering festival on the fourth Friday in September (open to the public). There are two short loop trails, one of which is interpreted, and year-round camping in 23 car-camping sites

> *Take a time warp walk through Monteverde General Store, looking exactly as it did when the owner closed up shop in 1971.*

> *Tiny Volcano may not have molten lava, but it does have spectacular cave formations, like these in Black Chasm Cavern.*

(first-come, first-served) and seven primitive bark houses that can be reserved up to 6 months in advance. ⏱ At least 1 hr. 14881 Pine Grove–Volcano Rd. (off Hwy. 88), Pine Grove. ☎ 209/296-7488. www.parks.ca.gov. Admission $8 per car, $7 with a senior; camping $25. Day use: sunrise–sunset. Museum: Mon–Fri 11am–3pm; Sat–Sun 10am–4pm; may be closed some weekdays in winter, call for hours.

Continue north on Pine Grove-Volcano Rd. for about 1½ miles, then make a sharp right turn on Volcano Pioneer Rd. to

⓫ ★ kids Black Chasm Cavern. This National Natural Landmark was almost mined for its marble until surveyors discovered it contained not only the usual cave formations like stalactites and stalagmites, but also rare and delicate helictite crystals; there are also marble arches and underground ponds. Fifty-minute walking tours are conducted daily (there are about 150 stairs); aboveground you can pan for gemstones. ⏱ 1 hr. 15701 Volcano Pioneer Rd. (off Hwy. 88), Volcano. ☎ 866/762-2837 or 209/736-2708. www.caverntours.com. Admission $14 adults, $7 kids 3–12. May–Sept 9am–5pm; Oct–Apr 10am–4pm.

Continue north on Pine Grove-Volcano Rd. (which becomes Rams Horn Grade Rd.); it's less than a mile to

⓬ ★ Volcano. It only has an official population of 85 now, but there was a time when Volcano was a hotbed of activity—it had 17 hotels, California's first lending library, the state's first theater company (the Volcano Thespian Society, 1845), a law school, and an observatory. The entire town is a registered California Historical Landmark; be sure to pay a call on the venerable ★ **St. George Hotel** and its classic **Whiskey Flat Saloon,** 16104 Main St. (☎ 209/296-4458; www.stgeorgehotel.com). If you're here in spring, head over to nearby ★ **Daffodil Hill.** This ranch has been owned by the same family since 1887—which was when the property's first daffodil bulbs were planted. It's now estimated there are more than 300,000 daffodils growing here. ⏱ At least 1 hr. Daffodil Hill: 13810 Shake Ridge Rd. (take Rams Horn Grade north from Volcano). ☎ 209/296-7048. Free admission. Amador County Chamber of Commerce: ☎ 209/223-0350. www.amadorcountychamber.com.

Where to Stay & Dine

★★ **The Foxes Inn** SUTTER CREEK
Chilled champagne awaits you (on request) at this luxury B&B, well located in a Victorian home dating from 1857. The spacious, elegant guest rooms all have private baths; some have private entrances. 77 Main St., Sutter Creek. ☎ 800/987-3344 or 209/267-5882. www. foxesinn.com. 7 units. Doubles $160–$325 w/ breakfast. AE, DISC, MC, V.

The Gate House Bed and Breakfast Inn JACKSON This 1-acre property has fun extras like a solar-heated swimming pool, table tennis, and a bocce court. There are four rooms in the main house (a Queen Anne Victorian with lots of period details), as well as a separate cottage with a Jacuzzi. Wine and hors d'oeuvres are served in the afternoon. 1330 Jackson Gate Rd., Jackson. ☎ 800/841-1072 or 209/223-3500. www.gatehouseinn.com. 5 units. Doubles $135–$215 w/ breakfast. AE, DISC, MC, V.

★ **Grey Gables Inn** SUTTER CREEK
With its leafy gardens and afternoon tea, this B&B has the look, feel, and charm of an English country manor. Each plushly furnished room, named for an English poet, has a fireplace and private bath. 161 Hanford St., Sutter Creek. ☎ 800/473-9422 or 209/267-1039. www. greygables.com. 8 units. Doubles $115–$200 w/ breakfast & afternoon tea. AE, DC, DISC, MC, V.

★★ **Imperial Hotel** AMADOR CITY
Dating from 1879, this delightful red-brick property sits on a hill overlooking quaint Amador City; in keeping with its Gold Rush–era heritage, there are no TVs or phones in the individually decorated rooms. The hotel restaurant serves fine California cuisine, and the Oasis Bar has a great selection of local wines. 14202 Hwy. 49, Amador City. ☎ 209/267-9172. www.imperialamador.com. 9 units. Doubles $105–$205 w/breakfast. AE, MC, V.

Mel and Faye's Diner JACKSON AMERICAN
Serving up pancakes and waffles, and "six-napkin" burgers and fountain drinks (try the peanut butter shake) since 1956, this busy

> In a region overflowing with lacy lodgings and B&Bs, Amador City's Imperial Hotel is an elegant standout.

place is your classic American roadside eatery. If you don't want to feel too guilty about ordering a slice of homemade cream pie, get something from the salad bar first. 31 Hwy. 49 (at Main St.). ☎ 209/223-0853. www.mel andfayesdiner.com. Menu items $4–$10. MC, V. Breakfast, lunch & dinner daily.

★★ **Taste** PLYMOUTH AMERICAN
Delivering a Napa-like foodie experience in the Sierra Wine Country, this acclaimed bistro serves contemporary American cuisine in an urbane setting. It's the perfect place to sample local vintages. Monday features a special prix-fixe menu for under $30; be sure to try the "mushroom cigar" (mushrooms, herbs, and goat cheese baked in phyllo dough). 9402 Main St. ☎ 209/245-3463. www.restaurant taste.com. Entrees $26–$37. AE, DISC, MC, V. Dinner Thurs–Mon.

Southern Gold Country

The southern portion of Gold Country offers a mother lode of adventure and fun. Its towns and attractions are some of Gold Country's best destinations—from the boutique wineries of Calaveras County to underworld caverns held sacred by Native Americans. You can live out your Wild West fantasies in a town that forgot to leave the 19th century, or gaze in awe at some of the world's biggest trees. Explore this area and you won't help but dig Gold Country.

> Mind-bogglingly big giant sequoias in Calaveras Big Trees State Park are especially stunning in spring, when framed by flowering dogwoods.

START Angels Camp is 77 miles southeast of Sacramento. A car is a must for this tour. **TRIP LENGTH** 4 days, about 125 miles.

1 ★ **Angels Camp.** For a town officially known as City of Angels, you'd think this former mining camp would have a fixation on celestial beings. In fact, it's frogs that dominate the cultural landscape. The town's fame (such as it is) stems from the fact it's the setting for Mark Twain's tall tale *The Celebrated Jumping Frog of Calaveras County.* An actual frog-jumping contest was begun in 1928, and the **Jumping Frog Jubilee** is still going strong, held in late May as part of the county fair. If you left your frog at home, no worries—you can rent one for the competition. See p. 174, **9**.

CALAVERAS

Dorrington

Stanislaus
National
Forest

Stanislaus R.

6

4

Hathaway
Pines

Mid Fk Stanislaus R.

4 13 14 15

Murphys

3

5

49

Angels
Camp

1

16

17 2

18

Vallecito

7

Columbia

8

Mi-Wuk Village

108

Twain Harte

Mono
Vista

Soulsbyville

Cherry L.

TUOLUMNE

19 20

Sonora

New Melones L.

Jamestown

10

Tuolumne

9

Stanislaus
National
Forest

Tuolumne R.

Tulloch Res.

Chinese Camp

120

Groveland

Don Pedro Res.

49

La Grange

STANISLAUS

Coulterville

Turlock L.

L. McClure

Midpines

MARIPOSA

Mariposa

11

Bootjack

12

140

49

Catheys Valley

Bridgeport

YOSEMITE N.P.

0   10 mi
0   10 km

> *Go down under at Ironstone Vineyards, where caverns dug by area gold miners are used to age wines.*

2 ★ **Gold Cliff Mine.** Unlike casual mine tours elsewhere in Gold Country, this is a mine adventure. It involves steep hiking, rappelling, climbing, and crawling on 45- to 50-degree slopes while hanging onto knotted hand lines, as well as rafting across a scary-deep underground lake. You actually get to explore two mines on this tour, both of which are in the Angels Camp area but whose exact locations won't be revealed to you until you make a reservation—and reservations are a must (claustrophobes need not apply). ⏱ 3 hr. ☎ 866/762-2837 or 209/736-2708. www.caverntours.com. Tours $99 per person. Tours daily. Minimum age 12 (16 if not accompanied by parent).

Take Hwy. 4 east; it's about 8 miles to

3 ★ **Murphys.** This picturesque hamlet was established in 1848 by two entrepreneurial brothers who wheeled and dealed from a tent trading post. Murphys' gold fields soon became one of California's richest "diggings," producing over $20 million in gold. See p. 175, **11**.

On Day 2, from Main St., head north on Sheep Ranch Rd.; it's less than 2 miles to

4 ★ **Mercer Caverns.** People have been touring these 3-million-year-old caverns since they were rediscovered by prospector Walter Mercer in 1885. Prior to that, the Yokut people

used them as burial chambers—a sacred place only the dead could enter. And this place is otherworldly, with unique formations like the nearly transparent Angels Wings and one of the world's most profuse displays of the rare, frostlike crystal known as Aragonite. The well-lit cavern's biggest chamber, the Gothic Chamber, is an impressive 234-feet long and nearly 60-feet high. Cavern tours take about 50 minutes, and there are some 170 steps to navigate. ⏱ 1 hr. 1665 Sheep Ranch Rd., Murphys (off Hwy. 4). ☎ 209/728-2101. www.mercercaverns.com. Admission $12 adults, $7 ages 3–12. Daily 10am–4:30pm (extended hours in summer).

Return to Main St. and turn left to the tasting rooms of

5 ★ **Calaveras County Wine Country.** There are more than two-dozen boutique wineries in the Calaveras County area, including many in and around Murphys. A handful have tasting rooms along Main Street, including ★ **Milliaire Winery,** 276 Main St. (☎ 209/728-1658; www.milliairewinery.com; daily 11am–5pm); **Black Sheep Winery,** 221 Main St. (☎ 209/728-2157; www.blacksheepwinery.com; daily 11am–5pm); and ★ **Zucca Mountain Winery,** with a cool cellar location at 431 E. Main St. (☎ 209/728-1623; www.zuccawisnes.com; daily noon–5pm). Nearby wineries worth

> *Vintage vehicles like this horse-drawn fire truck are a highlight at Columbia State Historic Park.*

checking out include ★ **Stevenot Winery,** 2690 San Domingo Rd. (☎ 209/728-0638; www.stevenotwinery.com; daily 11am–5pm), and ★ **Ironstone Vineyards Winery,** 1894 Six Mile Rd. (☎ 209/728-1251; www.ironstone vineyards.com; daily 10am–5pm). Stevenot has a tasting room in town, but you'll be happy you made the drive out to its historic location in a ranch house dating from 1870. Ironstone is a veritable wine theme park. **Calaveras Winegrape Alliance,** ☎ 866/806-9463 or 209/728-9467. www.calaveraswines.org.

Take Hwy. 4 east, 15 miles to

❻ ★★ Calaveras Big Trees State Park. Other white explorers had encountered giant sequoia trees previously, but it was hunter Augustus Dowd's "discovery" of these groves in 1852 that took root in the public's imagination. The trees became instant attractions and have remained so to this day. See p. 181, **❶❾**.

On Day 3, take Hwy. 4 west through Murphys, go left on Parrotts Ferry Rd., and right on Moaning Cave Rd.; it's about 21 miles total to

❼ ★ kids Moaning Cavern Park. Native Americans (who called this spot Samwel Cave) attributed it to the supernatural, but the moan sometimes emitted from this cavern is just a matter of acoustics (the sound of water dripping to the bottom of the cave echoes and gets distorted by wind). There are several underground tours available, as well as aboveground zip lines and panning for gemstones. See p. 175, **❶⓿**.

Turn right on Parrotts Ferry Rd.; it's about 9 more miles to

❽ ★★ kids Columbia State Historic Park. Stagecoach rides, a working blacksmith, banjo-playing minstrels, costumed shopkeepers—they're all part of the Wild West fantasy at this living museum, a National Historic Landmark. Shake the trail dust off at the **Jack Douglass Saloon** (☎ 209/533-4176) on Main Street and order yourself a locally made sarsaparilla or wild cherry soda. This classic saloon has been serving since 1857; it's open daily 10am to 6pm (till 7pm Fri), with occasional evening events. See p. 181, **❷⓿**.

Take Parrotts Ferry Rd. to Hwy. 49 south; go straight onto S. Washington St./Old Hwy. 108, turn left on Restano Way, right on Mono Way, and left on Greenley Rd. This is about a 6-mile trip to the Stanislaus National Forest office. Or continue on Hwy. 108 into the forest.

❾ ★★ Stanislaus National Forest. Those looking for a year-round wilderness experience, including hiking, fishing, backpacking, white-water rafting, and skiing, can head

> Ride the rails on a tour of handsome Gold Country foothills at Railtown 1897 State Historic Park.

up into this nearly 900,000-acre national forest which abuts the western side of ★★★ **Yosemite National Park** (p. 276). The wild and scenic Tuolumne River delivers world-class rapids for rafters and kayakers, and two ski facilities operate here: ★ **Bear Valley,** off Hwy. 4 (☎ 209/753-2301; www.bearvalley.com), and ★ **Dodge Ridge**, off Hwy. 108 (☎ 209/965-3474; www.dodgeridge.com). Pay a visit to the Stanislaus National Forest office in Sonora for maps and detailed information. 19777 Greenley Rd., Sonora. ☎ 209/532-3671. www.fs.fed.us/r5/stanislaus. Free admission to forest for day use. Mon–Fri 8am–4:30pm.

On Day 4 take Hwy. 49 south to Jamestown; go left on Fifth Ave. It's about 4 miles from Sonora to

⑩ ★ Railtown 1897 State Historic Park.
Sierra No. 3 is not a fragrance. It's a steam locomotive known as the "Movie Star" that has appeared in more than 100 film and television productions, from Clint Eastwood's *Unforgiven* to *Little House on the Prairie.* As of this writing it's being restored, but will hopefully be back on display at this museum and working rail yard, which has also had its share of big-screen exposure. You'll see locomotives, wooden passenger cars, as well as a still-functioning roundhouse; there's also an interpretive center and gift shop. On weekends, from April to October, there

are 40-minute steam-train excursions along a 6-mile route into the Sierra foothills (scheduled on the hour, 11am–3pm); throughout the year there are special themed rides, including winter holiday and spring wildflower trips. Railtown, which really does date back to 1897, is in ★ **Jamestown,** a quaint burg that offers historic pleasures of its own. ◷ At least 1 hr. Fifth Ave. at Reservoir Rd., Jamestown. ☎ 209/984-3953. www.parks.ca.gov or www.railtown1897.org. Admission $5 adults, $3 kids 6–17; Train rides $13 adults, $6 kids 6–17. Daily Apr–Oct 9:30am–4:30pm; Nov–Mar 10am–3pm.

Take Hwy. 49 south; when it merges with Hwy. 140 turn right. In Mariposa take the first right after Coakley Circle, then a left on Jessie St. Total trip is about 52 miles to the

⑪ ★ Mariposa Museum and History Center.
This great little museum interprets the history of Mariposa—a gateway to Yosemite National Park—and features an extensive collection of Miwok Indian artifacts, as well as items from Spanish colonial days up through the Gold Rush era. There are outdoor displays of mining equipment, plus relocated and re-created historic structures, including a one-room school, a miner's cabin, and a saloon. ◷ 45 min. 5119 Jessie St., Mariposa. ☎ 209/966-2924. www.mariposamuseum.com. Admission $4 adults, free for kids. Daily 10am–4pm.

Continue on Hwy. 140/49 through Mariposa. When they split, stay on Hwy. 49, then turn left on Fairgrounds Rd. Total trip is about 2½ miles to

⑫ ★ California State Mining and Mineral Museum.
This is the State of California's official mineral collection, begun in 1880. It has more than 13,000 items, including gems and minerals from around the globe, but only a small portion are on display at any given time. There is also a re-created assay office and a simulated mine tunnel that interprets the mining process. The star attraction, though, is the Fricot Nugget, a stupendous crystalline gold rock weighing nearly 14 pounds, discovered in the American River in 1864. ◷ 30 min. 5005 Fairgrounds Rd., Mariposa County Fairgrounds. ☎ 209/742-7675. www.parks.ca.gov. Admission $4 adults, kids 12 & under free. Thurs–Sun 10am–4pm (till 5pm in summer).

Where to Stay & Dine

★ **Best Western Cedar Inn & Suites** ANGELS CAMP No surprises here, just clean, spacious, pleasant accommodations with a good location and amenities like free Internet, a pool, and a fitness room. 444 S. Main St. ☎ 800/767-1127 or 209/736-4000. www.bestwesternangels camp.com. 38 units. Doubles $94–$139 w/ breakfast. AE, DC, DISC, MC, V.

★★ **Camps** ANGELS CAMP CALIFORNIAN Angels Camp's most upscale dining venue has a steak and seafood menu featuring seasonal specials as well as local beef. There's a lively bar with music on weekends. In the Greenhorn Creek golf resort, 676 McCauley Ranch Rd. (½ mile west of Hwy. 4/Hwy. 49 junction off Angel Oaks Dr.). ☎ 209/729-8181. www.greenhorn creek.com. Reservations recommended. Entrees $12–$31. AE, MC, V. Lunch & dinner Wed–Sun; brunch Sun.

★ **Crusco's Ristorante** ANGELS CAMP ITALIAN A family-run eatery with gracious service, featuring locally sourced products and house-made everything. Save room for dessert. 1240 S. Main St. ☎ 209/736-1440. www.cruscos.com. Reservations recommended. Entrees $15–$23. DISC, MC, V. Lunch & dinner Thurs–Mon.

★★ **Dunbar House, 1880** MURPHYS This luxury B&B, set in a lovely Italianate home built in 1880, is bright and cheerful and surrounded by beautiful gardens. Upscale amenities include fine linens, Wi-Fi, and a fireplace in every room. 271 Jones St. ☎ 800/692-6006 or 209/728-2897. www.dunbarhouse.com. 5 units. Doubles $190–$280 w/breakfast & afternoon appetizers. AE, DISC, MC, V.

★ **Firewood** MURPHYS ECLECTIC This casual, order-at-the-counter spot is in an old firehouse and serves wood-fired pizzas, burgers, and Mexican fare like fish tacos and burritos. It's all well executed and well priced, and when you toss in the local brew on tap— what's not to love? 420 Main St. ☎ 209/728-3248. www.firewoodeats.com. Entrees $6–$14. MC, V. Lunch & dinner daily.

> From burgers and fries to classier fare, Camps serves up good food every night and live music on weekends.

★★ **Grounds** MURPHYS ECLECTIC This locals' favorite is an all-day spot most of the week, serving everything from Belgian waffles to filet mignon. There's outdoor dining when the weather's nice. 402 Main St. ☎ 209/728-8663. www.groundsrestaurant. com. Dinner reservations recommended. Entrees $8–$29. AE, DISC, MC, V. Breakfast, lunch & dinner daily.

★ **Jamestown Hotel** JAMESTOWN Starting out as a boarding house in 1858, this historic property has been everything from a bus depot to a bordello. Loaded with antiques, the rooms come in varying sizes; several have sitting rooms equipped with TVs and some have claw-foot tubs. 18153 Main St. ☎ 800/205-4901 or 209/984-3902. www. jamestownhotel.com. 8 units. Doubles $90–$175 w/breakfast. AE, MC, V.

★ **National Hotel & Restaurant** JAMESTOWN One of the state's oldest continuously operating hotels, this cozy inn comfortably re-creates the Gold Rush days (but with modern amenities). Its restaurant serves up one of the best meals in town. 18183 Main St. ☎ 800/894-3446 or 209/984-3446. www.national-hotel. com. 9 units. Doubles $140 w/breakfast. AE, DC, DISC, MC, V.

HILLS OF FORTUNE

How the Gold Rush transformed California from a sleepy
U.S. territory to a thriving multicultural state

BY JENNIFER SENATOR

WHEN JAMES MARSHALL SPIED GOLD IN THE WATER at Sutter's Mill in 1848, he
forever altered the history of the then-U.S. territory of California. More than 300,000
people flooded the newly established "gold country," and within two years, California
became a state. By 1849, San Francisco was transformed from a sleepy settlement into
a bustling port city that was home to more millionaires than New York or Boston.

California's first millionaire wasn't a gold miner; he was a businessman named Samuel Brannan, who, after hearing of Marshall's discovery, shrewdly purchased mining
supplies and sold them at a substantial markup. The Gold Rush inspired other success
stories. Miners swore by the extra-durable canvas pants made by Bavarian tailor Levi
Strauss. Two other businessmen, Henry Wells and William Fargo, offered newly flush
miners secure banking services. And after little success in the mines, Italian confec-
tioner Domingo Ghirardelli decided to open a chocolate shop in San Francisco instead.

The Golden Years

1848
> On January 24, James Marshall, foreman of a crew building a sawmill in the Sierra Nevada foothills for Swiss-German immigrant John Sutter, discovers a ⅓-oz. nugget of gold while inspecting the mill's water flow. The nugget appraises for $5.12.
> Residents of Northern California descend on the area surrounding Sutter's Mill, collecting thousands of dollars' worth of gold each day. By the end of the year, travelers from across the U.S., Mexico, the Sandwich Islands, and China arrive in San Francisco.

1849
> Approximately 90,000 "forty-niners" descend on California, most of them Americans, in search of gold. Some arrive by land, via the Oregon-California Trail; others arrive by ship around the tip of South America. Immigrants from across Europe, Asia, Latin America, Australia, the Caribbean also arrive.

1850–51
> On September 9, 1850, California becomes the 31st state.
> The state legislature institutes a Foreign Miners Tax, charging non-American-born miners $20 per month. Banditry increases in the mines, and the tax is repealed within a year.

1852
> More than 20,000 Chinese immigrants arrive in San Francisco, the most since the rush began.
> California's annual gold production reaches $81 million.
> Hydraulic mining is introduced, bringing miners unparalleled success. But resulting floods endanger California's farmlands and ignite a battle that continues until 1884, when hydraulic mining is banned to protect the state's thriving wheat crop.

1853
> Levi Strauss arrives in San Francisco and opens a dry-goods business.

1854
> A 195-pound mass of gold—the largest yet discovered—is found in Calaveras County.

1855 & ON
> Gold production stabilizes in 1857 at around $45 million per year.
> The S.S. *Central America*, bound for New York, sinks in a hurricane off the coast of the Carolinas with approximately 10 tons of California gold onboard. In 1987, the ship and much of the gold (valued at more than $100 million) is recovered.
> In 1863, rails are laid for the western leg of the First Transcontinental Railroad, financed in part with Gold Rush money, and uniting California with the central and eastern U.S.

Immigration

THE EFFECTS OF THE FORTY-NINERS

More than 300,000 people came to California in hopes of finding fortune, a great many seeking relief from such calamities as the potato famine in Ireland and ongoing turmoil in Europe. Many remained in California after the Gold Rush, choosing to try their luck in business or farming the lush California terrain. Many Italians planted vineyards that would eventually make northern California one of the world's best wine-growing regions.

The largest number of immigrants (more than 100,000) came from China, after crop failure in southern China and the First Opium War. Because they were heavily taxed and banned from working the more profitable gold mines, the Chinese opened restaurants, laundries, and other stores in the surrounding cities, many amassing greater fortunes than the miners. Eventually, it was the Chinese who largely built the First Transcontinental Railroad.

However, the Gold Rush forced at least one group to emigrate from California. After the state passed The Act for the Government and Protection of Indians in 1850, which essentially allowed Native Americans to be enslaved by the miners, the tribes that weren't sold or killed left. While an estimated 150,000 Native Americans lived in California in 1845, by 1879, the population was less than 30,000.

Sacramento

California's state capital—but only its sixth-largest metropolis—is a thriving city that has been hailed as one of the country's most livable places. The past remains palpable here in River City (a nickname the city acquired because of its location at the confluence of the Sacramento and American rivers), thanks to a number of historic sites and museums, as well as the grand Victorian architecture you'll find along downtown's shady streets.

> *Inside the State Capitol, floor tiles bear the state motto, "Eureka," Greek for "I found it."*

START Old Sacramento State Historic Park, K and Second sts. **TRIP LENGTH** 3 days.

1 ★ **Old Sacramento State Historic Park.** What started out as a tent-city trading center for miners heading out to the mother lode is now California's largest restoration project. There are more than 50 Old West structures here (including the terminus of the famous Pony Express), some dating back to 1849, where you can shop, dine, and find lots of entertainment. See p. 172, **3**. Bus: 11, 30, 31, 36. or Downtown Trolley (route 143).

2 ★★★ kids **California State Railroad Museum.** You don't have to be a train buff to appreciate these beautifully restored locomotives and rail cars. From spring through summer, you can take a ride along the Sacramento River levee on one of the museum's historic trains. See p. 173, **4**. Bus: 11, 30, 31, 36 or Downtown Trolley (route 143).

3 **California State Military Museum.** California's official military museum and historical research center has more than 30,000 objects in its collection and covers the history of the state's fighting units from the Spanish and

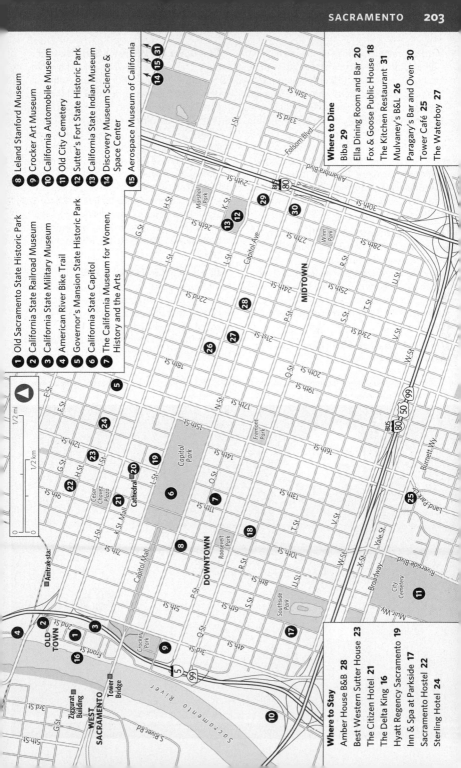

1 Old Sacramento State Historic Park
2 California State Railroad Museum
3 California State Military Museum
4 American River Bike Trail
5 Governor's Mansion State Historic Park
6 California State Capitol
7 The California Museum for Women, History and the Arts
8 Leland Stanford Museum
9 Crocker Art Museum
10 California Automobile Museum
11 Old City Cemetery
12 Sutter's Fort State Historic Park
13 California State Indian Museum
14 Discovery Museum Science & Space Center
15 Aerospace Museum of California

Where to Dine
Biba 29
Ella Dining Room and Bar 20
Fox & Goose Public House 18
The Kitchen Restaurant 31
Mulvaney's B&L 26
Paragary's Bar and Oven 30
Tower Café 25
The Waterboy 27

Where to Stay
Amber House B&B 28
Best Western Sutter House 23
The Citizen Hotel 21
The Delta King 16
Hyatt Regency Sacramento 19
Inn & Spa at Parkside 17
Sacramento Hostel 22
Sterling Hotel 24

Mexican colonial periods up to the conflict in Afghanistan. The museum takes pains to point out its purpose is not to glorify war, but to honor those Californians who served (including such notable warriors as Generals James Doolittle (1896–1993) and George S. Patton (1885–1945). This museum may not exist to rattle sabers, but it has a lot of them on display. 1119 Second St. ☎ 916/854-1900. www.militarymuseum.org. Tues–Sun 10am–4pm; Fri–Sat 10am–5pm. Admission $5 adults, $3 seniors and kids 6–17. Bus: 11, 30, 31, 36, or Downtown Trolley (route 143).

❹ ★★ American River Bike Trail. Running alongside the river for 32 miles from Old Sacramento to Folsom Lake, this paved path provides both bikers and pedestrians with an amazing recreational corridor right in the heart of the metropolitan area. See p. 178, ❻. Bus: 11, 30, 31, 36, or Downtown Trolley (route 143).

On Day 2, head to H St., between 15th and 16th sts. to the

❺ ★ Governor's Mansion State Historic Park. This ornate, wedding cake of a Victorian mansion—looking a little like the Addams family abode—was home to 13 California governors from 1903 to 1967. Ronald Reagan (1911–2004) lived here, as did Earl Warren (1891–1974), who would go on to become U.S. Supreme Court chief justice. Originally built in 1877, the house is filled with eclectic personal effects and mementoes of every first family that called the mansion home. Access is by guided tour only. ⏱ 1 hr. 1526 H St. ☎ 916/323-3047. www.parks.ca.gov. Admission $5 adults, $3 kids 6–17. Tours Tues–Sun 10am–4pm on the hour. Bus: Capital shuttle 141 (no service Sat–Sun).

❻ ★★★ California State Capitol. Perhaps it's the wonderful collection of art in this grand building that distracts state legislators from getting anything done. Whatever the case, you should definitely pay a visit here to marvel at the magnificent rotunda and stroll the grounds. The 40-acre park surrounding the

> *Strike a pose on a steam locomotive inside the California State Railway Museum, or catch a ride on one of the trains outside.*

capitol includes a World Peace Rose Garden with more than 150 varieties of roses, a camellia grove, a trout pond, and a slew of moving memorials and statues. See p. 172, ❷. Bus: 30, 31, 38, 50E, or Downtown Trolley (route 143).

❼ ★ **The California Museum for Women, History and the Arts.** Originally opened to display the state's vast archival holdings, this museum took a different turn under the guidance of First Lady Maria Shriver. It now celebrates the state's rich cultural heritage and the people who have made California history, with a special emphasis on the contributions of women. Exhibits might feature anything from Native American basketry to costumes made for Hollywood films and TV shows. A California Hall of Fame was initiated in 2006, highlighting the achievements of notable Californians—both living and dead—ranging from Walt Disney to NFL Hall of Fame coach and former broadcaster John Madden. ☉ At least 1 hr. 1020 O St. ☎ 916/653-7524. www. californiamuseum.org. Admission $8.50 adults, $7 seniors and students, $6 kids 6-13. Mon–Sat 10am–5pm; Sun noon–5pm. Light rail: Archives Plaza station.

> As goo-gawed as a wedding cake, the Governor's Mansion was purchased by the state in 1903—for $32,500.

❽ ★★ **Leland Stanford Mansion.** This splendiferous mansion has been home to three governors (including Mr. Stanford) and is currently used as California's official reception site for wining and dining visiting heads of state. A 14-year, $22-million restoration (1900–87 this was the Stanford Home for Children) completed in 2005 has brought the place to sparkling life. Originally built in 1856, it features elegant fixtures and period furnishings, incredible woodwork, and 17-foot ceilings. You can access the house by guided tour only, but you're free to check out the garden and visitor center on your own; there are exhibits, artifacts, and a gift shop. ☉ 1 hr. 800 N St. ☎ 916/324-0575 or 916/324-9266. www. parks.ca.gov or www.stanfordmansion.org. Tours $5 adults, $3 kids 6-17. Tours Tues–Sun 10am–4pm on the hour. Visitor center Tues–Sun 9:30am–5pm. Light rail: 8th & Capitol or 8th & O stations.

❾ ★ **Crocker Art Museum.** This fine museum, the oldest public art museum in the West, celebrates its 125th anniversary in 2010 with the opening of a new wing that will triple its

Sport of Kings

Sacramentans love their NBA basketball team the Kings, which has been a fixture in town since 1985. The Kings have struggled in recent years but you can still feel the love at ARCO Arena, 1 Sports Pkwy. (☎ 888/915-4647 or 916/928-0000; www.kings.com), from October to April; tickets are $25 to $965.

> *Go for the ghoulish at the 1849 Old City Cemetery; around Halloween, take a spooky lantern tour.*

current space. Though modern in style, the design of the new building echoes the architecture of the splendid Victorian-Italianate museum, which was commissioned in 1869 and dedicated to the city in 1885. See p. 176, ⑤. Bus: 38 or Capital shuttle 141.

Day 3 begins on Front St. at the

⑩ ★ **California Automobile Museum.** Even if you aren't a car buff, the fabulous design and detail of these vehicles is still something to behold. The collection includes more than 160 classic beauties, from a 1904 Ford Model C Runabout to a '58 Edsel to a NASCAR racer. And lest you think it's all about fawning over displays of conspicuous petroleum consumption, the museum also has a "Going Green" exhibition featuring a 1913 Rauch & Lang electric car, a 1972 electric Datsun, and more. ◷ 1 hr. 2200 Front St. ☎ 916/442-6802. www.calauto museum.org. Admission $8 adults, $7 seniors, $4 students, free for kids 4 & under. Daily 10am–6pm (3rd Thurs of the month till 9pm). Bus: 38.

⑪ ★ **Old City Cemetery.** Sacramento founder John Sutter donated 10 acres in 1849 to establish this Victorian-style graveyard. It now spreads over 44 acres, accommodating more than 25,000 "residents," and features colorful rose and perennial gardens, and creepy/beautiful monuments and statuary. Some notables interred here include John Sutter, Jr., who had a hand in establishing the city (in

fact, he named it Sacramento), railroad baron Mark Hopkins, Jr. (1813–78), and survivors of the ill-fated Donner Party. Stop by the Archives Mortuary Chapel (10am–3pm) to pick up a self-guided tour map, as well as souvenirs (yup, souvenirs) such as T-shirts and books. ◷ 1 hr. 1000 Broadway (main gate at 10th St. and Broadway). ☎ 916/448-0811. www.oldcity cemetery.com. Free admission. Summer daily 7am–7pm; winter Fri–Tues 7am–5pm. Guided tours Mar–Nov Sat 10am. Bus: 2, 51, or 53.

⑫ ★ **Sutter's Fort State Historic Park.** Swiss native John Sutter had dreams of creating an agricultural kingdom in a place he christened "New Helvetia" (New Switzerland). Establishing an adobe outpost in 1839 (and becoming a Mexican citizen in order to be awarded the land grant), Sutter was well on his way to making his plans a reality when in 1848 things spun out of control. Gold was discovered and New Helvetia's men abandoned the colony for the Sierra gold fields. Sutter's fort fell into disrepair, but even as far back as the 1890s it was seen as a historic resource worth preserving. It has now been restored to its 1846 appearance and is a treasure trove of California pioneer history. See p. 170, ❶. Bus: 30 or 31.

⑬ ★ **California State Indian Museum.** This small museum is adjacent to Sutter's Fort and has a great collection of Native American artifacts from various California tribes, with an emphasis on the First Peoples of the Central

Valley. There are examples of basketry and beadwork, as well as dance regalia, musical instruments, and tools. There is also an exhibit on Ishi, "the Wild Man of Oroville," who wandered out of the hills in 1911, the last surviving member of his tribe. He was befriended and studied by anthropologists, and lived out the remainder of his days in a museum in San Francisco. Ishi, in turn, observed that whites "were smart but not wise, knowing many things including much that is false." **Note:** The museum is in the process of transferring to the **California Indian Heritage Center** in West Sacramento—a major project that is going to take some years to complete. When finished, the 43-acre site will include a museum, a library, gardens, trails, and an amphitheatre and event space. Call ahead before visiting. ⏱ 30 min. 2618 K St. ☎ 916/324-0971. www.parks.ca.gov. Admission $3 adults, $2 kids 6–17. Tues–Sun 10am–5pm. Bus: 30 or 31.

⑭ ★ Discovery Museum Science & Space Center. This kid-friendly museum features lots of hands-on activities to stimulate interest and excitement about science and nature. There are live animals, from insects to reptiles, as well as planetarium shows. The ★ **Challenger Learning Center,** founded by the families of the space shuttle astronauts killed in 1986, is an interactive space-travel exhibit that features simulated voyages to Mars and the moon. ⏱ At least 1 hr. 3615 Auburn Blvd. ☎ 916/575-3942 or 916/575-3941. www.thediscovery.org. Admission $5 adults, $4 kids

13–17, $3 kids 4–12. $1 surcharge on weekends and holidays. Sept–June Tues–Fri noon–4:30pm, Sat–Sun 10am–4:30pm; July–Aug daily 10am–5pm. Planetarium shows Sept–June Sat–Sun 1 & 3pm; July–Aug Mon–Fri 3pm, Sat–Sun 1 & 3pm. Light rail: 533 Blue Line to Watt/I-80 station.

⑮ Aerospace Museum of California. A 20-minute drive from downtown, this indoor/outdoor collection of 40 military and civilian aircraft, from prop driven to jet powered, will appeal mostly to aficionados. There are also exhibits dedicated to the Apollo space program, restored engines (looking a little like industrial art), and a collection of artwork on loan from the U.S. Air Force. You can also go for a virtual ride in a flight simulator. ⏱ 1 hr. 3200 Freedom Park Dr., McClellan. ☎ 916/643-3192. www.aerospacemuseumofcalifornia.org. Admission $8 adults, $6 seniors and kids 13–18, $5 kids 6–12. Tues–Sat 9am–5pm; Sun 10am–5pm. Light rail: 533 Blue Line to Watt/I-80 station, transfer to bus 80.

> Simple cans turn into a lively display at the kid-friendly Discovery Museum, loaded with hands-on exhibits.

Putting the "H" into Theater

In 2003, Sacramento's H Street Theatre Project brought the city's beloved big-top tent musical series, the **Music Circus**, 1419 H St. (☎ 916/557-1999; www.calmt.com), into the 21st century. The summertime program of musical-theater productions, such as *Guys and Dolls* and *Into the Woods*, is now held in the state-of-the-art ★ **Wells Fargo Pavilion**, which offers arena-style seating and (to the relief of all) air-conditioning; tickets are $41 to $53. Next door, the **Sacramento Theatre Company** (☎ 916/443-6722; www.sactheatre.org) presents plays and musicals from September to May in its 300-seat main theater and a 90-seat black box theater; tickets are $28 to $46.

Where to Stay

> *As if the beds aren't elegant enough at Amber House B&B, you can request rose petals scattered on your pillows too.*

★★ **Amber House Bed-and-Breakfast** MID-TOWN A duo of historic homes—an 1895 Dutch colonial and a 1905 Craftsman—are the setting for this romantic, elegant, utterly tasteful B&B, which features top-notch service and a great location. Some rooms have fireplaces and whirlpool tubs for two; with advance notice you can arrange to have your room strewn with rose petals or have a candle-lit bath drawn. 1315 22nd St. ☎ 800/755-6526 or 916/444-8085. www.amberhouse.com. 10 units. Doubles $169–$279 w/breakfast. AE, DC, DISC, MC, V. Bus: 30, 31, 36, 38, or 62.

Best Western Sutter House DOWNTOWN You'll be pleasantly surprised by these accommodations—a great value—that are within walking distance of most of the major attractions in town. There is a more than passing attempt at comfort and style here, as well as free covered parking, free Wi-Fi, and a solar-heated swimming pool. 1100 H St. ☎ 888/256-8040 or 916/441-1314. www.the sutterhouse.com. 98 units. Doubles $79–$139 w/breakfast. AE, DC, DISC, MC, V. Bus: Capital shuttle 141. Light rail: 12th and I.

★★ **The Citizen Hotel** DOWNTOWN In its previous life this 1920s office building was home to lawyers and lobbyists, but in its new incarnation it's the city's coolest boutique hotel (law books and vintage political cartoons incorporated into the decor pay homage to its past). The rooms are all up-to-date, the location is great (you can walk to all the major sights), and the bar and restaurant are local hot spots. 926 J St. ☎ 916/447-2700. www. citizenhotel.com. 198 units. Doubles $149–$249. AE, DC, DISC, MC, V. Bus: 11, 15, or 86. Light rail: 8th and K.

> Giving a good name to hostels everywhere, the Sacramento Hostel impresses with beautiful gardens, great location, and free Wi-Fi.

★ The Delta King OLD SACRAMENTO

This place is kind of cheesy—but in a fun way. Delta King is an actual sternwheeler built in 1927 that ran the river from here to San Francisco. Lovingly refurbished, it's docked alongside Old Sacramento, steps from a plethora of shopping and dining options. If you want to splurge, go for the captain's quarters, a two-story suite with awesome views. 1000 Front St. ☎ 800/825-5464 or 916/444-5464. www.deltaking.com. 44 units. Doubles $99–$179; captain's quarters $550. Rates include breakfast. Riverside rooms are $15 extra. AE, DC, DISC, MC, V. Bus: 11, 30, 31, 36, or Downtown Trolley (route 143).

★★ Hyatt Regency Sacramento DOWNTOWN

Popular with politicos and conventioneers on expense accounts, this hotel is perfectly situated across the street from the capitol (opt for a corner room with a view of Capitol Park). The rooms are spacious, contemporary, and well maintained. 1209 L St. ☎ 800/233-1234 or 916/443-1234. www.sacramento.hyatt.com. 503 units. Doubles $149–$300; suites from $375. AE, DC, DISC, MC, V. Bus: 30, 31, 50E, or Downtown Trolley (route 143). Light rail: Cathedral Square.

★★★ Inn & Spa at Parkside DOWNTOWN

A Zen calm prevails over this upscale retreat, which includes a mansion that once served as the home for the Chinese ambassador. Located across the street from Southside Park, the individually decorated rooms are ranked from standard to extravagant, and all feature luxurious bedding and unique beds; some rooms have fireplaces. You can enhance your stay with a facial, stone massage, or botanical body wrap. 2116 Sixth St. ☎ 800/995-7275 or 916/658-1818. www.innatparkside.com. 11 units. Doubles $169–$339 w/breakfast and wine & cheese reception. AE, DC, DISC, MC, V. Bus: 38 or Capital shuttle 141.

★ Sacramento Hostel DOWNTOWN

This place is as impressively charming as a traditional B&B that would cost twice the price. A beautifully detailed mansion built in 1885, it has lovely grounds and is conveniently located near the capitol; it features a self-service full kitchen, game room, laundry, and free Wi-Fi. Both shared (gender-specific) and private rooms are available, and there's no curfew. 925 H St. ☎ 888/464-4872 or 916/443-1691. www.norcalhostels.org. 9 units. Dorm rooms $25, private rooms $55–$91. $3 daily fee for those not members of Hostelling International. AE, DISC, MC, V. Bus: 2, 6, 11, 15, or Capital shuttle 142.

★★ Sterling Hotel DOWNTOWN

This mansion was built in 1894 and has a great downtown location. Rooms are Victorian in style and are well cared for; each has a Jacuzzi. The hotel's ★ Chanterelle Restaurant has been a bastion of Sacramento fine dining since 1988. Note: The hotel's grand ballroom is a popular event space, so there may be events scheduled during your stay—call before booking. 1300 H St. ☎ 800/365-7660 or 916/448-1300. www.sterlinghotel.com. 17 units. Doubles $99–$257; suites $335. Rates include breakfast. AE, DISC, MC, V. Light rail: 12th and I.

Where to Dine

> It's showtime at The Kitchen, where 50 lucky diners per night enjoy the demos, food, and party atmosphere.

★★★ Biba MIDTOWN *ITALIAN*

Since 1986, Biba Caggiano, a native of Bologna, Italy, has been serving up authentic Italian fare at her eponymous eatery. She has also become a Sacramento culinary maven, publishing eight cookbooks and hosting her own cooking show. Look for prix-fixe meals at lunch and dinner (Mon–Fri), house-made pastas, classic *osso buco*, and live piano music nightly. 2801 Capitol Ave. ☎ 916/455-2422. www.biba-restaurant.com. Reservations recommended. Entrees $15–$32. AE, DC, MC, V. Lunch Mon–Fri; dinner Mon–Sat. Bus: 30, 31, 36, 67, or 68.

★★ Ella Dining Room and Bar DOWNTOWN

AMERICAN Foodie without being snooty, this contemporary American restaurant is modern and stylish, but also warm and inviting, with high ceilings whimsically adorned with battered shutters. Incorporating local, sustainable products, there are both small plates (hazelnut gnocchi, pan-seared scallops) and traditional entrees (wood-fired duck breast in huckleberry sauce) that emanate from the exhibition kitchen; there's also a knockout wine list and creative cocktails (try an elderberry gimlet). 1131 K St. ☎ 916/443-3772. www.elladiningroomandbar.com. AE, DISC, MC, V. Small plates $9–$15, entrees $15–$32. Lunch Mon–Fri; dinner Mon–Sat. Light rail: Cathedral Square.

★★ Fox & Goose Public House DOWNTOWN

PUB FARE Rule, Britannia—this pub has been a local institution since 1975. Breakfast is especially popular, and the self-serve coffee while you wait for a table is a nice touch. There's traditional British fare like bangers, fish and chips, ploughman's lunch, and Welsh rarebit—plus standard bar food and vegetarian items. Live music is scheduled 5 nights a week. 1001 R St. (at 10th St.). ☎ 916/443-8825. www.fox andgoose.com. Reservations not accepted. Entrees $5–$10. AE, MC, V. Breakfast daily; lunch Mon–Fri; dinner Mon–Sat. Bus: 2, 6, 38, 51, or Capital shuttle 142.

★★★ The Kitchen Restaurant ARDEN-ARCADE

AMERICAN Don't make plans to go out after this meal—this *is* your entertainment for the evening. This hybrid experience is part demonstration dinner, part culinary event, and one great party. There's one seating per evening for 50 people, and you're free to wander about, peer over the chef's shoulder, or even help out. The four-course menu is a seasonal, contemporary American affair, and you should plan on spending at least 4 hours working on it. 2225 Hurley Way, Ste. 101. ☎ 916/568-7171. www.thekitchenrestaurant.com. Reservations required. DISC, MC, V. $125 per person. Dinner Wed–Sun. Bus: 87.

★★ **Mulvaney's B&L** MIDTOWN *AMERICAN*
Set in an old firehouse and featuring outdoor dining, this Sacramento favorite expertly prepares local fare in a contemporary American style. You have to love a chef who would create a dessert like a White Russian *panna cotta* in the shape of a bowling pin, accompanied by a macaroon bowling ball, and dub it "The Dude Abides" in honor of Jeff Bridge's character from *The Big Lebowski*. **Note:** You'll find only bare bones information on the website. 1215 19th St. (off L St.). ☎ 916/441-1771. www.culinaryspecialists.com. Reservations recommended. Entrees $15–$30. AE, MC, V. Dinner Wed–Sat. Bus: 30, 31, 36, or 62.

★★ **Paragary's Bar and Oven** MIDTOWN *MEDITERRANEAN* Another longtime Sacramento favorite, it serves Italian and French fare, including pizzas from a wood-burning oven. The sweet outdoor patio, with its water features, olive trees, and fireplace, is the place to be. The Paragary Restaurant Group operates a dozen worthy restaurants and bars in the area; check the website for more information. 1401 28th St. ☎ 916/457-5737. www.paragarys.com. Entrees $11–$22. AE, DC, DISC, MC, V. Lunch Mon–Fri; dinner daily. Bus: 36, 67, or 68.

Tower Café DOWNTOWN *INTERNATIONAL*
An Art Deco spire marks the spot for this restaurant (once a movie house), which features globe-trotting cuisine and a decor scheme to match. Latin, Asian, Caribbean, Irish, and Southwestern items all find their way onto the menu; the French toast soaked in custard anchors breakfast. Although the experience here can be hit or miss, especially with service, you can't beat sitting out on the garden patio on a sunny day. 1518 Broadway. ☎ 916/441-0222. www.towercafe.com. Entrees $9–$18. AE, MC, V. Breakfast, lunch, & dinner daily. Bus: 6, 51, or Capital shuttle 141.

★★ **The Waterboy** MIDTOWN *FRENCH/ITALIAN* The decor is a bit dated but the execution of the Southern French/Northern Italian cuisine is excellent. Naturally raised meats; local,

> *Rarely do the chefs at Mulvaney's miss a step, with dishes focusing on local foods cooked with contemporary flare.*

organic produce; and a seasonal menu that changes monthly add up to one of the city's best dining experiences, and it's topped off by friendly, knowledgeable service. 2000 Capitol Ave. ☎ 916/498-9891. www.waterboyrestaurant.com. Entrees $16–$29. AE, DC, DISC, MC, V. Lunch Mon–Fri; dinner daily. Bus: 30, 31, 36, or 62.

Fast Facts

American Express

American Express Travel Service, 455 Market St., San Francisco (☎ 415/536-2600; www.amextravelresources.com), is the closest office. It's open Monday to Friday 9am to 5:30pm and Saturday 10am to 2pm. Or call ☎ 800/221-7282.

Dentists & Doctors

For a dental referral, call **1-800-DENTIST** (☎ 800/336-8422; www.1800dentist.com). For doctors, see "Emergencies," below.

Emergencies

In an emergency dial ☎ 911.

For medical emergencies in Sacramento, head for the **UC Davis Medical Center**, 4150 V St. (☎ 916/734-5010; www.ucdmc.ucdavis.edu). In Nevada City/Grass Valley, go to **Sierra Nevada Memorial Hospital**, 155 Glasson Way, Grass Valley (☎ 530/274-6000; www.snmh.org). In Placerville/Coloma, try the **Marshall Medical Center**, 1100 Marshall Way, Placerville (☎ 530/622-1441; www.marshallmedical.org). In the Amador City area, head for **Sutter Amador Hospital**, 200 Mission Blvd., Jackson (☎ 209/223-7500; www.sutteramador.org). In Angels Camp/Murphys, go to **Mark Twain St. Joseph's Hospital**, 768 Mountain Ranch Rd., San Andreas (☎ 209/754-3521; www.marktwainhospital.org). In Columbia/Jamestown, head for **Sonora Regional Medical Center**, 1000 Greenley Rd., Sonora (☎ 209/532-5000; www.sonoramedicalcenter.org). And in Mariposa, go to **John C. Fremont Hospital**, 5189 Hospital Rd., Mariposa (☎ 209/966-3631; www.jcfhospital.com).

Getting There

BY PLANE **Sacramento International Airport** (☎ 916/929-5411; www.sacairports.org) is located 12 miles northwest of downtown Sacramento and is served by about a dozen airlines, including Alaska, American, Continental, Delta, and JetBlue. **SuperShuttle** (☎ 800/258-3826 or 916/648-2505; www.supershuttle.com) runs from the airport to downtown for a flat rate of $14 ($11 each

additional rider in your party). In Terminal A, the SuperShuttle counter is in the baggage claim area; in Terminal B the booth is outside the food court, between Terminals B1 and B2. A taxi ride downtown will cost about $25. If you're looking for the cheapest way to town, **Yolobus** (☎ 530/666-2877; www.yolobus.com) route 42 will take you to the capitol area for $2, but the ride will take at least 1½ hr (a cab will take 15–20 min.). BY TRAIN The Sacramento **Amtrak** station is at 401 I St. (☎ 800/872-7245; www.amtrak.com). Rail and bus service connects to Auburn, Grass Valley, Mariposa, and Placerville. BY CAR Driving from San Francisco, Sacramento is about 90 miles east on I-80 (trip time: 1½ to more than 2hr., depending on traffic). From Los Angeles, take I-5 through the Central Valley directly into Sacramento (trip time: 6 hr.). From North Lake Tahoe, get on I-80 west, and from South Lake Tahoe take U.S. 50 (trip time: 2–2½ hr. from both, depending on road conditions). Hwy. 49 runs north and south through Gold Country, stretching from above Lake Tahoe to Yosemite's southern gateway.

Getting Around

IN SACRAMENTO The city sprawls, but the downtown area is well covered by **Sacramento Regional Transit District** (☎ 916/321-2877; www.sacrt.com) bus and light rail. The basic fare is $2.50 (exact change required) and no transfers are issued; your light-rail ticket, available at station vending machines, is good for 2 hours. Day passes ($6) provide unlimited rides on both the bus and light rail until 1:30am. They can be purchased on the bus, at the vending machines, or at the Customer Service Center, 1225 R St. (Mon–Fri 8am–6pm and Sat 10am–2pm). Discount single fares ($1.25) and daily passes ($3) are offered to seniors, students (ages 5–18), and persons with disabilities; up to two children under age 5 ride free with an adult.

Recommended taxi companies in Sacramento are **A1 Cab** (☎ 916/838-6474), **BC Cab** (☎ 916/338-1212; www.bccab.net). **Dave's Airport Shuttle** (☎ 916/879-6000; www.

davestaxiservice.com) will take you directly to the airport, without the hassle of additional shuttle stops for $14 (2-person minimum). Taxi rates are $3 at flag drop, $2.50 for each additional mile.

If you're driving in Gold Country (the best way get around the region), pick up a map from a visitor center or from your car-rental agency; motoring through the region is a relatively straightforward affair, but some roads go by multiple names, which can be a little confusing. In winter, be wary of icy conditions; as you gain elevation toward the Sierra, chains may be necessary. Also try to avoid Sacramento rush hour, from 7 to 9am and 5 to 7pm. For California road conditions call ☎ 800/427-7623 or go to www.dot.ca.gov.

Hospital
See "Emergencies," above.

Internet Access
Wi-Fi hotspots are plentiful; cybercafes are rare. In the Sacramento area is **An Internet Cafe**, 7734 Fair Oaks Blvd. (☎ 916/944-2299; www.aninternetstore.com); in Grass Valley there's **Flour Garden Cyber Cafe**, 999 Sutton Way (☎ 530/272-2043; www.flourgarden. com). Public libraries are another good option for those without a laptop.

Pharmacies
Walgreens has a 24-hour pharmacy at 2201 Arden Way (☎ 916/929-7341; www. walgreens.com) in Sacramento.

Post Office
In downtown Sacramento there's a post office at 801 I St. (☎ 916/556-3415); it's open Monday to Friday from 8am to 5pm. For other locations call ☎ 800/275-8777 or go to www. usps.com.

Safety
Gold Country is a safe destination. In Sacramento, observe the same precautions you would in any large city; the main areas of interest are generally visitor friendly (avoid the American River Bike Trail after dark, though). Do not leave valuables in your car anywhere in Gold Country.

In winery areas, beware of drunk drivers, and if you've been visiting tasting rooms, nominate a designated driver.

When hiking in wilderness parks, wear long pants to protect against ticks, which can carry Lyme disease. After a hike, do a thorough body search—if you do find a tick, use tweezers to remove it; don't crush it. Be sure to also carry sunscreen, water, and a hat; weather can change quickly in the Sierra foothills so be prepared with layers of clothing. Exercise extreme caution along snowmelt-fed rivers, which run fast and cold, and can easily claim lives.

Visitor Information
The **Sacramento Convention and Visitors Bureau**, 1608 I St., Sacramento, (☎ 916/808-7777; www. discovergold.org) is open Monday to Friday from 8am to 5pm. The Old Sacramento Visitor Center, 1002 Second St. (☎ 916/442-7644), in Old Sacramento, is usually open daily from 10am to 5pm.

Other sources for visitor information in Gold Country include the Nevada City Chamber of Commerce, 132 Main St., Nevada City (☎ 800/655-6569 or 530/265-2692; www.nevadacitychamber. com); Grass Valley/Nevada County Chamber, 248 Mill St., Grass Valley (☎ 800/655-4667 or 530/273-4667; www.grassvalleychamber.com); El Dorado County Chamber of Commerce, 542 Main St., Placerville (☎ 800/457-6279 or 530/621-5885; www.visit-eldorado.com); Amador Council of Tourism (☎ 877/868-7262; www.touramador. com); Sutter Creek Visitors Center, 71 Main St., Sutter Creek (☎ 800/400-0305 or 209/267-1344; www.suttercreek.org); Calaveras Visitors Bureau, 1192 S. Main St., Angels Camp (☎ 800/225-3764 or 209/736-0049; www.gocalaveras. com); Tuolumne County Visitors Bureau, 542 W. Stockton Rd., Sonora (☎ 800/446-1333 or 209/533-4420; www.tcvb.com); and Mariposa County Visitors Center, 5158 Hwy. 140, Mariposa (☎ 866/425-3366 or 209/966-7081; www. homeofyosemite.com).

The North

The Best of the North in 3 Days

From rugged, dramatic beaches to living cathedrals of soaring redwood trees, California's upper reaches offer some of the planet's most breathtaking natural environments. Leave the bright lights of the big city behind and immerse yourself in the cool calm of the state's Northern Coast, where the frequently foggy weather adds an air of primeval mystery and the towns offer an often sweet respite from urban living. Though some spots on this tour are accessible by public transportation, the remoteness of others means a car is a must for travel in this region.

> PREVIOUS PAGE *Waves laced with foam and strands of kelp roll in along wild and beautiful Bodega Head.* THIS PAGE *Thick marine fog helps redwoods thrive along the North Coast.*

START **Muir Woods National Monument is 11 miles north of San Francisco. Take Hwy. 101 to the Hwy. 1/ Stinson Beach exit, and then follow the signs to Muir Woods. TRIP LENGTH 206 miles, from Muir Woods to Ferndale.**

❶ **Muir Woods National Monument.** Part of the Golden Gate National Recreation area, this 559-acre haven—designated a national monument in 1908 by Teddy Roosevelt and named for naturalist John Muir—protects one of the few stands of old-growth coastal redwoods (*Sequoia sempervirens*) left in the region. These majestic trees (that start life as nothing more than a tiny seed) are a relative of the giant sequoia; they can grow as high as 380 feet and some are over 1,000 years old.

It's hard to remain unmoved by the beauty of the forest as you stroll beneath the old groves along the pedestrian trail that winds through the woods.

Crowds can be a problem here, especially on weekends, so I recommend hiking up the moderately difficult Ocean View trail, to avoid the masses. Also note that the woods are often foggy and cool (makes for very atmospheric photos), so dress appropriately. ⊙ At least 1 hr. Arrive early, especially Sat–Sun, as parking is scarce. Off Hwy. 1, Mill Valley. ☎ 415/388-2596. www.nps.gov. Admission $5 ages 17 & over. Daily 8am–6pm.

From Muir Woods, take the Panoramic Hwy. north and follow the signs to

② ★★ **Mount Tamalpais State Park.** Rising up through the coastal fog is 2,571-foot Mount Tamalpais, another beloved Bay Area escape and the birthplace of mountain biking (still a very popular sport in the park despite controversies over its environmental impact). Though it's not particularly imposing in height, Mount Tam (as it's known locally) is the highest peak in the Marin Hills and tall enough to usually get sunshine up top; if the weather is clear the views are amazing, stretching from San Francisco Bay to the Farallon Islands. Stop by the Pantoll ranger station along the Panoramic Highway to pick up a park map, then continue to the parking lot near Mount Tam's summit. It's a short but steep hike along a fire road to the peak. ⊙ At least 2 hr. 3801 Panoramic Hwy., Mill Valley. ☎ 415/388-2070. www.parks.ca.gov or www.mttam.net. Parking lots $8, seniors $7. Daily 7am–sunset.

Head southwest on the Panoramic Hwy. for 3.7 miles, then make a right onto Hwy. 1 and go north for 14 miles until you reach the Bear Valley Visitor Center, just north of Olema.

③ ★★★ **Point Reyes National Seashore.** Point Reyes is a 71,000-acre park that juts and curves into the Pacific, a peculiar appendage separated from much of the mainland by long and narrow Tomales Bay. Preserved from development in 1962, it not only is a spectacular natural setting, featuring 150 miles of trails, backcountry campgrounds, and numerous beaches, but also has three visitor centers, a replica of a Coast Miwok Native American

1 Muir Woods National Monument

2 Mount Tamalpais State Park

3 Point Reyes National Seashore

4 Cowgirl Cantina

5 Mendocino

6 Avenue of the Giants

7 Ferndale

> Straight out of Cape Cod, a tidy cottage in Mendocino reflects the town's history as settled by Easterners back in the 1850s.

village, and a historic lighthouse and ranch. The park's unique topography is a study in geology and plate tectonics—Point Reyes is the northernmost landmass on the Pacific Plate, sliced off from the North American Plate by the San Andreas Fault. It's actually sliding toward Alaska at a rate of about 2 inches per year; the massive earthquake of 1906 caused it to jump 20 feet in an instant, leveling San Francisco in the process.

Begin your visit at the **Bear Valley Visitor Center** (☎ 415/464-5100; Mon–Fri 9am–5pm, Sat–Sun & holidays except Dec 25 8am–5pm, extended hours in summer). You can pick up a park map here, as well as peruse exhibits on the park's diverse ecosystems and cultural heritage; you can also keep an eye on the resident seismograph for signs of earth movement. Before heading off for Point Reyes' most popular attraction, the 19th-century lighthouse, take some time to explore **Kule Loklo,** a replica of an indigenous village, and the **Earthquake Trail,** which allows you to get an up-close, interpreted look at the San Andreas Fault Zone. Both trail heads are located near

the visitor center and both are easy paths of .8 miles and .6 miles, respectively.

From the visitor center it's a 45-minute drive to the park's westernmost tip and the ★ **Point Reyes Lighthouse** (☎ 415/669-1534; visitor center Thurs–Mon 10am–4:30pm weather permitting), built in 1870. Be aware there are more than 300 steps down to the lighthouse, but even if you choose not to climb the stairs the scenery here is amazing, and this is the best place to scout for migrating gray whales (Jan–Apr). The Lighthouse Visitor Center has displays on whales, seals, maritime history, and more.

As you head back up Sir Francis Drake Boulevard from the lighthouse, drop down to ★ **Drakes Beach** and the **Kenneth C. Patrick Visitor Center** (☎ 415/669-1250; Sat–Sun & holidays 10am–5pm, extended hours in summer). Many believe the adjacent estuary, known as Drakes Estero, is the place where England's seafaring sinner/saint Sir Francis Drake spent 5 weeks in 1579, repairing and provisioning his ship *Golden Hind*. With its white sandstone cliffs, reminiscent of

England's Dover coast, Drakes Beach makes a compelling argument that this is indeed Drake's Nova Albion, or New England. At the visitor center you can learn more about 16th-century maritime exploration; there's also an excellent cafe.

Note: The weather here, and all along the Northern Coast, can turn nasty quickly—be prepared for damp, cold, and windy conditions. The 1980 horror flick, *The Fog* was filmed here because the park naturally provided the appropriate climate conditions. Water conditions can also be treacherous, featuring everything from frigid temperatures and rogue waves to severe undertows and great white sharks. Also note that on weekends in winter, portions of the park's major road are shut down to traffic, though a shuttle bus runs from the Ken Patrick visitor center at Drake's Beach to the major points of interest. At least 4 hr. www.nps.gov/pore. Free admission. Winter shuttle bus $5 17 & over (purchase tickets at the Ken Patrick visitor center). Daily sunrise–midnight. Overnight camping requires a permit ($15–$40).

From Point Reyes, head north to Mendocino. It's 132 miles along scenic, coast-hugging Hwy. 1; the drive takes 3½–4 hr. If you're running out of daylight, take the less winding road, U.S. 101 (3¼ hr.).

④ ★ **Cowgirl Cantina.** You'll encounter some amazing picnic sites along the road to Mendocino, so stop by this gourmet deli and wine shop operated by Cowgirl Creamery, makers of to-die-for cheeses. Set in a restored barn known as Tomales Bay Foods, there are all kinds of tasty local products for sale; you can also watch the cheese-making process from a glassed-in viewing area or even take a tour (Fri 11:30am). 80 Fourth St., Point Reyes Station. ☎ 415/663-9335. www.cowgirlcreamery.com. Items $8-$15.

❺ ★★★ **Mendocino.** This is the marquee destination on the Northern Coast—a postcard-perfect town, perched on a headland overlooking a jagged bay. The 19th-century, New England-style architecture might feel

> *Walk on the wild side in Pt. Reyes National Seashore, with miles of coast-hugging trails.*

> *Gingerbread houses like this 1899 beauty fill the coastal town of Ferndale, once the favored home of wealthy dairymen.*

somewhat incongruous here on the California coast, but Mendocino comes by its look honestly—many of the settlers who arrived here in the 1850s were lumbermen from Maine and Nova Scotia. In 1850, during a search for the cargo from a shipwreck, a different sort of loot was discovered: giant redwoods. The wood rush was on and Mendocino became the heart of a thriving logging industry, which fueled an especially appalling genocidal treatment of the local Native American tribes. Some 1 billion board feet were extracted from the surrounding forests and floated down the Big River to Mendocino Bay; much of the timber was used to build San Francisco (and rebuild it after the 1906 earthquake). Some estimates

put Mendocino's boomtown population at 20,000; there were eight hotels, 17 saloons, and more than a dozen brothels.

With the closing of the mill in 1939 the town struggled, but in the 1950s and '60s artists began paving the way for the town's rebirth as a center for art and culture, and eventually it emerged as a tourist magnet; the entire area was placed on the National Register of Historic Places in 1971. Today, there are only about 1,000 residents in Mendocino's village, but on any given summer weekend it will feel like those boomtown days all over again, with flocks of visitors roaming the charming streets and browsing through the boutiques and galleries. ⏱ 1 day. See p. 244.

The joy of the journey is the main point of Day 3, and getting there really is part of the fun. Head north on Hwy. 1, which merges onto U.S. 101 at Leggett; continue north to Phillipsville, where you can pick up the Avenue of the Giants (S.R. 254) and head north. The trip covers 85.7 miles and takes 2½ hr.

6 ★★ **Avenue of the Giants.** This 31-mile route, an officially designated scenic route, is one of the most spectacular drives in the West, cutting along the Eel River through ★ **Humboldt Redwoods State Park,** past a number of trail heads and quirky small towns with classically tacky roadside attractions. It all lies within a 51,000-acre forest of stately coastal redwoods, some more than 2,000 years old and soaring to more than 300 feet in height (more than 100 of the world's tallest trees can be found here).

About 9 miles along the route you'll find one of the state's oldest tourist traps—er, attractions—the **Shrine Drive-Thru Tree** (☎ 707/943-1658; $6) at Myers Flat; it's exactly what it sounds like—a hollowed out redwood that you can drive through. Another few miles down the road, in Weott, stop off at the **Humboldt Redwoods State Park Visitor Center** (☎ 707/946-2263; www.humboldtredwoods.org), where you can pick up a map and peruse some nature exhibits, and then make your way a few miles north to the Dyerville Loop Road and **Founders Grove Nature Trail.** This easy .5-mile trail meanders through the stand of trees that inspired a group of environmentalists to form the Save the Redwoods League in 1918. What was once thought to be the world's tallest redwood (it was 372 feet tall and over 1,600 years old), the Dyerville Giant, toppled to the ground here in 1991, but even supine, it's mighty impressive. ⏱ 2 hr. www.avenueofthegiants.net.

Continue along the Avenue of the Giants until it merges with U.S. 101 at Pepperwood; continue north to Hwy. 211 and head west to the time-warp town of Ferndale. The trip covers 24.6 miles and takes 30 min.

7 ★ **Ferndale.** Finish off your last day in the region with a walking tour of this perfectly preserved Victorian hamlet, a National Historic Landmark whose gingerbread architecture is mainly the result of dairy wealth accumulated by town residents in the 1880s.

> As soaring as any cathedral, coast redwoods, some over 300 feet tall, line quiet trails along Avenue of the Giants.

Main Street is a 3-block long trip back in time. A highlight is the **Kinetic Sculpture Museum,** the final resting place for some of the entries that participate in the Kinetic Grand Championship (www.kineticuniverse.com), a wonderfully wacky competition that's part performance art, part engineering project, and part Tour de France. It features people-powered, all-terrain contraptions in a cross-country race, held every Memorial Day weekend since 1969. The museum is located along with other galleries in the **Ferndale Art & Cultural Center,** 580 Main St. (daily 10am–5pm). ⏱ 4 hr. Ferndale Chamber of Commerce ☎ 707/786-4477. www.victorianferndale.com.

The Best of the North in 5 Days

Now that you've experienced the sublime coastline in your first 3 days in the North (p. 216), it's time to cut inland. It's a long journey from the Pacific shore to the dramatic landscapes of Lassen, but you'll be traveling some of the country's most scenic byways. Along the route you'll traverse Bigfoot country (yes, Bigfoot), see one of California's architectural icons, and encounter volcanic peaks and bubbling hot springs.

> Pretty in pink, this flamboyant 1889 Victorian in Eureka was actually a wedding gift from William Carson—to his son.

START **Eureka, 19.6 miles north of Ferndale.**
TRIP LENGTH **218 miles, from Eureka to Lassen Volcanic National Park.**

1 Eureka. This port city, the North Coast's most important, was originally populated by the Wiyot, but in 1850 Europeans arrived and struck gold—literally. The city's Greek name ("I have found it"—also the state motto of California) was bestowed on it by happy prospectors, who moved in and pushed out the indigenous tribe (the city has a history of ethnic conflict—it expelled all Chinese during the height of California's sinophobia in 1882, an act that wasn't repealed until 1959).

1 Eureka
2 Willow Creek–China Flat Museum
3 Turtle Bay Exploration Park
4 Café at Turtle Bay
5 Lassen Volcanic National Park

And when the gold ran out, the locals discovered timber and fishing made pretty good sources of income. The city's 19th-century prosperity is evident in its Old Town's historic Victorian architecture, much of which still stands today in its original splendor, though a January 2010 earthquake did do some damage to a number of buildings. To get an appreciation for the skill and techniques needed to create the town's beautifully detailed structures, check out the **Blue Ox Millworks**, 1 X St. (☎ 707/444-3437; Mon–Fri 9am–5pm; $7.50), where craftsmen still use old-style tools to produce Victorian-style woodwork and you'll also find a small historical museum. ⏱ 2 hr. See p. 251, ❸.

Head north on Hwy. 101 through Arcata for 9.6 miles, then exit onto S.R. 299 East toward Weatherville/Redding. Continue on S.R. 299 for 37 miles to

❷ **Willow Creek–China Flat Museum.** The mountain community of Willow Creek is known as the "Gateway to Bigfoot Country" and the Willow Creek–China Flat Museum is better known as the Bigfoot Museum. It's a repository of all things related to the legendary apelike creature said to lurk in the woods of the Pacific Northwest. The name Bigfoot was actually coined by a logger in these parts in 1958, after he and his crew began discovering enormous footprints in the freshly dug earth

roster of exhibits and interactive displays focusing on art, history, and science, as well as a cool aquarium providing a fish-eye view of the inhabitants of the adjacent Sacramento River. Spanning the river and connecting the museum to the 220-acre ★ **McConnell Arboretum & Gardens** on the north side of the campus is one of California's architectural gems: the ★★ **Sundial Bridge.** Designed by Spanish superstar architect Santiago Calatrava—who has described it as resembling a bird in flight—this 700-foot-long pedestrian bridge is not only a strikingly elegant creation but also literally a working sundial. A towering 217-foot pylon casts its shadow onto a dial plate at the bridge's north end; the ingenious suspension design .anchored to the pylon has also allowed the salmon spawning habitat beneath the bridge to remain undisturbed. ⏱ 3–4 hr. 840 Sundial Bridge Dr. (aka Auditorium Dr.), off S.R. 44. ☎ 800/887-8532. www.turtlebay.org. Admission (museum and gardens) $13 adults, $9 seniors and kids 4–12, free for kids 3 & under; gardens only $4 per person, free for kids 3 & under; free admission to bridge. Museum: mid-Mar to Sept daily 9am–5pm; Oct to mid-Mar Wed–Sat 9am–4pm, Sun 10am–4pm. Gardens: daily 9am–5pm. Bridge: daily 6am–midnight.

> *Walk in style in Redding, where the spectacular, pedestrian-only Sundial Bridge spans the Sacramento River.*

of a new road. The find dovetailed with local Native American lore about a creature that lived along the Klamath River. This museum and its Bigfoot souvenirs are a must for all cryptozoologists (and you know who you are). Plus, you're guaranteed a sighting of the nearly 25-foot redwood Bigfoot sculpture standing guard outside the museum. ⏱ 45 min. 38949 S.R. 299. ☎ 530/629-2653. www.bigfoot country. net. Free admission (donations appreciated). May–Oct, Wed–Sun 10am–4pm; Nov–Apr by appointment.

Follow S.R. 299 to Redding. Total driving distance is 100 miles and trip time is 2 hr.

❸ ★★ kids **Turtle Bay Exploration Park.** The star attraction of Redding, the largest city in the far north, is this 300-acre museum and park complex. The **museum** features a changing

④ 🍴 **Café at Turtle Bay.** Affording expansive views of the Sacramento River's riparian environment and the awe-inspiring Sundial Bridge, this handsome, airy cafe is a great place to cool down (or warm up). It serves creative sandwiches, pizzas, and salads and has an espresso bar. Dinner is served on summer Friday and Saturday nights, accompanied by live music. 840 Sundial Dial Bridge Dr. ☎ 530/242-3181. www.turtlebay.org. Entrees $7–$15.

Overnight in Redding, then head east on S.R. 44 on the morning of Day 5. Lassen Volcanic National Park is 48 miles away; the drive should take about an hour.

❺ ★★★ **Lassen Volcanic National Park.** One of the country's least-visited national parks (no crowds!), **Lassen Volcanic National Park** is home to Lassen Peak, a 10,457-foot dormant (albeit still very much alive) volcano, the southernmost in a chain of volcanoes that stretches all the way to British Columbia in Canada. Lassen last blew its top in 1915, and the park remains a hotbed of volcanic and geothermal activity, featuring bubbling mud pots, hot springs, fumaroles, and geysers. The 108,000-acre park is also home to glacial lakes, sprawling meadows, and lush forests—the diverse nature of the territory accounts for the very wide range of flora (715 species) and fauna (mule deer and black bears feed here in summer). Don't let the name fool you—there's a lot scenic beauty here.

From the western entrance follow S.R. 89 through the heart of the park; many of Lassen's highlights are easily seen or accessed from this 33-mile-long road. ★ **Bumpass Hell** is the signature hike, an easy 1.5-mile trail to the park's largest concentration of hydrothermal features. Named for a 19th-century mountain man who had an unfortunate accident at this location, Bumpass Hell offers a fascinating look at Mother Nature in action with steaming vents and boiling pools that are starkly beautiful, albeit sulfurously stinky (think rotten eggs).

Before exiting the park, stop off at the ★ **Kohm Yah-mah-nee Visitor Center,** a LEED-certified green facility that opened in 2008; there's a gift shop, exhibits, and a cafe, and it's the site of ranger-led programs. **Note:** This area receives upwards of 40 feet of snow in winter and S.R. 89 through the park is usually closed from November to May (the park itself stays open). If the road is closed, continue along S.R. 44 toward Old Station, then circle around the park on the **Volcanic Legacy Scenic Byway** (www.volcaniclegacy-byway.org) to S.R. 36 heading to Westwood and Chester. You can pick up S.R. 89 again at Chester. ⏱ 4–5 hr. ☎ 530/595-4480. www.nps.gov/lavo. Admission (good for 7 days) $10 per car. Daily 24 hr. Kohm Yah-mah-nee Visitor Center: daily 9am–5pm. Bumpass Hell trail usually opens July 1; call before you go.

> *Raised walkways snake through a sulphur-scented setting of Bumpass Hell, dotted with volcanic vents and boiling pools.*

GOLDEN PROSE

A bumper crop of Northern California writers

BY HARRIOT MANLEY

	Jack London 1876–1918	John Steinbeck 1902–1968	Dashiell Hammett 1894–1961	Wallace Stegner 1909–1993
CLAIM TO FAME	Heroic man vs. wild novels and short stories.	Novelist focusing on the land and the human spirit; awarded a Pulitzer in 1940, a Nobel Prize in 1962.	Pioneering writer of whodunit mysteries starring hard-boiled detectives.	Novelist, essayist, teacher; often called the "dean of Western writing." Pulitzer in 1972.
BORN AND RAISED	Son of a wealthy (but sickly) unwed mother in San Francisco who married John London the year Jack was born; largely raised in the Bay Area by ex-slave Virginia Prentiss.	Son of working-class parents, he grew up in the farmlands of the Salinas Valley, which strongly influenced his writing.	Born in Maryland, he was a school dropout at age 13, eventually working as a detective for the famed Pinkerton Agency, a gritty job that served as grist for much of his writing.	Stegner was born in Iowa to immigrant parents, but was shuttled to various Western states and Canada as his father tried out a host of get-rich-quick schemes.
WEST COAST HANGOUTS	As a firebrand young man in Oakland, he repeatedly ran for mayor (and lost) under the Socialist ticket. An adventurer and sailor, he traveled extensively before settling at his beloved Beauty Ranch in the Sonoma Valley.	Worked on ranches as a youth, entering Stanford University in 1919. After a brief stint in New York, he settled in Pacific Grove. Buried in Salinas.	Married with two children, in 1922 Hammett moved to San Francisco, where he penned the first Sam Spade stories. In the mid-'30s, he headed to Hollywood and became a successful rewriter—and long-time lover of author Lillian Hellman.	Teaching took him to Harvard and other universities, but he finally settled at Stanford, where he was director of creative writing. At age 84, he died from injuries suffered in a car crash while driving to a lecture in Santa Fe, New Mexico.
CLASSIC LINE	". . . there was about him a suggestion of lurking ferocity, as though the Wild still lingered in him and the wolf in him merely slept." (from *White Fang*)	"Men do change, and change comes like a little wind that ruffles the curtains at dawn, and it comes like the stealthy perfume of wildflowers hidden in the grass." (from *Of Mice and Men*)	"When you're slapped, you'll take it and like it." (from *The Maltese Falcon*)	"Some are born in their place, some find it, some realize after long searching that the place they left is the one they have been searching for." (from *The Sense of Place*)
MUST-READ WORK	*The Call of the Wild*	*The Grapes of Wrath*	*The Maltese Falcon*	*Angle of Repose*

ACCORDING TO SCREEN LEGEND GLORIA SWANSON, "All creative people should be required to leave California for three months every year." Apparently, these writers didn't get Ms. Swanson's memo. Each of them either grew up or lived here for long periods, and were creatively inspired by the land and life around them—the rich waters of Monterey Bay or the noisy streets of San Francisco's Chinatown. Reading their words, you can almost feel, smell, and even taste the beauty of the Golden State, an invitation and a love story in one.

Lawrence Ferlinghetti 1919–	Amy Tan 1953–	Joan Didion 1934–	Anne Lamott 1954–
Beat Generation poet, publisher, bookstore owner.	Novelist focusing on Chinese-American life, drawing heavily from her own mother's and grandmother's lives.	Novelist, essayist, screenwriter; known for elegant prose and fierce intelligence.	Novelist known for self-effacing humor and moving accounts of addiction and faith.
Raised by his French aunt in France and then New York, he eventually settled in San Francisco in the early '50s.	A child of Chinese immigrants, she grew up in San Francisco's Chinatown, and later obtained degrees from various Northern California universities, including U.C. Berkeley.	Born in Sacramento, she was inspired to write later about the region's sweltering summers: "August comes on so hot not like a month, but like an affliction."	Grew up north of San Francisco in the coastal hamlet of Bolinas in a chaotic but loving home. Struggled with bulimia, drugs, and alcohol; she has been sober since 1986.
His influential City Lights Bookstore, operating in San Francisco since 1953, was home base for Beat Generation authors Alan Ginsberg and Jack Kerouac, whose work he published.	With her main home in Sausalito, just north of San Francisco in Marin County, she often does local readings or talks at local venues like tiny 142 Throckmorton Theater in Mill Valley, and Book Passage independent bookstore in Corte Madera.	Attended U.C. Berkeley. After a stint in New York, she settled for many years in L.A. where she and husband John Gregory Dunne were a popular screenwriting duo.	Hugely popular in her home turf of Marin County, north of San Francisco, Lamott is a regular at her inspirational church, St. Andrew Presbyterian in Marin City. Frequent speaker on the region's lecture circuit.
"Poetry isn't a secret society, It isn't a temple either." (from *Populist Manifesto, No. 1*)	"I don't know why he thought this was good, to imitate what foreigners did, as if everything Western were good, everything Chinese not so good." (from *The Kitchen God's Wife*).	"Here is the last stop for all those who come from somewhere else, for all those who drifted away from the cold and the past and the old ways." (from *Slouching Towards Bethlehem*)	**"...laughter is carbonated holiness."** (from *Plan B*)
A Coney Island of the Mind	*The Joy Luck Club*	*Play It As It Lays*	*Operating Instructions: A Journal of My Son's First Year*

The Best of the Northern Coast

Though Southern California's beaches are, by and large, sunny and sandy fun zones, the northern coastline is tough, rugged, and mysterious, maybe even a little dangerous (when was the last time anyone saw a bear on Santa Monica beach?). The north is California's dark and brooding bad-boy coastline, the James Dean and Marlon Brando of seasides. Sure, there's family fun aplenty here, but the north keeps it cool, literally and figuratively.

> A lone bird strolls along Stinson Beach, a local favorite despite its treacherous surf and freezing water.

START **Stinson Beach, 23 miles northwest of San Francisco. Take U.S. 101 to the Stinson Beach/ Hwy. 1 exit, then head west and follow the signs.** TRIP LENGTH **at least 5 days, about 400 miles.**

❶ ★★ **Stinson Beach.** This wide, 3½-mile-long beach provides Bay Area residents with their most So Cal–like beach experience. City-weary urbanites flock here on the occasional sunny day to kick back in the sand or fire up one of the barbecue grills at the adjacent park. Some even brave the frigid waters to surf and swim; lifeguards are on duty from late May to mid-September. There's a great little beach town with plenty of cafes, too. Janis Joplin loved the area so much her ashes were scattered along the coast here. **Note:** There can be strong riptides and the beach is well within Northern California's "Red Triangle," where a healthy percentage of the world's great white shark attacks have occurred. ☺ At least 30 min. ☎ 415/868-1922. www.nps.gov or www.stinsonbeachonline.com. Free admission. Daily 9am–sunset.

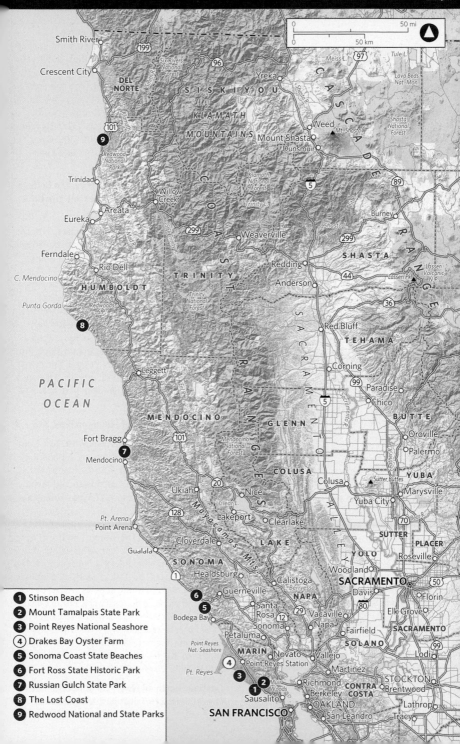

1 Stinson Beach
2 Mount Tamalpais State Park
3 Point Reyes National Seashore
4 Drakes Bay Oyster Farm
5 Sonoma Coast State Beaches
6 Fort Ross State Historic Park
7 Russian Gulch State Park
8 The Lost Coast
9 Redwood National and State Parks

> *Waves erode rocky cliffs into stranded formations called sea stacks, adding drama to the North Coast.*

Return to Hwy. 1 and head up Panoramic Highway, just south of Stinson Beach.

2 ★★ **Mount Tamalpais State Park.** See p. 217, **2**.

On Day 2, make your way north on Hwy. 1 to Point Reyes; it's about 14 miles from Stinson Beach.

3 ★★★ **Point Reyes National Seashore.** See p. 217, **3**.

④ 🦪 ★ **Drakes Bay Oyster Farm.** It's a real working oyster farm so don't expect much in the way of amenities, but if you want to slurp some superfresh bivalves, this is the place to come. You can either eat them at the picnic tables provided or take them to go. They'll show you how to properly shuck them, too. 17171 Sir Francis Drake Blvd. ☎ 415/669-1149. www.drakesbayfamilyfarms.com. $1–$2 per oyster.

On Day 3, continue north on Hwy. 1 to Bodega Bay. Distance is about 32 miles and trip time is 1 hr.

5 ★★ **Sonoma Coast State Beaches.** The 17 miles of beautiful and dramatic coastline from Bodega Bay to Jenner are collectively known as the Sonoma Coast State Beaches. Featuring rocky bluffs, secluded coves, natural arches, and sea stack formations, these are great beaches for tidepooling, strolling, and bird-watching, but water conditions are too dangerous for swimming. There are more than a dozen clearly marked access points along the highway, but even if you don't stop, this is a memorable drive. 🕐 At least 30 min. Off Hwy. 1 from Bodega Bay to north of Jenner. ☎ 707/875-3483. www.parks.ca.gov.

Drive 12 miles north of Jenner on Hwy. 1 to

6 ★ **Fort Ross State Historic Park.** The Cold War–era refrain of "the Russians are coming" was totally off the mark. The Russians had already been here. This reconstructed fort, originally established in 1812, was used as a base for Russian seal and otter hunting, and represented the farthest-flung outpost of the czarist empire. There are a handful of re-created buildings, including a Russian Orthodox chapel, and the only original structure, the Rotchev House. The park grounds also include a visitor center and museum, as well as beach trails and picnic grounds. 🕐 1 hr. 19005 Coast Hwy. 1. ☎ 707/847-3286. www.parks.ca.gov or www.fortrossstatepark.org. Admission $8 per car, $7 with a senior. Park: daily 30 min. before sunrise to 30 min. after sunset. Fort and visitor center: daily 10am–4:30pm.

Continue north on Hwy. 1 for about 80 miles (travel time: 2 hr.); just past Mendocino is

7 ★★ Russian Gulch State Park. This lush coastal canyon, perfectly framed by the arching span of the Frederick W. Panhorst Bridge, was named for the Russian fur trappers who founded Fort Ross (**6**) in the 19th century. It's highlighted by the **Devil's Punch Bowl,** a collapsed sea cave that forms a blowhole about 200 feet into the headland. When the tide is high, the huge punchbowl boils and bubbles. The bay here forms a sandy beach that's popular for swimming, diving, and fishing; inland, the **Waterfall Loop** trail (about 6 miles round-trip) leads to a 36-foot waterfall. Russian Gulch has a great campground, too. ⏲ At least 1 hr. ☎ 707/937-5804. www.parks.ca.gov. Admission $8 per car, $7 with a senior. Call for current hours.

On Day 4, head north on Hwy. 1 until it merges with U.S. 101; at Phillipsville you'll meet up with the Avenue of the Giants (p. 221, **6**). It's 85.7 miles and 2½ hr. to reach this legendary redwood grove. At Weott, head west on Mattole Rd. to start the Lost Coast loop.

8 ★★★ The Lost Coast. This part of the region isn't so much lost as it is stubborn—its daunting topography refused to yield to the engineers building Hwy. 1. It remains perhaps the most remote stretch of coastline in the contiguous United States, where bears forage on the black-sand beaches (the result of tectonic activity in the area). This route skirts the more impenetrable parts of the federally owned 60,000-acre King Range National Conservation Area, and though it passes through the tiny towns of Honeydew and Petrolia, it will still give you a taste of this untamed and largely undeveloped region. ⏲ 4 hr. www.redwoods.info or www.sheltercove-lostcoast.com.

Mattole Rd. becomes Petrolia Rd. which will take you to Ferndale (p. 221, **7**). You can overnight in the Ferndale area, then on Day 5 rejoin U.S. 101 and head north to the Thomas H. Kuchel Visitor Center, a mile south of Orick (p 253, **6**). Total distance is 62 miles (trip time 1¼ hr.).

9 ★★★ Redwood National and State Parks. An assemblage of several coastal redwood parks, these 132,000 acres comprise a designated World Heritage Site and International

> *Skyscraping coast redwoods shade the forest floor, which grows thick with ferns and moss.*

Biosphere Reserve filled with a variety of flora and fauna. Your first stop should be the **Thomas H. Kuchel Visitor Center** (daily 9am–6pm summer, 9am–4pm winter) to peruse its state-of-the-art nature exhibits and pick up a map. Highlights of the park include ★ **Lady Bird Johnson Grove,** a 1-mile loop trail through a lush grove of the park's famous towering giants that's named for the First Lady who dedicated it; the gray sands of ★ **Gold Bluffs Beach;** the primeval ★ **Fern Canyon,** whose lush, fern-covered walls have appeared in a number of films; the **Newton B. Drury Scenic Parkway,** a 10-mile-long rival of the Avenue of the Giants (p. 221, **6**) that passes by the **Big Tree Wayside** (whose namesake tree is 304 feet tall).

   Note: The park is generally cool (40°–60°F/4°–16°C) year-round and often foggy; dress appropriately. ⏲ At least 3 hr. ☎ 707/464-6101. www.nps.gov/redw. Free admission. Day use of campgrounds $8 per car, $7 with a senior. Daily 24 hr.

From the Newton B. Drury Scenic Byway, you can loop back onto Hwy. 101.

The Best of the Far North

In California's far north you'll encounter man-made marvels such as Shasta Dam and jaw-dropping natural ones like mystical Mount Shasta. Much of this route will take you along the Volcanic Legacy Scenic Byway, one of 31 federally designated "All-American Roads" celebrating the country's historic, scenic, and recreational highlights. From the educational wonders of Turtle Bay Exploration Park to the otherworldly landscape of Lava Bed National Monument, the state's northern reaches offer splendors you won't soon forget.

> *Erupting from the flat valley around it, 14,162-foot Mount Shasta is an undeniable jaw-dropper.*

START Redding is 158 miles north of Sacramento. **TRIP LENGTH** at least 6 days, about 363 miles.

1 ★★ kids **Turtle Bay Exploration Park.** This 300-acre campus explores man's relationship with the natural world through a museum focusing on science, nature, and Native American history (wander through a re-creation of a bark house); an underground aquarium; meticulously maintained gardens and walking trails; and a seasonal butterfly house. The complex is bisected by the Sacramento River, which is crossed by the sensational ★★ Sundial Bridge, a modernist wonder of engineering and design. See p. 224, **3**.

On Day 2, from Redding take I-5 north to Shasta Dam Blvd. (aka Hwy. 151) and head west to Shasta Dam. Distance: about 14 miles (trip time: 20 min.).

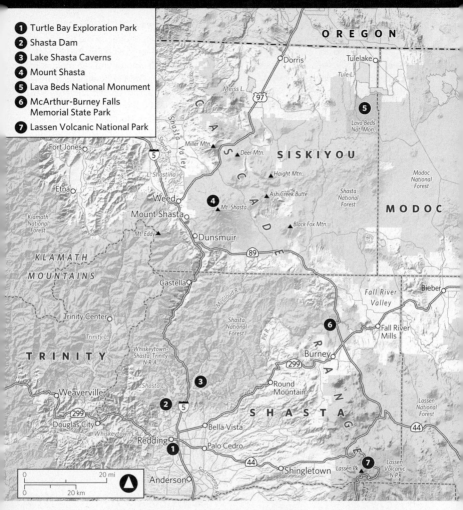

1 Turtle Bay Exploration Park
2 Shasta Dam
3 Lake Shasta Caverns
4 Mount Shasta
5 Lava Beds National Monument
6 McArthur-Burney Falls Memorial State Park
7 Lassen Volcanic National Park

2 ★ **Shasta Dam.** Whatever your feelings about dams (and this one did obliterate Native American homes and sacred spots)—this is truly an impressive sight. Shasta Dam is more than 3,400 feet long and 602 feet high (the second largest in the U.S.); when completed in 1944, it was one of the era's great feats of civil engineering. The overflow that cascades down the dam makes for the world's biggest man-made waterfall, some three times higher than Niagara Falls. You can walk across the dam's span and cast your gaze out on some of Shasta Lake's 365 miles of shoreline. Hour-long tours that take you within the bowels of the structure are offered daily (tours are free,

but require a ticket from the visitor center). ⏱ At least 1 hr. ☎ 530/275-4463. www. shastalake.com. Free admission. Visitor center daily 8am–4:30pm (5pm in summer). Tours daily 9am, 10:15am, 11:30am, 1pm, 2:15pm & 3:30pm summer; 9am, 11am, 1pm & 3pm winter.

Head north on I-5 for about 10 miles to exit 695 and go east on Shasta Caverns Rd. for 1½ miles; the road dead ends in the parking lot for the Lake Shasta Caverns concessionaire.

3 ★ **Lake Shasta Caverns.** You'll take a scenic 15-minute catamaran ride across Shasta Lake, then a short but steep bus ride to reach these limestone caves, dating back nearly 200

million years. With eight different "rooms," these caverns offer all the *Journey to the Center of the Earth* ambience you could ask for: stalactites, stalagmites, columns, and massive "draperies" that resemble melting wax. *Note:* There's lots of stair climbing involved. ⏱ 2 hr. 20359 Shasta Caverns Rd., Lakehead. ☎ 800/795-2283 or 530/238-2341. www.lakeshastacaverns.com. Admission $22 adults, $13 kids 3–15.Tours daily every 30 min. 9am–4pm Jun–Aug; every hour 9am–3pm Apr–May and Sept; 10am, noon & 2pm Oct–Mar.

Return to I-5 and head north about 45 miles (trip time: 45 min.), to Mount Shasta. Overnight here to get an early start on Day 3.

④ ★★★ Mount Shasta. Native American tribes revered it; Sierra Club founder John Muir said his "blood turned to wine" upon first seeing it; and New Agers celebrate it as an energy vortex. Capped in snow year-round, this mountain is as dramatic as they come—a 14,162-foot dormant volcano with a diameter of 20 miles that dwarfs everything around it. Exploring Shasta is easy thanks to the **Everitt**

Memorial Highway, which winds 14 miles up the mountain. Depending on the time of year, you may be able to go as far as **Bunny Flat** (mile 11); by midsummer you can make it to the road's end at **Old Ski Bowl,** which provides panoramic views from an elevation of 7,900 feet. You can set out on day hikes from either location. ⏱ At least 3 hr. ☎ 530/926-5555 for recorded weather and climbing information. www.mtshastachamber.com. Mount Shasta Ranger Station, 204 W. Alma St. ☎ 530/926-4511. www.fs.fed.us. Daily 8am–4:30pm (call to confirm).

On Day 4, travel north on I-5 to U.S. 97; at Weed, you are motoring along the Volcanic Legacy Scenic Byway. Just past Dorris, head east on U.S. 161, skimming the Oregon border, then go south on Hill Rd. into Lava Beds National Monument. Total distance is about 100 miles (trip time: 2¾ hr.).

⑤ ★★ Lava Beds National Monument. Established as a national monument in 1925, this remote and desolate high-desert plateau covering 46,000 acres is starkly beautiful,

> *Adventure deep into the earth at Lake Shasta Caverns, a spectacular limestone labyrinth dating back 250 million years.*

geologically rich, and culturally significant. More than 700 lava-tube caves (the largest concentration of them in North America) honeycomb this volcanically active region—begin your spelunking experience at **Mushpot Cave,** a lighted, easily accessed cave near the visitor center.

Despite the harsh environment, the ancient pictographs found at Lava Beds (**Symbol Bridge** and **Painted Cave** are good examples and close to the visitor center) bear witness to the fact this is one of the longest continuously inhabited sites in North America. It was also the location of the Modoc War (1872–73), California's only full-fledged Indian campaign, a brutal, costly affair that pitted Chief Kintpuash aka "Captain Jack" (1837–73) and his band of about 50 Modoc warriors against U.S. Army and Cavalry troops. Hike **Captain Jacks Stronghold,** a natural lava-rock fortress where Captain Jack and his men held out for 5 months against an army that outnumbered them 10 to 1. ☉ At least 3 hr. ☎ 530/667-8100. www.nps.gov/labe. Admission $10 per car (good for 7 days). No credit cards. Visitor center daily 8am–6pm summer; 8:30am–5pm remainder of year.

On Day 5, make your way back down U.S. 97 to I-5 South, and continue along the Volcanic Legacy byway south on U.S. 89 (distance: 152 miles; trip time: 4 hr.) past the town of Mount Shasta to

❻ ★★★ McArthur-Burney Falls Memorial State Park. Underground springs feed this park's achingly pretty twin waterfalls (Teddy Roosevelt allegedly called them the "Eighth Wonder of the World"), where each day 100 million gallons of water tumble 129 feet into an emerald-green pool. Cool off in the falls' iridescent mist or take a hike—there are 5 miles of hiking trails throughout the 910-acre park, which was considered a sacred site by the indigenous people of the region and is now a national landmark. ☉ At least 1 hr. 24898 Hwy. 89. ☎ 530/335-2777. www.parks.ca.gov. Admission $8 per car, $7 with a senior. Daily sunrise–sunset. Overnight camping available.

On Day 6, continue south on Hwy. 89 to Lassen Volcanic National Park. Distance is 42 miles (trip time: 1 hr.).

> Tumbling 129 feet, Burney Falls benefits from the region's porous volcanic soils, which quickly drain springs, creeks, and rivers.

❼ ★★★ Lassen Volcanic National Park. Lassen Peak, a 10,457-foot dormant volcano stands sentry over this park; aside from Mount St. Helens in Washington, it's the only Cascade volcano to erupt in the last century (1915). Evidence of that explosion can still be seen today in the aptly named Devastated Area, a swath of territory to the north of the mountain that's gradually being repopulated with conifer forests. Hwy. 89 cuts right through the park, but during winter and spring (snowfall in winter can exceed 600 inches in some parts of the park) you'll need to take a scenic detour along Hwy. 44 and Hwy. 36. See p. 224, ❺.

The North: Outdoor Adventures A to Z

Bicycling
★★ **Point Reyes Outdoors.** All the gear you need for biking through stunning Point Reyes National Seashore (p. 217, ❸); guided tours are available, too. 11401 State Route 1, Point Reyes Station. ☎ 415/663-8192. www.pointreyes outdoors.com. Rentals $15 per hour, $42 full day.

Boating/Whale-Watching
★ **All Aboard Adventures.** Two-hour whale-watching cruises aboard the 45-foot *Sea Hawk* (Dec–Apr); deep-sea fishing charters are also available. 32400 N. Harbor Dr., Fort Bragg. ☎ 707/964-1881. www.allaboard adventures.com. Cruises $35 per person.

★ kids **Humboldt Bay Harbor Cruise.** Narrated cruises aboard the *Madaket*, a ferry built in 1910, making it the country's oldest vessel in continuous service. Eureka Boardwalk at F St., Eureka. ☎ 707/445-1910. www.humboldtbay

maritimemuseum.com. Cruises $18 adults, $16 seniors and kids 13–17, $10 kids 5–12.

kids **Packers Bay Marina.** From May through September, Shasta Lake becomes "the house-boat capital of the west." Explore, swim, fish, or party on the lake aboard your own luxury houseboat. There's a 3-day minimum; mid-summer rates start around $1,300. 16814 Packers Bay Rd., Lakehead. ☎ 800/331-3137 or 530/275-5570. www.packersbay.com.

Camping
Many state and national parks offer opportunities for overnight stays, with facilities ranging from easily accessed car camping to remote, hike-in primitive sites. Some camp-grounds take reservations, others don't; some divide their inventory into reserved and first-come, first-served. Especially during the summer months, it's always worth trying to book

> On a roll in Pt. Reyes, a popular destination for pro and amateur cyclists.

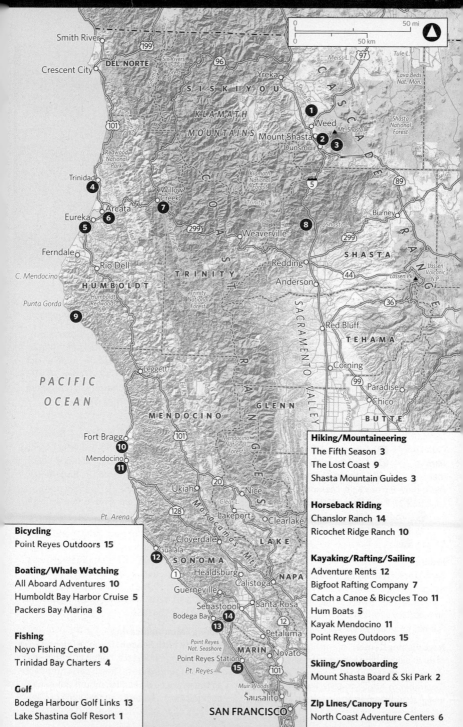

Hiking/Mountaineering
The Fifth Season **3**
The Lost Coast **9**
Shasta Mountain Guides **3**

Horseback Riding
Chanslor Ranch **14**
Ricochet Ridge Ranch **10**

Kayaking/Rafting/Sailing
Adventure Rents **12**
Bigfoot Rafting Company **7**
Catch a Canoe & Bicycles Too **11**
Hum Boats **5**
Kayak Mendocino **11**
Point Reyes Outdoors **15**

Skiing/Snowboarding
Mount Shasta Board & Ski Park **2**

Zip Lines/Canopy Tours
North Coast Adventure Centers **6**

Bicycling
Point Reyes Outdoors **15**

Boating/Whale Watching
All Aboard Adventures **10**
Humboldt Bay Harbor Cruise **5**
Packers Bay Marina **8**

Fishing
Noyo Fishing Center **10**
Trinidad Bay Charters **4**

Golf
Bodega Harbour Golf Links **13**
Lake Shastina Golf Resort **1**

> *With views this good, who cares if you make par at Bodega Harbor Golf Links.*

ahead; some park reservations can be made up to 6 months in advance. Fees are generally $15 to $35. For state campgrounds contact **Reserve America** (☎ 800/444-7275; www.reserveamerica.com), for national campgrounds contact the feds at ☎ 877/444-6777 or www.recreation.gov. When in doubt, check a park's website for camping info.

Some of the far north's best camping can be found at **Humboldt Redwoods State Park** (p. 221, ⑥), **Lassen Volcanic National Park** (p.224, ⑤), **Lava Beds National Monument** (p. 234, ⑤), **Mount Shasta** (p. 234, ④), **McArthur-Burney Falls Memorial State Park** (p. 235, ⑥), **Point Reyes National Seashore** (p. 217, ③), **Redwood National and State Parks** (p. 231, ⑨), and **Russian Gulch State Park** (p. 231, ⑦).

Fishing
Jack Trout Fly-Fishing Guide. Guided fly-fishing outings to the Klamath, Trinity, McCloud, and other rivers in the Mount Shasta area. ☎ 530/926-4540. www.jacktrout.com. Full-day excursions $375 for 1–2 people.

Noyo Fishing Center. Hit the high seas in search of tuna, halibut, and (when possible) salmon. Whale-watching excursions are available from December to April. 32440 N. Harbor Dr., Fort Bragg. ☎ 707/964-3000. www.fortbraggfishing.

com. Fishing expeditions $65–$100 per person.

Trinidad Bay Charters. All your gear is provided as you work the light tackle for black rockfish and lingcod aboard the **Jumpin' Jack**. Trinidad Harbor. ☎ 800/839-4744 or 707/839-4743. www.trinidadbaycharters.net. $100 per person. Two trips daily, May–Sept.

Golf
★★ **Bodega Harbour Golf Links.** A Scottish links-style course designed by Robert Trent Jones, Jr., and set on the distractingly beautiful Sonoma Coast. 21301 Heron Dr., Bodega Bay. ☎ 866/905-4657 or 707/875-3538. www.bodegaharbourgolf.com. Greens fees $45–$90.

★ **Lake Shastina Golf Resort.** The ubiquitous Robert Trent Joneses, senior and junior, teamed up on the design of this resort's main 18-hole course, where Mount Shasta looms in the background. There's also a 9-hole links course. 5925 Country Club Dr., Weed. ☎ 530/938-3205. www.lakeshastinagolf.com. Greens fees $24–$53.

Hiking/Mountaineering
★★★ **The Fifth Season.** If you're interested in climbing Mount Shasta, check in at this specialty outdoors outfit. They'll sell or rent you all the gear you'll need for mountaineering or backpacking. The professional staff can give you lots of great advice, too. 300 N. Mount

Shasta Blvd., Mount Shasta. ☎ 530/926-3606. www.thefifthseason.com.

★★★ The Lost Coast. Serious hikers may want to tackle a leg of the 35-mile Lost Coast Trail, which stretches along the forbiddingly named region that remains one of the country's most pristine coastal wildernesses. Isolated within the Sinkyone Wilderness State Park (www. parks.ca.gov) and the King Range National Conservation Area (www.blm.gov/ca/arcata), the trail is sometimes nothing more than just black-sand beach (and impassable at high tide). Day hikers can set out from the fishing hamlet of Shelter Cove; take the Briceland-Shelter Cove Road from Hwy. 101, 22 miles to Beach Road and turn right to the Black Sands Beach trail head (p. 250, ❶). Campers will need a tide chart and bear canisters.

★★★ Shasta Mountain Guides. Though it is physically strenuous (it takes about 8 hr.), you don't have to be a Sherpa to summit Mount Shasta. These folks can get you to the top. ☎ 530/926-3117. www.shastaguides.com. Rates start at $125 (a basic mountaineering expedition). 2-day climb about $450 per person.

Horseback Riding

★★ Chanslor Ranch. Ever dream of galloping along a deserted beach with your hair flying and the waves crashing? You can check that one off the list. 16702 Hwy. 1 (3 miles south of Bodega Bay at the Sonoma Coast Villa). ☎ 707/876-3374. www.chanslorranch.com . Rates start at $50 per person.

★★ kids Ricochet Ridge Ranch. Beginners and advanced riders can try the ranch's daily, multiday, or custom rides on English and Western saddles. Ride on a beach or through a redwood forest (or both) along the Mendocino Coast. 24201 N. Hwy. 1, Fort Bragg. ☎ 888/873-5777 or 707/964-7669. www.horse-vacation. com. Trail rides start at $45 per person.

Kayaking/Rafting/Sailing

★★ Adventure Rents. Single and tandem kayaks, as well as canoes, are available for paddling the Gualala River through a redwood forest. Hwy. 1 in Gualala. ☎ 888/881-4386 or 707/884-4386. www.adventurerents.com. Rates start at $30 per person for 2 hr.

★★ kids Bigfoot Rafting Company. White-water rafting trips along the Trinity and Klamath rivers, lasting from 3½ hours to 4 days. Inflatable kayaks and rafts are for rent, as well. Willow Creek. ☎ 800/722-2223 or 530/629-2263. www.bigfootrafting.com. Rentals start at $32. Tours start at $65 adults, $59 kids 12 & under (kids 10–16 on some trips).

★★★ kids Catch a Canoe & Bicycles Too. Canoes, kayaks, and cool outriggers can be rented here for exploring Mendocino's Big River; guided tours in a nine-person outrigger search out birds and (in summer) nighttime glow-in-the-dark bioluminescence. N. Hwy. 1 at Comptche Ukiah Rd. (at the Stanford Inn), Mendocino. ☎ 707/937-0273. www.catchacanoe.com. Rentals $28 for 3 hr. Tours $45 per person.

★ Hum Boats. Kayak rentals and guided tours (whale-watching, full-moon paddles) in the Humboldt Bay National Wildlife Refuge. Dock A, Woodley Island Marina, Eureka. ☎ 707/443-5157. www.humboats.com. Rentals start at $15 per hour. Tours start at $35 per person.

Kayak Mendocino. Guided sea-kayak tours into caves of the Mendocino coast; no experience necessary and all ages are welcome. ☎ 707/964-7480. www.kayakmendocino.com. Tours start at $50 per person.

★★★ Point Reyes Outdoors. A variety of naturalist-guided sea-kayaking tours through the waterways of the Point Reyes National Seashore. 11401 State Route 1, Point Reyes Station. ☎ 415/663-8192. www.pointreyesoutdoors.com. Tours $85–$120 per person.

Skiing/Snowboarding

★ Mount Shasta Board & Ski Park. There's a snowboarder-centric terrain park with challenging features such as "The Dragon" and "Wallaphant," but this ski park still has plenty of room for skiers and boarders of all skill levels. 104 Siskiyou Ave., Mount Shasta. ☎ 800/754-7427 or 530/926-8610. www. skipark.com. Adult lift tickets $39.

Zip Lines/Canopy Tours

★★ North Coast Adventure Centers. Climb, zip, and rappel 70 feet up through a redwood canopy. 1036 K St., Arcata. ☎ 800/808-2836. www.northcoastadventurecenters.com. Canopy tours start at $65.

The Sonoma Coast

This wind-swept coastline dotted with small towns is distinctly different from its more high-profile inland neighbor, the Sonoma Valley. Along the Sonoma Coast it's more about beachcombing than grape growing, and there are miles of dramatic beaches, bays, and coves to explore.

> *Pockets of soft sand make appealing—and often surprisingly empty—retreats on the coast of Bodega Head.*

START **Point Reyes National Seashore** is about 35 miles northwest of San Francisco. Drive north along U.S. 101 to the Stinson Beach/Hwy. 1 exit, then head north on scenic Hwy. 1. Note that the drive can take 90 min. because of slow traffic. TRIP LENGTH **2 days, about 95 miles.**

1 ★★★ **Point Reyes National Seashore.** This spectacular natural and cultural resource is separated from mainland California by the famous (and famously unstable) San Andreas Fault. See p. 217, **3**. ☉ At least 3 hr.

On Day 2, head north on Hwy. 1 for 33 miles to

2 **Bodega Bay.** Mostly a working fishing town supporting a fleet several hundred strong, Bodega Bay is nonetheless a tourist draw, too. There are shops and galleries to peruse, and the **Tides Wharf** is a fascinating and entertaining spot to watch the fishing boats unload their catch of the day.

Protecting the bay is ★ **Bodega Head State Park** (www.parks.ca.gov), a craggy headland that offers a great vantage point from which to watch the gray-whale migration that takes place January through April. **Doran Beach** (www.sonoma-county.org/parks), just south of Bodega Bay, offers 2 miles of sand and dunes, making it an important bird sanctuary, as well as the only beach safe for swimming for miles around. Parking is $6.

And speaking of birds, Bodega Bay is most famous as the setting for Alfred Hitchcock's 1961 ecohorror film, *The Birds*. Head inland a few miles on Hwy. 1 to the town of **Bodega,** where you'll find the **Potter Schoolhouse** and **St. Teresa's Church,** both featured locations in the film. ☉ 1½ hr. Bodega Bay Visitors Center, 850 Hwy. 1. ☎ 707/875-3866. www.bodegabay.com. Mon–Sat 9am–5pm; Sun 10am–5pm.

Head north on Hwy. 1 for about 22 miles to

3 ★ **Fort Ross State Historic Park.** This reconstructed fort shows what life was like for the Russian fur traders who lived here in the early19th century. See p. 230, **6**. ☉ 1 hr.

Drive 40 miles north on Hwy. 1 to

> A beacon blinking since 1908, the Point Arena
Lighthouse offers tours, views, and a chance to stay
in a light keeper's cabin.

❹ ★ Point Arena Lighthouse. Climb to the
top of this 115-foot (that's 145 steps!) working
lighthouse—the view is amazing. The original
lighthouse was built here in 1870 but was
destroyed in the 1906 earthquake; the current six-story lighthouse began operation in
1908. The impressive lens at the top is made
up of 666 separate prisms and worth about
$3.5 million. There are guided and self-guided
tours, as well as a museum and gift shop.
⏱ 45 min. 45500 Lighthouse Rd., Point Arena.
☎ 877/725-4448 or 707/882-2777. www.point
arenalighthouse.com. Admission $7.50 adults,
$1 kids 11 & under. Daily 10am–3pm.

Watch Your Back

The beaches of the Sonoma Coast, and
those all along the state's northern
reaches, are notorious for very dangerous
water conditions, including rogue waves.
Because of the shore's steep drop-off,
these large waves can appear suddenly
and sweep unsuspecting victims out to sea.
Always keep your eyes on the water when
you are anywhere near the shoreline, and
most definitely keep an eye on children at
all times.

❶ Point Reyes
National Seashore

❷ Bodega Bay

❸ Fort Ross State
Historic Park

❹ Point Arena Lighthouse

Where to Stay
Bodega Harbor Inn **7**
Jenner Inn & Cottages **6**
Manka's Inverness
   Lodge **9**
St. Orres **5**

Where to Dine
Nick's Cove
   Restaurant **8**
River's End **6**
St. Orres Restaurant **5**
Station House Café **10**

Where to Stay & Dine

> *Feel like a baron in the richly decorated rooms of Manka's Inverness Lodge, a turn-of-the-20th-century, Craftsman-style compound.*

★ Bodega Harbor Inn BODEGA BAY

Set on the bluffs overlooking Bodega Harbor, this impeccably kept property is one of the best values along the Sonoma Coast. Rooms are small, but well kept, and the lawns have fabulous water views. 1345 Bodega Ave. ☎ 707/875-3594. www.bodegaharborinn.com. 21 units. Doubles $80–$155 w/breakfast. MC, V.

★ Jenner Inn & Cottages JENNER

Popular with honeymooners, this collection of individually decorated rooms, suites, and cottages is located where the Russian River meets the Pacific Ocean—you can get views of either (or both). You can also get such amenities as kitchens, fireplaces, and hot tubs. 10400 Hwy. 1. ☎ 800/732-2377 or 707/865-2377. www.jennerinn.com. 23 units. Doubles $118–$378. AE, MC, V.

★★★ Manka's Inverness Lodge INVERNESS

Adjacent to the Point Reyes National Seashore, this collection of luxuriously rustic and romantic accommodations was once a hunting-and-fishing-lodge compound, dating back to the early 1900s. Amenities include fireplaces, outdoor showers, and private gourmet meals. 30 Callendar Way (at Argyle St., off Sir Francis Drake Blvd.). ☎ 415/669-1034. www.mankas.com. 14 units. Doubles $215–$385. AE, MC, V.

★★★ Nick's Cove Restaurant MARSHALL

NORTH COAST CUISINE This old roadhouse complex from the 1930s has been renovated by renowned restaurateur Pat Kuleto into something special. Set along the Tomales Bay, Nick's features fresh, local seafood and oysters, and every table has a view. 23240 Hwy. 1. ☎ 866/636-4257 or 415/663-1033. www.nickscove.com. Entrees $8–$29. AE, DISC, MC, V. Breakfast, lunch & dinner daily. Map p. 241.

★ River's End JENNER *INTERNATIONAL*

You can come here for the gorgeous view

> *A sun-splashed day at St. Orres Restaurant, where daily dishes might feature local salmon or freshly foraged mushrooms.*

alone, but the memory of its excellent international cuisine will linger. The menu incorporates local everything: crab, halibut, lamb, poultry, cheese, wine, and beer. 11048 Hwy. 1. ☎ 707/865-2484, ext. 111. www.ilove sunsets.com. Entrees $13–$37. DISC, MC, V. Dinner Thurs–Mon; lunch only in summer.

★★ **St. Orres** GUALALA
Uncle Vanya would feel right at home at this fantastic, rough-hewn Russian-style property, complete with onion domes. A full breakfast is included, but you might have to share a bathroom. 36601 Hwy. 1. ☎ 707/884-3303. www. saintorres.com. 22 units, 8 rooms share 3 bathrooms. Doubles $95–$135; cottages $140–$445. Rates include breakfast. MC, V.

★★ **St. Orres Restaurant** GUALALA *NORTH COAST CUISINE* This acclaimed restaurant at the whimsical Russian-themed St. Orres hotel works with local purveyors, who supply it with fresh, seasonal product. Chef Rosemary Campiformio has dubbed her fare North Coast cuisine—look for rich, sophisticated items such as pan-roasted wild salmon or pheasant breast stuffed with andouille sausage. 36601 Hwy. 1. ☎ 707/884-3335. www.saintorres.com. Prix-fixe dinner menu $45 (does not include appetizers or dessert). MC, V. Dinner daily.

★ **Station House Café** POINT REYES STATION *AMERICAN* After working up an appetite hiking through Point Reyes National Seashore, fill up here on local, organic, sustainable products, such as a Niman Ranch beef burger. There's a full bar and an outdoor garden dining area, too. 11180 State Route 1. ☎ 415/663-1515. www.stationhousecafe.com. Entrees $7–$18. AE, DISC, MC, V. Breakfast, lunch & dinner Thurs–Tues.

The Mendocino Coast

The Mendocino Coast has it all: small-town charm and urbane sophistication, killer campgrounds and high-end B&Bs, surging seas and towering redwoods. The star of the region is the town of Mendocino itself where a Victorian past is perfectly preserved, seasoned with plenty of 21st-century amenities.

> With real-town grit and a gorgeous setting, Fort Bragg has become a sneaky favorite of in-the-know travelers.

START Mendocino, 155 miles north of San Francisco. TRIP LENGTH 3 days.

SITE GUIDE
PAGE 247

❶ ★★★ **Mendocino.** Set atop a headland surrounded by the Pacific, beautiful Mendocino looks so much like an old New England fishing town, it was used as a stand-in for Cabot Cove, Maine, the fictional home of TV sleuth Jessica Fletcher (played by Angela Lansbury) in the long-running series *Murder, She Wrote*.

From Mendocino, on Day 2 head south on Hwy. 1 for 3 miles to

❷ ★★ **Van Damme State Park.** With the collapse of the local lumber industry, the once-thriving lumber town and port of Little River (birthplace of Charles Van Damme, a ferry operator and the park's namesake) was swallowed up by the forest and became official state parkland in 1934. Today, there's a beach popular for abalone diving and kayaking (a concession is on-site), a campground, and 10 miles of trails. The lush Fern Canyon Trail

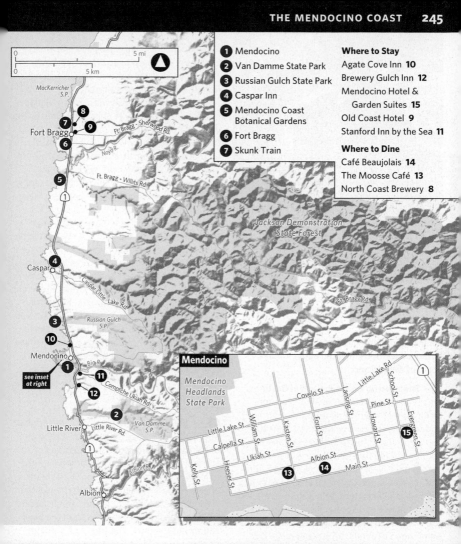

1 Mendocino
2 Van Damme State Park
3 Russian Gulch State Park
4 Caspar Inn
5 Mendocino Coast Botanical Gardens
6 Fort Bragg
7 Skunk Train

Where to Stay
Agate Cove Inn 10
Brewery Gulch Inn 12
Mendocino Hotel & Garden Suites 15
Old Coast Hotel 9
Stanford Inn by the Sea 11

Where to Dine
Café Beaujolais 14
The Moosse Café 13
North Coast Brewery 8

parallels the Little River; the unique Pygmy Forest features a stymied grove of mature cypress and pine trees that range in height from 6 inches to 8 feet. ⏱ At least 1 hr. 8125 N. Hwy. 1. ☎ 707/937-5804. www.parks.ca.gov. Admission $8 per car, $7 with a senior.

Two miles north of Mendocino on Hwy. 1. is

3 ★★ **Russian Gulch State Park.** Another stellar coastal park and campground, it's highlighted by a 36-foot waterfall (reached via an abandoned logging road) and the **Devil's Punch Bowl,** a collapsed sea cave that has formed a natural cauldron 100 feet in diameter and 60 feet deep. At high tide this

blowhole roils and bubbles with seawater. ⏱ At least 1 hr. See p. 231, 7 .

Two miles north of the park, from Hwy. 1, make a left on Caspar St., then a left on Caspar Rd.

4 ★ **Caspar Inn.** This roadhouse dating from 1906 would be a great find anywhere, but along the nightlife-deprived Mendocino Coast, it's especially welcome. You'll find live music and DJs nightly, playing everything from hip-hop and reggae to rock and bluegrass. 14957 Caspar Rd., Caspar. ☎ 707/964-5565; www.casparinn. com. Cover $5-$10. Tues-Sat 5pm-2am; Sun 8:30pm-1:30am.

> *Earlier versions of the Skunk Train got the railway its name, with locals saying you could "smell 'em before you see 'em."*

On Day 3, continue up Hwy. 1 to the Coast Botanical Gardens, located about 7 miles north of Mendocino.

⑤ ★ Mendocino Coast Botanical Gardens. This relaxing and contemplative bluff-top facility grows everything from fragrant rhododendrons (blooming in spring) to heaths and heathers, to fuchsias and azaleas—just about anything that can thrive in the region's coastal fog. There's also a sculpture garden and vegetable patch. The lovely and easy hiking trails are also great for birders—some 150 species have been spotted here. 18220 N. Hwy. 1. ☎ 707/964-4352. www.gardenbythesea.org. Admission $10 adults, $7.50 seniors, $4 kids 13–17, $2 kids 6–12, free for kids 5 & under. Daily Mar–Oct 9am to 5pm; Nov–Feb 9am–4pm.

Continue north on Hwy. 1, for 2 miles to

⑥ Fort Bragg. The commercial hub of the Mendocino Coast, Fort Bragg was founded as an Indian reservation and military post in the mid-19th century. By the 1870s, the reservation was disbanded and the land sold to settlers for $1.25 an acre. Lumber and fishing became the town's bread and butter, with tourism now playing a key role. You can learn about Fort Bragg's history at the **Guest House Museum,** 343 N. Main St. (☎ 707/964-4251; www.fortbragg history.org; hours vary, so call ahead), a fine old redwood mansion once used as a guesthouse for lumber company executives. Nearby at 430 N. Franklin St. is the only remaining building from the town's days as a fort.

While not as precious and artsy as Mendocino, there is still plenty to enjoy here. Stop by the local Chamber of Commerce, 332 N. Main St. (☎ 707/961-6300; www.mendocinocoast.com) for maps and information about special events. Then, spend some time wandering the town's main shopping district, a collection of galleries, boutiques, and antiques stores between Main and Franklin and Redwood and Fir streets.

At the south end of town is pretty **Noyo Harbor,** where you can join a whale-watching excursion (Dec–Apr) or fishing charter, or rent a kayak. At the north end of town is **Glass Beach** (head west on Elm St.), where Mother Nature has turned trash to treasure. Beginning in 1949, and for nearly 20 years thereafter, this place was a dump. Literally. Garbage was thrown over the cliff and left for the tides to claim. Decades of pounding wave action have turned broken glass and refuse into smooth, colorful rocks and pebbles (with the occasional piece of junk still visible); you'll find tide pools here, too. ⏱ At least 2 hr.

⑦ ★★ Skunk Train. It may lack name appeal, but this is Fort Bragg's biggest draw and one of the most popular tourist attractions on the Northern Coast. A fleet of locomotives—the coolest being a mint-condition 1924 steam engine—takes passengers along the old Redwood Route, a logging rail line established in 1885 to transport felled trees from the backcountry to the port. The trains cut through remote redwood groves, traveling through two mountain tunnels and across more than 30 bridges and trestles along the evergreen Noyo River Canyon. A special treat is the summertime sunset barbecue ride. And if you're wondering about that funky name: It was bestowed in 1925 when the line switched from steam to gas engines, and you could "smell them before you saw them." ⏱ 4 hr. Fort Bragg Depot at the foot of Laurel St. ☎ 866/457-5865 or 707/459-1060. www.skunktrain.com. Tickets $47–$70 adults, $22–$35 kids 3–11. Daily Mar–Nov; Sat Dec–Feb. Schedules vary, particularly during holidays; call for details. Reservations recommended in summer.

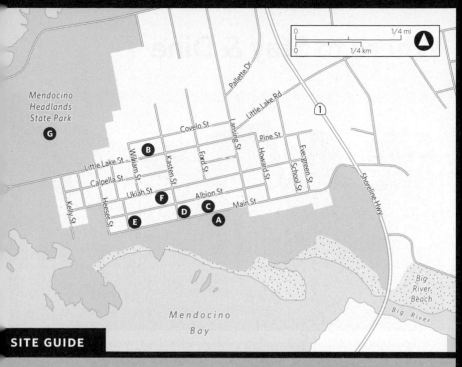

① Mendocino

Start at the **Ⓐ Ford House Visitor Center,** 735 Main St. (☎ 707/937-5397; www.mendoparks. org; daily 11am–4pm). Built in 1854, it features both historical and current information on the area, including photographic displays, seasonal exhibits, maps, brochures, and books. Next, get an overview of the town's artistic life at the **Ⓑ Mendocino Art Center,** 45200 Little Lake St. (☎ 707/937-5818; www.mendocinoartcenter. org; daily 10am–5pm; free admission). Founded in 1959, this is Mendocino's unofficial cultural headquarters, sponsoring numerous events, conducting classes, and showcasing local art and crafts in its galleries, shops, and sculpture garden. The town may be small, but it's jampacked with shoppers' delights. Highlights include the aptly named **Ⓒ Highlight Gallery,** 45052 Main St. (☎ 707/937-3132; www. thehighlightgallery.com), featuring handmade furniture, pottery, and crafts; **Ⓓ Gallery Bookshop & Bookwinkle's Children's Books,** at the corner of Main and Kasten streets (☎ 707/937-2665; www.gallerybooks.com), one of the best independent bookstores in Northern California; and **Ⓔ Mendocino Jams & Preserves,** 440 Main St. (☎ 707/937-1037; www.mendojams. com), which offers free tastes of its gourmet fruit spreads. Musicians and music lovers will want to check out **Ⓕ Lark in the Morning Musique Shoppe,** 45101 Ukiah St. (☎ 707/937-5275; www.larkinthemorning.com), purveyor of musical instruments from around the world. **Ⓖ ★ Mendocino Headlands State Park** envelops the town, so after exploring the shops take a walk on the wild side. There are 3 miles of trails, offering panoramic views of sea arches and hidden grottoes; behind the Mendocino Presbyterian Church on Main Street there's a trail that leads to a set of stairs that will take you down to a small, picturesque beach. ⊕ At least 3 hr. www. parks.ca.gov.

Where to Stay & Dine

> *Catch the sunset with glasses of local wine and incredible hors d'oeuvres at Brewery Gulch Inn.*

★★ **Agate Cove Inn** MENDOCINO
Sweeping views from 125 feet above the crashing waves of Agate Cove highlight this cheery property. It's comprised of a farmhouse built in 1860 and a lineup of single and duplex cottages. Even the foggiest night stands no chance against the fireplaces and cozy down comforters. 11201 N. Lansing St. ☎ 800/527-3111 or 707/937-0551. www.agatecove.com. 10 units. Doubles $159–$329 w/breakfast. MC, V.

★★ **Brewery Gulch Inn** MENDOCINO
Built of redwood reclaimed from the bottom of the Big River, this handsome and luxurious inn is on the east side of the highway but still affords smashing views of Smuggler's Cove and the coast. The complimentary late-afternoon happy hour, featuring multicourse heavy hors d'oeuvres and local wine and beer, can definitely suffice as dinner. 9401 N. Hwy. 1. ☎ 800/578-4454 or 707/937-4752. www.brewerygulchinn.com. 10 units. Doubles $210–$465 w/breakfast. AE, MC, V.

★★ **Café Beaujolais** MENDOCINO AMERICAN/ FRENCH One of Mendocino's pre-eminent dining spots, this intimate and unpretentious restaurant is set within a charming farmhouse built in 1893 and is surrounded by gardens (the atrium dining room takes full advantage of the view). The product here is organic and humanely harvested, including free-range meat and poultry and locally line-caught or farmed seafood. 961 Ukiah St. ☎ 707/937-5614. www.cafebeaujolais.com. Reservations recommended. Entrees $24–$42. DISC, MC, V. Lunch Wed–Sun; dinner daily.

★ **Mendocino Hotel & Garden Suites** MEN-DOCINO Right smack on Main Street, close to everything in town, is this Old West false-front Victorian, dating from 1878. Stepping through the doors is a trip back in time. The best rooms have views of the headlands, fireplaces, modern bathrooms, and sitting rooms or balconies. 45080 Main St. ☎ 800/548-0513 or 707/937-0511. www.mendocinohotel.com. 51 units, 37 with private bathroom. Doubles $100–$120 with shared bathroom; $115–$295 with private bathroom. AE, MC, V.

★★ **The Moosse Café** MENDOCINO CALIFOR-NIA It looks like an old New England sea captain's house (and maybe it was), so come out of

> *Locals like the comfortable elegance of Café Beaujolais; stroll out back to see the pretty kitchen garden.*

the fog, slip off your peacoat and order up some savory cioppino brimming with local seafood. **Note:** When the place is full, quarters are a might cramped. 390 Kasten St. ☎ 707/937-4323. www.themoosse.com. Reservations recommended for dinner. Entrees $8–$30. MC, V. May–Oct lunch & dinner daily; Feb–May Thurs–Mon lunch & dinner. Winter schedule varies, but usually closed Jan; call ahead.

★ **North Coast Brewery** FORT BRAGG AMERICAN This hugely popular spot serves up craft beers such as Old Rasputin Stout and Red Seal Ale. The food ranges from standard brewpub fare (the garlic fries will definitely keep the vampires at bay) to more upscale items like scallops, T-bone steak, and local catch of the day. Across the street at the brewery, free tours are offered every Saturday at noon. 455 N. Main St. ☎ 707/964-2739. www.northcoast brewing.com. Entrees $17–$25. DISC, MC, V. Lunch & dinner daily.

Old Coast Hotel FORT BRAGG
Restored to its Victorian glory days, this B&B,

built in 1892, is located in the heart of Fort Bragg. Each room is individually decorated, and some include fireplaces; there's also a garden and sun deck. 101 N. Franklin St. ☎ 888/468-3550 or 707/961-4488. www.old coasthotel.com. 15 units. Doubles $120–$205 w/breakfast. AE, DISC, MC, V.

★★ **Stanford Inn by the Sea** MENDOCINO There's so much for the conscious traveler to love about this retreat, set on 11 acres alongside the Big River. There are yoga classes and massage therapy; there's ★★ **Ravens' Restaurant,** an outstanding vegan and vegetarian eatery (serving breakfast and dinner), and there is the hotel's commitment to sustainable practices. If that's not enough, the first-class amenities such as the awesome indoor pool, in-room fireplaces, and the supercool outrigger canoes available for rent will sway you. N. Hwy. 1 and Comptche Ukiah Rd. ☎ 800/331-8884 or 707/937-5615. www.stanfordinn.com. 33 units. Doubles $198–$308 w/breakfast. AE, DC, DISC, MC, V.

The Redwood Coast

Half of the world's old-growth forests are located along this wild coastline. You will find sun-dappled primeval landscapes where the planet's tallest trees form living cathedrals that inspire awe and reverence. You'll also find time-warped towns that look much the same as they did in the 19th century, with elaborate Victorian buildings housing galleries, boutiques, and antiques stores.

> *Hold tight to the wheel in Redwood National Park, where it's easy to get distracted by breathtaking views.*

START **Shelter Cove.** From U.S. 101 take the Redway/Garberville exit, then go west on Briceland-Shelter Cove Rd., a 23-mile serpentine route that will take about an hour to drive. TRIP LENGTH at least 3 days, about 160 miles.

1 Shelter Cove. This fishing enclave, accessible by land by only a single mountain road, is the gateway to the ★★★ **Lost Coast,** perhaps the most wild and remote coastline in the lower 48 states. Day-trippers can hike part of the Lost Coast Trail at Black Sands Beach, just north of town on Beach Road. Featuring tide pools and unusual rock formations, this

trail continues for 25 miles before running into anything resembling a road. Back in Shelter Cove you can pick up a fishing charter or even play a round of 9-hole golf. The par-33 course operates on the honor system and you can rent clubs from the nearby surf shop (yes, there's a surf break here). See p. 231, **8**. ☺ At least 4 hr. www.redwoods.info or www.shelter cove-lostcoast.com.

As you head back up Briceland Rd., make a left on Wilder Ridge Rd. Go left on Mattole Rd. at the tiny town of Honeydew. Continue along the scenic Mattole-Ferndale-Petrolia Rd. It's about 75 miles and 2¾ hr. to

2 ★ **Ferndale.** Founded in 1852, this entire town is a National Historic Landmark. Thanks to its dairy history, Ferndale is called the Cream City, a place where prosperous 19th-century farmers built ornate Victorian homes that became known as Butterfat Palaces. As if preserved in amber (if not butter), the town is still chock full of fanciful architecture. You can catch up on local history at the well-curated **Ferndale Museum,** 515 Shaw Ave. (☎ 707/786-4466; www.ferndale-museum.org; Wed–Sat 11am–4pm, Sun 1–4pm, closed Jan), which boasts a number of artifacts and exhibits, including a working blacksmith shop and an active seismograph (which no doubt came in handy when an earthquake measuring 6.5 on the Richter scale struck Ferndale-just off the town's shore in Jan 2010).

There's more history at Ferndale's pioneer **cemetery,** located on Bluff Street, as well as vistas of the town, the Eel River Valley, and the ocean. Three miles outside of town, **Fern Cottage,** 2121 Centerville Rd. (☎ 707/786-4835; www.ferncottage.org; tours Wed–Sun 11am–4pm, year-round by appt.; $10 per person) is listed on the National Register of Historic Places and was the home of local entrepreneur and three-time state assemblyman Joseph Russ.

Charming and quirky boutiques and galleries are located along Main Street; highlights include the old-fashion general store, **Golden Gait Mercantile,** 421 Main St. (☎ 707/786-4891), and the **Blacksmith Shop,** 455 Main St. (☎ 707/786-4216; www.ferndaleblacksmith.com), specializing in hand-forged metalwork. See p. 221, **7**. ☺ At least 2 hr. ☎ 707/786-4477. www.victorianferndale.com.

Overnight in Ferndale. On Day 2 take Hwy. 211 to U.S. 101 north; it's about 20 miles and 30 min. to

3 ★ **Eureka.** You've found it—the most prominent city on the far north coast (pop. 27,000), featuring one of the best-preserved Victorian commercial districts in the country. Eureka was once a rough and tumble timber, gold mining, and fishing port, but the wealth that flowed into the city in the 19th century led to the construction of opulent, ostentatious Victorian buildings, a rich legacy that

1 Shelter Cove
2 Ferndale
3 Eureka
4 Arcata
5 Trinidad
6 Redwood National and State Parks

Where to Stay
Benbow Inn **15**
Carter House Inns **12**
Hotel Arcata **9**
Shaw House Inn B&B **14**
Trinidad Bay B&B **7**

Where to Dine
Folie Douce **10**
Larrupin Café **8**
Restaurant 301 **13**
Samoa Cookhouse **11**

> *Bring binoculars when you visit Arcata Marsh, a lush haven for a wide array of birds.*

survives to this day. The king (or queen?) of all these structures is the ★ **Carson Mansion** (located on the corner of Second and M sts.), arguably the most exquisite Victorian home in the country. Built between 1884 and 1886, it was commissioned by lumber baron William Carson (1770–1843), apparently as a way to keep idled craftsmen and mill workers busy during a slow period. It has been a private club since 1950, so you'll have to admire it from the sidewalk. Across the street at 202 M St. is another historic home, the aptly named **Pink Lady,** a wedding gift for Carson's son.

Old Town Eureka is listed as an official Historic District in the National Register of Historic Places; in all, the city has some 1,500 buildings that have qualified for the register. This waterfront area offers all manner of engaging shops and restaurants, and is fronted by a boardwalk that provides expansive views of Humboldt Bay. You can also join a scenic bay cruise from here. Extending from the boardwalk along F Street to Seventh Street is the Cultural Arts District, where the festive **Arts Alive!** art walk takes place the first Saturday of every month.

The **Morris Graves Museum of Art,** 636 F St. (☎ 707/442-0278; www.humboldtarts. org; Wed–Sun noon–5pm; donation suggested), showcases the art and artists of the Pacific Northwest in its seven galleries; it also hosts a roster of classes, workshops, and special events. The **Clarke Historical Museum,**

240 E St. (☎ 707/443-1947; www.clarke museum.org; Wed–Sat 11am–4pm; donation suggested), has a fine collection of Native American baskets and other artifacts, as well as Victorian relics. **Fort Humboldt State Historic Park,** 3431 Fort Ave. (☎ 707/445-6567; www.parks.ca.gov; daily 8am–5pm; free admission), relates the local military and logging history, as well as the tragically familiar story of rapacious white settlers and their indigenous foes. ◷ At least 2 hr. Eureka Chamber of Commerce, 2112 Broadway. ☎ 800/356-6381 or 707/442-3738. www.eurekachamber.com. Mon–Thurs 8:30am–5; Fri 8:30am–4pm.

It's less than 8 miles and 15 min. up U.S. 101 to

❹ ★ **Arcata.** The home of Humboldt State University, Arcata is as creative, lively, and progressive as you would expect a college town to be. It's also as pretty as you'd expect a Victorian town to be. There's great people-watching at the town square, **Arcata Plaza,** which is surrounded by boutiques, bookstores, and restaurants set in historic buildings. In June and July the **Crabs** come out to play— that would be the beloved semipro baseball team that plays at Arcata Ballpark at Ninth and F streets (☎ 707/826-2333; www. humboldtcrabs.com; tickets $5–$7).

Just south of town is the ★ **Arcata Marsh and Wildlife Sanctuary** (daily 4am to 1 hr. after sunset), a wetland that also innovatively acts as the town's wastewater treatment system. The 307-acre sanctuary is part of the Pacific Flyway, visited by 270 species of birds; the Audubon Society leads birding tours every Saturday at 8:30am. Visitors can learn more about the ecological and political aspects of this project at the interpretive center, 569 S. G St. (☎ 707/826-2359; www.arcatamarsh friends.org; Tues–Sun 9am–5pm, Mon 1–5pm). ⏱ At least 2 hr. Arcata Chamber of Commerce, 1635 Heindon Rd. ☎ 707/822-3619. www. arcatachamber.com or www.redwoods.info. Daily 9am–5pm.

On Day 3, take U.S. 101 north 15 miles to

⑤ ★ Trinidad. With a population of about 300, Trinidad is one of the smallest—and also one of the oldest and most westerly—cities in the state. The spectacular coastline features tide pools and dramatic sea stack formations and is prime territory for whale-watching (Dec–Apr) and fishing. The small **Trinidad Museum,** 400 Janis Ct. (☎ 707/677-3883; www.trinidadmuseum.org), is in a restored bungalow dating from 1899 and explores Native American and natural history.

To the north of the city is ★★ **Patrick's Point State Park,** 4150 Patrick's Point Dr. (☎ 707/677-3570; www.parks.ca.gov; $8 per car, $7 with a senior), where you'll find campgrounds, epic scenery, and a re-created Yurok Indian village and garden. At its amazing ★★ **Agate Beach,** volcanic and tidal activity has left behind a beach strewn with semiprecious agate, jade, and moonstone. ⏱ At least 1 hr. Trinidad Chamber of Commerce, ☎ 707/677-1610. www.discovertrinidadca.com.

Take U.S. 101 N. 20 miles to Orick

⑥ ★★★ Redwood National and State Parks. Just south of the town of Orick you'll find the park's **Thomas H. Kuchel Visitor Center**—stop here for maps and info and to take a peek at the exhibits. Alas, poor Orick, there's really not much here, otherwise. You will find it handy for supplies, groceries, or roadside souvenirs as you head onward to explore the magnificent groves and trails of this UNESCO World Heritage Site. See p. 231, ❾. ⏱ At least 3 hr. www.redwoods.info.

> Beach comb and romp at Patrick's Point, where Agate Beach is naturally strewn with semiprecious gemstones.

Where to Stay & Dine

> *Snuggle up in the big fluffy beds at Carter House Inn, made up of four unique properties.*

★ Benbow Inn GARBERVILLE

This elegant and romantic Tudor-style lodge along the Eel River has been welcoming visitors since 1926. Amenities include a 9-hole golf course, RV sites, and a complimentary decanter of sherry in every room. 445 Lake Benbow Dr. ☎ 800/355-3301 or 707/923-2124. www.benbowinn.com. 55 units. Doubles $99–$405. AE, DISC, MC, V.

★★★ Carter House Inns EUREKA

This classy collection of four Victorian properties (the Hotel Carter and Carter House are reproductions, but Belle Cottage and Carter Cottage are restored originals) offers luxury, sophistication, and excellent service. Antiques mix with modern amenities at all of the inns, though if your budget allows ($615 a night), the Carter Cottage is worth the splurge. 301 L St. ☎ 800/404-1390 or 707/444-8062. www.carterhouse.com. 32 units. Doubles $155–$385 w/breakfast & afternoon hors d'oeuvres. AE, DC, DISC, MC, V.

★★ Folie Douce ARCATA *BISTRO*

Organic, local, and seasonal are the catchwords for this hip and creative bistro. Influences are eclectic, ranging from Asian (wasabi steak) to Mediterranean (wood-fired pizzas); there's also a daily vegetarian special. 1551 G St. ☎ 707/822-1042. www.holyfolie.com. Reservations suggested. Entrees $12–$37. AE, DISC, MC, V. Dinner Tues–Sat.

Hotel Arcata ARCATA

Run by a local Native American tribal organization this well-kept, comfortable hotel opened in 1915 and is still the town's most prominent option. It's conveniently located right on Arcata's main plaza, but noise can be a factor (the minisuites, a bargain at $100, are the quietest option). 708 Ninth St. ☎ 800/344-1221 or 707/826-0217. www.hotelarcata.com. 32 units. Doubles $85–$136 w/breakfast. AE, DC, DISC, MC, V.

★★ Larrupin Café TRINIDAD *AMERICAN*

Since the mid-1980s this gem has been a locals' favorite for its exotic decor, mesquite-

> *The smoky scent of wood-fired pizza at Folie Douce hints at greatness to come—in fancier dishes too.*

barbecued fare, seasonal and organic produce, and house-made mustard-dill sauce (available for sale). 1658 Patrick's Point Dr. ☎707/677-0230. www.larrupincafe.com. Reservations recommended. Entrees $15–$22. No credit cards. Dinner Thurs–Mon.

★★ **Restaurant 301** EUREKA *CALIFORNIAN* This attractive, airy space in the Hotel Carter (above) is Eureka's best choice for fine dining. The fare is seasonal, featuring garden-to-table fresh products; your best bet is to journey along with the chef on the Discovery tasting menu with wine pairings. 301 L St. ☎800/404-1390 or 707/444-8062. www.carterhouse.com. Reservations recommended. Entrees $18–$29. AE, DC, DISC, MC, V. Dinner daily.

★ **Samoa Cookhouse** SAMOA *AMERICAN* You might be forgiven if you start singing the Monty Python lumberjack song here—this is North America's last lumber camp-style cookhouse. It's been serving huge portions of hearty fare since 1890, when it was a company-town mess hall; tables are still communal

with red-checkered tablecloths. There's a logging museum next door. Cookhouse Rd. ☎707-442-1659. www.samoacookhouse.net. Entrees $8–$12. AE, DISC, MC, V. Breakfast, lunch, & dinner daily.

★★ **Trinidad Bay Bed & Breakfast** TRINIDAD Overlooking Trinidad's beautiful bay and lighthouse, this Cape Cod-style property is homey without being fussy. All rooms have ocean views; one has a kitchenette. 560 Edwards St. ☎707/677-0840. www.trinidadbaybnb.com. 4 units. Doubles $200–$300 w/breakfast. AE, MC, V.

★★ **Shaw House Inn Bed and Breakfast** FERNDALE Dripping with historical charm, this splendid Victorian inn surrounded by lush gardens was built in 1854. All the antiques-filled rooms have private bathrooms; some have their own balconies and private entrances. 703 Main St. ☎800/557-7429 or 707/786-9958. www.shawhouse.com. 8 units. Doubles $105–$260 w/breakfast. DISC, MC, V.

The Best of the Shasta Cascade Region

California's vast northern reaches feature dramatic landscapes of massive volcanoes, sparkling lakes, trout-filled streams, and thundering waterfalls, along with small towns where Old West pioneer history lives on. The Shasta Cascade region will entrance hard-core outdoor enthusiasts and casual fun seekers alike.

> Rent a boat and explore hundreds of miles of shoreline on California's largest reservoir, Shasta Lake.

START Redding, 162 miles north of Sacramento. TRIP LENGTH at least 5 days, about 480 miles.

1 Redding. Incorporated in 1887, the far north's major city and transportation hub, Redding serves mostly as a base from which to enjoy the region's outdoor adventures and natural wonders, but it is home to several prime attractions, including ★★ **Turtle Bay**

Exploration Park and the ★★ **Sundial Bridge** (p. 224, **3**). ⊙ At least 2 hr. Redding Chamber of Commerce, 777 Auditorium Dr. ☎ 800/874-7562 or 530/225-4100. www.visitredding. com. Mon–Fri 9am–5pm (and Sat 10am–5pm in summer).

Drive west on Hwy. 299 for about 45 miles to

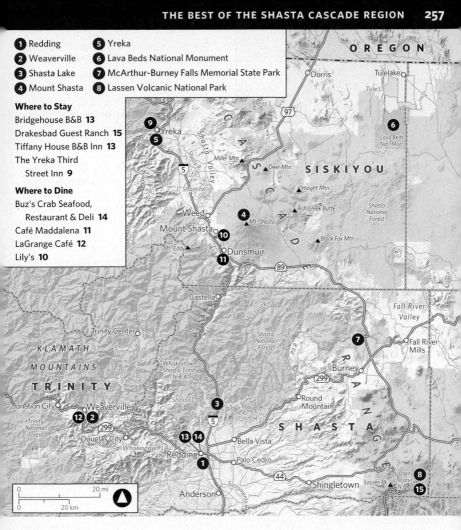

1 Redding
2 Weaverville
3 Shasta Lake
4 Mount Shasta
5 Yreka
6 Lava Beds National Monument
7 McArthur-Burney Falls Memorial State Park
8 Lassen Volcanic National Park

Where to Stay
Bridgehouse B&B **13**
Drakesbad Guest Ranch **15**
Tiffany House B&B Inn **13**
The Yreka Third
    Street Inn **9**

Where to Dine
Buz's Crab Seafood,
    Restaurant & Deli **14**
Café Maddalena **11**
LaGrange Café **12**
Lily's **10**

2 ★ **Weaverville.** A Gold Rush town that eventually became known for logging and marijuana cultivation, Weaverville was also notable for its large population of 19th-century Chinese prospectors. Their legacy survives at **Joss House State Historic Park,** Hwy. 299 and Oregon St. (☎ 530/623-5284; www.parks.ca.gov; Thurs–Sun 10am–5pm), the location of "The Temple of the Forest Beneath the Clouds," the oldest continuously used Chinese temple in California, built in 1874. The **Jake Jackson Memorial Museum,** 508 Main St. (☎ 530/623-5211; www.trini-tymuseum.org) examines the town's mining history; hours vary seasonally, so call ahead.

Weaverville is also the gateway to the ★★ **Trinity Alps,** the state's second-largest wilderness area, and the ★★ **Whiskeytown National Recreation Area.** For more info, including directions to ★ **Whiskeytown Falls,** a 220-foot waterfall rediscovered in 2004, visit the ranger station in Weaverville at 360 Main St. (☎ 530/623-2121; www.fs.fed.us). ★ **Trinity Lake,** one of the state's largest with 147 miles of shoreline, is a great alternative to more popular Shasta Lake. ☉ At least 1 hr. www.weavervilleinfo.com or www.shasta cascade.com.

On Day 2, from Redding, head north on I-5 for 15 miles to

> *Wearing a white cloak year-round, Mount Shasta is a magnet for downhill and cross-country skiing and snowshoeing.*

3 ★ **Shasta Lake.** This artificial lake—created by the building of the Shasta Dam (p. 223, **2**) is California's largest reservoir, covering nearly 30,000 acres. It's also a mecca for outdoor recreation. ◷ At least 2 hr. See p. 236 for recreational options in the area.

Take I-5 north for 51 miles to the Mount Shasta City exit.

4 ★★★ **Mount Shasta.** The magnificent, perennially snowcapped Mount Shasta is another magnet for outdoor recreation in many forms. ◷ At least 3 hr. See p. 234, **4**. Mount Shasta Visitors' Bureau, 300 Pine St. ☎ 800/926-4865 or 530/926-4865. www.mtshastachamber.com. Daily 10am–4pm.

On Day 3, head north on I-5 for 43 miles to the Central Yreka exit.

5 ★ **Yreka.** This Gold Rush town, once known as "the richest square mile on earth," has a colorful history, including once being proposed as the capital of the secessionist State of Jefferson in the 1940s. The historic downtown district features dozens of Victorian buildings; pick up a walking-tour map from the chamber of commerce, 117 W. Miner St. (☎ 530/842-1649; www.yrekachamber.com).

The town's wild past is covered at the **Siskiyou County Museum,** 910 S. Main St. (☎ 530/842-3836; www.co.siskiyou.ca.us; Tues–Fri 9am–5pm, Sat 10am–4pm). To see what kick-started Yreka in 1852, check out the huge chunks of local gold on display (the biggest collection south of Alaska) in the **Siskiyou County Courthouse,** 311 Fourth St. (daily 8am–5pm).

The town is also a handy base for exploring the 2-million-acre ★★ **Klamath National Forest,** which is laced by the Klamath River and its tributaries. It offers some of Northern California's best rafting, kayaking, and fishing. The ranger headquarters at 1312 Fairlane Rd. (☎ 530/842-6131; www.fs.fed.us) has all the info you need on activities in the park, as well as an interpretive museum. ◷ At least 1 hr.

Head south on I-5 for 39 miles, then head east on Hwy. 89 for 24 miles. Take Forest Route 15 to Forest Route 49/Medicine Lake Rd. and follow that for 26 miles. From that point, follow signs to

6 ★★ **Lava Beds National Monument.** Native American history, volcanic rock formations, and lava-tube caves make this far-flung park endlessly fascinating. See p. 234, **5**.

On Day 4, go down U.S. 97 to I-5 South, and continue along the Volcanic Legacy byway south on U.S. 89 (distance: 152 miles; trip time: 4 hr.) past the town of Mount Shasta to

7 ★★★ **McArthur-Burney Falls Memorial State Park.** A host of recreational opportunities can be found at this picturesque park, named for pioneer settlers. You'll also find a good variety of wildlife and flora, though the major draw remains the park's gorgeous year-round waterfalls. See p. 235, **6**.

On Day 5, continue south on Hwy. 89 to Lassen Volcanic National Park. Distance is 42 miles (trip time: 1 hr.).

8 ★★★ **Lassen Volcanic National Park.** Named for Peter Lassen (1800–59)—a Danish blacksmith and rancher who guided settlers through the region—this park bubbles with geothermal activity. But there's more to the park than just its dormant volcano—you'll also find picturesque lakes, meadows, and forests. See p. 224, **5**.

Where to Stay & Dine

★★ **Bridgehouse Bed and Breakfast** REDDING Redding isn't exactly known for its highly rated accommodations, so this place really stands out. Bright, classy, and elegant, it also has the unusual B&B amenity of a workout room. 1455 Riverside Dr. ☎ 530/247-7177. www.redding bridgehouse.com. 4 units. Doubles $119–$179 w/breakfast. AE, MC, V.

★★ **Buz's Crab Seafood, Restaurant & Deli** REDDING *SEAFOOD* Since 1968 Buz's has been hooking fans with such tasty fare as salmon burgers, prawn and scallop kabobs, house-baked bread, and the popular seafood combo baskets. 2159 East St. ☎ 530/243-2120. www. buzscrab.com. Entrees $2.50–$14. MC, V. Lunch & dinner daily.

★★ **Café Maddalena** DUNSMUIR *MEDITER-RANEAN* This rustic-chic bistro artfully melds the flavors of Italy, Spain, France, and North Africa, and pairs them with an artisanal wine list. This would be a great find anywhere, let alone a small town. 5801 Sacramento Ave. ☎ 530/235-2725. www.cafemaddalena.com. Entrees $17–$25. DISC, MC, V. Dinner Thurs–Sun; closed Jan.

★★★ **Drakesbad Guest Ranch** LASSEN VOL-CANIC NATIONAL PARK Hosting visitors since 1900, this rustic operation (most rooms have no electricity and utilize kerosene lamps) is right in the park. It books up to 2 years in advance; try getting on the waiting list or calling for last-minute cancellations. c/o California Guest Services, 2150 N. Main St., no. 5, Red Bluff. ☎ 866/999-0914 or 530/529-1512. www.drakesbad. com. 19 units. $155–$201 per person, double occupancy. Rates include all meals. DISC, MC, V.

★★ **LaGrange Café** WEAVERVILLE *AMERICAN* Big-city technique and flair meets rural country cuisine in the form of seasonal, creative dishes such as braised rabbit or venison bratwurst; there's an excellent wine list, too. 226 Main St. ☎ 530/623-5325. Entrees $10–$25. AE, DISC, MC, V. Lunch & dinner daily.

★ **Lily's** MOUNT SHASTA *INTERNATIONAL* Most popular for its breakfast and brunch,

> *There's a skillful hand in the kitchen at Café Maddalena, a surprisingly chic eatery in sleepy Dunsmuir.*

Lily's also serves a globe-trotting dinner menu that has wide appeal. You'll find Asian, Mexican, and Italian dishes, as well as vegetarian offerings. 1013 S. Mount Shasta Blvd. ☎ 530/926-3372. www.lilysrestaurant.com. Entrees $7–$23. AE, DISC, MC, V. Breakfast, lunch, & dinner daily.

Tiffany House Bed and Breakfast Inn RED-DING This charming Victorian inn is set on a hill above the city, affording each room a view of Mount Lassen. The swimming pool is an added bonus not usually associated with country-style inns. 1510 Barbara Rd. ☎ 530/244-3225. www.tiffanyhousebb.com. 4 units. Doubles $125–$170 w/breakfast. AE, DISC, MC, V.

★ **The Yreka Third Street Inn** YREKA This perfectly turned-out Victorian property has a fine, shady garden and maintains its period feeling without being overly frilly. It's just a stone's throw from Yreka's historic Main Street. 326 Third St. ☎ 530/598-0615. www. yrekabedandbreakfast.com. 4 units. Doubles $95–$120 w/breakfast. MC, V.

Fast Facts

American Express
American Express Travel Service, 455 Market St., San Francisco (☎ 415/536-2600; www.amextravelresources.com), is the closest office. It's open Monday to Friday 9am to 5:30pm and Saturday 10am to 2pm. Or call ☎ 800/221-7282.

Dentists & Doctors
For a dental referral, call **1-800-DENTIST** (☎ 800/336-8422; www.1800dentist.com). For doctors, see "Emergencies," below.

Emergencies
In an emergency dial ☎ 911.

In the event of a medical emergency on the Sonoma Coast, head to **Palm Drive Hospital,** 501 Petaluma Ave., Sebastopol (☎ 707/823-8511; www.palmdrivehospital.com). On the Mendocino Coast head to **Mendocino Coast District Hospital,** 700 River Dr., Fort Bragg (☎ 707/961-1234; www.mcdh.org). On the Redwood Coast try **St. Joseph's Hospital,** 2700 Dolbeer St., Eureka (☎ 707/445-8121; www.stjosepheureka.org). In the Shasta/Cascade region, head for **Shasta Regional Medical Center,** 1100 Butte St., Redding (☎ 530/244-5400; www.srmc.phcs.us), or **Fairchild Medical Center,** 444 Bruce St., Yreka (☎ 530/842-4121; www.fairchildmed.org).

Getting There
BY PLANE The three major airports serving the north are **Oakland International Airport** (☎ 800/247-6255 or 510/563-3300; www.oaklandairport.com), **Sacramento International Airport** (☎ 916/929-5411; www.sacairports.org), and **San Francisco International Airport** (☎ 650/821-8211; www.flysfo.com). Regional airports serving the north include **Redding Municipal Airport** (☎ 530/224-4320; www.ci.redding.ca.us) and **Arcata/Eureka Airport** (☎ 707/839-5401; www.co.humboldt.ca.us). No matter where you land, you'll need to rent a car to get efficiently around in this region. All of the airports have car-rental desks. BY BUS **Greyhound** buses (☎ 800/231-2222; www.greyhound.com) serve such northern points as Arcata, Crescent City, Eureka, Redding, and Truckee.

BY TRAIN **Amtrak** (☎ 800/872-7245; www.amtrak.com) can deliver you to Redding and Truckee; rail and bus service is available to such places as Arcata, Eureka, Mount Shasta, and Yreka. BY CAR I-5 is the state's main north–south corridor; U.S. 101 is the fastest way to reach most areas on the Northern Coast. The most spectacular, and slowest, route is the coast-hugging Hwy. 1. From the Bay Area, the fastest-route drive time to Mendocino is 4 hours, to Eureka it's 5 hours, to Redding it's 3½ hours, and to Yreka it's 5 hours.

Getting Around
The absolute best and most efficient way to get around this region is with a car, and I strongly recommend you rent one if you didn't arrive in your own vehicle. That said, for travel within some towns and smaller areas, you can try public transit if you so choose.

Mendocino Coast: For bus service, the **Mendocino Transit Authority** (☎ 800/696-4682; www.4mta.org) serves Mendocino County, including Point Arena, Mendocino, and Fort Bragg. Fares are based on a zone system and range from $1 to $2.50; up to two children ages 6 and under ride free with a paying adult. In Fort Bragg you can call for door-to-door van service (☎ 707/964-1800; $4 for central zone, $4 for additional zones).

Fort Bragg–based **Hey Taxi** (☎ 707/962-0800; www.heytaxiinc.com) serves several locations in the North. Call for fares.

Redwood Coast: Eureka Transit Service (☎ 707/443-0826; www.eurekatransit.org) provides bus service Monday to Friday and limited Saturday service in Eureka; fares are $1.40 adults and $1.10 kids 3 to 17. **Redwood Transit Service** (☎ 707/443-0826; www.redwoodtransit.org) runs from Eureka to Trinidad (Mon–Sat) and from Arcata to Willow Creek (Mon–Fri); fares are $2.50 adults and $2.25 kids 3 to 17. **Arcata & Mad River Transit System** (☎ 707/822-3775; www.arcatatransit.org) serves Arcata Monday to Friday with limited Saturday operation; fares are $1.40 adults and 75¢ kids 3 to 17. **Del Norte County. Public Transportation** (☎ 707/464-6400; www.redwoodcoasttransit.org) runs from Arcata to

Crescent City, and runs bus lines within Crescent City; fares range from 75¢ to $25, depending on how far you go. Up to two children ages 6 and under ride free with a paying adult.

For taxi service, in Arcata/Eureka try **Arcata Dial-a-Ride** (☎ 707/822-3775; www.arcatatransit.org) and **City Cab** (☎ 707/442-4551; www.cityambulance.com). In Crescent City, call **Comfort Cab** (☎ 707/464-7788).

Shasta/Cascade: Redding Area Bus Authority (☎ 530/241-2877; www.rabaride.com) serves the Redding and Shasta Lake area Monday through Saturday; fares are based on a zone system and run $1.50 to $3, kids 5 and under travel free.

If you need a taxi in Redding, call **Redding Yellow Cab** (☎ 530/222-1234) or **ABC Cab** (☎ 530/244-5909).

Hospital
See "Emergencies," above.

Internet Access
Cybercafes are few and far between in the North; two good options are **Moody's Organic Coffee Bar,** 10450 Lansing St., Mendocino (☎ 707/937-4843; www.moodyscoffeebar.com); and **Old Town Coffee & Chocolates,** 211 F St., Eureka (☎ 707/445-8600; www.oldtowncoffeeeureka.com). Except in wilderness areas, those with laptops won't have trouble finding Wi-Fi hotspots.

Pharmacies
Chain drugstores with pharmacies, like **CVS** (☎ 800/746-7287; www.cvs.com) and **Rite Aid,** (☎ 800/748-3243; www.rite-aid.com), are common; 24-hour pharmacies are not. An exception is the **Walgreens** in Redding, 980 E. Cypress Ave. (☎ 530/221-5028; www.walgreens.com).

Post Office
The Mendocino office is at 10500 Ford St. (☎ 707/937-5282); it's open Monday to Friday 7:30am to 4:30pm. The Eureka office is at 514 H St. (☎ 707/442-0856); hours are Monday to Friday 8:30am to 5pm. For other locations call ☎ 800/275-8777 or go to www.usps.com.

Safety
In this region, where outdoor recreation rules, it pays to be prepared. Bring along a hat, sunscreen, plenty of water, and dress in layers—weather can change quickly from fair to bad. And whether you're hiking, skiing, or swimming in the ocean, don't do it alone. If you are going solo, let someone know where you are headed and what time you'll be back. And do recognize your own limitations.

Most the of the northern coastline is unsuitable for swimming—the temperatures are frigid, the rip currents wicked, and great white sharks are a very real presence. Even when just strolling along the shoreline, keep your eyes on the water (and on your children)—rogue waves can appear suddenly and sweep victims off the beach.

Hikers, particularly in the coastal foothills, should wear long pants and light-colored clothing to protect against ticks, which can carry Lyme disease. After a hike, do a thorough search of your body—if you find one of the buggers, use tweezers to remove it; don't crush it. California's forests are also black bear country; campers need to properly stow all food and any scented items (including canned goods, cosmetics, toiletries, trash, and so forth). Cars are not bear proof.

Visitor Information
There's an outpost of the **Sonoma County Tourism Bureau** (☎ 800/576-6662, www.sonomacounty.com) at 850 Hwy. 1 in Bodega Bay. **The Mendocino Coast Chamber of Commerce** (☎ 707/961-6300, www.mendocinocoast.com) is at 217 S. Main St. in Fort Bragg. For the Redwood Coast, call or visit the website of the **Humboldt County Convention & Visitors Bureau** (☎ 800/346-3482, www.redwoods.info). In the Shasta/Cascade region, visit the **Redding Chamber of Commerce,** 77 Auditorium Dr., Redding (☎ 800/874-7562 or 530/225-4100; www.visitredding.com), or try the **Mount Shasta Visitors' Bureau,** 300 Pine St., Mount Shasta (☎ 800/926-4865 or 530/926-4865; www.mtshastachamber.com).

7
The High
Sierra

The Best of the High Sierra in 3 Days

The Sierra Nevada extends 400 miles like a spine along California's eastern border. Words can barely do justice to the majesty and beauty of this region, known informally as the High Sierra (or just the Sierras). From the amazing, glacier-scrubbed granite valley of Yosemite to the alluringly bizarre formations of Mono Lake, this itinerary will give you a feel for California's backbone. Be advised that you'll need a car for some of this tour, though within Yosemite National Park, you should take advantage of the park's shuttle system.

> PREVIOUS PAGE *Tiny Fannette Island rises from exquisite Emerald Bay.* THIS PAGE *Swollen by spring snowmelt, Bridalveil Fall cascades 620 feet to the Yosemite Valley floor.*

START Southern entrance of Yosemite National Park, 190 miles east of San Francisco. From Fresno-Yosemite International Airport, head north on Hwy. 41 for about 68 miles; upon entering the park, head right on Mariposa Grove Rd. TRIP LENGTH about 200 miles.

❶ ★ **Mariposa Grove.** This grove of giant sequoias will leave you awestruck. Not as tall as their coastal redwood cousins—though they can reach heights of 285 feet—sequoias have a ridiculous girth and can live upward of 3,500 years. The ★ **Grizzly Giant** is the oldest in the grove and has a base circumference of

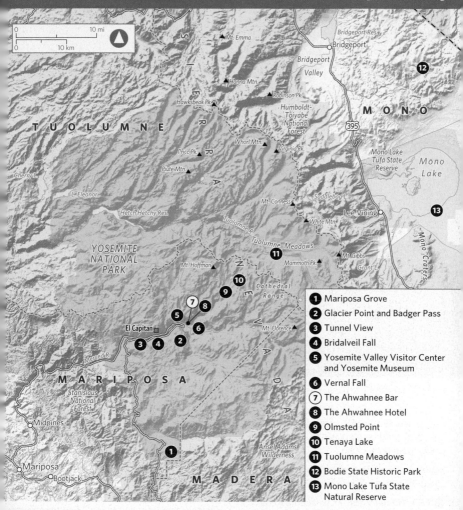

0 ——— 10 mi
0 ——— 10 km

1 Mariposa Grove
2 Glacier Point and Badger Pass
3 Tunnel View
4 Bridalveil Fall
5 Yosemite Valley Visitor Center and Yosemite Museum
6 Vernal Fall
7 The Ahwahnee Bar
8 The Ahwahnee Hotel
9 Olmsted Point
10 Tenaya Lake
11 Tuolumne Meadows
12 Bodie State Historic Park
13 Mono Lake Tufa State Natural Reserve

an astonishing 96.5 feet; take the 1.6-mile hike to pay your respects to this humongous tree. **Note:** The road to the grove is closed approximately November to April. In summer, the small parking lot may be full; consider taking the free Wawona–Mariposa Grove shuttle. ⏱ At least 1 hr. ☎ 209/372-0200. www.nps.gov/yose. Admission $10 per person or $20 per car (valid for 7 days); senior lifetime pass $10.

Return to Hwy. 41/Wawona Rd. and go right; it's about an hour's drive to Glacier Point Rd., where you will turn right. It takes another 30 min. to drive the 16 miles to Glacier Point.

2 ★★ **Glacier Point and Badger Pass.** Time for your next "wow" moment. At road's end, it's a short walk to an overlook some 3,000 feet above Yosemite Valley. Stretched out before you is the granite mountain ★★★ **Half Dome** (p. 280, **11**), three waterfalls, and the High Sierra range; the view is stupendous. Much of this road is closed November to May, but from mid-December to early April it is plowed as far as the ★ **Badger Pass Ski Area.** Opened in 1935, this is California's oldest ski operation, offering downhill (mainly beginner and intermediate-level runs) and cross-country skiing. In winter, Glacier Point

> *Few views compare to the epic sweep of Yosemite Valley as seen from Tunnel View.*

can be reached via ski or snowshoe, available for rental. ⏱ At least 30 min. ☎ 209/372-8430. www.yosemitepark.com.

Return to the main road and turn right; in about 30 min. you'll reach

❸ ★★★ **Tunnel View.** As you come to the exit of the tunnel, slow down and pull into the parking lot on your left. This is it—the money shot. Yosemite's most iconic image—captured in the famous Ansel Adams photo—featuring the sheer granite face of ★★ **El Capitan** (p. 280, ⑫), **Half Dome** (p. 280, ⑪), and ★★ **Bridalveil Fall** (p. 266, ❹) comes vividly to life here. *Note:* You'll most likely be jockeying for position to get the perfect picture at this very crowded viewpoint. ⏱ At least 15 min.

Within a few minutes you'll come to the parking area for Bridalveil Fall on the right-hand side of the road.

❹ ★★ **Bridalveil Fall.** This 620-foot waterfall flows year-round, but is best in late spring.

From the parking area, you can make the short but steep hike (½ mile) along a paved trail to the base of the fall. If it's a hot day, the spray will be very refreshing; if it's winter, beware of icy conditions. ⏱ 30 min. See p. 278, ❺.

From here it's about 6 miles to Yosemite Village, where in summer you'll find the crowds and traffic you were trying to escape by coming here in the first place. It's time to park your car and start taking advantage of Yosemite's shuttle buses.

❺ ★ **Yosemite Valley Visitor Center and Yosemite Museum.** Take a moment to catch your breath and learn about the park and its history. The visitor center will educate you about the titanic geological forces that scraped this valley and tell you about the wildlife that calls this area home. The adjacent museum has interpretive displays about Yosemite's cultural history from 1850 to the present, including that of the Miwok and

> *Original stained-glass panels top the floor-to-ceiling windows in the Great Lounge of the 1927 Ahwahnee Hotel.*

Paiute peoples, with demonstrations of craft making (baskets and beadwork) and traditional games. There's also a reconstructed village behind the museum. The on-site gallery also has occasional exhibits showcasing a vast collection of archaeological artifacts, artwork, and photography. ⏱ 30 min. Daily 8am–6pm.

Take the park shuttle to Happy Isles and the Mist Trail trail head.

❻ ★ Vernal Fall. Take the ★ **Mist Trail** up to this 317-foot waterfall, where the melting snowpack powers its best flow in spring and early summer. Make your way to the top of the fall via 600 thigh-burning granite steps—the Mist Trail really earns its name along this route; if you're here during peak flow, you are going to get sprayed, so watch your footing. This section is closed in winter. ⏱ 3 hr.

Take the shuttle to the Ahwahnee Hotel.

⑦ 🍷 ★ **The Ahwahnee Bar.** With its classic cocktails, piano entertainment, and knowing bartenders, this is the kind of old-school lounge you'd expect to find in an urban downtown hotel—but in the middle of a national park? Sweet. In the Ahwahnee Hotel. ☎ 209/372-1489. www.yosemitepark.com. Entrees $5–$20.

❽ ★★★ **The Ahwahnee Hotel.** This magnificent hotel, a National Historic Landmark, opened in 1927 and has remained an enduring and hugely popular destination. With an Art Deco/Arts and Crafts timberland style, massive **Great Lounge** with roaring fireplace, and floor-to-ceiling windows with views of the park's top features, the Ahwahnee is one of California's most romantic hotels. If you feel like splurging, have dinner in the fabulous (and expensive) dining room (p. 281). ⏱ 1 hr. ☎ 209/372-1489. www.yosemitepark.com. See p. 281.

> *Like a bizarre twist on drip castles, ghostly tufa towers rise out of Mono Lake's alkaline waters.*

On Day 2, take the Tuolumne Meadows Hikers Bus from Yosemite Valley along Tioga Rd./Hwy. 120; the bus runs from June to mid-Sept. Round-trip tickets are $23 maximum (if you go to the end of the line at Tuolumne Meadows Lodge). The bus leaves around 8am and the drive takes 2–2½ hr. (it makes several photo stops along the way); it departs around 2pm from the lodge. Reservations are recommended (☎ 209/372-4386; www.yosemitepark.com). *Note:* Tioga Rd./Hwy. 120 is closed to all traffic Nov–May.

9 ★ **Olmsted Point.** From this vantage point, you'll get a whole new perspective on the Yosemite Valley. You'll be looking at Half Dome from behind, facing west. The hikers bus stops here on its way to rustic **Tuolumne Meadows Lodge;** there's also a free shuttle that runs every 30 minutes between here and the lodge, June to mid-September (7am–7pm). ⏱ 15 min. See p. 272, **6**.

10 ★ **Tenaya Lake.** One of the park's most accessible lakes—both the hikers bus and Tuolumne shuttle stop here—this pretty lake is popular for picnics and canoeing. Some folks even brave the chilly water for a swim. ⏱ At least 1 hr.

At this point, switch over to the Tuolumne Meadows Shuttle Bus, which runs at half-hour intervals, and has pickup points at the east and west ends of the lake.

11 ★★ **Tuolumne Meadows.** This huge, sub-alpine meadow sits between the meandering Tuolumne River and a line of imposing granite peaks and domes. Tuolumne (pronounced "to-*all*-o-me") Meadows is at an elevation of 8,500 feet and is the gateway to Yosemite's backcountry; if you want to get away from the crowds of Yosemite Village, this is where to do it. Just west of the lodge (shuttle stop 2), is the Dog Lake parking area; from here you can make the trek to the top of ★ **Lembert Dome.** This moderately difficult hike is 2.8 miles round-trip and will reward you with a spectacular vista of Tuolumne Meadows, where a profusion of wildflowers bloom in late summer. *Note:* Weather can be unpredictable here; stay off domes during thunderstorms. ⏱ At least 3 hr.

On Day 3, head out through the park's eastern entrance along Tioga Rd./Hwy. 120, over 9,945-foot Tioga Pass to Lee Vining. Go north on U.S. 395 for about 18 miles and east on Hwy. 270 for 13 miles to Bodie State Historic Park. If you're coming from Yosemite Village, it's about 107 miles and 2¾ hr.; if you've stayed over in Tuolumne Meadows you can cut the mileage in half and save about 1½ hr. in trip time. Note that Hwy. 120 and Hwy. 270 are both closed approximately Nov–May.

12 ★ **Bodie State Historic Park.** Mayhem was a daily occurrence in this wild and wicked boomtown where as many as 10,000 people lived after a major gold vein was discovered in 1875. Since 1962 Bodie has been preserved in a state of "arrested decay"—you can take a self-guided tour through the weather-beaten, truly ghostly remains of the town. The church, the saloons (there were reportedly as many as 65 at one time), the schoolhouse, the hotel, even the morgue—it's all still here, with furnishings and personal belongings left as they were. Gas up the car, purge your camera's memory card (this is a photographer's paradise), pack some food and water (there's a small museum, but no stores, restaurants, or service stations), bring your sunscreen, and whistle some Ennio Morricone tunes as you take an eerie trip through the past. **Note:** The last 3 miles of the road are not paved. This park is at very high elevation (8,375 ft.), and the weather is very unpredictable. Although Hwy. 270 closes in winter, the park stays open and is accessible by snowmobile, skis, and snowshoes (it's best to let the ranger know you're coming). ⏱ At least 1 hr. ☎ 760/647-6445. www.parks.ca.gov or www.bodie.com. Admission $5 adults, $3 kids 7–16, free for kids 6 & under. Daily 9am–6pm summer; 10am–3pm Oct–spring. Museum daily 9am–5pm in summer only.

> The reward for a climb to the top of Tenaya Peak in Tuolomne Meadows? Fabulous vistas of Yosemite's backcountry.

Return to U.S. 395 and head south through Lee Vining and back to Hwy. 120; go east on Hwy. 120 for about 5 miles to the signed turnoff for South Tufa Area/Mono Lake Tufa State Reserve. Turn left here and proceed down a maintained gravel road for about 1 mile.

⑬ ★ **Mono Lake Tufa State Natural Reserve.** Why spend billions on a space program, when it's possible to explore extraterrestrial landscapes right here at Mono Lake? Mono Lake (pronounced "moe-no") is a 65-square-mile body of water that's more than 1 million years old, making it one of the oldest lakes in North America. It's made cameo appearances in everything from Clint Eastwood's *High Plains Drifter* to the inner sleeve of Pink Floyd's *Wish You Were Here,* and it is famous for the bizarre towers and spires that rise up out of the water and dot the landscape. Known as tufas, these limestone formations have been created by freshwater springs bubbling up into the highly alkaline lake. Mono Lake is 2½ times as salty and 80 times as alkaline as the ocean and supports bountiful populations of algae, brine shrimp, and alkali flies (which utilize air bubbles to scuba dive); these in turn make the lake a favored stopover for some 2 million birds annually (some 300 different species) and a favorite of birders.

Look for the **Mono Basin Scenic Area Visitors Center** (☎ 760/647-3044) on Hwy. 395, about a ½ mile north of Lee Vining. You can pick up maps and take a free tour (3 times daily in summer) here; the center is closed in winter. The interpreted walk along the **South Tufa Trail** is about 2 miles round-trip and includes a stop at **Navy Beach,** the lake's best swimming area. Many people tout the healing properties of the water, but don't go in if you have any cuts—you'll definitely be adding salt to the wound; there are also no shower facilities and you'll come out of the lake salty as a pretzel. There's no shade either, so make sure you have sunscreen, a hat, and water, too. ⏱ At least 1 hr. ☎ 760/647-6331. www.parks.ca.gov. Admission $3 adults for South Tufa Trail area; free for kids 17 & under. Call for current hours.

The Best of the High Sierra in 9 Days

An extended journey through the High Sierra will give you time to explore more of wondrous Yosemite National Park, as well as bask in the sublime beauty of Lake Tahoe. As you head down the far side of California along the Eastern Sierra, you'll encounter amazing recreational areas, an evocative ghost town, surreal landscapes, and the planet's oldest living things.

> See in double vision at aptly named Mirror Lake, also a good place to spot wildlife.

START Southern entrance of Yosemite National Park, 190 miles east of San Francisco. From Fresno-Yosemite International Airport, head north on Hwy. 41 for about 68 miles; upon entering the park, head right on Mariposa Grove Rd. **TRIP LENGTH** about 590 miles.

❶ ★★★ Yosemite National Park. It won't take long for this incredible national treasure to blow you away. For a summary of your first day's itinerary, see p. 264, ❶–❽.

❷ ★ Mirror Lake. Start Day 2 with an easy walk along this small lake; take the free shuttle to the **Mirror Lake trail head** (shuttle stop 17) to embark on a gentle 2-mile hike along a paved trail. The lake is in the process of silting up and becoming a meadow, but in spring and early summer it lives up to its name, reflecting the incredible landscape around it in the shallow, glassy water. ⏱ 1 hr.

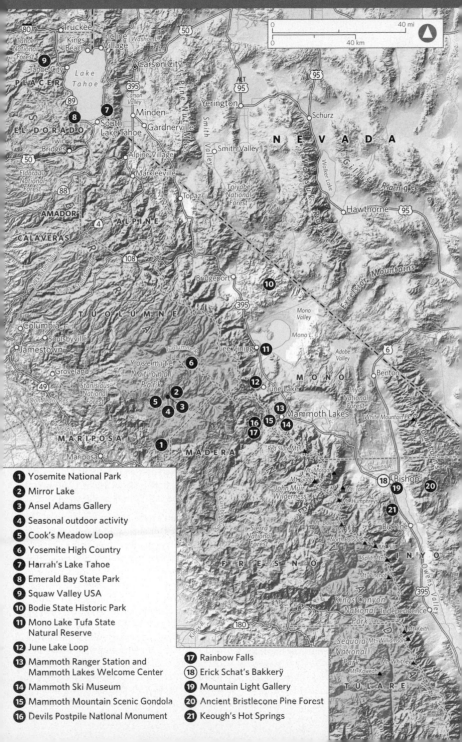

1. Yosemite National Park
2. Mirror Lake
3. Ansel Adams Gallery
4. Seasonal outdoor activity
5. Cook's Meadow Loop
6. Yosemite High Country
7. Harrah's Lake Tahoe
8. Emerald Bay State Park
9. Squaw Valley USA
10. Bodie State Historic Park
11. Mono Lake Tufa State Natural Reserve
12. June Lake Loop
13. Mammoth Ranger Station and Mammoth Lakes Welcome Center
14. Mammoth Ski Museum
15. Mammoth Mountain Scenic Gondola
16. Devils Postpile National Monument
17. Rainbow Falls
18. Erick Schat's Bakkerÿ
19. Mountain Light Gallery
20. Ancient Bristlecone Pine Forest
21. Keough's Hot Springs

> As lonely as the sound of the wind in the sagebrush hills, Bodie leaves an eerie and unforgettable impression.

③ Ansel Adams Gallery. Back in the village, pop into this longtime Yosemite staple (this family-owned business is currently run by the famed photographer's grandson). It's really more gift shop than gallery, and a great place to pick up some souvenirs, but you will find the work of contemporary photographers as well as some by the master himself. You can also participate in photo workshops and pick up photography supplies. ⊕ 20 min. ☎ 209/372-4413. www.anseladams.com. Daily 10am–5pm.

④ ★★ Seasonal Outdoor Activity. Take advantage of the park concessions for some seasonal recreation. From May to July, **rafting** is one of the best, most-fun ways of seeing the sights. It's a 3-mile, self-guided trip in inflatable rafts down the Merced River through the heart of the valley. You'll start out at **Curry Village** and end up at **Sentinel Beach,** with transportation provided to return you to the starting point. If conditions aren't right for rafting, consider a half-day **mule or horseback ride** to **Clark Point,** where you'll get awesome views of ★ **Vernal Fall** (novice riders should opt for the 2-hour **Mirror Lake** ride). Both mules and horses are used on these trails and

riders usually don't have a choice of mount. If there's snow on the ground, shuttle up to the ★ **Badger Pass Ski Area,** California's oldest ski operation. Badger Pass is especially good for novice and intermediate skiers and snowboarders; there's also cross-country skiing and snowshoeing out to the fabulous ★★ **Glacier Point** vista. Lessons and all the equipment you might need are available. ⊕ At least 3 hr. ☎ 209/372-4386. www.yosemitepark.com. Rafts: $26 adults, $16 kids 12 & under (kids weighing less than 50lb. are not permitted—and they do check). Daily in season 10am–6pm. Mule and horseback outings: ☎ 209/372-8348. Rides $60–$80 (ages 7 & up). Badger Pass lift tickets: $35–$42 adults, $35–$37 kids 13–17, $16–$20 kids 7–12, free for kids 6 & under.

⑤ ★ Cook's Meadow Loop. End your day with a relaxed stroll along a boardwalk through a meadow. The highlight is a stop at ★ **Sentinel Bridge,** where you can watch the sunset reflect off the face of **Half Dome.** Ansel Adams shot one of his most famous images from this very spot. ⊕ 30 min.

⑥ ★★★ Yosemite High Country. On Day 3, it's time to leave the crowds behind and head out to the high country. ★ Olmstead Point (p. 268, ⑨), ★ Tenaya Lake (p. 268, ⑩) and ★★ Tuolumne Meadows (p. 268, ⑪) are all on the day's agenda. ⊕ At least 5 hr.

On Day 4, head west along Big Oak Flat Rd./ Hwy. 120 and exit the park. Go north on Hwy. 49, then east on U.S. 50 to South Lake Tahoe. Trip time is about 5½ hr. (200 miles). Continue on U.S. 50 to Stateline and

⑦ ★ Harrah's Lake Tahoe. Baby needs a new pair of shoes, or at least to recoup some gas money, so try your luck at this glitzy casino, just on the other side of the California/Nevada border. You won't confuse Tahoe's South Shore with the Las Vegas Strip, but you'll find plenty of action here at Harrah's: 24-hour gaming (craps, blackjack, poker, and more); a glam nightclub, **VEX,** featuring aerialists swinging from the ceiling and topless go-go dancers; and big-name entertainment—from comedy to classic rock—in the **South Shore Room.** Whatever happens in Tahoe stays in Tahoe. 18 Hwy. 50. ☎ 800/427-7247 or 775/588-6611. www.harrahslaketahoe.com.

On Day 5, from Stateline, return through South Lake Tahoe on Lake Tahoe Blvd. (U.S. 50) and go north 12⅓ miles on Hwy. 89 to Emerald Bay. Trip time: 25 min.

8 ★★ **Emerald Bay State Park.** Designated a National Natural Landmark in 1968, Emerald Bay shows off Lake Tahoe at its absolute best and makes for a spectacular photo-op. Inside the park, and accessible via a great short hike, is ★ **Vikingsholm,** a 38-room castle built in 1929 by the couple who financed Charles Lindbergh's trans-Atlantic flight in 1927. Especially in snowy winter, the authentically rendered medieval Scandinavian design will convince you you're tromping along some Norwegian fjord. Tours of the mansion are offered from Memorial Day weekend through September 30, 10am to 4pm. **Note:** Emerald Bay's popularity can mean a scarcity of parking on weekends. ⏲ At least 1 hr. ☎ 530/541-3030. www.parks.ca.gov. Parking $7. Vikingsholm: ☎ 530/541-6498. Tours $5 adults, $3 kids 6–17.

Continue north on Hwy. 89 and turn left at Squaw Valley Rd.; it's about 45 min. and 27 miles to

9 ★★★ **kids** **Squaw Valley USA.** In February 1960, more than 800 athletes descended on Squaw Valley for the VIII Winter Olympics, making this resort an international star. If you're here in winter, you're in for some of the best alpine skiing in the world. There are six peaks, the highest of which, Granite Chief, soars to almost 10,000 feet; there are more than 170 trails on 4,000 skiable acres that see some 450 inches of snow annually. If you're a nonskier or have arrived in summer, you're still in luck—Squaw Valley has a wide assortment of year-round activities and attractions. Take the cable car up to ★★ **High Camp,** elevation 8,200 feet, where you'll find ice skating, a climbing wall, a collection of Olympic memorabilia, and five restaurants to go along with the breathtaking views. There's even a huge free-form pool and spa (spring and summer only). In 2009, the resort dropped more than $5 million on improvements and renovations to spruce up for its 50th anniversary Olympic celebration. ⏲ At least 3 hr. ☎ 530/583-6985. www.squaw.com. Cable car ride: $24 adults, $18 seniors and kids 13–18, $6 kids 12 & under. See p. 304.

On Day 6, return south on Hwy. 89 and make a right on U.S. 395; continue on U.S. 395 to Hwy. 270 and turn left to Bodie State Historic Park. **TRIP LENGTH** around 145 miles, about 3¼ hr.

10 ★ **Bodie State Historic Park.** The story is told two ways: A little girl whose family was moving from San Francisco to this wild, high-desert boomtown wrote, "Goodbye, God; I'm going to Bodie." Or was it: "Good, by God; I'm going to Bodie." You should go with the latter interpretation—this is one of the coolest, creepiest ghost towns in the country. ⏲ At least 1 hr. See p. 268, **12** .

Head south on U.S. 395 through the town of Lee Vining, and turn east on Hwy. 120. Proceed to the signed turnoff for South Tufa Area/ Mono Lake Tufa State Reserve. Turn left and drive down a maintained gravel road for about 1 mile. The reserve is about 40 miles from Bodie; trip time is less than an hour.

11 ★ **Mono Lake Tufa State Natural Reserve.** ⏲ At least 1 hr. See p. 269, **13** .

On Day 7 take Hwy. 158, the June Lake Loop; it's about 5 miles south of Lee Vining and just north of the Hwy. 120 Mono Lake turnoff.

> *Sometimes nicknamed Sierra cement, the deep drifts that blanket the region are still irresistible to boarders and skiers.*

> *For a perfect paddle, head to the June Lake Loop, where a series of aspen-ringed lakes sparkle beneath Sierra peaks.*

⓬ ★ **June Lake Loop.** This 16-mile drive skirts along the edge of the ★★ **Ansel Adams Wilderness,** taking you past ★ **Grant** (p. 283, ❹), **Silver** (p. 283, ❺), **Gull** (p. 284, ❼), and **June Lakes** (p. 284, ❽). The drive is at its best in early to mid-October, when this alpine area bursts out in fall colors of yellow, orange, and red. Boating and trout fishing are major pursuits here (particularly Grant Lake, the largest of the quartet, known as the "home of the German brown" trout). In winter, the excellent and uncrowded ★ **June Mountain Ski Area** (p. 284, ❻) springs into action, offering 35 trails over more than 500 acres of skiable territory. You'll find a number of campgrounds, as well as other options for lodging and dining, along the road. ⏱ At least 1 hr. www.junelakeloop.org. See p. 284, ❸.

Hwy. 158 rejoins U.S. 395; from here it's less than 30 min. south to the Hwy. 203 turnoff and Mammoth Lakes.

⓭ **Mammoth Ranger Station and Mammoth Lakes Welcome Center.** A joint operation by the Inyo National Forest, the National Park Service, the Eastern Sierra Interpretive Association, and the town of Mammoth Lakes, the ranger station and welcome center offer all the specific info you need about anything from lodging (special hotel hot lines are set up) to tours to recreational activities. There's a bookstore on-site as well, where you can score field guides or tomes on local history. ⏱ 15 min. Hwy. 203, just before the town of Mammoth Lakes. ☎ 760/924-5500. www.fs.fed.us/r5/inyo. Daily 8am–5pm.

From Hwy. 203, make a left on Meridian Blvd. to College Pkwy.

⓮ **Mammoth Ski Museum.** The art of skiing takes on a whole new meaning at this museum that celebrates 500 years of skiing heritage. It features vintage posters, paintings, sculptures, photos, and literature, from artists ranging from Ansel Adams and Andrew Wyeth to extreme-skiing filmmaker Warren Miller. Lovers of Art Deco graphics will appreciate the cool old promotional posters, reproductions of which are for sale. ⏱ 30 min. 100 College Pkwy, Mammoth Lakes. ☎ 760/934-6592. www.mammothskimuseum.org. Admission $5 adults, $3 kids 12–18. Wed–Sat 10am–5pm (hours may vary, call ahead). Closed Sept–Nov.

Continue on Meridian Blvd. and go right on Minaret Rd. to the Mammoth Mountain main lodge.

⓯ ★★ **Mammoth Mountain Scenic Gondola.** You may literally need to catch your breath when you get to the top of 11,053-foot ★★ **Mammoth Mountain,** the highest ski resort in California. Year-round, stunning views of the Eastern Sierra await you, and once you arrive after a 15-minute ride on the gondola, you can learn about what you're seeing at the **Sierra Interpretive Center.** It covers the cultural and geological history of the Mammoth Lakes area (although it may give you pause to realize you're standing in a still-active volcanic region). In summer there are hiking and biking trails to explore; in winter, you better be a darn good skier if you don't plan on taking the gondola back down. ⏱ At least 1 hr. ☎ 800/626-6684. www.mammothmountain.com. Gondola $22 adults, $16 kids 13–18, $11 kids 7–12. Summer 9am–4:30pm; winter 7:30am–2pm (weather permitting).

On Day 8, catch the shuttle from the Mammoth main lodge to Devils Postpile National Monument. If you've arrived in fall, you can drive in via S.R. 203 from Mammoth (about 18 miles).

⑯ ★ Devils Postpile National Monument. Looking like the remains of a giant stockade, this geological curiosity was nearly blasted to pieces in 1911 to make way for a dam. These long (some as tall as 60 ft.), hexagonal basalt columns seem almost sculpted, but were actually formed about 100,000 years ago by a combination of volcanic and glacial activity. In summer, unless you're camping here, you have to take a shuttle to get to the park; the ride is about 45 minutes. In the fall, you can drive in. ⊙ At least 1 hr. ☎ 760/924-5500. www.nps.gov/depo. Summer shuttle (available at Mammoth Mountain's Adventure Center) $7 adults, $4 kids 3–15; fall admission $10 per car. Daily approx. June–early fall. Summer shuttle 7:30–9:30am every 45 min., 9:30am–4pm every 20–30 min., 4–7:45pm every 40 min.

From Devils Postpile National Monument hike 2 miles to

⑰ ★ Rainbow Falls. Your Devils Postpile experience is not complete until you make your way to this wide and roaring waterfall. The San Joaquin River tumbles 101 feet to the pool below, throwing up prismed rainbows in the process; there's a cutoff trail that will take you to the base of the falls for an awesome vantage point. Be sure to bring a hat, sunscreen, and water, as the trail is exposed. ⊙ At least 1½ hr.

On Day 9, go south on U.S. 395 to the high desert town of Bishop; it will take about 45 min. (43 miles).

⑱ ☙ ★★ Erick Schat's Bakkerÿ. Crowds line up here for an overwhelming array of baked goods. Famous for its sheepherder bread, you'll also find all manner of specialty loaves, pastries, cookies, preserves, and honey. 763 N. Main St., Bishop. ☎ 866/323-5854 or 760/873-7156. www.erickschatsbakery.com. Items $2.25–$10.

⑲ ★ Mountain Light Gallery. While in Bishop, drop by this gallery displaying the stirring nature photography of Galen and Barbara Rowell, featuring images from the Sierra and around the world. There's a good selection of prints, posters, books, cards, DVDs, and more. ⊙ 30 min. 106 S. Main St., Bishop. ☎ 760/873-7700. www.mountainlight.com. Daily 10am–6pm.

From Bishop go south 15 miles to Hwy. 168, then go east about 12 miles and turn left on White Mountain Rd.; from here it's 10 miles to the Ancient Bristlecone Pine Forest, a 1-hr. drive from Bishop.

⑳ ★ Ancient Bristlecone Pine Forest. Bristlecone pines are believed to be the earth's oldest living single organisms, with a life span of nearly 5,000 years. Resembling huge pieces of driftwood, these gnarled trees cling to a surreal moonscape, somehow surviving the harsh conditions found at 10,000 feet above sea level. This forest is located inside the vast Inyo National Forest and has three interpreted trails; somewhere in this grove is **Methuselah,** the world's oldest living tree (left unidentified to prevent vandalism) at about 4,750 years old. The park visitor center, operating out of a temporary structure following a fire in 2008, is open mid-May to October; in summer it hosts lectures and ranger-led programs. Even in summer, be prepared for chilly temps, and bring a hat, sunscreen, and water. ⊙ At least 1½ hr. ☎ 760/873-2500. www.fs.fed.us. Admission $3 adults (free for kids 17 & under) or $5 per vehicle.

Back on U.S. 395, midway between Big Pine and Bishop, head west on Keough Hot Springs Rd. Total drive time is about 45 min. (30 miles) to

㉑ ★ Keough's Hot Springs. After 9 days of hard traveling, treat yourself and your body to a soak at this natural hot springs pool (massages are available too), where the water temp in the Hot Pool is maintained at a comfy 104°F year-round. This rustic facility has been in business since 1919, when it was first established as a health resort. If you forgot to pack a swimsuit, there's a gift shop on-site. 800 Keough Hot Springs Rd. ☎ 760/872-4670. www.keoughshotsprings.com. Admission $8 adults, $6 kids 12 & under. Summer Mon–Thurs 9am–8pm, Fri–Sat 9am–9pm and Sun 9am–7pm; rest of the year Mon and Wed–Fri 11am–7pm, Sat–Sun 9am–8pm.

The Best of Yosemite National Park

Naturalist and early Yosemite advocate John Muir (1838–1914) described this incomparable wilderness as "the grandest of all the special temples of nature I was ever permitted to enter." Most of the 3.5 million visitors per year who make pilgrimages to Yosemite National Park these days probably have sentiments similar to Mr. Muir's. With its iconic granite edifices, lush meadows, epic waterfalls, sparkling lakes, and towering sequoias, this UNESCO World Heritage Site indeed lives up to its reputation. ***Note:*** Enhance the park experience for all by parking your car and utilizing the free park shuttle whenever possible.

> *Looking like the feet of rust-colored dinosaurs, giant sequoia trunks loom in Yosemite's Mariposa Grove.*

START Southern entrance of Yosemite National Park, 190 miles east of San Francisco. From Fresno-Yosemite International Airport, head north on Hwy. 41 for about 68 miles; upon entering the park, head right on Mariposa Grove Rd. **TRIP LENGTH** 6 days (including Half Dome ascent).

1 Mariposa Grove
2 Sentinel Dome
3 Glacier Point
4 Tunnel View
5 Bridalveil Fall
6 Yosemite Valley Visitor Center and Yosemite Museum
7 Sentinel Bridge
8 The Awahnee Hotel
9 Yosemite Falls
10 Mist Trail
11 Half Dome
12 El Capitan
13 Olmsted Point
14 Tenaya Lake
15 Tuolumne Meadows

Where to Stay

The Ahwahnee Hotel 20
Curry Village 18
Wawona Hotel 16
Yosemite Lodge at the Falls 17

Where to Dine

Ahwahnee Dining Room 20
Curry Village Pizza Deck 18
Degnan's Deli 19

> *Tunnel View may be the ultimate Yosemite photo-op but it's also a prime spot for seeing how glaciers carved Yosemite's granite monoliths.*

1 ★ **Mariposa Grove.** Just minutes past the park's southern entrance you'll find this landmark stand of more than 500 giant sequoias. Though the ★ Grizzly Giant is the oldest tree (dating back about 2,400 years), the tallest (here and in the park) is the Columbia Tree, which tops out at close to 285 feet. See p. 264, **1**.

2 ★★ **kids Sentinel Dome.** The trail here is flat, easy, and only about a mile long, making this a great choice for families. Despite the ease of the hike, though, there's a huge payoff— scramble up the side of the granite dome and behold the unobstructed vistas from 1,000 feet higher than nearby Glacier Point (**3**). ⏱1 hr. About 13 miles down Glacier Point Rd. to the Taft Point/Sentinel Dome trail head.

3 ★★ **Glacier Point.** From this vantage point you'll get a jaw-dropping look at Yosemite Valley, Half Dome, and a trio of waterfalls from a height of 3,000 feet. See p. 272, **4**.

4 ★★★ **Tunnel View.** It's often mobbed by gawkers and shutterbugs, but this is Yosemite's most iconic vista, as made famous by photographer Ansel Adams (1902–84). See p. 266, **3**.

5 ★★ **Bridalveil Fall.** The indigenous Ahwahneechee tribe placed great mystical importance on this 620-foot waterfall. Not only did they believe it to be the home of the "Spirit of the Puffing Wind" (so named because in heavy winds the water appears to be moving to the side instead of down), it was also said breathing in the waterfall's mist improved one's chance of finding a mate. See p. 266, **4**.

6 ★ **Yosemite Valley Visitor Center and Yosemite Museum.** Add some context to the beauty you see around you by learning about Yosemite's unique geological and cultural history. The museum, founded in 1926, focuses on the indigenous art and culture of the Yosemite Valley. Don't miss the free film that provides an introductory look at the park's scenic wonders; it plays every 30 minutes in the visitor center. See p. 266, **5**.

7 ★ **Sentinel Bridge.** This scenic spot along the valley floor is where Ansel Adams took another of his most famous Yosemite shots— this one of Half Dome looming overhead. Though it's a stunning vista at any time of day, it's particularly breathtaking at sunset. See p. 272, **5**.

8 ★★★ **The Ahwahnee Hotel.** Even if you aren't staying here, be sure to pay a visit to this magnificent hotel, designed by Gilbert Stanley Underwood, who also did lodges for several other national parks, including the Grand Canyon. Movie buffs shouldn't be surprised if some of the hotel decor looks familiar—the interior of the Overlook Hotel in *The Shining* was modeled on the Ahwahnee. See p. 281.

9 ★ **Yosemite Falls.** Three separate falls combine to make this North America's tallest waterfall (and the world's sixth highest), a dizzying 2,425 feet. The hike to the top on the Upper Yosemite Falls Trail is no less head spinning—and challenging. This is an all-day affair, covering 7.2 miles round-trip—but gaining 2,700 feet in elevation— as you trudge up one of Yosemite's oldest trails, carved out in the 1870s. The falls run from November to July and are at their peak in May. ☺ At least 6 hr. www.nps.gov/yose. Start from Yosemite Falls trail head at shuttle stop 7.

10 ★ **Mist Trail.** Follow this moderately challenging trail, one of the park's most popular, for a thrilling look at the top of ★ **Vernal Fall** as the torrent plunges 317 feet below. If you do this in spring, you're almost guaranteed to get wet, so take some time at the top to admire the views and dry off. See p. 267, **6**.

The Life & Times of John Muir

Over the course of his illustrious 75 years, John Muir earned a nickname: "Father of Our National Parks." In the late 19th century, he pushed for conservation of the pristine wilderness and helped establish Yosemite, Sequoia, and Kings Canyon as national parks.

Born in Scotland in 1838, Muir immigrated with his family to Wisconsin at the age of 11. After an accident nearly blinded him about a decade later, he dropped everything to pursue his fascination with the natural world and decided to go to the Amazon—on foot. He didn't make it, but traveling became a way of life for Muir, and his journeys eventually took him west. He discovered the Sierra Nevada area in 1868 and worked as a shepherd in the Yosemite area. He later ran a sawmill nearby.

Muir began writing about the Sierra Nevada the moment he arrived, and his passionate words started finding an audience in the late 1800s. He wrote a number of books, contributed to numerous periodicals, and became a leading voice in the budding environmentalist movement. In 1892, Muir helped found the Sierra Club. In 1903, he took President Theodore Roosevelt camping in the Yosemite backcountry and catalyzed Roosevelt's vision of an entire system of national parks.

Muir is a legend not only for his words and his deeds, but also for being something of an eccentric. He never shaved, making way for an impressive beard. He experienced nature to its fullest—he climbed a tree during an incredible storm, sledded down Yosemite Valley's steep walls on his rump to avoid an avalanche, and chased a bear so he could study the animal's stride. (Not surprisingly, these actions have since been banned by the National Park Service.)

From the first moment a politician pondered Hetch Hetchy Reservoir, Muir fought it. Damming and drowning a place whose beauty rivaled that of Yosemite Valley was sacrilege to him. But San Francisco needed water to drink, and Congress passed legislation approving Hetch Hetchy Reservoir in 1913. John Muir died the very next year— some say of a broken heart.

> *Cast a fly (all fishing is catch-and-release in the national park) into the Tuolumne River as it snakes through Yosemite's high country.*

⓫ ★★★ **Half Dome.** Despite being described in 1865 as "perfectly inaccessible," thousands of people summit this nearly 5,000-foot granite monolith every year. The 14- to 16-mile hike takes most trekkers 10 to 12 hours, and requires fitness and some preparation. You'll need sturdy footwear with good traction, plenty of food and water (1 gallon per person), gloves, and a flashlight (in case you return after sundown; camping is not allowed on Half Dome). No special climbing equipment or skills are needed—the final 400 feet of the ascent features a pair of cables that allow you to steady and pull yourself up. Consider camping at Little Yosemite Valley (wilderness permit required) to shorten the journey. *Note:* You should not attempt this hike if the ground is wet or if storm clouds are approaching. ⊙ At least 1 day. John Muir or Mist Trail from Happy Isles; take the shuttle to stop 16. www.nps.gov/yose.

⓬ ★★ **El Capitan.** Its Spanish name means "the chief" and it definitely lives up to the moniker: This is the world's largest hunk of granite. A magnet for rock climbers, "El Cap" was first conquered in 1958, when it took 47 days to make the ascent (today it takes 4–7 days to do the job). Unless you're an experienced climber, its sheer 3,000-foot face is best admired from afar. ⊙ 15 min. El Capitan Meadow, along Northside Dr., on the west side of Yosemite Village.

⓭ ★ **Olmsted Point.** Half Dome (⓫) and Tenaya Lake (⓮) are just some of the scenic marvels you'll see from this viewing area, named for noted landscape artist and conservationist Frederick Law Olmsted, Jr. (1870–1957). See p. 268, ❾.

⓮ ★ **Tenaya Lake.** The native Miwok people called this sapphire body of water the "Lake of the Shining Rocks," and its current moniker honors Chief Tenaya (d. 1853), who led the natives of the Yosemite Valley. See p. 268, ❿.

⓯ ★★ **Tuolumne Meadows.** This subalpine meadow is surrounded by domes and steep granite formations that are great for sightseeing and/or climbing. If you face north on this grassy expanse, at roughly two o'clock you'll see Lembert Dome; at eight o'clock is Unicorn Peak, and at ten o'clock is Fairview Dome. The section of the Tuolumne River here is a popular place to fish. See p. 268, ⓫.

Where to Stay & Dine

> Kick off the hiking boots and put on the fancy duds for a dinner in the ultra-elegant—and pricey—Ahwahnee Dining Room.

★★ **Ahwahnee Dining Room** *CALIFORNIAN*
With its 34-foot ceilings, floor-to-ceiling windows, chandeliers, and granite columns, this dining room is designed to impress. The menu features traditional dishes prepared with organic and local product. Dinner dress code: collared shirts for men, no shorts or T-shirts; other meals are more casual. In the Ahwahnee Hotel. ☎ 209/372-1489. www.yosemitepark.com. Reservations recommended. Entrees $8–$40; Sun brunch $32 adults, $17 kids. DC, DISC, MC, V. Breakfast, lunch & dinner daily.

★★★ **The Ahwahnee Hotel** *YOSEMITE NATIONAL PARK* Art Deco, Arts and Crafts, and Native American elements are woven together to create one of California's premier lodgings. With its murals, fireplaces, stained glass, and wood and stone accents, the Ahwahnee, which opened in 1927, is a romantic and stylishly rugged luxe experience. ☎ 209/372-1489. www.yosemitepark.com. 99 units, 24 cottages. Doubles $408–$984. AE, DC, DISC, MC, V.

Curry Village *YOSEMITE NATIONAL PARK* Opened in 1899 and still fulfilling the goal of its original owners to provide affordable lodgings in the park, Curry Village offers a variety of family-friendly options. There are standard motel rooms and cabins, but the primary accommodations are the more than 300 large canvas tents with wooden frames. Most cabins are not heated and have shared bathroom/shower facilities. ☎ 801/559-5000. www.yosemitepark.com. 499 units. Doubles $85–$207. AE, DC, DISC, MC, V.

★ **Curry Village Pizza Deck** *PIZZA*
If you need to do some carb loading, this is your place. Pizzas, salads, beers on tap, and the view-enhanced deck make this a popular spot; this is also where to come to catch a sporting event on the big-screen TV. Pizza $8–$16. DC, DISC, MC, V. In season lunch & dinner daily; winter lunch Sat-Sun, dinner daily.

★★ **Degnan's Deli** *DELI*
All things considered, this might be the best food in Yosemite—Quick, healthy fare, as well as groceries—including a good selection of beer and wine—make this the go-to spot before any day hike. In Yosemite Village. Most items $1–$7. DC, DISC, MC, V. Breakfast, lunch & dinner daily.

★ **Wawona Hotel** *YOSEMITE NATIONAL PARK* What began as a log-cabin way station in 1856 has grown into an elegant and charming Victorian inn at the park's southern entrance. To enhance your time-traveling experience, the rooms don't have telephones or TVs; in season, there's golf, swimming, horseback riding, and tennis. ☎ 801/559-5000. www.yosemitepark.com. 104 units, 52 with private bathroom. Doubles $126 without private bathroom; $198 with private bathroom. AE, DC, DISC, MC, V.

kids Yosemite Lodge at the Falls *YOSEMITE NATIONAL PARK* With its large "lodge" rooms, featuring dining tables and sofa sleepers, this modern complex is a great choice for families. The on-site activities desk can also set up tours, transportation, classes, and recreation for you. ☎ 801/559-5000. www.yosemitepark.com. 249 units. Doubles $113–$180. AE, DC, DISC, MC, V.

The Best of Mammoth Lakes Region

With more than 100 lakes, the Mammoth Lakes region is one of California's best destinations for fishing, boating, hiking, and biking. As the weather turns chilly, the aspen leaves turn fiery red and golden orange, heralding the approach of winter—which means some of the state's best skiing is just around the corner.

> *A quick swing off U.S. 395 reveals a surprisingly secluded corner of Sierra beauty, with watersports, hiking, and fishing.*

START Bodie State Historic Park is 60 miles north of Mammoth Lakes, which is 40 miles east of Yosemite. From U.S. 395, go east on Hwy. 270. *Note:* Hwy. 270 is closed in winter, but the park stays open. **TRIP LENGTH** 4 days, about 80 miles.

❶ ★ Bodie State Historic Park. This National Historic Landmark is California's Official State Gold Rush Ghost Town, with some 200 buildings still standing from its boomtown days. ☺ At least 1 hr. See p. 268, **⓬** .

Go south on U.S. 395 through the town of Lee Vining, and turn east on Hwy. 120. Proceed to the signed turnoff for South Tufa Area/ Mono Lake Tufa State Reserve. Turn left and drive down a maintained gravel road for about 1 mile. The reserve is about 40 miles from Bodie; trip time is less than an hour.

❷ ★ Mono Lake Tufa State Natural Reserve. Mark Twain called this ancient lake "one of the strangest freaks of Nature found in any land." It's an alien-looking landscape of bizarre

1. Bodie State Historic Park
2. Mono Lake Tufa State Natural Reserve
3. June Lake Loop
4. Grant Lake
5. Silver Lake
6. June Mountain Ski Area
7. Gull Lake
8. June Lake
9. Mammoth Mountain Ski Area
10. Devils Postpile National Monument
11. Rainbow Falls

Where to Stay

Mammoth Mountain Inn **12**
Tamarack Lodge & Resort **13**
Westin Monache Resort **14**

Where to Dine

Nevados **15**
The Restaurant at Convict Lake **17**
Skadi **16**

limestone formations—and a sight you won't soon forget. **Note:** "Mono" translates as "flies" in the native Yokut language. Enough said. ⏲ At least 1 hr. See p. 269, ⑬.

On Day 2, take Hwy. 158, the June Lake Loop; it's about 5 miles south of Lee Vining and just north of the Hwy. 120 Mono Lake turnoff.

❸ ★ **June Lake Loop.** Hwy. 158 loops off U.S. 395 for a lovely 16-mile detour along a horse-shoe-shaped canyon that features blazing fall colors in autumn and takes you past four lakes popular for fishing and boating as well as the ★ **June Mountain Ski Area** (❻). ⏲ At least 1 hr., not including stops. www.junelakeloop.org.

❹ ★ **Grant Lake.** If you want to wet a line in search of trout, this is a great place to do it. Long known as "the Home of the German Brown," this lake is devoted to fishing until 10am; the **Grant Lake Marina and Campground** (☎ 760/648-7964) can set you up with a fishing boat and gear. After 10am, Grant Lake is turned over to recreational boaters, water-skiers, and jet-skiers. Other than the marina and campground, this lake is undeveloped, so there's good hiking, too. ⏲ At least 1 hr. Inyo National Forest. ☎ 760/873-2400. www.fs.fed.us/r5/inyo. Marina and campground daily late Apr to mid-Oct.

❺ ★ **Silver Lake.** Not to be confused with L.A.'s hipster neighborhood of the same name

> *Peek inside the lonely buildings in the ghost town of Bodie to read decades-old newspapers once used for wallpaper.*

(as if), this lake is home to one of the oldest fishing resorts in the Sierra, the **Silver Lake Resort,** first opened in 1916 (when it was known as "Carson's Camp"). Even if you aren't staying in one of the cabins, you can rent boats and kayaks (rentals start at $18); there's also a cafe (daily 7am–2pm) and a general store. Across the road you'll find the ★ **Rush Creek trail head,** which leads into the ★★ **Ansel Adams Wilderness.** This is the start of a demanding but rewarding backcountry trek, but you can make a great day hike out of it by just going the 3 miles to beautiful ★ **Gem Lake.** You'll also find **Frontier Pack Train** (☎ 888/437-6853; www.frontierpacktrain.net) here, offering horseback and mule trail rides (1 hr. rides start at $30). ⏲ At least 1 hr. Inyo National Forest. ☎ 760/873-2400. www.fs.fed.us/r5/inyo. Silver Lake Resort ☎ 760/648-7525. www.silverlakeresort.net. Daily late Apr to mid-Oct.

After about 12 miles along the loop you will come to

⑥ ★ **June Mountain Ski Area.** In the proverbial shadow of the much larger Mammoth Mountain, June Mountain more than holds its own with excellent conditions and shorter lift lines. The 500 skiable acres offer something for all levels of skiers, and there's also a terrain park for boarders. Skiers and snowboarders can also arrange for a backcountry guide. ⏲ At least 3 hr. 3819 Hwy. 158. ☎ 888/586-3686 or 760/648-7733. www.junemountain.com. One-day lift tickets $64 adults, $54 kids 13–17, and $32 kids 7–12.

Coming up immediately on your left will be Gull Lake, and within 2 miles, the town of June Lake.

⑦ ★ **Gull Lake.** This is the smallest lake on the loop, but perhaps the most popular with fishermen. It also has some of the best campsites in the area at the small (11 sites), first-come, first-served campground. ⏲ 30 min. Inyo National Forest. ☎ 760/873-2400. www.fs.fed.us/r5/inyo.

⑧ ★ **June Lake.** This quaint town offers services, lodgings, and dining choices. The mile-long lake has two marinas, and fishing boats are available for rent; the lake is also favored by sailors and sailboarders. The ★ **Oh! Ridge Campground** (which accepts reservations) is at the eastern end of the lake and is a good stop for a lakeshore photo-op; it's also near June Lake's swimming beach. ⏲ At least 1 hr. Inyo National Forest. ☎ 760/873-2400. www.fs.fed.us/r5/inyo.

On Day 3, make a right on U.S. 395, then go right on Hwy. 203 to Mammoth Lakes; make a right on Minaret Rd. It's about 20 miles (30 min.) to

⑨ ★★ **Mammoth Mountain Ski Area.** With 150 trails on more than 3,500 skiable acres and a 3,100-foot vertical drop, Mammoth Mountain is the state's tallest ski area (11,053 ft.), and more than lives up to its name. And with 400 inches of snow annually, Mammoth has a 6-month season. Skiers and nonskiers alike can make use of the ★★ **Scenic Gondola** to the mountaintop; in summer it transports hikers and mountain bikers (p. 274, **⑮**). The **Adventure Center** at the main lodge can outfit you with all the gear you need for summer or winter fun. ⏲ At least 2 hr. 1 Minaret Rd., Mammoth Lakes. ☎ 800/626-6684 or 760/934-2571. www.mammothmountain.com. One-day lift tickets $87 adults, $64 kids 13–17, $43 kids 7–12. Bike park pass $39 adults, $20 kids 12 & under.

From Mammoth's main lodge, a shuttle (summer only) can take you on Day 4 to

⑩ ★ **Devils Postpile National Monument.** ⏲ At least 1 hr. See p. 275, **⑯**.

From Devils Postpile, it's a 2-mile hike to

⑪ ★ **Rainbow Falls.** Don't just stop at the Upper Falls of this shutterbug's dream, be sure to see the Lower Falls as well. ⏲ At least 1½ hr. See p. 275, **⑰**.

Where to Stay & Dine

> Nevados is one of the classiest ways to carbo-load in the ski town of Mammoth Lakes.

★ kids **Mammoth Mountain Inn** MAMMOTH LAKES Location, location, location—roll out of bed and onto the lifts. There's a wide variety of rooms available, and families will love the big condo units and the well-stocked game room. There's also a courtesy shuttle down to the village. 1 Minaret Rd. ☎ 800/626-6684 or 760/934-2581. www.mammothmountain. com. 173 units, 40 condos. Doubles $165–$315 winter, $125–$179 summer; condos $170–$545. AE, MC, V.

★★ **Nevados** MAMMOTH LAKES *CALIFORNIAN* One of Mammoth's best restaurants, this casual, bustling eatery shows sophisticated flair with fish, meat (including game), and pasta dishes. The prix-fixe meal is a good way to go. 3950 Main St. ☎ 760/934-4466. Entrees $21–$30; prix-fixe meal $40. AE, DC, DISC, MC, V. Dinner daily.

★★ **The Restaurant at Convict Lake** MAMMOTH LAKES *FRENCH* Known for its beef Wellington, fresh rainbow trout, and extensive wine list, this is one the area's most famous restaurants; better make a reservation. 2000 Convict Lake Rd. ☎ 760/934-3803. www.con victlake.com. Entrees $22–$50. AE, MC, V. Dinner daily; lunch daily in summer; brunch Sun.

★★ **Skadi** MAMMOTH LAKES *ECLECTIC* Locals and visitors alike rave about Skadi's exacting standards and urban vibe, a combination that makes for one of Mammoth's top dining experiences. 587 Old Mammoth Rd. ☎ 760/934-3902. Entrees $22–$32. AE, MC, V. Dinner daily.

★ **Tamarack Lodge & Resort** MAMMOTH LAKES Built as a celebrity retreat in 1924 by the famous Foy vaudevillian family, this rustic and woodsy property offers a variety of cabins and lodge rooms (only 6 have private bathrooms). Even if you aren't a guest, the **Lakefront Restaurant** is worth checking out. Twin Lakes Rd. (off Lake Mary Rd.). ☎ 800/626-6684 or 760/934-2442. www.tamaracklodge.com. 45 units. Doubles $94–$300; cabins $135–$485. AE, MC, V.

★★ **Westin Monache Resort** MAMMOTH LAKES A full-on upscale resort with all the bells and whistles; these are the nicest digs in the area. A great location, too—close to the village and an express gondola to the mountain. 50 Hillside Dr. ☎ 866/716-8132 or 760/934-0400. www.westin.com/mammoth. 230 units. Doubles $199–$395. AE, DC, DISC, MC, V.

The Best of Sequoia and Kings Canyon National Parks

In 1873, Sierra Club founder John Muir described the Sequoia and Kings Canyon national parks region as every bit the rival to Yosemite. These two conjoined parks indeed display a spectacular diversity—from their massive old-growth trees and an extensive system of subterranean caverns, to Mount Whitney, the highest mountain in the contiguous United States.

> Imagine—it's 130 feet before you get to the first branch on the staggeringly enormous General Sherman giant sequoia.

START Kings Canyon National Park. It's about 60 miles east of Fresno on Hwy. 180. **TRIP LENGTH** 2 days, about 35 miles.

❶ ★ **General Grant Grove.** Stop off at the **Kings Canyon Visitor Center,** located 3 miles past the park's Big Stump entrance on Hwy. 180, for a crash course in giant sequoia and Kings Canyon natural history. Then head down the road about a mile to this easily accessed sequoia grove, home to what is believed to

be the world's third largest tree, ★ **General Grant.** Some 267 feet tall, with a circumference of 107 feet, not only is this tree enormous, but it also carries emotional weight, as well. In 1926, President Calvin Coolidge declared it to be our National Christmas Tree, and 30 years later President Dwight D. Eisenhower dedicated it as a National Shrine, honoring the nation's military killed in action. ⏱ At least 30 min. Kings Canyon Visitor Center

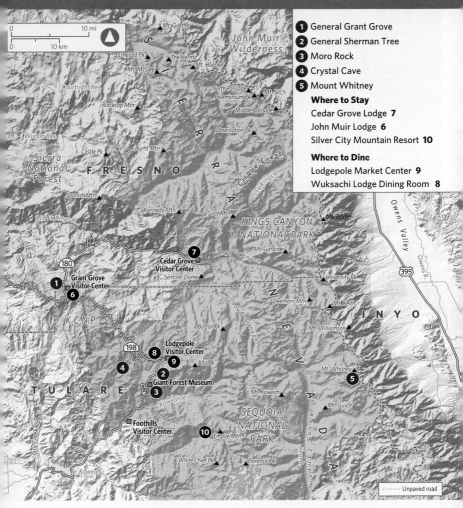

1 General Grant Grove
2 General Sherman Tree
3 Moro Rock
4 Crystal Cave
5 Mount Whitney

Where to Stay
Cedar Grove Lodge 7
John Muir Lodge 6
Silver City Mountain Resort 10

Where to Dine
Lodgepole Market Center 9
Wuksachi Lodge Dining Room 8

☎ 559/565-4307. www.nps.gov/seki. Daily 9am–4:30pm (hours vary seasonally; call ahead). Admission $10 per person or $20 per car (valid for 7 days); senior lifetime pass $10.

❷ ★ **General Sherman Tree.** This is it— *número uno,* top dog, the übertree. The General Sherman tree is taller than a 26-story building and has a base circumference of 103 feet, making it (by volume, not height) the biggest known tree in the world. The ★ **Congress Trail** is a 2.1-mile loop that begins and ends at General Sherman; the crowds gather to salute the general, so pay your respects and move on for some solitude in the ★ **Giant Forest.** You can pick up an interpretive brochure and learn

about the area's indigenous people and animals at the **Lodgepole Visitor Center.** ⏲ At least 1 hr. Lodgepole Visitor Center, 2 miles north of the General Sherman tree and 21 miles from the Sequoia Park entrance on Hwy. 198/ Generals Highway. ☎ 559/565-4436. Daily early spring–late fall; Sat–Sun winter (call for hours). Free park shuttle stops here May–Sept. Nov–May Hwy. 198/Generals Highway subject to closure due to snow; call ☎ 559/565-3341 for road conditions.

❸ ★★ **Moro Rock.** If your joints and thighs will allow you only one burst of exertion, this is the place to spend it. The trail is less than a mile, but gains 300 feet in elevation, with the

> *Grab a sweatshirt before exploring the 3½-mile Crystal Cave network—temperatures hover at 48°F/9°C year-round.*

last ¼ mile to the summit being a flight of 380 steps carved out of the pointy granite dome. This stairway to heaven offers simply majestic views of the Great Western Divide, the middle fork of the Kaweah River, and beyond. It's an awesome place to catch a sunset (but don't make the climb if there's snow or ice on the stairs). ☺ 1 hr. In Giant Forest, Crescent Meadow Rd., off Hwy. 198/Generals Highway.

④ ★ Crystal Cave. There are more than 200 marble caverns in the parks, a magical underworld of stalactites, stalagmites, waterfalls, and pools. You can explore this cool (literally, the temperature stays at a constant 48°F/9°C), 3½-mile cave on a variety of daily guided tours, May to September. The main tour is a 45-minute, 1.5-mile hike that is moderately strenuous (there's a 320-ft. elevation gain). There are also a limited number of more in-depth tours, including a 1½-hour hike, and an extreme 4- to 6-hour journey that will have you spelunking off trail. ☺ At least 2½ hr. Off Hwy. 198/Generals Highway btw. Ash Mountain park entrance and Giant Forest; from the parking lot it's a ½ mile walk to the cave. ☎ 559/565-3135. www.nps.gov/seki. Purchase tickets at the Lodgepole Visitor Center (❷) or the Foothills Visitor Center, located 1 mile from the Sequoia park entrance on Hwy. 198/Generals Highway. Allow 1½ hr. to reach the cave. For more information contact the Sequoia Natural History Association. ☎ 559/565-3759. www.sequoiahistory.

org. Tickets for main tour are $11 adults, $6 kids 6–12; 1½-hour tour $19 per person; extreme 4- to 6-hour trail $129 for ages 16 & up.

❺ ★★ Mount Whitney. At 14,497 feet, this craggy peak is the tallest point in the Lower 48, named in 1864 for geologist Josiah Whitney (1819–96). From about mid-July to October it is possible to hike the mountain without any special gear or training, and that might explain why this is the most frequently climbed mountain in the country. But standing between you and Mount Whitney is the Great Western Divide, a Sierra range that no road traverses. Unless you are already in the Eastern Sierra (say, heading to or from Mammoth Lakes or Tahoe) or are willing to undertake a 10-day backpacking trip, visiting Whitney is not going to be worth your time. If you are on the eastern side, pull into the **Eastern Sierra InterAgency Visitor Center,** where you can either gaze at the mountain or plan your assault. Needless to say, this trek requires fitness and some preparation; even day hikers need to secure a wilderness permit (available at the visitor center). Because of the altitude, a 1-day hike (22 miles) up the **Mount Whitney Trail** is not recommended, although people do it. InterAgency Visitor Center, U.S. 395 at Hwy. 136 (1 mile south of Lone Pine). ☎ 760/876-6222. www.fs.fed.us or www.nps.gov/seki. Daily 8am–5pm with extended summer hours.

Where to Stay & Dine

> *Modern amenities (like Wi-Fi) blend with rustic touches in the comfortable John Muir Lodge.*

★ **Cedar Grove Lodge** KINGS CANYON NA-
TIONAL PARK The rooms are motel basic but
the Kings River that flows past this property,
located deep in the heart of the park, is one
heck of an amenity. Try to snag one of the
three rooms with riverside patios. The lodge is
open May to October. Hwy. 180, Cedar Grove,
Kings Canyon National Park. ☎ 866/522-6966
or 559/522-6966. www.sequoia-kingscanyon.
com. 18 units. Doubles $119-$180. AE, DISC,
MC, V.

★★ **John Muir Lodge** KINGS CANYON
NATIONAL PARK Those looking for comfortable, modern digs in the park will definitely
appreciate this year-round lodge, built in 1998.
It's located in the Grant Grove Village where
there's a cafe (with free Wi-Fi), espresso bar,
gift shop, and visitor center. Hwy. 180, Grant
Grove Village, ☎ 866/522-6966 or 559/522-
6966. www.sequoia-kingscanyon.com. 36 units.
Doubles $89-$180; suites $270. Register at
Grant Grove Village Registration Center, btw the
restaurant & gift shop. AE, DISC, MC, V.

★ **Lodgepole Market Center** SEQUOIA NA-
TIONAL PARK DELI/AMERICAN You'll find a
seasonal deli (May-Oct), as well as a grill serving up burgers, pizza, and the like year-round at
this market complex near the Wukasachi Lodge
(below). You can also pick up supplies to make
your own meals here. 63204 Lodgepole Rd.

☎ 559/565-3301. www.visitsequoia.com. Most
items $5-$8. AE, MC, V. Daily 8am-8pm (shorter
hours in winter).

★ **Silver City Mountain Resort** SEQUOIA
NATIONAL PARK Accommodations run the
spectrum from "historic" 1930s cabins with
shared bathhouses to contemporary chalets
with fireplaces, full kitchens, and bathrooms
with showers. Mineral King, Sequoia National
Park. ☎ 559/561-3223 or 559/734-4109 in winter. www.silvercityresort.com. 14 units, 7 with
shared central bathhouse. Cabins $130-$395
(2-8 guests). Discounts June 1-15 and after
Sept 18. MC, V. Closed Nov-May. Take Hwy. 198
through Three Rivers to the Mineral King turnoff. Silver City is a little more than halfway btw.
Lookout Point & Mineral King.

★ **Wuksachi Lodge Dining Room** SEQUOIA
NATIONAL PARK AMERICAN Dining choices are
pretty limited in the park, which makes it easy
to pick this place as the standout choice. The
restaurant uses local, organic products, sustainable seafood and has a full bar, majestic views,
and a roaring fireplace. 64740 Wuksachi Way.
☎ 559/565-4070. www.visitsequoia.com. Dinner
reservations required. Entrees $10-$35. AE, DC,
DISC, MC, V. Breakfast, lunch & dinner daily. From
Hwy. 180 park entrance, veer right at "Y" intersection; it's 25 miles to the lodge.

WATER WARS

The battle over California's
most precious resource

BY HARRIOT MANLEY

IT'S NOT QUITE THE YANKEES VERSUS THE CONFEDERATES, but California has long had tensions between the north and south, with one of the key thorns being the fight over water: The parched south wants it; the wetter north has it. The fight dates back to around 1900, when powerful men cooked up a plan to divert plentiful Sierra Nevada snowmelt from the north and transport it to the arid Los Angeles Basin, boosting land values. Under a cloud of bribes and crooked deals, the 223-mile Los Angeles Aqueduct was built, opening its valves in 1913. As regions to the north dried up, irate ranchers and farmers tried to blow up the aqueduct. The plot failed, and by the 1930s, regions like the once-lush Owens Valley were green no more. Water wars still rage in California, especially between thirsty agribusiness in the Central Valley and environmentalists keen on protecting native species. And frequent droughts and increasing population put pressure on communities to develop new sources of potable water, such as pricey desalinization plants.

Something Fishy

As human demands on water rise in California, wildlife experts have raised a red flag for native fish and moved the state's water wars into the court room. First up, the delta smelt, found only in the Sacramento-San Joaquin River Delta. The tiny minnow used to thrive here, but numbers dived in the '80s. Scientists found the smelt needed a good mix of cold, fresh water to spawn—and the smelt wasn't getting it. In a legal battle that continues today, environmental experts argue that agribusiness drains too much water, while farmers say they need it to survive. The smelt isn't alone. Historically, wild salmon have spawned in the waterways feeding San Francisco Bay. But no more—and native salmon are now endangered. While suspects range from logging to overfishing, the demand for water has undoubtedly played a role in the decline of the once-abundant salmon.

Water-Wise Tips

PLANT DROUGHT-TOLERANT SPECIES. Native plants, such as sage and ceonothus (California lilac), need little watering.

NIX LAWNS. Reduce water-guzzling lawns and replace them with hardscape and drought-tolerant plants.

USE MULCH. A thick layer retains moisture, so the garden needs less watering.

INSTALL DRIP IRRIGATION. Specially designed tubes and emitters deliver water to plants—no wasteful sprinkling. ▼

Chinatown

Sneering Jack Nicholson, sultry Faye Dunaway, evil John Houston—this 1974 Roman Polanski masterpiece, which garnered 11 Academy Awards, splashed the dirty secrets that came out of the early 1900s Southern California water wars all over the silver screen.

The Best of Lake Tahoe

Mark Twain referred to Lake Tahoe as "the fairest picture the whole earth affords." Indeed, this stunningly blue lake—the largest alpine lake in North America, famous for its deep, clear water—is one of the country's standout destinations. A year-round sports paradise whose history as a first-class resort dates back to the 1860s, Tahoe also offers top-notch dining, boutique shopping, and glitzy Vegas-style action.

> The paddle wheeler may be straight out of Mississippi, but the view of Emerald Bay at dusk is pure Sierra.

START Tahoe City is 107 miles east of Sacramento, reached by car via I-80 and Hwy. 89. Many visitors, however, fly into Reno, Nevada, then drive 45 miles (also via I-80 and Hwy. 89) to the lake. **TRIP LENGTH** 4 days, about 75 miles.

1 ★ **Tahoe City.** Founded in 1864 as a retreat for the wealthy folks of Virginia City, Nevada, who'd struck it rich with the Comstock silver lode, this North Shore town represents Tahoe's sedate side. It's close to some of the best resorts, but far from Tahoe's best casinos and entertainment (and the drive from one end of the lake to the other can take more than an hour in summer and can be dicey in winter).

The North Lake Tahoe Historical Society operates the ★ **Gatekeeper's Museum/ Marion Steinbach Indian Basket Museum,** 130 W. Lake Blvd. (☎ 530/583-1762; www. northtahoemuseums.org; $3 adults, $1 kids 6–12, free for kids 5 & under. Summer daily

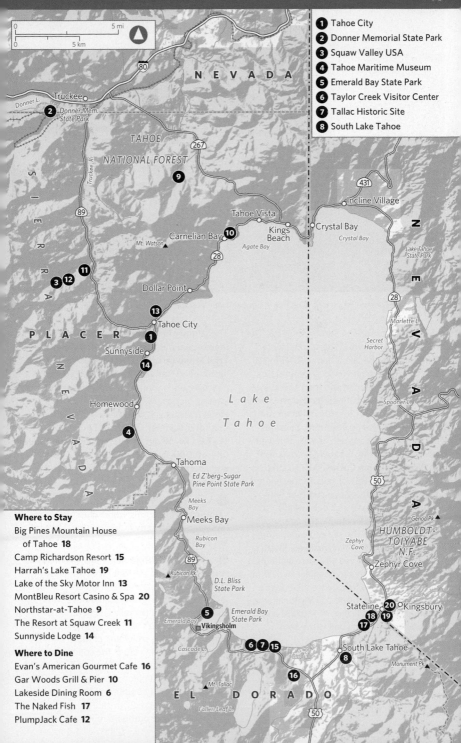

1 Tahoe City
2 Donner Memorial State Park
3 Squaw Valley USA
4 Tahoe Maritime Museum
5 Emerald Bay State Park
6 Taylor Creek Visitor Center
7 Tallac Historic Site
8 South Lake Tahoe

Where to Stay

Big Pines Mountain House
of Tahoe **18**

Camp Richardson Resort **15**

Harrah's Lake Tahoe **19**

Lake of the Sky Motor Inn **13**

MontBleu Resort Casino & Spa **20**

Northstar-at-Tahoe **9**

The Resort at Squaw Creek **11**

Sunnyside Lodge **14**

Where to Dine

Evan's American Gourmet Cafe **16**

Gar Woods Grill & Pier **10**

Lakeside Dining Room **6**

The Naked Fish **17**

PlumpJack Cafe **12**

> *Get a shot of adrenaline on a thrilling ride in Squaw Valley's wraparound-window gondola.*

11am–5pm; Oct–Apr Sat–Sun 11am–3pm). The Gatekeeper's Museum is the reconstructed log cabin where the lake's dam keeper lived, and it includes exhibits on local natural history, indigenous people, and the 1960 Winter Olympic Games held at nearby Squaw Valley. The adjacent basket museum holds more than 800 woven baskets representing 85 tribes from throughout the West, as well as jewelry, pottery, and clothing. A satellite museum store, **Watson Cabin Curios,** 560 N. Lake Blvd. (☎ 530/583-8717), sells Tahoe-related, vintage-style gifts; it's open summer only noon to 4pm (days vary, so call ahead).

At **Fanny Bridge,** located at the intersection of Hwy. 28 and Hwy. 89, you can watch trout as they swim along the Truckee River. There's no fishing allowed but you will catch sight of an assortment of derrières as people lean over to observe and feed the fish, hence the bridge's name. ⏱ At least 1 hr. Tahoe City Visitor Information Center, 380 N. Lake Blvd. ☎ 530/581-6900. www.gotahoenorth.com. Daily 9am–5pm.

❷ ★ **Donner Memorial State Park.** This park offers camping, easy hiking, fishing, and boating, but its popularity is fired more by interest in the luckless pioneers who were stranded here in the winter of 1846–47, resorting to murder and cannibalism in order to survive.

The Donner Party story (complete with creepy mannequins) is told at the park's **Emigrant Trail Museum** (daily 9am–4pm), along with natural and Native American history; the nearby grand monument of a westward-looking pioneer family sits atop a 22-foot stone base, which was the height of the snow that fateful winter. ⏱ At least 1 hr. 12593 Donner Pass Rd. (about 15 miles northwest of Tahoe City, off I-80, in Truckee). ☎ 530/582-7892. www.parks.ca.gov. Admission $8 per car, $7 with a senior.

❸ ★★★ **Squaw Valley USA.** Site of the 1960 Winter Olympics, this world-class resort offers year-round activities and entertainment. See p. 304.

❹ ★ **Tahoe Maritime Museum.** This handsome, 5,800-square-foot facility opened in 2008 and documents Lake Tahoe's rich maritime history, dating back to the days when steamers worked the lake and gentleman millionaires raced their mahogany-accented boats for glory. A collection of more than 25 vessels is rotated through the space, along with memorabilia and photographs. Highlights include a Victorian launch salvaged from the lake bottom, mint condition racing boats from the early days of the 20th century, and a collection of vintage outboard motors. ⏱ 45 min.

5205 W. Lake Blvd., Homewood. ☎ 530/525-9253. www.tahoemaritimemuseum.org. Admission $5 adults, free for kids 11 & under. Summer Thurs–Tues 10am–5pm; fall and spring Fri–Sat 10am–5pm; various weekends in winter (call for schedule).

❺ ★★ Emerald Bay State Park. One of the lake's most popular spots—not only are the views spectacular, but there's also a historic Scandinavian-style castle to tour. See p. 273, ❽.

❻ ★ Taylor Creek Visitor Center. You can load up on maps and souvenirs, take part in ranger-led programs, or start out on several self-guided nature walks from the center, but the big draw is the ★ **Stream Profile Chamber.** Featuring floor-to-ceiling aquarium windows, it gives you an underwater look at a diverted section of Taylor Creek, where rainbow trout and crayfish go about their business. October is the best month for viewing, when kokanee salmon fight their way upstream to spawn. ☉ At least 30 min. Hwy. 89, 3 miles north of Hwy. 50. ☎ 530/543-2674. www.fs.fed.us. Free admission. Daily June–Sept 8am–5:30pm; Oct 8am–4:30pm (Stream Profile Chamber closes 30 min before visitor center).

❼ ★★ Tallac Historic Site. This lakefront monument to Tahoe's gilded age includes the remnants of "the grandest resort in the world" and the summer homes of several rich and powerful families. The largest of the mansions, the **Pope Estate** (1894) is now the interpretive center for the park; the **Baldwin Estate** (1921) houses a museum. Tallac provides more than just look back at Tahoe's privileged class—it has become the lake's vibrant center for arts and culture. A renovated boathouse is now a community theater and the annual **★★ Valhalla Festival** (☎ 530/541-4975; www.valhallatahoe.com) presents music and arts programming on the grounds every summer; there are also local arts and crafts for sale in twin cabins known as the **Cultural Arts Store.** The buildings are shuttered in winter but the area is popular for cross-country skiing and snowshoeing. ☉ At least 1 hr. Hwy. 89, 2½ miles north of Hwy. 50. ☎ 530/541-5227 or 530/543-0956. www.tahoeheritage.org. Free admission, except for concerts. Grounds daily dawn–dusk. Estates summer 10am–4:30pm daily.

> Stunning views make it hard to keep your eyes on the trails circling sapphire blue Lake Tahoe.

❽ ★ South Lake Tahoe. This is where the action is, with a plethora of shopping and dining options, and some Vegas-style casinos just across the state line in Nevada. If you're not too busy recreating (see p. 298 for outdoor options), stop by the ★ **Lake Tahoe Historical Society Museum,** 3058 Lake Tahoe Blvd. (☎ 530/541-5458; free admission; Jun–Aug Wed–Mon 11am–3pm, Sept–May Sat–Sun 11am–3pm), for a comprehensive journey through the region's past. Exhibits cover the indigenous Washoe people, the white explorers—John C. Frémont (1813–90) and Kit Carson (1809–68)—who came upon the lake in 1844, and Tahoe's mining, logging, and railroad history. Lake Tahoe Visitors Authority, 3066 Lake Tahoe Blvd. ☎ 530/544-5050. www.bluelaketahoe.com. Daily 9am–5pm.

Where to Stay & Dine

> Take a turn on the ice at Northstar, where the lively village makes a prime spot for après-ski fun.

North Shore

★ Gar Woods Grill & Pier CARNELIAN BAY
You have to love a place with free boat valet docking and a drink called a Wet Woody. Named for a legendary boating pioneer, this grill offers good food, and the views and vibe are great. 5000 N. Lake Blvd. ☎ 800/298-2463 or 530/546-3366. www.garwoods.com. Entrees $9–$30. AE, DISC, MC, V. Lunch & dinner daily.

Lake of the Sky Motor Inn TAHOE CITY
Kick it old school—1960s motel style—at this quiet, clean, thoroughly affordable spot. There's a pool in summer, ski packages in winter. 955 N. Lake Blvd. ☎ 530/583-3305. www.lakeofthesky inn.com. 23 units. Doubles $89–$167. AE, DC, DISC, MC, V.

★ Lakeside Dining Room TAHOE CITY AMERICAN Sublime alfresco dining along the lakeside is the hallmark of this popular hotel steakhouse. In the Sunnyside Lodge, 1850 W. Lake Blvd. ☎ 800/822-2754 or 530/583-7200. www.sunnysideresort.com. Entrees $7–$34. Dinner daily; lunch daily in summer. AE, DISC, MC, V.

★★ Northstar-at-Tahoe TRUCKEE
There's no need to leave this self-contained, family-friendly resort, which has everything from boutique shopping to ice-skating. This village features a number of different kinds of accommodations, from simple hotel rooms to four-bedroom condos; for a taste of real luxury, check out the **Ritz-Carlton Highlands,** which opened midmountain in 2009. 100 Northstar Dr. ☎ 800/466-6784 or 530/562-1010. www.north

starattahoe.com. 250 units. Doubles $209–$349. AE, DISC, MC, V.

★★ **PlumpJack Cafe** SQUAW VALLEY AMERICAN With sister restaurants in San Francisco, Napa, and elsewhere, this place has serious standards to live up to—and with its seasonal, contemporary menu this sexy and intimate eatery is more than up to the challenge. In the PlumpJack Squaw Valley Inn, 1920 Squaw Valley Rd. ☎ 530/583-1576. www.plumpjack.com. Entrees $14–$45. AE, MC, V. Breakfast, lunch & dinner daily.

★★★ kids **The Resort at Squaw Creek** OLYMPIC VALLEY You'll find just about every creature comfort, recreational activity, and hotel amenity you could ask for at this deluxe property—one of the country's top resorts. 400 Squaw Creek Rd. ☎ 800/327-3353 or 530/583-6300. www.squawcreek.com. 403 units. Doubles $309–$395. AE, DC, DISC, MC, V.

★★ **Sunnyside Lodge** TAHOE CITY This classic lakefront lodge was built as a home in 1908 and has been a resort since the 1950s, featuring its own minimarina and gravel beach. 1850 W. Lake Blvd. ☎ 800/822-2754 or 530/583-7200. www.sunnysideresort.com. 23 units. Doubles $135–$295 w/breakfast & afternoon tea. AE, MC, V.

South Shore

Big Pines Mountain House of Tahoe SOUTH LAKE TAHOE These basic accommodations are pet friendly and every room has free Wi-Fi, a microwave, and a fridge. It's within walking distance of a private beach, shopping, dining, and the Heavenly Gondola. 4083 Cedar Ave. ☎ 800/288-4083 or 530/541-5155. www.bigpinesmountainhouse.com. 76 units. Doubles $56–$119. AE, DC, DISC, MC, V.

★ **Camp Richardson Resort** SOUTH LAKE TAHOE There's fun for all seasons at this property that fronts a long, sandy beach. The sports center and marina has for rent any equipment you might need, from skis to kayaks; the on-site ice cream parlor will provide the calories

you need to keep your energy up. Jameson Beach Rd. ☎ 800/544-1801 or 530/541-1801. www.camprichardson.com. 76 units, over 300 camping and RV sites. Doubles $95–$195; weekly cabin rates available in summer. Camping or RV hookup $25–$40 per day. DISC, MC, V.

★★ **Evan's American Gourmet Cafe** SOUTH LAKE TAHOE INTERNATIONAL Fresh daily seafood specials and an extensive wine list highlight this casually sophisticated restaurant, where Pacific Rim and classic French cuisine blend beautifully. Save room for dessert, too. 536 Emerald Bay Rd. ☎ 530/542-1990. www.evanstahoe.com. Reservations required (must confirm by 4pm). Entrees $20–$32. AE, DISC, MC, V. Dinner daily.

★ **Harrah's Lake Tahoe** STATELINE This Vegas-like property screams glitz with large, amenity-filled guest rooms; a casino; nightclub; and big-name entertainment. 18 Hwy. 50, Stateline, Nevada. ☎ 800/427-7247 or 775/588-6611. www.harrahs.com. 525 units. Doubles $159–$349. AE, DC, DISC, MC, V.

★ **MontBleu Resort Casino & Spa** LAKE TAHOE A glam makeover has allowed the former Caesar's Tahoe to channel its inner Vegas, complete with contemporary guest rooms, casino, celebrity performers, nightclubs, indoor pool, and spa. 55 U.S. 50, Lake Tahoe, Nevada. ☎ 888/829-7630 or 775/588-3515. www.montbleuresort.com. 437 units. Doubles $99–$330. AE, DC, MC, V.

★★ **The Naked Fish** SOUTH LAKE TAHOE SUSHI For the best experience, sit at the sushi bar and check the "specials" board to see what the creative chefs have (un)cooked up for the day. For a decadent dessert try the tempura cheesecake. 3940 Lake Tahoe Blvd. ☎ 530/541-3474. www.thenakedfish.com. Entrees $14–$21; sushi $4–$12. AE, DC, DISC, MC, V. Dinner daily; lunch Sat–Sun.

Outdoor Adventures A to Z

Ballooning

★★ **Lake Tahoe Balloons.** Unique boat-launched flights over Lake Tahoe from May to October; trips over the picturesque Carson Valley are available April to December. ☎ 800/872-9294 or 530/544-1221. www.laketahoeballoons.com. $250 per person.

★★ **Mammoth Balloon Adventures.** Up, up, and away over Mammoth Lakes and the Eastern Sierra. Flight time is 1–1½ hours; brunch can be arranged, as well. 2593 W. Line Blvd., Bishop. ☎ 760/937-8787. www.mammothballoonadventures.com. $165 per person.

Bicycling

★ **Anderson's Bike Rentals.** Conveniently located near a bike path trail head, this family-owned operation has been in business in Tahoe since 1978 (daily Apr–Nov). 645 Emerald Bay Rd., South Lake Tahoe. ☎ 877/720-2121 or 530/541-0500. www.andersonsbicyclerental.com. Rentals $9 per hour.

★★ **Mammoth Mountain Bike Park.** From go-for-broke downhill plunges to nice-and-easy dirt tracks, Mammoth Mountain segues from killer skiing in winter to awesome mountain biking in summer. The Scenic Gondola (p. 274, ⑮) can take you to midmountain or the summit for bike trails with a view (9am–4:30pm). The Adventure Center at the main lodge has all the rental gear you'll need; a bike shuttle is available from the village, too. 1 Minaret Rd., Mammoth Lakes. ☎ 800/626-6684 or 760/934-2571. www.mammothmountain.com. Bike park pass $39 adults, $20 ages 12 & under; packages (pass and rental bike) start at $54 adults, $27 kids 12 & under for 2 hr.

Yosemite Lodge and Curry Village. Yosemite National Park has more than 12 miles of easy bike paths, making biking not only a great way to see the park, but also an excellent way to beat the summer traffic. Yosemite Valley. ☎ 209/372-4386. www.yosemitepark.com. Bikes available spring–late fall, weather permitting. Rentals $9.50 per hour, $26 per day.

Boating

★ **Tahoe City Marina.** A one-stop location for all your Lake Tahoe water recreation: crewed or bareboat sailing charters, powerboat and water-skiing rentals, fishing boats, and parasailing adventures. 700 N. Lake Blvd., Tahoe City. ☎ 530/583-1039. www.tahoecitymarina.com. Fishing boats start at $50 per hour, 3 hr. maximum.

> *Summer warms Lake Tahoe's chilly snowmelt waters just enough for zooming, sailing, swimming, and splashing.*

Horseback Riding

Alpine Meadows Stables **6**
Camp Richardson Corral **8**
Mammoth Lakes Pack Outfit **18**
Sequoia and Kings Canyon
    National Parks **20**
Yosemite National Park **11**

Ice Skating

Curry Village Ice Rink **11**
Olympic Ice Pavilion **2**

Rafting/Kayaking/Sailing

Caldera Kayaks **14**
Kayak Tahoe **8**
Tahoe Adventure Company **4**
Yosemite National Park **11**

Skiing/Snowboarding/Snowshoeing

Alpine Meadows **6**
Badger Pass Ski Area **12**
Heavenly Resort **9**
June Mountain Ski Area **15**
Kirkwood **10**
Mammoth Mountain Ski Area **17**
Northstar-at-Tahoe **3**
Royal Gorge Cross-Country
    Ski Resort **1**
Sequoia and Kings Canyon
    National Parks **20**
Squaw Valley USA **2**
Tamarack Cross-Country
    Ski Center **18**

Zip Lines/Canopy Tours

Heavenly Flyer **8**

Ballooning

Lake Tahoe Balloons **8**
Mammoth Balloon Adventures **19**

Bicycling

Anderson's Bike Rentals **8**
Mammoth Mountain Bike Park **16**
Yosemite Lodge and Curry Village **11**

Boating

Tahoe City Marina **6**
Tahoe Gal **6**
Tahoe Queen **8**

Camping

Sequoia and Kings Canyon
    National Parks **20**
Yosemite National Park **11**

Fishing

Tahoe Sportfishing **8**
The Trout Fly Guide Service **16**
Yosemite National Park **11**

Golf

Edgewood Tahoe **7**
Incline Village Championship Course **5**
Resort at Squaw Creek **2**
Wawona Golf Course **13**

Hiking/Mountaineering

Tahoe Trips & Trails **6**
Yosemite Mountaineering School **11**

★ *Tahoe Gal.* Operating out of north Lake Tahoe (May–Oct), this riverboat-style vessel offers a variety of brunch, lunch, and dinner trips, as well as specialty cruises featuring wine tasting, magicians, or comics. **952 N. Lake Blvd., Tahoe City. ☎ 800/218-2464. www.tahoegal.com. Most cruises $35 adults, $16 kids.**

★ *Tahoe Queen.* Year-round this 144-foot Mississippi River-style paddle-wheeler plies Lake Tahoe, taking guests on daytime sightseeing runs ($39 adults, $15 kids) and sunset dinner-dance cruises ($75 adults, $41 kids). **900 Ski Run Blvd., South Lake Tahoe. ☎ 800/238-2463. www.zephyrcove.com.**

Camping

★★ **Sequoia and Kings Canyon National Parks.** These parks have 800 campsites in 14 campgrounds, only two of which take reservations (☎ 877/444-6777; www.recreation.gov). Count on campgrounds being filled on weekends in July and August, so plan ahead; three campgrounds are open year-round.

For backcountry camping, trail quotas are in effect late September to late May; 75% of the quota is filled by advance reservations, accepted from March to mid-September, and they must be made at least 2 weeks prior to your arrival. You can download the form at www.nps.gov/seki and fax it to (fax) 559/565-3730, or mail it to Sequoia and Kings Canyon National Parks, 47050 Generals Hwy., Three Rivers, CA 93271-9700. The remainder of the first-come, first-served permits are available prior to the day of your trip from the permit station **closest to your trail head** (call ☎ 559/565-3341 or go to www.nps.gov/seki for locations). Wilderness permits are $15 in quota season and are free (but still required) the rest of the year.

You can rent camping equipment from REI in Fresno, 7810 N. Blackstone Ave. (☎ 559/261-4168; www.rei.com).

★★ **Yosemite National Park.** There are 13 campgrounds in the park, 7 of which operate on a reservation system. If you want to stay in the park anytime from April to September, you should plan on making a reservation. Reservations can be made up to 5 months in advance, and summer availability tends to sell out quickly, sometimes even within minutes of coming online. Make reservations at www.

recreation.gov or ☎ 877/444-6777 (outside the U.S. or Canada call ☎ 518/885-3639). First-come, first-served campsites often fill by noon from May through September and cost $10 to $20 per night.

If you are backpacking you need a free wilderness permit—there is a trail head quota system to prevent overcrowding. For treks from May to September, 60% of the quota is filled by advance reservation, the remainder is available on a first-come, first-served basis beginning 1 day prior to your planned trip; reservations are not necessary November through April. To make a reservation (up to 24 weeks in advance) download the form from www.nps.gov/yose and fax it to (fax) 209/372-0739; mail the form to Wilderness Permits, PO Box 545, Yosemite, CA 95389; or call ☎ 209/372-0740 during regular business hours. Reservations are $5, plus $5 per person.

Catered backcountry camping is one of the parks most popular experiences. The High Sierra Camps, a string of five hike-in (or pack-in) camps, 5 to 10 miles apart, feature tent cabins with dormitory-style bunks and include full breakfast and dinner, with sack lunches available on request; some camps have hot showers. Space is awarded via lottery, with applications available September 1 to November 1; check www.yosemitepark.com for details. Lottery winners are notified in January; any remaining spaces can be had on a first-come, first-served basis by calling ☎ 801/559-4909 in February. A limited number of meals-only spaces are available, too. Meals and lodging cost $153 for adults and $99 for kids ages 7 to 12 (campers must be at least 7); meals only cost $40 for adults and $21 for kids ages 7 to 12.

You can rent camping, backpacking, and climbing gear from the Yosemite Mountaineering School (☎ 209/372-8344; www.yosemitepark.com).

Fishing

★ **Tahoe Sportfishing.** With the largest fleet on the lake, Tahoe Sportsfishing has been leading fishing tours here since 1953. Trips include all the necessary gear and bait. **900 Ski Run Blvd., South Lake Tahoe. ☎ 800/696-7797 or 530/541-5448. www.tahoesportfishing.com. $85–$95 per person for 4–5 hr. trip; kids 4 & under ride free if sharing adult pole.**

★ **The Trout Fly Guide Service.** Offers half-and full-day outings to Eastern Sierra lakes and streams for beginners or experts. Troutfitter, the guide service's retail component, has a huge selection of fishing gear and supplies. In the Shell Mart Center, Main St./Hwy. 203 at Old Mammoth Rd., Mammoth Lakes. ☎ 760/934-2517. www.thetroutfly.com. Half-day fishing trip $310 (1 or 2 people).

Yosemite National Park. Trout season is generally the last Saturday in April until November 15; fishing in lakes and reservoirs is allowed year-round. The Merced River from Happy Isles downstream to the Pohono Bridge is catch and release only for native rainbow trout, and barbless hooks are required. A California fishing license is required for anyone age 16 and above ($13); you can get a license and gear at the Yosemite Village Sport Shop (☎ 209/372-1286).

Golf

★★ **Edgewood Tahoe.** This is the home of the annual Celebrity Golf Championship. After a round at the dramatic lakeside 18-hole course, designed by George Fazio, you can repair to the superstylish stone-and-wood accented clubhouse. 100 Lake Pkwy., Stateline. ☎ 888/881-8659 or 775/588-3566. www.edgewood-tahoe.com. Greens fees $110–$220.

★★ **Incline Village Championship Course.** Robert Trent Jones, Sr., is the mastermind behind this challenging course—once voted best in the state by *Golf Digest*—featuring towering pines and Lake Tahoe views. 955 Fairway Blvd., Incline Village. ☎ 866/925-4563. www.golfincline.com. Greens fees $99–$175.

★ **Resort at Squaw Creek.** Surrounded by the epic peaks of Squaw Valley, this tough 18-hole championship course is green in more ways than one—it's pesticide free. 400 Squaw Creek Rd., Olympic Valley. ☎ 800/327-3353 or 530/583-6300. www.squawcreek.com. Greens fees $95–$110 nonguests, $85–$95 guests.

★ **Wawona Golf Course.** The Sierra's first regulation golf course, this 9-hole, par-35 course opened in 1918 and blends right into the natural surroundings of Yosemite National Park. These environmentally green links are pesticide free and use reclaimed gray water. It's open spring through fall, weather permitting;

> *Whether you're a newbie or a seasoned rock hound, Yosemite Mountaineering offers classes to suit your skills.*

club rental is available. At the Wawona Hotel. ☎ 209/375-6572. www.yosemiteparks.com. Greens fees $22–$26. See p. 281.

Hiking/Mountaineering

★★★ **kids** **Southern Yosemite Mountain Guides.** This top-drawer outfit has a wide range of itineraries, from backpacking weekends to the extreme 26-day, 195-mile Kings Canyon to Yosemite trek. There are also rock-climbing, fly-fishing, and custom trips for all levels of experience and for families. ☎ 800/231-4575. www.symg.com. 3-day backpacking trips start at $485.

> Catch big air in the half-pipe and on other tricked-out features in Mammoth Mountain's terrain parks.

★★ **Tahoe Trips & Trails.** This outfit offers 3- and 5-day guided hiking trips to Lake Tahoe and the North Coast; custom and specialty tours featuring hiking, biking, kayaking, and photography are available as well. ☎ 800/581-4453 or 530/583-4506. www.tahoetrips.com. Trips start at $1,100.

★★★ **Yosemite Mountaineering School.** This park institution leads everything from beginner classes to hair-raising ascents of El Capitan. It also offers women-only classes and backpacking outings. ☎ 209/372-8344. www.yosemitepark.com. Intro class $117.

Horseback Riding

kids **Alpine Meadows Stables.** Guided trail rides through shady Tahoe National Forest, and pony rides for the little ones (5 & under). 355 Alpine Meadows Rd., Tahoe City. ☎ 530/583-3905. Trail rides start at $30.

★ kids **Camp Richardson Corral.** Guided trail rides, as well as breakfast, dinner, and overnight outings. Seasonal hay rides and sleigh

rides, too. 4 Emerald Bay Rd., South Lake Tahoe. ☎ 530/541-3113. Trail rides start at $30.

★ **Mammoth Lakes Pack Outfit.** Operating June to September, this family-run business has been around since 1915. It offers hourly excursions, multiday wilderness pack trips, even a 4-day ride to the ghost town of Bodie. Lake Mary Rd. past Twin Lakes. ☎ 888/475-8747 or 760/934-2434. www.mammothpack.com. Rides start at $45 for a 1-hr. ride.

Sequoia and Kings Canyon National Parks. In Kings Canyon, Cedar Grove Pack Station (☎ 559/565-3464) is a mile east of Cedar Grove Village, and Grant Grove Stables (☎ 559/335-9292) is near Grant Grove Village. In Sequoia, Horse Corral Pack Station is on Big Meadows Road, 10 miles east of Generals Highway (☎ 559/565-3404; www.horsecorralpackers.com). The pack stations offer hourly rides as well as overnight treks; the stables offer dayrides only. Stables are open from spring to early fall; a half-day ride is $50 per person.

★★ **Yosemite National Park.** Saddle up for mule and horseback rides at Yosemite Valley Stables (☎ 209/372-8348; daily spring–fall), Wawona (☎ 209/375-6502), or Tuolumne Stables (☎ 209/372-8427), the latter two operating in summer only. Rides generally range in duration from 2 hours to a full day; 4- to 6-day backcountry and custom pack-and-saddle trips are also available. www.yosemitepark.com. Rides $60 per person for 2 hr., $80 per person for a ½ day, $119 per person for a full day.

Ice-Skating

★★ kids **Curry Village Ice Rink.** An outdoor seasonal ice rink has made an appearance in Yosemite Valley since 1930. After your skate session you can make s'mores at the adjacent fire ring. ☎ 209/372-8319. www.yosemitepark.com. Mid-Nov to early Mar, daily noon–9:30pm. Admission $8 adults, $6 kids. Skate rental $3.

★★ kids **Olympic Ice Pavilion.** Year-round outdoor ice-skating with a million-dollar view at Squaw Valley Resort's High Camp, perched at 8,200 feet above sea level and reached via aerial cable car. 1960 Olympic Valley Rd., Olympic Valley. ☎ 530/583-6985. www.squaw.com. Cable car/skate package $29 adults, $24 seniors and kids 13–18, $15 kids 12 & under.

Rafting/Kayaking/Sailing

★★ **Caldera Kayaks.** Get up close and personal with the bizarre tufa formations and bird life of Mono Lake on guided kayak tours; kayak rentals for Mammoth's Crowley Lake, too. ☎ 760/934-1691. www.calderakayak.com. Mono Lake tours $75 per person.

★★ **Kayak Tahoe.** Kayak and paddle-board rentals, as well as paddling classes for all levels and guided day tours. Timber Cove Marina, 3411 Lake Tahoe Blvd., South Lake Tahoe. ☎ 530/544-2011. www.kayaktahoe.com. Kayak rentals start at $15 per hour.

★★ **Tahoe Adventure Company.** A variety of kayaking tours, including multiday "lodge to lodge" trips, paddling from one lakefront hotel to another. 7010 N. Lake Blvd., Tahoe Vista. ☎ 866/830-6125 or 530/913-9212. www.tahoe adventurecompany.com. Tours start at $49 per person.

★★ **Whitewater Voyages.** Running rapids since 1975, this company offers 1- to 3-day trips on the Tuolumne, Merced, Kings, Kaweah, and Kern rivers, from May to September. ☎ 800/400-7238. www.whitewater voyages.com. One-day trips start at $129 per person.

★★ kids **Yosemite National Park.** Paddle a 3-mile stretch of the Merced River through the heart of Yosemite Valley. Curry Village. ☎ 209/372-4386. www.yosemitepark.com. Canoe rental $26 adults, $16 kids 12 & under (kids weighing less than 50 lb. are not permitted). May–July daily 10am–6pm.

★★ **Zephyr Whitewater Expeditions.** Working the rapids since 1973, this company runs ½- to 3-day trips along the Tuolumne, Merced, and Kings rivers from April to September. ☎ 800/431-3636 or 209/532-6249. www.zraft ing.com. Half-day trips start at $105 for adults.

Skiing/Snowboarding/Snowshoeing

★★ kids **Alpine Meadows.** With more than 100 runs over 2,400 acres, this low-key resort is a locals' favorite; it offers a variety of ski and snowboarding classes, as well as programs for disabled skiers. 2600 Alpine Meadows Rd., Tahoe City. ☎ 530-583-4232. www.skialpine. com. 1-day lift tickets start at $59 for adults, $52 for teens 13–18, $15 for kids 5–12.

kids **Badger Pass Ski Area.** California's oldest ski area, this Yosemite facility is great for families; there's even a terrain park designed with beginner/intermediate snowboarders in mind. Cross-country skiing and snowshoeing is huge here; make a reservation for the way-cool Glacier Point Hut, with its incredible views (☎ 209/372-8444; www.yosemite park.com; 1-night guided tour $192, 1-night self-guided stay $121). Reservations are also recommended for the 25-bunk Ostrander Hut (☎ 209/379-2646; www.ostranderhut.com; $30–$50 per night). Badger Pass ☎ 209/372-8430. www.yosemitepark.com. Lift tickets $35–$42 adults, $35–$37 teens 13–17, $16–$20 for kids 7–12, free for kids 6 & under.

★★ kids **Heavenly Resort.** Tahoe's highest resort (more than 10,000 ft.); it's spread over 4,800 acres and will appeal to skiers and boarders of all levels. There's plenty of action in Heavenly Village, too. 3860 Saddle Rd., South Lake Tahoe. ☎ 775/586-7000. www. skiheavenly.com. One-day lift tickets $83 adults, $71 kids 13–17, $46 kids 5–12.

★ **June Mountain Ski Area.** Twenty minutes north of Mammoth, June Mountain lacks the immensity of its sister ski area but often has better conditions, not to mention smaller crowds. From Hwy. 158 go about 4 miles down June Lake Junction. ☎ 888/586-3686 or 760/648-7733. www.junemountain.com. 1-day lift tickets $64 adults, $58 ages 19–23, $48 kids 13–18, $32 kids 7–12. See p. 284, ❻.

★★ kids **Kirkwood.** About 30 miles south of South Lake Tahoe, Kirkwood is one of Tahoe's best ski resorts. It's a great place for cross-country skiing (guided tours and lessons available). 1501 Kirkwood Meadows Dr., Kirkwood. ☎ 209/258-6000. www.kirkwood.com. 1-day lift tickets start at $74 for adults, $59 for kids 13–17, $19 for kids 5–12.

★★ kids **Mammoth Mountain Ski Area.** One of California's top ski destinations, this aptly named mountain's 11,053-foot summit makes it the state's loftiest ski zone—and 30% of its runs are black diamonds. Lots of other snow-play activities, too, from snowmobiling to dog-sled rides. 1 Minaret Rd., Mammoth Lakes. ☎ 800/626-6684 or 760/934-2571. www. mammothmountain.com. One-day lift tickets

> Be a kid again on the super-fast, family-friendly tubing hill at Badger Pass.

$69–$87 adults, $51–$64 teens 13–18, $34–$43 kids 7–12. See p. 284, **9**.

★★ **kids Northstar-at-Tahoe.** Backcountry terrain, instruction and coaching, child care, tubing, sleigh rides, ice-skating—this hugely popular resort has it all. 100 Northstar Dr., Truckee. ☎ 800/466-6784 or 530/562-1010. www.northstarattahoe.com. 1-day lift tickets $84 adults, $74 kids 13–17, $32 kids 5–12.

★★★ **Royal Gorge Cross-Country Ski Resort.** North America's largest cross-country ski resort, covering more than 9,000 acres, features two overnight lodges and eight warming huts. 9411 Hillside Dr., Soda Springs. ☎ 800/500-3871 or 800/666-3871. www.royalgorge.com. Adult passes start at $25.

★★ **kids Sequoia and Kings Canyon National Parks.** Cross-country skiing and snowshoeing are popular activities in the parks. Ski rentals are available at Wuksachi Lodge in the Giant Forest and at the Grant Grove Market in Grant Grove. There are snow-play and sledding areas here, too; you can buy gear at the lodge and market. Advanced skiers and snowshoers can make the steep 6-mile trip from Wolverton Meadow to the Pear Lake Ski Hut (☎ 565/565-4222; www.sequoiahistory.org), which sleeps 10 ($30–$38 per person; reservations required). Free 2-hour, 1-mile ranger-guided snowshoe programs are conducted on Saturday, weather permitting, at Wuksachi Lodge and Grant Grove. Make a reservation at any park visitor center or call ☎ 559/565-4480 for the Wuksachi walk, or ☎ 559/565-4307 for the Grant Grove program. ☎ 559/565-3341. www.nps.gov/seki.

★★★ **kids Squaw Valley USA.** Go for the gold at this 1960 Winter Olympics site, Tahoe's most famous ski resort. Thirty percent of the terrain here is designed for the no-guts, no-glory crowd. 1960 Olympic Valley Rd., Olympic Valley. ☎ 800/545-4350 or 530/583-6985. www.squaw.com. One-day lift tickets $83 adults, $61 kids 13–17, $10 kids 5–12.

★★ **Tamarack Cross-Country Ski Center.** This 1920s lodge has 19 miles of cross-country and snowshoeing track; lessons (starting at $33 for 1 hr.) and rentals available. Twin Lakes Rd. (off Lake Mary Rd.), Mammoth Lakes. ☎ 760/934-2442. www.tamaracklodge.com. Nov–Apr daily 8:30am–5pm. Trail pass $26 adults, $20 kids 13–18, $14 kids 7–12.

Zip Lines/Canopy Tours
★ **Heavenly Flyer.** More than a ½ mile in length, this year-round option is the longest zip ride in the Lower 48. You'll hit speeds of up to 50 mph as you drop more than 525 vertical feet. 3860 Saddle Rd., South Lake Tahoe. ☎ 775/586-7000. www.skiheavenly.com. $40 per ride.

Fast Facts

Emergencies

In an emergency dial ☎ **911.** In wilderness areas (except for Yosemite Valley) cellphones may not work; note where the nearest pay phone may be.

In **Yosemite,** you can call Park Dispatch (☎ 209/379-1992). For medical emergencies, there's a 24-hour clinic in Yosemite Valley on Ahwahnee Drive (☎ 209/372-4637).

For medical emergencies in Mammoth Lakes, head to **Mammoth Hospital,** 85 Sierra Park Rd., Mammoth Lakes (☎ 760/934-3311; www.mammothhospital.com).

In **Sequoia and Kings Canyon national parks,** you can call Park Dispatch (☎ 559/565-3341). For medical emergencies, go to **Kaweah Delta Medical Center,** 400 W. Mineral King, Visalia (☎ 559/624-2000; www.kaweahdelta.org).

For medical emergencies in Lake Tahoe, on the North Shore, your best bet is **Tahoe Forest Health System,** 10121 Pine Ave., Truckee (☎ 530/587-6011; www.tfhd.com); on the South Shore it's **Barton Health,** 2170 South Ave., South Lake Tahoe (☎ 530/541-3420; www.bartonhealth.org).

Getting There

BY PLANE Regional airports that serve the area include **Fresno Yosemite International Airport** (☎ 800/244-2359 or 559/621-4500; www.fresno.gov) and **Mammoth Yosemite Airport** (☎ 760/934-3825; www.ci.mammoth-lakes.ca.us); both airports have car-rental counters. If you're headed for Lake Tahoe, your best bet is **Reno-Tahoe International Airport** (☎ 775/328-6400; www.renoairport.com) in Nevada; it's a 45-minute drive from the North Shore and 3 hours from Mammoth Lakes. **North Lake Tahoe Express** (☎ 866/216-5222 or 530/581-3922; www.northlaketahoeexpress.com) operates a shuttle from Reno-Tahoe International to Truckee and Tahoe City resorts ($40 one-way, $75 round-trip). **South Tahoe Express** (☎ 866/898-2463 or 775/325-8944; www.southtahoeexpress.com) makes trips from the airport to the South Shore hotels ($26

one-way, $47 round-trip). You can also rent a car at the airport. BY CAR There are five entrances to Yosemite; the most popular are the west entrance, **Big Oak Flat,** via Hwy. 120, the best option from San Francisco (trip time: 4 hr.); **Arch Rock,** via Hwy. 140 from Merced (trip time: 2 hr.), the easiest route from central California; and the **South Entrance** at Wawona, via Hwy. 41, north of Fresno (trip time: 2¼ hr.), the best inroad from Southern California (trip time from Los Angeles is 6 hr.). The park is not accessible from the east on Hwy. 120 in winter. Call ☎ 209/372-0200 for current Yosemite driving conditions.

To get to **Mammoth Lakes,** it's a 6-hour drive from San Francisco via Hwy. 120 over the Tioga Pass in Yosemite (summer only), 5 hours from Los Angeles via Hwy. 14 and U.S. 395, and 2¾ hours from South Lake Tahoe via U.S. 395. In winter, Mammoth is accessible via U.S. 395 from the north or the south. For road conditions call ☎ 800/427-7623.

Kings Canyon National Park can be entered on Hwy. 180; it's 2¼ hours from Yosemite's southern Wawona entrance, 4½ hours from Los Angeles, and 4 hours from the Bay Area. **Sequoia National Park** is accessed via Hwy. 198 from Hwy. 65 or Hwy. 99; it's 2¾ hours from Yosemite's Wawona entrance, 3¾ hours from Los Angeles, and 4½ hours from the Bay Area. The parks' main road, the Generals Highway, loops from one entrance to the other (no roads enter the park from the east). For road conditions call ☎ 559/565-3341.

To reach **Lake Tahoe** from the Bay Area, take I-80 east to Sacramento, and then U.S. 50 to the South Shore, or I-80 east to Hwy. 89 or Hwy. 267 to the North Shore; it's about a 4-hour drive (be prepared with chains in winter; for road conditions call ☎ 511). BY BUS **Yosemite Area Regional Transportation System** (☎ 877/989-2787 or 209/388-9589; www.yarts.com) operates service from Merced to Yosemite ($25 round-trip; fare includes park admission) and summer service from the Mammoth Lakes region ($30 round-trip, including park admission). In summer, the

Sequoia Shuttle (☎ 877/287-4453; www. sequoiashuttle.com) runs between Visalia and Sequoia National Park ($15 round-trip; includes park admission). BY TRAIN **Amtrak** (☎ 800/872-7245; www.amtrak.com) operates rail and bus service to Yosemite, June Lake, and Mammoth Lakes, as well as direct rail service to Merced, Fresno, and Visalia. Amtrak also services Truckee, 10 miles north of Lake Tahoe.

Getting Around

BY CAR Park and ski-resort shuttles are a great way to get around—once you arrive at your destination. Touring the Sierras, though, is best done in your own vehicle.

There are no gas stations in Yosemite, Sequoia, or Kings Canyon, so make sure to gas up before you enter the parks. Don't speed on park roads—it's a hazard to wildlife and yourself. Be prepared to use tire chains in winter throughout the region. BY BUS In summer, Yosemite, Sequoia, and Kings Canyon have free shuttles that can take you just about anywhere you need to go within the parks. Yosemite Valley in particular suffers from traffic congestion in summer, making the shuttles the best way to get around. A variety of guided bus tours are scheduled in Yosemite, most are seasonal from spring to summer (☎ 209/372-4386; www.yosemitepark.com; $25–$82 adults).

The **Eastern Sierra Transit Authority** (☎ 800/922-1930; www.easternsierratransit authority.com) serves the Mammoth Lakes area with local and regional transportation. Several of the local routes are free of charge, others cost $1.25.

Tahoe Area Regional Transit, aka TART (☎ 800/736-6365 or 530/550-1212; www. placer.ca.gov or www.laketahoetransit.com), operates daily 6am to 7pm in Lake Tahoe along 30 miles of Tahoe's North Shore, as well as in Truckee; the fare is $1.75. Additional service (9am–midnight) is offered in summer by the free **Tahoe Trolley,** which also makes shuttle runs from Tahoe City to Emerald Bay. In winter, many resort ski shuttles connect to the routes. The **South Tahoe Area Transit Authority** (☎ 530/541-7149; www.bluego. org) covers the South Shore round-the-clock (though frequency varies by route); basic fare is $2. Seasonal summer trolleys service Emerald Bay and connect to TART routes; in winter there are eight free ski-shuttle routes. BY TAXI In the Mammoth Lakes region, try **Mammoth Taxi/Sierra Express** (☎ 760/934-8294; www.mammoth-taxi.com). For Lake Tahoe, on the North Shore, try **Anytime Taxi** (☎ 877/808-8294 or 530/414-4187; www. anytimetaxi.net) or **North Tahoe Checker** (☎ 775/833-0707). On the South Shore **Sunshine Yellow Cab** (☎ 530/544-5555) or **Paradise Taxi** (☎ 530/577-4708) are good options. *Note:* Particularly in Lake Tahoe, waits for a cab can be long, and rates can be soberingly high.

Internet Access

Internet kiosks are available in Yosemite Village at **Degnan's Cafe** (☎ 209/372-8454; www.yosemitepark.com), open April to September; year-round you'll find kiosks at **Yosemite Lodge at the Falls** (☎ 801/559-5000; www.yosemitepark.com). In South Lake Tahoe, try **Alpina Cafe,** 822 Emerald Bay Rd. (☎ 530/541-7449; www.alpinacafe.com).

Pharmacy

The closest 24-hour pharmacy is **Walgreens,** 626 Clovis Ave., Fresno (☎ 559/251-0163; www.walgreens.com).

Post Offices

There are several post offices in Yosemite, including Yosemite Village, 9017 Village Dr. (☎ 209/372-4475); it's open Monday to Friday 8:30am to 5pm and Saturday 10am to noon. In South Lake Tahoe, there's a post office at 1046 Al Tahoe Blvd. (☎ 530/544-8133); hours are Monday to Friday 8:30am to 5pm and Saturday noon to 2pm.

Safety

WILDERNESS SAFETY Be prepared and know your limitations. Weather can change quickly so dress in layers, and bring along a hat, sunscreen, plenty of water, and insect repellent (ticks and mosquitoes can be problematic). Avoid hiking or jogging alone in the wilderness—mountain lion attacks are rare but not unprecedented. When going on an outing, let someone know where you are headed and when you expect to return and carry a whistle and flashlight with you. Be alert for rock and tree falls, even pine cones dropping from tall trees can cause serious injury. In case of lightning, seek shelter immediately or crouch down (don't lie down) and don't stand under a solitary tree. Most park deaths are the result of drowning—rivers fed by snowmelt are cold and dangerous; use extreme caution around them. Never swim or wade upstream from the edge of a waterfall, even if the water looks calm and shallow.

Black bears are common in the Sierra (the grizzly bear may be on the state flag, but the last known grizzly bear in California was killed south of Yosemite in the 1920s). Proper food storage is crucial in order to keep both bears and campers safe. Canned goods; cosmetics; toiletries; empty ice chests; and anything that goes in your mouth, on your skin, or has a scent needs to be stowed properly (communal food lockers are available in campgrounds; backpackers need to carry bear-proof food canisters). *Cars are not bear-proof.* Food can be stored in cars during daylight hours only; at night vehicles should be cleaned of trash, food wrappers, and crumbs. *NEVER feed any wild animal.* It's a violation of federal law and can result in the impounding of your food or car and/or a $5,000 fine. If a bear does make an appearance in your camp, make a lot of noise to scare it away. Bears that become too dependent on raiding campgrounds for food may become aggressive and must be destroyed. Do your part to spare a bear.

DRIVING SAFETY The Sierra's steep, winding roads may lead you to ride your brakes—don't! Prolonged braking can cause brake failure. Even in automatics, downshift to low gears rather than relying solely on the brakes. Don't stop on grassy areas—use paved turnouts only—as hot mufflers and brakes can start fires.

In winter, make sure your vehicle's antifreeze is cold-weather ready; make sure the heater and defroster work; carry tire chains, an ice scraper, and a blanket. Winter can last well into spring; call ☎ 800/427-7623 for road conditions anywhere in California.

Visitor Information

The **Yosemite Chamber of Commerce** is at 18653 Hwy. 120, Groveland (☎ 800/449-9120 or 209/962-0429; www.groveland. org). The **Yosemite Sierra Visitors Bureau** is at 41969 Hwy. 41, Oakhurst, (☎ 559/683-4636; www.yosemitethisyear.com). The **Yosemite-Mariposa County Tourism Bureau** (☎ 866/425-3366; www.homeofyosemite. com) operates visitor centers at 5158 Hwy. 140, Mariposa (☎ 209/966-7081) and 5007 Main St., Coulterville (☎ 209/878-3074). For Yosemite National Park vacation and lodging information, call ☎ 801/559-4884 or head online to www.yosemitepark.com.

The **Mammoth Lakes Visitors Bureau** is at 2520 Main St., Mammoth Lakes (☎ 888/466-2666 or 760/934-2712; www.visitmammoth. com). Another good source of information for the region is the **Mono County Tourism and Film Commission** (☎ 800/845-7922; www. monocounty.org).

For information when visiting Sequoia and Kings Canyon national parks, contact the **Visalia Chamber of Commerce,** 220 N. Santa Fe Ave., Visalia (☎ 559/734-5876; www.visaliachamber.org) or the **Bishop Area Chamber of Commerce and Visitors Bureau,** 690 N. Main St., Bishop (☎ 888/395-3952 or 760/873-8405; www.bishopvisitor.com).

In Lake Tahoe, try the **Tahoe City Visitor Information Center,** 380 North Lake Blvd., Tahoe City (☎ 530/581-6900; www.go tahoenorth.com), or contact the **Lake Tahoe Visitors Authority** (☎ 530/544-5050; www. bluelaketahoe.com).

Monterey Peninsula & Big Sur

The Best of the Monterey Peninsula & Big Sur in 3 Days

A whirlwind tour of this scenic region starts at its northern end with a visit to Santa Cruz, whose oceanfront boardwalk is a sunny blast of Americana. Then you're off to say "hi" to the fish at the world-class Monterey Bay Aquarium before heading off to dazzling Carmel, with its Spanish missions, fairy-tale cottages, and white sandy beaches. Your reward for making it to the finish line? Big Sur, home to some of the most spectacular coastline in the United States.

> PREVIOUS PAGE *Have wetsuit, will surf is the mantra of Monterey surfers, who brave icy waters for some hot waves.* THIS PAGE *Look familiar? Bixby Bridge on the north end of Big Sur has been used in countless commercials.*

START Santa Cruz, **77 miles southeast of San Francisco.** TRIP LENGTH **about 150 miles.**

❶ Santa Cruz. With less than a full day in Santa Cruz, it's best to stick close to the beach and its old-fashioned amusement park, ★★★ **Santa Cruz Beach Boardwalk** (p. 332,

❶). Two of the vintage rides are National Historic Landmarks: the rollicking, rickety ★★ **Giant Dipper** wooden roller coaster from 1924 and the ★ **Looff Carousel** from 1911, with 73 hand-carved wooden horses and music provided by a 342-pipe organ built in 1894.

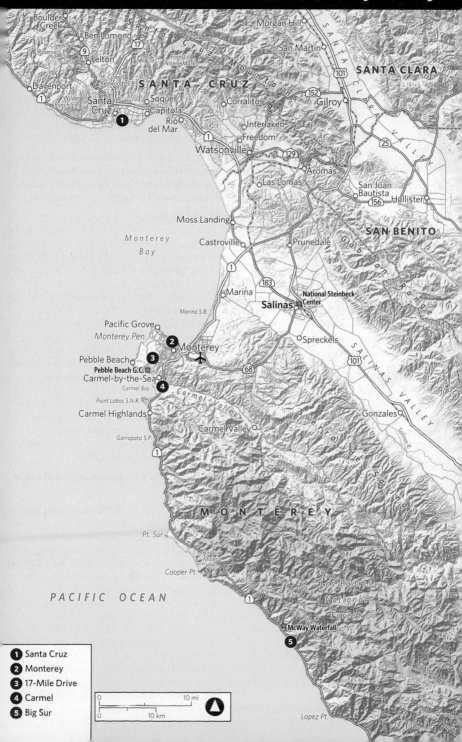

1 Santa Cruz
2 Monterey
3 17-Mile Drive
4 Carmel
5 Big Sur

> Sip and savor vintages from over 70 regional wineries at Taste of Monterey on Cannery Row.

There are plenty of new rides (thrillers like the Sea Swings, Skyglider, and Hurricane), a bowling alley, a miniature golf course, arcade games (classic and video), and some of the junkiest junk food (fried Twinkies) you'll ever find. Stop at **Marini's** candy store (☎ 831/423-7258; www.mariniscandies.com) for delicious saltwater taffy, a boardwalk staple since 1915.

Check out the ★ **Santa Cruz Surfing Museum** (p. 332, ④) tucked into a tiny lighthouse. From the bluffs near the lighthouse, watch the locals shredding at the world-famous **Steamers Lane** surf spot. Or snap a photo in front of the iconic surfer statue.

Cruise down scenic **West Cliff Drive** to ★★ **Natural Bridges State Park** (p. 333, ⑥) where you can romp in the water near the striking arches carved by the wind and sea, or investigate the tide pools on the rocks north of the natural bridge.

Before hitting the road, grab lunch at **Walnut Avenue Café** (p. 335), a local favorite. ☺ half-day.

Head south on Hwy. 1 for nearly 40 miles to Monterey.

❷ **Monterey.** The biggest attraction is the renowned ★★★ **Monterey Bay Aquarium** (p. 316, ❷). Its ingenious design links the aquarium ecologically with the bay by a system that continually pumps 2,000 gallons of ocean water per minute into over 100 exhibit tanks.

Stroll up touristy ★ **Cannery Row** (p. 336, ❸), made famous by John Steinbeck's novel about the saints and sinners working amidst the sardine canning industry that once stunk up this street. Look for the **bust of Steinbeck,**

Ed Ricketts' lab, and the **Cannery Workers' Shacks.**

To see how much the once-gritty Cannery Row has changed, sample the excellent wines of Monterey County at the ★ **Taste of Monterey** (p. 338, ⑥), before sitting down to fine dining at the nearby **Sardine Factory** (p. 339). Or head to the **Fisherman's Wharf** and grab a bowl of **clam chowder** (p. 337, ④). ☺ half-day.

Start Day 2 with a spin around 17-Mile Drive. From Monterey head south on Hwy. 1, then exit 399A for Hwy. 68 toward Pacific Grove/Pebble Beach. Turn right at 17-Mile Drive.

❸ **17-Mile Drive.** A private toll road ($9.75) is the only access to this famously scenic drive past cypress-covered coastline, the Del Monte Forest, a few of the world's finest golf courses, and gated palatial estates. Enter at any of five gates, grab a brochure of highlights, then follow the red-dotted road. **Spanish Bay** is where **Gaspar de Portolà** (1716–1784), the Spanish explorer, camped in 1769, and it now makes a great picnic spot. **Point Joe** is a treacherous rocky patch of the coast that sank many a ship. **Bird Rock** and **Seal Rock** draw hordes of their respective namesakes. **Cypress Grove** is a lovely 13-acre grove of the world's largest and oldest Monterey cypresses. The drive's most famous landmark (due to its trademarked image as a logo) is the **Lone Cypress,** a spectacular specimen of cypress that rises over the sea from its rocky perch. ☺ 2 hr.

Return to Hwy. 1, then head south and exit at Ocean Ave.

❹ **Carmel.** It may look like an absurdly quaint village of gingerbread houses, but Carmel has a rich Spanish history and a century-old artistic tradition. Founded in 1771 as the second Spanish mission in California, the ★★★ **Carmel Mission** (p. 342, ❶) served as headquarters for the other 20 missions; today, it's a National Historic Landmark and the final resting place of the chain's founder, Father Junípero Serra (1713–1784). Take the self-guided tour; docents sometimes give informal tours at 10am and/or 2pm.

Carmel has no shortage of enchanting homes and gardens, but the stone-stacked **Tor House and Hawk Tower** (p. 343, ❷) take the cake. Make advance reservations for the

> *The signature tree of the region, Monterey cypress cut a filigreed profile at sunset.*

tour where you'll learn about the house and its owner and builder, Robinson Jeffers (1887–1962), a passionate poet who listened closely to the land around him.

Stroll among the pricey **boutiques,** especially near Ocean Avenue, and you'll start to get a sense of the exclusivity of the community. You'll also pass many art galleries; the best is the **Weston Gallery** (p. 331, ④), which displays the masterly photography of Edward Weston and Ansel Adams, both Carmel residents. Finish the day down at **Carmel City Beach** (p. 344, ⑤), where you can stroll along the white sandy beach, the perfect place to take in the sunset.

After dinner, linger on the patio of the restaurant at **Mission Ranch,** Clint Eastwood's charming farmhouse-style inn. With a little moonlight, you may be able to make out beautiful and mysterious **Point Lobos** (p. 344, ⑦) in the distance. ⏲ 6 hr.

On Day 3, head south on Hwy. 1 to

⑤ **Big Sur.** Completed in 1937, the 72-mile stretch of **Hwy. 1** through Big Sur is an official National Scenic Byway and considered one of the most spectacular stretches of highway in the world. You'll pass two man-made landmarks that deserve a photo: **Bixby Bridge** (p. 346, ❶), built in 1932, and the **Point Sur Lighthouse** (p. 346, ❷), built in 1889.

★★ **Pfeiffer Big Sur State Park** is Big Sur's most popular park, with coastal redwood trees, the Big Sur River, and a short hike to the 60-foot-high Pfeiffer Falls. Heading south for a mile (the turnoff at Sycamore Canyon to easy to miss) is ★★ **Pfeiffer Beach** (p. 348, ⑤), a pocket beach with crashing waves and purplish sand.

The next two stops are steeped in local history. The **Henry Miller Library** (p. 348, ❼) celebrates the controversial writer and one-time resident of Big Sur, but it also serves as an artsy community center. Check to see if it has any events—movies or music—scheduled for the evening. At ★ **Nepenthe** (p. 349), a property once by Orson Welles and Rita Hayworth, enjoy a drink on the patio with stunning views of the coast.

Continue south to ★★★ **Julia Pfeiffer Burns State Park** and make sure you get a photo—it's practically mandatory—of the ★★ **McWay Falls,** which plummets over a rocky cliff onto a pristine beach.

If you want to cap your 3 days with a world-class dining experience, head back north to the **Restaurant at the Ventana** (p. 349) or **Sierra Mar** (p. 349) at the Post Ranch Inn. ⏲ 1 day.

Driving Tip

If you're traveling along Hwy. 1 during summer, especially on weekends, traffic can get very heavy. Take advantage of the frequent turnouts to let any ornery drivers pass—as an added bonus, these stops will also let you take in the scenic vistas (a must!).

The Best of the Monterey Peninsula & Big Sur in 1 Week

A full week allows you to delve deeper. Explore towering redwoods in the Santa Cruz Mountains; see some of California's most historic buildings in Monterey; learn about Steinbeck Country; discover the haunting beauty of Carmel's Point Lobos; chase monarch butterflies in Pacific Grove, a quiet and charming town; and hike more of Big Sur's glorious state parks.

> *The Outer Bay exhibit has some of the largest and fastest ocean animals at the Monterey Bay Aquarium.*

START **Santa Cruz, 77 miles southeast of San Francisco.** TRIP LENGTH **about 184 miles.**

1 Santa Cruz. For the first half of the day, see p. 310, **1**. In the afternoon, head into the Santa Cruz Mountains, filled with coastal redwoods. Visit the hokey tourist trap, the ⋆ **Mystery Spot** (p. 334, **9**), where kids love watching physical oddities like a ball rolling

uphill, while adults roll their eyes. At **Henry Cowell Redwoods State Park** (www.santa cruzstateparks.org), you can visit old-growth redwoods, some of which are up to 1,800 years old and nearly 300 feet tall. The best way to breeze through the trees is on an open-air steam train at **Roaring Camp Railroads** (p. 334, **10**), also a favorite of kids. Spend the night in Santa Cruz.

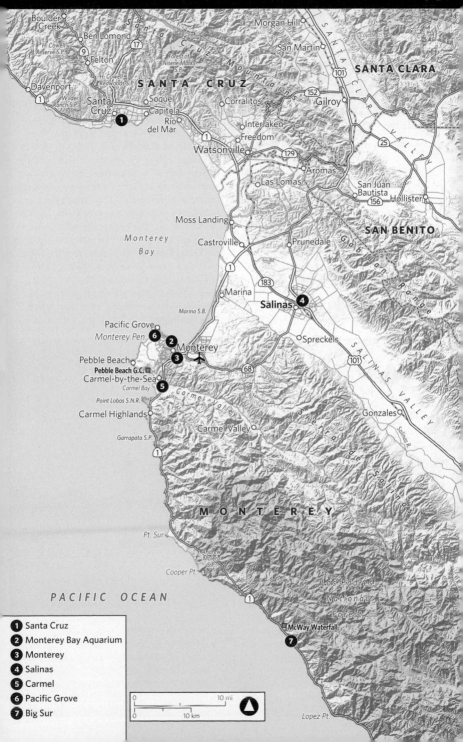

1 Santa Cruz
2 Monterey Bay Aquarium
3 Monterey
4 Salinas
5 Carmel
6 Pacific Grove
7 Big Sur

On the morning of Day 2, head a few miles north on Hwy. 1 to ★ **Wilder Ranch State Park** (p. 334, ⓫), a favorite among hikers and mountain bikers. Or if you feel like slowing down for a few hours, relax on one of Santa Cruz's many **beaches** (p. 316). ☺ 1½ days.

In the afternoon, head south for 40 miles on Hwy. 1 to the

❷ ★★★ 🅚🅘🅓🅢 **Monterey Bay Aquarium.** One of the biggest and best aquariums in the world, with 35,000 plants and animals and over 600 different species, Monterey's main attraction reels in nearly 2 million visitors a year. On summer weekends, the aquarium—formerly the site of the town's largest cannery—packs visitors in like sardines. The 28-foot-tall **Giant Kelp Forest** tank displays leopard sharks, bizarre-looking wolf eels, and giant sea bass drifting through swaying kelp. The **Outer Bay** may be the most dazzling attraction—a 1.2-million-gallon tank with clear walls that showcases big tuna, dolphinfish, hammerhead and Galapagos sharks, barracudas, and schools of silvery sardines. Have your camera ready for the brilliant orange **sea nettles (jellyfish),** which radiate an ethereal beauty; the display is so perfectly lit that even cellphone photos will look like *National Geographic* spreads. Don't miss the **giant octopus** exhibit, presenting the mysterious, complex, and surprisingly intelligent creatures. The **Secret Lives of Seahorses** shows 15 species of seahorses—some ghostly, others like twigs with eyeballs. The **sea otters** are the party animals of the aquarium, drawing crowds with their playful romping. At the **Touch Pool,** an indoor tide pool, kids can explore the tactile sensations of slippery bat rays, warty sea cucumbers, and spikey starfish. Step out onto the **Outer Deck** which looks out at the Monterey Bay, part of a National Marine Sanctuary stretching from Cambria to Marin; harbor seals and sea otters are visible year-round. The aquarium's newest guests are the **hot pink flamingos.** Feeding time for the animals

Santa Cruz Beaches

The most popular beach is Main Beach in front of the boardwalk. The best beaches for surfing are Steamers Lane (Lighthouse Point, West Cliff Dr.) and Pleasure Point (East Cliff at Pleasure Point Dr.). Great all-around beaches include Twin Lakes State Beach (pic-tured above), East Cliff Drive at 7th Ave., Capitola (☎ 831/429-2850; www. santacruzstateparks.org), and New Brighton State Beach, 1500 Park Ave., Capitola (☎ 831/464-6330; www.santacruzstateparks. org), which has popular campgrounds. In Davenport (17 miles north of Santa Cruz on Hwy. 1), Waddell Beach is always hopping with daring kite surfers. For current water and weather conditions, visit www.surfingsantacruz.com.

Car Crazy

The Monterey Peninsula has had a long love affair with the automobile. Since 1950, the **Pebble Beach Concours d'Elegance** (French for "competition of elegance"; ☎ 831/372-8026; www.pebblebeachconcours.net; admission $150–$175) has been one of the premiere collector car exhibitions in the world. On the third Sunday in August auto aficionados descend onto the Pebble Beach Golf Course to drool over vintage Duesenbergs, Bentleys, and Bugattis. For faster-paced fun, visit the **Laguna Seca Raceway** at 1021 Salinas Hwy., Monterey (☎ 800-327-7322; www.mazdaraceway.com), also a tradition over 50 years old, to catch racing events like American Le Man Series and the Rolex Monterey Motorsports Reunion, an event showcasing historic race cars.

> *California's first constitution was signed in 1849 at Monterey State Historic Park. Be sure to check out the whalebone sidewalks.*

is a lively affair, especially for the **blackfooted penguins** (10:30am and 3pm) in the Splash Zone. *Note:* On weekdays, it's quieter in the afternoon after buses of young students have departed. ⏱ At least 2 hr. 886 Cannery Row. ☎ 831/648-4800 or 831/648-4888 or 866/963-9645 for advance tickets (recommended). www.montereybayaquarium.org. Admission $30 adults, $28 seniors and students, $18 kids 3–12, free for kids 2 & under. Daily 10am–6pm; extended summer hours.

Spend the remainder of your day in Monterey, following the itinerary on p. 312, ➋ (minus the aquarium). Base yourself in Monterey or Pacific Grove for the next 2 nights.

➌ **Monterey.** On the morning of Day 3, learn about Monterey's role as capital of Alta California during the Spanish and Mexican colonial era. Take the self-guided **Path of History** tour at the **Monterey State Historic Park** (p. 338, ➐), a collection of historic buildings including **Colton Hall,** where California ratified its first state constitution in 1849; and the **Royal Presidio Chapel,** a National Historic Landmark and the oldest surviving building from the Monterey Presidio. You can download an accompanying audio tour from www.seemonterey.com. ⏱ 4 hr.

Head east on Hwy. 68 for 21 miles to Salinas.

➍ **Salinas.** This little agricultural town, known as the Salad Bowl of the World, is also the hometown of John Steinbeck, the first American writer to win both a Pulitzer Prize and a Nobel Prize. The innovative, 37,000-square-foot ★ **National Steinbeck Center** (p. 328, ➊) is the largest museum in the U.S. devoted to a single writer. Patrons will also learn about the history of the Salinas River valley, where Steinbeck found so much inspiration, once saying, "I would like to write the story of this whole valley, of all the little towns and all the farms . . . it would be the valley of the world."

Also, visit the beautiful Victorian home where Steinbeck was born and raised; the **Steinbeck House** (p. 329) offers tours as well as lunch and an afternoon tea. ⏱ At least 3 hr.

Head west on Hwy. 68 to Hwy. 1, then continue south to Carmel. Base yourself in Carmel or Pacific Grove for the next 2 nights.

➎ **Carmel.** For your Day 4 itinerary, see p. 312, ➍. On the morning of Day 5, go to ★★★ **Point Lobos State Natural Reserve** (p. 344, ➐) and spend a couple of hours meandering the trails among the Monterey cypress trees and jutting rocks lashed by the sea. Try to see why creative souls—Robert Louis Stevenson, Robinson Jeffers, Edward Weston—found the reserve so inspiring.

> *Point Pinos Lighthouse has always been a photographer's favorite, especially at sunset. Bundle up against chilly fog.*

Take the scenic drive through the **Carmel Valley** (p. 344, **8**) to **Carmel Valley Village,** where there are several wine-tasting rooms within walking distance. ⏲ 1½ days.

Return to Hwy. 1 and head north for 1 mile. Exit 399A for Pacific Grove and continue onto Hwy. 68, which turns into Forest Ave.

6 Pacific Grove. Unlike its well-touristed neighbors, Pacific Grove manages to stay fairly quiet, perhaps a remnant of its roots as a religious retreat.

One of the best ways to experience Pacific Grove is to walk or bike along **Pacific Grove Recreational Trail** (p. 340, **1**), especially in the spring when it's lined with bright pink flowers. Start at **Lover's Point** (p. 340, **2**)—perfect for picnicking, watching sea otters or tidepooling—and continue up to the historic **Point Pinos Lighthouse** (p. 340, **3**), which first shone its light in 1855.

Walking around the tip of Point Pinos, you can reach **Asilomar State Beach** (p. 340, **4**), a beautiful mile-long beach, which backs up

on 25 acres of restored sand dunes. Nearby is the **Asilomar Conference Center,** a complex of Arts and Crafts buildings designed by Julia Morgan (1872-1957) that is now a National Historic Landmark.

Check out the **Pacific Grove Museum of Natural History** (p. 340, **5**), a great way to learn about the Native Americans of Monterey Bay—the Esselen, Ohlone, and Salinan tribes. The most popular attraction, at least for kids, is the life-size sculpture of a gray whale named Sandy.

Because the town calls itself "Butterfly Town, U.S.A.," you must stop at **Monarch Grove Sanctuary** (p. 340, **6**), where butterflies cluster on the branches of eucalyptus trees between October and February. Look, but do not touch these striking black and orange creatures—"molestation of butterflies" carries a $1,000 fine. ⏲ half-day.

On Day 6, take Hwy. 1 south to Big Sur.

7 Big Sur. See p. 313, **5** for your day in Big Sur. Late that night, take a soak in the healing

> *Soak up the view from the hot spring baths at Esalen (only open to non-guests from 1am to 3am).*

natural hot springs baths at the renowned ★ **Esalen Institute** (p. 348, **9**). You have to book far in advance, and the only times available are between 1am and 3am. It's highly

Back Roads of Big Sur

Just north of the Bixby Bridge, you can access **Old Coast Road,** which before the bridge was completed in 1932, was the main road through the area. It jogs inland, presenting a panorama of the entire bridge, then heads south through the valley to Andrew Molera State Park. **Nacimiento-Fergusson Road** is a lonely stretch that turns off Hwy. 1 north of Gorda and runs inland, twisting and climbing over the 5,000-foot-high Santa Lucia Range, then continues to Fort Hunter Liggett, home of **Mission San Antonio de Padua,** and all the way to U.S. 101. The remote road is a favorite among motorcyclists. Be sure to read and follow road signs; some roads are unpaved and rains can make them impassable.

rewarding for those with a sense of adventure.

Start Day 7 with a tour ★ **Point Sur Lighthouse** (p. 346, **2**). Take a spin on the catwalk around the lamp tower, and you might well imagine a lighthouse keeper's sense of isolation.

At 4,800 acres, the largely underdeveloped ★ **Andrew Molera State Park** (p. 347, **3**) is the largest state park on the Big Sur coast and is usually less crowded than adjacent Pfeiffer Big Sur State Park. Hike (you'll find 20 miles of trails in a variety of ecosystems), look for California condors, or take a horseback ride through the meadows and onto the beach (p. 324, **7**).

At the north end of **Julia Pfeiffer Burns State Park** (p. 348, **8**), you can gain rare access to Big Sur's shoreline at the secluded little beach called **Partington Cove.** Or head 18 miles south to two other favorites—**Sand Dollar Beach** (daily 9am–8pm; $5 parking) and its neighbor to the south, **Jade Cove** (no services). ⏱ 2 days.

The Best of the Outdoors

For nature lovers, the Monterey Peninsula and surrounding area is an embarrassment of riches. Yes, we'll gallivant through Big Sur's many state parks, but we'll also wander under towering old redwoods, drift through preserved wetlands, climb among volcanic peaks, and hunt for hidden coves with aquamarine waters.

> A ghost inside the barn at Elkhorn Slough? No, It's just a family of barn owls, who nest here annually.

START **Big Basin Redwoods State Park, 24 miles north of Santa Cruz via Hwy. 9.** TRIP LENGTH **3 days, about 260 miles.**

❶ ★★ **Big Basin Redwoods State Park.** California's oldest state park, Big Basin was created in 1902 following the efforts of conservationists to save the tall coast redwoods from the voracious logging industry. There are 80 miles of trails that traverse 18,000 acres on the coastal side of the Santa Cruz Mountains. The **Redwood Loop** is an easy .5-mile loop through some of the park's most noteworthy specimens: Mother of the Forest is the tallest at 329 feet; Father of the Forest is the oldest at around 2,000 years; and the Chimney Tree is completely hollowed out. Hard-core hikers attack the 10-mile **Berry Creek Falls Trail,** which runs across creeks and fern-covered glens and through groves of old-growth redwoods to a cascade of waterfalls. ⊕ At least 2 hr. 21600 Big Basin Way, Boulder Creek. ☎ 831/338-8860. www.bigbasin.org. Parking $10. Daily 6am–10pm.

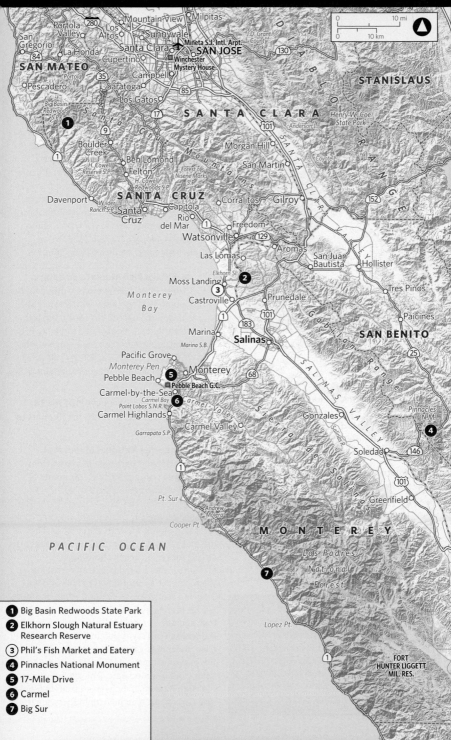

1 Big Basin Redwoods State Park
2 Elkhorn Slough Natural Estuary Research Reserve
3 Phil's Fish Market and Eatery
4 Pinnacles National Monument
5 17-Mile Drive
6 Carmel
7 Big Sur

> *Scramble up the weird rock formations—remnants of an ancient volcano—at Pinnacles National Monument.*

Return to Santa Cruz by heading 24 miles south on Hwy. 9. Head south on Hwy. 1 for 19 miles to Salinas Rd., then head east for 1½ miles. At Elkhorn Rd., turn right and head south for 5 miles to

❷ ★ Elkhorn Slough National Estuarine Research Reserve. One of California's largest coastal wetlands, Elkhorn Slough (pronounced "slew") is the natural habitat for an estimated 700 species of plants and animals. There are 340 species of birds, making it one of the state's best spots for birding, and recently, there have been sightings of wintering flamingos. You'll also see seals, sea lions, and the never-shy sea

Nature Tip

As you roam through the redwoods in Santa Cruz County, keep your eyes peeled for the banana slug—a slimy, yellow, gastropod mollusk that can grow up to nearly 10 inches long and is the mascot of the University of Santa Cruz. Please don't pick them up, as the salt on your skin can harm them.

otters, but leopard sharks and bat rays roaming the muddy waters can be harder to spot. Admission to the visitor center is free and they'll even loan you binoculars. To explore the trails costs $2.50 for adults (kids are free), and docent-led tours are available on weekends at 10am and 1pm at no additional charge.

Kayaking is a popular way to explore the calm waters (**Kayak Connection;** ☎ 831/724-5692; www.kayakconnection.com), but I prefer taking ★ **Elkhorn Slough Safari** (☎ 831/633-5555; www.elkhornslough.com; $32 adults, $24 kids 3–14), a 2-hour pontoon boat tour that explains the slough's unique ecology and its use by its native inhabitants. ⏱ 2½ hr. (including boat tour). 1700 Elkhorn Rd., Watsonville. ☎ 831/728-2822. www.elkhornslough.org. Wed–Sun 9am–5pm.

---

③   ➧ ★ **Phil's Fish Market and Eatery.** Owner Phil DiGirolamo is famous for his cioppino—a fish stew with fresh crab, squid, and lingcod. His recipe bested celebrity chef Bobby Flay's in a head-to-head competition on the Food Network. 7600 Sandholdt Rd. ☎ 831/728-2822. www.philsfishmarket.com. Cioppino $19. AE, DC, MC, V.

On Day 2, head south on U.S. 101 for 34 miles, then east on Hwy. 146 for 10 miles to the west entrance of

❹ ★★ **Pinnacles National Monument.** This often-overlooked park gets its name from the hundreds of rocky spires, remnants of an ancient volcano carried 200 miles north by movement along the San Andreas fault. The unusual geologic formations of volcanic rock—including monoliths with sheer faces, and jumbles of boulders—make the park a favorite choice for serious **rock climbing.**

There's also 30 miles of trails crossing the rolling, chaparral-covered hills and dipping into talus caves—formed when boulders wedge into narrow ravines creating dark tunnels and caverns below. The gentle, 2.5-mile **Balconies Trail** takes you to the west-side cave, **Balconies Cave** (you'll need a flashlight); the east-side cave, Bear Gulch, is home to a colony of big-eared bats. The jagged crags of the **High Peaks** can be viewed from the west-side parking area, or hike up to them via the

The Heavenly Greens of Pebble Beach

Pebble Beach (pictured above) is a golfer's paradise, with several world-class golf courses set along the famous 17-Mile Drive. It's easier to get a tee time if you're staying at one of the high-priced golf resorts, but do note that greens fees here are costly.

The best of the best is ★★★ **Pebble Beach Golf Links,** 1700 17-Mile Dr. (☎ 800/654-9300; www.pebblebeach.com; greens fees $495, plus cart fee), of which Jack Nicklaus said, "If I could play only one course for the rest of my life, this would be it."

Ranked among the finest public courses in the country, ★ **Spyglass Hill,** Stevenson Drive and Spyglass Hill Road (☎ 800/654-9300; www.pebblebeach.com; greens fees $340, plus cart fee), is also known as one of the toughest; the first 5 holes have ocean views, while the others run deep into the pine forest.

Perhaps the most easily booked course, ★ **Links at Spanish Bay** at Inn of the Spanish Bay, 2700 17-Mile Dr. (☎ 800/654-9300; www.pebblebeach.com; greens fees $260, plus cart fee), is modeled after a traditional Scottish links course.

Juniper Canyon Trail, a hearty 6-mile loop. During your visit, scan the skies for the wide wings of the endangered **California condor.** The park has been a part of the California Condor Recovery Program since 2003. But also, stay on the lookout for poison oak on the trails. Summers are intensely hot; fall and spring, during wildflower season, make the best times for visiting. ⏱ 2 hr. 5000 Hwy. 146, Paicines. ☎ 831/389-4485. www.nps.gov/pinn. Admission $5 per car. West gate 7:30am–8pm.

Return to U.S. 101 and head north for 33 miles. Follow signs for Monterey Peninsula and head west on Hwy. 156. Continue onto Hwy. 1 south. Exit 402B and head west on Del Monte Ave. to Alvarado St.

❺ ★★ 17-Mile Drive. The best way to cruise scenic 17-Mile Drive is on a bicycle with the wind in your hair. If you wear a backpack stuffed with picnic supplies and a camera, even better. Rent a bike at **Adventures by the Sea,** 201 Alvarado St. (☎ 831/372-1807; www.adventures bythesea.com; $7 per hr.; $20 per 4 hr.). You can follow the **Monterey Recreation Trail** up the shoreline from Cannery Row, past Lover's Point, around the tip of the peninsula, and onto Sunset Drive where you can enter (for free) the gate to 17-Mile Drive. ⏱ 2 hr. See p. 312, ❸.

> *It's a dog's life on the beach at Carmel, paws down one of the pet-friendliest towns anywhere.*

6 Carmel. Carmel City Beach (p. 344, **5**) and **Carmel River Beach** (p. 344, **6**) are both excellent, but the town's most alluring nature retreat is the **Point Lobos State Reserve** (p. 344, **7**), commonly called the crown jewel of California's state parks.

From ocean vistas along the park's many easy trails (maps are available at the information station at the Sea Lion Point parking area), you'll often spot otters, sea lions, and migrating whales. The **Cypress Grove** and **North Shore Trails** are favorites, but **Bird Island Trail** lets you dip down to two incredible little beaches, **China Cove** and **Gibson Beach,** white sandy pockets tucked against the cliffs. The best tidal pools are at **Weston Beach,** named for the photographer who found so much inspiration here.

Check out **Whaler's Cabin,** a ramshackle building from the 1850s that once housed Japanese and Chinese fishermen and now serves as a small museum on the area's former whaling industry.

If you're qualified to **scuba dive,** explore the 750 acres of pristine marine life among the 70-foot-high ropes of kelp at Whaler's or Bluefish Coves (reservations are recommended; ☎ 800/624-8413). ⏱ At least 2 hr.

On Day 3, from Point Lobos, head south on Hwy. 1 for 5 miles to Garrapata State Park; there is no visitor center, so use the turnouts marked 1 to 19 on the east side of Hwy. 1.

7 Big Sur. You could easily spend days rambling through the breathtaking coastline where the Santa Lucias plunge dramatically into the Pacific Ocean. To hit only some of the following highlights in a single day will take stamina and good hiking shoes.

Enjoy spectacular coastal hiking at easy-to-miss ★ **Garrapata State Park** (☎ 831/624-4909; www.parks.ca.gov) featuring 3,000 acres with 2 miles of rocky shoreline, redwood canyons, and steep mountainsides that erupt with color during wildflower season. The strenuous 5-mile **Rocky Ridge** and **Soberanes Canyon** loop is a popular choice for fitness fanatics, but there are gentler trails along **Soberanes Point,** from which you can scan the ocean for sea mammals. **Garrapata Beach,** though often foggy, makes an idyllic spot for a picnic.

A great way to explore ★ **Andrew Molera State Park** (p. 347, **3**) is by horseback; **Molera Big Sur Trail Rides** (☎ 831/625-5486; www.molerahorsebacktours.com; tours are seasonal) offers a small variety of coastal horseback tours starting at $40 for a 1-hour ride. Tent-only campgrounds are also available and are walk in only.

Look for California condors—the largest

> *Get your giddy-up at Andrew Molera State Park, where you can trail ride right down to the beach.*

flying bird in North America and still a critically endangered species—soaring in the skies above Big Sur. The Ventana Wildlife Society (☎ 831/455-9514; www.ventanaws.org) offers a condor viewing tour ($50 per person); you can visit the society's Discovery Center (Fri–Sun, 9am–4pm) at Andrew Molera State Park for information on condors and other birds and wildlife.

★★★ **Julia Pfeiffer Burns State Park** (p. 348, ⑧) has the pretty-as-a-picture ★★ **McWay Falls,** but once you get the picture, hit the trails. From the parking area, you can access one of Big Sur's best hikes, the 4.5-mile ★ **Ewoldsen Trail,** which winds through McWay Canyon, with creek crossings, lush fern growth, mature redwoods, and stunning coastal views. At the park's northern edge (on Hwy. 1, north of Partington Bridge), pick up the trail which runs through a 200-foot (and 100-year-old) tunnel, then down to ★★ **Partington Cove,** one of the few accessible beaches in Big Sur, and where rum-runners are rumored to have docked during Prohibition.

Camping in Big Sur

Pfeiffer Big Sur State Park (☎ 800/444-7275; www.reserveamerica.com; campsites $35–$50) offers Big Sur's best-equipped campgrounds, with restrooms, showers, laundry, a convenience store, and Wi-Fi. The cool spots on the banks of the river are hotly contested during summer; reservations are recommended. See p. 347, ④ for more information.

Big Sur Campground and Cabins, 47000 Hwy. 1. (☎ 831/667-2322; www.bigsurcamp.com; tent sites from $34), is a family-friendly camping complex offering tent sites, RV sites, tent cabins, and cabins with private bathrooms as well as a playground, river access, and inner-tube rentals.

An experience between camping and a hotel, ★ **Treebones Resort,** 71895 Hwy. 1 (☎ 877/424-4787; www.treebonesresort.com; yurts $165–$230), offers comfortable ocean-side yurts (circular fabric tent/cabins), a pool and hot tub with ocean views, and a sushi and tapas bar.

CALIFORNIA MUSIC

A Down and Dirty Guide to the Sounds and the Scenes

BY DAN TUCKER

	BAKERSFIELD SOUND	CALIFORNIA FOLK ROCK	SURF MUSIC
THE SOUND	Stripped down country: a reaction against the slick Nashville sound	Smooth vocal harmonies, generous helpings of slide guitar, pedal steel, and dobro	Upbeat melodies, 4/4 rhythms, guitars with reverb and tremolo, sweet vocal harmonies (or pure instrumentals)
LEADERS	Merle Haggard, Buck Owens & the Buckaroos	Mamas and the Papas, Gram Parsons, The Byrds, Joni Mitchell, Crosby, Stills & Nash, The Eagles	Dick Dale, Duane Eddy, The Beach Boys, The Ventures, Surfaris, Jan & Dean
INFLUENCES	Jimmie Rodgers, Hank Williams. Soulful, storytelling country music.	Southern country blues, cowboy songs, Appalachian bluegrass, and country ballads. Oh—and marijuana.	Early rock instrumentation gets a pinch of Latin and jazz riffs and a tsunami of So Cal flavor.
EPICENTER	Bakersfield honky-tonks like the Blackboard	Laurel Canyon in L.A.	The beach, man! Orange and San Diego Counties
ICONIC ALBUM	*Branded Man* (Merle Haggard)	*Hotel California* (Eagles)	*Pet Sounds* (Beach Boys)
TELLING SCANDAL	Merle Haggard attends Johnny Cash's legendary San Quentin concert as an inmate (three years for attempted robbery).	Sex, drugs, and bickering: founding Eagles guitarist Leadon "resigns" by pouring beer on Glen Frey's head	Beach Boy and Brian Wilson cousin Mike Love dismisses Wilson's "Good Vibrations" as "avant-garde shit."

A REMARKABLE VARIETY OF MUSICAL GENRES has flourished in California, most often transplanted from elsewhere and then transformed: country music from the Southeastern U.S., folk, punk, and hardcore from the U.K., New York, and elsewhere. Hip-hop artists maintained a mutual influence and rivalry, sometimes deadly, with the genre's originators in New York. But one category—surf music—could only have originated here, and it's hard to imagine more fertile ground for psychedelia than San Francisco in the 1960s. Following is an overview of the movements that have emanated from various parts of California since the late 1950s.

WEST COAST PSYCHEDELICA	PUNK	HARDCORE	HIP-HOP
Soaring guitar solos, feedback, wah-wah pedals, fuzzboxes, dreamlike lyrics, long jams	Propulsive, fast-paced rhythms, urgent melodic vocals—three chord pop-music taken off the Zoloft	Short, aggressive songs, slapping, out-front basslines, hatchet guitar work, shouted vocals	Slow, heavy, beats, flowing rhymes, background vocals used as percussion, melodic samples.
The Grateful Dead, Jefferson Airplane, The Doors, Carlos Santana, Janis Joplin, Moby Grape	X, Red Hot Chili Peppers, Dead Kennedys, NOFX, Rancid, Social Distortion, Green Day, The Offspring	Black Flag, The Dickies, Circle Jerks, the Germs, Agent Orange, The Descendents, Bad Religion	Dr. Dre, Ice Cube, Ice T, Snoop Dogg, Tupac Shakur, NWA, Cypress Hill
Lead Belly and blues classics, Aldous Huxley, Timothy Leary, LSD.	Rockabilly meets funk meets surf music meets William Burroughs	Anarchist philosophers, angry garage bands, DIY support groups.	Eldridge Cleaver, George Clinton, Bootsy Collins, Malcolm X
Haight-Ashbury, San Francisco, Sunset in L.A.	San Francisco, East Bay, Los Angeles and Orange Counties	Anywhere there's disaffected youth.	South Central L.A., East Bay
Surrealistic Pillow (Airplane)	*Los Angeles* (X)	*Damaged* (Black Flag)	*Straight Outta Compton* (NWA)
Jimi Hendrix, Janis Joplin, Jim Morrison all die at age 27.	Former Dead Kennedy bandmates sue Jello Biafra for unpaid royalties as he refuses to license "Holiday in Cambodia" for a Levi's Dockers commercial.	Recurring violent confrontations between Black Flag, audiences, and police; band is dropped by label for being "antiparent."	Tupac murdered in a drive-by... after being severely injured in a shooting two years previously.

Monterey & Big Sur for Culture Lovers

Monterey County, which includes the fertile valley around the Salinas River, inspired the socially conscious novels of native son John Steinbeck (1902–68), who was familiar with its farmhands and migrant workers. Carmel's natural beauty drew poet and early environmentalist Robinson Jeffers, (who called the craggy coastline his "inevitable place") as well as photographers such as Edward Weston (1886–1958) and Ansel Adams (1902–84). Big Sur's roots are more bohemian, perhaps owing to the remoteness and wildness of its geography.

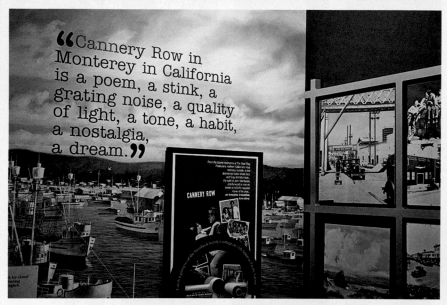

"Cannery Row in Monterey in California is a poem, a stink, a grating noise, a quality of light, a tone, a habit, a nostalgia, a dream."

> *A swirl of high-tech media brings a master's literature to life at the National Steinbeck Center.*

START Salinas, 107 miles southeast of San Francisco. **TRIP LENGTH** 2 days, about 68 miles.

❶ Salinas. The ★ **National Steinbeck Center,** 1 Main St. (☎ 831/775-4721; www.steinbeck. org; $11 adults, $9 seniors 61 and over, $8 kids 13–17, $6 kids 6–12, free for kids 5 & under; daily 10am–5pm) is a modern museum in historic Old Town Salinas. High-tech interactive exhibits bring Steinbeck's written words to life, but they also describe how his own personal history, and the agricultural history of the surrounding land (sometimes called Steinbeck Country), so deeply informed his novels, such as *East of Eden, Of Mice and Men,* and *The Red Pony.* Catch a short film on Steinbeck and

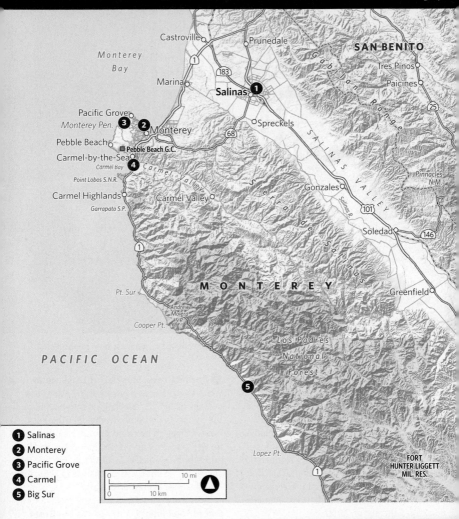

1 Salinas
2 Monterey
3 Pacific Grove
4 Carmel
5 Big Sur

clips from several movies based on his works such as *The Grapes of Wrath* and *Cannery Row*. The center promotes serious scholarship and research with access to the Steinbeck Archive featuring over 45,000 items.

Take the 2-block walk to the **Steinbeck House,** 132 Central Ave. (☎ 831/424-2735; www.steinbeckhouse.com; tours Sun 1–3pm in summer; $5 adults, $4 kids), Steinbeck's birthplace and childhood home, now a National Historic Landmark. It's also a cafe serving lunch, with a menu accentuating Salinas produce, as well as a Victorian tea (reservations required; entrees $10–$13, tea $25; Mon–Sat 11am–2:30pm). ⏱ At least 2 hr.

From Salinas, head west on Hwy. 68 for 21 miles.

2 Monterey. Originally called Ocean View Avenue, **Cannery Row** was officially renamed in 1958 in honor of Steinbeck's 1945 novel of the same name, which immortalized the stretch of sardine-canning factories that thrived here in the first half of the 20th century. The memorable first line of the book refers to Cannery Row as "a poem, a stink, a grating noise, a quality of light, a tone, a habit, a nostalgia, a dream."

Steinbeck based the main character Doc on his close, and intellectually influential, friend Ed

> *With cozy courtyards and snugly B&Bs, Carmel-by-the-Sea might be the quaintest town on the planet.*

Ricketts, a prominent and charismatic marine biologist whose laboratory occupied 800 Cannery Row (the small shack remains there today). **Ricketts' lab** was the site of informal gatherings of local artists and philosophers, including Steinbeck, Henry Miller, and Joseph Campbell.

In 1940 Ricketts and Steinbeck departed **Fisherman's Wharf** for the Gulf of California on an expedition to collect biological specimens; the trip yielded a nonfiction collaboration called the *Sea of Cortez.*

The Scottish novelist Robert Louis Stevenson lived in Monterey for several months in 1879 at a boardinghouse, now called the **Stevenson House,** 530 Houston St. (state budget cuts have affected tour times and costs; for the latest information, call ☎ 831/649-7118 or visit www.parks.ca.gov/mshp), where he wrote a memoir called *The Old Pacific Capital* while waiting to be reunited with his soon-to-be wife. Scholars believe that Stevenson began work on *Treasure Island* after being inspired by his walks through Point Lobos. His former room contains memorabilia—furniture, books, manuscripts, and personal keepsakes—donated by his family. ⏱ 2 hr.

❸ **Pacific Grove.** Steinbeck spent several years struggling as a writer at the Steinbeck cottage at 147 11th St. His father, who had built the house as a summer home, let Steinbeck live rent free so he could pursue his craft. Here he wrote several books, including *The Red Pony* and Monterey-based *Tortilla Flats,* his first real success. The book was published in 1935, just months after his father's death.

At the northern tip of the peninsula, at the foot of Point Pinos Lighthouse, is the **Great Tide Pool,** where Ricketts used to collect specimens, as Steinbeck vividly describes in *Cannery Row.* ⏱ 20 min.

On Day 2, take Forest Ave. south and continue onto Hwy. 68. Head south on Hwy. 1, then exit at Ocean Ave. Total trip is 6 miles.

❹ **Carmel.** Despite Carmel's present-day image—with its exclusive real estate prices and chichi boutiques—it began as a humble artists' colony at the turn of the 20th century, attracting such writers as Jack London, a young Sinclair Lewis, ringleader George Sterling, and poet Robinson Jeffers.

A must stop is at Jeffers' handcrafted

home, the ★★ **Tor House and Hawk Tower** (p. 343, ❷), constructed with a technique he described as "stone love stone." Jeffers did all of his writing here, and much of his work reflects his intense relationship with the physical world. Today the Robinson Jeffers Tor House Foundation, created by his friend Ansel Adams, seeks to preserve Jeffers' literary legacy. A tour may include a brief recitation of his work, allowing you a moment to imagine Jeffers' visitors back in the day—admirers like Charlie Chaplin, Charles Lindbergh, Langston Hughes, and George Gershwin.

Some people joke that Carmel has the highest number of art galleries per capita in the United States. Peruse local artwork at the **Carmel Art Association,** Dolores Street, between 5th and 6th streets, (☎ 831/624-6176; www.carmelart.org), Carmel's oldest gallery, founded in 1927. My favorite gallery is the **Weston Gallery,** 6th Avenue between Dolores and Lincoln streets (☎ 831/624-4453; www.westongallery.com; daily 10:30am–5:30pm), which displays vintage and contemporary photographs by Edward Weston (as well as his sons, Brett and Cole), Ansel Adams, and other giants who contributed to the history of the art form.

The jutting, jagged, wave-battered coastline at ★★★ **Point Lobos State Reserve** has inspired countless artists—Robert Louis Stevenson, Robinson Jeffers, and Edward Weston, who while succumbing to Parkinson's disease, shot his last photographs here. After Weston's death in 1958, his ashes were scattered on Lobos' Pebbly Beach, later renamed Weston Beach. ☉ At least 3 hr.

From Point Lobos to Bixby Bridge, head south on Hwy. 1 for 11 miles to

❺ **Big Sur.** In 1960 at the height of his fame following the publication of *On the Road,* Jack Kerouac (1922–69) retreated to a cabin (owned

> *Not your typical book nook, Henry Miller Library in Big Sur has art shows, film screenings, and music.*

by Lawrence Ferlinghetti, poet and cofounder of San Francisco's legendary City Lights Bookstore; p. 83, ❹) in Bixby Canyon, below the **Bixby Bridge.** Drunk, depressed, paranoid, and lonely in the remote cabin, Kerouac suffered a nervous breakdown, which he chronicled in his semiautobiographical novel *Big Sur.*

On a property once owned by Orson Welles and Rita Hayworth, the small complex of **Nepenthe** (p. 349) is home to a couple of restaurants with sensational views and a gift shop with Big Sur–related art and books. The restaurant has always drawn artist and writers, especially Henry Miller, whose cabin was nearby.

Writer and artist Henry Miller, inspired by Robinson Jeffers, based himself in Big Sur from 1944 to 1962, and wrote, at times rhapsodically, of this period in *Big Sur and the Oranges of Hieronymus Bosch.* Stop by the **Henry Miller Library** (p. 348, ❼) to delve into more of his books and artwork. If you don't have time to bang your way through *Sexus, Plexus,* and *Nexus,* check the schedule for eclectic events like outdoor summer film screenings, and off-beat musical performances (Patti Smith, Animal Collective).

Not far from Nepenthe is the **Coast Gallery** 49901 Hwy. 1 (☎ 831/667 2301; www.coastgalleries.com), which displays art by Miller, Marc Chagall and others in galleries made of huge recycled redwood water tanks. ☉ At least 2 hr.

A Bit of Photo History

In 1932 Edward Weston and Ansel Adams, friends and colleagues, cofounded Group f/64, dedicated to the straight, sharp-focused aesthetic of photography. Both lived out their days at their respective homes and workplaces in the Carmel Highlands.

Santa Cruz

Santa Cruz is perhaps best known for its old-school beachside boardwalk and its south-facing beaches, which make the most of the 300 days a year of sunshine. It's family friendly, surf crazy, and proudly nonconformist ("Keep Santa Cruz weird" is one of its mottoes).

> In a town that wetsuit-inventor Jack O'Neill calls home, it's only appropriate to have the Santa Cruz Surfing Museum housed in a former lighthouse.

START **Santa Cruz Beach Boardwalk.** Santa Cruz is 77 miles southeast of San Francisco and 44 miles north of Monterey.

1 ★★★ kids **Santa Cruz Beach Boardwalk.** Opening in 1907 as Coney Island of the West, Santa Cruz's boardwalk is one of the last remaining old-fashioned seaside amusement parks in the world. On Friday nights during the summer, enjoy a free concert, usually by a nostalgia-tripping band from the '80s. ⏱ 2 hr. ☎. 831/423-5590. www.beachboardwalk.com. Free admission, but rides $3–$5 each; all-day unlimited-ride pass $30. Summer daily; rest of the year and holidays Sat–Sun.

2 ★ **Municipal Wharf.** Sea lions bark on the beams below you as you walk, shop, fish, or eat along the wharf, which extends a ½ mile into Monterey Bay. Arrange whale-watching or scenic tours, fishing trips, or private charters with **Stagnaro's** (☎ 831/427-2334; www.stagnaros.com). If you're visiting near the end of June, check out **Woodies on the Wharf** (www.santacruzwoodies.com), a free event celebrating "woodies," the wood-paneled, surfboard-friendly cars from the '50s and a vibrant part of California surf culture. ⏱ 15 min. ☎ 831/420-6025. Daily 5am–2am.

3 ★★ **West Cliff Drive.** Walk, bike, or, if you must, drive along the coastal bluff between the wharf and Natural Bridges State Beach. Out on the water, surfers catch waves, sailboats catch breezes, and seabirds claim rocky outposts. ⏱ 30 min.

4 ★ **Santa Cruz Surfing Museum.** Opened in 1986 as the first museum devoted to surfing, the museum traces the 100-year history of surfing in Santa Cruz through photographs, surfboards, and other memorabilia. ⏱ 30 min.

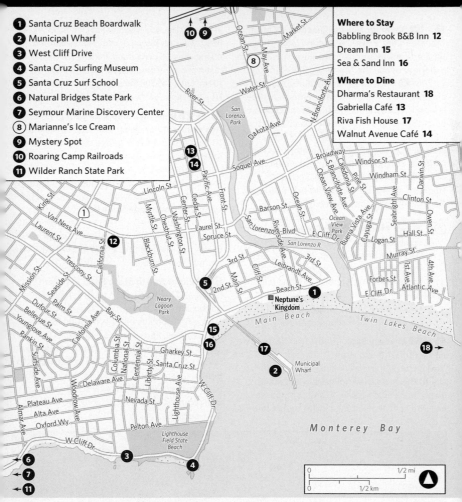

1. Santa Cruz Beach Boardwalk
2. Municipal Wharf
3. West Cliff Drive
4. Santa Cruz Surfing Museum
5. Santa Cruz Surf School
6. Natural Bridges State Park
7. Seymour Marine Discovery Center
8. Marianne's Ice Cream
9. Mystery Spot
10. Roaring Camp Railroads
11. Wilder Ranch State Park

Where to Stay
Babbling Brook B&B Inn 12
Dream Inn 15
Sea & Sand Inn 16

Where to Dine
Dharma's Restaurant 18
Gabriella Café 13
Riva Fish House 17
Walnut Avenue Café 14

701 West Cliff Dr. ☎ 831/420-6289. www.santa cruzsurfingmuseum.org. Free admission, donations welcome. Summer Wed–Sun 10am–5pm; winter Thurs–Mon noon–4pm.

5 ★ **Santa Cruz Surf School.** Inspired by the town's surfing legacy? Learn to ride the gentle waves at Cowell's Beach with patient and positive instructors, who are equally good with kids and adults. ⏱ 2 hr. 322 Pacific Ave. ☎ 831/426-7072. www.santacruzsurfschool.com. 2 hr. group lessons $80 per person.

6 ★★ **Natural Bridges State Park.** This soft-sand beach, one of my favorites, is best known

for its striking sandstone arch carved by wind and sea, once a series of arches forming a natural bridge. The rocks north of the bridge are perfect for tide pooling during low tide, with plenty of starfish, crabs, and sea anemones. The park also features a small eucalyptus grove, which draws thousands of migrating monarch butterflies from October to February. Park amenities include a picnic area, restrooms, and an excellent visitor center, which provides free docent-led tours of the tide pools and monarch groves. ⏱ 1 hr. 2531 W. Cliff Dr. ☎ 831/423-4609. www.parks.ca.gov. Parking $10. Daily 8am–sunset.

7 ★ **kids** **Seymour Marine Discovery Center.** Modeled after a working marine laboratory, this center offers a cheaper, more manageable experience than the Monterey Bay Aquarium (p. 316, **2**). Budding marine biologists are encouraged to "think like a scientist" as they interact with exhibits. Be sure to meet Ms. Blue, the world's largest blue whale skeleton, which measures 18-feet high and 87-feet long. ⏱ 45 min. At Long Marine Laboratory, 100 Shaffer Rd. ☎ 831/459-3800. http://seymourcenter. ucsc.edu. Admission $6 adults; $4 seniors, students, and kids 4–16; free for kids 3 & under. Tues–Sat 10am–5pm; Sun noon–5pm.

8 🍦 ★★ **Marianne's Ice Cream.** This local institution serves delicious ice cream in a wild assortment of over 70 flavors, including garlic, blueberry cheesecake, baby coconut, oatmeal cookie, and the favorite 10-20—a blend of caramel, fudge, and Oreos. 1020 Ocean St. ☎ 831/458-1447. Cash only. Double scoop under $5.

9 ★ **kids** **Mystery Spot.** Tourist trap? Yep. Pseudoscientific mumbo jumbo? That too. Still, it's a hoot to visit this dizzying place where (they claim) the normal laws of gravity and physics do not apply: Balls roll up a ramp, compasses go haywire, and people can stand at preposterous angles. ⏱ 1 hr. 465 Mystery Spot Rd. ☎ 831/423-8897. www.mysteryspot.com. Admission and 45 min. tour $5 per person. Parking $5. Online reservations recommended. Summer Mon–Fri 10am–6pm, Sat–Sun 9am–7pm; rest of year Mon–Fri 10am–4pm, Sat–Sun 9am–5pm.

10 ★★ **kids** **Roaring Camp Railroads.** There are two wonderful open-air train rides available: a 100-year-old, narrow-gauge steam train that takes a 75-minute loop north through pristine groves of towering redwood groves and a "beach" train that takes a 3-hour round-trip to the Santa Cruz boardwalk, by way of the **Henry Cowell Redwoods State Park** (www.santa cruzstateparks.org)—a worthy destination in itself—and the San Lorenzo River Gorge. 5355 Graham Hill Rd., Felton. ☎ 831/335-4400. www. roaringcamp.com.

11 ★ **Wilder Ranch State Park.** Excellent hiking and biking close to town can be found on these 7,000 acres of reclaimed ranch land, with 34 miles of trails through forests and canyons, and along coastal bluffs with stunning views of Monterey Bay. A great hike follows Old Cove Landing Trail to **Fern Grotto Beach.** ⏱ 2 hr. 1401 Coast Rd. (at Hwy. 1, 1 mile past Western Dr.). ☎ 831/426-0505. www. santacruzstateparks.org. Parking $10. Daily 8am–sunset.

"The Real Surf City USA"

The fact that the phrase "Surf City, USA" is a registered trademark of the Huntington Beach Conference and Visitors Bureau roils many locals who insist that surfing was brought to Santa Cruz and the mainland from Hawaii in 1886 when three Hawaiian princes tried the waves near the mouth of the San Lorenzo River on 15-foot, 100-pound redwood planks. In 2009 the royal family of Hawaii donated a bronze plaque to Santa Cruz to commemorate the event. Earlier in 2009 *Surfer* magazine named Santa Cruz "the real Surf City USA."

Where to Stay & Dine

> *Crowds spill out of Walnut Avenue Café, a hugely (and justifiably) popular eatery, especially on weekends.*

★ **Babbling Brook Bed & Breakfast Inn**
Santa Cruz's first B&B remains one of its most charming, with a babbling brook drowning out the city noise, and simple, tasteful rooms. 1025 Laurel St. ☎ 800/866-1131 or 831/427-2437. www.babblingbrookinn.com. 13 units. Doubles $209–$289 w/breakfast & afternoon wine. AE, DISC, MC, V.

★ **Dharma's Restaurant** *VEGETARIAN*
Sometimes called McDharma's for its fast-food style efficiency, this organic vegetarian restaurant has been a hit with healthy eaters for nearly 30 years. 4250 Capitola Rd., Capitola. ☎ 831/462-1717. www.dharmasrestaurant.com. Entrees $5–$11. Breakfast, lunch & dinner daily. AE, MC, V.

★★ **Dream Inn**
This beachfront hotel, on Cowell Beach near the boardwalk, is a satisfying blend of corporate efficiency, laid-back beach vibe, and groovy design. Each room has an ocean view. There's also a heated pool, hot tub, and children's wading pool. 175 W. Cliff Dr. ☎ 831/426-4330. www.dreaminnsantacruz.com. 165 units. Doubles $169–$389. AE, MC, V.

★ **Gabriella Café.** *CAL-ITALIAN*
The small but welcoming dining room presents a sophisticated Cal-Italian menu—potato gnocchi with bone marrow confit, cinnamon braised lamb shank—with an emphasis on seasonal, local, and organic ingredients. 910 Cedar St. ☎ 831/457-1677. www.gabriellacafe.com. Entrees $18–$28. Lunch Tues–Fri; dinner daily; brunch Sat–Sun. AE, MC, V.

★ **Riva Fish House** *SEAFOOD*
This no-frills spot on the wharf offers quick and delicious seafood staples like clam chowder and fried calamari, as well as great views, and a brilliant Bloody Mary. 31 Municipal Wharf, Ste. 500. ☎ 831/429-1223. Entrees $5–$10. Lunch & dinner daily. Cash only.

★ **Sea & Sand Inn**
This upscale motel on the water is a popular choice for its ocean views, proximity to the boardwalk and wharf, and comfortable rooms. 201 W. Cliff Dr. ☎ 831/427-3400. www.santacruzmotels.com. 20 units. Doubles $109–$319. AE, DISC, MC, V.

★★ **Walnut Avenue Café** *AMERICAN*
Locals crowd this downtown brunch joint for its savory scrambles (like chilaquiles), serious home fries, and fruit-topped French toast and Belgian waffles, as well as light lunches. 106 Walnut Ave. ☎ 831/457-2307. www.walnutavenuecafe.com. Entrees $6–$10. Breakfast & lunch daily. AE, MC, V.

Monterey

The acting capital of California while it was under Spanish and Mexican rule, Monterey claims a unique spot in the state's history. In the early 1900s sardine fishing and canning became the town's main industry, as illustrated by John Steinbeck in his gritty novel *Cannery Row*. These days the fish at the Monterey Bay Aquarium—sitting atop a National Marine Sanctuary—are the town's biggest stars.

> Nothing fishy about Cannery Row, once a main source for canned sardines and now an appealing if touristy strip.

START **Monterey Bay Aquarium. Monterey is 45 miles south of Santa Cruz, 72 miles south of San Jose, and 116 miles south of San Francisco.**

❶ ★★★ kids **Monterey Bay Aquarium.** See p. 316, ❷.

❷ ★ **Monterey Bay Kayaks.** Kayaking is an excellent way to explore a small patch of the 6,094 square miles of the Monterey Bay National Marine Sanctuary. Equipment and instruction are provided. You're likely to meet sea lions, harbor seals, and cute sea otters during your journey. ⏲ At least 3hr. 693 Del Monte Ave. ☎ 831/373-5357. www.monterey baykayaks.com. Rentals from $30 a day; guided tours from $60 for 3 hr.

❸ ★ **Cannery Row.** A touristy hodgepodge of souvenir shops and restaurants has replaced

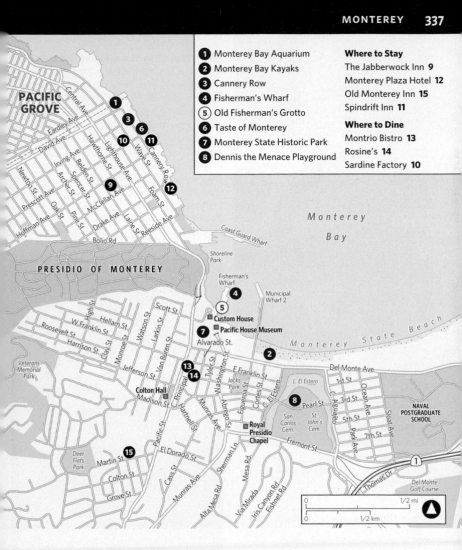

1 Monterey Bay Aquarium
2 Monterey Bay Kayaks
3 Cannery Row
4 Fisherman's Wharf
5 Old Fisherman's Grotto
6 Taste of Monterey
7 Monterey State Historic Park
8 Dennis the Menace Playground

Where to Stay
The Jabberwock Inn 9
Monterey Plaza Hotel 12
Old Monterey Inn 15
Spindrift Inn 11

Where to Dine
Montrio Bistro 13
Rosine's 14
Sardine Factory 10

the sardine canning factories that dominated the waterfront in the first half of the 20th century. Upon returning to Cannery Row many years after he portrayed it in his classic 1945 novel, Steinbeck noted, "They fish for tourists now, not pilchards, and that species they are not likely to wipe out." Check out the bust of Steinbeck near Prescott Avenue. At 800 Cannery Row see the weathered shack that once housed **Ed Ricketts' lab,** made famous by Steinbeck. Across the street are the preserved **Cannery Workers Shacks,** small rooms which originally housed immigrant laborers. ⏱ 30 min. Btw. David & Drake aves. www.canneryrow.com.

4 **Fisherman's Wharf.** Afraid to run the gauntlet of thick crowds, tacky gift shops, candy stores, and seafood markets? I say eat your way through it—clam chowder in a sourdough bowl (see below), fresh and cheap oysters, crabs, and ceviche. You can also catch a whale-watching tour year-round at **Monterey Bay Whale Watch,** 84 Fisherman's Wharf (☎ 831/375-4658; www.gowhales.com; tickets $23–$45 depending on season and tour length). ⏱ 15 min. 99 Pacific Ave. www.montereywharf.com.

> *Charming kids for over a half-century, Dennis the Menace Playground is a great place to romp along Monterey Bay.*

⑤   🍴 ★ **Old Fisherman's Grotto.** Amidst heavy competition, this place offers the best cup of clam chowder around. **39 Fisherman's Wharf.** ☎ 831/375-4604. www.oldfishermansgrotto.com. Cup $5, sourdough bowl $11.

❻ ★ **Taste of Monterey.** This "wine visitor center" is the easiest way to sample over 200 local wines from Monterey County's 70 vintners, and the panorama of the Pacific Ocean through the windows adds to the enjoyment. If you like what you try, buy a few bottles, or better yet, grab one of their handy maps and head for the tasting rooms in the countryside. ⏱ 30 min. **700 Cannery Row, 2nd Floor.** ☎ 831/646-5446. www.tastemonterey.com. Wine tastings $10–$15. Daily 11am–6pm.

❼ ★★ **Monterey State Historic Park.** Pick up a map (or look for the little yellow circles in the sidewalk) and follow the **Path of History,** a 2-mile self-guided walking tour of Monterey's many historic adobe buildings. The state's oldest government building (designated State Historic Monument No. 1), the **Custom House** (Custom Plaza) was built in 1827 to process incoming goods into Monterey, then the capital of Alta California. In 1846 Commodore John D. Sloat raised the American flag here to claim California for the United States. **Pacific House Museum** (Customs Plaza), built in 1847, houses a tidy museum on Monterey

Monterey Jazz Festival

The longest-running annual jazz festival in the world debuted in 1958 with a lineup that included Billie Holiday and Louis Armstrong. Today the festival features over 500 artists, performing on eight stages across 20 acres. The action takes place at the Monterey Fairgrounds, 2000 Fairground Rd. (☎ 831/373-3366; www.montereyjazzfestival.org) on the third weekend in September. Tickets run $35 to $66 per person per day; family and multiday discounts are also available.

history with plenty of Native American artifacts. An English sailor built **California's First Theatre** (Pacific and Scott sts.) as his private home in 1846, and a few years later, added a stage and benches to produce melodramas. The two-story **Larkin House** (464 Calle Principal) from 1835 is considered the prototype of the Monterey colonial style of architecture, with its wooden balconies and adobe walls. In 1849 California ratified its first state constitution at **Colton Hall** (Pacific St. btw. Jefferson and Madison); check out the museum on the second floor. The **Royal Presidio Chapel** (550 Church St.), completed in 1794, is the oldest building on the peninsula and the oldest continuously functioning church in California. The **Stevenson House** (530 Houston St.) is where Robert Louis Stevenson lived in 1879 while he

reportedly worked on Treasure Island. ⏱ 2 hr. Custom House Plaza. ☎ 831/649-7118. www. parks.ca.gov/mshp. Due to budget cutbacks, free public tours are cancelled until further notice; self-guided tours are available, but some buildings are closed or have severely limited hours. Consult website for latest information.

⑧ ★★ kids Dennis the Menace Playground. A family favorite for over 50 years, this colorful playground is the perfect place to let the kids run amok. Created by Dennis the Menace cartoonist and Pacific Grove resident Hank Ketcham (1920–2001), the park has a long roller slide, bridges and tunnels, a railroad engine to explore, a lake with ducks and paddle boats, and a snack stand. ⏱ 30 min. 777 Pearl St. ☎ 831/646-3860. Daily 10am–sunset.

Where to Stay & Dine

The Jabberwock Inn
Lovingly decorated in a whimsical Lewis Carroll theme, this hilltop B&B charms guests with its warm hospitality. 598 Laine St. ☎ 800/428-7253 or 831/372-4777. www.jabberwock inn.com. 7 units. Doubles $169–$299 w/breakfast, afternoon wine & snacks. AE, MC, V

★★ Monterey Plaza Hotel
With sweeping views of Monterey Bay, this large, upscale, if slightly corporate, waterfront hotel boasts elegant decor, two quality restaurants, a cafe, a spa, and a rooftop sun deck with hot tubs. 400 Cannery Row. ☎ 800/334-3999 or 831/646-1700. www.montereyplazahotel.com. 290 units. Doubles $215–$760. DC, DISC, MC, V.

★★ Montrio Bistro NEW AMERICAN
Enjoy ambitious (and sustainably produced) bistro fare—boeuf bourguignon, Dungeness crab cakes, roasted duck breast—and a great wine list in a lively space, once the Monterey firehouse. 414 Calle Principal. ☎ 831/648-8880. www.montrio.com. Reservations recommended. Entrees $14–$38. Dinner daily. AE, DISC, MC, V.

★★★ Old Monterey Inn
This three-story Tudor manor built in 1929 for Monterey's first mayor is one of the top-rated B&Bs in the country, with romantic and luxurious rooms, an immaculate garden, and excellent service. 500 Martin St. (off Pacific Ave.). ☎ 800/350-2344 or 831/375-8284. www.oldmonterey inn.com. 10 units. Doubles $220–$380 w/breakfast, afternoon wine & snacks. MC, V.

★ kids Rosine's AMERICAN
This local favorite is best known for its homey breakfasts, cakes, generous portions, and great value across the board. 434 Alvarado St. ☎ 831/375-1400. www.rosinesmonterey.com. Entrees $4–$20. Breakfast, lunch & dinner daily. AE, DC, DISC, MC, V.

★★ Sardine Factory STEAK/SEAFOOD
A Cannery Row institution for over 40 years, this fancy-pants steak and seafood restaurant has four dining rooms, the most elegant being the glass-domed Conservatory, and live piano music in the lounge on most nights. 701 Wave St. ☎ 831/373-3775. www.sardinefactory.com. Entrees $25–$47. Dinner daily. AE, DISC, MC, V.

★★ Spindrift Inn
Between the calming ocean and chaotic Cannery Row, this elegant boutique hotel offers rooms with hardwood floors, wood-burning fireplaces, and ocean views (well worth the extra dough). 652 Cannery Row. ☎ 800/841-1879 or 831/646-8900. www.spindriftinn.com. 42 units. Doubles $190–$330 w/breakfast. AE, DC, DISC, MC, V.

Pacific Grove

This is a charming, strollable little town (pop. 15,000)

that's best known for its picturesque coastline, visiting monarch butterflies, and several hundred century-old Victorian and Craftsman homes.

> The fog, as Robert Frost noted, comes in on little cat feet, softening the edges of Asilomar State Beach.

START Pacific Grove Recreational Trail. Pacific Grove is 2 miles west of Monterey and 113 miles south of San Francisco.

1 ★★★ **Pacific Grove Recreational Trail.** This gorgeous stretch showcases the town's dramatic rocky coastline and its multitude of parks, small beaches, and rich animal life, from sea otters to shorebirds to butterflies. ⊕ 1 hr. Ocean View Blvd. from Lover's Point to Point Pinos.

2 ★★ **Lovers Point.** Don't get seduced by the name; it was originally Lovers of Jesus Point, named in the late 1800s when the entire area

was a Methodist retreat camp. There's a large grassy lawn with cypress trees, a sandy cove, and thriving tide pools among its rocky outcroppings. ⊕ 1 hr. Ocean View Blvd. & 17th St.

3 ★ **Point Pinos Lighthouse.** Flashing since 1855, this is the oldest continuously working lighthouse on the Pacific Coast. Its 1,000-watt bulb is amplified by a lens and prisms to create a 50,000-candlepower beacon with a visibility of 15 miles. ⊕ 1 hr. Lighthouse Ave. & Asilomar Blvd. ☎ 831/648-5716. www.pgmuseum. org/Lighthouse.htm. Free admission, requested donation $2 adults, $1 kids. Thurs–Sun 1–4pm.

4 ★ **Asilomar State Beach.** This narrow mile-long stretch of white sandy beach is punctuated by rocky outcroppings, and the sunsets are often dazzling. Across Sunset Drive you can roam through the 25 acres of restored sand dunes. ⊕ 30 min. Adjacent to Sunset Dr. ☎ 831/646-6440. www.parks.ca.gov.

5 ★ **kids Pacific Grove Museum of Natural History.** With roots going back to the 1880s, this museum features permanent exhibits on native plants, animals (especially seabirds and, yes, butterflies), geology, and the native tribes of Monterey Bay. ⊕ 1 hr. 165 Forest Ave. ☎ 831/648-5716. www.pgmuseum.org. Free admission. Tues–Sun 10am–5pm.

6 **Monarch Grove Sanctuary.** Pacific Grove proudly calls itself "Butterfly Town, U.S.A." in honor of the tens of thousands of overwintering butterflies that cluster in its pine and eucalyptus groves every year seeking the perfect balance of temperature, humidity, light, and wind protection. Please don't disturb the precious creatures—the town police can slap you with a $1,000 fine for "molestation of butterflies." ⊕ 30 min. Ridge Rd., (btw. Lighthouse Ave. & Short St.). ☎ 831/648-5716. Free admission. Oct–Feb dawn–dusk.

Where to Stay & Dine

★ **First Awakenings** *AMERICAN*
In what was once the American Tin Cannery building, this brunch spot near the aquarium offers a variety of egg dishes (omelettes, frittatas, scrambles, skillets with potatoes) and made-from-scratch pancakes, as well as well as lunch salads and sandwiches. **125 Ocean View Blvd.** ☎ 831/372-1125. www.firstawakenings.net. Entrees $4–$11. Breakfast & lunch daily. AE, DISC, MC, V.

★★ **Passionfish** *SEAFOOD*
True to its name, this restaurant is passionate about fish, presenting fresh sustainable (and reasonably priced) seafood in a relaxed setting. **701 Lighthouse Ave.** ☎ 831/655-3311. www.passionfish.net. Entrees $15–$24. Dinner daily. AE, DISC, MC, V.

★★★ **Seven Gables Inn**
For B&B lovers, it rarely gets better than this. This beautiful, yellow Victorian, built in 1886, dazzles with its opulent interior and luxurious rooms—all have ocean views, high-end amenities, and big, comfy beds. **555 Ocean View Blvd.** ☎ 831/372-4341. www.thesevengablesinn.com. 25 units. Doubles $210–$360 w/breakfast, afternoon wine & snacks. AE, MC, V.

Carmel-by-the-Sea

The center for all Spanish missions in Alta California in the early 1800s, Carmel reemerged as an artists' retreat in the early 1900s, its natural beauty drawing the bohemian set—Jack London, Sinclair Lewis— from San Francisco (especially following the 1906 earthquake). Today it's a romanticized version of a seaside village, with fairy-tale cottages nestled beneath cypress trees, and while it may strike some as too precious (and too expensive), Carmel is one of the state's biggest tourist destinations.

> As inspiring a setting as any poet could want, Tor House was the waterfront compound of Robinson Jeffers.

START **Mission San Carlos Borroméo del Carmelo. Carmel-by-the-Sea is 5 miles south of Monterey, 121 miles south of San Francisco, and 33 miles north of Big Sur.**

❶ ★★★ **Mission San Carlos de Borroméo del Carmelo.** This stone mission features a Moorish-style facade, with a star window and domed bell tower, and is flanked by bougainvillea-filled courtyards. Be sure to see the kitchen, Father Junípero Serra's sparse living quarters, and California's first library—Serra's collection of 600 books. In the curved-ceiling chapel, an ornate altar serves an active parish today. Buried in the cemetery are thousands of Native Americans, who converted to Christianity and worked on the mission. ☺ 1 hr. Basilica Rio Rd. (at Lasuen Dr.) ☎ 831/624-1271. www.carmelmission.org. Admission $6.50 adults, $4 seniors, $2 kids 7 & older, free for kids 5 & under. Mon–Sat 9:30am–5pm; Sun 10:30am–5pm.

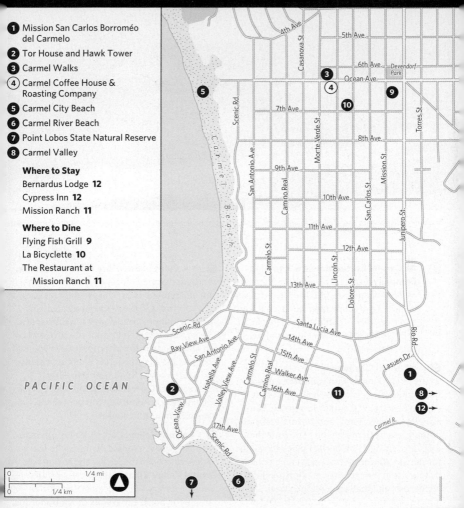

1 Mission San Carlos Borroméo del Carmelo

2 Tor House and Hawk Tower

3 Carmel Walks

4 Carmel Coffee House & Roasting Company

5 Carmel City Beach

6 Carmel River Beach

7 Point Lobos State Natural Reserve

8 Carmel Valley

Where to Stay
Bernardus Lodge **12**
Cypress Inn **12**
Mission Ranch **11**

Where to Dine
Flying Fish Grill **9**
La Bicyclette **10**
The Restaurant at
    Mission Ranch **11**

2 ★ **Tor House and Hawk Tower.** The Tor House—named for its position atop a tor (a rocky peak)—was constructed for poet Robinson Jeffers in 1919 using granite boulders hauled by horse from the rocky shoreline below. Jeffers, inspired by ancient Irish castles, erected the 40-foot Hawk Tower as a magical retreat for his wife, Una, and twin sons. ⏲ 45 min. 26304 Ocean View Ave. ☎ 831/624-1813. www.torhouse.org. Reservations required. Admission $7 adults, $4 college students, $2 high-school students. Kids 11 & under not admitted. Hourly docent-led tours Fri–Sat 10am–3pm.

3 ★ **Carmel Walks.** A 2-hour walk with a local photographer takes you through many of Carmel's most notable buildings: homes of artists and writers, whimsical cottages by builder Hugh Comstock, and Arts and Crafts homes designed by Julia Morgan and Charles S. Greene. You'll also see famous movie locations and hidden pathways and become acquainted with Carmel's idiosyncrasies, like its dogged devotion to all things canine. **Tours begin at the Pine Inn (Ocean Ave. & Monte Verde St.).** ☎ 831/642-2700. www. carmelwalks.com. Reservations required. Tours $25 per person. Tues–Fri 10am; Sat 10am & 2pm.

> *Where river meets sea, Carmel River Beach makes a spectacular—and surprisingly uncrowded—picnic spot.*

④ ☕ **Carmel Coffee House & Roasting Company.** Coffee brewed from freshly roasted beans (on-site) keeps the locals loyal. It's a great pit stop with a courtyard and free Wi-Fi. Ocean Ave. & Lincoln St. ☎ 831/626-2095. www.carmelcoffee. com. Coffee $2.

❺ ★★ **Carmel City Beach.** This slope of soft white sand is ringed with windswept cypress trees, and in the distance, the lawns of the Pebble Beach Golf Course glow green. Families play, couples stroll, and surfers surf, but nothing seems to match the good time the dogs are having. It's a perfect place to watch the sunset. *Beware:* The beach can be crushed by tourists in the summer, making parking a nightmare, and that aquamarine water that looks so inviting is quite cold. ⏱ 1 hr. End of Ocean Ave.

❻ ★★ **Carmel River Beach.** If you're looking for less people and more nature, head south of Carmel City Beach to this sandy mile-long beach where the Carmel River meets the sea, creating an inland lagoon and bird sanctuary. Diving and kayaking are popular here, especially at the southern end called Monastery Beach, just north of Point Lobos. Along the entire beach, swimming can be dangerous and is not recommended. A cross at the beach commemorates the one Spanish explorer Sebastián Vizcaíno (1548–1624) planted here in 1602. ⏱ 1 hr. Carmelo St. & Scenic Rd. ☎ 831/649-2836. www.parks.ca.gov. Sunrise–sunset.

❼ ★★★ **Point Lobos State Natural Reserve.** Landscape artist Francis McComas' estimation of Point Lobos as "the greatest meeting of land and water in the world" may sound hyperbolic, but no one disagrees in these parts. The parking lot often fills up, so arrive early in the day, or late in the afternoon. Give yourself enough time to discover its haunting beauty and hidden coves. ⏱ At least 2 hr. Hwy. 1, 3 miles south of Carmel. ☎ 831/624-4909. www. pointlobos.org. Admission $10 per vehicle. Daily 8am to 30 min. after sunset.

❽ ★ **Carmel Valley.** Carmel Valley refers to the inland valley cradled by the Santa Lucia Range, with open meadows and rolling hills. At **Carmel Valley Village,** there are several wine-tasting rooms within blocks of each other; sample the bordeaux blends of ★★ **Benardus,** 5 West Carmel Valley Rd. (☎ 831/659-1900; www.bernardus.com), or enjoy the garden setting of ★ **Georis,** 4 Pilot Rd. (☎ 831/659-1050; www.georiswine.com), best known for merlot and cabernet sauvignon. For something a little more heart pumping, head to ★ **Garland Ranch Regional Park,** 700 W. Carmel Valley Rd. (☎ 831/659-4488; www. mprpd.org), which offers 50 miles of hiking trails across 4,500 acres of creeks, canyons, and woodlands. During the spring months, the park comes alive with colorful wildflowers. ⏱ 2 hr. From Hwy. 1 head east on Carmel Valley Rd. for 13 miles.

Where to Stay & Dine

> *Make your day—and night—with a stay at Mission Ranch, a dairy-farm-turned-inn deftly created by Clint Eastwood.*

★★★ **Bernardus Lodge** CARMEL VALLEY
Tucked away in the verdant Carmel Valley, this destination resort draws lovers, wine tasters, and spa seekers. Rooms are understated, but luxuriously appointed, each with a fireplace, oversize tub, and complimentary "wine grotto" minibar. **415 Carmel Valley Rd. ☎ 831/659-3131. www.bernardus.com. 57 units. Doubles $295–$615. AE, DISC, MC, V.**

★★ **Cypress Inn** CARMEL VALLEY
This Mission-style boutique hotel is co-owned by Doris Day, which should explain the kitschy movie posters in the lounge. Canine pals are treated like kings here, yet the decor remains tasteful and upscale. Afternoon tea is a warm touch. **Lincoln St. & 7th Ave. ☎ 800/443-7443 or 831/624-3871. www.cypress-inn.com. 44 units. Doubles $165–$445 w/breakfast and afternoon tea. AE, DC, DISC, MC, V.**

★★ **Flying Fish Grill** SEAFOOD
Dine on Asian-fusion seafood in a cozy atmosphere. Standouts include the (complimentary) fried wonton chips with ginger tomato salsa, rare peppered *ahi* tuna, and the pan-fried almond sea bass. **In Carmel Plaza, Mission St. (btw. Ocean & 7th aves.). ☎ 831/625-1962. Reservations recommended. Entrees $15–$28. Dinner daily. AE, DISC, MC, V.**

★ **La Bicyclette** FRENCH
This tiny bistro cooks up rustic French cuisine including heirloom tomato salad, roasted chicken, and filet mignon with Gorgonzola. Be sure to finish with the chocolate mousse. **Dolores St., at 7th Ave. ☎ 831/622-9899. www.labicycletterestaurant.com. Reservations recommended. Entrees $10–$37. Lunch & dinner daily. AE, DISC, MC, V.**

★★ **Mission Ranch** CARMEL
An 1850s dairy farm restored by Clint Eastwood, this sprawling property offers a range of accommodations from simple rooms to detached cottages—all surrounded by sheep pastures, wetlands, and views of the coastline. Rustic, relaxed, and utterly charming. **26270 Dolores St. ☎ 800/538-8221 or 831/624-6436. www.missionranchcarmel.com. 31 units. Doubles $120–$265. AE, MC, V.**

★★ **The Restaurant at Mission Ranch** AMERICAN On summer days, grab a table on the patio and enjoy the views along with hearty American fare like steaks, short ribs, salmon, and duck. There's nightly entertainment at the piano bar; on Sunday, there's a jazz and champagne brunch. **26270 Dolores St. ☎ 831/625-9040. www.missionranchcarmel.com. Entrees $20–$40. Dinner daily; brunch Sun. AE, MC, V.**

Big Sur

Novelist Henry Miller (1891–1980) referred to Big Sur as "nature smiling at herself in the mirror of eternity"—a testament to Big Sur's breathtaking beauty, but also a reference to the sense of mysticism its inhabitants feel creeping like fog over the 90 miles of coastline where the Santa Lucia Range plunges into the Pacific Ocean.

> Don't lean over too far when ogling the Big Sur coast, where cliffs plunge hundreds of feet to the sea.

START ★ **Bixby Bridge on Hwy. 1, 13 miles south of Carmel. Big Sur stretches along Hwy. 1 and begins 3 miles south of Carmel and 123 miles south of San Francisco. TRIP LENGTH about 30 miles.**

❶ ★ **Bixby Bridge.** Created by a WPA project in 1932, this is one of the world's highest single-arch bridges, looming nearly 270 feet above the surf. It's also one of the most photographed spans—just north of the bridge, there's a small parking area where shutterbugs can get a good shot. ⏱ 15 min. Hwy. 1, 13 miles south of Carmel.

❷ ★ **Point Sur State Historic Park.** The prominent feature in this park is Point Sur Lightstation, a 40-foot-tall lighthouse built in 1889. Sitting atop Point Sur, a large volcanic peak, the lighthouse still lights the way for ships at sea, and it has seen its fair share of shipwrecks off the treacherous coastline. Listed on the National Register of Historic Places, the lighthouse is the only one of its kind open to the public in California. It and other lightstation buildings can be explored on 3-hour tours, which require some minor exertion—walking uphill, climbing stairs. ⏱ 3 hr.

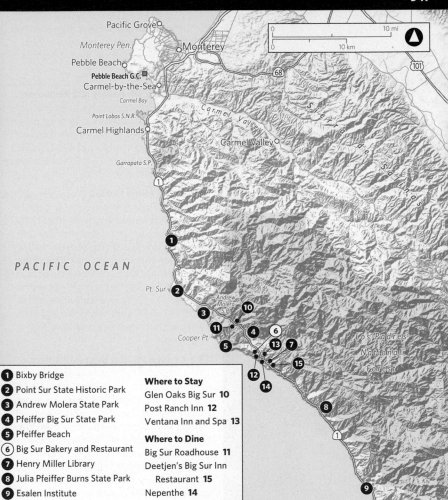

① Bixby Bridge
② Point Sur State Historic Park
③ Andrew Molera State Park
④ Pfeiffer Big Sur State Park
⑤ Pfeiffer Beach
⑥ Big Sur Bakery and Restaurant
⑦ Henry Miller Library
⑧ Julia Pfeiffer Burns State Park
⑨ Esalen Institute

Where to Stay
Glen Oaks Big Sur **10**
Post Ranch Inn **12**
Ventana Inn and Spa **13**

Where to Dine
Big Sur Roadhouse **11**
Deetjen's Big Sur Inn
    Restaurant **15**
Nepenthe **14**

Hwy 1, ¼ miles north of Point Sur Naval Facility.
☎ 831/625-4419. www.pointsur.org. Tours $10
adults, $5 kids 6–17, free for kids 5 & under. Summer Wed and Sat 10am and 2pm, Thurs and Sun
10am; winter Wed 1pm, Sat–Sun 10am. Moonlight tours available, check the website.

③ ★ **Andrew Molera State Park.** A lovely
mile-long path, Beach Trail, runs parallel to
the Big Sur River and ends at a long stretch of
driftwood-covered beach, perfect for beachcombing; return via the Creamery Meadow
Trail. ⏱ 1 hr. Hwy. 1, 3 miles south of the lighthouse. ☎ 831/667-2315. www.parks.ca.gov.
Parking $8. Daily 30 min. before sunrise to 30
min. after sunset.

④ ★★ **Pfeiffer Big Sur State Park.** This
visitor-friendly, amenity-filled park in the
coastal redwood forest is Big Sur's most popular park, with plenty of activities, including
fishing, swimming, and picnicking along the
Big Sur River, and outstanding hiking. Make
the ¾-mile trek through the towering trees
to the rocky 60-foot **Pfeiffer Falls** that runs
from winter to spring; if you have more energy,
continue another ½ mile to the **Valley View**
overlook with vistas of the Big Sur River gorge,
Point Sur, and the Pacific. ⏱ 2 hr. 47225 Hwy.
1. ☎ 831/667-2315. www.bigsurcalifornia.org.
Parking $8. Daily 30 min. before sunrise to 30
min. after sunset.

> *Wave-carved rocks at Pfeiffer Beach make for dramatic photos—but beware of rogue waves and frigid water.*

5 ★★ **Pfeiffer Beach.** This crescent of sandy beach has bright blue water, cypress trees, and dramatic rock formations highlighted by crashing waves. Notice the beach's distinct purplish sand (from manganese garnate particles washed down the hills), but avoid swimming in the water—it's too cold and dangerous. ***Warning:*** The road down to the beach, Sycamore Canyon, is unmarked and easy to miss. ⏱ 1 hr. Off Hwy. 1, 1 mile south of Pfeiffer

Big Sur State Park and north of the post office. ☎ 831/667-2315. www.campone.com. Parking $5. Restrooms, but no other services. Daily 9am–8pm.

6 🍴 ★ **Big Sur Bakery and Restaurant.** Grab a strong cup of joe, and one of the fresh-baked goodies at this friendly joint. It also serves soups, sandwiches, and tasty wood-fired pizzas. 47540 Hwy. 1. ☎ 831/667-0520. www.bigsurbakery.com. Entrees $13–$36.

7 ★ **Henry Miller Library.** This warm-spirited memorial to Henry Miller, writer and Big Sur resident (4 miles south of here) from 1944 to 1962, displays his artwork and books, including his first editions, and select titles that influenced him. Sip some coffee or tea, peruse the literature, meditate, or just use the free Wi-Fi (though Henry might not approve). ⏱ 30 min. Hwy. 1, ¼-mile south of Nepenthe. ☎ 831/667-2574. www.henrymiller.org. Free admission, donations welcome. Wed–Mon 11am–6pm.

8 ★★★ **Julia Pfeiffer Burns State Park.** Often less crowded than Pfeiffer Big Sur, this 3,000-plus-acre park presents some of Big Sur's most magnificent coastline. When friends ask about your trip to Big Sur, you'll want to show them your pics of ★★ **McWay Falls,** the 80-foot waterfall that cascades off green cliffs onto the shoreline of a picture-perfect beach cove. ⏱ 1 hr. Entrance is on the east side of Hwy. 1. ☎ 831/667-2315. www.parks. ca.gov. Parking $8. Daily ½ hr. before sunrise to ½ hr. after sunset.

9 ★ **Esalen Institute.** Surely after all that hiking, your muscles could use a good soak. Stop into this world-famous New Age center to luxuriate in the natural **hot springs baths** perched on cliffs high above the ocean. If you're not participating in any of their workshops (meditation, massage, yoga), you can only make a reservation for their "late night bathing" between 1am and 3am (yeah, that's right). One more thing: It's clothing optional, meaning that nudity is common, and while it may not be everyone's cup of tea, the experience is one you'll never forget. 55000 Hwy. 1, (11 miles south of Nepenthe). ☎ 831/667-3047. www.esalen.org. Bathing $20 per person. MC, V.

Where to Stay & Dine

> *Luxury meets world-class views at Ventana Inn and Spa, where you can feel like a celeb (and maybe even see one).*

★ kids **Big Sur Roadhouse** *ECLECTIC*
This is a warm and casual place to enjoy such Latin American–influenced California cuisine as stuffed peppers, barbecued chicken breast, and skirt steaks. Hwy. 1, 1 mile north of Pfeiffer Big Sur State Park. ☎ 831/667-2264. www. bigsurroadhouse.com. Entrees $13–$36. Dinner Wed–Mon. AE, MC, V.

★★ **Deetjen's Big Sur Inn Restaurant**
AMERICAN This farmhouse-style, candle-lit dining room makes for a romantic dinner, but it's best known for breakfast—eggs Benedict, huevos rancheros, and blueberry pancakes. 48865 Hwy. 1. ☎ 831/667-2377. www.deetjens. com. Reservations recommended. Entrees $13–$24. Breakfast & dinner daily. MC, V.

★★ **Glen Oaks Big Sur**
One of the more affordable options in steeply priced Big Sur, this '50s-era motor lodge is made of adobe bricks and redwood beams, and refers to its sensibility as "rustic-modern." Hwy. 1, about 1 mile north of Pfeiffer Big Sur State Park. ☎ 831/667-2105. www.glenoaksbig sur.com. 17 units. Doubles $155–$275. MC, V.

★ **Nepenthe** *AMERICAN*
You pay for the view, but what a stunning view it is, as you sit on a terrace perched high over the coast. Stick to the lunch menu, or better yet, the wine list. Downstairs, the outdoor Café Kevah is cheaper and more casual, but with a similarly killer view. 48510 Hwy. 1. ☎ 831/667-2345. www.nepenthebigsur.com. Entrees $14–$35. Lunch & dinner daily. AE, MC, V.

★★★ **Post Ranch Inn**
Dramatic, eco-friendly architecture rides the woody cliff tops high above the Pacific Ocean, imbuing this 100-acre luxe property with a romantic otherworldliness. Soaking in the hot-water infinity pools is a must, and the restaurant Sierra Mar provides an unforgettable dinner. Hwy. 1, 1½ miles south of Pfeiffer Big Sur State Park. ☎ 831/667-2200. www.post ranchinn.com. 30 units. Doubles $550–$1,485 w/breakfast. AE, MC, V.

★★★ **Ventana Inn and Spa**
Rustic yet elegant, a wilderness retreat yet supremely luxurious—a stay at this celeb fave never fails to rejuvenate. If your pockets run deep enough, stop by the spa, as well as the world-class Restaurant at Ventana. Hwy. 1, about 1 mile south of Pfeiffer Big Sur State Park. ☎ 831/667-2331. www.ventanainn.com. 62 units. Doubles $500–$1,100 w/breakfast and wine & cheese. AE, DC, DISC, MC, V.

Fast Facts

American Express

If you're in Monterey and Big Sur and need to see an American Express travel representative in person, head to San Jose to **Mundi Travel,** 13785 Story Rd. (☎ 408/272-1753; Mon–Fri 9:30am–5:30pm, Sat 9:30am–2pm). **Note:** This office does not provide financial services; for that you'll need to go to the San Francisco office (p. 166).

Dentists & Doctors

For a dentist, call **1-800-DENTIST** (☎ 800/336-8422; www.1800dentist.com). For doctors, see "Emergencies," below.

Emergencies

In an emergency, dial ☎ **911.**

To contact the police in nonemergency situations, in Santa Cruz, contact the **City of Santa Cruz Police Department,** 155 Center St. (☎ 831/471-1131).

In Monterey or Pacific Grove, contact the **Monterey Police Department,** 351 Madison St. (☎ 831/646-3914).

In Carmel or Big Sur, contact the **Carmel Police Department,** Junipero Street and 4th Avenue (☎ 831/624-6403).

To seek medical assistance, in Santa Cruz, go to the **Dominican Hospital,** 1555 Soquel Dr. (☎ 831/462-7700).

In Monterey, Carmel, Pacific Grove, or Big Sur, head to **Community Hospital of the Monterey Peninsula,** 23625 Holman Hwy., Monterey (☎ 831/624-45311; www.chomp.org).

In Big Sur, you can also get medical attention at the **Big Sur Health Center,** 46896 Hwy. 1 (☎ 831/667-2580; www.bigsurhealth center.org; Mon–Fri 10am–1pm, 2–5pm).

Getting There

BY PLANE The most convenient airport is the **Monterey Peninsula Airport** (MRY; ☎ 831/648-7000; www.montereyairport. com), which is 3 miles east of Monterey on Hwy. 68. American Eagle, Northwest, United, and US Airways run daily flights in and out of Monterey. Many hotels in the area offer free airport shuttle service. A taxi will cost $14 to $20 to get to a peninsula hotel. If you'd prefer

to rent a car, **Dollar** (☎ 800/800-3665; www. dollar.com) and **Hertz** (☎ 800/654-3131; www.hertz.com) are available at the airport.

BY CAR Santa Cruz is 43 miles north of Monterey and 77 miles southeast of San Francisco. Hwy. 1 offers a beautiful scenic route to Santa Cruz from San Francisco. The fastest route is Hwy. 17, which you can access near San Jose from I-280, I-880, or U.S. 101 and takes you straight to the boardwalk. Weekend mornings can be a popular time to head to the beach; Hwy. 17 tends to be slower, while Hwy. 1 is less crowded.

The town of Monterey is 45 miles south of Santa Cruz, 116 miles south of San Francisco, and 335 miles north of Los Angeles. Carmel is 5 miles south of Monterey and 33 miles north of Big Sur. Pacific Grove is 2½ miles north of Monterey.

Big Sur is 3 miles south of Carmel, 123 miles south of San Francisco, and 87 miles north of Hearst Castle. Although there is an actual Big Sur Village 25 miles south of Carmel, "Big Sur" generally refers to the entire 90-mile stretch of coastline between Carmel and San Simeon, with the Santa Lucia Range to the east and the rocky Pacific coastline to the west. **BY TRAIN** With a great deal of patience it's possible, if a bit cumbersome, to access the Monterey Bay area via train and bus. Amtrak's Coast Starlight stops in Salinas and San Jose, where you can catch buses (see "Getting Around," below) to other areas. For scheduling and price information, call ☎ 800/872-7245 or consult www.amtrak.com.

Getting Around

In Santa Cruz, local buses are run by the **Santa Cruz Metropolitan Transit District.** Check routes and schedules at www.scmtd.com.

In Monterey, the **Waterfront Area Visitor Express (WAVE)** trolley is free and takes passengers to and from the aquarium and other waterfront attractions from Memorial Day to Labor Day. It departs from the downtown parking garages at Tyler Street and Del Monte Avenue every 10 to 12 minutes from 10am to 7pm Monday to Friday and 10am to

8pm Saturday to Sunday. Other WAVE stops include many hotels and motels in Monterey and Pacific Grove. For further information, call **Monterey Salinas Transit** at ☎ 831/899-2555 (www.mst.org).

In Pacific Grove, Lighthouse Avenue is the main thoroughfare, running from Monterey to the lighthouse at the point of the peninsula. Lighthouse Avenue is bisected by Forest Avenue, which runs from Hwy. 1 (where it's called Holman Highway, or Hwy. 68) to Lovers Point, an area of the bay in the middle of Pacific Grove.

Big Sur is accessible almost entirely off of Hwy. 1, which hugs the ocean. Most of this stretch is state park and includes restaurants, hotels, and sights. Situated directly along the highway, they're relatively easy to spot.

To truly explore the Monterey Peninsula and Big Sur, driving a car is a must. In fact, zipping along the Big Sur coastline on Hwy. 1 is one of the great thrills of the region. But traffic can be an issue, especially during summer weekends when Hwy. 1 can become maddeningly congested. Heavy traffic or not—if you find yourself frustrated by drivers either in front of you or behind you, pull off at one of the many scenic outlooks and regain some composure.

Hospitals
See "Emergencies," above.

Internet Access
Many hotels and many cafes have wireless access. In the wilderness of Big Sur, a reliable place to get Internet service is the **Henry Miller Library,** Hwy. 1, ¼-mile south of Nepenthe (☎ 831/667-2574; www.henrymiller. org).

Pharmacies
A centrally located pharmacy in Monterey is **Rite Aid** at 1301 Munras Ave. (☎ 831/375-8900; daily 8am–9pm). A centrally located pharmacy in Santa Cruz is **Rite Aid** at 901 Soquel Ave. (☎ 831/426-4303; daily 8am–10pm). The major chains—**Rite Aid, CVS, Walgreens**—are well represented throughout the Monterey Bay area, although none of them have a 24-hour pharmacy.

Post Office
In **Big Sur,** the main post office is at 47500 Hwy. 1 (☎ 831/667-2305; Mon–Fri 8:30–11am, noon–4pm). In **Monterey,** the main post office

is at 565 Hartnell St. (☎ 831/372-4063; Mon–Fri 8:30am–5pm, Sat 10am–2pm). In **Santa Cruz,** the main post office is at 850 Front St. (☎ 831/426-0144; Mon–Fri 9am–5pm).

Safety
Road conditions in the winter are sometimes affected by mudslides caused by rains; before you head out, check the website for the **California Department of Transportation** (www. dot.ca.gov), for road and weather conditions. The twists and turns of Hwy. 1 require good visibility, so if possible, avoid driving at night or during thick fog.

Taxes
Sales tax in Monterey, Carmel, and Big Sur is 8.25%. In Pacific Grove, sales tax is 9.25%. In Santa Cruz, sales tax ranges from 9% to 9.25%. Hotel tax is charged on the room tariff only (which is not subject to sales tax) and ranges from 10% to 15%.

Visitor Information
In Santa Cruz, contact the **Santa Cruz County Conference and Visitors Council,** 1211 Ocean St. (☎ 800/833-3494 or 831/425-1234; www. santacruzca.org; Mon–Sat 9am–5pm, Sun 10am–4pm).

In Monterey, contact the **Monterey County Convention and Visitors Bureau** (☎ 877/666-8373; www.seemonterey.com), which has two visitor centers: one in the lobby of the Maritime Museum at Custom House Plaza near Fisherman's Wharf, the other at Lake El Estero on Camino El Estero. Both locations, open daily, offer good maps and free pamphlets and publications, including the *Monterey County Weekly* and an excellent visitors' guide.

In Carmel, the **Carmel Business Association** (☎ 831/624-2522; www.carmelcalifornia. org), is on San Carlos Street between Fifth and Sixth streets, and it distributes local maps, brochures, and publications. Hours are 10am to 5pm daily.

In Pacific Grove, the **Chamber of Commerce,** located on the corner of Forest and Central avenues (☎ 800/656-6650 or 831/373-3304; www.pacificgrove.org), dispenses information about the town of Pacific Grove.

For information on Big Sur, contact the **Big Sur Chamber of Commerce** (☎ 831/667-2100; www.bigsurcalifornia.org).

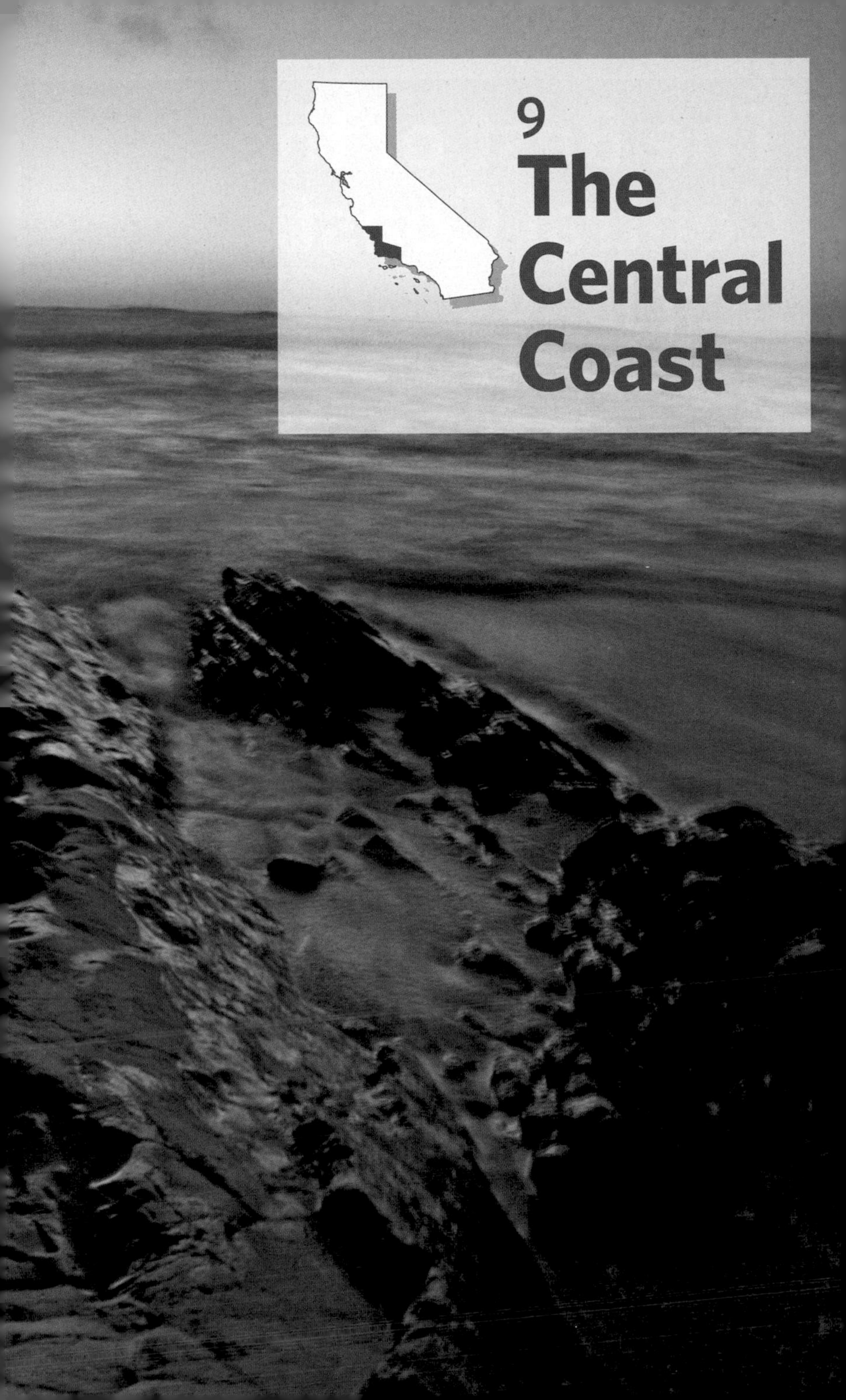

9 The Central Coast

The Best of the Central Coast in 3 Days

With its scenic drives and sleepy beach towns, the Central Coast is a great place for slowing down. With only 3 days, however, you'll need to keep moving to tour the state's only castle, explore an old Spanish mission or two, stroll along the uncrowded beaches, sample farm-fresh cuisine, and experience the American Riviera known as Santa Barbara.

> *PREVIOUS PAGE Dusk falls on the edge of the sea at Montana de Oro State Park. THIS PAGE Visit a mogul's personal kingdom at Hearst Castle, whose centerpiece Neptune Pool includes intricate mosaics and marble statues.*

START **Hearst Castle in San Simeon. San Simeon is 240 miles south of San Francisco.** TRIP LENGTH **About 166 miles.**

❶ ★★★ **Hearst Castle.** The dream home of media magnate William Randolph Hearst (1863–1951), La Cuesta Encantada (the Enchanted Hill) is an ode to ostentation, a sprawling hilltop complex with 165 rooms overflowing with centuries-old European art and antiquities—truly one of California's great destinations.

The main house, **Casa Grande,** boasts the striking, twin-towered facade of a Spanish cathedral and over 100 rooms, including 22 for houseguests, who included VIPs like Winston Churchill and Charles Lindbergh, as well as countless Hollywood celebrities. Highlights

include the **Assembly Room,** an opulent gathering area lined with Flemish tapestries and choir stalls from an Italian monastery; the **Refectory,** a medieval dining hall with a long, narrow table where W.R. would position his guests around him in order of their importance; a 50-seat **private theater;** the **Celestial Suite,** two hexagonal bedrooms—one a favorite of Clark Gable and Carole Lombard—that occupy the tops of the bell towers; and the indoor **Roman Pool,** a glittering mosaic of gold-leaf and glass tiles.

The grounds include 127 acres of lush, Mediterranean-inspired gardens, with terraces and fountains, fruit trees, colorful flowers year-round, and most unforgettably, the **Neptune Pool,** a spring-fed, white-marble pool, surrounded by a pair of colonnades, cascading steps, an ancient Roman temple, and spectacular views.

The Hearst Castle can only be experienced on guided tours; four different tours are available daily, each lasting approximately 1 hour and 45 minutes. The **Experience Tour (Tour 1)** is recommended for first-time visitors and showcases the most noteworthy rooms on the ground floor of Casa Grande. Your ticket also includes admission to an IMAX screening of the 40-minute *Hearst Castle: Building the Dream* (without a Tour 1 ticket $8 for adults

> *Wacky? Weird? Whatever it is, Nitt Witt Ridge is sure to entertain with its found-object version of an "anti-Hearst Castle."*

and $6 for kids 6–17). **Tour 2** explores Casa Grande's upper floors, including a fascinating peek into the Gothic Suite—Hearst's private suite, library, and study. **Tour 3** and **Tour 4** focus on the guest suites, guesthouses, and gardens. The **Evening Tour (Tour 5),** available on most Fridays and Saturdays in the spring and fall, is a delightful 2-hour and 10-minute trip back in time. Docents in period costume foster the illusion that you've stumbled into one of the castle's parties in the 1930s. ⏱ 4 hr. 750 Hearst Castle Rd., San Simeon. ☎ 800/444-4445 or 805/927-2020. www.hearstcastle.org. Tours 1–4 $24 adults, $12 kids 6–17; tour 5 $30 adults, $15 kids. Reservations strongly recommended. Mar–Sept daily 8am–6pm; Oct–Feb Mon–Fri 9am–5pm, Sat–Sun 9am–3pm.

From San Simeon, head south on Hwy. 1 for 8 miles.

Hearst vs. Kane

The castle at San Simeon isn't the only lasting monument to Hearst—there's also the Orson Welles 1941 masterpiece, *Citizen Kane,* considered by many critics to be the greatest film ever made. The brash wunderkind Welles quite deliberately, and perhaps naively, chose to base his title character—the ruthless, vindictive, megalomaniacal Charles Foster Kane—on Hearst. Kane, like Hearst, is a newspaper magnate who gets his start in yellow journalism, manipulates public opinion on the Spanish-American War, loses a high-profile political campaign, ruins his marriage, tries and fails to make a star out of his mistress, then retreats to his vast, baroque palace.

It's ironic that Hearst—a man who had built an empire on slagging public figures, a man who once said that he preferred the newspaper business to filmmaking because "you can crush a man with journalism, and you can't with motion pictures"—so feared the film's impact on his own reputation that he attempted to block its release. Hearst bullied his Hollywood cronies, studio brass such as Louis B. Mayer and Irving Thalberg (frequent guests at San Simeon), into trying to buy the film negative in order to burn it. When that failed, Hearst strong-armed the major theater chains, dependent on Hearst's newspaper for publicity, into refusing to book the film. The result: *Citizen Kane* was eventually released, garnering brilliant reviews, but no business, and Welles' golden boy status was forever tarnished in Hollywood.

> *Moody and beautiful, Morro Rock looms out of expansive Morro Bay, perfect for renting a kayak and exploring.*

2 Cambria. If you arrive in this quaint artists' colony in the afternoon, you'll have just enough time to tour the "anti–Hearst Castle" called ★★ **Nitt Witt Ridge** (p. 388, **2**), a ramshackle folk-art palace made of found objects such as abalone shells, beer cans, car parts, and washed-up lumber. Enjoy a leisurely, sunset stroll along the crashing surf of ★★ **Moonstone Beach** (p. 389, **4**), before dining at one of the town's excellent restaurants (p. 389).

On the morning of Day 2, peruse the antiques and local, handcrafted glass art and jewelry at the cluster of small boutiques and galleries along Main Street. Ever taste an olallieberry? No? Then you must make a short detour into the countryside to ★ **Linn's Fruit Bin Original Farmhouse** (p. 388, **3**) to sample, preferably in pie form, this delicious, locally grown fruit. ◷ At least 4 hr.

Head south on Hwy. 1 for 20 miles.

3 Morro Bay. Approaching Morro Bay on Hwy. 1, you'll spot a State Historic Landmark, the photogenic Central Coast icon Morro Rock, a nearly 600-foot-high stone dome, named El Morro (Spanish for "crown-shaped hill") by 16th-century Portuguese explorer Juan Cabrillo (1499–1543). Used for centuries as a navigational tool by mariners, the rock (and surrounding estuary) is now a protected bird sanctuary for peregrine falcons and over 200 species of birds. ◷ 30 min. See p. 374, **1**.

Head south on Hwy. 1 for 1½ miles, and exit Baywood Park/Los Osos. Turn right at Bay Blvd. and go 4 miles. Turn right at Los Osos Valley Rd. and go 1½ miles. Continue onto Pecho Valley Rd. for 3½ miles.

4 ★★ Montana de Oro State Park. Near the visitor center at Spooner's Cove, a sandy beach and picnic area, several hiking trails are accessible, the most popular being the relatively easy Bluff Trail which clings to the cliff's edge and dips down into pocket beaches perfect for tidepooling. ◷ 2 hr. See p. 375, **2**.

Head back north on Pecho Valley Rd. for 3½ miles. Continue onto Los Osos Valley Rd. for 10½ miles. Turn left at Madonna Rd. for 1½ miles. Turn left onto Higuera St. for a ½ mile. Turn left at Nipomo St., then right on Monterey St.

5 San Luis Obispo. Once known as a halfway-point stopover between San Francisco and Los Angeles, this small agricultural and college town has a historical background and a charming pedestrian-friendly downtown area that make it a destination in itself.

Start at the heart of the downtown, **Mission Plaza,** a lovely, leafy area along the San Luis Creek. California's fifth mission, the **Mission San Luis Obispo de Tolosa** (p. 392, **1**), was founded here in 1772 by Father Junípero Serra and remains an active parish today. A small museum, formerly the padres' quarters,

> *Step inside the Santa Barbara Mission, established in 1786, to discover glorious archways and richly decorated walls.*

details the mission's rich history and includes artifacts from the Spanish settlers and the Native American Chumash people. For more history, head across the street to the **San Luis Obispo County Historical Museum** (p. 392, ❷).

If you're able, time your visit for Thursday night so you can experience the region's biggest and best ★ **farmers market** (p. 394), which fills 4 blocks along Higuera Street with straight-from-the-farm produce, smoky barbecues, political kiosks, and street entertainment. For more local flavor, dash through **Bubblegum Alley** (p. 393, ❹), a narrow passage with walls painted in several decades' worth of colorful blobs of chewed gum.

Even if you're not checking in here, you'll want to check out the garish, so-bad-it's-good appeal of the ★★ **Madonna Inn** (p. 395), a local institution for over 50 years. Every room is individually and deliriously decorated, many with rock walls and waterfall showers, and the dining room is so pink that it hurts. Cap Day 2 with a drink at the Silver Bar Cocktail Lounge and soak up the surreal atmosphere. ☺ At least 4 hr.

On Day 3, from San Luis Obispo, head south on U.S. 101 for about 105 miles. Exit Mission St., turn left and go 1 mile. Turn left at Laguna St.

❻ **Santa Barbara.** To enjoy one of California's most beautiful towns, you'll need (at the very least) a full day, so arrive as early as possible.

Begin the day with a self-guided tour of the Queen of the Missions, the grand ★★★ **Old Mission Santa Barbara** (p. 380, ❶), tenth of the 21 California missions built by the Spanish Franciscans and a National Historic Landmark. Take the short drive uphill to the serene

Dining Tip

One of the best ways to taste the delicious bounty of the region is to shop at one of the many farmers markets. In Santa Barbara and San Luis Obispo counties, one or more are available every single day of the week. It's an excellent way to connect to the land, support small farmers, eat healthy, and even save a few dollars. For more information, visit www.sbfarmersmarket.org and www.countryfarmandcraftmarket.com.

★ **Santa Barbara Botanic Garden** (p. 380, **2**), which features miles of foot trails across 65 acres of gorgeous, native California flora.

After a quick bite downtown (for dining recommendations, see p. 387), take the Red Tile Tour, a self-guided walking tour of the historic downtown area, which highlights the town's Spanish mission-revival architecture with its archways, white adobe facades, and terra-cotta rooftops. You can pick up a map and begin your tour at the magnificent ★ **Santa Barbara County Courthouse** (p. 382, **4**). Be sure to see the stunning Mural Room and catch the views from the balcony of El Mirador, the 85-foot-high clock tower. Historical highlights of the tour include ★ **El Presidio de Santa Barbara** (p. 383, **8**), the site of the last Spanish military outpost in California; El Cuartel, the second-oldest adobe building in California; and **Casa de la Guerra** (p. 382, **7**),

the U-shape courtyard home of the presidio's commander. Stop by the **Santa Barbara Historical Museum** (p. 383, **9**) to learn more about the town's rich history, beginning with the region's earliest inhabitants, the Chumash.

Cruise along the Cabrillo beachfront path, 3½ miles from Shoreline Park to the **Andrew Clark Bird Refuge** (you can rent bikes, surreys, and Rollerblades at Wheel Fun, 23 E Cabrillo Dr.; ☎ 805/966-2282; daily 8am–8pm). Or explore ★ **Stearns Wharf** (p. 384, **12**), the oldest working wharf in California with shops, fishing, and the Ty Warner Sea Center, where children can get up close and personal with cute sea critters. Catch the day's final rays at the pretty and very popular ★ **East Beach** (p. 385), a wide, sandy stretch that has something for everyone—picnic tables, volleyball courts, swings, and great facilities.

Santa Maria–Style Barbecue

Mouthwatering barbecue from the Santa Maria Valley is a true California culinary tradition dating back to the mid-1800s when rancheros would rustle up a feast for their cattle-tending vaqueros. The classic recipe that evolved over time is simple (and copyrighted by the local chamber of commerce): season top sirloin or tri-tip with coarse salt, pepper, and garlic salt, then grill over an open fire of local red oak; serve with salsa, pinquito beans, and grilled French bread dipped in butter. The Food Network's resident grill master Bobby Flay is a big fan, as was President Ronald Reagan, who

hosted several Santa Maria–style barbecues on the south lawn of the White House.

The quaint ★★ **Far Western Tavern,** 899 Guadalupe St., Guadalupe (☎ 805/343-2211), was recently named one of the top 10 barbecue restaurants in the West by *Sunset* magazine. Frank Ostini's ★ **Hitching Post II** (pictured above) 406 E. Hwy. 246, Buellton (☎ 805/688-0676), featured in *Sideways,* is a Wine Country favorite. The lively ★ **Jocko's Steak House,** 125 N. Thompson St., Nipomo (☎ 805/929-3686), serves big ol' steaks in a no-frills setting.

The Best of the Central Coast in 1 Week

A leisurely weeklong pace offers more time at must-sees like the Hearst Castle, Spanish missions, and the sun-scrubbed resort community of Santa Barbara and also allows you to take the scenic highways, such as Hwy. 46 and Hwy. 154, especially while traversing the wine trails of Paso Robles and Santa Ynez. You'll scope out small towns with big city cuisine, and explore natural sanctuaries, which many residents, particularly the busy urbanites to the north or south, sometimes forget are right in their own backyard.

> Naptime at Piedras Blancas, a favored hangout for shockingly large (up to 5 tons each) elephant seals.

START Hearst Castle in San Simeon. San Simeon is 240 miles south of San Francisco. **TRIP LENGTH** about 245 miles.

❶ ★★★ Hearst Castle. William Randolph Hearst inherited this 250,000-acre ranch, the site of his favorite boyhood camping trips, in 1919. With the help of architect Julia Morgan (1872–1957), the first female graduate of the famous Ecole des Beaux-Arts in Paris, Hearst spent the next 28 years trying to fulfill his grandiose vision, constantly revising to fit

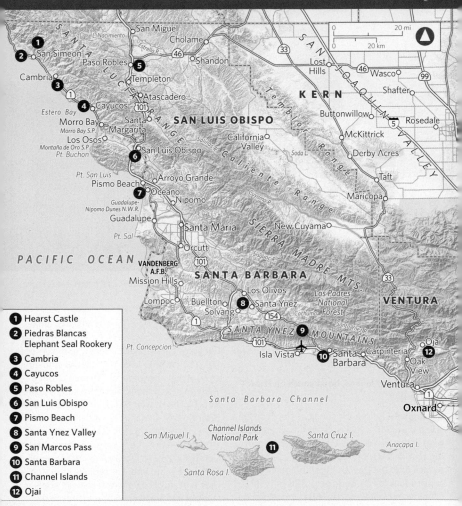

1. Hearst Castle
2. Piedras Blancas Elephant Seal Rookery
3. Cambria
4. Cayucos
5. Paso Robles
6. San Luis Obispo
7. Pismo Beach
8. Santa Ynez Valley
9. San Marcos Pass
10. Santa Barbara
11. Channel Islands
12. Ojai

his aesthetic whims and ever-expanding art collection, before shelving his efforts in 1947 following a heart attack. The result is spectacular and certainly worth the best chunk of your day.

Take one of several available tours, each lasting 1 hour and 45 minutes. If you're curiosity is piqued (and it likely will be), take another, more in-depth tour (you'll have to return to the visitor center btw. tours). Give yourself 2 hours between tours—time to snack and catch the IMAX movie about Hearst and the castle's construction. See p. 354, **1**.

From Hearst Castle, head north on Hwy. 1 for 4 miles.

2 ★ **Piedras Blancas Elephant Seal Rookery.** Over 100 years ago, elephant seals were hunted for their blubber to the brink of extinction, their numbers dwindling to around 30. These days they're back in a big way. In this breeding colony, a windy beach just south of the Piedras Blancas lighthouse, there are over 15,000, each weighing between 3,000 to 5,000 pounds. The seals laze about in the sand, frolic in the water, and, in the case of the would-be alpha males called bulls, battle one another with their giant proboscis and violent honking. Volunteer docents are usually on-site with plenty of pertinent information, such as friendly reminders to keep a respectable

> *The brown pelicans will probably outnumber the people on stretches of Central Coast beach, like this one in Cambria.*

distance from the animals as they, though seemingly docile, can be very unpredictable. ⊕ 1 hr. ☎ 805/924-1628. www.elephantseal.org. Free admission. Daily 24 hr.

From Piedras Blancas, head south on Hwy. 1 for 16 miles.

❸ **Cambria.** Before the sun goes down on Day 1, you'll want to arrive in Cambria, where you'll bunk down for the next 2 nights. Aside from the tour of Nitt Witt Ridge (which you'll have to tack onto the Day 2's itinerary), follow the suggestions for Cambria on p. 388 for your evening and following day. After lunch, get on the road. ⊕ At least 4 hr.

On the afternoon of Day 2, head south on Hwy. 1 for 12 miles.

❹ **Cayucos.** Hop on over to the classic little beach town of Cayucos and make the rest of Day 2 about the easy-breezy beach life. The wide, white sandy beaches are perfect for sunning and strolling, and the gentle surf goes easy on boogie boarders, inexperienced surfers, and kayakers (rent equipment from Good Clean Fun Surf and Sport, 136 N Ocean Ave.; ☎ 805/995-1993; www.gcfsurf.com). The 953-foot-long pier is great for fishing or taking in views of **Morro Bay** (p. 374, ❶), including Morro Rock.

You might have expected a lack of dining options in such a no-fuss, no-stoplight village, but you'd be mistaken. Ruddell's Smokehouse, 101 D St. (☎ 805/995-5028; www.smokerjim.com) slings phenomenal fish tacos from a walk-up beach shack. For more sophisticated fare, try the cozy and elegant **Hoppe's Garden Bistro,** 78 N. Ocean Ave. (☎ 805/995-1006; www.hoppesbistro.com). An absolute must stop for treats is the ★ Brown Butter Cookie Company, 250 N. Ocean Ave. (☎ 805/995-2076; www.brownbuttercookies.com) for their amazing brown butter sea salt cookies (tucked into small cube boxes, they make great gifts). ⊕ At least 2 hr.

On the morning of Day 3, head inland to Paso Robles. From Cambria, head south on Hwy. 1 for 2 miles, then go east on Hwy. 46 for 22 miles. A slower, more scenic route is to take Santa Rosa Creek Rd. 16½ miles to Hwy. 46.

❺ **Paso Robles.** Rambling through the rolling hills surrounding Paso Robles—Spanish for "pass of the oaks"—you'll see plenty of oak trees, but also equestrian farms, almond orchards, lavender fields, olive groves, and vineyards. With only a half-day day to explore, you should visit a couple of the many **wine-tasting** rooms strung along the bucolic back roads such as Vineyard Drive and Adelaida Road

> *Roll down the window and take in the graceful beauty of vineyards lining Highway 46.*

(see p. 366 for specific recommendations and routes). You should also sample some olive oil, an emerging regional export, at **Pasolivo,** 8530 Vineyard Dr. (☎ 805/227-0186; www. pasolivo.com).

Head downtown to Paso's town square, so idyllic you might mistake it for a movie set. **City Park** fills 5 acres with shady oaks, a large gazebo, a playground, and a stately public library built in 1907. Fanning out from the park are charming, blocks of boutiques, excellent restaurants, and yep, more wine-tasting rooms.

Time permitting, indulge in the Paso Robles tradition of "taking the cure," soaking in the sulphur-rich natural hot springs. Your best bet is the **River Oaks Hot Springs Spa** at 800 Clubhouse Dr. (☎ 805/238-4600; www.river oakshotsprings.com), unless you're staying at the historic **Paso Robles Inn** (p. 391), whose deluxe rooms feature private hot springs tubs. ⏱ half-day. See p. 390.

On the afternoon of Day 3, head south on U.S. 101 for 27 miles.

❻ **San Luis Obispo.** For the remainder of Day 3, see p. 357, ❺. You'll call San Luis Obispo home for the next 2 nights; after all, it was here that the first motor hotel, or motel, was born in 1925.

Kick-start Day 4 with a hike up to **Bishop Peak,** the tallest of the Nine Sisters, a row of volcanic plugs extending from San Luis Obispo to Morro Bay. From the summit admire the line of "little sisters" and the sweeping views of the valley. ⏱ 2 hr. See p. 392.

Dining Tip

For a truly unique Central Coast dining experience, head to the ★★ **Range in Santa Margarita,** an Old West–flavored village 8 miles north of San Luis Obispo. Don't let the casual, retro-cowpoke decor fool you—a sophisticated menu mixes Southern comfort and French preparation, with an emphasis on fresh, local ingredients such as Hearst Ranch beef. An outdoor patio rumbles with honky-tonk music on weekend nights. 22317 G St., Santa Margarita. ☎ 805/438-4500. Entrees $17–$31. Cash only. Lunch Sat; dinner Tues–Sat.

> *Raised boardwalks protect the shifting sands of Guadalupe-Nipomo Dunes, a fascinating—and delicate—ecosystem.*

Head south on U.S. 101 for 12 miles. Take the Hwy. 1 exit and head south for 13½ miles. At Oso Flaco Lake Rd., take a right and go 3 miles until you reach the self-pay parking lot for the Oso Flaco Natural Area. Another slower but more scenic route involves taking Hwy. 227 south, skirting Wine Country and passing through Old Edna. Take a right on Price Canyon Rd. and follow for 5 miles.

❼ Pismo Beach. One of Pismo's prettiest attractions is seasonal: Every year from late October to February, monarch butterflies by the tens of thousands descend upon the eucalyptus groves at the North Beach Campground. You can observe the striking orange and black clusters at the **Monarch Butterfly Grove** (p. 376, ❸) where volunteer docents are usually on-site to guide you.

The ★★★ **Guadalupe-Nipomo Dunes Complex** (p. 376, ❹) is one of the largest and most pristine coastal dune ecosystems in the country. At the Oso Flaco entrance, a 1-mile walk (2 miles round-trip) takes you across a footbridge spanning a freshwater lake dotted with ducks, along a wooden boardwalk through gorgeous coastal scrub, then finally to the beach. Give yourself at least an hour, depending on how deep in the dunes you wish

to get. A few miles south in Guadalupe is the ★ **Guadalupe-Nipomo Dunes Complex** (p. 376, ❹) where you can learn more about the dunes, other access points, and activities, including guided walks.

Wind down the rest of the day on the wide, sandy beaches of Pismo State Beach or venture a couple miles north to the more rugged Shell Beach set against the bluffs. ⏱ At least 6 hr.

From Pismo Beach, take U.S. 101 north for 13 miles to San Luis Obispo for the night. On Day 5, head south on U.S. 101 to Hwy. 246 and go left. Head east for 3½ miles.

❽ ★ Santa Ynez Valley. Best known for its star turn in the wine-soaked 2004 film *Sideways,* the scenic Santa Ynez Valley is a geographic triangle formed by U.S. 101, Hwy. 246 and Hwy. 154, and encompasses several small towns. Solvang, founded by Danish immigrants in 1911, is a cutesy community that cranks up its Scandinavian heritage—windmills, thatched roofs, flags, clogs, and pastries (look for ebelskivers that are as fun to eat as they are to say). The Mayberryesque Los Olivos offers wine-tasting rooms (for more on Santa Ynez wine tasting, see p. 366) and excellent dining options along Grand Avenue, its main drag.

Kids love to say howdy to the miniature horses at **Quicksilver Ranch,** 1555 Alamo Pintado Rd. (☎ 805/686-4002), and to feed the ostriches at **OstrichLand USA,** 610 E. Hwy. 246, Buellton (☎ 805/686-9696; www.ostrichlandusa.com; admission $4, ostrich food $1).

Old Mission Santa Inés, 1750 Mission Dr. (☎ 805/688-4815; www.missionsantaines.org) stands close to the tourist bustle in Solvang, but history buffs will appreciate the short detour to Lompoc to experience the living history museum of **La Purisima Mission** (p. 396, ❸), the only complete mission complex in California. ⏱ 4 hr.

Take Hwy. 246 east to Hwy. 154, and head south.

❾ San Marcos Pass. Sure, U.S. 101 is the fastest way to Santa Barbara, but the San Marcos Pass, a former stagecoach route turned state highway (Hwy. 154), is far prettier, winding through the Santa Ynez Mountains and past the silver-green Lake Cachuma. Do not miss ★★ **Cold Spring Tavern,** 5995 Stagecoach Rd. (☎ 805/967-0066; www.coldspringtavern. com). Established in 1876 as a stagecoach stop and still drenched in Old West nostalgia, the rustic property combines an upscale restaurant with a casual, lively bar and patio that, on weekends, serves music and tri-tip beef sandwiches. You'll also want to stop at the **Chumash Painted Caves,** Painted Cave Road, 2 miles north of Hwy. 154 (☎ 805/733-3713; free admission; dawn–dusk), to get a glimpse of the striking pictographs made on the sandstone walls by the Chumash over 400 years ago. Be aware that a metal screen restricts access. ⊕ 2 hr.

🔟 **Santa Barbara.** Hit the harbor for a sailboat cruise on the *Double Dolphin* from the **Santa Barbara Sailing Center** (p. 384, ⑭); check its website for times and the types of cruises (sunset, dinner, jazz, whale-watching) offered. If you miss the boat, you can always check out the **Santa Barbara Maritime Museum** (p. 384, ⑭) which celebrates California's seafaring heritage.

For dinner, eat along the water. The best option is at the harbor, where the always-crowded **Brophy Brothers** (p. 387) offers fresh and tasty seafood along with stellar harbor views.

On Day 6, follow the Santa Barbara itinerary on p. 358, ⑥, and try to squeeze in the **Santa Barbara Zoo** (p. 383, ⑪) in the afternoon, especially if you have kids in tow. ⊕ 1½ days. See p. 380.

On Day 7, take U.S. 101 south for 28 miles. Take exit 68 toward Seaward Ave., then go left (south) on Harbor Blvd. for 2 miles. Take a right on Spinnaker Dr.

⑪ ★★ **Channel Islands.** Plan ahead to make a ½-day excursion to the most accessible of the rugged Channel Islands, Anacapa, and be sure to get a shot of the iconic natural land bridge Arch Rock. Adventure seekers, or photo hounds, may want the whole day to explore the larger and more diverse island of Santa Cruz, home to the ★★ **Painted Cave,** one the largest sea caves in the world and accessible only by kayak. ⊕ half-day. See p. 378, ⑨.

Retrace your route back to U.S. 101 North and go north for 2½ miles. Take the Hwy. 33 North exit, and follow Hwy. 33 for a total of

> *Technicolor macaws, slender-tailed meerkats, and over 500 other animals are on display at the Santa Barbara Zoo.*

13½ miles. Continue onto Ojai Ave. for a mile.

⑫ **Ojai.** Nestled in a remote valley at the foothills of Los Padres National Forest, Ojai is a small, laid-back community with a long tradition as an artistic and spiritual retreat. On Ojai Avenue snack and shop along the Spanish-style arcade, admire the post office campanile, stroll through the pergola-lined park, or duck into the **Ojai Valley Museum** (p. 398, ③).

With the sun setting fast on your Day 7, drive past the citrus and avocado groves up to Meditation Mount (p. 398, ⑤) to take in the ★ **Pink Moment,** a local phenomenon which bathes the distant Topa Topa bluffs in a majestic pinkish glow. ⊕ At least 2 hr. See p. 398.

Wine Trails of the Central Coast

The winemaking regions of the Central Coast are unstuffy and approachable, with scenic, virtually traffic-free roads; sleepy but sophisticated towns; and most importantly, perhaps surprisingly, world-class wines. Our 3-day tour starts in Paso Robles, the state's fastest-growing wine region. Then we'll drift south to San Luis Obispo and the Edna Valley and finally finish up north of Santa Barbara in the greater Santa Ynez Valley, made famous by the 2004 Oscar-nominated film *Sideways*.

> Twenty-first-century barmaids pour local vintages in the 140-year-old mahogany bar at saloon-style *Tobin James*.

START Paso Robles. **TRIP LENGTH** 3 days, about 190 miles.

From Paso Robles, head south on U.S. 101. The first two wineries are located about 4 miles away, just off Hwy. 46, in an area with hillsides known for their rich, chalky soil.

❶ Peachy Canyon. Big zin lovers, here ya go. At its tasting room, the Old Bethel School House dating back to 1886, this winery pours several different zinfandels, some estate grown and all sourced from the Paso Robles AVA. The serene grounds are perfect for picnicking, with an open, green lawn; a large gazebo; and tables beneath towering oak trees. ⏱ 1 hr. 1480 N. Bethel Rd., Templeton. ☎ 805/237-1577 or 800/315-7908. www.peachycanyon.com. Tastings $5 (waived w/ purchase of bottle). Daily 11am–5pm.

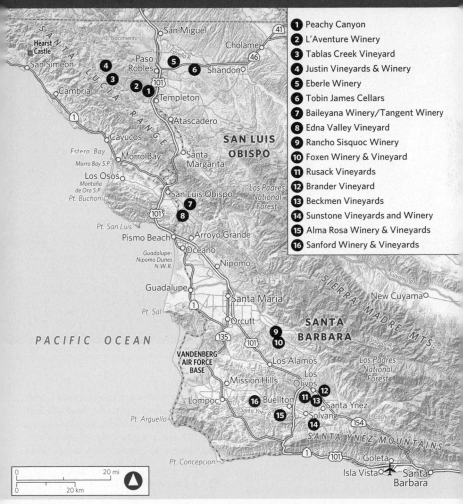

1. Peachy Canyon
2. L'Aventure Winery
3. Tablas Creek Vineyard
4. Justin Vineyards & Winery
5. Eberle Winery
6. Tobin James Cellars
7. Baileyana Winery/Tangent Winery
8. Edna Valley Vineyard
9. Rancho Sisquoc Winery
10. Foxen Winery & Vineyard
11. Rusack Vineyards
12. Brander Vineyard
13. Beckmen Vineyards
14. Sunstone Vineyards and Winery
15. Alma Rosa Winery & Vineyards
16. Sanford Winery & Vineyards

2 ★ **L'Aventure Winery.** The simple tasting room at this winery is all about the tasting (although the winery prefers the term "degustation"). Innovative vintner Stephan Asseo, frustrated by the strict wine regulations in his native Bordeaux, came to Paso in the late nineties eager to experiment with the combination of bordeaux and Rhône varietals. His Optimus and Estate Cuvée—both are blends of cabernet, Syrah, petit verdot—are legendary. ⏱ 1 hr. 2815 Live Oak Rd., Paso Robles. ☎ 805/227-1588. www.aventurewine.com. Tastings $10 (includes souvenir glass). Thurs-Sun 11am-4pm.

Head west on Hwy. 46, then north on Vineyard Dr. Turn left on Adelaida Rd.

Go slow enough to soak up the bucolic scenery surrounding these wineries off the beaten path, the self-proclaimed "Far Out Wineries."

3 ★★ **Tablas Creek Vineyard.** The union of importer Robert Haas and the Perrin family of

Travel Tip

Don't drink and drive! If you aren't able to have a designated driver in your party, you can always practice the four S's—"swirl, smell, sip, and spit"—like a true evaluator of fine wines.

> *The charming Old World look of Sunstone Winery contrasts with the cutting edge organic techniques used to produce its wines.*

Château de Beaucastel, this winery hews to the Châteauneuf-du-Pape tradition of blending specific Rhône varietals. Their signature wines are the highly acclaimed Esprit de Beaucastel and Esprit de Beaucastel Blanc. ⏱ 1 hr. 9339 Adelaida Rd., Paso Robles. ☎ 805/237-1231. www.tablascreek.com. Tastings $10 (waived w/ purchase of bottle). Daily 10am–5pm.

❹ ★ **Justin Vineyards & Winery.** This family-run winery is a popular stop that has it all: friendly dogs, a tasting room stocked with gourmet nibbles, a garden and picnic area, a variety of tours and seminars (which include tastings), fine dining with patio seating at Deborah's Room, even a luxurious B&B called the Just Inn. Most importantly, it also makes excellent bordeaux-style wines, including an award-winning cabernet blend called Isosceles. ⏱ 1 hr. 11680 Chimney Rock Rd., Paso Robles. ☎ 805/238-6932 or 800/726-0049. www.justinwine.com. Tastings $10 (includes souvenir glass). Tours start at $15. Daily 10am–6pm.

Trace your route back to Vineyard Dr. and head south. At Adelaida Rd. head left (east), then turn right on 24th St. Continue across U.S. 101, and onto Hwy. 46. Heading east, you'll pass many of the area's largest wine producers.

❺ ★★ **Eberle Winery.** The history of the Paso wine region cannot be written without the name Gary Eberle, a pioneering force who swept into town nearly 40 years ago. In 1978 he became the first winemaker in the country to produce a 100% Syrah, and in 1980, he cofounded the Paso Robles Appellation. He cemented his reputation with an award-winning Estate Cabernet Sauvignon. Take the VIP Tour through the underground wine caves (*Wine Spectator* calls it "one of the best tours on the Central Coast"), or enjoy a gourmet picnic lunch (preordered through the website) on the scenic redwood deck overlooking the vineyards. ⏱ 1 hr. 3810 E. Hwy. 46, Paso Robles. ☎ 805/238-9607. www.eberlewinery.com. Free tasting. VIP tour & tasting $25. Summer daily 10am–6pm; winter daily 10am–5pm.

Head east on Hwy. 46 for 5½ miles and take a right on Union Rd.

6 ★ Tobin James Cellars. Wine snobbery is strictly outlawed at this saloon-style tasting room built on the site of an old stagecoach stop. Pony up to the 140-year-old mahogany bar and sample some big, straight-shooting reds like zinfandel and cabernet in a rowdy and rustic atmosphere meant to channel the ghosts of the James gang, who once passed through these parts. ⏱ 30 min. 8950 Union Rd., Paso Robles. ☎ 805/239-2204. www.tobin james.com. Tastings free. Daily 10am–6pm.

From Hwy. 46, head south on U.S. 101 for 30 miles. Exit Marsh St. and head east to Broad St., then take a right. Take a left on Orcutt Rd., and follow for 3½ miles.

7 ★ Baileyana Winery/Tangent Winery. At the historic and utterly charming Independence Schoolhouse (originally erected by local farmhands in 1909), you can sample the fruits of two wineries, both certified sustainable and both run by Burgundy-born Christian Roguenant. Baileyana presents chardonnays, pinot noirs and Syrahs from its Firepeak Vineyards, while Tangent focuses exclusively on "alternative" whites like pinot gris, pinot blanc, Viognier, and Riesling. ⏱ 1 hr. 5828 Orcutt Rd., San Luis Obispo. ☎ 805/269-8200. www. baileyana.com. Tastings $5. Daily 10am–5pm.

8 ★★ Edna Valley Vineyard. Best known for its estate-grown chardonnay, this winery welcomes guests with a polished tasting room that offers wine-related goodies (gourmet chocolates, picnic baskets, books) and a gorgeous panorama of its vineyards and the volcanic peak Islay Hill in the distance. You can also take a stroll through the "demonstration vineyard" which has 14 rows of grapes, each featuring a different varietal or trellis design. ⏱ 1 hr. 2585 Biddle Ranch Rd., San Luis Obispo. ☎ 805/544-5855. www.ednavalleyvineyard. com. Tastings $5, reserve wine tastings $10. Daily 10am–5pm.

Head west on Biddle Ranch Rd. Take a left on Hwy. 227, and head south through Arroyo Grande. At U.S. 101, head south for 17½ miles. Exit Betteravia Rd. and take a left. Continue onto Foxen Canyon Rd., a winding road that is home to 16 tasting rooms.

> *Cowboys don't just drink whiskey; they quaff Edna Valley Vineyard's gold-medal vintages just like the rest of us.*

9 Rancho Sisquoc Winery. Ramble down a couple miles of farm road, past the quaint, white San Ramon Chapel, a State Historic Landmark, and sample some big reds and bordeaux blends, many of which pair nicely with the local, Santa Maria–style barbecue. The winery also takes pride in being the only California producer of Sylvaner, a refreshing white wine blended with a splash of Riesling, making it perfect for a summer picnic. ⏱ 30 min. 6600 Foxen Canyon Rd., Santa Maria. ☎ 805/934-4332. www.rancho sisquoc.com. Tastings $8 (includes souvenir glass). Mon–Fri 10am–4pm; Sat–Sun 10am–5pm.

10 ★★ Foxen Winery & Vineyard. Foxen now offers two different wine-tasting experiences a ½-mile apart: A new modern solar-powered tasting room presents burgundy and Rhône-style wines; the original roadside tin-roofed tasting shack has been renamed Foxen 7200 and showcases bordeaux and Cal Ital–style wines. Recently the winery has earned rave reviews for its pinot noirs from the Sea Smoke Vineyard in the Santa Rita Hills. ⏱ 1 hr. 7200 & 7600 Foxen Canyon Rd., Santa Maria. ☎ 805/937-4251. www.foxenvineyard.com. Tastings $10 (includes souvenir glass). Daily 11am–4pm.

> *Thin wires, here strung at Rusack Vineyards, tempt grapevines to twine when new shoots grow in spring.*

Take Foxen Canyon Rd. south for 12 miles, cross over Hwy. 154. Take a right onto Ballard Canyon Rd. and follow it for 3⅓ miles.

⑪ ★ Rusack Vineyards. This boutique winery tucked away in picturesque Ballard Canyon produces less than 7,000 cases a year and garners stellar reviews for its Syrahs, pinot noirs, and chardonnays. If it's warm outside, linger on the shady, tree-canopied deck overlooking the vineyards and the oak-dotted hills which turn golden in the late-afternoon sun. ⏱ 1 hr. 1819 Ballard Canyon Rd., Solvang. ☎ 805/688-1278. www.rusack.com. Tastings $6 (includes souvenir glass). Daily 11am–5pm.

Retrace your route back to Hwy. 154 and take a right. After 2 miles, take a left onto Roblar Ave., then another left onto Refugio Rd.

⑫ Brander Vineyard. The low-wattage charm of the pink château-style tasting room may not bowl you over, but the wines might, especially if you're a fan of crisp sauvignon blancs. Fred Brander has been producing award-winning (and reasonably priced) vintages of the varietal for over 30 years. ⏱ 30 min. 2401 Refugio Rd., Los Olivos. ☎ 805/688-2455. www.brander.com. Tastings $10 (includes souvenir glass). Summer daily 10am–5pm; winter daily 11am–4pm.

Head south on Refugio Rd. to Roblar Ave. and take a right. After ¼ mile, continue onto Ontiveros Rd.

⑬ ★★ Beckmen Vineyards. This is a small, family-owned winery with a nifty outdoor deck and a beautiful pond ringed by gazebos, a perfect setting for splitting a bottle—the estate-grown grenache is excellent—between friends and taking in the rural beauty. ⏱ 1 hr. 2670 Ontiveros Rd., Los Olivos. ☎ 805/688-8664. www.beckmenvineyards.com. Tastings $10, reserve tastings $15. Daily 11am–5pm.

⑭ Sunstone Vineyards and Winery. Sunstone is one of the largest organic vineyards in Santa Barbara County, and its tasting room draws crowds for its Rhône varietals such as Viognier and old-world charm. With its lavender-scented courtyard and barrel-aging caves built into the hillside, the winery is designed to make visitors feel as if they've stumbled upon a countryside manor in Provence, and it nearly succeeds. ⊕ 1 hr. 125 N. Refugio Rd., Santa Ynez. ☎ 805/688-9463. www.sunstonewinery.com. Tastings $10 (includes souvenir glass). Daily 10am–4pm.

Head west on Hwy. 246 for 6 miles. Take U.S. 101 south, exit Santa Rosa Rd. and take a right. As you drive 5 miles, take in the Santa Rita Hills, an area known for its cooler, pinot noir–friendly climate.

⑮ ★ Alma Rosa Winery & Vineyards. Although pioneering vintner Richard Sanford and wife, Thekla, left their namesake winery (below) in 2005, they've maintained the appealingly rustic tasting room, where *Sideways* shot a memorable scene with tasting room manager Chris Burroughs. Their new winery concentrates on organic farming and sustainable agriculture (Sanford was the first in Santa Barbara County to plant 100% organic vineyards) as well as food-friendly, well-balanced wines. ⊕ 1 hr. 7250 Santa Rosa Rd., Buellton. ☎ 805/688-9090. www.almarosawinery.com. Tastings $10. Daily 11am–4:30pm.

⑯ ★ Sanford Winery & Vineyards. Sample some first-rate pinot noirs and chardonnays at this winery's new expansive tasting room, crafted in the California–mission style, including handmade adobe bricks and local stones. The back patio provides panoramas of the estate vineyards and the Santa Rita Hills and makes a relaxing spot for a quick picnic. ⊕ 1 hr. 5010 Santa Rosa Rd., Lompoc. ☎ 805/735-5900. www.sanfordwinery.com. Tastings $10 (includes souvenir glass). Daily 11am–5pm.

> As pretty as a sunset, the rosy color of a Rhone varietal tempts at Beckmen Vineyards.

Pack a Picnic

There's no shortage of great restaurants in the Central Coast Wine Country, but packing a picnic lets you be more spontaneous in your dedicated pursuit of fine wines. Plus, few restaurants can match the ambience you'll find at these wineries, surrounded by endless acres of sun-dappled grapes. In the Santa Ynez Valley, **Panino** (2900 Grand Ave., Los Olivos; ☎ 805/688-9304; www.paninorestaurants.com) makes delicious sandwiches such as Italian combos or curry chicken salad. My favorite food supply stop is **Los Olivos Grocery** (2621 Hwy. 154, Los Olivos; ☎ 805/688-5115; www.losolivosgrocery.com), a small country store that stocks basic staples (don't forget water!), fresh local produce, gourmet cheeses, and tri-tip sandwiches from their deli. In Paso Robles, head for the retail shop at **Mt. Olive Organic Farm** (3445 Adelaida Rd., Paso Robles; ☎ 805/237-0147; www.mtoliveco.com), which grows its own organic fruits and vegetables; the store has an organic bakery, and sandwiches and boxed lunches to go.

THE
ROYAL ROAD
California Missions BY MEGAN MCFARLAND

CALIFORNIA'S 21 MISSIONS PROVIDE an admittedly romantic window into the state's Spanish-colonial past. Here visitors will find bougainvillea-draped court-yards, bubbling fountains, intimate chapels, and impressive collections of Mexican and Spanish-colonial art. Founded between 1769 and 1823 by Franciscan padres, or friars, first led by Father Junipero Serra, the missions link San Diego to Sonoma along a route known as El Camino Real, or the Royal Road.

In many ways the missions were self-supporting cities, with the humble Franciscans iron-ically administering vast and profitable holdings of land and livestock. The missions were largely secularized and abandoned by the 1840s; reporter Helen Hunt Jackson dramatized the plight of Mission Indians in her bestselling novel *Ramona* (1844), which jumpstarted ongoing restoration efforts and pride in California's Spanish–Mexican heritage.

Windows on Colonial California

SAN FRANCISCO DE ASÍS (MISSION DOLORES)
LOCATION: San Francisco
FOUNDED: 1776
With 4-foot-thick walls, the original chapel is the oldest building in the city and one of a few structures to have miraculously survived the 1906 earthquake. Its three original bells hang above the entryway and are still in use.
See p. 88, **10**.

SAN CARLOS BORROMÉO DE CARMELO
LOCATION: Carmel
FOUNDED: 1770
Originally established at the presidio in Mon-terey, the mission was relocated to Carmel—"two gunshots" from the ocean—in 1771 after soldiers repeatedly harassed the Indian residents. The church was designated a Minor Basilica in 1969. See p. 342, **1**.

SANTA BARBARA
LOCATION: Santa Barbara
FOUNDED: 1786
The "Queen of the Missions" is the only one continu-ously operated by the Franciscans since its founding, and one of only three stone missions in California (the others are San Juan Capistrano and Carmel). The church contains a ca. 1790 abalone-encrusted altar built by Chumash Indians. See p.380, **1**.

SAN JUAN CAPISTRANO
LOCATION: San Juan Capistrano (Orange County)
FOUNDED: 1776
The ruins of the Great Stone Church dominate the entrance to one of the most storied of the missions, famed for the annual return of the swallows (*golondrinas*) from Argentina.
See p. 504, **8**.

SAN LUIS REY DE FRANCÍA
LOCATION: East of Oceanside (San Diego County)
FOUNDED: 1798
Known as "King of the Missions," the white-washed complex is framed by palm trees, with a three-story bell tower topped by a sky-blue dome. California's first pepper tree, planted in 1830, still graces the quadrangle. See p. 580.

Mission Revival Architecture

The quintessential elements of mis-sion architecture—red-tile roofs, whitewashed adobe walls, arcaded patios, arched doorways, and graceful bel-fries—have been copied in Califor-nia by everyone from William Randolph Hearst to Taco Bell. The style enjoyed huge popularity in California between 1890 and 1940, as romantic accounts of Spain flourished in American popular culture. Early California real-estate devel-opers also seized on an "authentic" and romantic building tradition to promote in a young state where American history held little sway. It didn't hurt that several silent films featured mission- and Spanish-style sets, including *The Mark of Zorro* (1920), with Doug-las Fairbanks—who also lived in a Spanish-revival-style estate in Beverly Hills.

Central Coast for Nature Lovers

The natural attractions of the Central Coast may lack the marquee appeal of, say Yosemite or Death Valley, but frankly, that's part of their appeal. The rugged coastline of Montana de Oro, the majestic Guadalupe dunes, the wild and uninhabited Channel Islands—these jewels will surprise you, not only by their beauty, but also their accessibility. In a single day, you could scale an ancient volcanic peak, kayak into sea caves, and go surfing.

> Now home to nesting peregrine falcons, 576-foot-tall Morro Rock is all that's left of an ancient volcano.

START Morro Bay, 232 miles south of San Francisco. TRIP LENGTH 5 days, about 150 miles.

❶ ★ **Morro Bay.** Get the lay of the land by perusing the interactive exhibits at the **Morro Bay State Park Museum of Natural History,** State Park Road (☎ 805/772-2694; www. slostateparks.com/natural_history_museum; daily 10am–5pm; $3 adults, free for kids 16 & under), perched on a bluff overlooking Morro Bay and Morro Rock, the "Gibraltar of the Pacific" and the town's star attraction. The 576-foot dramatic monolith is the last of a series of long-dormant, ancient volcanic peaks known as the Nine Sisters stretching from San Luis Obispo to Morro Bay.

The **estuary** at Morro Bay is one of the state's largest saltwater marshes, and a natural habitat for a rich variety of shorebirds, wading birds, and during winter, migratory waterfowl. Other great bird-watching spots nearby include the El Moro Elfin Forest (S. Bay Rd. at Santa Ysabel Ave.), the Heron Rookery (north of the museum), and the Sweet Springs Nature Preserve (Ramona Ave., west of Fourth St.)

1 Morro Bay
2 Montana de Oro
3 Pismo Beach
4 Guadalupe-Nipomo
   Dunes Complex
5 Lompoc
6 Santa Ynez Valley
7 Santa Barbara
8 Lotusland
9 Channel Islands
   National Park

The best way to experience Morro Bay—the birds, the sea mammals (seals, sea otters, sea lions), the small pockets of sandy beach, and of course, the Rock—is by kayak. ★ **Central Coast Outdoors,** 10 State Park Rd., Morro Bay State Park Marina (☎ 805/528-1080; www.central coastoutdoors.com) offers a variety of guided tours with rates beginning at $65 for 3 hours. If you prefer to roam on your own, try the **Kayak Shack,** also at 10 State Park Rd., Morro Bay State Park Marina (☎ 805/772-8796; www. morrobaykayakshack.com), where rates start at $12 an hour. ☉ At least 4 hr.

From Morro Bay State Park Marina, head east on State Park Rd. until Bay Blvd., then take a right and continue south for 3⅓ miles. At Los Osos Valley Rd., take a right and go 1½ miles. Continue onto Pecho Valley Rd. for 3¾ miles.

2 ★★ **Montana de Oro.** You'll find fantastic hiking among the dramatic coastal bluffs of this 8,000-acre state park, and if you're traveling in the spring, you'll also find hillsides glowing with yellow and orange wildflowers (hence the park's name—Spanish for "Mountain of Gold").

The visitor center is uphill from an ancient Chumash settlement called ★ **Spooner's Cove,** a sandy inlet bracketed by dramatic rock formations and a popular swimming and picnicking spot. A popular hike is the 1½-hour

> *Windswept and wild, Guadalupe-Nipomo Dunes was the sandy setting for Cecil B. DeMille's* The Ten
  Commandments.

trek along ★ **Bluff Trail,** which follows the craggy coastline where you can watch the surf thunder against the rocky outcroppings or scramble down to the clear tide pools of Corallina Cove and Quarry Cove. For those with more oomph in their lungs and legs, make the 4-mile, round-trip to 1,347-foot-high ★★ **Valencia Peak,** with its stunning 360-degree views of the entire park, the Nine Sisters, Morro Bay, and the coast from Piedras Blancas to Point Sal. ⊙ At least 2 hr. End of Pecho Valley Rd., Los Osos. ☎ 805/528-0513.

Retrace your route back to Los Osos Valley Rd. and continue east to Hwy. 101 (about 15 miles total). Head south on Hwy. 101 for 9 miles.

Dining Tip

It's been decades since clamming was king on Pismo Beach, but fear not, you can still grab a delicious cup of clam chowder. A Clam Festival with a chowder cook-off is held every October. On any other day queue up at the always-packed ★ **Splash Café,** 197 Pomeroy Ave. (☎ 805/773-4653; www.splashcafe.com), where the chowder is served hot and creamy in sourdough bowls ($6.75).

❸ **Pismo Beach.** Every winter from late October to February, monarch butterflies migrate south, some flying over 1,000 miles, to the eucalyptus trees of ★ **Monarch Butterfly Grove**, one of the largest monarch colonies in the country. Scientists have yet to solve the mystery of how successive generations, born months later and many miles north, inherit the knowledge needed to return to the same wintering location. ⊙ 1 hr. North Beach Campground, Dolliver St. (Hwy. 1), 1½ miles south of U.S. 101. ☎ 800/443-7778. www.monarchbutterfly.org. Docents available for information and tours daily 10am–4pm, Nov-Feb. Free admission daily.

Head south on Hwy. 1 for 2 miles.

❹ ★★★ **Guadalupe-Nipomo Dunes Complex.** Rolling 18 miles along the coast from Pismo State Beach to Point Sal, this National Natural Landmark is a biologically diverse ecosystem that supports over 100 species of rare and endangered plants, like the wonderfully named dunedelion flower, and animals, such as the silvery legless lizard and the western snowy plover.

The northern end offers high-octane recreation: the ★ **Oceano Dunes State Vehicular Recreation Area,** end of Pier Avenue, Oceano (☎ 805/773-7170; www.ohv.parks.ca.gov), is the only state park that allows vehicles onto the beach, and 1,500 acres of dunes are open to thrill seekers on motorcycles, dune buggies, and all-terrain vehicles (rent ATVs at **BJ's ATV Rentals,** 197 W. Grand Ave., Grover Beach; ☎ 805/481-5411; www.bjsatvrentals.com).

A quieter place to commune with the dunes is ★★ **National Wildlife Refuge,** the most protected area of the complex. At the Oso Flaco Lake entrance (at the end of Oso Flaco Lake Rd.), take the lovely mile-long boardwalk to the beach and enjoy views of a rare coastal freshwater lake and thriving coastal scrub vegetation. Or head farther south to ★ **Rancho Guadalupe Dunes County Park** (at the end of Hwy. 166), better known as Guadalupe Beach, where you can reach **Mussel Rock** and the tallest dunes (upwards of 500 ft.) on the West Coast. Access to some areas is limited between March and October.

The Guadalupe-Nipomo Dunes Center, 1055 Guadalupe St., (☎ 805/343-2455; www. dunescenter.org; Wed–Sun 10am–4pm), arranges educational walks and provides information on the dunes unique flora and fauna. Check out the fascinating exhibit of artifacts from what appears to have been a mighty ancient Egyptian civilization—actually just the remnants of the enormous plaster sphinxes and pharaoh statues from Cecil B. DeMille's 1923 epic *The Ten Commandments,* filmed in the windswept dunes where many of the sets are still buried today. ⌚ At least 4 hr.

Head south on Hwy. 1 for 35 miles. Take a right on Jalama Beach Rd. and go 14 miles.

⑤ Lompoc. Although hard-core surfers clamor for the famous curls at ★ **Rincon Beach** in Carpenteria, most folks will prefer the beautiful and remote ★★ **Jalama Beach** at the end of a rolling and winding road that's lined with yellow wildflowers in the spring. ⌚ At least 2 hr. End of Jalama Beach Rd., Lompoc.

Return to Hwy. 1, then head south for 25 miles, merging with Hwy. 101. Exit Refugio Rd. for Circle Bar B Ranch.

⑥ Santa Ynez Valley. The pastoral valley is home to some of the country's top horse breeding, training, and rehabilitation facilities, most notably, **Flag Is Up Farms,** 901 E. Hwy. 246 (☎ 805/688-4382; www.montyroberts.

com; daily 9am–5pm), which welcomes visitors and is run by Monty Roberts, known as the "Man Who Listens to Horses."

The best place to saddle up and hit the trail is ★ **Circle Bar B Guest Ranch & Staples,** 1800 Refugio Rd., Goleta (☎ 805/968-3901; www. circlebarbstables.com; rides start at $37 per person), next to President Reagan's old ranch overlooking the Pacific Ocean. ⌚ At least 2 hr.

From Refugio Rd. head south on Hwy. 101 for 22 miles.

The Birth of Earth Day

In early 1969 an underwater pipe of a Union Oil platform in the Santa Barbara Channel burst, releasing 100,000 gallons of crude oil into the channel, marring the coastline from Ventura to Goleta, as well as the Channel Islands, and killing 10,000 sea birds. Senator Gaylord Nelson, an environmental activist from Wisconsin, witnessed the spill's devastation and then conceived a grass-roots effort, a national "teach-in" with the goal of preventing such ecological disasters. The first Earth Day was celebrated on April 22, 1970.

> Cowboy up and head out for a Circle Bar B trail ride in Refugio Canyon, with sweeping views of the Santa Ynez region.

7 **Santa Barbara.** Immerse yourself in the lush native vegetation of the **Santa Barbara Botanic Garden** (p. 380, **2**), then head to the nearby **Museum of Natural History** (p. 382, **3**) which offers captivating dioramas on animal wildlife.

Santa Barbara's best hike is ★ **Seven Falls/ Inspiration Point.** At the end of Tunnel Road, follow the Tunnel Trail to Jesusita Trail, then watch for signs (if you get confused, just ask a local—there are always many on the trails). The 3.7-mile round-trip takes you to a handful of small cascading pools along Mission Creek, then onto a 1,750-foot overlook that rewards you with a glorious panorama of the entire town and the coast.

Watch the whales from **Shoreline Park** (p. 385), or get closer to the action and take a catamaran cruise on the *Double Dolphin* at ★ **Santa Barbara Sailing Center** (p. 384, **14**). ⏱ At least 6 hr. See p. 380.

8 ★★ **Lotusland.** Created by Madame Ganna Walska (1887–1984), an opera diva turned landscape designer, this 37-acre estate and botanic garden displays a fiery sense of showmanship, mixing natives with rare exotic specimens, including some prehistoric plants that are no longer found in the wild. Manicured paths wind through several types of gardens—cacti, rare cycads, ferns, playful topiaries, water lilies, Japanese style, and even a monochromatic blue garden. ⏱ 2 hr. 695 Ashley Rd., Montecito. ☎ 805/969-9990. www.lotusland.org. Reservations required. 2-hr. guided tours $35

adults ($25 in the fall), $10 kids 5–18, free for kids 4 & under. Mid-Feb to mid-Nov Wed–Sat 10am–1:30pm.

Head south on Hwy. 101 for 28 miles to exit 68, then head south on Harbor Blvd. for 2 miles. Take a right onto Spinnaker Dr.

9 ★★★ **Channel Islands National Park.** Twenty-five miles off the mainland, Channel Islands National Park feels utterly remote— rugged, wild, and pristine, with 150 species of plants and animals (such as the island fox) found nowhere else in the world, earning the nickname America's Galapagos. The park, comprised of the northernmost five islands in an archipelago of eight, offers visitors a thrilling opportunity to discover a part of the California coast that looks much the same as it did centuries ago.

Visiting the Channel Islands takes planning and access is limited. Learn about the islands' history, unique ecology, and the distinct experiences offered by each at **Channel Islands National Park Visitor Center,** 1901 Spinnaker Dr. Ventura (☎ 805/658-5730; www.nps. gov/chis; daily 8:30am–5pm). Nearby is the best choice for visiting the islands by boat, **Island Packers,** 1691 Spinnaker Dr. Ste. 105B, Ventura (☎ 805/642-1393; www.island packers.com; tickets $28–$48; check the website for times and tour options). If you're departing from Santa Barbara, you can use **Truth Aquatics,** 301 W. Cabrillo Blvd. (☎ 805/962-1127; www.truthaquatics.com).

> *Join a guided kayak cruise and take in the spectacular Channel Islands, including Arch Rock off Anacapa.*

The most popular trip is the ½-day jaunt to the three islets of Anacapa, home of the striking natural land bridge ★ **Arch Rock,** icon of the islands. Also popular is the day trip to the largest and most geographically diverse Channel Island, Santa Cruz. Kayak into one of the largest and deepest sea caves in the world, ★★ **Painted Cave** (named for its colorful, lichen-lined walls), measuring ¼-mile long and 100-feet wide, its entrance curtained by a cascading waterfall in the spring. More intrepid explorers will want to venture farther out to the wilder, windier, and more remote islands—Santa Rosa, westernmost San Miguel, and tiny Santa Barbara.

The park offers spectacular hiking, snorkeling, diving, kayaking, and whale-watching. Primitive camping is available on each island (reservations required; ☎ 877/444-6777; www.recreation.gov). Be aware that no goods or services are offered in the park. Weather is unpredictable; temperatures are fairly consistent, but winds, fog, and precipitation can fluctuate wildly, so plan accordingly. ☺ 1 day.

Roughing It (and Not So Roughing It)

Here are the three best options for camping on the Central Coast. Except for Jalama Beach (which is first-come, first-served), book well ahead, since these sites are very popular, especially during the summer.
Montana de Oro State Park (☎ 805/444-7275; www.parks.ca.gov; $20 per night)
Refugio State Beach (☎ 805/444-7275; www.parks.ca.gov; $35-$45 per night)
Jalama Beach County Park (☎ 805/736-6316; $20 per night)

At ★ **El Capitan Canyon,** 11560 Calle Real, Goleta (☎ 866/352-2729 or 805/685-3887; www.elcapitancanyon.com), the key word is *glamping* (glamorous camping), which describes the trend of retreating into nature, but not without a few choice amenities like down comforters, space heaters, and Wi-Fi. Choose from simple safari tents or cedar cabins with kitchenettes. Tents and cabins run $135 to $350.

Santa Barbara

The rugged Santa Ynez Mountains to the north, the sparkling Pacific Ocean to the south, harmonious Spanish mission-revival architecture, and a sun-drenched Mediterranean climate—Santa Barbara more than lives up to its billing as the "American Riviera."

> With pools and peaceful gardens, the Old Mission Santa Barbara makes a quiet retreat above the city bustle.

START Old Mission Santa Barbara. From U.S. 101, exit Mission St. and head northeast. Follow the signs for the mission. Santa Barbara is 95 miles north of Los Angeles and 106 miles south of San Luis Obispo. **TRIP LENGTH** 2 days.

❶ ★★★ Old Mission Santa Barbara. With its stately, pink sandstone facade and twin bell towers, the aptly nicknamed Queen of the Missions occupies a verdant hill overlooking the town and the Channel Islands in the distance. Father Fermín Francisco de Lasuén (1736–1803) established the mission in 1786 using the labor, as well as the artistic craftsmanship, of the native Chumash whom they were trying to convert. Over the years, the original humble-looking adobe buildings have seen substantial additions and renovations—earthquakes in 1812 and 1925 caused serious damage. Take the self-guided tour or the 90-minute docent guided tour. ⏱ 1½ hr. 2201 Laguna St. (at Los Olivos St.). ☎ 805/682-4149. www.santabarbaramission.org. Self-guided tours $5 adults, $1 kids 5–15, free for kids 4 & under. Docent guided tours $8 per person; Thurs–Fri 11am & Sat 10:30am. Daily 9am–5pm.

❷ Santa Barbara Botanic Garden. A devastating fire in May 2009 may have burned 60 of these 78 lush acres of indigenous California plants, but the wildflower meadow, redwood grove, and the administration buildings were spared. The gardens, established in 1926, are regenerating nicely, thanks in large part to an effective irrigation system installed shortly before the 2009 fires. ⏱ 30 min. 1212 Mission Canyon Rd. ☎ 805/682-4726. www.sbbg.org. Admission $8 adults, $6 seniors and kids 13–17, $4 kids 2–12, free for kids 1 & under. Daily 9am–5pm.

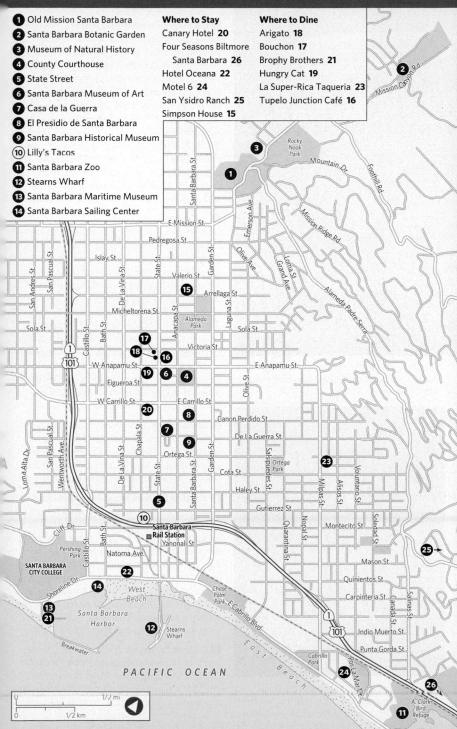

1. Old Mission Santa Barbara
2. Santa Barbara Botanic Garden
3. Museum of Natural History
4. County Courthouse
5. State Street
6. Santa Barbara Museum of Art
7. Casa de la Guerra
8. El Presidio de Santa Barbara
9. Santa Barbara Historical Museum
10. Lilly's Tacos
11. Santa Barbara Zoo
12. Stearns Wharf
13. Santa Barbara Maritime Museum
14. Santa Barbara Sailing Center

Where to Stay
Canary Hotel **20**
Four Seasons Biltmore
   Santa Barbara **26**
Hotel Oceana **22**
Motel 6 **24**
San Ysidro Ranch **25**
Simpson House **15**

Where to Dine
Arigato **18**
Bouchon **17**
Brophy Brothers **21**
Hungry Cat **19**
La Super-Rica Taqueria **23**
Tupelo Junction Café **16**

> *Intricate patterns add elegance to Chumash Indian baskets on display at the Santa Barbara Natural History Museum.*

> *The colorful wildflower meadow at the Santa Barbara Botanic Garden was spared destruction in a 2009 fire that struck the Santa Ynez Mountains.*

③ kids Museum of Natural History. Nature lovers should stop at this Spanish mission–style complex full of fine displays on local animal life, especially birds, insects, and mammals, as well as prehistoric fossils (be sure to check out the dwarf mammoths). The biggest attraction is the outdoor 72-foot-long skeleton of a blue whale. There's also a planetarium and an informative exhibit on native Chumash life, including an excellent collection of Chumash basketry. ⏱ 40 min. 2559 Puesta del Sol. ☎ 805/682-4711. www.sbnature.org. Admission $10 adults, $7 seniors and kids 13–17, $6 kids 3–12, free for kids 2 & under. Daily 10am–5pm.

④ ★ County Courthouse. Built in 1929 in the Spanish-Moorish style, this National Historic Landmark features a grand archway, turrets, wrought-iron balconies, mosaic tiles, hand-carved doors, hand-painted ceilings, striking murals that illustrate the history of the land, and a grassy sunken garden. At the top of the 85-foot El Mirador clock tower, you can admire magnificent views of the mountains, coastline, and the sea of red-tile roofs. ⏱ 45 min. 1100 Anacapa St. ☎ 805/962-6464. www. santabarbaracourthouse.org. Free admission. Free guided tours Mon–Tues & Fri at 10:30am, Mon–Sat at 2pm. Courthouse Mon–Fri 8am–5pm, Sat–Sun 10am–4:30pm.

⑤ State Street. The town's main drag is populated by restaurants, loud bars, movie theaters, art galleries, and countless shops selling souvenir trinkets to high-end fashion. State St., from Victoria St. to the beach.

⑥ ★ Santa Barbara Museum of Art. This small but excellent museum boasts an eclectic permanent collection featuring classical antiquities; 19th- and 20th-century paintings; contemporary Latin American art; photography; and most impressively, Asian art from India, Tibet, China, Japan, and Southeast Asia. ⏱ 1 hr. 1130 State St. ☎ 805/963-4364. www. sbmuseart.org. Admission $9 adults; $6 seniors, students, and kids 6–17; free for kids 5 & under; free for all Sun. Tues–Sun 11am–5pm.

⑦ Casa de la Guerra. It's all too easy to overlook this city and state landmark located just off State Street near the Paseo Nuevo mall. The adobe home was built in the 1820s by the fifth Presidio comandante, José de la Guerra

(1779–1858). Following the city's devastating earthquake in 1925, the Casa served as a model of style and architecture for the city's rebuilding process. ⏱ 20 min. 15 E. De la Guerra St., Santa Barbara. ☎ 805/965-0093. www.sbthp.org. Admission (includes admission to El Presidio, see below) $5 adults, free for kids 16 & under. Sat–Sun noon–4pm.

⑧ ★ El Presidio de Santa Barbara. The last of four Spanish military outposts built in California was founded on this site in 1782. Over the years only two buildings have survived the earthquakes and downtown expansion: El Cuartel, the second-oldest adobe building in the state, and Canedo Adobe, a remnant of the barracks. The other standing structures, including the chapel, bell tower, and padres' quarters, were fastidiously reconstructed after 30 years of research and archaeological excavations. ⏱ 30 min. 123 E. Canon Perdido St. ☎ 805/965-0093. www.sbthp.org. Admission (includes admission to Casa de la Guerra, see above) $5 adults, free for kids 16 & under. Daily 10:30am–4:30pm.

⑨ ★ Santa Barbara Historical Museum. This first-rate museum traces the vibrant history of Santa Barbara from the early Chumash, through the Spanish explorers and Mexican settlers, American acquisition, and the ruinous 1925 earthquake, which ultimately paved the way for the town to reinvent itself. ⏱ 30 min. 136 E. De la Guerra St. ☎ 805/966-1601. www.santabarbaramuseum.com. Free admission, donations appreciated. Tues–Sat 10am–5pm; Sun noon–5pm.

Start Day 2 at

⑩ ☕ ★ Lilly's Tacos. This barebones taco joint serves them fast, cheap and seriously tasty. I put my money on the beef and marinated pork, but true taco connoisseurs opt for the cow eye—chopped, cooked and steamed. If you want to participate in the town's vigorous ongoing "best taco" debate, also try the favorite of the late Julia Child, **La Super-Rica Taqueria** (p. 387). 310 Chapala St. ☎ 805/966-9180. www.lillystacos.com. Tacos $1.40. AE, MC, V. Lunch & dinner Wed–Mon.

> Get into the spin along State Street, where clubs and cafes keep things hopping into the night.

⑪ ★★ kids Santa Barbara Zoo. Considered one of the best small zoos in the country, this zoo presents 500 animals (160 different species) on 30 acres of botanic gardens overlooking the Pacific Ocean. Exhibits include the popular Humboldt penguins and several endangered species, such as Asian elephants, snow leopards, white-handed gibbons, and western lowland gorillas. ⏱ 1 hr. 500 Niños Dr. ☎ 805/962-5339. www.sbzoo.org. Admission $12 adults, $10 seniors and kids 2–12, free for kids 1 & under. Daily 10am–5pm.

Getting Around

The electric **Downtown-Waterfront Shuttle** (☎ 805/963-3366; www.sbmtd.gov) is a handy way to cruise around town. The downtown shuttle runs along State Street from Sota Street to Stearns Wharf every 15 minutes (every 10 min. in summer) from 10am to 6pm. The waterfront shuttle runs along Cabrillo Boulevard from the harbor to the zoo every 30 minutes (every 15 min. in summer) from 10am to 6pm. The fare is 25¢.

> Like the real dolphins that frequent the waters here, this bronze trio near Stearns Wharf arcs in a playful jump.

⑫ Stearns Wharf. The longest and oldest working wooden wharf in California is located at the very bottom of State Street (look for the statue of three dolphins), and reels in five million visitors a year. Eat, shop, go pier fishing, or visit the **Ty Warner Sea Center,** full of interactive exhibits on marine education, the most entertaining being the live shark touch pool. ⏱ 45 min. End of State St. www.stearnswharf. org. Ty Warner Sea Center, 211 Stearns Wharf. ☎ 805/962-2526. www.sbnature.org. Admission $8 adults, $7 seniors and kids 13–17, $5 kids 2–12, free for kids 1 & under. Daily 10am–5pm.

⑬ kids Santa Barbara Maritime Museum. Occupying an old navy training facility in the harbor, this hands-on museum explores Santa Barbara's seafaring history, offering exhibits on shipwrecks, whaling, surfing, oil drilling, environmentalism, the Channel Islands, andthe coast's first settlers some 10,000 years ago, the Chumash Indians. Check out the 23-foot wooden tomol, a Chumash canoe used to cross from Santa Barbara to the Channel Islands. Kids will want to peek through an operating periscope, and try to reel in the big one on the sport-fishing simulator. ⏱ 30 min. 113 Harbor Way, Ste. 190. ☎ 805/962-8404. www.sbmm.org. Admission $7 adults; $4 seniors, students, and kids 6–17; $2 kids 1–5; free for kids under 1. Thurs–Tues 10am–6pm.

⑭ ★ Santa Barbara Sailing Center. Sail into the Santa Barbara Channel aboard the 50-foot catamaran, the *Double Dolphin*, which offers several different cruises: coastal, sunset, dinner, and whale-watching (the Pacific gray whale or the less-common blue whale, one of Earth's largest animals). Private charters and small boat and kayak rentals are also available. ⏱ 2–2½ hr. 133 Harbor Way. ☎ 805/962-2826. www.sbsail.com. Cruises $20–$30 adults, $10 kids. Fall & winter daily 9am–5pm; spring & summer daily 9am–6pm.

Old Spanish Days

Every August Santa Barbara proudly celebrates its Spanish heritage with Old Spanish Days (www.oldspanishdays-fiesta.org), a cultural tradition dating back 85 years. Also called Fiesta, the celebration includes several days of parades, arts and crafts displays, authentic eats, flamenco music, colorful dancing, horse shows, and rodeos.

Santa Barbara Beaches & Parks A to Z

★★ **Arroyo Burro Beach.** This slightly out-of-the-way beach, called Hendry Beach by locals, boasts a small sandy stretch backed against rugged cliffs (from which you'll often see fearless paragliders taking flight). It also has a restaurant, the Boat House; a creek to explore; and an area for dogs to romp off leash. Cliff Dr., ⅛ miles W. of Las Positas Rd. Daily 8am–sunset.

★ **Butterfly Beach.** This lovely, low-key beach across from the Four Seasons is big with locals, but not so big on amenities, which is fine because it probably helps keep the crowds at bay. The best feature: the beach faces slightly to the west, allowing for gorgeous sunsets over the water. Olive Mill Rd., at Channel Dr., Montecito. Daily sunrise–sunset.

★ kids **Chase Palm Park.** This long, narrow, grassy park bordering East Beach features an antique carousel and a playground built like a shipwreck. Both sides of E. Cabrillo Blvd., next to East Beach. Daily sunrise–10pm.

Douglas Family Preserve. Saved from development by actors Kirk and Michael Douglas, these 70 woodland acres sit atop a 150-foot-high mesa with views of Arroyo Burro Beach below and the Channel Islands in the distance. 2551 Medcliff Rd. (at Selrose Lane). Daily sunrise–10pm.

★★ **East Beach.** Santa Barbara's best all-around beach has a wide, sandy beach with volleyball courts, a rollerblading path, picnic areas, a playground, and restrooms, all hemmed in by a green lawn under swaying palm trees. It's also one of the most accessible, located across from the zoo and stretching all the way to the pier. East of Stearns Wharf. Sunrise–10pm.

★ **Leadbetter Beach.** Between Santa Barbara Harbor and Santa Barbara Point, this always-active beach is crawling with surfers, windsurfers, sailboaters, swimmers, and families enjoying the grassy picnic area. Shoreline Dr. at Loma Alta Dr. Daily sunrise–10pm.

> *It's not a stretch to say that East Beach epitomizes Santa Barbara, with volleyball courts, rollerblading, palm trees, and room to run.*

Shoreline Park. This manicured grassy hilltop is the perfect place to whale-watch, fly kites, or picnic. Wooden steps lead down to Mesa Beach, accessible during low tide only. Shoreline Dr. San Rafael Ave & La Marina Dr. Daily sunrise–10pm.

West Beach. This accessible sandy beach is good for launching kayaks or watching the boats drift in and out of the harbor. It also plays host to an AVP Pro Volleyball Tournament and an annual music festival. West of Stearns Wharf. Daily sunrise–10pm.

Hit the Links

The challenging and picturesque ★ **Sandpiper Golf Course**, 7925 Hollister Ave. (☎ 805/ 968-1541; www.sandpipergolf.com), is known as one of the best public golf courses in the country. Perched above the ocean, the course spreads 18 holes across 7,000 yards. Greens fees run up to $159 at peak times.

Where to Stay

> *Shangri-La on the American Riviera—the rooftop pool at the Canary Hotel gets it right.*

★★ **Canary Hotel** DOWNTOWN
The Spanish island decor is breezy and chic, and the hotel's central location, tucked just off State Street, is ideal. The rooftop pool area, complete with Jacuzzi and fireplace, provides 360-degree views of the town's fabled red-tiled roofs, the Santa Ynez mountains, and the shimmering Pacific Ocean. 31 W. Carrillo Dr. ☎ 877/468-3515. www.canarysantabarbara. com. 97 units. Doubles $280–$580. AE, MC, V.

★★★ **Four Seasons Biltmore Santa Barbara**
AROUND TOWN Overlooking the beautiful and secluded Butterfly Beach, with grand Spanish-colonial architecture, and lush gardens fringed by palms, this luxury hotel has been Santa Barbara's gold standard for beachside elegance since its opening in 1927. The hotel's restaurant, Bella Vista, hosts a classy Sunday brunch, adored by locals and day-tripping Angelenos. 1260 Channel Dr. ☎ 800/819-5053 or 805/969-2261. www.fourseasons.com/santabarbara. 207 units. Doubles $525–$1,800. AE, DC, MC, V.

★ **Hotel Oceana** AROUND TOWN
This oceanfront hotel (or perhaps, more ac-curately motel complex) has a mission-style exterior and simple, bright, and cheery rooms. Ceiling fans and ocean breezes cover for the lack of air-conditioning with mixed results. 202 W. Cabrillo Blvd. ☎ 800/965-9776 or 805/965-4577. www.hoteloceana.com. 122 units. Doubles $195–$350. AE, DC, DISC, MC, V.

★ **Motel 6** AROUND TOWN
This is the original Motel 6 that opened in 1962 (not that you go to Motel 6 for history, or for unnecessary extras, like linens with a high thread count). If you want dirt-cheap (by Santa Barbara standards), squeaky clean, and a minute walk to the beach, this is the best option. Book early. 443 Corona Del Mar. ☎ 805/564-1392. www.motel6.com. 51 units. Doubles $74–$114. AE, DC, DISC, MC, V.

★★★ **San Ysidro Ranch** MONTECITO
Routinely rated among America's finest hotels, this romantic retreat set in the foothills of the Santa Ynez offers secluded rooms with stone fireplaces and private patios. The idyllic setting among flowering gardens, in-room spa services, and the Stonehouse Restaurant make it hard for guests to leave the grounds. The hotel prides itself on its "discreet pampering," making it a favorite of celebrities and dignitaries since the 1930s. 900 San Ysidro Lane. ☎ 805/565-1700. www.sanysidroranch.com. 41 units. Doubles from $685; cottages from $1,195. AE, MC, V.

★★★ **Simpson House** DOWNTOWN
A beautiful 1874 Victorian in a garden setting, this luxurious B&B charms with its period de-tails, attentive staff, and extras like afternoon hors d'oeuvres and wine and loaner bikes. 121 E. Arrellaga St. ☎ 800/676-1280 or 805/963-7067. www.simpsonhouseinn.com. 15 units. Doubles $235–$615 w/breakfast. AE, DISC, MC, V.

Where to Dine

★ **Arigato** *JAPANESE*
Expect a wait at this popular sushi joint with killer rolls and a warm, lively ambience. 1225 State St. ☎ 805/965-6704. Reservations not accepted. Sushi rolls $9–$15. AE, MC, V. Dinner daily.

★★ **Bouchon** *CALIFORNIAN*
For a quintessential Central Coast dining experience, try this cozy, romantic spot whose menu changes with the seasons, but always offers a sophisticated preparation of the freshest local ingredients—organic whenever possible. Signature dishes include seared duck breast with confit of duck thigh, and for dessert, chocolate molten lava cake. The wine list offers over 100 wines from Santa Barbara County. 9 W. Victoria St. ☎ 805/730-1160. Reservations recommended. Entrees $28–$38. AE, DC, MC, V. Dinner daily.

★★ **kids** **Brophy Brothers** *SEAFOOD*
It can be noisy and crowded, with sometimes indifferent service, but you're here for the superfresh seafood, consistently voted by locals as the best in Santa Barbara. Ask for an outdoor table to savor the harbor views, but if the wait is killing you, don't hesitate to plop down at the bar. Some favorites include the clam chowder, the beer-boiled shrimp, and the garlic-baked clams. In the Waterfront Center, 119 Harbor Way. ☎ 805/966-4418. Reservations not accepted. Entrees $9–$19. AE, MC, V. Lunch & dinner daily.

★ **Hungry Cat** *SEAFOOD*
Smaller, warmer, and more intimate than the original Hungry Cat in Hollywood, this upscale seafood restaurant, from the formidable husband and wife team of David Lenz and Suzanne Goin, showcases a range of local catches, from sea bass to urchin. There's also a raw bar and cocktails with fruit obtained fresh from the farmers market. 1134 Chapala St. ☎ 805/884-4701. www.thehungrycat.com. Reservations not accepted. Entrees $16–$25. AE, MC, V. Lunch & dinner Tues–Sun; brunch Sun.

> Cozy up to an incredible meal at Bouchon, where ultra-fresh ingredients pair up with an impressive selection of local wines.

★ **La Super-Rica Taqueria** *MEXICAN*
Rarely do little *taquerías* create this much hoopla. Blame it on Julia Child, who used to queue up for her favorite tacos in town. Authentic, spicy, and cheap—everything is delicious, so feel free to gamble on the daily specials even if you trip on the pronunciation. 622 N. Milpas St. ☎ 805/963-4940. Most items $4–$10. Cash only. Lunch & dinner Thurs–Tues.

★★ **kids** **Tupelo Junction Café** *SOUTHERN*
This homey, Southern-style restaurant is best known for its knockout brunch, with such options as cinnamon apple beignets, Dungeness crab cake over roasted potatoes with avocado salsa and poached eggs, and my favorite—pumpkin oatmeal waffle with caramelized bananas and candied pecans. 1218 State St. ☎ 805/099-3100. Entrees $6–$33. AE, MC, V. Breakfast, lunch & dinner daily.

Cambria

Cambria sprung to life in the 1860s as a mining and lumber town. It's now a tourist-driven artists' colony and makes a good seaside base while exploring Hearst Castle, the Piedras Blancas elephant seals, or the Paso Robles wine region.

> *An eccentric comment on the excess of nearby Hearst Castle, Nitt Witt Ridge is built of cast-offs and trash.*

START Main Street. Cambria is about 6 miles south of San Simeon and 22 miles west of Paso Robles.

1 ★ **Main Street Shopping.** Cambria's main thoroughfare is divided into two sections: the newer West Village, and the more historic East Village, lined with Victorian buildings from the 1870s. Browse antiques shops, independent boutiques, and galleries, most specializing in locally crafted glass art, sculpture, and jewelry. Two favorites tucked away on Burton Drive are **Seekers Glass Gallery,** 4090 Burton Dr. (☎ 805/927-3447; www.seekersglass.com) and **Moonstones Craft Gallery,** 4070 Burton Dr. (☎ 805/927-3447; www.moonstones.com). ⏱ 1 hr.

2 ★ **Nitt Witt Ridge.** Art Beal's castle of junk, a State Historic Landmark, makes a fascinating juxtaposition with another obsessively built estate a few miles north, Hearst Castle (p. 354, **1**). For 50 years beginning in 1928, Beal, town trash hauler and poet, clawed at the hillside with a pick and shovel, stitching together a ramshackle palace with beer cans, driftwood, car rims, abalone shells, toilet seats, and rumor has it, some construction scraps from Hearst Castle. An engrossing tour makes you wonder if the penniless Beal and all-mighty Hearst were so different after all. ⏱ 1 hr. 881 Hillcrest Dr. ☎ 805/927-2690. Tours $10 adults, $5 kids. Admission by tour only, daily 10am–4pm; call for appointment.

3 ★ **Linn's Fruit Bin Original Farmhouse.** There's a cluster of Linn shops along Main Street, but take a scenic jaunt up a country road to the original location to taste the locally

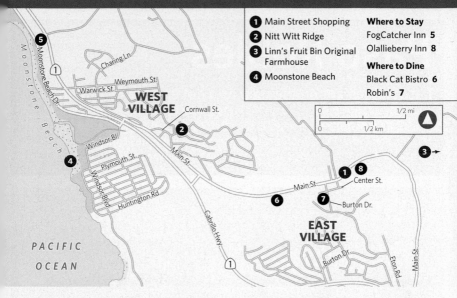

1 Main Street Shopping	**Where to Stay**
2 Nitt Witt Ridge	FogCatcher Inn **5**
3 Linn's Fruit Bin Original Farmhouse	Olallieberry Inn **8**
4 Moonstone Beach	**Where to Dine**
	Black Cat Bistro **6**
	Robin's **7**

grown specialty known as the olallieberry—the sweet, tart offspring of a blackberry, raspberry, and dewberry. Enjoy a slice a pie baked with "more fruit, less sugar." ⏱ 30 min. 6275 Santa Rosa Creek Rd. ☎ 805/927-8134. Daily 10am–5pm.

4 ★★ **Moonstone Beach.** Take a sunset stroll along the wooden boardwalk atop the ocean bluffs with windswept cypress and pines. Listen to the waves crash the rugged shoreline and watch for sea lions, sea otters, and migrating California gray whales. Shuffle down to the beach below where unspoiled coves provide excellent rock hunting and tidepooling. ⏱ 1½ hr. Btw Leffingwell Landing & Santa Rosa Creek.

Where to Stay & Dine

★ **Black Cat Bistro** *AMERICAN*
The staff at this intimate restaurant takes pleasure in pairing the right wine with sophisticated, well-prepared dishes like seared sea scallops with corn pudding or braised short ribs. 1602 Main St. ☎ 805/927-1600. www.black catbistro.com. Reservations recommended. Entrees $17–$36. MC, V. Dinner Thurs–Mon.

★ **FogCatcher Inn**
An excellent choice among the row of motels on Moonstone Beach Drive. Some rooms have intoxicating ocean views, some not so much, and the price varies accordingly. Amenities include free Wi-Fi, heated outdoor pool and hot tub, and gas fireplaces in every room. 6400 Moonstone Beach Dr. ☎ 805/927-1400. www.fogcatcherinn.com. 60 units. Doubles $170–$280 w/breakfast. AE, DISC, MC, V.

★★ **Olallieberry Inn**
A historic home built in 1873 along the Santa Rosa Creek, this cute-as-pie B&B delights guests with wine and hors d'oeuvres in the evening and a gourmet breakfast (olallieberry stuffed French toast!) in the morn. 2476 Main St. ☎ 805/927-3222. www.olallieberry.com. 9 units. Doubles $135–$200 w/breakfast. AE, MC, V.

★ **Robin's** *INTERNATIONAL*
In a charming Craftsman with a patio and flowery garden, this local favorite presents a multiethnic menu of meat, fish, and especially tasty vegetarian options. 4095 Burton Dr. ☎ 805/927-5007. www.robinsrestaurant.com. Reservations recommended. Entrees $9–$32. MC, V. Lunch & dinner daily; brunch Sun.

Paso Robles

Paso Robles got on the map as a hot springs retreat in the mid–19th century, but these days it's getting back to its deeper roots. Wine grapes were first planted locally in the 1790s by the padres at Mission San Miguel, and today Paso Robles is the fastest-growing wine region in the state, with more than 180 wineries across 26,000 acres of vineyards.

> *A former workhorse finds a final resting spot in a field along scenic Highway 46.*

START Downtown. Paso Robles is about 200 miles from San Francisco and Los Angeles and 30 miles from San Luis Obispo.

❶ ★★ **Historic Downtown.** City Park, with its 5 acres of shady oaks, gazebo, library, and playground, functions as the town square and is often abuzz with a community event: biweekly farmers markets, concerts, holiday celebrations, and festivals like the **Paso Robles Wine Festival** in late May. Stroll the surrounding blocks whose historic buildings, most dating to the 1870s, are filled with boutiques, high-quality restaurants, and a dozen wine-tasting rooms. ⏲ 1½ hr.

❷ ★ **Mission San Miguel.** Only a few years ago this 1818 mission was listed among the country's most endangered historic sites after being nearly destroyed by a 6.5 magnitude earthquake in 2003 (one of several

debilitating quakes over the years). It reopened in late 2009 following a costly restoration. Particularly arresting are the colorful murals painted on the adobe walls by the native Salinan people nearly 2 centuries ago. ⏲ 45 min. 775 Mission St. ☎ 805/467-2131. www.missionsanmiguel.org. Free admission, $2-$5 donation suggested. Daily 10am–4:30pm.

❸ **James Dean Memorial Junction.** The 30-mile stretch of Hwy. 46 from Paso to Cholame used to be known as Blood Alley for its high rate of accidents, but James Dean fans may be tempted to make the trek (rest assured, it's much safer now) out to the junction with Hwy. 41. In 1955 the 24-year-old star was killed when his Porsche Spyder was struck by an oncoming vehicle. A stainless steel memorial monument, strangely poignant, sits in the parking lot of the Jack Ranch Café. ⏲ 20 min. www.jamesdeanmemorialjunction.com.

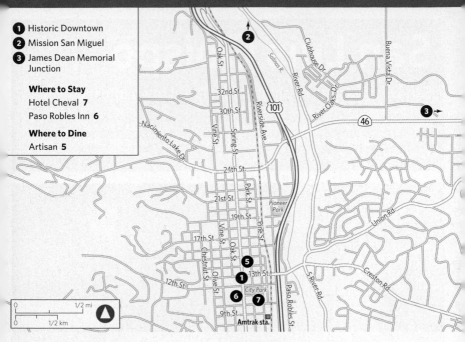

Where to Stay & Dine

★★ Artisan AMERICAN

Big-city culinary chops in a small town setting. Standouts from the evolving menu include fried calamari, gazpacho, and Hearst Ranch flatiron steak. 1401 Park St. ☎ 805/237-8084. www.artisanpasorobles.com. Entrees $12–$28. AE, MC, V. Lunch Mon–Sat; dinner daily; brunch Sun.

★★ Hotel Cheval

The luxe rooms of this equestrian-themed boutique hotel circle a charming courtyard, perfect for relaxing by the outdoor fireplaces after sampling Paso wines at the Pony Club, the hotel's horseshoe-shaped wine bar. 1021 Pine St. ☎ 805/226-9995. www.hotelcheval. com. 16 units. Doubles $242–$342 w/breakfast. AE, MC, V.

★ Paso Robles Inn

At this historic hotel (the earliest incarnation was built in 1864 around the natural hot springs), you can splurge on a deluxe room featuring a private hot springs tub (some

> Making magic on a plate, the Kobayashi brothers imbue Artisan with incredible taste and style.

are on the balcony). The room decor may be slightly faded, but the hotel's manicured grounds and its perfect location, on the edge of town square, compensate. 1101 Spring St. ☎ 805/238-2660. www.pasoroblesinn.com. 98 units. Doubles $109–$239. AE, MC, V.

San Luis Obispo

San Luis Obispo is a small agricultural town infused with youthful vigor from the local California Polytechnic State University. Located between the Paso Robles and Santa Barbara wine regions and accessible to gorgeous beaches and coastal hikes, San Luis Obispo makes an ideal base for exploring the Central Coast.

> *Franciscan monks, led by Father Junipero Serra, created the striking Mission San Luis Obispo in 1772.*

START **Mission San Luis Obispo. The mission is in the heart of downtown, located at the junction of Hwy. 1 and U.S. 101. San Luis Obispo is 190 miles north of Los Angeles.**

❶ ★ **Mission San Luis Obispo.** Father Junípero Serra founded his fifth Franciscan mission in 1772 on the banks of the San Luis Obispo Creek in hopes of hunting enough California grizzly bears in the area (plenty then, zero now) to provide meat for his other starving missions. Of architectural note: This was the first mission to adopt the now-iconic red-tile roof after the thatched roof was repeatedly torched by hostile natives. A small museum occupies the former padres' quarters and includes information and artifacts from both the Spanish settlers and the Chumash. The mission is part of ★ **Mission Plaza,** which functions as the town square, hosting events like Concerts in the Plaza—free musical

performances every Friday night in the summer. Lining the plaza is a shady, lush creekside area where kids love to tiptoe in the shallow water. ◷ 1 hr. 751 Palm St. ☎ 805/781-8220. www.missionsanluisobispo.org. Free admission, donations requested. Daily 9am–5pm.

❷ **San Luis Obispo County Historical Museum.** Housed in the Carnegie Library building, an elegant sandstone built in 1905, this museum offers a glimpse of local history through old photographs and rotating exhibits. ◷ 20 min. 696 Monterey St. ☎ 805/543-0638. www.slochs.org. Free admission. Wed–Sun 10am–4pm.

❸ **Historic Walking Tour.** Pick up a map for a self-guided walking tour of the town's historic buildings, including the **Ah Louis Store** at 800 Palm St., erected in 1874 as the center for the town's burgeoning Chinese community

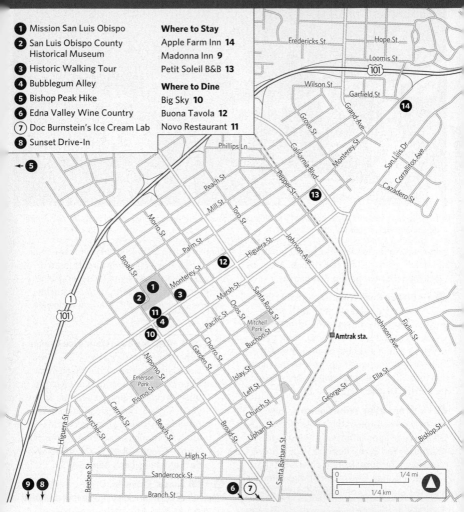

1. Mission San Luis Obispo
2. San Luis Obispo County Historical Museum
3. Historic Walking Tour
4. Bubblegum Alley
5. Bishop Peak Hike
6. Edna Valley Wine Country
7. Doc Burnstein's Ice Cream Lab
8. Sunset Drive-In

Where to Stay
Apple Farm Inn **14**
Madonna Inn **9**
Petit Soleil B&B **13**

Where to Dine
Big Sky **10**
Buona Tavola **12**
Novo Restaurant **11**

of railroad laborers, and surprisingly, a minor gem from Frank Lloyd Wright—a medical office at 1106 Pacific St. ⏱ 30 min. Start at Visitor Center, 1039 Chorro St. ☎ 805/781/2651. www. visitslo.com.

④ ★ **Bubblegum Alley.** For around 50 years, folks (usually college kids from Cal Poly) have been "decorating" the brick walls of this alleyway with blobs of chewed gum. Consider it an ongoing, ever-changing community project on a 15-by-70-foot canvas where you might find declarations of love, fraternity letters, or a goopy portrait. The city has attempted to scrub the walls afresh a few times over the years, but the wads have always returned,

> *Thumb through history at the San Luis Obispo County Historical Society, home to vintage photographs and memorabilia.*

> *Early evening strollers check out what's fresh and delicious or just entertaining at San Luis Obispo's Thursday night farmers' market.*

proving the alley to be a sticky tradition. Look, but definitely don't touch. ⊕ 15 min. **Alleyway off Higuera St. btw. Garden & Broad sts.**

5 ★★ **Bishop Peak Hike.** Explore this 20-million-year-old volcanic peak with a moderately strenuous 4.5-mile round-trip hike, which takes you to the rocky summit, the highest point in all of the Nine Sisters. For a shorter, less dramatic hike, bear to the right and follow the Felsman Loop. ⊕ 2 hr. **Start at the Patricia Dr. trail head.**

6 ★★ **Edna Valley Wine Country.** Take a leisurely drive through this southern San Luis Obispo wine appellation only minutes from downtown San Luis. The Edna Valley, only 5 miles from the coast, is far cooler than the Paso Robles area, and is sometimes referred to as the "Burgundy of the Pacific" for its concentration of chardonnay and pinot noir vineyards. Traveling along Orcutt Road or Hwy. 227, you'll see signs for several wine-tasting rooms. For information on specific wineries, see p. 366. ⊕ 1½ hr. www.slowine.com.

7 🍦 ★★ kids **Doc Burnstein's Ice Cream Lab.** When traveling Hwy. 227—especially before, after, or during an Edna Valley excursion—continue on to the quaint village of Arroyo Grande, where you'll find this old-fashioned ice cream parlor with handcrafted cold treats and a loopy, toy train theme. **114 W. Branch Dr., Arroyo Grande.** ☎ 805/474-4068. www.docburnsteins.com. Items $4-$9.

8 ★ kids **Sunset Drive-In.** Drive-ins are a dying breed all over America, so movie lovers should jump at the chance to catch a flick (or two, since it's always a double feature) at this family-owned favorite, built in 1950. It ain't fancy, but there's a nostalgic charm that no modern-day megaplex can match. And it's a cheap way to entertain a carload of kids. **255 Elks Lane.** ☎ 805/544-4475. www.rodkey.net. Double feature $6 adults, $2 kids 5-11, free for kids 4 & under.

Farmers' Market

Every Thursday night between 6pm and 9pm, 4 blocks of Higuera Street (btw. Osos and Nipomo sts.) are blocked off for the region's biggest farmers market with a lively street-fair atmosphere. Peruse fresh produce from nearby farms in Edna and Osos valleys, sample barbecued tri-tip or hand-pressed cider, shop for nuts and flowers, join a political movement, or just enjoy the street entertainment—a variety of local musicians, mimes, and hand-puppet shows. Some summer nights can draw upwards of 20,000 people.

Getting Around

For a mere quarter, catch a ride on the Old SLO Trolley that loops conveniently through downtown every 15 minutes. It runs Thursday 3:30pm to 9pm, Friday and Saturday noon to 9pm, and Sunday noon to 5:30pm.

Where to Stay & Dine

> Kitschy cool, the themed rooms and restaurants at the Madonna Inn are so bad they're great.

★ Apple Farm Inn

The operating word for this hotel is "sweet," from its decor, which it calls country Victorian, to its service. The Apple Farm complex—the inn; Trellis Court, a motel with smaller, cheaper rooms; and the popular, namesake restaurant—is conveniently accessible from U.S. 101. 2015 Monterey St. ☎ 805/544-2040. www.applefarm.com. 104 units. Doubles $109–$329. AE, DISC, MC, V.

★ kids Big Sky AMERICAN

Filled with locals and the easy thrum of San Luis life, this casual restaurant fills its menu with international flavors: Caribbean, Cajun, Southwestern, and Mediterranean. Breakfast is especially popular thanks to dishes like Devil's Mess (spicy scrambled eggs), Mexican-style posole, and beignets. 1121 Broad St. ☎ 805/545-5401. www.bigskycafe.com. Entrees $5–$18. AE, MC, V. Breakfast, lunch & dinner daily.

★ Buona Tavola ITALIAN

Savor the homemade pasta at this authentic Italian restaurant with an impressive wine list and an inviting garden patio. Their best-prepared dish is tortellini stuffed with pumpkin and ricotta cheese in a sage and mascarpone cheese sauce. 1037 Monterey St. ☎ 805/ 545-8000. www.btslo.com. Reservations recommended. Entrees $9–$34. AE, DISC, MC, V. Lunch Mon–Fri; dinner daily.

★★ Madonna Inn

Travelers seeking one-of-a-kind experiences, should check into this inn's one-of-a-kind rooms, including the Caveman, with rock walls and a waterfall shower; the Love Nest, with a hot-pink, shag-carpet spiral staircase; and the Buffalo Room, with an enormous mounted buffalo head and a tree-limbed, four-poster bed. If you can't manage a stay here, at least drop by the kitschtastic Gold Rush Steak House and Silver Bar cocktail lounge for a bite. 100 Madonna Rd. ☎ 805/543-3000. www.madonnainn.com. 104 units. Doubles $179–$269. AE, DISC, MC, V.

★★ Novo Restaurant INTERNATIONAL

You cannot beat the ambience at a table on the patio with views overlooking the lazy San Luis Creek and Mission Plaza through the trees. The eclectic menu—salads, stir-fry, tapas, curries, seafood—has something for everyone. 726 Higuera St. ☎ 805/543-3986. www.novorestaurant.com. Reservations recommended. Entrees $8–$18. AE, MC, V. Lunch & dinner daily; brunch Sun.

★ Petit Soleil Bed et Breakfast

What's essentially a motel lodge with a French-country makeover wins you over with its warmth and whimsy. There's wine tasting in the evening and complimentary bicycles to explore downtown. 1472 Monterey St. ☎ 805/549-0321. www.petitsoleilslo.com 15 units. Doubles $159–$219 w/breakfast. AE, DISC, MC, V.

Santa Ynez Valley

This beautiful Wine Country getaway, especially popular since *Sideways* hit theaters in 2004, is full of rolling hills of green vineyards, golden grazing pastures, small wineries, quaint restaurants, Spanish missions, and horse ranches.

> With windmills and fake wood storks perched on thatched rooftops, Solvang aims to mirror the town's Danish roots.

START Solvang. The Santa Ynez Valley, 30 miles north of Santa Barbara, is a triangle formed by U.S. 101, Hwy. 246, and Hwy. 154. Solvang lies 3 miles east of U.S. 101 on Hwy. 246. **TRIP LENGTH 30 miles.**

① Solvang. Solvang (Danish for "sunny field") bills itself as the "Danish Capital of America," and projects an admittedly Disneyfied version of a traditional Scandinavian village. Stroll among the windmills, kitschy shops, and bakeries peddling pastries like kringles, *kransekages,* and my favorite, *ebelskivers,* rounded puffs of pancake. The best bakery is ★ **Olsen's Danish Village Bakery,** 1529 Mission Dr. (☎ 805/688-6314; www.olsensdanishvillage bakery.com). To learn about Solvang's Danish heritage, drop by the ★ **Elverhoj Museum** in a pristine, handcrafted Danish-style farmhouse, 1624 Elvorhoy Way (☎ 805/686-1211; www.elverhoj.org; free admission, donations requested; Wed–Thurs 1–4pm, Fri–Sun noon–4pm). There's also the **Hans Christian Andersen Museum,** 1680 Mission Dr., upstairs at the Book Loft Building (☎ 805/688-2052; daily 10am–5pm), where you can learn about the Danish master of the fairy tale. ⏱ 1½ hr.

② ★ Los Olivos Tasting Room & Wine Shop. The staff here knows their stuff, and you can sample a variety of excellent wines from several smaller vintners. If your palette is piqued, try another along the block, or better yet, pick up a Santa Ynez wine-tasting map (or go to www.sbcountywines.com) and head into the countryside. For Santa Ynez winery recommendations, see p. 366. ⏱ 40 min. 2905 Grand Ave., Los Olivos. ☎ 805/688-7406. Tastings $10. Daily 11am–5pm.

③ ★ La Purisima Mission State Historic Park. La Purisima Mission is the most evocative of mission life in the 1820s, the peak of the Spanish missions. The 2,000-acre park boasts the only complete mission complex in California, with 10 of the original buildings fully restored and furnished; even the original aqueduct system has been recreated. ⏱ 1½ hr. 2295 Purisima Rd., Lompoc. ☎ 805/733-3713. www.lapurisima mission.org. Admission $5 per vehicle. Tours free. Daily 9am–5pm. Tours daily 1pm.

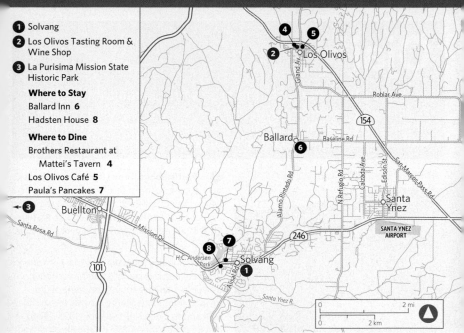

1. Solvang
2. Los Olivos Tasting Room & Wine Shop
3. La Purisima Mission State Historic Park

Where to Stay
Ballard Inn 6
Hadsten House 8

Where to Dine
Brothers Restaurant at
   Mattei's Tavern 4
Los Olivos Café 5
Paula's Pancakes 7

Where to Stay & Dine

★★ **Ballard Inn** BALLARD
A wraparound porch with wicker rockers, a cozy restaurant, weekend wine tasting, relentless hospitality, and warm, country-style guest rooms—this nabs my vote for the most charming B&B in the Santa Ynez Valley. 2436 Baseline Ave. ☎ 805/688-7770. www.ballard inn.com. 15 units. Doubles $245–$315 w/breakfast. AE, MC, V.

★★ **Brothers Restaurant at Mattei's Tavern**
LOS OLIVOS AMERICAN At this former stage-coach stop, built in 1886, settle into a slow-roasted prime rib or rack of lamb, then chase it with a sinful dessert like mud pie with Kahlúa-caramel sauce. 2350 Railway Ave. (near Grand Ave. & Hwy. 154). ☎ 805/688-4820. www.matteistavern.com. Reservations recommended. Entrees $18–$44. AE, MC, V. Dinner daily.

Hadsten House SOLVANG
Rooms have a sleek, vaguely European decor and upscale amenities. There's also a spa and a indoor heated pool. 1450 Mission Dr. ☎ 800/457-5473. www.hadstenhouse.com. 75 units. Doubles $164–$254 w/breakfast. AE, MC, V.

★ **Los Olivos Café** LOS OLIVOS CALIFORNIAN/MEDITERRANEAN Seen in *Sideways*, this restaurant presents seasonal Mediterranean cuisine (spinach gnocchi, paella, rustic pizzas) and a superb wine list in a casually elegant setting. The lovely wisteria-covered patio is perfect for a sunny lunch. 2879 Grand Ave. ☎ 805/688-7265. www.losolivoscafe.com. Entrees $12–$29. AE, DISC, MC, V. Lunch, dinner & wine tasting daily.

★ **kids Paula's Pancakes** SOLVANG AMERICAN/DANISH Sure, the place may be touristy and crowded, but the Danish pancakes—thin and wide, preferably topped with fresh strawberries—make it more than worth your while. 1531 Mission Dr. ☎ 805/688-2867. Entrees $10 & under. AE, DC, MC, V. Breakfast & lunch daily.

Ojai

Ever since the Chumash, the area's first inhabitants, called it *Ojai*, meaning "valley of the moon," this land has been known for its beauty and metaphysical pull. In 1937, the valley shined in the part of Shangri-La, the mythical utopia, in Frank Capra's film *Lost Horizon*.

> Framed by the dramatic Toga Toga Mountains, the town of Ojai feels like an inside secret for people in the know.

START The Downtown Arcade on Ojai Ave. Ojai is 35 miles south of Santa Barbara (take Hwy. 150, which becomes Ojai Ave., the town's main drag) and 84 miles north of Los Angeles.

1 ★ **Downtown Arcade.** The Spanish-style arcade built in 1917 houses many boutiques, galleries, and restaurants—the perfect introduction to Ojai's small-town charms. Across the street is the pergola-lined Libbey Park and the post office's striking campanile. ⏲ 1 hr. Ojai Ave., btw. Signal & Montgomery sts.

2 ★ **Bart's Books.** Browse the nooks of books on the shady patio of this local institution, which likes to call itself the "world's greatest outdoor bookstore." ⏲ 45 min. 302 W. Matilija St. ☎ 805/646-3755. www.bartsbooksojai.com. Daily 9:30am–sunset.

3 ★ **Ojai Valley Museum.** The museum offers excellent displays on early Chumash culture, as well as changing exhibits on some of the town's famous inhabitants, such as the spiritual philosopher Jiddu Krishnamurti (1895–1986), and Beatrice Wood (1893–1998), the artist and potter called the "Mama of Dada." You can also find information on historical walking tours. ⏲ 45 min. 130 W. Ojai Ave. ☎ 805/640-1390. Admission $4 adults, $1 kids 6–18, free for kids 4 & under. www.ojaivalleymuseum.org. Thurs–Fri 1–4pm; Sat 10am–4pm; Sun noon–4pm.

4 ★ **kids Lake Casitas.** Host to the 1984 Olympic rowing and canoeing events, this placid 2,700-acre lake with 32 miles of shoreline offers great largemouth bass fishing, small motorboat rentals, and camping. There's a shoreside water park (Casitas Water Adventure $12 per person; $5 after 5pm; Sun–Thurs 11am–6pm, Fri–Sat 11am–7pm, closed in winter), an elaborate jungle gym in a pool that kiddies can't get enough of. ⏲ 2 hr. Hwy. 150, 3 miles west of the Hwy. 33 intersection. ☎ 805/649-2233. www.lakecasitas.info. Check the website for fishing, boating, and camping info.

5 ★★ **Meditation Mount.** In a serene garden setting overlooking the entire valley, observe Ojai's best-known attraction, the ★ **Pink Moment,** as the setting sun paints the Topa Topa bluffs in warm light causing the whole valley to radiate a faint, pinkish glow. ⏲ 1 hr. 10340 Reeves Rd. ☎ 805/646-5508. www.meditation.com. Free admission, donations accepted. Daily sunrise–sunset; office Mon–Fri 9am–5pm.

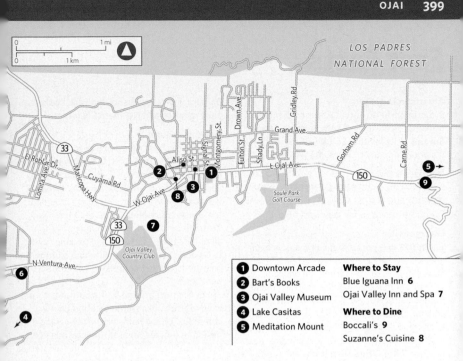

- 1 Downtown Arcade
- 2 Bart's Books
- 3 Ojai Valley Museum
- 4 Lake Casitas
- 5 Meditation Mount

Where to Stay
Blue Iguana Inn **6**
Ojai Valley Inn and Spa **7**

Where to Dine
Boccali's **9**
Suzanne's Cuisine **8**

Where to Stay & Dine

★ Blue Iguana Inn

Old mission-style architecture funked up with local artistic flair, including a blue iguana mosaic tile fountain, make this cozy inn a popular choice. Light sleepers may balk at the proximity to Hwy. 33, but overall a great value. 11794 N. Ventura Ave. ☎ 805/646-5277. www.blue iguanainn.com. 23 units. Doubles $119–$169. AE, DC, DISC, MC, V.

★★ kids Boccali's *ITALIAN*

This pizza and pasta house on the east side of town (skip the Oak View location) keeps it simple and delicious: excellent lasagna, fresh salad with tomatoes straight from the restaurant's own garden, and the best strawberry shortcake I've ever eaten. 3277 Ojai Ave. ☎ 805/646-6116. Entrees $9–$35. Cash only. Lunch & dinner Wed–Sun; dinner Mon–Tues.

★★★ kids Ojai Valley Inn and Spa

Many folks, especially luxury-seeking Angelenos, regard this historic resort—check out Wallace Neff's 1923 Spanish colonial–style clubhouse—as the reason to visit Ojai. The sumptuous grounds include an excellent golf course and tennis facilities, three swimming pools, an 800-acre ranch, and a world-class 31,000-square-foot spa. 905 Country Club Rd. ☎ 805/646-1111 or 888/697-8780. www.ojai resort.com. 308 units. Doubles $350–$600. AE, DC, DISC, MC, V.

★ Suzanne's Cuisine *CONTEMPORARY EUROPEAN*

A creative take on seasonal French-Italian cuisine, this mom and daughter operation is both homey and romantic—ask for a table on the lovely garden patio. 502 W. Ojai Ave. ☎ 805/640-1961. Reservations recommended. Entrees $9–$35. AE, DC, MC, V. Lunch & dinner Wed–Mon.

Fast Facts

American Express
In Santa Barbara, obtain America Express travel services at the **Santa Barbara Travel Bureau** at 1028 State St. (☎ 805/966-3166). It's open Monday to Friday 9am to 5pm.

Dentists & Doctors
For a dentist, call **1-800-DENTIST** (☎ 800/336-8422; www.1800dentist.com). For doctors, see "Emergencies," below.

Emergencies
Call ☎ **911** to report a fire, call the police, or get an ambulance anywhere in the United States. This is toll free from any phone.

For nonemergency police matters, in **Paso Robles** call ☎ 805/237-6464, in **San Luis Obispo** dial ☎ 805/781-7317, and in **Santa Barbara** call ☎ 805/897-2300.

In Paso Robles, you can seek medical assistance at **Twin Cities Hospital,** 1100 Las Tablas Rd., Templeton (☎ 805/434-3500; www.twincitieshospital.com). In San Luis Obispo, there's the **Sierra Vista Regional Center,** 1010 Murray Ave. (☎ 805/546-7600; www.sierra vistaregional.com). In Santa Barbara, head for **Cottage Hospital,** Bath and Pueblo sts. (☎ 805/682-7111; www.sbch.org).

Getting There
Many visitors access the Central Coast by driving up or down Hwy. 101 after flying into either Los Angeles (p. 494) or San Francisco (p. 128). It is possible to fly into the Santa Barbara Airport (SBA; ☎ 805/967-7111; www.flysba.com) or into the smaller San Luis Obispo County Regional Airport (SLO; ☎ 805/781-5205; www.sloairport.com); both airports have on-site car rentals.

If rail is more your speed, Amtrak (☎ 800/USA-RAIL (872-7245); www.amtrak.com) makes several stops along the Central Coast. Amtrak stations are located in Santa Barbara at 209 State St. (☎ 805/963-1015), in San Luis Obispo at 1011 Railroad Ave. (☎ 805/541-0505), and in Paso Robles at 800 Pine St. (no phone). The Pacific Surfliner connects Santa Barbara and San Luis Obispo to Los Angeles and San Diego. The Coast Starlight connects Santa Barbara, San Luis Obispo, and Paso Robles to San Francisco and Northern California.

Getting Around
Cars are the best mode of transportation within the Central Coast. **U.S. 101** is the main north–south artery connecting Paso Robles, San Luis Obispo, and Santa Barbara. **Hwy. 1** is slower, more scenic, and clings mostly to the coast, connecting Cambria, Morro Bay, Pismo Beach, and San Luis Obispo. Within all of these towns, traffic and parking tend to be quite manageable, although summer weekends can get congested with tourists and beachgoers.

For hopping around Santa Barbara, it's possible to use public transportation (www.sbmtd.gov), especially when staying and playing in the downtown area. Several bus lines branch out from the Transit Center located at 1020 Chapala St. Especially handy for tourists are the downtown and waterfront shuttles, electric open-air buses that run regularly along State Street and the waterfront, and a ride only costs a quarter each way. Also, there's a nifty website (www.santabarbara carfree.org) with information on how to enjoy Santa Barbara without a car.

The downtown areas of San Luis Obispo and Paso Robles are pedestrian friendly. For bus routes between San Luis Obispo and Paso Robles (as well as Morro Bay and Pismo Beach), visit www.slorta.org.

Hospitals
See "Emergencies," above.

Internet Access
Many hotels and cafes have wireless access. Check www.wififreespot.com for a comprehensive list of Wi-Fi hotspots present in the larger towns of Paso Robles, San Luis Obispo, and Santa Barbara. **Santa Barbara Central Library** at 40 East Anapamu St. (☎ 805/962-7653; www.sbplibrary.org) offers computers with Internet access as well as free Wi-Fi. It's open Monday to Thursday from 10am to 8pm, Friday and Saturday 10am to 5:30pm, and Sunday from 1 to 5pm.

Pharmacies

A centrally located pharmacy in Santa Barbara is **Rite Aid** at 825 State St. (☎ 805/966-2760). The major chains—**Rite Aid, CVS, Walgreens**—are well represented throughout the Central Coast, although none of them have a 24-hour pharmacy.

Post Office

In Santa Barbara, the main post office is at 836 Anacapa St. (☎ 805/564-2226; Mon–Fri 9:30am–6pm, Sat 10am–2pm). In San Luis Obispo, the main post office is at 893 Marsh St. (☎ 805/541-9138; Mon–Fri 8:30am–5:30pm, Sat 9am–2pm). In Paso Robles, the main post office is at 800 Sixth St. (☎ 805/237-8342; Mon–Fri 8:30am–5:30pm, Sat 9am–2pm). In Cambria, the main post office is at 4100 Bridge St. (☎ 805/927-1385; Mon–Fri 9am–5pm). For more information, including the closest post office, go to www.usps.com.

Safety

Be very careful when driving in this region. Driving under the influence is a very serious offense in the Central Coast—if you choose to go wine tasting, have a designated driver. Roads in the Central Coast, especially in the countryside, may be scenic, but are dangerous enough with frequent curves and hairpin turns.

If you're navigating some of the less-populated areas of the Central Coast, such as the wine country or parks, don't be surprised if your cellphone—and its nifty GPS tracking—drops out of coverage.

If you smoke, be extremely careful when lighting up (or when dealing with any sort of fire) outdoors while hiking or camping. California has endured many devastating fires in recent years.

The Central Coast towns—Santa Barbara, Ojai, San Luis Obispo, Paso Robles, Cambria—are generally safe places. But don't let a small town atmosphere obscure your common sense, and don't leave valuables unattended in your car.

Taxes

Sales tax in San Luis Obispo and Santa Barbara counties varies between 8.25% and 8.75%. Hotel tax is charged on the room tariff only (which is not subject to sales tax) and ranges from 10% to 12% on the Central Coast.

Visitor Information

In Cambria, the **Cambria Chamber of Commerce** is at 767 Main St. (☎ 805/927-3624; www.cambriachamber.org). In Paso Robles, the **Paso Robles Visitors and Conference Bureau** is at 1225 Park St. (☎ 805/238-0506; www.pasorobleschamber.com); for information, including maps, on Paso Robles wine country, visit www.pasowine.com. In Morro Bay, the **Morro Bay Chamber of Commerce and Visitor Center** is at 845 D Embarcadero Rd., Ste. D (☎ 805/772-4467; www.morrobay.org). In San Luis Obispo, the **San Luis Obispo Visitors Center** is at 1039 Chorro St. (☎ 805/781-2670; www.visitslo.com). In Pismo Beach, the **Pismo Beach Visitors Information Center** is 581 Dolliver St. (☎ 800/443-7778; www.classiccalifornia.com). For information on the Santa Ynez Valley, visit www.syvva.com or www.solvangusa.com; for information, including maps, on Santa Ynez wine country, visit www.sbcountywines.com. In Santa Barbara, the **Santa Barbara Conference and Visitors Bureau** is at 1601 Anacapa St. (☎ 805/966-9222; www.santabarbaraca.com). For more information about Santa Barbara, visit www.santabarbara.com. In Ojai, the **Ojai Valley Chamber of Commerce and Visitor Bureau** is at 201 S. Signal St. (☎ 805/646-8126; www.ojaichamber.org).

10
Los Angeles

Our Favorite L.A. Moments

Constantly adapting to new identities, Los Angeles is a great actor, impossible to pin down. I love the way that, within a single block, the city can switch from gritty to glitzy, capable of embodying both the American dream of endless opportunity ("Go west, young man") and the American nightmare of not being cool enough ("You're not on the guest list, man"). Here's a highlight reel of some of L.A.'s best roles, from star-making turns to bit parts.

> PREVIOUS PAGE *The dazzling glitter of the Los Angeles metropolis spreads out below Griffith Observatory, a 1930s Art Deco gem.* THIS PAGE *A little night music at the Hollywood Bowl, where you can put out your own picnic spread during the show.*

❶ Pack a picnic for the Hollywood Bowl. The nation's largest natural amphitheater is a lovely place to enjoy dinner with a bottle of wine under the stars. Summer home to the L.A. Philharmonic and its ebullient and energizing conductor Gustavo Dudamel, the Bowl also hosts touring heavyweights like Willie Nelson and Radiohead. See p. 412, ❿.

❷ Catch a flick at the Hollywood Forever Cemetery. Join Rudolph Valentino, Douglas Fairbanks, and the other unemployed actors here any Saturday night in summer for the Cinespia outdoor film series. You can spread a blanket, rest your head against a headstone, and enjoy the show, usually something classic and creepy. And feel free to scream—you won't wake anybody. See p. 433.

❸ Shop like a starlet. Stay on the cutting edge of fashion by inspecting the trendy boutiques on paparazzi-littered Roberston Boulevard, the independently owned shops along Third Avenue, or the big-name, high-end designers around Melrose Place. Make celeb-fave Fred Segal your first stop. See p. 467.

1 Hollywood Bowl
2 Hollywood Forever
3 Fred Segal
4 Huntington Botanical Gardens
5 Chateau Marmont
6 Dodger Stadium
7 Sunset Strip
8 Walt Disney Concert Hall
9 Venice Boardwalk
10 El Matador Beach
11 Walk of Fame
12 Griffith Observatory
13 Getty Center
14 Mulholland Drive
15 Santa Monica Farmers Market
16 Warner Bros. Studios VIP Tour

> *The King of Pop finds stardom on the Hollywood Walk of Fame, commemorating the luminaries of film, music, TV, and radio.*

④ Stop and smell the roses in the Huntington Botanical Gardens. The Rose Garden is my favorite among these 150 green acres, which manage to appear both manicured and sprawling. Applaud nature's sense of humor in some of the strange, ballooning succulents of the Desert Garden, or Zen out in the quiet retreat of the Japanese Garden. See p. 421, ⑦.

⑤ Soak up some Old Hollywood glamour with your highball. The lobby of the infamous Chateau Marmont may be a costly place for a cocktail, but it buys you a chance to stargaze on the sly. This legendary hideaway prides itself on its exclusivity; to gain entry, you'll need either a globally recognized face or a hard-won reservation at the hotel or restaurant. See p. 483.

⑥ Down a Dodger Dog. Dodger Stadium welcomed the boys from Brooklyn back in 1962. While newer sports stadiums strain to manufacture a vintage vibe, Dodger Stadium is a So Cal classic, sunny and laid-back, with swaying palm trees framing panoramic views of the San Gabriel Mountains and downtown. See p. 422, ⑧.

⑦ Rock the Sunset Strip. Take in some live entertainment at one of the storied venues on the Sunset Strip: Rock out at Whisky a Go Go, the Viper Room, or the Roxy; or bust a gut at the Laugh Factory or Comedy Store. Or try the other end of Sunset Boulevard (and the musical spectrum) by catching the more under-the-radar acts working the Silver Lake scene. You never know about that little band you've never heard or the stand-up who's still perfecting his act—they just might be the next big things. See p. 411, ⑦.

⑧ Experience the majesty of the Walt Disney Concert Hall. This is the other home of the L.A. Philharmonic (those lucky dogs). Frank Gehry's audacious exterior looks gift-wrapped by God in curvilinear steel, a stunning catalyst for the revitalization of downtown. But the hall is no hollow shell—the acoustics within are flawless. A must-see and a must hear. See p. 438, ④.

⑨ Rollerblade up Venice Boardwalk. C'mon, there's no shame in trying. Matter of fact, there's no shame in anything on this kitschy stretch of street performers, leathery-skinned exhibitionists, tacky trinket peddlers, break dancers, soothsayers, and doomsayers. If you've got a freak flag, this is the spot to fly it. See p. 445, ⑤.

⑩ Tiptoe in the tide pools. Pick the right time—early on weekdays, off season—to explore the rocky coves of El Matador Beach, a remote enclave backed against the cliffs of Malibu, and, with a little luck, you'll get what many locals hold so dear—a little privacy. See p. 454.

⑪ Walk the Walk of Fame. The front of Grauman's Chinese Theatre may look like a zoo of tacky tourism, but don't let that fool you—this is some of Hollywood's most hallowed ground. Snap a couple of shots of the celebrity impersonators—say a sweaty Charlie Chaplin

> *Load up on produce, flowers, prepared foods, and crafts at Santa Monica Farmers Market, one of the country's best.*

or an ill-tempered Marilyn Monroe—and try to imagine the flashbulbs a-popping on their real-life versions walking the red carpet all those years ago. See p. 409, **5**.

12 Celebrate some lesser-known stars. At the recently renovated Griffith Observatory, it's easy to get caught up in the scientific exhibits, the planetarium, or the spectacular views of the city and the HOLLYWOOD Sign, but don't forget to direct some of that wonder skyward. Mounted on both copper domes are telescopes, free for public use, to help us (in the words of the park's benefactor Griffith J. Griffith) broaden our human perspective. See p. 421, **5**.

13 Get sketchy at the Getty Center. Feast your eyes on Monet's Impressionistic gems or on *Irises* by Vincent van Gogh, and once you're sufficiently inspired, head over to the sketching gallery, where you can try your hand at mimicking the masters. See p. 411, **8**.

14 Cruise Mulholland Drive. A great way to get the lay of the land is to drive the winding ridgeline of the Santa Monica Mountains, which separates the city from the valley. Pull off onto one of the many overlooks for stunning panoramas. See p. 412, **9**.

15 Savor the local flavors. Shop at one of the city's many farmers markets. The Santa Monica Farmers Market on Wednesday mornings is known as the secret weapon of fresh-ingredient-driven California cuisine, and you may find yourself picking over seasonal organic produce alongside some of the city's best chefs.

16 Peek behind the curtain. Take a tour of a working movie studio. On the Warner Bros. Studios VIP tour, you can see where Bogie bid farewell to Bacall in **Casablanca**, or sit on the couch where the cast of **Friends** traded zingers. See p. 408, **1**.

The Best of Los Angeles in 1 Day

Seeing the country's largest city in a single day takes preparation. It's best to secure reservations in advance for the Warner Bros. Studios VIP tour, your first stop, as well as tickets to the Hollywood Bowl for the day's finale. In between, you'll see landmarks in pop culture, experience the majestic Getty Center, and wind along the city's most scenic and historic roads.

> The street of dreams, Sunset Boulevard twists for nearly 25 miles through L.A.'s most iconic neighborhoods.

START From Riverside Dr. take Avon St. south to Warner Blvd. Go left and follow the signs to VIP Tour parking.

❶ ★★ Warner Bros. Studios VIP Tour. Start the day early in Burbank because that's how the ghost of studio chief Jack Warner would want it. Warner Bros., the third-oldest movie studio (founded in 1918), took over 110 acres from First National Pictures in 1928 with the payout from betting big on the first "talkie," *The Jazz Singer.* The 2½-hour tour takes you behind the scenes of the working lot, and with roughly 35 soundstages and outdoor sets, there's a lot of work going on. The hit television show *ER* was shot here, as were *The Dukes of Hazzard, The West Wing,* and *Friends.* But it's the studio's film history that boggles the mind—*My Fair Lady, Rebel Without a Cause,* and *Bonnie and Clyde* were all made here. Standing on the hallowed ground where *Casablanca* was shot, take a moment to imagine Bogie telling Ingrid Bergman, "We'll always have Burbank." Children 7 and under are not admitted. Reservations are recommended and can be made online. ⏱2–3 hr. 3400 Riverside Dr., Burbank. ☎ 818/972-8687. www.wbstudiotour.com. VIP tour $48 per person. Mon–Fri continuously 8:20am–4pm (extended hours in spring & summer).

> *The ultimate temple to the stars, Grauman's Chinese Theater has over 200 celebrity foot and handprints outside its pagoda-style entrance.*

2 ★ **Hollywood & Highland.** After languishing for years as flypaper for runaways and hustlers, Hollywood Boulevard has Times Squared itself in the past decade and is now a polished link to Tinseltown's heyday. The centerpiece of the area's revitalization is the retail and entertainment behemoth at Hollywood & Highland, which includes the grand Kodak Theatre, the first permanent home of the Academy Awards. Explore the multitiered Babylonian-style courtyard, inspired by D. W. Griffith's silent film epic *Intolerance,* and you'll find photo-ready views of the HOLLYWOOD Sign perched atop Mount Lee in the distance. ⏲ 30 min. 6801 Hollywood Blvd., at Highland Ave. ☎ 323/817-0200. www.hollywoodandhighland.com. Mon–Sat 10am–10pm; Sun 10am–7pm.

③ 🍮 **Beard Papa Sweets Café.** Grab one exquisitely calibrated cream puff to go. And I do mean go—if you stay, you might not be able to stop eating. 6801 Hollywood Blvd., no. 153. ☎ 323/462-6100. Cream puffs $2 apiece.

4 ★★ **Grauman's Chinese Theatre.** "Over the top" would be an understatement. The bronze pagoda roof, garish columns, leering gargoyles, and fiery dragons—for mad impresario Sid Grauman, these were only half the fun. According to the apocryphal story, silent-film star Norma Talmadge accidentally stepped in a patch of wet cement at the theater's opening (the 1927 premiere of Cecil B. DeMille's *The King of Kings*) and the great imprinting tradition was born. A less-dramatic version says Grauman got the idea when he observed his chief mason signing his work (look for "J.W.K."). Today, the Forecourt of the Stars is cemented in history, crammed with the handprints and footprints of more than 200 movie legends. Ask yourself: Is there a more famous movie theater on the planet? ⏲ 45 min. 6925 Hollywood Blvd. ☎ 323/464-8111. www.manntheatres.com. Free admission to forecourt. Daily 24 hr.

5 ★ **Walk of Fame.** On 18 blocks of pink terrazzo stars, you can find more than 2,000 names—some unforgettable, some already forgotten, and others perhaps less than

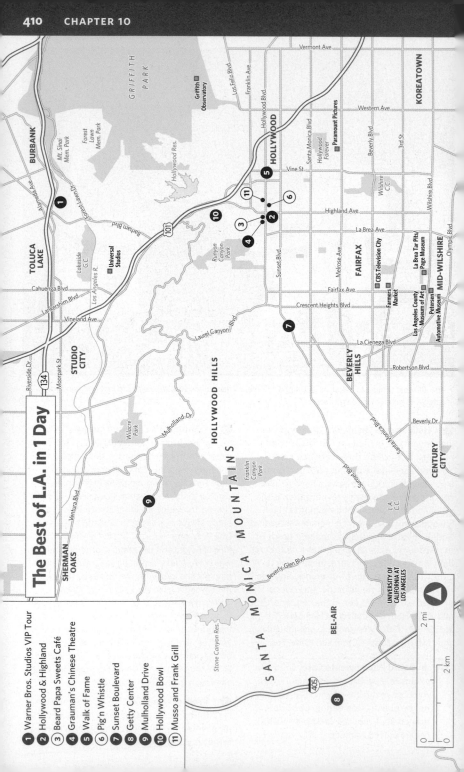

The Best of L.A. in 1 Day

1. Warner Bros. Studios VIP Tour
2. Hollywood & Highland
3. Beard Papa Sweets Café
4. Grauman's Chinese Theatre
5. Walk of Fame
6. Pig'n Whistle
7. Sunset Boulevard
8. Getty Center
9. Mulholland Drive
10. Hollywood Bowl
11. Musso and Frank Grill

deserving (sorry, I just don't think Godzilla is much of an actor). Joanne Woodward received the first star in 1960, and Gene Autry received the most, one for each of the five categories: film, television, music, radio, and theater. Immortality doesn't come cheap; the honoree must fork over $25,000 (a "sponsorship fee") to cover installation and maintenance. Be sure to poke your head up every once in a while as you shuffle along, or you could miss other landmarks: the immaculate El Capitan Theatre (6838 Hollywood Blvd.), which premiered *Citizen Kane* in 1941; the Hollywood Roosevelt (7000 Hollywood Blvd.), where the first Academy Awards were held; and another Sid Grauman inspiration, the Egyptian Theatre (6712 Hollywood Blvd.), now home to the American Cinematheque. ⏱ 30 min.; best times are Mon–Fri mornings. Hollywood Blvd. from La Brea Ave. to Gower St. and down Vine St. from Yucca St. to Sunset Blvd.

---

⑥ 🍴 **Pig'n Whistle.** Food options abound at the Hollywood & Highland Center, but if you're looking for old-school ambience, duck in here for slightly upscale pub fare. 6714 Hollywood Blvd. ☎ 323/463-0000. Soups, salads, sandwiches $7–$15.

⑦ ★★ Sunset Boulevard. If you have to choose only one road by which to see the city of Los Angeles, this is the one. Beginning near El Pueblo, the historic core of downtown, and stretching nearly 25 miles west to the Pacific Ocean, Sunset links working-class ethnic communities (Hispanic, Armenian, Thai), bohemian Silver Lake, historic Hollywood, the always rockin' Sunset Strip, exclusive Beverly Hills and Bel Air, UCLA, and the Pacific Palisades.

For an abbreviated tour, start in Hollywood at Sunset and Vine and head west. You can't miss the Cinerama Dome (6360 Sunset Blvd.), which anchors the ArcLight Cinemas complex, where serious cineastes get their fix. When you hit Crescent Heights, you're officially on the world-famous Sunset Strip. Keep your eyes peeled—the names are going to jump out at you hard and fast: Chateau Marmont (no. 8221), the Standard (no. 8300), the Sunset Tower (no. 8358), the Viper Room (no. 8852), and Whisky a Go Go (no. 8901), to name just a few. By the time you reach the pink palace of the Beverly Hills Hotel (no. 9641), you're loving the lushness of Beverly

> *Marilyn slept here. Originally a star-studded apartment complex, the 1921 Sunset Tower now offers refined lodgings for all.*

Hills. Continue on past the gates of Bel Air and the UCLA campus until you reach Sepulveda Blvd. ⏱ 45 min.

⑧ ★★★ 🧒 Getty Center. Money can't buy happiness, but J. Paul Getty's $1.2 billion bought plenty of world-class art (works by van Gogh, Monet, and Man Ray, among others) and an architectural marvel in which to display it—that makes you a little happy, right? Ascend the acropolis and admire the way Richard Meier ballasts his modern, airy design with textured travertine blocks. But don't forget about the art on the inside. Grab a *GettyGuide* ($5), your own personal digital docent, and go.

SITE GUIDE
PAGE 413

> *Retro glam and a mean martini make Musso & Frank, L.A.'s oldest restaurant, still worth a visit.*

⑨ ★ Mulholland Drive. Rolling east along the ridge of the Santa Monica Mountains and away from the setting sun, you can watch the canyons pooling with diffuse golden light. It can be hard to keep your eyes on the road, so pull off into one of the many overlooks to take in vistas of the Los Angeles basin to the south and the San Fernando Valley to the north. Repeat as necessary, because an overload of these curves (or worse, tailgating cars) can be as disorienting as watching David Lynch's *Mulholland Drive*. ⏱ 45 min.

⑩ ★★★ Hollywood Bowl. Fantastic music, a cool summer evening, a lush green hillside, and an arresting venue steeped in entertainment history—a night at the Hollywood Bowl is a consummate Los Angeles experience. The Bowl derives its name not from its famous backdrop of concentric arches, but from the way Mother Nature cups her hands into a 60-acre canyon once known as Daisy Dell. One of the world's largest natural amphitheaters, the Bowl was built in 1922 and holds nearly 18,000 people. The bleachers can be a blast, but if you decide to splurge on box seats, you won't regret it.

You can even have a multicourse meal brought right to your box (buy tickets well in advance and order your dinner the day before by 4pm). A diverse schedule—including acts as distinct as the L.A. Philharmonic and Willie Nelson—makes it easy to pick the right night for you. Be sure to come early to check out the Bowl Museum, take a self-guided Bowl Walk, or just relax with a bottle of wine. ⏱ At least 2 hr. 2301 N. Highland Ave. ☎ 323/850-2000. www.holly woodbowl.com. Tickets $1–$147. June–Sept.

⑪ ☕ ★★ Musso & Frank Grill. Need a nightcap? The town's oldest restaurant (established in 1919) was once a workday watering hole for such writers as F. Scott Fitzgerald, William Faulkner, Dorothy Parker, and Raymond Chandler, who they say wrote *The Big Sleep* while boozing in a red-leather booth in the back. Plop onto a seat at the counter, order one of their mean martinis, and let yourself slowly drift back in time. When you start calling the bartender "doll face," he'll let you know it's time to go. 6667 Hollywood Blvd. ☎ 323/467-7788. Martinis start at $8.50.

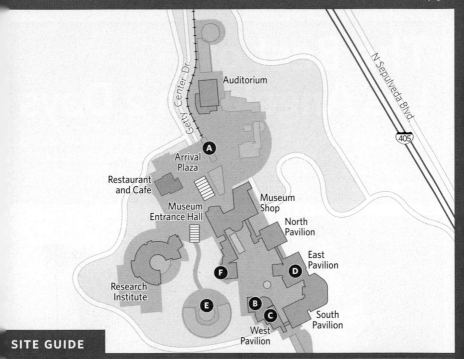

8 Getty Center

A 5-minute **Ⓐ tram ride** transports you from the parking area up the hill to the museum and provides the first of many excellent views; for now, just pity those poor saps on the 405 freeway. Head across the courtyard to the terrace of the West Pavilion for the **Ⓑ photography collection,** which traces the history of the medium and includes many Man Ray (1890–1976) prints, such as the famous *Tears.* Take the elevator two floors to the upper level to **Ⓒ paintings** (after 1800). On your right are a couple of Impressionist gems by Claude Monet: *Wheatstacks, Snow Effect, Morning* and *The Portal of Rouen Cathedral in Morning Light.* Screaming at you from the next wall is the room's rock star, Vincent van Gogh's *Irises,* created in a Saint-Rémy asylum the year before he died. If your creative juices are flowing, make for the **Ⓓ sketching gallery** in the upper level of the East Pavilion. Here you can borrow a pencil and a sketch pad to re-create the artwork on display in the studio. Afterward, take a stroll through the delightful and

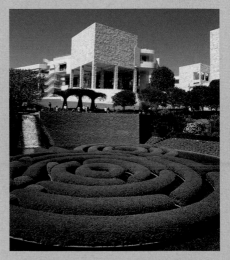

ever-evolving **Ⓔ Central Garden.** Then relax at the **Ⓕ Garden Terrace Café** with a coffee or snack and get your fill of scenic wonder. ⊙ 2 hr. 1200 Getty Center Dr. ☎ 310/440-7300. www. getty.edu. Free admission. Tues–Thurs & Sun 10am–6pm; Fri–Sat 10am–9pm. Closed major holidays. Parking $8.

The Best of Los Angeles in 2 Days

If you made it through Day 1, you've earned a few hours at the beach. Catch the buzz of bustling Venice Boardwalk, then drift up the Pacific Coast Highway past Santa Monica, and splash in the waves of Malibu. Finish up with some hoity-toity shopping on Beverly Hills' Rodeo Drive.

> *A slice of Italy in L.A., the Venice canals wind around charming bungalows and manicured mansions.*

START **Venice Blvd. & Ocean Ave.**

❶ ★ **Venice Canals.** Today only a handful of canals and bridges remain of Abbot Kinney's elaborate quest to build a fantastic European-style resort. Cute, decades-old bungalows and modernist McMansions flank the canals, which are dotted with ducks and small boats. The perfect setting for a peaceful morning stroll. ⏱ 30 min. See p. 444, ❷.

❷ ★★★ **Venice Boardwalk.** When I say it's a "complete freak show," I mean that lovingly. L.A. has a rich history of people who require a lot of attention, and the Venice Boardwalk is where exhibitionists come to out-exhibit each other: messiahs in Reeboks; amateur acrobats; jewelry-bedecked pit bulls; and a ubiquitous rollerblading, electric guitar-playing dude who seems to be everywhere at once. Join a drum

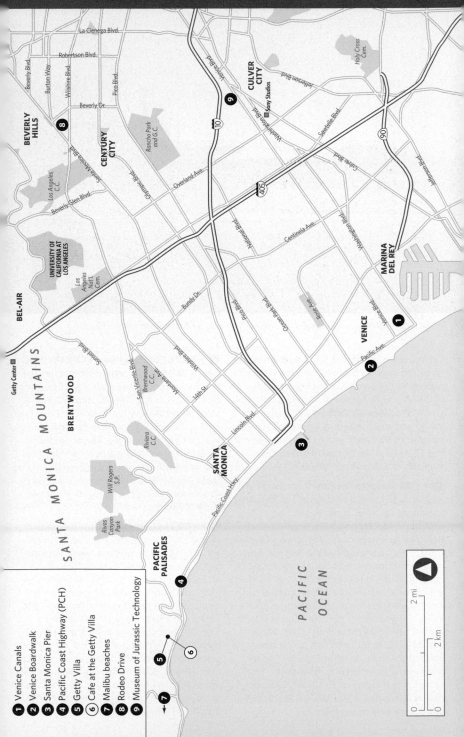

1 Venice Canals
2 Venice Boardwalk
3 Santa Monica Pier
4 Pacific Coast Highway (PCH)
5 Getty Villa
6 Cafe at the Getty Villa
7 Malibu beaches
8 Rodeo Drive
9 Museum of Jurassic Technology

> The neon-bright Ferris wheel and other rides add a dose of fun to the Santa Monica Pier.

circle, get a henna tattoo, join a political movement you've never heard of, help the skate rats make a YouTube video, or even join the grunts of the Muscle Beachheads. Or take a front-row seat at the **Sidewalk Café** (1401 Ocean Front Walk) and watch it all through a pair of cheap sunglasses that you'll lose by the end of your trip. ⏱ At least 1 hr. Ocean Front Walk (btw. Venice Blvd. & Rose Ave.), Venice.

3 ★★ kids **Santa Monica Pier.** This century-old slice of Americana is considered the end of the legendary Route 66. If you're catching a Coney Island vibe, that might be because it was designed by amusement-park pioneer Charles Looff, the man who carved the first wooden carousel at Coney Island. Today the pier's gorgeous Looff Hippodrome Carousel building is a National Historic Landmark (and not just for its plum roles in film and television, such as in the opening credits of *Three's Company*). For a great panorama of the entire Santa Monica Bay, head to the far end of the pier or, even better, take a spin on the world's first solar-powered Ferris wheel, which sends you nine stories above the water. ⏱ 30 min. Colorado Ave. at Ocean Ave., Santa Monica. ☎ 310/458-8900. www.santamonicapier.org.

4 ★ **Pacific Coast Highway (PCH)**, aka Highway 1, California 1. If you haven't dropped the top of your convertible, now might be a good time. The PCH hugs the dramatic California coastline all the way to the San Francisco Bay area and beyond. But we don't need to go that far to get the picture. The ocean shimmers to the west, the warm wind whips your hair, and you finally find a song you dig on the radio—it's little moments like this that keep Angelenos addicted to their cars. ⏱ 30 min. Pacific Coast Hwy.

5 ★★ kids **The Getty Villa.** Little (but older) sibling of the Getty Center, the Getty Villa is entirely dedicated to ancient Greek, Roman, and Etruscan art. In 1974, when J. Paul Getty's art collection overran his Malibu ranch home (don't you hate it when that happens?), he had a museum built next door and modeled it after the Roman Villa dei Papiri in Herculaneum. The collection grew and, in 1997, moved into bigger digs: the celebrated Getty Center a few miles away in Brentwood. Reopened in 2006 after a 9-year, $275-million makeover, the Villa displays roughly 1,200 artifacts from 6500 B.C. to A.D. 600 (from a total collection of 44,000 items). Fittingly, you enter the lavish grounds from an elevated walkway, as if stumbling across an archaeological dig. Wander the sun-drenched formal gardens (even the smelly one, the Herb Garden, which grows herbs popular with the ancient Romans), and soak in the magnificent Pacific views. Admission is limited to around 1,200 people a day, so reservations are a must. ⏱1 hr. 17985 Pacific Coast Hwy., Malibu. ☎310/440-7300. www.getty.edu. Reservations strongly recommended. Free admission. Thurs–Mon 10am–5pm. Parking $8.

⑥ 🍽 ★ **Cafe at the Getty Villa.** The Mediterranean-inspired lunch fare is simple, but it's made tastier by an outdoor patio with a killer view. **Lunch entrees $7-$14.**

❼ **Malibu beaches.** Malibu has several great beach options depending on what floats your boat. The most popular and most accessible choice is ★ **Zuma Beach,** a wide, family-friendly stretch with plenty of activities, snack shacks, and restrooms. Just south is my favorite beach, ★★ **Point Dume,** which lacks the Zuma amenities, but also its crowds. The ★★ **Robert H. Meyer Memorial State Beach** is a few miles north and is actually three mini-beaches: **El Matador, La Piedra,** and **El Pescador.** Each of these rocky coves has little parking and no facilities and can only be reached by trails and tricky stairways. Set against the Malibu cliffs, these beaches are both cozy and rugged. You might have a hard time choosing between splashing in the waves, climbing the rocks, or exploring the tide pools. ⏱2 hr. Point Dume, 7103 Westward Rd., Malibu. Zuma Beach, 30000 Pacific Coast Hwy., Malibu. Robert H. Meyer Memorial State Beach, 33000 Pacific Coast Hwy., Malibu. Daily 7am–10pm.

❽ ★★ **Rodeo Drive.** If the beach doesn't have the cure for what ails you, perhaps some serious retail therapy is in order. In the "Golden Triangle" of Beverly Hills (Santa Monica Blvd., Wilshire Blvd., and Crescent Dr.), the doctor is in, though his rates are sky-high. No street says "beautiful things I can't afford" quite like fabled Rodeo Drive. Gucci, Versace, Cartier, and Tiffany—all the biggest names in fashion and jewelry design are here. The most popular spot for "look, I was there" snapshots is the "Spanish Steps" that descend from the pedestrian-only cobblestone path, Via Rodeo, to

> Leave the clunker at home when you head for Rodeo Drive, home to some of the country's ritziest boutiques.

Wilshire Boulevard. Directly across the street stands the Beverly Wilshire, where Julia Roberts was swept off her feet in *Pretty Woman.* ⏱30 min. 200–500 Rodeo Dr. (at Wilshire Blvd.), Beverly Hills. Most shops Mon–Sat 10am–6pm, Sun noon–5pm. Public parking $2 per hour.

❾ ★★ **Museum of Jurassic Technology.** You start with the enigmatic name and become more baffled the deeper you delve into this museum's intricacies—which is precisely what creator/curator David Wilson wants. A 2001 recipient of a MacArthur Fellowship, also known as "the Genius Award," Wilson promotes confusion as "a vehicle to open people's minds." If this sounds like gobbledygook, wait until you see the Eye of the Needle exhibit, featuring a sculpture of Pope John Paul II placed within the eye of a needle. ⏱30 min. 9341 Venice Blvd., Culver City. ☎310/836-6131. www.mjt.org. Suggested donation $5 adults, $3 seniors and ages 12–21, free for kids 11 & under. Thurs 2–8pm; Fri–Sun noon–6pm.

The Best of Los Angeles in 3 Days

After 2 jampacked days, it's time to stop and smell the hydrogen sulfide (bubbling up from the La Brea Tar Pits). Then you'll sample the city's most extensive collection of art at the Los Angeles County Museum of Art, have lunch at the Farmers Market, and scope out the sparkling Griffith Observatory. Cap your 3 days with a blast downtown at Dodger Stadium.

> Crude oil might be black gold now, but in prehistoric times it was a trap for Ice Age animals at La Brea Tar Pits. Excavation of these pits has unearthed more than 200 species of vertebrates, many exctinct today.

START **At Wilshire Blvd. and Curson Ave. (park in the lot at southwest corner of Curson Ave. and Sixth St.).**

❶ ★ kids The La Brea Tar Pits and the Page Museum. Ready for some stinky pools of tar? Well, actually, it's asphalt, and it's been seeping out of the ground here on 23 acres of Hancock Park for the last 40,000 years. In the last Ice Age, animals roaming the Los Angeles basin would sometimes get trapped by the sticky pools and sucked into the ground where the asphalt would eventually fossilize the remains.

The first written account of the asphalt seepage was in 1770 by a Franciscan friar, who theorized that the goo was the cause of the area's earthquakes. Native Americans used the sticky substance for thousands of years as waterproof caulking for baskets and canoes. The first excavations occurred in 1906, and the search for fossils continues to this day.

Today the collection at the Page Museum holds around a million bones from more than 200 species of vertebrates, including the long-extinct Columbian mammoth and saber-toothed cat. If you visit during July and August, there's a good chance you can observe scientists at work on Pit 91. The gift shop has great toys for budding paleontologists. ⏱ 1 hr. 5801 Wilshire Blvd. ☎ 323/934-7243. www.tarpits.org. Admission $7 adults, $4.50 seniors and students, $2 kids 5–12, free for kids 4 & under. Mon–Fri 9:30am–5pm; Sat–Sun 10am–5pm.

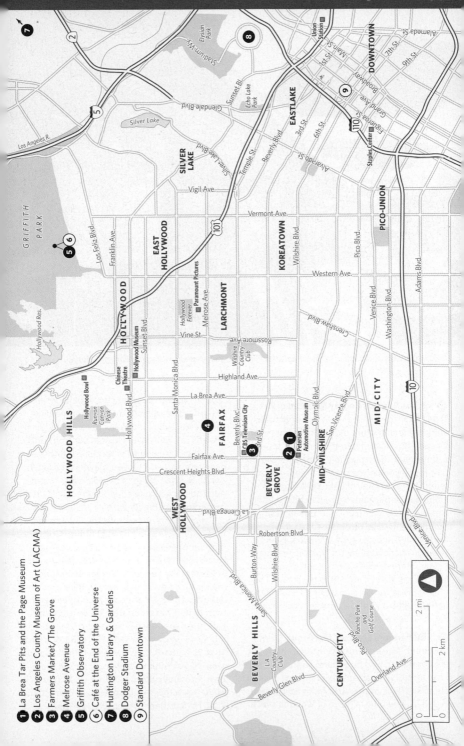

Union Station

DOWNTOWN

Alameda St.

7th St.

9th St.

Main St.

6th St.

3rd St.

Broadway

Grand Ave.

Figueroa St.

EASTLAKE

Staples Center

PICO-UNION

Elysian Park

Stadium Wy.

Echo Lake Park

Sunset Bl.

Glendale Blvd.

Silver Lake

Los Angeles R.

SILVER LAKE

Vigil Ave.

Vermont Ave.

KOREATOWN

Wilshire Blvd.

Pico Blvd.

Western Ave.

Adams Blvd.

GRIFFITH PARK

Los Feliz Blvd.

Franklin Ave.

EAST HOLLYWOOD

Temple St.

Beverly Blvd.

Alvarado St.

Hollywood Res.

Paramount Pictures

LARCHMONT

Melrose Ave.

Hollywood Forever

Vine St.

Wilshire Country Club

Rossmore Ave.

Crenshaw Blvd.

Venice Blvd.

Washington Blvd.

MID-CITY

Hollywood Bowl

Runyon Canyon Park

Chinese Theatre

Hollywood Museum

Sunset Blvd.

Santa Monica Blvd.

Highland Ave.

La Brea Ave.

Hollywood Blvd.

FAIRFAX

CBS Television City

Petersen Automotive Museum

Olympic Blvd.

San Vicente Blvd.

MID-WILSHIRE

Fairfax Ave.

Beverly Blvd.

3rd St.

BEVERLY GROVE

Crescent Heights Blvd.

WEST HOLLYWOOD

La Cienega Blvd.

Robertson Blvd.

Burton Way

Wilshire Blvd.

Santa Monica Blvd.

BEVERLY HILLS

L.A. Country Club

Beverly Glen Blvd.

CENTURY CITY

Rancho Park and Golf Course

Pico Blvd.

Overland Ave.

Venice Blvd.

HOLLYWOOD HILLS

HOLLYWOOD

1 La Brea Tar Pits and the Page Museum
2 Los Angeles County Museum of Art (LACMA)
3 Farmers Market/The Grove
4 Melrose Avenue
5 Griffith Observatory
6 Café at the End of the Universe
7 Huntington Library & Gardens
8 Dodger Stadium
9 Standard Downtown

2 mi

2 km

> *Pull up a stool at dozens of open-air eateries filling the year-round Los Angeles Farmers Market.*

② ★★ **Los Angeles County Museum of Art (LACMA).** The LACMA may not boast the stunning architecture of the Getty Center or its easy-flow layout, but it does offer more art than you could possibly hope to see in 1 day. Heck, you can run out of breath just attempting to list the collections: American (John Singer Sargent, Mary Cassatt), Latin American (Diego Rivera), European, Islamic, Japanese, modern (Picasso, Chagall, Matisse, Kandinsky), photography (Weston, Evans, Arbus), and several more. One piece of particular interest is David Hockney's exuberant *Mulholland Drive: The Road to the Studio*. The offerings are too diverse to simply start wandering—grab a guide and make a game plan. ◷ 1 ½ hr. See p. 438, **❾**.

❸ ★ **kids Farmers Market/The Grove.** During the Great Depression, on a dirt parking lot at the corner of Third Street and Fairfax Avenue, local farmers began selling their fresh produce out of the back of their trucks. Folks poured in and, before long, a maze of wooden stalls sprung up, with butcher shops, bakeries, and restaurants adding to the mix. Surprisingly, the market today manages to retain its folksy charms (as well as its clock tower from 1941). Sure, there are plenty of tourists, but there are even more locals—power players on a lunch break, Russian retirees playing chess, mommies pushing strollers, and solitary artsy types contemplating big ideas.

Favorite eateries include the Gumbo Pot for Cajun-style gumbo, and Loteria! Grill for authentic Mexican food. You can ride the Disney-like trolley a few hundred feet to your next stop, the Grove, an elaborate outdoor mall, which has been hugely popular since its debut in 2002. With its faux-European architecture and water fountain that mesmerizes kids, the experience is equal parts fab and prefab. ◷ 45 min. Farmers Market, 6333 W. Third St. ☎ 323/933-9211. www.farmersmarketla.com. Mon–Fri 9am–9pm; Sat 9am–8pm; Sun 10am–7pm. The Grove, 189 The Grove Dr. ☎ 323/900-8080. www.thegrovela.com. Mon–Thurs 10am–9pm; Fri–Sat 10am–10pm; Sun 11am–8pm.

> *Shedding light on an extraordinary array of artists, Los Angeles County Museum of Art should be a must see on any art fan's list.*

❹ Melrose Avenue. In dire need of vintage tees, tattoos, or tips on how to chop/sculpt/dye your hair? The blocks between Fairfax and La Brea avenues make a fascinating cruise of scruffy shops and restaurants. Also, see "Hottest Blocks for Shopping," on p. 422. ⏱ 10 min.

❺ ★★ kids Griffith Observatory. Like so many iconic beauties in Los Angeles, the Griffith Observatory had a teensy amount of work done—about 4 years' and $93 million's worth, finished up in 2006. Architectural details were spit shined to their original 1930s grandeur; a 40,000-square-foot expansion added slick but accessible exhibits like the Edge of Space, which displays Martian and lunar meteorites, and the 200-seat Leonard Nimoy Event Horizon multimedia theater for presentations, films, and lectures; the Samuel Oschin Planetarium underwent a massive overhaul (sorry, no more Pink Floyd laser shows).

One of the most popular features, and part of the original building in 1935, is the Foucault Pendulum, a 240-pound brass ball that hangs in the Central Rotunda and demonstrates Earth's rotation. Entrance to the observatory is free; planetarium tickets are available on-site and often sell out. Before you step inside, circle the grounds and admire the building's beautiful Art Deco architecture and the stellar views of the city stretched out below. Parking is very limited at the top of the hill in front of the observatory; you may have to park along the road, then walk uphill. ⏱ 1–2 hr. 2800 E. Observatory Rd. ☎ 213/473-0800. www.griffithobservatory.org. Free admission. Planetarium tickets $7 adults, $5 seniors and students, $3 kids 5–11. Tues–Fri noon–10pm; Sat–Sun 10am–10pm.

❻ 🍽 Café at the End of the Universe. The views may trump the menu, but you can't go wrong snacking it up on this sunny terrace catered by Wolfgang Puck. **In the Griffith Observatory. Entrees $7–$12.**

SITE GUIDE PAGE 423

❼ ★★ kids Huntington Library & Gardens. Upon his death in 1927, railroad and real-estate tycoon Henry E. Huntington willed that his private 207-acre estate, near Pasadena, be opened to the public as a library, museum, and botanical gardens—now a triple shot of world-class attractions. With 15,000 species of plants landscaped across 120 acres, the magnificent gardens are best enjoyed at a leisurely pace.

> *Hang out with the boys of summer at 56,000-seat Dodgers Stadium, an L.A. institution since 1962.*

8 ★★ kids **Dodger Stadium.** Don't underestimate the simple pleasure of taking in a baseball game in Southern California on a spring or summer evening. Since 1962 Angelenos have rooted for the Dodgers at classic Dodger Stadium, the third-oldest stadium in the league. Kick back with a Dodger Dog in cushy box seats, or whoop it up with the die-hards in the bleachers. If it's not baseball season, check out what's scheduled at the Walt Disney Concert Hall (p. 438, **4**). 1000 Elysian Park Ave. ☎ 866/DODGERS (363-4377). www.dodgers.com. Tickets $10–$225. Most night games 7:10pm; most day games 1:10pm. Check the schedule on the website for specific dates & times.

9 🍸 ★ **Standard Downtown.** This groovy nightspot single-handedly launched the city's rooftop bar trend. A swimming pool, skyscraper views, and space-pod waterbeds—your head is spinning before you can order your first cocktail. 550 S. Flower St., at Sixth St. ☎ 213/892-8080. www.standardhotel.com. Cocktails start at $8.

Hottest Blocks for Shopping

If you've already conquered the Grove, the Beverly Center, and the Third Street Promenade, then try the following shopping areas on for size. The übertrendy shops of **Robertson Boulevard** (btw. Beverly Blvd. and Third St.) cater to the "young and love-to-be-in-the-tabloids" set. Gals duck into Curve, Lisa Kline, and Kitson for the latest fashions. Guys can try John Varvatos, Lisa Kline for Men, and the rocker outfits at Logan Riese.

Melrose Heights (btw. La Cienega Blvd. and Fairfax Ave.) is the spiffier side of Melrose, west of Fairfax, where big-name designers line the blocks, especially along Melrose Place: Marc Jacobs, Diane von Furstenberg, Chloe, and Oscar de la Renta. Anchored by the legendary Fred Segal, a must stop for shopping, there's also Cynthia Rowley, Paul Smith, and the splashy Betsey Johnson. **Third Street** (btw. La Cienega Blvd. and Fairfax Ave.) offers a refreshing stretch of independently owned boutiques. Smart, stylish, eccentric—these shops specialize in the "I had no idea I needed that" experience: fashion boutiques like Noodle Stories and Satine. vintage wear at Polka Dots & Moonbeams, design-heavy gifts at OK and Plastica.

True to Venice's bohemian roots, **Abbot Kinney** boasts an eclectic mix of funky art, health-conscious eats, and beach-chic vibe. Check out Surfing Cowboys for its retro surf home decor, and Equator Books & Vinyl, a pulsing space with art, records, and first-edition books. Or have Strange Invisible Perfume customize a scent for you. Next to a lovely Santa Monica neighborhood, the shops of **Montana Avenue** (7th & 17th sts.) are all about maintaining the good life: Dermalogica and Kiehl's for skin care; the oft-imitated linens of Shabby Chic; and Every Picture Tells a Story, a gallery for illustrators of children's books.

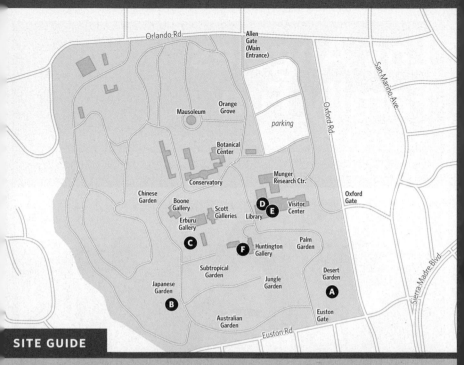

❼ Huntington Library & Gardens

In the Ⓐ **Desert Garden** two dozen families of succulents, many imported from the Southwest and Mexico, occupy 10 acres, making it one of the largest collections of its kind in the world. True to Japanese tradition, the Ⓑ **Japanese Garden** is a harmonious and multifaceted retreat, created through the disciplined interplay between the elements of water, rocks, and plants. Highlights include a stroll garden, picturesque moon bridge, Shoin-style house, and Bonsai court. In the Ⓒ **Rose Garden** are 1,200 cultivars in a kaleidoscope of colors. To catch them in full bloom—between late April and early June—is breathtaking. The Huntington is home to more than six million rare books and manuscripts; in the Library Exhibition Hall you'll find two items of literary note, including a 1455 Ⓓ **Gutenberg Bible.** It's 1 of only 12 vellum (fine parchment, as opposed to paper) copies in the world. Created around 1410, the Ellesmere manuscript of Chaucer's Ⓔ *Canterbury Tales* features 464 pages of cursive text with floral borders and other meticulous decorations.

Scholars consider it to be one of the most significant English-language manuscripts in existence. Your final stop is the Ⓕ **Huntington Gallery**, whose highlights include two portraits that seem to be checking each other out: Thomas Gainsborough's *The Blue Boy* and Thomas Lawrence's *Pinkie*. ⏲ 2 hr. 1151 Oxford Rd., San Marino. ☎ 626/405-2100. www.huntington.org. Mon and Wed–Fri noon–4:30pm; Sat–Sun 10:30am–4:30pm; Tues closed. Admission $15–$20 adults, $12–$15 seniors 65 & up, $10 kids 12 & up, $6 kids 5–11, free for kids 4 & under.

Los Angeles Family Fun

Let's be honest: Kids' moods can be as unpredictable as Los Angeles traffic. By no means do I recommend trying to hit every stop on this list. Let your kid be the guide.

> *Give the kids a hare-raising experience on the spit-and-polish sparkling Santa Monica Carousel.*

1 ★★ kids **California Science Center.** This interactive museum about science and technology never fails to dazzle kids of all ages. Watch an IMAX movie in 3-D on L.A.'s biggest screen (seven stories high!), or investigate exhibits such as Ecosystems and Timescapes: California from the Air. Take a spin on a high-wire bicycle, or strap into the Millennium Falcon flight simulator. Tess, a 50-foot woman with a see-through body, teaches kids about homeostasis, how the body keeps its system in balance. There are also hands-on areas for younger kids. Check the website for current exhibits and IMAX movies. ⏱ 1–2 hr. 39th & Figueroa sts. ☎ 323/724-3623. www.california-sciencecenter.org. Free admission. IMAX movie $4.75–$8. Parking $8. Daily 10am–5pm.

2 ★ kids **Natural History Museum.** Opened in 1913, this museum is the largest of its kind in the western United States. A scrapbook documenting the history of Mother Earth and her inhabitants, the museum holds 33 million specimens and artifacts, including the Megamouth, the world's rarest shark (only 17 have ever been discovered). But it's the dinosaurs that are the real rock stars among the rocks and fossils; the T. rex skull on display is considered one of the finest anywhere. ⏱ 1 hr. 900 Exposition Blvd., Exposition Park. ☎ 213/763-DINO (3466). www.nhm.org. Admission $9 adults; $6.50 seniors, students and kids 13–17; $2 kids 5–12; free for kids 4 & under. Free for everyone 1st Tues of the month. Daily 9:30am–5pm.

1 California Science Center
2 Natural History Museum
3 Bob Baker Marionette Theater
4 E! Capitan Theatre
5 Disney Soda Fountain
6 Page Museum at La Brea Tar Pits
7 Petersen Automotive Museum
8 Pacific Park, Santa Monica Pier
9 Santa Monica Carousel

> *Still dazzling after all these years, the 1926 El Capitan Theatre—now fully restored—makes a pretty classy place to spill your popcorn.*

3 kids **Bob Baker Marionette Theater.** With all the high-tech wizardry out there competing for kids' attention, sometimes it's nice to enjoy the good, old-fashioned fun of watching wooden puppets spring to life with string. Founded in 1963 by puppeteer pioneer Bob Baker, this children's theater company is the oldest in Los Angeles. You'll have to forgive its less-than-pristine exterior; this labor of love is the real deal. ⏱1 hr. 1345 W. First St. ☎ 213/250-9995. www.bobbakermarionettes.com. Reservations required. Tickets $20 per person, free for kids 2 & under. Tues–Fri 10:30am; Sat–Sun 2:30pm.

4 ★ kids **El Capitan Theatre.** This is the spot to catch the latest summer blockbuster from Disney/Pixar. Debuting in 1926 as "Hollywood's First Home of Spoken Drama," the theater has been fully restored to its original grandeur by the Walt Disney Company. El Capitan is one of three themed theaters—along with the Chinese and the Egyptian—from the team of Charles Toberman and Sid Grauman. It boasts a Spanish colonial facade; a lively, East Indian–influenced interior; and a 2,500-piped organ from the 1920s called the Mighty Wurlitzer. Get there early for the preshow song-and-dance numbers by costumed characters. ⏱2 hr. 6838 Hollywood Blvd. ☎ 800/347-6396. Tickets $13 adults, $10 seniors and kids. $2 discount on adult tickets for matinees.

5 🍴 kids **Disney Soda Fountain.** Your kids are going to beg you for a milkshake or a movie-themed sundae at the old-fashioned ice cream parlor next door to El Capitan Theatre. 6834 Hollywood Blvd. ☎ 323/939-9024. Shakes and sundaes $4–$9.

6 ★ kids **Page Museum at La Brea Tar Pits.** In a town that's not always reverential toward history (much less prehistory), the La Brea Tar Pits capture life as it was in the Los Angeles basin tens of thousands of years ago. ⏱1 hr. See p. 418, **1**.

7 ★ kids **Petersen Automotive Museum.** There could be no better city than Los Angeles to house a museum about the automobile and how it's shaped American culture. There's an ongoing exhibition of Hollywood star cars, including the original 1966 Batmobile and a 1942 Cadillac that Clark Gable gave to his

> *From bugs to Model Ts, the Petersen Automotive Museum showcases over 150 rare and classic cars.*

Universal Studios Hollywood

Although this high-tech theme park may not have the same magical allure as Disneyland, it is close to Hollywood, and it packs an entertaining, if sanitized, hour-long tour of its moviemaking facilities. In 1915, Carl Laemmle bought 230 acres of farmland just north of Hollywood and built the world's largest motion picture production facility, Universal City Studios (eventually expanding to 420 acres). In the early years, the studio figured the burgeoning film industry needed all the publicity it could get and happily opened its doors to spectators; today the tradition continues (albeit at a much higher price).

Popular thrill rides and attractions include the new *The Simpsons* virtual-reality ride flying through Krustyland with Homer and the gang, the *Revenge of the Mummy* roller coaster, the *Backdraft* simulated warehouse fire, and—my favorite for a hot summer day—the water-soaked *Jurassic Park* river ride. Lines can get long; consider splurging on a "Front of the Line" pass ($139), which eliminates the wait for any ride, or a VIP pass ($239), which combines the "Front of the Line" pass with a private studio tour. Multiday discounts are available on Universal's website.

Universal Studios (☎ 818/662-3801; www.universalstudioshollywood.com) is located at 100 Universal City Plaza (off the 101 Hollywood Fwy.). Admission costs $69 for adults, $59 for children under 48 inches tall, and free for kids 2 and under. Call for current hours.

wife, Carole Lombard. Kids flock to the Discovery Center, where they can learn about how a car works with Professor Lugnut or hop on a police motorcycle in the Vroom Room. ⏲ 1 hr. 6060 Wilshire Blvd., at Fairfax Ave. ☎ 323/930-CARS (2277). www.petersen.org. Admission $10 adults, $5 seniors and students, $3 children 5–12, free for kids 4 & under. Parking $5. Tues–Sun 10am–6pm.

8 **kids** **Pacific Park, Santa Monica Pier.** It might not be Disneyland, but, hey, it's on the water and does a good job hearkening back to the turn-of-the-20th-century amusement piers. The Ferris wheel is the high point, literally and figuratively. ⏲ 45 min. On the Santa Monica Pier. ☎ 310/260-8744. www.pacpark.com. Free admission; cost varies per ride. Summer Sun–Thurs 11am–11pm, Fri–Sat 11am–12:30am; rest of the year Mon–Fri noon–midnight, Sat 11am–midnight, Sun 11am–9pm.

9 **kids** **Santa Monica Carousel.** Built by Charles Looff in 1916, the Looff Hippodrome Carousel building is a National Historic Landmark. The carousel is a spinning spectacle of lights, hand-carved ponies, and brightly colored chariots. The original 1909 merry-go-round was replaced by this "new" one built in 1922. ⏲ 15 min. On the Santa Monica Pier. ☎ 310/394-8042. www.santamonicapier.org. Rides $1 adults, 50¢ kids. Mon–Thurs 11am–5pm; Fri–Sun 11am–7pm. Rides $1 adults, 50¢ kids.

That's Entertainment!

Have you done your homework by devouring countless hours of movies, television, and music? Well, no one said that was a spectator sport—you'll need to start early and finish strong to cram the following tour into a single blockbuster day.

> *Walk the same red-carpet route as Clooney and Streep when you walk into the Kodak Theatre, site of the annual Academy Awards.*

❶ ★ Hollywood Museum. Don't make the mistake of lumping this in with tourist traps like the Hollywood Wax or Ripley's Believe It or Not! museums. This museum—occupying the historic Max Factor building, restored to its full Art Deco loveliness—traces the history of film with 5,000 displays of rare Hollywood memorabilia, including Hannibal Lecter's cell block, Indiana Jones's whip, Rita Hayworth's makeup case, Cary Grant's Rolls-Royce, and the earliest film cameras. ⏱ 30 min. 1660 N. Highland Ave. (at Hollywood Blvd.). ☎ 323/464-7776. www.thehollywoodmuseum.com. Admission $15 adults, $12 seniors and kids 11 & under. Parking $2 w/validation. Thurs–Sun 10am–5pm.

❷ ★ Larry Edmund's Bookshop. This Hollywood mainstay and Quentin Tarantino favorite is a film geek's paradise with stacks of books on the craft and history of filmmaking, thousands of vintage movie posters, and a bottomless well of movie stills, lobby cards, and publicity shots. ⏱ 15 min. 6644 Hollywood Blvd. (at Cherokee Ave.). ☎ 323/463-3273. www.larryedmunds.com. Mon–Fri 10am–5:30pm, Sat 10am–6pm, Sun noon–5:30pm.

❸ ★ Kodak Theatre. If you're a person who hosts an Oscar party every year at home with your own printed ballots, a 30-minute walking tour of the Kodak Theatre will tickle your fancy. You'll see the grand entrance (you'll

1 Hollywood Museum
2 Larry Edmund's Bookshop
3 Kodak Theatre
4 Egyptian Theatre
5 Capitol Records
6 Sunset & Gower
7 Paramount Studios
8 Cinerama Dome/ ArcLight Cinemas
9 Amoeba Music
10 Charlie Chaplin Studios
11 Formosa Cafe
12 Guitar Center's Rockwalk and Museum
13 Andaz West Hollywood (Riot House)
14 Whisky a Go Go
15 Troubadour

> *Forget CDs and iPods—the 1956 building of record-ing mecca Capitol Records resembles a stack of 45-rpm records.*

have to imagine the red carpet), a few Oscar statuettes, the 3,300-seat auditorium inspired by a European opera house, and the backstage VIP area. ⏲ 30 min. 6801 Hollywood Blvd. (at Highland Ave.). ☎ 323/308-6300. www.kodak theatre.com. Admission $15 adults, $10 seniors and kids 3 & up, free for kids 2 & under. Jun–Aug Mon–Sun 10:30am–4pm; Sept–May Mon–Sun 10:30am–2:30pm.

❹ ★ **Egyptian Theatre.** In 1922, as the hunt closed in on King Tut's tomb, Sid Grauman un-veiled the Egyptian Theatre, the second of his spectacular, themed movie palaces. Reopened in 1998 following a multimillion-dollar restora-tion, the theater is now the home of the non-profit American Cinematheque, which caters to

serious film enthusiasts. It offers fresh, 70mm prints of classics (*Lawrence of Arabia, The Sound of Music*); programs of national cinema (classic Italian, Russian fantastik, and British new wave); director retrospectives (Douglas Sirk, Orson Welles); and in-person tributes to actors and filmmakers (George Clooney, Quentin Taran-tino). If you're lucky you can catch the monthly screening of *Forever Hollywood*, an hour-long look at a century of cinema. ⏲ 1 hr. 6712 Holly-wood Blvd. ☎ 323/466-FILM (3456). www.egyp-tiantheatre.com. Forever Hollywood $7 adults, $5 seniors and students.

❺ ★ **Capitol Records.** The 13-story landmark 2 blocks north of the world-famous corner of Hollywood and Vine looks like a gigantic stack of 45 rpm records on a turntable (a heap of mp3s doesn't have the same magic, does it?), but it was actually designed by modern-ist architect Welton Becket to be the world's first circular office building when it debuted in 1956. Frank Sinatra banged out 19 albums in these hallowed studios, which also recorded the likes of Nat King Cole, Ella Fitzgerald, Dean Martin, and the Beach Boys. The first record company based on the West Coast, Capitol Records also imported British acts such as the Beatles, Pink Floyd, Duran Duran, and Radiohead. ⏲ 10 min. 1750 Vine St. ☎ 323/462-6252.

❻ **Sunset & Gower.** In an old tavern on the northwest corner of Sunset and Gower, the Nestor Company launched the first film studio in Hollywood in 1911. Using natural California sunshine and a small wooden stage, several one reelers were shot each week: one West-ern, one drama, one comedy. In 1912 Nestor merged with Carl Laemmle's Universal Film Company. The original building was razed in 1936 to make room for the CBS Columbia Square radio studio, which can be seen today. On the southeast corner of the same intersec-tion sits the Sunset-Gower studios, formerly the home of Columbia Pictures Studios (1921–72), which produced countless gems such as *It Happened One Night, From Here to Eternity, Dr. Strangelove,* and *Funny Girl.* On the southwest corner known as Gower Gulch, cowboy extras used to loiter in hopes of gaining work on the many Westerns filming nearby. ⏲ 10 min.

> *Wrap yourself in some of the most luxurious movie theaters around at ArcLight Complex, including the retro-cool Cinerama Dome.*

7 ★ **Paramount Studios.** Paramount Studios traces its origins to a rented horse barn near Sunset and Vine in 1913. Thirteen years later, it moved to its current location and never left, unlike the rest of the major studios in Hollywood. The back lot eventually gobbled up neighboring R.K.O. Pictures, and the distinctive globe is still visible in the southwest corner. Book tickets in advance for a 2-hour golf cart tour, which scoots you through the "living history" of the film and television soundstages. This is where the stars punch the clock, so keep your eyes peeled for sightings. Don't get so caught up gawking that you forget whose footsteps you're walking in: Rudolph Valentino, Mary Pickford, W. C. Fields, Alfred Hitchcock, the Marx Brothers, and many more. Before leaving, make sure to get a photo of yourself in front of the famous Bronson Gate, the arched gateway you may remember Gloria Swanson driving through in *Sunset Boulevard*. ⏱ 2 hr. 5555 Melrose Ave. ☎ 323/ 956-1777. www.paramount.com. Tours $35 per person. Kids 11 & under not admitted. Mon–Fri 10am–2pm.

8 ★★ **Cinerama Dome/ArcLight Cinemas.** Built in 1963 to showcase the widescreen format, the landmark Cinerama Dome now belongs to the state-of-the-art ArcLight Complex of 14 theaters. While the Dome is the coolest with its curving screen, all of the theaters feature sumptuous assigned seating, immaculate sound, and detail-oriented service. ⏱ 2 hr. 6160 W. Sunset Blvd. (btw. Vine St. and Ivar Ave.). ☎ 323/464-1478. www.arclightcinemas.com. Tickets $7.75–$15. Parking $2 for 4 hr. w/validation.

9 ★★ **Amoeba Music.** A mecca for music lovers, this independently owned store spans an entire block of Sunset and offers the biggest and baddest selection of tunes in town. ⏱ 30 min. See p. 470.

10 **Charlie Chaplin Studios.** In 1917, on acres of orange groves at Sunset and La Brea, Charlie Chaplin built himself a studio, a row of English-style cottages, where he shot many of his classics, such as *The Gold Rush, City Lights*, and *Modern Times*. Today Jim Henson Productions occupies the building, which explains the statue of Kermit the Frog dressed as The Little Tramp. ⏱ 10 min. 1416 N. La Brea Ave.

> *Get your groove on at gigantic Amoeba Music—if you can't find what you want to hear here, look again.*

⑪ 🍽 ★★ **Formosa Cafe.** The shiny, strip-mall surroundings may throw you, but trust me: This is a vintage Hollywood watering hole. Formosa Cafe has always attracted celebrity lunchtimers and late-nighters. Marilyn Monroe and Clark Gable shared a red-leather booth while taking a break from shooting *The Misfits*. Bogie, Sinatra, Brando, and, in recent years, Bono, have all sidled up to this bar. The food is nothing special, but the atmosphere you can eat with a spoon. 7156 Santa Monica Blvd. (at Formosa Ave.). ☎ 323/850-9050. Entrees $12–$19.

⓬ **Guitar Center's Rockwalk and Museum.** The Rockwalk, the sidewalk in front of the Guitar Center, is the rock equivalent of the forecourt of Grauman's Chinese Theatre. The concrete has been high-fived by the talented hands of Chuck Berry, Jerry Lee Lewis, Jimmy Page, Eddie Van Halen, and more. There's also an awesome display of memorabilia such as Eddie's homemade red Kramer guitar, Stevie Ray Vaughn's denim jacket, Keith Moon's drum kit, and platform boots from KISS. Oh yeah, you can buy a guitar here, too. ⏱ 15 min. 7425 Sunset Blvd. ☎ 323/874-1060. www.rockwalk.com. Mon-Fri 10am–9pm; Sat 10am–8pm; Sun 11am–8pm.

> *Led Zep, Van Halen, and the Doors are some of the rock legends who have played at Whisky a Go Go.*

⓭ **Andaz West Hollywood (Riot House).** This monument to mayhem began life innocently enough in 1958 as the Gene Autry Hotel. By the mid-'60s, the hotel became the stomping

> *Putting their heavy-metal mark in cement, The Scorpions leave a lasting impression for the Guitar Center's Rockwalk.*

grounds (literally) of rock 'n' rollers who came to play nearby clubs on the Strip. Over the years the Riot House, as it came to be called, became a sort of bad-boy finishing school; members of Led Zeppelin rode their motorcycles up and down the hallways, and, on separate occasions, Keith Richards of the Rolling Stones and Keith Moon of the Who hurled televisions out of 10th-floor windows. ⏲10 min. See p. 481.

⑭ ★ **Whisky a Go Go.** Aside from its footnote as the birthplace of go-go dancing, the Whisky opened in 1964 and was the epicenter of the Los Angeles rock scene for 3 decades. The 1960s saw the Doors, the Byrds, Love, and Buffalo Springfield. The 1970s imported Led Zeppelin, the Who, and Roxy Music. The lineup in the later '70s edged toward the homegrown punk rock of the Germs, the Runaways, and X. Then came the pop metal of Van Halen, followed by Mötley Crüe, and Guns N' Roses in the '80s. ⏲10 min. See p. 493.

⑮ ★★ **Troubadour.** In the 1960s the Troubadour was a hotbed for folkies such as Bob Dylan and Joni Mitchell. Over the years, the small club helped launch the careers of other singer-songwriters: James Taylor, Elton John, Randy Newman, and Tom Waits. And in 1985, during the heyday of heavy metal, Guns N'

Roses made its debut on this stage and caught the eye of a Geffen A&R rep. My favorite wish-I-was-there moment happened in 1974, when John Lennon (on his 18-month-long "lost weekend" in Los Angeles) and Harry Nilsson were tossed out for drunkenly heckling the Smothers Brothers. ⏲10 min. See p. 493.

Cinespia

No one with a pulse can resist a classic movie projected on a mausoleum wall. Classic and campy, creepy and cool—**Cinespia** is a summer screening series set on the tomb-strewn grounds of the Hollywood Forever Cemetery. With rabid word-of-mouth and national press coverage (*Vanity Fair, USA Today,* and NPR), the scene at this boneyard is anything but underground. Pack a picnic basket and get there early to claim a choice spot (or is it plot?) on the grass and enjoy a glass of wine as the sun sets and the DJ spins. Parking and getting in can be a slog, but the crowd's enthusiasm—cheering a crackling line from Cary Grant or Jack Nicholson—is downright refreshing.

Cinespia, 6000 Santa Monica Blvd., at Gower St. (www.cinespia.org), is on Saturday in the summer; gates open at 7:30pm, film begins at 9pm. Admission is $10.

L.A. NOIR

Hard-boiled Crime Fiction in
the City of Angels

BY DAN TUCKER

SUNSHINE. PALM TREES. ORANGE GROVES. MOVIE STARS. What is it about this town that gets so many writers and filmmakers to dwell on the seamy side of life?

The darker aspects of human nature—and of Los Angeles itself—come to high-contrast, nihilistic life in the hardboiled crime fiction of writers such as Raymond Chandler and James M. Cain, both transplants to the city (Cain only briefly) whose novels form the backbone of the great 1930s and 1940s noir genre. Both men were regular contributors to the classic pulp magazine *Black Mask* launched by the great literary editors H.L. Mencken and George Jean Nathan. And both worked as Hollywood screenwriters, exploring through their writing the sinister forces running from downtown flophouses to the highest reaches of L.A. society, politics, and law enforcement. Above all, both elevated the genre with intelligent plots; snappy, clipped dialogue; and a streetwise, world-weary nobility.

Chandler's and Cain's contemporary heirs are writers such as Walter Mosley and James Ellroy, each of whom rejuvenated the noir genre with hard-boiled crime fiction set safely in the past, but with themes of duplicity and corruption—and the power of hard-nosed, uncompromising pursuit of the truth—that are timeless: A forthcoming video game, L.A. Noire, promises to carry the aesthetic, if not the spirit, of hardboiled Los Angeles crime fiction into the next generation.

Classic L.A. Film Noir

Cinema purists insist that film noir must be black-and-white, but when it comes to Los Angeles, it's more a frame of mind. Here's a selection of top-notch film noir each of which is either set in Los Angeles or written by an L.A.-based writer.

Double Indemnity (1944). An L.A. insurance man (Fred MacMurray) plots the perfect murder with femme fatale housewife Phyllis Dietrichson (Barbara Stanwyck)... but will she betray him? Is his boss (Edward G. Robinson) on to him? Raymond Chandler and director Billy Wilder wrote the screenplay from the James M. Cain novel.

Murder My Sweet (1944). A freed convict hires Philip Marlowe (Dick Powell) to track down his ex-girlfriend, and the trail of murder and corruption leads to the highest echelon of L.A. society. Has its finale on the Santa Monica Pier. Based on the Chandler novel *Farewell My Lovely*.

The Big Sleep (1946). The wealthy General Sternwood hires Marlowe (Humphrey Bogart) to keep an eye on his wayward youngest daughter, and trouble ensues as Marlowe uncovers a trail of drugs, pornography, and murder. Marlowe falls hard for the General's older daughter, played by Lauren Bacall. From a novel by Chandler.

Kiss Me Deadly (1955). An enigmatic and doomed hitchhiker (Cloris Leachman) leads Mike Hammer (Ralph Meeker) first off a cliff and then onto the thug-strewn trail of a small, mysterious valise filled with a radioactive substance. From a novel by Mickey Spillane, who cowrote the screenplay.

L.A. Confidential (1997). Three L.A. cops (Russell Crowe, Guy Pearce, and Kevin Spacey) and a sleazy tabloid reporter (Danny DeVito) try to untangle a web of intrigue involving the L.A.P.D. brass, the DA's office, and a prostitution ring of movie star lookalikes, including "Veronica Lake" (Kim Basinger)—while simultaneously tangling with each other. From a novel by James Ellroy.

Devil in a Blue Dress (1995). Ezekiel "Easy" Rawlins (Denzel Washington), an African-American World War II veteran in 1948 Los Angeles, deals with mobsters, small-time hoods, crooked politicians, and thuggish cops as he trolls the juke joints of South Central L.A. and the Hollywood Hills in his pursuit of the mysterious girlfriend (Jennifer Beals) of the wealthy man likely to become L.A.'s next mayor (Terry Kinney). From a novel by Walter Mosley.

Raymond Chandler

If Dashiell Hammett was the chancellor of American hardboiled detective writers, Chandler was certainly the hard-drinking dean of its Los Angeles school. Chandler used "the detective story to create the whole of Los Angeles in much the same way that Dickens and Balzac created London and Paris for future generations," according to his biographer Frank MacShane.

Chandler, who led an impoverished life in L.A. until he gained financial success as a screenwriter in the late 1940s, was exceedingly familiar with the best and worst the city had to offer, and he made extensive use of both in his fictional settings. Chandler's best-known hero, Philip Marlowe, prowls real L.A. locations, some given fictitious names—"Bay City" for Santa Monica, e.g.—and some still in existence, such as the Musso & Frank Grill in Hollywood.

Los Angeles Art & Architecture

The city isn't just red carpet flashbulbs and Botox jobs. Visit these six architectural landmarks and three world-class museums to dispel the myth that "Los Angeles culture" is an oxymoron.

> Like soaring wings of a giant sailing ship, the stainless steel-clad Walt Disney Concert Hall adds drama downtown.

START Orange Grove Ave., 3 blocks north of Hwy. 134.

❶ ★★ Gamble House. This 1908 masterpiece in the American Arts and Crafts style was designed by Charles and Henry Greene, masters of the Craftsman bungalow. Commissioned by David and Mary Gamble (of Proctor and Gamble) to be their winter residence in California, the house is a National Historic Landmark. The exterior uses Japanese-style proportions, low and horizontal, in an open, California setting. The interior is especially impressive with stained-glass doors and windows and intricately crafted woodwork. In the home's original garage structure, the bookstore (Tues–Sat 10am–5pm; Sun 11:30am–5pm) carries a fantastic selection of architectural books and guides. ⏱ 1 hr. 4 Westmoreland Place, Pasadena. ☎ 626/793-3334. www.gamblehouse.org. Tours $10 adults, $7 seniors and students, free for kids 11 & under. Thurs–Sun noon–3pm.

❷ ★★★ Norton Simon Museum. This stunning private collection of art boasts major pieces by Picasso, Matisse, Diego Rivera, van Gogh, Rembrandt, and Rodin. The museum holds a significant collection of works by Impressionists, including Monet and Renoir, and over 100 works by Edgar Degas. ⏱ 1 hr. 411 W. Colorado Blvd. ☎ 626/449-6840. www.nortonsimon. org. Admission $8 adults; $4 seniors; free for

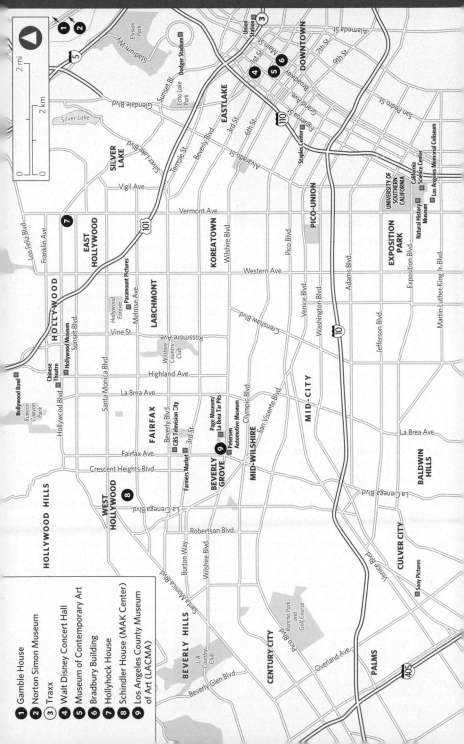

> *Step into a world of priceless artwork, the private collection of multinational businessman and philanthropist Norton Simon.*

students and kids 17 & under; free for everyone 1st Fri of the month 6–9pm. Mon, Wed–Thurs & Sat–Sun noon–6pm; Fri noon–9pm; Tues closed.

③ 🍴 **Traxx.** Tucked into Union Station, Traxx is a surprisingly swanky restaurant with a separate, intimate bar area. Choose from a tasty menu of is tapas, soups, salads, and sandwiches. Or order up the excellent house martini. 800 N. Alameda St. ☎ 213/625-1999. Entrees $13–$24.

④ ★★★ **Walt Disney Concert Hall.** Frank Gehry's instant classic is a Rorschach test for lovers of architecture. What do you see as you gaze upon its steel waves? Circle the 22 million pounds of steel and try to find an angle that doesn't stretch your imagination like taffy. The audio tour is a great primer, but you'll have to come back for a show to experience the auditorium and its stunning acoustics. ⏱ 1 hr. 111 S. Grand Ave. ☎ 323/850-2000. www.laphil.com. Free self-guided audio tours most days 10am–2pm; free guided tours Thurs–Sun 10am–1pm (times vary).

⑤ **Museum of Contemporary Art.** In a striking red sandstone building designed by acclaimed Japanese architect Arata Isozaki, the museum's permanent collection contains 5,000 pieces, including work by Andy Warhol, Mark Rothko, and David Hockney. ⏱ 45 min. 250 S. Grand Ave. ☎ 213/626-6222. www.moca.org. Admission $10

adults, $5 seniors and students, free for children 11 & under; free for all Thurs 5–8pm. Mon & Fri 11am–5pm; Thurs 11am–8pm; Sat–Sun 11am–6pm.

⑥ ★★ **Bradbury Building.** The ordinary brick facade of this 1893 structure, the city's oldest commercial building, masks one of the most striking interior spaces you'll ever find. A peaked glass ceiling makes for a dramatic dance of sunlight and shadow in the five-story atrium, which has two open-cage elevators, suspended mail chutes, marble staircases, and spidery, wrought-iron railings. Its inexperienced architect George Wyman took more inspiration from science fiction than from formal architectural training. ⏱ 10 min. 304 S. Broadway. ☎ 213/626-1893. Mon–Fri 9am–6pm; Sat–Sun 9am–5pm.

⑦ ★ **Hollyhock House.** The exalted Frank Lloyd Wright designed this private residence for oil heiress Aline Barnsdall, who envisioned it as the centerpiece of a large arts complex. The hilltop structure is modeled after a Mayan temple, with exterior walls tilting back slightly, and a roofline with symmetrical reliefs based on a geometric abstraction of the owner's favorite flower, the hollyhock. ⏱ 1 hr. 4800 Hollywood Blvd. ☎ 323/644-6269. www.hollyhockhouse.net. Tours $7 adults, $3 students and seniors, free for kids 11 & under. Wed–Sun 12:30, 1:30, 2:30 and 3:30pm.

⑧ ★ **Schindler House (MAK Center).** An Austrian architect who worked under Frank Lloyd Wright, Rudolph Schindler came west to work on the Hollyhock House before launching his own practice with the design of his home in 1922. Modern and modular, with interlocking L shapes, the house was conceptualized as shared living and work space for multiple households. ⏱ 30 min. 835 N. King's Rd. ☎ 323/651-1510. www.makcenter.org. Admission $7 adults, $6 seniors and students, free for kids 11 & under. Free tours Sat–Sun 11am–6pm. Wed–Sun 11am–6pm.

SITE GUIDE PAGE 439

⑨ ★★ **Los Angeles County Museum of Art (LACMA).** The city's largest collection of art (with 110,000 pieces) is spread across a series of buildings, stylistically unified by internationally acclaimed architect Renzo Piano.

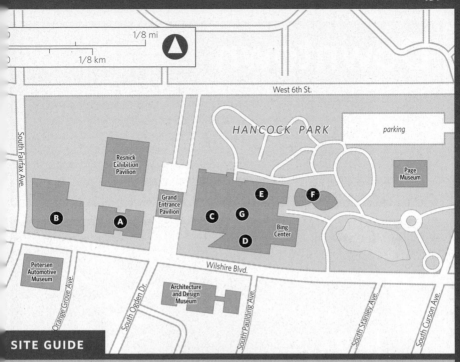

West 6th St.

HANCOCK PARK

parking

South Fairfax Ave.

Resnick Exhibition Pavilion

Page Museum

Grand Entrance Pavilion

E

F

B

A

C

G

D

Bing Center

Petersen Automotive Museum

Wilshire Blvd.

Orange Grove Ave.

South Ogden Dr.

Architecture and Design Museum

South Paulding Ave.

South Stanley Ave.

South Curson Ave.

SITE GUIDE

9 Los Angeles County Museum of Art

The **A** **Broad Contemporary Art Museum** is the home of the museum's 20th-century paintings and sculptures, including works by Hockney, Kadinsky, Magritte, and Matisse. If you're with kids, head next door to the **B** **LACMA West** (in the 1939 Art Deco building that used to be the May Company department store) to play in the Boone Children's Gallery, where kids can make art of their own. Head back to the entrance and continue on to the **C** **Ahmanson Building,** where you can meander for days in an astounding array of galleries: Chinese, Korean, African, Islamic, pre-Columbian, South and Southeast Asian, European Painting, and the Decorative Arts. In the **D** **Art of the Americas Building,** which has the American and Latin American collections, you'll find work by Winslow Homer (*The Cotton Pickers*), Mary Cassatt (*Mother About to Wash Her Sleepy Child*), and Diego Rivera. The **E** **Hammer Building** houses Chinese and Korean art, as well as the museum's photography collection.. Next door, the serene **F** **Japanese**

Pavilion displays Buddhist and Shinto sculpture, woodblock prints, Edo paintings, and intricately carved sculptures called netsuke. Time your visit to catch the free **G** **Friday Night Jazz** series, which features Californian jazz artists playing in the courtyard (Apr–Nov Fri 6–8pm). ⏱ At least 1 hr. 5905 Wilshire Blvd. ☎ 323/857-6000. www.lacma.org. Admission $12 adults, $8 seniors, free for kids 17 & under; free for all after 5pm and all day the 2nd Tues of the month. Parking $5–$8. Mon–Tues and Thurs noon–8pm; Fri noon–9pm; Sat–Sun 11am–8pm.

Downtown

Downtown Los Angeles has seen a remarkable resurgence in recent years. Old architectural marvels (City Hall, the Orpheum, and the Eastern Columbia) have been gussied up, while new marvels (Walt Disney Concert Hall and Cathedral of Our Lady of Angels) have been added. Even an economic downturn and a precipitous drop in California real estate have not slowed the steady influx of überhip bars (the Edison, the Varnish) and scene-stealing restaurants (Rivera, Church and State, Bottega Louie).

> The golden age of train travel still lives on in the soaring, cathedral-like waiting room of 1939 Union Station.

START N. Main St. & Cesar Chavez Ave.

❶ ★★ El Pueblo de Los Angeles. As the birthplace of Los Angeles, this makes an *excelente* start to a downtown tour. Forty-four Mexican settlers founded a pueblo in 1781 on the orders of Carlos III of Spain, who needed food for the troops guarding Alta California, this faraway Spanish province. The 44-acre historical park contains the city's oldest house, **Avila Adobe** (1818); the city's oldest church, **Old Plaza Church** (1822); and the city's first fire station, **Old Plaza Firehouse** (1884). Wander the brick path of **Olvera Street,** a pedestrian marketplace bursting like a piñata with Mexican knickknacks. Keep an eye out for the **Pelanconi House** (1855), the first brick building in Los Angeles, and home to the popular **La Golondrina** restaurant since 1930. The visitor center is located in a Victorian building from 1887 called the **Sepulveda House,** where tours, maps, brochures, and gifts are available, as well as a free screening of a short film, *Pueblo of Promise.* ⏱ 1 ½ hr. Visitor center, 622 N. Main St. ☎ 213/628-1274. www.elpueblo.lacity.org. Park Mon–Sat 10am–3pm. Most historic buildings Mon–Sat 10am–3pm.

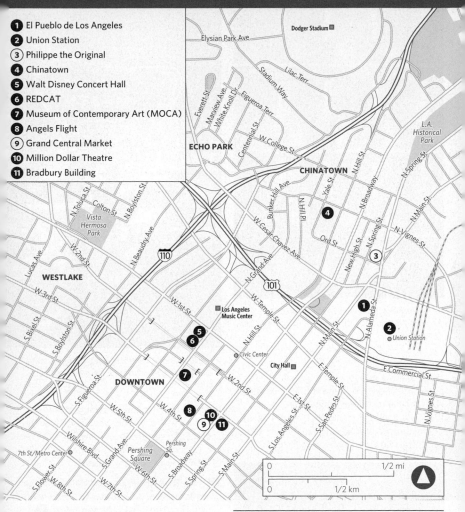

1. El Pueblo de Los Angeles
2. Union Station
3. Philippe the Original
4. Chinatown
5. Walt Disney Concert Hall
6. REDCAT
7. Museum of Contemporary Art (MOCA)
8. Angels Flight
9. Grand Central Market
10. Million Dollar Theatre
11. Bradbury Building

Olvera St. market daily 10am–7pm. La Golondrina restaurant daily 9am–9pm.

2 ★ **Union Station.** Considered to be the last great railway station built in America, this 1939 terminal used to see 7,000 folks a day, coming and going on three different railroads. Although still a vital transportation hub (subway, light rail, Metrolink, and Amtrak all stop here), today the station is better known as a time capsule of the golden age of train travel. A quiet seat in the glamorous waiting room— with a cathedral ceiling, twinkling chandeliers, and marble and tile finishes—is a trip back in time. ⏱ 20 min. 800 N. Alameda St. ☎ 213/683-6979. Daily 24 hr.

③ 🍴 ★ **Philippe the Original.** Since this legendary eatery opened its doors a century ago, the big seller has been the French dipped sandwich, which the restaurant claims to have invented (after taking a bite, you're not going to question it). With sawdust floors and dirt-cheap prices, this is an everyman's paradise. And just to prove that they're keeping it real, a cup of joe is a dime—you heard right: 10¢. 1001 N. Alameda St. (at Ord St.). ☎ 213/628-3781. Sandwiches $5–$7.

4 ★ **Chinatown.** Lacking the scope and vibrancy of the Chinese communities in San Francisco and New York, the "new"

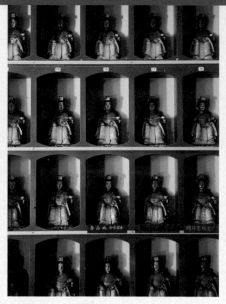

> Peek into another culture in L.A.'s Chinatown, a mix of Old World traditions, mom-and-pop shops, and restaurants.

Chinatown—sadly, the "old" Chinatown was razed to make way for Union Station—juxtaposes a reverence for ancient traditions with an appreciation for the vanguard, such as the experimental art galleries blossoming on Chung King Road. Poke through the tiny shops in Central Plaza, and look for my favorite

Downtown Art Walk

On the second Tuesday night of the month from 7 to 11pm, local artists of all ages, gadabouts, students, and scenesters gather in downtown's Historic Core to stroll through the 45 or so participating galleries along Gallery Row. Five years ago, the first event drew less than 100 folks; the most recent art walk drew over 10,000. If your feet start to flag before your sense of fun does, hop on the Hippodrome, a shuttle bus (although the driver prefers "floating salon featuring live music and art happenings") that loops along the row.

The action takes place on Main and Springs streets, between Second and Ninth streets. For more information, see www.downtownartwalk.com.

> Dig in at Grand Central Market, the largest and oldest food hall in Los Angeles, big on ethnic cuisine.

building, the Hop Louie Restaurant, a 1941 structure with a five-tier pagoda roof. Serenity seekers can visit the lovely new Buddhist temple, Cam Au, a few blocks away at 750 Yale St. ⏱ 40 min. www.chinatownla.com.

5 ★★★ **Walt Disney Concert Hall.** Frank Gehry's masterpiece is often credited with revitalizing downtown L.A. ⏱ 1 hr. See p. 438, **4**.

6 ★ **REDCAT.** Tucked away in the southwest corner of the Walt Disney Concert Hall, REDCAT (the Roy and Edna Disney/CalArts Theater) presents experimental films, plays, and art exhibitions. Equally provocative is the lounge's signature drink, the Cat-a-tonic. 631 W. Second St. ☎ 213/237-2800. www.redcat.org Tues-Fri 9am-9pm; Sat-Sun noon-9pm. Check website for events.

7 ★★ **Museum of Contemporary Art (MOCA).** A must-see for fans of the modern masters. ⏱ 45 min. See p. 438, **5**.

8 ★ **Angels Flight.** The "shortest railway in the world" (actually a two-car funicular) was built in 1901 so that the wealthy residents of the Victorian mansions of Bunker Hill could take a penny-ride down to the town's main shopping district. Eventually the well-heeled headed for the suburbs and the Bunker Hill enclave degenerated into slums; by 1969, the cars were put into storage. In 1996, after a 27-year hiatus, the Los Angeles landmark was restored and reopened; unfortunately, a fatal accident in 2001 shut it down once again. But as of spring 2010, Angels Flight is finally back on track; a one-way, 1-minute jaunt costs only 25¢. Hill St. (btw. Third & Fourth sts.). Daily 6:45am–10pm.

⑨ 🍴 **Grand Central Market.** Since 1917 this open-air market has been a lively place to pick up coffee, ice cream, or tasty ethnic grub on the cheap—Hawaiian barbecue, Cuban sandwiches, Persian kebabs, *pupusas* (deep-fried pastries filled with meat, beans, and cheese), and empanadas. 317 S. Broadway. ☎ 213/624-2378. www.grandcentralsquare.com. Most items $3–$9.

⑩ ★ **Million Dollar Theatre.** Built for (gasp!) $1 million, Sid Grauman's first take on a movie palace opened in 1918 with Mary Pickford and Charlie Chaplin on hand. The lavishly ornamented interior resembles a Mexican cathedral; in fact, for many years a Spanish-speaking church held services in the 2,100-seat auditorium, and today it presents Spanish-speaking live theater. The once-mighty Broadway District was comprised of a dozen movie

> *Like a Jules Verne dream, the Bradbury Building's Victorian-style courtyard features open-air elevators and wrought-iron railings.*

palaces within several blocks, making it a monument to escapism during the lean years of the Depression. Other spectacular theaters still standing are **Los Angeles Theatre** (615 S. Broadway), the **Palace** (630 S. Broadway), and the **Orpheum** (842 S. Broadway). ⏱ 10 min. 307 S. Broadway. www.milliondollartheater.com.

⑪ ★★ **Bradbury Building.** The awe-inspiring courtyard has starred in numerous films, including *Blade Runner.* ⏱ 20 min. See p. 438, ⑥.

L.A. Conservancy Tours

A nonprofit organization dedicated to preserving the city's architectural and cultural heritage, the **Los Angeles Conservancy** (☎ 213/623-2489; www.laconservancy. org) offers a variety of downtown walking tours: Art Deco, Little Tokyo, Union Station, Angelino Heights, Historic Core, Broadway Historic Theatre, and more. The informative, docent-led tours ($10 adults, $5 kids) run on Saturday; start between 10am and 2pm; and most last 2 ½ hours. For more information, check out the website, which also provides free self-guided tour maps and downloadable podcasts.

Venice

No area of the sprawling Los Angeles metropolis has as colorful a history as Venice. Before it was a place, it was a grand concept: first the "Coney Island of the Pacific," then "Venice of America." At the end of the 1920s, it was an oil boomtown; a few years later, it was a ghost town. The '50s brought the Beatniks; the '60s, the hippies; the '70s, the surfers and skateboarders. In recent years, as the canals cleaned up, gourmet restaurants moved in, and real estate soared, Venice has somehow managed to maintain its bohemian edge.

> Anything goes along the Venice Boardwalk, a people-watching gold mine with joggers, roller-bladers, and skateboarders.

START Venice Blvd. at Venice Way.

❶ ★ Venice Farmers Market. A morning stroll through a farmers market is a quintessential Southern California experience and can offer a revealing look at the market's neighborhood and residents. While Venice's market may not be the city's best (that title goes to Santa Monica's on Wed and Sat), it's friendly and brimming with adventurous fruits and vegetables like persimmons and squash blossoms. ⏲ 30 min. 502 Venice Blvd. (at Venice Way). www.venicefarmersmarket.com. Fri 7–11am.

❷ ★ Venice Canals. The image of these canals, like the HOLLYWOOD Sign is a Los Angeles icon

born of a busted real-estate venture. In the early 1900s, entrepreneur Abbot Kinney dreamt up "Venice of America," 16 miles of canals connecting piers, theaters, restaurants, and hotels; he even imported a couple dozen gondoliers from Italy. Cars or gondolas: Guess which won out in the long run? Only 6 canals remain of Kinney's original 16; most were paved over in 1929 to make room for automobiles, while the few remaining canals were neglected for half a century. In 1994 the city dredged the canals and added small bridges and sidewalks. Tossing a few crumbs to the ducks in the placid water, you might wonder whether Kinney's vision was so crazy after all. Let yourself wander and take in

1 Venice Farmers Market
2 Venice Canals
3 Norton House
4 L.A. Louver
5 Venice Boardwalk
6 Jody Maroni's Sausage Kingdom
7 Muscle Beach
8 Venice Art Walls
9 Venice Beach Skate Park
10 Venice Murals by Rip Cronk
11 Abbot Kinney Boulevard
12 Jin Patisserie

the eclectic homes that line the canals. ⏱ 30 min. Venice Blvd. (btw. Pacific and Ocean aves.), Venice. Start at the Grand Canal and follow the bridges.

3 ★ **Norton House.** This residential design by Frank Gehry fascinates me, mainly because of its awfulness, as if a 9-year-old boy replaced the blueprints with his crayon sketch of a treehouse. If, however, you side with the architect's opinion that "buildings under construction look nicer than buildings finished," you'll love this odd duck. ⏱ 10 min. 2509 Ocean Front Walk.

4 ★ **L.A. Louver.** The 8,000-square-foot gallery displays the work of such established contemporary artists as David Hockney and Ed Moses, as well as cutting-edge up-and-comers. ⏱ 30 min. 45 N. Venice Blvd. ☎ 310/822-4955. www.lalouver.com. Free admission. Tues–Sat 10am–6pm.

5 ★★★ **Venice Boardwalk.** In most places, it's not polite to stare, but on the boardwalk, it's the highest compliment you can pay a performer (without actually paying a performer). The endless stream of tacky shops are perfect for buying gifts for (a) someone with a sense of humor, or (b) someone you don't really like. For a more relaxing time, rent Rollerblades or a bike and roll up the path to Santa Monica. ⏱ At least 1 hr. Ocean Front Walk (btw. Venice Blvd. & Rose Ave.).

> *Graffiti goes legit on the Venice Art Walls, aiming to add a highbrow edge to a controversial art form.*

⑥ 🌭 **Jody Maroni's Sausage Kingdom.** Although Jody Maroni, self-proclaimed Sausage King, assures his customers that he's not making health food, these "haut dogs" are all natural, preservative free, and boast fancy flavorings such as cilantro, orange, fig, and apple. Only vegetarians will leave disappointed. 2011 Ocean Front Walk (north of Venice Blvd.). ☎ 310/822-5639. www.jodymaroni.com. Hot dogs $3–$8.

❼ ★ **Muscle Beach.** This famous outdoor gym originally resided just south of the Santa Monica Pier from the 1930s through the 1950s. Fitness gurus Jack LaLanne and Joe Gold worked out here, as well as celebrities such as Clark Gable, Kirk Douglas, and Jayne Mansfield. Later the gym migrated to facilities in Venice, where a young Arnold Schwarzenegger would stop in to pump up. Today the gym is still going strong. ⊙ 10 min. Ocean Front Walk (2 blocks north of Venice Blvd.).

❽ ★ **Venice Art Walls.** These walls are the only remnants of "The Pit," an area popular with graffiti artists from 1961 to 1999. Today a permit is required to paint on the walls (Sat–Sun only). The goal is to nurture high-quality street art while minimizing the vandalism sometimes associated with it. ⊙ 10 min. Ocean Front Walk (btw. Windward & Market sts.). www.veniceartwalls.com.

Venice Beach on Celluloid

Since the earliest days of the silent film comedies in the 1910s, moviemakers have embraced Venice's unique atmosphere. Charlie Chaplin's debuted his Little Tramp character in *Kid Auto Races at Venice* (1914), filmed on a dirt track along one of the many canals, with a roller coaster—part of the elaborate (and long-gone) amusement pier—in the background. In the 1950s the canals and the good times dried up, and Venice doubled convincingly for a seedy Mexican border town in Orson Welles's 1958 classic *Touch of Evil*. During the chase scenes, look for the oceanfront oil derricks, which used to line the beach south of Washington Street. The 1979 not-so-classic *Roller Boogie* is an unintentionally hilarious snapshot of the boardwalk's roller-disco days. Steve Martin's 1991 *L.A. Story* captures Venice's present-day image as a colorfully kooky, bohemian fun house.

> *Retro cool blends with kickback surf culture at Surfing Cowboys, a hip shop in funky-fun Venice Beach.*

> *Hang around the outdoor gym at Muscle Beach for an eyeful of buffed and polished beefcake.*

⑨ ★★ Venice Beach Skate Park. Venice surfers-turned-boarders, the Z-boys, popularized skateboarding in the '70s largely by perfecting their techniques on the smooth concrete banks and dips of drained swimming pools. Therefore it's fitting that the park's design would mimic these pools, as well as a streetscape with steps, ramps, and rails. ⏱10 min. Ocean Front Walk (at Windward St.).

⑩ ★★ Venice Murals by Rip Cronk. Venice loves its street murals. Some of the most memorable ones were created in the late '80s and early '90s by an artist named Rip Cronk. Look for the following: *Morning Shot* (at Speedway and 18th Court), which features a towering Jim Morrison; *Venice Reconstituted* (25 Windward at Speedway), a loose interpretation of Botticelli's *The Birth of Venus;* and *Homage to a Starry Night,* Cronk's nod to van Gogh (Wavecrest Ave. and Ocean Front Walk). ⏱20 min.

⑪ ★★ Abbot Kinney Boulevard. Compared to the sea of humanity on the boardwalk, this stretch of funky-chic shops and small cafes

is refreshingly laid-back. But if you see something you gotta have, you better grab it—these stores specialize in the hard to find and one of a kind. Trawl for home furnishings and decor at **Tortoise General Store, French 50s-60s,** and **Surfing Cowboys** (1208, 1103, and 1624 Abbot Kinney Blvd.). The new kid on the block, **Linus Bikes** (1413½ Abbot Kinney Blvd.), sells the coolest (and fairly affordable) bikes that look like they've been plucked out of a French new wave film. Quality restaurants also dot the block: Joe's Restaurant (1023 Abbot Kinney Blvd.) has been considered the best on the block for nearly 20 years, sophisticated and unpretentious newcomer Gjelina (1429 Abbot Kinney Blvd.) draws raves for its spectacular small plates. ⏱1 hr. Btw. Broadway St. & Venice Blvd.

⑫ 🍴 **★ Jin Patisserie.** Relax in the tranquil garden of this Asian-influenced cafe. An afternoon tea offers French teas, finger sandwiches, scones (yes, with clotted cream), cookies, and cakes—all made fresh in the store. Many folks claim that the chocolate truffles are the best in the city. 1202 Abbot Kinney Blvd., Venice. ☎310/399-8801. www.jinpatisserie. com. Afternoon tea $10–$19.

Silver Lake

Silver Lake is a bohemian enclave east of Hollywood. Once home to the first movie studios (Mack Sennett, Vitagraph, and Walt Disney) and later modernist architects (Neutra, Schindler), this hipster haven now offers one-of-a-kind shopping, eclectic eats, and a music scene that has arguably become a brand name (much like Brooklyn's Williamsburg). You can't see all of Silver Lake on foot, but the Sunset Junction makes for a happening hub.

> Bring your leather jacket, coolest hair, and a laptop to fit into the hipster-cool cafe scene in Silver Lake.

START At Sunset and Santa Monica blvds.

❶ ★ Cheese Store of Silverlake. At this quaint shop, you can grab all the fixings for a gourmet picnic: artisanal cheeses, hard-to-find wines, cured meats, and chocolates. ⏱ 10 min. 3926 W. Sunset Blvd. ☎ 323/644-7511. www.cheese storesl.com. Mon 10am–6pm; Tues–Sat 10am–6:45pm; Sun 11am–5pm.

❷ ★ Silverlake Conservatory of Music. It's only fitting that Silver Lake, with its thriving indie music scene, would have its own school of rock. Flea, local music hero and bassist for the Red Hot Chili Peppers, founded the not-for-profit organization, which offers affordable lessons on singing and a variety of musical instruments to kids and adults. ⏱ 10 min. 3920 W. Sunset Blvd. ☎ 323/665-3363. www. silverlakeconservatory.com. Fri noon–9pm; Sat 10am–6pm.

❸ ★ Bar Keeper. If you're looking to set up a *Mad Men*-esque bar at home, get a load of this amazing array of bar paraphernalia—vintage glassware, seltzer bottles, martini shakers, old-school cocktail manuals, absinthe fountains, and bitters galore. ⏱ 10 min. 3910 W. Sunset Blvd. ☎ 323/669-1675. www.barkeeper silverlake.com. Mon–Thurs noon–6pm; Fri–Sat 11am–7pm; Sun 11am–6pm.

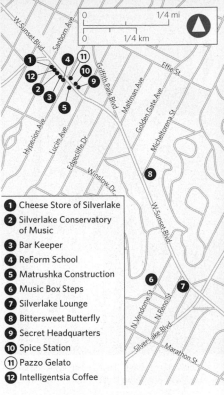

1 Cheese Store of Silverlake
2 Silverlake Conservatory of Music
3 Bar Keeper
4 ReForm School
5 Matrushka Construction
6 Music Box Steps
7 Silverlake Lounge
8 Bittersweet Butterfly
9 Secret Headquarters
10 Spice Station
11 Pazzo Gelato
12 Intelligentsia Coffee

> *Tune in to the region's revered music scene at Silverlake Conservatory of Music, with low-cost instruments and classes.*

4 ★ **ReForm School.** Designers, crafters, and DIYers make a beeline for this store's handmade gifts, eco-friendly home decor, and sense of community. The Handmade Nation shall rise! ⏱ 10 min. 3902 W. Sunset Blvd. ☎ 323/906-8660. www.reformschoolrules.com. Mon–Fri noon–7pm; Sat 11am–7pm; Sun 11am–6pm.

5 ★ **Matrushka Construction.** If you want to pick up some local fashion flavor, you won't do better than the dresses made by Silver Laker Laura Howe. She'll even tailor them for you right there in her store, which *Los Angeles Magazine* recently named the "Best Boutique for a Sunset Junction Outfit." ⏱ 10 min. 3822 W. Sunset Blvd. ☎ 323/665-4513. www. matrushka.com. Mon–Fri noon–7pm; Sat–Sun 11am–6pm.

6 ★ **Music Box Steps.** This small detour combines two of the neighborhood's hallmarks: steps (seriously, there are websites devoted to cataloging them all—like train spotting for steps) and moviemaking history (Mack Sennett's Keystone Studios was just around the corner). It was here that the comedic duo Laurel and Hardy shot their 1932 Oscar-winning short, *The Music Box*, in which Stan and Ollie had to deliver a piano up this ludicrously long stairway. ⏱ 10 min. Btw. 923 & 925 Vendome St.

7 ★★ **Silverlake Lounge.** A funky hole in the wall with a cash-only bar, this neighborhood favorite segues from on-the-cusp bands (Elbow, Vampire Weekend) on weekday nights to drag queens on weekends without ever skipping a beat. Hipster-hero Beck has been known to pop in for a secret after-show performance. Don't be afraid to roll the dice on shows, especially on Monday, when it won't cost a thing to get in. 2906 Sunset Blvd. ☎ 323/663-9636. www.foldsilverlake.com. Cover $8 Tues–Thurs. Mon–Fri 5pm–2am, Sat–Sun 3pm–2am.

8 ★ **Bittersweet Butterfly.** Gentlemen, if you're looking to get out of trouble with your lady (or perhaps into some trouble), try this cute boutique chock-full of fresh-cut flowers and high-end lingerie. ⏱ 10 min. 1406 Micheltorena St. ☎ 323/660-4303. www.bittersweetbutterfly.com. Mon–Sat noon–8pm; Sun noon–5pm.

> A piano up 131 steps? That's what happened at the Music Box Steps, made famous in a Laurel and Hardy movie.

9 ★★ **Secret Headquarters.** Comic book collecting gets a sophisticated spin at this quiet and orderly store, whose leather armchairs and rich wood racks create a leisurely, library-like atmosphere. ⏱ 20 min. 3817 W. Sunset Blvd. ☎ 323/666-2228. www.thesecretheadquarters. com. Mon–Sat 11am–9pm; Sun noon–7pm.

10 ★★ **Spice Station .** Follow your nose into this aromatic sanctum for exotic spices—Szechuan peppercorns, Indian fenugreek, ghost pepper salt (the hottest in the world), sassafras bark—where the friendly owners will encourage you to explore and sample. ⏱ 10 min. 3819 W. Sunset Blvd. ☎ 323/660-3565. www.spice stationsilverlake.com. Mon & Wed 11am–6pm; Thurs & Fri 11am–8pm; Sat 10am–8pm; Sun noon–5pm.

11 🍨 ★ **Pazzo Gelato.** Cold treats face fierce competition in sunny Los Angeles, but this gelato and espresso bar recently earned "Best of L.A." from *L.A. Weekly.* Pazzo Gelato prides itself on its daring flavors (chocolate coconut curry, green tea with ginger), so put those sample spoons to good use. 3827 W. Sunset Blvd. ☎ 323/662-1410. www.pazzogelato.net. Double scoop $4.

Modernist Masterworks

Silver Lake is known for its healthy concentration of homes designed by the some of the world's best modernist architects—Richard Neutra, R. M. Schindler, John Lautner, Gregory Ain, and Raphael Soriano.

Neutra set up shop in Silver Lake and designed several residences along the Silver Lake Reservoir, including his own at 2300 Silver Lake Blvd., which is available for tours (www.neutra-vdl.org; Sat 11am–3pm; $10 admission). A block south at the intersection with Earl Street is "Neutra Colony," a clutch of Neutra designs: 2226, 2232, 2238, 2242, and 2250 Silver Lake Blvd. and 2218, 2210, and 2200 Neutra Place.

My favorite modernist home in the area is John Lautner's curvilinear masterpiece called Silvertop, which sits atop a hill at 2138 Micheltorena St. on the west side of the reservoir.

The Silver Lake Music Scene

If you want to see Silver Lake with its personality cranked up to eleven, come in August for the annual Sunset Junction Street Fair (www.sunsetjunction.org)—now over 30 years old—a 2-day barnburner of music, food, and people-watching that takes over Sunset Boulevard. Past performers have included local bands (Rilo Kiley, Silversun Pickups) along with bigger indie acts (Sonic Youth, Camper Van Beethoven, the Buzzcocks). The festival runs for one weekend in August, noon to midnight. Parking is at 4400 Sunset Blvd. Tickets run $15 to $20.

If you miss the fair, no worries—there's plenty of entertainment year-round. Sure, the Sunset Strip is littered with rock-'n'-roll history, but the East Side is the beating heart of the city's music scene these days. Hipsters can catch an up-and-coming band almost every night of the week. In the mid-1990s Beck broke through and put Silver Lake on the map. Later came the Eels, the late great Elliot Smith, Earlimart, Sea Wolf, and countless more. The best indie venues are the stalwart The Satellite (p. 492), the new Bootleg Theater (2220 Beverly Blvd.; ☎ 213/389-3856; www.bootlegtheater. org), the Echo, and the Echoplex—the latter two share a building, but not an address (1822 W. Sunset Blvd. and 1154 Glendale Blvd. respectively; ☎ 213/413-8200; www. attheecho.com).

> *Tap into the cool scene at Pazzo Gelato, where you can dip into outrageous flavors like Guinness Extra Stout.*

⑫ ★★ Intelligentsia Coffee. Okay, now that you're fully acclimated to the Silver Lake scene, take a seat at this cafe and order one of the finest cups of java in town. Every cup is made fresh to order using the mighty Clover, the single-blast coffee machine with a cult-like following. Cup in hand, take a seat on the bustling patio and blend in among the locals: Grow your beard, ruminate, work on turning your screenplay into a concept album, or vice versa. Take a moment to observe the creative creatures in their own habitat. ⊕ 30 min. 3922 W. Sunset Blvd. ☎ 323/663-6173. www. intelligentsiacoffee.com. Mon–Wed 6am–8pm; Thurs–Sat 6am–11pm; Sun 6am–8pm.

L.A.'s Best Beaches A to Z

★ **Hermosa Beach.** Like its neighbor, Manhattan Beach, this beach community is proud of its surfing and volleyball. A few years ago, the Hermosa Beach Surfer's Hall of Fame was created on the pier to help support the town's claim as the birthplace of surfing in California. Pro volleyball tournaments are a regular feature and draw huge crowds. When the sun goes down, the bar scene on Pier Avenue heats up. **Hermosa Ave. at 33rd St., Hermosa Beach.**

★ **Leo Carrillo State Beach.** Named after the actor who played Pancho, sidekick to the Cisco Kid in the 1950s television show, Leo Carrillo is a 1½-mile-wide sandy beach where Hollywood used to shoot beach blanket flicks, earning the nickname Movie Beach. Kids love searching for hermit crabs in the tide pools and coastal caves. Family-friendly campgrounds are available; Wi-Fi is free for campers, and a Starbucks is a short drive away. Ahh, roughing it. **35000 W. Pacific Coast Hwy., Malibu.**

★ **Malibu Lagoon State Beach.** Malibu Creek meets the Pacific Ocean at this lagoon, and the wetlands create a unique bird sanctuary, a pit stop for more than 200 species during their annual migrations. Watch the birds, watch the surfers, go fishing on the Malibu Pier, or lounge on the beach. When you're ready to reengage your mind, pop into the **Adamson House** (☎ 310/456-8432; www.adamsonhouse.org; Wed–Sat 11am–3pm; guided tours $5 adults, $2 kids), renowned for its display of Malibu tiles; or try the **Malibu Lagoon Museum** (free admission), which traces the history of the area from the days of the Chumash Indians. **23200 Pacific Coast Hwy. (at Cross Creek Rd.), Malibu.**

Manhattan Beach. Surfing and volleyball are the two big draws on this big beach with small-town friendliness. More than 150 volleyball courts (for both pros and amateurs) dot the 2 miles of wide, flat beach. Surfers catch killer waves at El Porto at the north end of the beach. **Manhattan Beach Blvd. at Highland Ave., Manhattan Beach.**

> *Find the perfect hangout at Leo Carrillo State Beach, named after the actor who played Poncho on TV's The Cisco Kid.*

Nicholas Canyon Beach. Called Zeroes by locals, this sandy spot is usually far less crowded than nearby beaches such as Leo Carrillo or Zuma; perhaps the lack of a sign on Pacific Coast Highway has something to do with it. It's certainly no secret to local surfers, who dig the left point break on south swells. Families enjoy the easy access and picnic tables. **33850 W. Pacific Coast Hwy., Malibu.**

Paradise Cove. This is technically a private beach, so it'll cost you $25 to drive in ($5 if validated with a $20 purchase at the Paradise Cove Cafe), or $5 to walk in. Families love—and on weekends, can overrun—this small, scenic cove where television's *Gidget* was filmed, while others enjoy drinking and dining with their toes in the sand. **28128 Pacific Coast Hwy., Malibu. ☎ 310/457-9791. www.paradise covemalibu.com.**

★★ **Point Dume Beach.** Don't tell anybody, but this is my favorite beach in Los Angeles. The Point lies just south of Zuma, but it lacks Zuma's crowds (and, frankly, its amenities and activities, as well). Frolic in the surf or hike up into the Point Dume State Preserve and take in the views (perfect for whale-watching during the Dec–Mar migration season). From the

> *Dig in at Manhattan Beach, where 150 beach volleyball courts line the sandy shore.*

summit, you can descend to a smaller, isolated beach called Pirate's Cove. **7103 Westward Rd. (at the PCH), Malibu.**

> Another day in paradise comes to a close at Will Rogers State Beach, a tranquil family favorite.

> Brought back from the brink of extinction, brown pelicans are now commonly seen at Malibu Lagoon State Beach.

★★ Robert H. Meyer Memorial State Beach (El Pescador, La Piedra, and El Matador). These three hidden coves are gems tucked against the Malibu cliffs. If you can manage your way down a short trail and/or rickety staircases, clean pockets of sand and alluring sea caves await you. Crowded summer weekends can kill the magical vibe, but if you make it mid-week or, better yet, off season, you might be able stake out a patch of paradise. No lifeguard on duty. 32900, 32700 and 32350 W. Pacific Coast Hwy. (btw. Broad Beach & Decker Canyon rds.), Malibu.

Santa Monica State Beach. White sands, restrooms, easy access with ample parking, hot dogs, and in full view of the Santa Monica Pier—sheesh, how much more can you ask of

General Beach Information

Most beaches are operated by the Los Angeles County Department of Beaches & Harbors (☎ 310/305-9503; www.la beaches.info).

For the surf report on Malibu beaches, call ☎ 310/457-9701. For the surf report on South Bay beaches, call ☎ 310/379-8471.

Beaches are generally open daily sunrise to sunset. Parking lots for county-run beaches typically charge $5 to $12.

Water pollution can be a factor, especially after heavy rains, when storm drains empty into the ocean. Before you head out, check www.watchthewater.org to make sure a specific beach has a current clean bill of health.

a beach so close to all the action? While it may not be a "get there early and camp out all day" type beach, it's a great way to combine beach time with other activities such as eating or shopping in Santa Monica. **400-2900 blocks of Ocean Ave., Santa Monica.**

Surfrider Beach. Next to the Malibu Pier is this surfing hot spot, probably the most-surfed break in the county. Arguably the birthplace of surfing in California, Surfrider still enjoys a fine reputation for the consistency of its summer waves, although local surfers aren't fond of sharing them with out-of-towners. **Part of Malibu Lagoon State Beach, 23200 Pacific Coast Hwy. (at Cross Creek Rd.), Malibu.**

★★ **Venice Beach.** Consider the beach to be a sandy extension of wild Venice Boardwalk. It's about entertainment, not relaxation—the

> Carving it up off the Malibu Coast, where surfers flock for arguably some of the best breaks in California.

Malibu Beach Eats

A tasty meal, fresh seafood perhaps, a glass of wine, and gorgeous views of the sun dipping into the Pacific Ocean—for many people this is the perfect way to cap a relaxing day at the beach. Malibu offers the best options for oceanfront dining.

Sunset Restaurant, 6800 Westward Beach Rd. (☎ 310/589-1007; www.thesunsetrestaurant.com), sits between Zuma and Point Dume, and faces due west with perfect, unobstructed views (hence the name). The elegant **Geoffrey's Malibu**, 27400 Pacific Coast Highway (☎ 310/457-1519; www.geoffreysmalibu.com) has a lovely, glass-walled patio perched over the crashing ocean. On the east side of the PCH, **Malibu Seafood** (p. 477) is a casual, walk-up shack crowded with surfers and beachgoers clamoring for fresh fish. On the recently renovated Malibu Pier, the **Beachcomber**, 23000 Pacific Coast Highway (☎ 310/456-9800; www.thebeachcombercafe.com) offers casual dining, beachy cocktails, and views of the action on Surfrider Beach. **Duke's**, 21150 Pacific Coast Highway (☎ 310/317-0777; www.dukesmalibu.com) and **Moonshadows**, 20356 Pacific Coast Highway (☎ 310/456-3010; www.moonshadowsmalibu.com) are lively places to grab a beer and munchies.

sound of waves crashing isn't quite as soothing when accompanied by an impromptu drum circle. You may as well rent some skates or a bike (try Venice Bike & Skates at 21 Washington Blvd.), and join the streams heading up and down the boardwalk. **3100 Ocean Front Walk, Venice.**

Will Rogers State Beach. This 3-mile-long beach, a favorite for families, provides playground and gymnastic equipment, plenty of new restrooms, volleyball courts (especially near Chautauqua Blvd.), and the start of the South Bay Bike Path that ends 22 miles south in Torrance County Beach. **16000 Pacific Coast Hwy., Pacific Palisades.**

★ **Zuma Beach County Park.** This huge and hugely popular stretch of white, sandy beach has the proverbial "something for everyone": swimming, surfing, body boarding, fishing, volleyball, snack bars, playground swings, restrooms, and plenty of parking. Weekends are a zoo, but weekdays are surprisingly tame. **30000 W. Pacific Coast Hwy. (btw. Kanan Dume & Encinal Canyon rds.), Malibu.**

L.A.'s Best Hikes A to Z

★★ **Angeles National Forest: Cooper Canyon.** North of the Los Angeles basin loom the rugged San Gabriel Mountains, which make for great hiking in the late spring after the winter snow melts, creating lovely waterfalls like the 40-foot Cooper Canyon Falls. Take the Burkhart Trail for a relatively easy 3-mile loop to the falls and back; or if you're really adventurous (and fit), continue on Burkhardt Trail toward the Devil's Punchbowl and the edge of the "High" Mojave Desert. Hwy. 2, or Angeles Crest Highway, at Burkhart Campground entrance road. ☎ 818/880-0350. Daily 7am–10pm.

Franklin Canyon: Hastain Trail. Tucked away between the San Fernando Valley and Beverly Hills, these 605 chaparral-covered acres are home to a lake (originally a reservoir built in 1914 by William Mulholland), a small duck pond, and 5 miles of hiking trails—the most popular being the pretty Hastain Trail, a hearty 2.3-mile workout. Grab a map near the park's entrance at the Sooky Goldman Nature Center. 2600 Franklin Canyon Dr. (at Mulholland Dr.), Beverly Hills. ☎ 310/858-7272. Head north on Beverly Dr., turn left on Coldwater/Beverly Dr. and turn left again on Beverly Dr. Go right at Franklin Canyon Dr.

Griffith Park: Mount Hollywood. A wide sandy trail takes you to the top of Mount Hollywood, undoubtedly the best view in all of Griffith Park. Being the most popular hike in the city's most popular park, it can get crowded. Take the Charlie Turner trail head, which begins across from the Griffith Observatory, for a 2.5-mile loop. For a 5-mile version, start at the Fern Dell Trail near the Ferndell Nature Museum. Griffith Observatory, 2800 E. Observatory Rd. ☎ 213/473-0800. www.griffith observatory.org. Ferndell Nature Museum, Ferndell Dr. (north of Los Feliz Blvd.). ☎ 323/666-5046. Trails daily 6am–dusk.

Griffith Park: Mount Lee and the HOLLYWOOD Sign. This is my favorite way to experience the

> Get away from it all at Point Mugu State Park, a bit of a drive from L.A. but oh so worth it.

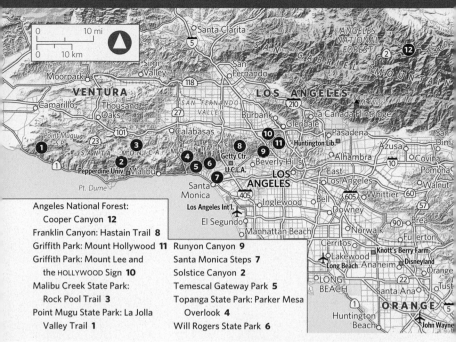

Angeles National Forest:
  Cooper Canyon **12**
Franklin Canyon: Hastain Trail **8**
Griffith Park: Mount Hollywood **11**
Griffith Park: Mount Lee and
  the HOLLYWOOD Sign **10**
Malibu Creek State Park:
  Rock Pool Trail **3**
Point Mugu State Park: La Jolla
  Valley Trail **1**

Runyon Canyon **9**
Santa Monica Steps **7**
Solstice Canyon **2**
Temescal Gateway Park **5**
Topanga State Park: Parker Mesa
  Overlook **4**
Will Rogers State Park **6**

sign, looking over the tops of the 45-foot-high letters at the city sprawled out below. Think about all the people who could be looking up at the HOLLYWOOD Sign right now for inspiration and wave at them. Take Beachwood Dr. north to Hollyridge Dr. Follow the Hollyridge Trail northeast. After ½ mile, take Mulholland Trail west. At Mount Lee Dr., head north and follow the trail to the back of the sign.

Malibu Creek State Park: Rock Pool Trail.
Former owner Twentieth Century Fox fully exploited the park's "so close, yet so far away" quality, using it as a backdrop for movies (*Planet of the Apes, Tarzan*) and television shows (*M*A*S*H*). An easy walk brings you to a refreshing Rock Pool, although it can get overcrowded on summer weekends. Try rock climbing along its volcanic rock walls. For a more serene water setting, head along the trail to Century Lake, set in a grove of redwoods. *M*A*S*H* fans might want to trek farther down Crags Road to visit "Korea," where a couple of rusty jeeps appear to be the only casualties of the war. 1925 Las Virgenes Rd. (at Mulholland Dr.), Malibu. ☎ 818/880-0367. Daily sunrise–sunset.

> This look like Korea? TV producers thought so—Malibu Creek State Park was the Asian stand-in on M.A.S.H.

> Get an L.A. 360—ocean, city, hills, and sky—from Parker Mesa Overlook, within sprawling Topanga State Park.

> Dog park to the stars, Runyon Canyon is an off-leash sagebrush-dotted heaven for designer pooches.

★★ **Point Mugu State Park: La Jolla Valley Trail.** A longer drive from Los Angeles than the other options, Point Mugu throws in plenty of incentives: 70 miles of hiking trails, 13,300 acres of state park, and miles of jagged coastline. The La Jolla Valley Trail cuts through rolling grasslands, lush canyons, and, in spring, blooming wildflowers and burbling waterfalls. The most dramatic vistas are along the oceanside hills on the way to Mugu Peak. 9000 W. Pacific Coast Hwy., Malibu. ☎ 818/880-0350. Daily 7am–10pm.

★ **Runyon Canyon.** An off-leash dog park just a bone's throw from Hollywood & Highland, the canyon's trails are always packed with people and their pooches. Make it to the highest point in the park, Indian Rock, and you'll earn a lovely panorama of Hollywood and beyond Plus, there's something refreshing about spotting a celeb, baseball cap pulled low, dutifully picking up after his or her dog. 2000 N. Fuller Ave. (at Hillside Ave.), Hollywood. ☎ 323/666-5046. Daily dawn–dusk.

> *Send in the clouds at Temescal Gateway Park, where cooling marine fog often sweeps in on summer evenings.*

Santa Monica Steps. Enjoy hiking except for that pesky back-to-nature business? Here's a popular urban hike—actually more of a nightmarishly long set of stairs that will burn your legs and lungs. Locals come for an intense workout, with lovely views of the ocean—and of each other. Try the loop: Go up the concrete steps, jog a few hundred feet east on Adelaide Street, and come down the wooden steps. Repeat ad nauseam. **Fourth St. (btw. Adelaide St. & San Vicente Blvd.).**

Solstice Canyon. For centuries, Chumash Indians used this beautiful coastal canyon for food and shelter, but a hike along the Solstice Canyon Trail will yield evidence of not-so-ancient ruins—an architecturally significant residence designed by the renowned Paul Williams that burned down in 1982. The area, called Tropical Terrace, also features a lovely 30-foot waterfall and lush foliage. Play archaeologist or simply sun on the large boulders in the creek. **Corral Canyon Rd. (at PCH), Malibu. ☎ 805/ 370-2301. Daily 8am–sunset.**

★ Temescal Gateway Park. The popular Canyon Loop follows a scenic ridgeline, then dips into a woodsy canyon, at the bottom of which is a small waterfall (don't get too excited—it barely trickles during the dry summer season). A steep climb out of the canyon yields expansive ocean views, and the adventurous can climb another ½ mile up to Skull Rock, where the views are even better; both offer gentle ocean breezes to cool your brow. **15601 Sunset Blvd. (at Temescal Canyon Rd.), Pacific Palisades. ☎ 310/454-1395. Daily sunrise–sunset.**

★★ Topanga State Park: Parker Mesa Overlook. The largest state park within the boundaries of a major city, Topanga is a whopper: 11,000 acres of grassland, live oak groves, and sandstone cliffs overlooking the Pacific Ocean. With 36 miles of trails (including some backbreakers that extend into the neighboring parks of Will Rogers and Point Mugu), you've got plenty of options. I recommend the hike from Trippet Ranch to the Parker Mesa Overlook, where you can absorb the stunning 360-degree view. **20825 Entrada Dr. ☎ 310/ 455-2465. Daily 8am–sunset. From Pacific Coast Highway, travel north on Topanga Canyon Blvd., and then turn right on Entrada Rd.**

Will Rogers State Park. Good ol' Will Rogers (1879–1935) left us his ranch, 186 acres at the western edge of the Santa Monica Mountains, to enjoy. A relatively easy hike lifts you into the countryside along the ranch's perimeter, where highlights include **Inspiration Point;** from here you can take in the gorgeous ocean and mountain views. **1501 Will Rogers Park Rd. (off Sunset Blvd.), Pacific Palisades. ☎ 310/454-8212. Daily 8am–sunset.**

Griffith Park

Welsh mining millionaire Griffith J. Griffith (1850–1919) believed every great city needs a great park, and for Christmas in 1896, he gave 3,015 acres to the people of Los Angeles to create "a place of rest and relaxation for the masses, a resort for the rank and file." Today it is one of the largest urban parks in the United States and beloved by Angelenos. It's open daily 6am to 10pm.

> Star power takes center stage at Griffith Observatory at monthly "star parties," with telescopes set up for all comers.

START Take the Canyon Dr. entrance to Griffith Park, then hike ¼ mile past the Bronson Canyon parking lot.

❶ **Bronson Caves.** To the Batcave! These man-made caves, actually short tunnels, are the result of quarry operations to gather crushed rock for paving Sunset Boulevard and other major roads. Most folks will recognize the caves from the 1960s' *Batman* television series. The "exotic" location has appeared in countless films, as well—from sci-fi B-movies (*Teenagers from Outer Space*), to Westerns (*The Searchers*), to historical epics (*Julius Caesar*). ⏱ 20 min. Canyon Dr. & Brush Canyon Trail.

❷ ★★ kids **Griffith Observatory.** After trying out a powerful telescope at nearby Mount Wilson, Griffith experienced an epiphany: "If all mankind could look through that telescope, it would change the world!" With that noble goal, he left the city money to create this observatory, which debuted in 1935. The original 12-inch Zeiss refracting telescope, which more people have looked through than any other on Earth, remains in prime condition and serves up to 600 visitors nightly. In the other copper-topped dome is the triple-beam solar telescope, which is used to observe the sun safely. ⏱ 1 hr. See p. 421, ❺.

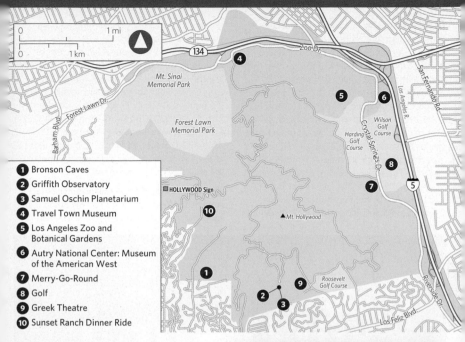

1 Bronson Caves
2 Griffith Observatory
3 Samuel Oschin Planetarium
4 Travel Town Museum
5 Los Angeles Zoo and Botanical Gardens
6 Autry National Center: Museum of the American West
7 Merry-Go-Round
8 Golf
9 Greek Theatre
10 Sunset Ranch Dinner Ride

3 ★ kids **Samuel Oschin Planetarium.** This planetarium offers a state-of-the-art, star-studded experience called Centered in the Universe, which lets the viewer experience the Big Bang, travel distant galaxies, and observe the overall structure of the universe—all without leaving his or her cushy seat. Tickets can only be purchased at the observatory, and they often sell out; try to buy tickets immediately upon your arrival. ⏲ At least 1 hr. Tickets $7 ages 13 & over, $5 seniors, $3 kids 5–12. Kids 4 & under are not admitted. Tues–Fri noon–10pm; Sat–Sun 10am–10pm. Check www.griffithobservatory.org for show times. See p. 421.

4 ★ kids **Travel Town Museum.** In the late 1940s, park employee Charley Atkins and a few of his train-loving pals decided to create a "railroad petting zoo" to encourage kids to become engineers. Young kids, especially Thomas the Tank Engine fans, love exploring the steam-powered engines and cabooses. A miniature-train ride costs $2.50. For more train fun, head over to the Griffith Park & Southern Railroad (4400 Crystal Springs Dr.) on the other side of the park. ⏲ 30 min. 5200 Zoo Dr. ☎ 323/662-9678. www.traveltown.org. Free admission. Mon–Fri 10am–4pm; Sat–Sun 10am–5pm.

> Go ape at the Los Angeles Zoo, where western lowland gorillas strut their stuff in an expansive naturalized enclosure.

5 kids **Los Angeles Zoo and Botanical Gardens.** Smaller and more manageable than the famous San Diego Zoo, this zoo continues to improve its exhibits: As of this writing the Pachyderm Forest, which will expand the elephant space into one of the largest in the country, is scheduled to open in November 2010, and Rainforest of the Americas, scheduled to open in 2012, will present mixed species (mammals, reptiles, birds, and insects) in a tropical setting intended to immerse the visitor in a sensory experience, with a central theme of water, the rainforest's key ingredient. Current highlights include the junglelike Campo Gorilla Reserve, with western lowland gorillas; the Sea Life Cliffs, where you can watch the underwater antics of the sea lions through a glass tank; and Chimpanzees of Mahale Mountains, home to one of the largest groups of chimpanzees in the United States. Less exotic animals, goats, and sheep greet the kiddies at the Winnick Family Children's Zoo. ⏱ 1 hr. 5333 Zoo Dr., Griffith Park. ☎ 323/644-4200. www.lazoo.org. Admission $13 adults, $10 seniors, $8 kids 2–12, free for kids 1 & under. Labor Day to June daily 10am–5pm; July to Labor Day daily 10am–6pm.

6 **Autry National Center: Museum of the American West.** This is no Podunk outpost, but a well-kept museum that explores the "real"

The HOLLYWOOD Sign

Nine letters, 45-feet high—the HOLLYWOOD Sign stands on Griffith Park's Mount Lee as an enduring symbol of the glitz and glamour of the entertainment industry and is one of the most recognizable signs on the planet. It began in 1923 as a billboard for a housing development called "Hollywoodland," and since this is Hollywood, a town booming with an energetic film industry, the developers had a sense of showmanship—4,000 blinking 20-watt bulbs lit the letters at night.

In 1932 Peg Entwistle, a struggling actress, exposed the dark reality of the Hollywood dream when she climbed to the top of the letter H and jumped to her death. The sign languished over the years, and in 1949 city boosters repaired and rebuilt the sign as "Hollywood" without the "land" and the light bulbs. By the 1970s the wood and sheet-metal structure was falling apart, and an unlikely alliance of private donors—Hugh Hefner, Alice Cooper, and Gene Autry—came to its rescue.

In 2002 a group of cagey real estate investors bought 138 acres adjacent to the sign (long held by the Howard Hughes estate) and aimed to build luxury homes on the ridgeline behind the sign. Preservationists seeking to keep the iconic landscape as is launched a massive public campaign to raise $12.5 million to buy the developers out. In the spring of 2010—after donations by the major studios and individuals like Steven Spielberg, Tom Hanks, and once again, Hugh Hefner—the land was saved and given to Griffith Park.

One of the best places to view the sign is from the lawn in front of the Griffith Observatory; other choice spots are the Hollywood & Highland Center, up Beachwood Canyon Drive, and Lake Hollywood. Or simply check out the webcams—and much more information—at www.hollywoodsign.org.

> *Horse around above Hollywood, where Sunset Ranch trail rides let you explore Griffith Park (Tip: avoid midday heat).*

Old West as well as the mythology perpetuated by movies and television. Past exhibits include George Catlin's Indian Gallery, hundreds of paintings from the 1830s by the first artist to document the Plains Indians in their own territories; Dazzling Firearms, decorative pistols from the 19th and 20th centuries; and the Art of Native American Basketry, a dazzling selection from nearly 14,000 baskets, the largest collection in the world, at the Southwest Museum of the American Indian, also part of the Autry National Center. ⏱ 40 min. 4700 Western Heritage Way. ☎ 323/667-2000. www.autrynational center.org. Admission $9 adults, $5 seniors and students, $3 kids 3–12, free for kids 2 & under. Tues–Fri 10am–4pm; Sat–Sun 11am–5pm.

⑦ kids Merry-Go-Round. This carousel has delighted families since 1937. Jumping horses, bejeweled and brightly colored, spin around to the sounds of marches and waltzes from a Stinson band organ. A quick and easy way to make a kid happy. ⏱ 20 min. Park Center (off Crystal Springs Dr. btw. the zoo & the Los Feliz entrance). ☎ 323/665-3051. Rides $1.50 per person. Summer daily 11am–5pm; rest of year Sat–Sun 11am–5pm.

⑧ Golf. Got time to hit the links? The park is home to two popular 18-hole public golf courses, Wilson and Harding, as well as a driving range and practice putting greens. There's also the 9-hole Roosevelt course at 2650 N. Vermont Ave. (greens fees $15–$22). 4730 Crystal Springs Dr. ☎ 323/663-2555. Greens fees $26–$39. Daily sunrise–11pm. Head east on Los Feliz Blvd. and north at the Riverside entrance.

⑨ ★ Greek Theatre. Another gift from Griffith J. Griffith, this 5,700-seat venue debuted in 1930. Tree lined and nestled in the hills, the award-winning theater feels like an intimate version of the Hollywood Bowl. If you find one of your favorites playing there, jump on the opportunity. Recent acts include the Flaming Lips, Phish, and a Super '70s Soul Jam Spectacular. The only downside is the stacked parking ($15) that can make exiting a show a long slog. ⏱ 2–2½ hr. 2700 Vermont Canyon Rd. ☎ 323/665-1927. www.greektheatrela.com. Tickets $30–$155.

⑩ Sunset Ranch Dinner Ride. Mount up and mosey through the twilight over the hills to a Mexican restaurant in Burbank. Take it easy on the margaritas, cowboy—you still have to ride the horse back. Day rides ($25–$40 per person) are also available and provide great photo-ops for the HOLLYWOOD sign. ⏱ 4 hr. 3400 Beachwood Dr. ☎ 323/469-5450. www.sunsetranch hollywood.com. Reservations required. Dinner ride begins btw. 4–5pm daily. Dinner ride $105 per person. Head north up Beachwood Dr.

Los Angeles Shopping Best Bets

Hippest Store for Guys & Gals
American Rag Cie, 150 S. La Brea Ave. (p. 467)

Best Music Store
Amoeba Music, 6400 Sunset Blvd. (p. 470)

Best Cheese Shop
Beverly Hills Cheese Shop, 419 N. Beverly Dr. (p. 471)

Best Bookstore
Book Soup, 8818 Sunset Blvd. (p. 465)

Best Shopping for Tiny Dogs
Fifi & Romeo Boutique, 7282 Beverly Blvd. (p. 469)

Best Old-World Charm
Santa Maria Novella, 8411 Melrose Place (p. 469)

Biggest Celeb Scene
Fred Segal, 8100 Melrose Ave. (p. 467)

Best Bargain Hunting
Rose Bowl Flea Market, 1001 Rose Bowl Dr. (p. 468)

Best Kids' Clothing Store
La La Ling, 1810 N. Vermont Ave. (p. 470)

Best Funky Gift Shop
OK, 8303 W. Third St. (p. 469)

Best Men's Boutique
Lisa Kline for Men, 143 S. Robertson Blvd. (p. 468)

Best Kids Bookstore
Storyopolis, 12348 Ventura Blvd. (p. 465)

Best Women's Shoes
Neiman Marcus, 9700 Wilshire Blvd. (p. 467); and **Sigerson Morrison,** 8307 W. Third St. (p. 468)

Best Place to Find a Party Dress in a Jiffy
Betsey Johnson, 8050 Melrose Ave. (p. 467)

Best Wine Store
Silverlake Wine, 2395 Glendale Blvd. (p. 471)

Sexiest Shop
Agent Provocateur, 7961 Melrose Ave. (p. 470)

> *Early birds definitely get the worm at Rose Bowl Flea Market, with 2,500 vendors selling, well, everything.*

Los Angeles Shopping A to Z

Beauty

★ Larchmont Beauty Supply LARCHMONT
This may be the city's best collection of pre-mium shampoos, soaps, candles, makeup, hair products, and more. 208 N. Larchmont Blvd. (btw. Third St. & Beverly Blvd.). ☎ 323/461-0162. www.larchmontbeauty.com. AE, DISC, MC, V. Map p. 466.

★★ Ole Henriksen WEST HOLLYWOOD
Luxurious facials and a superb line of skin-care products make this spa a hit among celebrities like Charlize Theron, Prince, and Leonardo Di-Caprio. 8622 W. Sunset Blvd. (west of Alta Loma Rd.). ☎ 310/854-7700. www.olehenriksen.com. AE, MC, V. Map p. 466.

Books

★★ Book Soup WEST HOLLYWOOD
The city's favorite independent bookstore has an amazing stock of books crammed into its nooks and crannies, a monstrous magazine rack, an interesting clientele, and in-store author events that have included appearances by James Ellroy, Sarah Vowell, and Werner

Herzog. 8818 Sunset Blvd. (at Larabee St.). ☎ 310/659-3110. www.booksoup.com. AE, DISC, MC, V. Map p. 466.

★ Skylight Books LOS FELIZ
This independent bookstore specializes in literary fiction, film, and Los Angeles history. The staff recommendations are always intelligent and spot on. 1816K N. Vermont Ave. (at Melbourne Ave.). ☎ 323/666-2202. www.skylightbooks.com. AE, DISC, MC, V. Map p. 467.

★ Storyopolis STUDIO CITY
Storyopolis, a children's bookstore, is best known for its story-time events and its Oprah-endorsed "Book Bushels," custom-made gift baskets of books. An art gallery with original art and limited-edition prints from top illustrators is also on-site. 12348 Ventura Blvd. (at Laurel Grove Ave.). ☎ 818/509-5600. www.storyopolis.com. AE, DISC, MC, V. Map p. 467.

Department Stores

★★ Barneys New York BEVERLY HILLS
Fashion mavens navigate five luxurious floors of ready-to-wear from every designer on the

> *Page-turners pack Skylight Books, an excellent independent bookstore (catch excellent author events too).*

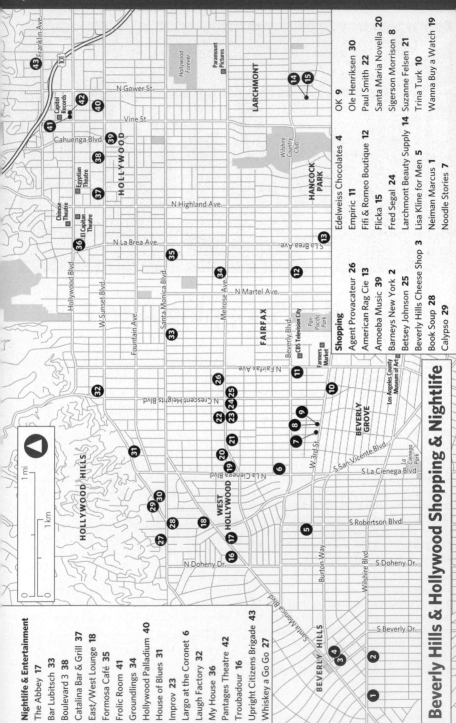

Beverly Hills & Hollywood Shopping & Nightlife

Nightlife & Entertainment

The Abbey 17
Bar Lubitsch 33
Boulevard 3 38
Catalina Bar & Grill 37
East/West Lounge 18
Formosa Café 35
Frolic Room 41
Groundlings 34
Hollywood Palladium 40
House of Blues 31
Improv 23
Largo at the Coronet 6
Laugh Factory 32
My House 36
Pantages Theatre 42
Troubadour 16
Upright Citizens Brigade 43
Whiskey a Go Go 27

Shopping

Agent Provacateur 26
American Rag Cie 13
Amoeba Music 39
Barneys New York 2
Betsey Johnson 25
Beverly Hills Cheese Shop 3
Book Soup 28
Calypso 29
Edelweiss Chocolates 4
Empiric 11
Fifi & Romeo Boutique 12
Flicka 15
Fred Segal 24
Larchmont Beauty Supply 14
Lisa Kline for Men 5
Neiman Marcus 1
Noodle Stories 7
OK 9
Ole Henriksen 30
Paul Smith 22
Santa Maria Novella 20
Sigerson Morrison 8
Suzanne Felsen 21
Trina Turk 10
Wanna Buy a Watch 19

Nightlife & Entertainment
Ahmanson Theater **22**
Brig **4**
Copa d'Oro **2**
Dodger Stadium **23**
Dorothy Chandler Pavilion **22**
The Dresden **10**
4100 Bar **14**

Geffen Playhouse **7**
Hollywood Bowl **9**
Home Depot
  Center **28**
La Cita Bar **24**

HOLLYWOOD
Sunset Blvd.
Santa Monica Blvd.
BEVERLY HILLS
Burton Wy
FAIRFAX
Highland Ave.
Western Ave.
LOS FELIZ
SILVER LAKE
EAST HOLLYWOOD
BRENTWOOD
San Vicente Blvd.
Santa Monica Blvd.
Wilshire Blvd.
MID-WILSHIRE
Olympic Blvd.
see large map
Robertson Blvd.
San Vicente Blvd.
Alvarado St.
DOWNTOWN
Pico Blvd.
Grand Ave.
Main St.
Wilshire Blvd.
Olympic Blvd.
Venice Blvd.
Culver Blvd.
SANTA MONICA
CULVER CITY
VENICE

Mark Taper Forum **22**
Nokia Theatre L.A. Live **20**
The Satellite **17**
Staples Center **19**
Tiki-Ti **15**
The Varnish **25**
Walt Disney Concert Hall **21**
Shopping
H.D. Buttercup **8**
La La Ling **12**

McCabe's Guitar Shop **5**
Obsolete **3**
Panty Raid **13**
PuzzleZoo **1**
Rose Bowl Flea Market **27**
Silverlake Wines **17**
Skylight Books **11**
Storyopolis **26**
Wally's Wines **6**
Wee Soles **16**

0   2 mi
0   2 km

L.A. Shopping & Nightlife

---

planet. The women's shoes, bags, and beauty departments are especially alluring. Try the hoity-toity deli on the rooftop. 9570 Wilshire Blvd. (at N. Camden Dr.). ☎ 310/276-4400. www.barneys.com. AE, MC, V. Map p. 466.

★ **Neiman Marcus** BEVERLY HILLS
At this monument to retail escapism, a woman can rampage through the Manolo Blahniks in the highly regarded shoe department while her man waits patiently at the bar on the fourth floor. 9700 Wilshire Blvd. (btw. Santa Monica Blvd. & Brighton Way). ☎ 310/550-5900. www.neimanmarcus.com. AE, MC, V. Map p. 466.

Fashion
★ **American Rag Cie** HOLLYWOOD
This popular store features up-and-coming designers, well-selected vintage wear, retro sneakers, hip accessories, and a massive denim selection at their World Denim Bar—all guaranteed to make you cooler. 150 S. La Brea Ave. (btw. W. First & W. Second sts.). ☎ 323/935-3154. www.americanragcie.co.jp. AE, MC, V. Map p. 466.

★ **Betsey Johnson** WEST HOLLYWOOD
If you're looking for a sexy little number to wear to a party, check out the famous designer's colorful bouquet of playful, vintage-inspired dresses. 8050 Melrose Ave. (at N. Laurel Ave.). ☎ 323/852-1534. www.betseyjohnson.com. AE, MC, V. Map p. 466.

★ **Calypso** WEST HOLLYWOOD
Christiane Celle's elegant, French-inspired designs are comfortable and flowing, perfect for the warm So Cal weather. 8635 W. Sunset Blvd. (at Sunset Plaza Dr.). ☎ 310/652-4454. Also in Santa Monica, 225 26th St. (at San Vicente Blvd.). ☎ 310/434-9601. www.calypso-celle.com. AE, MC, V. Map p. 466.

★★★ **Fred Segal** WEST HOLLYWOOD
No clothing store draws more celebrity shoppers than this ivy-covered landmark. The only thing reasonably priced is the parking, which is free. 8100 Melrose Ave. (at Crescent Heights Blvd.). ☎ 323/651-4129. Also in Santa Monica, 500 Broadway (at Fifth St.). ☎ 310/394-9814. www.fredsegalfun.com. AE, MC, V. Map p. 466 & p. 405.

> *Fashionistas flock to Fred Segal, open for decades but still a magnet for trend-setting celebs.*

> *If this guy parks his bike and walks into Paul Smith, he'll walk out looking like a million bucks.*

★★ Lisa Kline for Men BEVERLY HILLS

Men going for that L.A. look shop here for the "right" kind of shirts, jeans, and jackets. Assuring fellas that shopping is indeed a manly pursuit, the clubhouse decor features comfy couches, big-screen TVs, and a complimentary bar. 143 S. Robertson Blvd. (at Alden Dr.). ☎ 310/385-7113. www.lisakline.com. AE, MC, V. Map p. 466.

★ Noodle Stories WEST HOLLYWOOD

This collection of women's clothing emphasizes subtlety, simplicity, and sophistication. Designers include Comme des Garçons, Martin Margiela, and Yohji Yamamoto. 8323 W. Third St. (at N. Flores St.). ☎ 323/651-1782. AE, MC, V. Map p. 466.

★★ Paul Smith WEST HOLLYWOOD

Designer Paul Smith is celebrated for his snappy, British style; his slightly mod shirts and suits will make any man look like a million bucks. 8221 Melrose Ave. (at N. La Jolla Ave.). ☎ 323/951-4800. www.paulsmith.co.uk. AE, DC, DISC, MC, V. Map p. 466.

★ Sigerson Morrison WEST HOLLYWOOD

This NYC export showcases sleek bags, shoes, and boots, and its sexy flat sandals have inspired a passionate legion of fans. 8307 W. Third St. (at S. Sweetzer Ave.). ☎ 323/655-6133. www.sigersonmorrison.com. AE, DISC, MC, V. Map p. 466.

★ Trina Turk WEST HOLLYWOOD

This California designer is known for her retro-glam style that marries brightly colored patterns with classic silhouettes. 8008 W. Third St. (at S. Edinburgh Ave.). ☎ 323/651-1382. www.trinaturk.com. AE, DISC, MC, V. Map p. 466.

Flea Market

★★★ Rose Bowl Flea Market PASADENA

On the second Sunday of every month, locals flock to this massive outdoor marketplace with over 2,500 vendors to hunt for antique furniture, hard-to-find collectibles, and vintage clothing. *Tip:* If you happen to be in town on the "wrong" Sunday, try Melrose Trading Post at the corner of Melrose and Fairfax avenues. 1001 Rose Bowl Dr. ☎ 323/651-1382. www.rgcshows.com. Admission $8 adults, kids 11 and under free with an adult. Cash only. Second Sun of the month 9am–5pm. Map p. 467.

> *Good scents abound at Santa Maria Novella, an elegant boutique with perfumes based on centuries-old Italian blends.*

Gifts

★ Fifi & Romeo Boutique WEST HOLLYWOOD

This luxury boutique for little pooches offers cashmere and angora sweaters, faux fur–trimmed coats, jewel-encrusted collars, and that sense of validation that tiny canines sometimes need. 7282 Beverly Blvd. (at N. Poinsettia Place). ☎ 323/857-7214. www.fifiandromeo.com. AE, MC, V. Map p. 466.

★ OK WEST HOLLYWOOD

Blown-glass vases, Japanese ceramics, vintage phones, modernist clocks, and a well-curated array of art and design books—unusual gift ideas abound at this gallery-like store. 8303 W. Third St. (at S. Sweetzer Ave.). ☎ 323/ 653-3501. www.okthestore.com. AE, MC, V. Map p. 466.

★ Santa Maria Novella WEST HOLLYWOOD

On Melrose Place, take a side trip to Florence, Italy. This boutique carries soaps, lotions, and scents based upon the same recipes used 400 years ago by the Dominican friars of Santa Maria Novella. 8411 Melrose Place (at N. Orlando Ave.). ☎ 323/651-3754. www.smnovella.it. AE, MC, V. Map p. 466.

Home Decor

★★ Empiric WEST HOLLYWOOD

This store offers an eclectic mix of home furnishings: midcentury lamps, industrial steel desks and bookcases, and accessories (apothecary jars, phrenological charts, a frog skeleton) that'll make you think you've wandered into a mad scientist's estate sale. 7918 Beverly Blvd. (at N. Hayworth Ave.). ☎ 323/634-7373. www.empiricstudio.com. AE, MC, V. Map p. 466.

★ H.D. Buttercup CULVER CITY

Fifty or so vendors present a wide array of high-end furniture and arty home decor in a 150,000-square-foot Art Deco building that was once home to the historic Helms Bakery. 3225 Helms Ave. (at Washington Ave.). ☎ 310/558-8900. www.hdbuttercup.com. AE, DISC, MC, V. Map p. 467.

★ Obsolete SANTA MONICA

This art store/gallery carries visually arresting, creepy-cool pieces such as antique models of the human brain and sculptures made of found objects. Pottery Barn this ain't. 222 Main St. (btw. Rose Ave. & Marine St.). ☎ 310/399-0024. www.obsoleteinc.com. AE, MC, V. Map p. 467.

> *Check out life in miniature at Flicka, a trendy shop for oh-so-cute baby clothes and gifts.*

Jewelry

★ Suzanne Felsen WEST HOLLYWOOD
Giving unusual gemstones a modern twist, this native Angeleno is one of the city's most popular jewelry designers. 8332 Melrose Ave. (at N. Kings Rd.). ☎ 323/653-5400. Also in Santa Monica, 2525 Michigan Ave, No. G3. ☎ 310/315-1972. www.suzannefelsen.com. AE, MC, V. Map p. 406 & p. 466.

★★ Wanna Buy a Watch WEST HOLLYWOOD
Take the time to check out this shop's selection of high-end vintage watches by such names as Rolex, Patek Philippe, and Cartier. 8465 Melrose Ave. (at La Cienega Blvd.). ☎ 323/653-0467. www.wannabuyawatch.com. AE, DISC, MC, V. Map p. 466.

Kids

★ Flicka LARCHMONT
The clothes for infants and toddlers are sweet, trendy, and well made. Finding the perfect baby shower or birthday gift is a snap, and the free wrapping helps. 204 N. Larchmont Blvd. (btw. Beverly Blvd. & First St.). ☎ 323/466-5822. AE, MC, V. Map p. 466.

★ La La Ling LOS FELIZ
If your kid simply has to have what the Jolie-Pitt kids are wearing this season, hit this funky shop stuffed with such designer duds as Paul Frank galoshes and rocker tees. 1810 N. Vermont Ave. (at Melbourne Ave.). ☎ 323/664-4400. www.lalaling.com. MC, V. Map p. 467.

★ Puzzle Zoo SANTA MONICA
Conveniently located on the Third Street Promenade, this lively toy store specializes in puzzles (naturally) as well as collectibles, such as action figures from *Star Wars, Lord of the Rings,* and *Austin Powers.* 1413 Third St. Promenade (at Arizona Ave.). ☎ 310/393-9201. www.puzzlezoo.com. AE, DISC, MC, V. Map p. 467.

★ Wee Soles SILVER LAKE
Where hip parents go to buy hip shoes for their hip kids. 3827 W. Sunset Blvd., Ste. E (at Lucile Ave.). ☎ 323/667-0774. AE, MC, V. Map p. 467.

Lingerie

★ Agent Provocateur WEST HOLLYWOOD
The grande dame of Los Angeles lingerie, this sexy boutique sells high-end lingerie with sky-high price tags. You'll love the service you get from the ladies dressed in matching frocks. 7961 Melrose Ave. (at N. Hayworth Ave.). ☎ 323/653-0229. www.agentprovocateur.com. AE, MC, V. Map p. 466.

★ Panty Raid SILVER LAKE
Eastside hipsters shop here for the fun and affordable variety of frilly underthings from designers like Hanky Panky, Mary Green, and Cosabella. 1953 Hillhurst Ave. (at Franklin Ave.). ☎ 323/668-1888. www.pantyraidshop.com. AE, DISC, MC, V. Map p. 467.

Music & Musical Instruments

★★ Amoeba Music HOLLYWOOD
In the war of music retailers, score one for the little guy—and by "little," I mean *huuuge* but independently owned. The extra-large music store's staff—walking encyclopedias of music—don't mind you asking, "What's the name of that band . . . with that song; it kinda goes like . . . ?" 6400 Sunset Blvd. (at Ivar Ave.). ☎ 323/245-6400. www.amoeba.com. DISC, MC, V. Map p. 466.

★ McCabe's Guitar Shop SANTA MONICA
Faithfully serving local and itinerant musicians

> *Tune in to the amazing guitar selection (and surprise performances from master artists) at venerable McCabe's Guitar Shop.*

in Los Angeles for over 50 years, this homey shop sports the largest selection of stringed instruments in the state and is known for its intimate, backroom concerts featuring rootsy performers such as M. Ward, Steve Earle, and Lucinda Williams. 3101 Pico Blvd. (at 31st St.). ☎ 310/828-4497. www.mccabes.com. AE, DISC, MC, V. Map p. 467.

Specialty Foods & Wines

★★ **Beverly Hills Cheese Shop** BEVERLY HILLS
Cheese lovers have flocked here since 1967 for a staggering selection of heavenly cheeses—more than 500 varieties from around the globe. 419 N. Beverly Dr. (at Brighton Way). ☎ 310/278-2855. www.cheesestorebh.com. AE, DC, DISC, MC, V. Map p. 466.

★ **Edelweiss Chocolates** BEVERLY HILLS
This old-fashioned chocolate shop, a Beverly Hills landmark since 1942, stays fresh by creating all its delectables on the premises. Happy customers have included Katharine Hepburn, Lauren Bacall, and Steven Spielberg.

The fudge rocks. 444 N. Canon Dr. (at Burton Way). ☎ 310/275-0341. www.edelweiss chocolates.com. AE, MC, V. Map p. 466.

★★ **Silverlake Wine** SILVER LAKE
This neighborhood shop focuses on top-notch, small-batch wines for all budgets. On Friday evenings in summer, they host popular wine-tasting events on the lovely grounds of the historic Hollyhock House at the Barnsdall Art Park ($20)—I highly recommend them. They also offer in-store tastings on Monday, Thursday, and Sunday ($12–$20). 2395 Glendale Blvd. (at Brier Ave.). ☎ 323/662-9024. www. silverlakewines.com. AE, MC, V. Map p. 467.

★ **Wally's Wines** WESTWOOD
Lovers of the grape know to hit this Westside warehouse for its vast selection and friendly, knowledgeable staff. Great gift baskets are also available. 2107 Westwood Blvd. (at Mississippi Ave.). ☎ 310/475-0606. www.wallywine. com. AE, DISC, MC, V. Map p. 467.

Los Angeles Restaurant Best Bets

Best Italian
Angelini Osteria, 7313 Beverly Blvd. (p. 473)

Best of the Best
Lucques, 8474 Melrose Ave. (p. 477)

Best Burger
Father's Office, 3229 Helms Ave. (p. 475)

Best Brunch
Campanile, 624 S. La Brea Ave. (p. 475)

Best Movie Set Interior
Cicada, 617 S. Olive St. (p. 475)

Best Steak
Mastro's Steakhouse, 246 N. Canon Dr. (p. 478)

Best Dim Sum
Empress Pavilion, 988 N. Hill St. (p. 475)

Best Date Night
Grace, 7360 Beverly Blvd. (p. 476)

Best Fine Dining
Patina, 141 S. Grand Ave. (p. 478)

Best Sushi
Sushi Katsu-Ya, 11680 Ventura Blvd. (p. 479)

Best Lunch at the Farmers Market
Loteria! Grill, 6333 W. Third St. (p. 477)

Best Seafood
Providence, 5855 Melrose Ave. (p. 478)

Best Hot & Spicy Thai
Jitlada, 5233K W. Sunset Blvd. (p. 477)

Most Worth the Wait
Pizzeria Mozza, 641 N. Highland Ave. (p. 478)

Best Wine Selection
A.O.C., 8022 W. Third St. (p. 473)

Best Korean BBQ
Soot Bull Jeep, 3136 Eighth St. (p. 478)

Best Cupcakes
Sprinkles Cupcakes, 9635 Little Santa Monica Blvd. (p. 479)

Best Tacos
Kogi, various locations. (p. 477)

> *Get your grill on at Campanile, with exceptional dining, and 12 types of grilled-cheese sandwiches on Tuesdays.*

Los Angeles Restaurants A to Z

★★ **Angelini Osteria** WEST HOLLYWOOD *ITALIAN* Chef/owner Gino Angelini brings Roma right to your plate with fresh ingredients and his mamma's authentic recipes. A great sign: The crowd in this small, unpretentious room usually includes Italians and off-duty chefs. 7313 Beverly Blvd. (at Poinsettia Place). ☎ 323/297-0070. www.angeliniosteria.com. Reservations recommended. Entrees $13–$38. AE, MC, V. Lunch Tues–Fri; dinner Tues–Sun. Map p. 474.

★ **Bay Cities Italian Deli & Bakery** SANTA MONICA *DELI* You'll swear off assembly-line, chain restaurant sandwiches once you sink your teeth into the legendary Godmother - fresh baked Italian bread stuffed with Genoa salami, mortadella, capicola, ham, prosciutto, and provolone - at this locals' favorite since 1925. 1517 Lincoln Blvd., (at Broadway). ☎ 310/395-8279. www.baycitiesitaliandeli.com . Sandwiches $6-$12. MC, V. Lunch & dinner Tues–Sun. Map p. 475.

★★ **A.O.C.** WEST HOLLYWOOD *CALIFORNIA/ FRENCH* Foodies huddle over small plates—charcuterie, cheese (French, Italian, Spanish), skirt steak, fried oysters—and sip on sublime

wines in a casual, chic setting. 8022 W. Third St. (at Crescent Heights Blvd.). ☎ 323/653-6359. www.aocwinebar.com. Reservations recommended. Small plates $9–$18. AE, MC, V. Dinner daily. Map p. 474.

★ **Border Grill** SANTA MONICA *LATIN* The Food Network's *Too Hot Tamales*, Mary Sue Milliken and Susan Feniger, present gourmet Mexican cuisine in a fiesta-like atmosphere. The *tres leches* cake is a must for dessert. 1445 Fourth St., (btw. Broadway & Santa Monica blvds.). ☎ 310/451-1655. www.bordergrill.com. Entrees $14–$30. AE, MC, V. Dinner daily. Map p. 475.

★ **Bottega Louie** DOWNTOWN *ITALIAN* You can't help but love a place that does so much and so well: modern Italian dishes, pizzas, small plates, desserts like gelato and macaroons, a bustling weekend brunch, a stylish bar, and a gourmet market and take-away. 700 S. Grand Ave. (at W. Seventh St.). ☎ 213/802-1470 or 310/395-3200. www.bottegalouie.com. Entrees $9–$40. AE, MC, V. Lunch Mon–Fri; dinner daily; brunch Sat–Sun. Map p. 475.

> *Don't skip dessert at Bottega Louie; its patisserie turns out tasty Italian treats that are worth every calorie.*

Beverly Hills & Hollywood Restaurants

A.O.C. **9**
Angelini Osteria **12**
Campanile **13**
Grace **11**
Hungry Cat **18**
In-N-Out Burger **17**
Ivy **4**
Jar **7**
Joan's on Third **8**

Loteria! Grill **10**
Lucques **5**
Mastro's Steakhouse **2**
M Café de Chaya **14**
Pizzeria Mozza **15**
Providence **16**
Spago **3**
Sprinkles Cupcakes **1**
Sweet Lady Jane **6**

Franklin Ave.
101
Capitol Records
N Gower St.
Vine St.
Cahuenga Blvd.
HOLLYWOOD
Hollywood Forever
Paramount Pictures
LARCHMONT
Egyptian Theatre
Chinese Theatre
El Capitan Theatre
Hollywood Blvd.
W Sunset Blvd.
Santa Monica Blvd.
N Highland Ave.
N La Brea Ave.
Melrose Ave.
N Martel Ave.
FAIRFAX
Pan Pacific Park
Farmers Market
Beverly Blvd.
Wilshire Country Club
HANCOCK PARK
S La Brea Ave.
Wilshire Blvd.
La Brea Tar Pits/Page Museum
Los Angeles County Museum of Art
Hancock Park
Petersen Automotive Museum
MID-WILSHIRE
S Fairfax Ave.
Fountain Ave.
W 3rd St.
N Fairfax Ave.
CBS Television City
N Crescent Heights Blvd.
BEVERLY GROVE
N La Cienega Blvd.
S La Cienega Blvd.
La Cienega Park
WEST HOLLYWOOD
S San Vicente Blvd.
HOLLYWOOD HILLS
Greystone Park
N Doheny Dr.
S Robertson Blvd.
Burton Way
Wilshire Blvd.
S Doheny Dr.
W Olympic Blvd.
Santa Monica Blvd.
W Sunset Blvd.
BEVERLY HILLS
Rodeo Dr.
S Beverly Dr.

1 mi
1 km

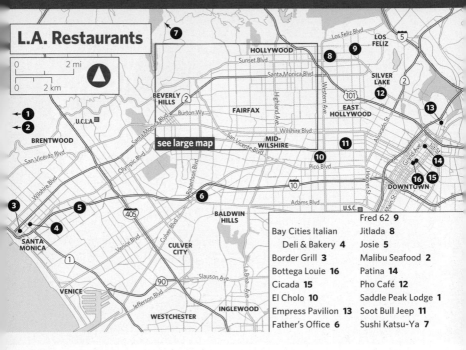

L.A. Restaurants

Bay Cities Italian Deli & Bakery **4**	Fred 62 **9**
	Jitlada **8**
Border Grill **3**	Josie **5**
Bottega Louie **16**	Malibu Seafood **2**
Cicada **15**	Patina **14**
El Cholo **10**	Pho Café **12**
Empress Pavilion **13**	Saddle Peak Lodge **1**
Father's Office **6**	Soot Bull Jeep **11**
	Sushi Katsu-Ya **7**

★★ **Campanile** HOLLYWOOD *CALIFORNIA/ MEDITERRANEAN* In a 1928 Tuscan-style building that once belonged to Charlie Chaplin, Mark Peel's restaurant has made history on its own for nearly 20 years as one of the city's best restaurants. Grilled Cheese Night is a popular draw on Thursday, but nothing beats the delicious weekend brunch in the sunny courtyard. 624 La Brea Ave. (at Wilshire Blvd.). ☎ 323/938-1447. www.campanilerestaurant. com. Reservations recommended. Entrees $16–$38. AE, MC, V. Lunch Mon–Fri; dinner Mon–Sat; brunch Sat–Sun. Map p. 474.

★ **Cicada** DOWNTOWN *NORTHERN ITALIAN* Enjoy fine Italian dining in one of the city's most stunning Art Deco environments, adorned with Lalique glass doors, rich wood columns and paneling, a gold-leaf ceiling, and a grand stairway. 617 S. Olive St. (btw. Sixth & Seventh sts.). ☎ 213/488-9488. www.cicada restaurant.com. Reservations recommended. Entrees $23–$42. AE, MC, V. Dinner Tues–Sun. Map p. 475.

★ **El Cholo** KOREATOWN *MEXICAN* Try the green corn tamales at L.A.'s oldest Mexican restaurant, which has drawn its share of celebs since 1927. 1121 S. Western Ave. (btw. 11th & 12th sts.). ☎ 323/734-2773. www.elcholo. com. Entrees $10–$16. AE, MC, V. Lunch & dinner daily. Map p. 475.

★ **Empress Pavilion** CHINATOWN *DIM SUM* For dim sum this good, you may end up waiting for a table even though the massive dining room seats 600 people. 988 N. Hill St. (at Bernard St.). ☎ 213/617-9898. www.empress pavilion.com. Entrees $8–$28. AE, MC, V. Dinner daily. Map p. 475.

★ **Father's Office** CULVER CITY *CONTEMPORARY CALIFORNIAN* Finding a seat is competitive, and the menu inflexible—absolutely no substitutions and no ketchup. All is forgiven, however, when you sink your teeth into Sang Yoon's famous burger: dry-aged beef, Gruyere and Maytag blue cheese, caramelized onions, and smoked bacon compote on a French roll. 3229 Helms Ave. (at Venice Blvd.).

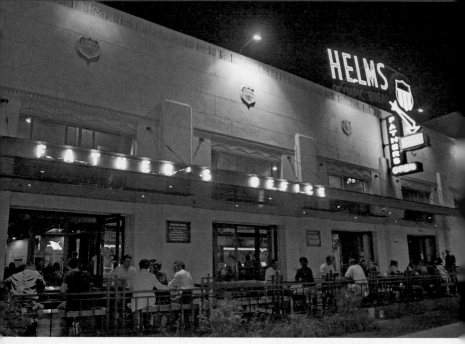

> *Step inside the intriguingly named Father's Office for extraordinary burgers (think Maytag blue cheese) and the 40 beers on tap.*

☎ 310/736-2224. www.fathersoffice.com. Reservations not accepted; minors not admitted. Entrees $5–$16. Lunch Sat; dinner daily. AE, MC, V. Map p. 475.

★ **Fred 62** LOS FELIZ *DINER*
A favorite among eastside hipsters, this retro-styled 24-hour diner always hits its mark—Bearded Mr. Frenchy (cornflake-encrusted French toast), Thai Cobb salad, or a mean tuna melt to quell the late-night munchies. 1850 N. Vermont Ave. (at Russell Ave.). ☎ 323/667-0062. www.fred62.com. Entrees $8–$12. AE, MC, V. Breakfast, lunch & dinner daily. Map p. 475.

★★ **Grace** WEST HOLLYWOOD *NEW AMERICAN*
Neal Fraser's lovely restaurant has earned a reputation as one of best dining experiences in town, with fine cuisine in a warm, relaxed atmosphere. Try Doughnut Shoppe Night (Wed; 6pm). 7360 Beverly Blvd. (at Fuller Ave.). ☎ 323/934-4400. www.gracerestaurant.com. Reservations recommended. Entrees $26–$38. AE, MC, V. Dinner Tues–Sun. Map p. 474.

★ **The Hungry Cat** HOLLYWOOD *SEAFOOD*
Enjoy fantastic cocktails and fresh, well-executed seafood, such as Maine lobster rolls, in the heart of Hollywood. 1535 N. Vine St. (at Sunset Blvd.). ☎ 323/462-2155. www.thehungry cat.com. Entrees $13–$45. AE, MC, V. Lunch & dinner daily. Map p. 474.

★ **In-N-Out Burger** HOLLYWOOD *BURGERS*
With the freshest ingredients and no micro-waves or freezers, this is the best fast-food burger in California. 7009 Sunset Blvd. (at Orange Dr.). ☎ 800/786-1000. www.in-n-out. com. Burgers $4. AE, MC, V. Lunch & dinner daily. Map p. 474.

★ **Ivy** BEVERLY HILLS *NEW AMERICAN*
With the paparazzi camped outside the white picket-fenced patio, this spot serves upscale comfort food to stars, power brokers, and tourists. 113 N. Robertson Blvd. (btw. Beverly Blvd. and Third St.). ☎ 310/274-8303. Reservations recommended. Entrees $22–$38. AE, MC, V. Lunch & dinner daily. Map p. 474.

★★ Jar WEST HOLLYWOOD *NEW AMERICAN*
Stylish and elegant, Suzanne Tracht's steak-house offers superb service and a refined take on pork chops, pot roast, and filet of beef. The Sunday brunch, featuring chilaquiles with crème fraîche, corn pancakes, and pecan sweet bread is a knockout. 8225 Beverly Blvd. (at Harper Ave.). ☎ 323/655-6566. www.thejar. com. Entrees $21–$48. AE, MC, V. Dinner daily; brunch Sun. Map p. 474.

★★ Jitlada HOLLYWOOD *THAI*
This humble, strip-mall restaurant with authentic Southern Thai cuisine is celebrated for its flavorful curries, which will make your taste buds pop and your eyes water. 5233 K W. Sunset Blvd. (at N. Harvard Blvd.). ☎ 323/667-9809. www.jitladala.com. Entrees $6.95–$17. AE, MC, V. Lunch Tues–Sun; dinner Mon–Sun. Map p. 475.

★ Joan's on Third WEST HOLLYWOOD *BAKERY/ SANDWICHES* This bakery and deluxe deli stocks a variety of gourmet salads and sandwiches and to-die-for cupcakes. A perfect pit stop when shopping on Third Street. 8350 W. Third St. (at Kings Rd.). ☎ 323/655-2285. www. joansonthird.com. Sandwiches & salads $10–$13. AE, MC, V. Lunch & dinner daily. Map p. 474.

★ Josie SANTA MONICA *NEW AMERICAN*
Gourmands seek out Josie Le Balch's nuanced American cuisine, prepared with French and Mediterranean flair. 2424 Pico Blvd. (at 25th St.). ☎ 310/581-9888. www.josierestaurant. com. Reservations recommended. Entrees $26–$38. AE, MC, V. Dinner daily. Map p. 475.

★ Kogi *KOREAN*
These taco trucks have launched a mobile restaurant movement. Savor their signature taco, Korean short ribs, the popular spicy pork taco, or something a little more offbeat, like kimchi quesadillas. Various locations; check http://kogibbq.com or http://twitter.com/kogi bbq. Tacos & burritos $5–$7 . Cash only. Lunch & dinner daily.

★ Loteria! Grill FARMERS MARKET *MEXICAN*
For years this unassuming stand has drawn lines of locals for its authentic Mexican fare. A new outpost in Hollywood, a "real" restaurant you might say, is spacious and modern with a grande selection of tequilas. 6333 W. Third St. (at Fairfax Ave.). ☎ 323/930-2211.

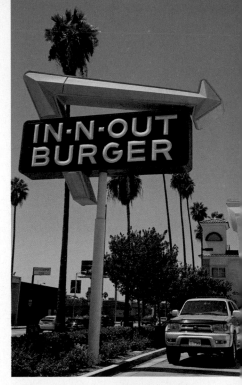

> *Pull over at In-N-Out for surprisingly good fast food, including burgers, fresh-cut fries, and super-thick shakes.*

wwwloteriagrill.com. Entrees $7–$21. MC, V. Breakfast Sat–Sun; lunch & dinner daily. Map p. 474.

★★★ Lucques WEST HOLLYWOOD *CALIFORNIAN*
Suzanne Goin's revered restaurant offers a small but sophisticated menu of French-Mediterranean dishes. Request a table on the lovely patio. 8474 Melrose Ave. (at La Cienega Blvd.). ☎ 323/655-6277. www.lucques.com. Reservations recommended. Entrees $16–$44. AE, DC, MC, V. Lunch Tues–Sat; dinner daily. Map p. 474.

★ Malibu Seafood MALIBU *SEAFOOD*
Just a stone's throw from the Pacific, this walk-up-and-order shack serves some of the freshest seafood on the coast. You can't miss with fish and chips or lobster. BYOB and no corkage fee. 25653 Pacific Coast Hwy. (1½ miles north of Malibu Canyon Rd.). ☎ 310/456-3430. www. malibuseafood.com. Entrees $5–$20. MC, V. Lunch & dinner daily. Map p. 475.

> Nothing fishy at Providence, Los Angeles's preeminent seafood restaurant (if you've never tried sea urchin, do it here).

★ **Mastro's Steakhouse** BEVERLY HILLS *STEAK*
Score a martini and a perfectly grilled double porterhouse at this swank, low-lit steakhouse in the heart of Beverly Hills. Somewhere, the Rat Pack is smiling. 246 N. Canon Dr. (btw. Clifton & Dayton ways). ☎ 310/888-8782. www.mastrosrestaurants.com. Reservations recommended. Entrees $26–$84. AE, DC, MC, V. Dinner daily. Map p. 474.

★ **M Café de Chaya** WEST HOLLYWOOD
VEGETARIAN If "flavorful macrobiotic" sounds oxymoronic to you, prepare to be surprisingly satisfied by the panini and rice bowls at this hot spot for starlets and the health obsessed. 7119 Melrose Ave. (at La Brea Ave.). ☎ 323/525-0588. www.mcafedechaya.com. Entrees $5–$14. AE, MC, V. Breakfast, lunch & dinner daily. Map p. 474.

★★ **Patina** DOWNTOWN *NEW AMERICAN*
For a world-class dining experience, sample Joachim Splichal's New American cuisine in this stunning space tucked inside the Walt Disney Concert Hall. In Walt Disney Concert Hall, 141 S. Grand Ave. (at Second St.). ☎ 213/972-3331. www.patinagroup.com. Reservations recommended. Entrees $32–$54. AE, MC, V. Dinner Tues–Sun. Map p. 475.

★ **Pho Café** SILVER LAKE *VIETNAMESE*
The Vietnamese noodle soups and crepes are fresh, cheap, and unbelievably tasty. The lack of a sign lets you know it's too cool for its random strip-mall location. 2841 W. Sunset Blvd. (at Silver Lake Blvd.). ☎ 213/413-0888. Entrees $5–$10. Cash only. Lunch & dinner daily. Map p. 475.

★★ **Pizzeria Mozza** HOLLYWOOD *PIZZA*
Since opening with a bang in 2006, this high-brow pizzeria has had foodies fighting for tables. The pizza's distinctive crust—puffy, crispy, yet chewy—sets the stage for artisanal toppings such as squash blossoms with Burrata, littleneck clams, or (my favorite) fennel sausage. 641 N. Highland Ave. (at Melrose Ave.). ☎ 323/297-0101. www.mozza-la.com. Reservations recommended. Entrees $10–$25. AE, MC, V. Lunch & dinner daily. Map p. 474.

★★ **Providence** HOLLYWOOD *SEAFOOD*
Known for its exquisitely prepared seafood, Michael Cimarusti's restaurant is considered one of the best in the country. 5955 Melrose Ave. (at Cole Ave.). ☎ 323/460-4170. www.providencela.com. Entrees $21–$49. AE, MC, V. Lunch Fri; dinner daily. Map p. 474.

★ **Saddle Peak Lodge** CALABASAS *NEW AMERICAN/GAME* This former hunting lodge is worth the drive to the Malibu hills for its rustic beauty and fabulous game dishes. 419 Cold Canyon Rd. (at Piuma Rd.). ☎ 818/222-3888. www.saddlepeaklodge.com. Reservations recommended. Entrees $29–$45. AE, DC, MC, V. Dinner Wed–Sun; brunch Sun. Map p. 475.

★ **Soot Bull Jeep** KOREATOWN *KOREAN BBQ*
Indifferent service, thick air, and a no-frills interior—none of this matters; the charcoal grill at your table gives the marinated meat a sensational, smoky flavor. 3136 Eighth St. (at Catalina St.). ☎ 213/387-3865. Entrees $12–$25. AE, MC, V. Lunch & dinner daily. Map p. 475.

> Don't ask why it's called Soot Bull Jeep, just order meat at this no-frills, do-it-yourself Korean barbecue joint.

★ **Spago** BEVERLY HILLS *CALIFORNIA*
Wolfgang Puck's legendary, groundbreaking restaurant continues to dazzle. Make it easy on yourself and order the tasting menu. 176 N. Canon Dr. (at Wilshire Blvd.). ☎ 310/385-0880. www.wolfgangpuck.com. Reservations recommended. Entrees $17–$66; tasting menu $125. AE, MC, V. Lunch & dinner daily. Map p. 474.

★ **Sprinkles Cupcakes** BEVERLY HILLS *DESSERT*
This cute cupcakery with a cult following has lines spilling out onto the sidewalk and some of the most delectable cupcakes you'll ever stuff in your mouth. Careful, the red velvet might melt your brain. 9635 Little Santa Monica Blvd. (2 blocks west of Rodeo Dr.). ☎ 310/274-8765. www.sprinkles.com. Cupcakes $3.25. Daily. Map p. 474.

★★ **Sushi Katsu-Ya** STUDIO CITY *SUSHI*
Before teaming up with SBE Entertainment to launch a string of glammed-up sushi joints on prime L.A. real estate (like Hollywood and Vine), Katsuya Uechi, one of four master sushi chefs in Los Angeles, made waves in the valley with his flawless sushi, amazing baked crab rolls, and signature spicy tuna on crispy rice. 11680 Ventura Blvd. (at Colfax Ave.). ☎ 818/985-6976. www.katsu-yagroup.com. Reservations recommended. Sushi & rolls $4–$12. AE, MC, V. Dinner daily. Map p. 475.

> It's bite-size love at Sprinkles Cupcakes, where the frosted sensations have fans lining up in Beverly Hills.

★ **Sweet Lady Jane** WEST HOLLYWOOD *DESSERT* The scrumptious cakes and cupcakes are big hits for parties and gifts. Try the Tripleberry. 8360 Melrose Ave. (at N. Kings Rd.). ☎ 323/653-7145. www.sweetladyjane.com. Sandwiches & desserts $8.50–$10. AE, MC, V. Breakfast & lunch daily. Map p. 474.

Los Angeles Hotel Best Bets

Most Romantic
Hotel Bel Air, 701 Stone Canyon Rd. (p. 485)

Best Service
Four Seasons Beverly Hills, 300 S. Doheny Dr. (p. 484)

Best Value
Elan Hotel, 8010 Beverly Blvd. (p. 483)

Best Spot for Shopaholics
Beverly Wilshire, 9500 Wilshire Blvd. (p. 483)

Best Bed & Breakfast
Bissell House Bed and Breakfast, 201 Orange Grove Ave. (p. 483)

Most Iconic
Beverly Hills Hotel & Bungalows, 9641 Sunset Blvd. (p. 481)

Most Exclusive
Chateau Marmont, 8221 Sunset Blvd. (p. 483)

Quirkiest Decor
Farmer's Daughter, 115 S. Fairfax Ave. (p. 484)

Best Boutique Hotel
Maison 140, 140 S. Lasky Dr. (p. 485)

Most Historic
Hollywood Roosevelt Hotel, 7000 Hollywood Blvd. (p. 484)

Best Sunday Brunch
The Langham Huntington, 1401 S. Oak Knoll Ave. (p. 485)

Best Views
Shutters on the Beach, 1 Pico Blvd. (p. 486)

Hottest Hotel
SLS Hotel, 465 S. La Cienega Blvd. (p. 486)

Most Rock 'n' Roll
Sunset Marquis Hotel & Villas, 1200 Alta Loma Rd. (p. 487)

Best Hotel Bar
Millennium Biltmore Hotel, 506 S. Grand Ave. (p. 485)

Best Pool Scene
W Los Angeles, 930 Hilgard Ave. (p. 487)

Best Hotel Spa
The Peninsula Beverly Hills, 9882 S. Santa Monica Blvd. (p. 486)

> *A refined oasis in the San Gabriel foothills, the elegant Langham Huntington holds court on 23 lush acres.*

Los Angeles Hotels A to Z

★ **Andaz West Hollywood** WEST HOLLYWOOD
This is the infamous "Riot Hyatt" where rock
'n' roll will never die, although it will get older
and more sophisticated, with sedate decor,
and a refined restaurant featuring French-
inspired cuisine and master mixologists behind the bar. Check out the views of the Strip
and beyond from the rooftop pool. 8401 Sunset Blvd. (at Kings Rd.). ☎ 323/656-1234. www.
westhollywood.hyatt.com. 262 units. Doubles
$245–$340. AE, DC, DISC, MC, V. Map p. 482.

★★ **Avalon Hotel** BEVERLY HILLS
Formerly the apartments of starlets such as
Marilyn Monroe, the building has been redone
in a winking '50s style with designer accessories (Charles Eames, George Nelson). The
pool courtyard is a groovy scene; if you seek
peace and quiet, ask for a room in the Canon
building across the street. 9400 W. Olympic
Blvd. (at S. Canon Dr.). ☎ 310/277-5221. www.
avalonbeverlyhills.com. 84 units. Doubles $280–
$320. AE, DC, MC, V. Map p. 482.

★ **Best Western Hollywood Hills Hotel**
HOLLYWOOD All the contemporary-style
rooms feature a fridge, a microwave, and Wi-
Fi. Downstairs is the 101 Coffee Shop, typically
packed with scruffy hipsters. Hollywood is a
short walk, and a Metro Line stop is 3 blocks
away. 6141 Franklin Ave. (btw. N. Gower St. &
Argyle Ave.). ☎ 323/464-5181. www.best
westerncalifornia.com. 84 units. Doubles $116–
$149. AE, DISC, MC, V. Map p. 482.

kids **Beverly Garland's Holiday Inn** UNIVERSAL
CITY A pool, tennis courts, free Wi-Fi, friendly
staff, easy freeway access, and a free shuttle
to Universal Studios make this a great option
for families. 4222 Vineland Ave. (at Hwy. 101).
☎ 818/980-8000. www.beverlygarland.com.
255 units. Doubles $159–$209. AE, MC, V. Map
p. 483.

★★★ **Beverly Hills Hotel & Bungalows** BEVERLY
HILLS The legendary "Pink Palace" opened in
1912 and still retains its golden-age glamour,
ritziness, impeccable service, and that famous
pink facade, which was immortalized on the
cover of the Eagles' album *Hotel California*.

> *High-class hip finds a perfect package in the style-conscious Avalon Hotel, fortunately as comfortable as it
> is stunning.*

Beverly Hills & Hollywood Hotels

Four Seasons Beverly Hills **6**
Hollywood Roosevelt Hotel **15**
Maison 140 **3**
Mondrian **11**
Peninsula Beverly Hills **2**
SLS Hotel **7**
Sunset Marquis Hotel & Villas **10**
Sunset Tower Hotel **13**

Andaz West Hollywood **12**
Avalon Hotel **5**
Best Western Hollywood Hills Hotel **16**
Beverly Hills Hotel & Bungalows **1**
Beverly Wilshire **4**
Chateau Marmont **14**
Elan Hotel **8**
Farmer's Daughter **9**

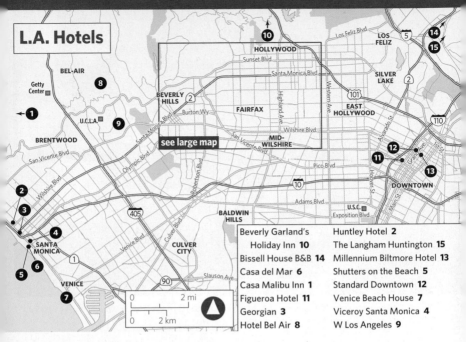

L.A. Hotels

Beverly Garland's Holiday Inn **10**
Bissell House B&B **14**
Casa del Mar **6**
Casa Malibu Inn **1**
Figueroa Hotel **11**
Georgian **3**
Hotel Bel Air **8**

Huntley Hotel **2**
The Langham Huntington **15**
Millennium Biltmore Hotel **13**
Shutters on the Beach **5**
Standard Downtown **12**
Venice Beach House **7**
Viceroy Santa Monica **4**
W Los Angeles **9**

9641 Sunset Blvd. (at Beverly Dr.). ☎ 310/276-2251. www.thebeverlyhillshotel.com. 204 units. Doubles $480–$590. AE, DC, DISC, MC, V. Map p. 482.

★★ **Beverly Wilshire** BEVERLY HILLS
Directly across from Rodeo Drive stands this swanky, Four Seasons-managed hotel, originally built in 1928. The hotel's restaurant, Wolfgang Puck's hit steakhouse, CUT, is a ma-jor celebrity magnet. 9500 Wilshire Blvd. (at Beverly Dr.). ☎ 310/275-5200. www.fourseasons.com/beverlywilshire. 395 units. Dou-bles $395–$575. AE, DC, DISC, MC, V. Map p. 482.

★ **Bissell House Bed and Breakfast** PASADENA
Set in a historic and architecturally rich neighborhood, this restored, antiques-filled Victorian built in 1887 is a comfy and cozy alternative to the typical L.A. hotel experience. 201 Orange Grove Ave. (at Columbia St.). ☎ 626/441-3535. www.bissellhouse.com. 5 units. Doubles $195–$350. AE, MC, V. Map p. 483.

★★ **Casa del Mar** SANTA MONICA
This resort hotel recaptures the glamour of its past as a 1920s beach club, with a rooftop pool and a sumptuous, velvet-draped lobby.

Rooms offer ocean views, chaise longues, and large, white-marble bathrooms with whirlpool tubs and Murad products. 1910 Ocean Way (at Pico Blvd.). ☎ 310/581-5533. www.hotelcasadelmar.com. 129 units. Doubles $365–$630. AE, DC, DISC, MC, V. Map p. 483.

★ **Casa Malibu Inn** MALIBU
Book well in advance to snag these simple and clean beachfront digs that won't blow your budget. 22752 Pacific Coast Hwy. (at Sweetwater Canyon Dr.). ☎ 310/456-2219. 21 units. Doubles $129–$299. AE, MC, V. Map p. 483.

★★★ **Chateau Marmont** WEST HOLLYWOOD
Built in 1927 in the mold of a Loire Valley castle, this landmark hotel prides itself on its exclusivity and privacy, which is probably why so many celebrities feel comfortable misbehaving here. The rooms, suites, cottages, and bungalows are individually decorated (Gothic, Arts and Crafts, midcentury, Spanish), but all bask in the glow of Hollywood's golden era. 8221 Sunset Blvd. (at Havenhurst Dr.). ☎ 323/656-1010. www.chateaumarmont.com. 63 units. Doubles $370–$480. AE, DC, MC, V. Map p. 482.

★ **Elan Hotel** WEST HOLLYWOOD
This small, clean, modern and perfectly

> Bad boys and naughty starlets have long-favored the exclusive seclusion of the charmingly quirky Chateau Marmont, a landmark of Hollywood's Golden Age.

located boutique hotel does the little things to keep its campers happy; there's complimentary wine and cheese in the afternoons and free Wi-Fi throughout the hotel. 8435 Beverly Blvd. (at N. Croft Ave.). ☎ 323/658-6663. www.elanhotel.com. 49 units. Doubles from $155. AE, DC, MC, V. Map p. 482.

★ **Farmer's Daughter** WEST HOLLYWOOD
You can't help but smile at this budget motel's crazy-cowpoke style: plaid curtains, denim bedspreads, thrift-store art, a recurring rooster motif, and a better-than-average supply of rusty pitchforks. And, boy, howdy—it's right across from the Farmers Market and CBS Television Center, where many guests try out for *The Price Is Right.* 115 S. Fairfax Ave. (at W. First St.). ☎ 323/937-3930. www.farmersdaughterhotel.com. 66 units. Doubles $175–$255. AE, DISC, MC, V. Map p. 482.

★ **Figueroa Hotel** DOWNTOWN
Downtown adventurers might enjoy this moderately priced hotel with eclectic, exotic decor such as Moroccan chandeliers, Indian fabrics, Mexican tiles, and hand-woven Afghani kilims. A pool and patio bar complete the urban oasis. 939 S. Figueroa St. (at Olympic Blvd.). ☎ 213/627-8971. www.figueroahotel.com. 285

units. Doubles $144–$205. AE, DC, MC, V. Map p. 483.

★★★ **Four Seasons Beverly Hills** BEVERLY HILLS
Fabulousness and impeccable service in the heart of Beverly Hills—this is for those who are living the dream, baby. 300 S. Doheny Dr. (at Burton Way). ☎ 800/332-3442. www.fourseasons.com/beverlyhills. 285 units. Doubles $385–$450. AE, DC, DISC, MC, V. Map p. 482.

★ **Georgian** SANTA MONICA
This Art Deco masterpiece facing Santa Monica beach combines a lot of luxury and a bit of history—during Prohibition Bugsy Siegel opened a speak-easy in the hotel's basement. 1415 Ocean Ave. (btw. Santa Monica Blvd. & Broadway). ☎ 800/538-8147 or 310/395-9945. www.georgianhotel.com. 84 units. Doubles $220–$265. AE, DC, DISC, MC, V. Map p. 483.

★ **Hollywood Roosevelt Hotel** HOLLYWOOD
This hotel, site of the first Academy Awards in 1929, has been restored to its former glory—just ask the ghost of Montgomery Clift, who some say still haunts the building. Teddy's Lounge and the Tropicana poolside bar draw throngs of young partiers. 7000 Hollywood Blvd. (at N. Orange Dr.). ☎ 800/950-7667 or

> *The best lodging for less might be Farmer's Daughter, which offers a funky, playful style for less ka-ching.*

> *Slip into something comfortable at the Penthouse, an ultra-hot bar inside the postmodern-cool Huntley Hotel.*

323/466-7000. www.hollywoodroosevelt.com. 302 units. Doubles $230–$316. AE, DC, DISC, MC, V. Map p. 482.

★★★ Hotel Bel Air BEL AIR

Pink stucco buildings are nestled among 12 tranquil acres with manicured gardens, canopies of bougainvillea, old-as-dirt sycamores and live oaks, fragrant flowers, and a swan lake. In the fall of 2009 the one-of-a-kind hotel began a massive multiyear renovation to update rooms and add a spa as well as additional villas. 701 Stone Canyon Rd. (north of Sunset Blvd.). ☎ 800/648-4097 or 310/472-1211. www.hotelbelair.com. 91 units. Doubles $485–$600. AE, DC, DISC, MC, V. Map p. 483.

★ Huntley Hotel SANTA MONICA

Bed down in postmodern coolness at this hotel close to the beach and prime Santa Monica shopping. It may be worth a stay just to score a white-leather seat at the white-hot bar, the Penthouse. 1111 Second St. (at California Ave.). ☎ 310/394-5454. www.thehuntleyhotel.com. 209 units. Doubles $215–$399. AE, DC, DISC, MC, V. Map p. 483.

★★ The Langham Huntington PASADENA

Set on 23 acres among lush gardens in the foothills of San Gabriel Mountains, this beautiful hotel, built in 1906, makes a great base for exploring downtown L.A., as well as the museums and architectural homes of Pasadena. . The Terrace Restaurant offers a wonderful,

relaxed Sunday brunch. 1401 S. Oak Knoll Ave. (at Hillcrest Ave.). ☎ 626/568-3900. www. pasadena.langhamhotels.com. 380 units. Doubles $279–$399. AE, DC, MC, V. Map p. 483.

★★ Maison 140 BEVERLY HILLS

Originally a boarding house owned by Lillian Gish, this superchic boutique hotel blends elements that are French, Far East, and far out. Stroll nearby Rodeo Drive and then cozy up in the dark and velvety Bar Noir, the trystiest hotel bar around. 140 S. Lasky Dr. (btw. Wilshire & Charleville blvds.). ☎ 800/670-6182 or 310/281-4000. www.maison140beverlyhills. com. 43 units. Doubles $225–$275. AE, DC, MC, V. Map p. 482.

★ Millennium Biltmore Hotel DOWNTOWN

Architecture lovers should consider a stay at this 1923 historic landmark for its stunning lobby, halls, and ballrooms, which have been used for Oscar ceremonies, JFK's 1960 DNC headquarters, and, of course, movie locations (*Ghostbusters, Beverly Hills Cop*). The rooms,

> The ultimate getaway might just be a vacation overlooking Santa Monica sands from Shutters on the Beach.

9882 S. Santa Monica Blvd. (at Wilshire Blvd.). ☎ 800/462-7899 or 310/551-2888. www. peninsula.com. 196 units. Doubles $395–$555. AE, DC, DISC, MC, V. Map p. 482.

> Versailles meets L.A. in the lavishly embellished Millennium Biltmore's Gallery Bar, dubbed one of L.A.'s sexiest bars.

while elegant, are rather small. 506 S. Grand Ave. (at W. Fifth St.). ☎ 213/624-1011. www. millenniumhotels.com. 683 units. Doubles $159–$375. AE, DC, DISC, MC, V. Map p. 483.

★ Mondrian WEST HOLLYWOOD
This stylish white-on-white high rise is best known for its poolside bar, the exclusive Skybar, which maintains its status as one of Hollywood's hottest see-and-be-seen scenes. A $20-million renovation has spruced up the rooms. 8440 W. Sunset Blvd. (at Queens Rd.). ☎ 800/606-6090 or 323/650-8999. www. mondrianhotel.com. 237 units. Doubles $305–$405. AE, DC, DISC, MC, V. Map p. 482.

★★ The Peninsula Beverly Hills BEVERLY HILLS
You'll get an opulent, European-style room and flawless service if you can fork out the cash to stay at this gardenlike oasis.

★★ Shutters on the Beach SANTA MONICA
This shingled building on the sand combines the luxury of a fine hotel with the breeziness of a beach cottage. Watch the sun set on the ocean from your own private balcony. 1 Pico Blvd. (at Neilson Way). ☎ 800/334-9000 or 310/458-0030. www.shuttersonthebeach.com. 198 units. Doubles $395–$575. AE, DC, DISC, MC, V. Map p. 483.

★ SLS Hotel BEVERLY HILLS
The first luxury hotel from relentless nightlife impresario Sam Nazarian buzzes with energy. Philippe Starck spearheaded the design, both sophisticated and over-the-top, mixing clean lines and muted tones with larky elements like a mounted glass deer head. 465 S. La Cienega Blvd. (btw. Colgate Ave & Clifton Way). ☎ 310/274-7777. www.slshotels.com. 297 units. Doubles $169–$350. AE, DC, DISC, MC, V. Map p. 482.

★ Standard Downtown DOWNTOWN
Accommodations are cheeky and modern, but you come here to groove at the retro-style rooftop pool and bar, with its red pod beds and

skyscraper views. 550 S. Flower St. (btw. W. Fifth & W. Sixth sts.). ☎ 213/892-8080. www. standardhotel.com. 205 units. Doubles $245–$285. AE, DC, DISC, MC, V. Map p. 483.

★ **Sunset Marquis Hotel & Villas** WEST HOLLYWOOD A Mediterranean oasis off the Sunset Strip, this all-suite hotel has long catered to the high-profile musician crowd (Stones, U2, Eminem); there's even a state-of-the-art recording studio in the basement. The Bar 1200 can be impossible to get into, unless you're a hotel guest or famous or both. 1200 Alta Loma Rd. (btw. Sunset Blvd. & Halloway Dr.). ☎ 310/657-1333. www.sunsetmarquishotel. com. 114 units. Doubles $345–$530. AE, DC, DISC, MC, V. Map p. 482.

★ **Sunset Tower Hotel** WEST HOLLYWOOD A 1929 Art Deco landmark that has seen tenants such as Frank Sinatra, Marilyn Monroe, and Howard Hughes, this hotel takes a straight-faced look back at Hollywood's heyday, and presents a grown-up's version of the Sunset Strip. Rooms have views, comfortable beds, and Kiehl's toiletries. 8358 W. Sunset Blvd. (btw. Crescent Heights & La Cienega blvds.). ☎ 323/654-7100. www.sunsettower hotel.com. 74 units. Doubles $225–$325. AE, DISC, MC, V. Map p. 482.

★ **Venice Beach House** VENICE No designer decor, no high-end amenities, but most importantly, no attitude—this charming B&B occupies a historic Craftsman bungalow just a block from Venice Beach. Half of the rooms have private bathrooms. 15 30th Ave. (at Speedway). ☎ 310/823-1966. www.venice beachhouse.com. 9 units, 5 w/private bathroom. Doubles $145–$235. AE, MC, V. Map p. 483.

★ **Viceroy Santa Monica** SANTA MONICA This glamorous retreat features what I'd call groovy-colonialism decor, two outdoor pools with swank cabanas, and the destination bar Cameo. 1819 Ocean Ave. (at Pico Blvd.). ☎ 800/670-6185 or 310/260-7500. www. viceroysantamonica.com. 162 units. Doubles $340–$415. AE, DC, DISC, MC, V. Map p. 483.

★ **W Los Angeles** WESTWOOD This sleek, all-suite hotel near UCLA makes a good base for exploring the Westside. Enjoy WET, the heated outdoor pool ringed by chaise longues and cabanas. During the summer, movies screen poolside. 930 Hilgard Ave. (at Le Conte Ave.). ☎ 800/W-HOTELS (946-8357) or 310/208-8765. www.starwood.com/ whotels. 258 units. Doubles from $299. AE, DC, DISC, MC, V. Map p. 483.

> *Pool parties are huge at L.A. hotels, and the rooftop oasis at the Standard Downtown adds edgy style to the trend.*

Los Angeles Nightlife & Entertainment Best Bets

Best One-Man Band
Jon Brion at Largo at the Coronet, 366 N. La Cienega Blvd. (p. 492)

Best Happy Hour
Copa d'Oro, 217 Broadway. (p. 489)

Best Dive Bar
Frolic Room, 6245 Hollywood Blvd. (p. 490)

Best Lounge Act
Marty and Elaine at the Dresden, 1760 N. Vermont Ave. (p. 489)

Most Historic Bar
Formosa Cafe, 7156 Santa Monica Blvd. (p. 489)

Best Prohibition-Era Cocktails
The Varnish, 118 E. Sixth St. (p. 490)

Best Indie Rock
The Satellite, 1717 Silver Lake Blvd. (p. 492)

Best Gay Bar
The Abbey, 692 N. Robertson Blvd. (p. 492)

Best Acoustics
Walt Disney Concert Hall, 111 S. Grand Ave. (p. 490)

Best Chance to Do the Wave
Dodger Stadium, 1000 Elysian Park Ave. (p. 493)

Best Theater for a Hit Broadway Musical
Pantages Theatre, 6233 Hollywood Blvd. (p. 493)

Best Concert Under the Stars
Hollywood Bowl, 2301 N. Highland Ave. (p. 490)

Best Ongoing *Saturday Night Live* Auditions
Groundlings, 7307 Melrose Ave. (p. 491)

Best Slam Dunk
Los Angeles Lakers at the Staples Center, 1111 S. Figueroa St. (p. 493)

Most Unpredictable Comedy
Upright Citizens Brigade, 5919 Franklin Ave. (p. 491)

> *Not-so-subtle signage announces the kinda-divey Frolic Room, where the jukebox cranks and drinks are stiff.*

Los Angeles Nightlife & Entertainment A to Z

Bars & Cocktail Lounges

★★ Bar Lubitsch WEST HOLLYWOOD
This dimly-lit Russian-themed vodka parlor offers you and your comrades over 200 kinds of vodka and the Red Room in back to dance off the effects. 7702 Santa Monica Blvd. (at Spaulding Ave.). ☎ 323/654-1234. Map p. 466.

★ Brig VENICE
A friendly, mixed crowd downs drinks in a hip and modern space with a DJ spinning on most nights. 1515 Abbot Kinney Blvd. (at California Ave.). ☎ 310/399-7537. Map p. 467.

★ Copa d'Oro SANTA MONICA
You've probably never tasted anything like these creative cocktails, made with the freshest ingredients—fruits and herbs straight from the Santa Monica Farmers Market. The "Happy Depression" menu is a bargain: $5 cocktails from 6pm to 8pm. 217 Broadway (at Second St.). ☎ 310/576-3030. www.copadoro.com. Map p. 467.

★ The Dresden LOS FELIZ
Check out the musical stylings of Marty and Elaine, the legendary lounge act you might remember from the movie *Swingers*. Don't leave before they do their version of "Stayin' Alive." 1760 N. Vermont Ave. (at Kingswell Ave.). ☎ 323/665-4294. www.thedresden.com. Map p. 467.

★★ Formosa Cafe WEST HOLLYWOOD
Built in 1939 and declared a city landmark in 1991, this trolley car bar is perfect if you like your drinks dripping with nostalgia—Marilyn, Sinatra, and Elvis have all tippled here. 7156 Santa Monica Blvd. (at Formosa Ave.). ☎ 323/850-9050. Map p. 466.

★ 4100 Bar SILVER LAKE
Snake through the velvet curtain, kick back in the red glow of the vaguely Asian decor, and take in the eclectic crowd and the sounds of the stellar jukebox. 4100 Sunset Blvd. (at Manzanita St.). ☎ 323/666-4460. Map p. 467.

Map Note
For a map denoting the locations of all listings in this section, see p. 466-67.

> *Pictures paint a thousand words inside Formosa Cafe, where stars have sipped martinis since 1939.*

> *Don't say "Hey bartender" at The Varnish, where "mixologists" craft seriously stylized cocktails.*

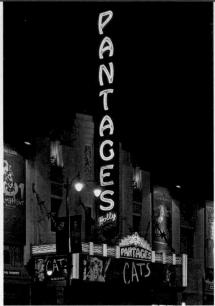

> *The richly restored Art Deco–style Pantages Theatre presents top-name acts and Broadway shows.*

★ Frolic Room HOLLYWOOD

Slumped next to the high-flying Pantages Theatre, this bar is refreshingly untouched by Hollywood's wave of regentrification. It's got an exuberant neon sign on the outside and a fading wallpaper mural of yesteryear celebrities on the inside. 6245 Hollywood Blvd. (at Argyle Ave.). ☎ 323/462-5890. Map p. 466.

★ Tiki-Ti LOS FELIZ

Try the exotic cocktails—the Blood and Sand, the Great White Shark, Ray's Mistake—at what may be the world's tiniest Tiki hut, serving loyal locals since 1961. 4427 W. Sunset Blvd. (at Virgil Place). ☎ 323/669-9381. www.tiki-ti.com. Map p. 467.

★★★ The Varnish DOWNTOWN

The mixologists at this speak-easy-style bar—the entrance is an unmarked door in the back of Cole's restaurant—craft meticulous cocktails like the Penicillin, a single-malt Scotch with honey, lemon, and crystallized ginger, on a single slab of ice. 118 E. Sixth St. (at Main St.). ☎ 213/622-9999. www.thevarnishbar.com. Map p. 467.

Classical Music & Opera

★ Dorothy Chandler Pavilion DOWNTOWN

The 3,200-seat auditorium is home to the nation's fourth-largest opera company, which continues to garner acclaim under the bold guidance of artistic director Plácido Domingo. Also, Dance at the Music Center hosts touring dance troupes such as the American Ballet Theatre. 135 N. Grand Ave., (btw. W. Temple & First sts.). ☎ 213/972-8001 or 213/972-0711. www.musiccenter.org. Tickets $20–$220. Map p. 467.

★★★ Hollywood Bowl HOLLYWOOD

In 1922 the city's finest musicians, the Los Angeles Philharmonic, played the city's finest outdoor venue, the Hollywood Bowl. Thankfully, the tradition continues. Nonclassical acts fill out the rest of the schedule. 2301 N. Highland Ave. ☎ 323/850-2000. www.hollywoodbowl.com. Tickets $1–$147. Map p. 467.

★★★ Walt Disney Concert Hall DOWNTOWN

Charismatic Venezuelan conductor Gustavo Dudamel has reinvigorated the performances of the L.A. Philharmonic at this first-rate hall, a masterpiece for the eyes and ears. 111 S. Grand Ave. (at First St.). ☎ 323/850-2000. www.laphil.com. Tickets $15–$142. Map p. 467.

> *Exquisite music and architecture join forces at the Walt Disney Concert Hall, home to the Los Angeles Philharmonic.*

Comedy

★ Groundlings HOLLYWOOD

For improv and sketch comedy in L.A., nothing beats Groundlings, whose long list of funny alumni includes Will Ferrell, Lisa Kudrow, Phil Hartman, and Maya Rudolph. **7307 Melrose Ave. (at Poinsettia Place). ☎ 323/934-4747. www. groundlings.com. Tickets $11–$22. Map p. 466.**

★ Improv WEST HOLLYWOOD

At some point in their careers, all the big-time stand-ups have played Bud Friedman's club: Seinfeld, Cosby, Leno, Crystal, Carlin, et al. **8162 Melrose Ave. (at N. Kilkea Dr.). ☎ 323/651-2583. www.improv2.com. Tickets $13–$18. Map p. 466.**

★ Laugh Factory HOLLYWOOD

Aside from Michael "Kramer" Richards' infamous meltdown in 2006, Jamie Masada's club has been consistently bringing the funny since 1979, when Richard Pryor headlined the first show. **8001 Sunset Blvd. (at Laurel Ave.). ☎ 323/656-1336. www.laughfactory.com. Tickets $20–$45. Map p. 466.**

★★ Upright Citizens Brigade HOLLYWOOD

This tiny theater rivals Groundlings for sketch-comedy supremacy, and the yuks per bucks ratio cannot be beat. **5919 Franklin Ave. (at Bronson Ave.). ☎ 323/908-8702. www.ucb theatre.com. Tickets $1–$8. Map p. 466.**

Dance Clubs and DJ Music

★ Boulevard 3 HOLLYWOOD

At the former Hollywood Athletic Club (established in 1924 with charter members such as Chaplin and DeMille), this club offers a huge dance floor as well as a courtyard retreat with cozy cabanas. Call ahead for reservations, but you may still have to rely on the kindness of bouncers, if there is such a thing. **6523 W. Sunset Blvd. (at N. Hudson Ave.). ☎ 323/466-2144. www.boulevard3.com. Cover $20. Map p. 466.**

★★ La Cita Bar DOWNTOWN

Saturday and Sunday offer authentic salsa and ranchera-style dancing, while the rest of the week, especially Thursday nights, features DJs spinning for shimmying hipsters from Echo Park and Silver Lake. **336 S. Hill St. (at W. Third St.). ☎ 213/687-7111. www.lacitabar.com. Cover Thurs-Fri $5–$10. Map p. 467.**

★ My House HOLLYWOOD

This hot spot feels like a rock star's mansion and caters to young Hollywood and their entourages. Bottle service reservations, which are costly, are the only guaranteed way through the door. **7080 Hollywood Blvd. (at N. La Brea Ave.). ☎ 323/960-3300. www. myhousehollywood.com. Cover $20–$30. Map p. 466.**

> Catch the colorful scene at The Satellite, once home to classic Indie rock acts, but now a major dance club.

The Satellite SILVER LAKE
In a former incarnation, this was the home of the Indie Rock mecca, Spaceland. Nowadays electro bands and DJs rule the dance floor. 1717 Silver Lake Blvd. (at Effie St.). ☎ 323/661-4380. www.clubspaceland.com. Cover $5–$15, free Mon. Map p. 466.

Gay & Lesbian Bars
★★ **The Abbey** WEST HOLLYWOOD
This indoor/outdoor cafe and bar has long been considered ground zero of West Hollywood's gay and lesbian nightlife. 692 N. Robertson Blvd. (at Santa Monica Blvd.). ☎ 310/289-8410. www.abbeyfoodandbar.com. Map p. 466.

★ **East/West Lounge** WEST HOLLYWOOD
Gay professionals chill at this upscale club, which serves specialty drinks (like puréed-fruit martinis) in a plush, conversation-friendly setting. 801 Larrabee St. (at Santa Monica Blvd.). ☎ 310/360-6186. www.eastwestlounge.com. Map p. 466.

Live Music
★ **Catalina Bar and Grill** HOLLYWOOD
Cooking up classic jazz in Hollywood for 20 years, this 250-seat dinner club has hosted such legends as Dizzy Gillespie, Art Blakey, and Wynton Marsalis. 6725 W. Sunset Blvd. (at Highland Ave.). ☎ 323/466-2210. www.catalinajazzclub.com. Cover $10–$35. 2-drink or dinner minimum. Map p. 466.

★**Hollywood Palladium** HOLLYWOOD
This large streamline-moderne venue has been a fixture on the Hollywood music scene since Frank Sinatra topped the bill at its opening in 1940. Recent acts include Jay-Z, Bob Dylan, and the Pixies. 6215 W. Sunset Blvd. (Btw. Vine & Gower sts.). ☎ 323/962-7600. Tickets $20–$150. Map p. 466.

★ **House of Blues** HOLLYWOOD
This slick, well-run venue hosts major acts from all genres. Try the Sunday gospel brunch, which serves up live gospel music and a buffet of Southern cuisine. 8430 W. Sunset Blvd. (at N. Olive Dr.). ☎ 323/848-5100. www.hob.com. Tickets $20–$50. Map p. 466.

★★ **Largo at the Coronet** WEST HOLLYWOOD
This is a quiet, sit-down venue for intimate musical performances (Eels, Fiona Apple) and comedic acts (Sarah Silverman, Patton Oswalt). Friday nights with producer, performer, and musical mad scientist Jon Brion are extraordinary. 366 N. La Cienega Blvd. (at Oakwood Ave.). ☎ 310/855-0350. www.largo-la.com. Cover $10–$30. Map p. 466.

★ **Nokia Theatre L.A. Live** DOWNTOWN
Part of a massive entertainment complex, this 7,100-seater presents major acts like Pink Floyd, Neil Young, and Mary J. Blige, as well as special events like the Emmy Awards. 777 Chick Hearns Court (at the Staples Center). ☎ 213/763-6030. www.nokiatheatrelalive.com. Cover $10–$30. Map p. 467.

> Holding court, Lakers' super-fan Jack Nicholson cheers on Kobe Bryant and other big boys at the Staples Center.

★★ Troubadour WEST HOLLYWOOD
Opened in 1957, this club has played a vital role in the careers of Elton John, Tom Waits, Guns N' Roses, and countless more. Today's lineup veers toward indie sensations like Clap Your Hands Say Yeah, the Fiery Furnaces, and Art Brut. 9081 Santa Monica Blvd. (at N. Doheny Dr.). ☎ 310/276-6168. www.troubadour.com. Tickets $10–$15. Map p. 466.

★ Whisky a Go Go HOLLYWOOD
This legendary venue still presents a variety of musical acts—mostly hard rockin'—including tribute bands to the greats that once played here: Led Zeppelin, Van Halen, and the Doors. 8901 W. Sunset Blvd. (at N. San Vicente Blvd.). ☎ 310/652-4202. www.whiskyagogo.com. Tickets $8–$40. Map p. 466.

Sports Venues
★★ Dodger Stadium DOWNTOWN
Built in 1962 to welcome the Dodgers from Brooklyn, this is one of Major League Baseball's classic stadiums, and currently the third oldest in use. 1000 Elysian Park Ave. (at Stadium Way). ☎ 866/DODGERS (363-4377). www.dodgers.com. Tickets $6–$225. Map p. 467.

★ Home Depot Center CARSON
This 27,000-seat soccer-only stadium is the home field for both Chivas U.S.A. and the Los

Angeles Galaxy. 1000 E. Victoria St. (at Tamcliff Ave.). ☎ 213/480-3232. www.homedepotcenter.com. Tickets $10–$250. Map p. 467.

★ Staples Center DOWNTOWN
This state-of-the-art sporting palace plays home to the NHL's Los Angeles Kings, as well as the NBA's Los Angeles Clippers and 2010 World Champion Los Angeles Lakers. 1111 S. Figueroa St. (at 11th St.). ☎ 213/742-7300. www.staplescenter.com. Tickets $10–$275. Map p. 467.

Theaters
★ Ahmanson Theater DOWNTOWN
Supported by the largest theatrical subscription base on the West Coast, this venue presents exclusive Los Angeles engagements of Tony Award-winning productions such as *Death of a Salesman, Doubt,* and *Jersey Boys.* 135 N. Grand Ave. (at W. Temple St.). ☎ 213/628-2772. www.centertheatregroup.org. Tickets $20–$100. Map p. 467.

★★ Geffen Playhouse WESTWOOD
This striking venue near UCLA is known for showcasing film and television actors (Annette Bening, David Hyde Pierce) in a shuffling between classic works (Arthur Miller) and edgier fare (Terrence McNally, Wendy Wasserstein). 10886 Le Conte Ave. (at Westwood Blvd.). ☎ 310/208-5454. www.geffenplayhouse.com. Tickets $35–$110. Map p. 467.

★ Mark Taper Forum DOWNTOWN
This intimate, 750-seat theater benefits from its thrust stage, which projects into the audience, allowing the action to be viewed from three sides. Sparkling from a $30-million overhaul, the internationally acclaimed venue presents innovative works by contemporary playwrights such as David Mamet, John Patrick Shanley, and John Guare. 135 N. Grand Ave. (at W. Temple St.). ☎ 213/628-2772. www.centertheatregroup.org. Map p. 467.

★ Pantages Theatre HOLLYWOOD
Home to the Academy Awards ceremony from 1949 to 1959, this lavishly restored Art Deco landmark presents hit Broadway musicals such as *Wicked, Stomp, Cats,* and *Chicago.* 6233 Hollywood Blvd. (at Argyle Ave.). ☎ 323/468-1770. www.broadwayla.org. Tickets $81–$300. Map p. 466.

Fast Facts

American Express

There is an office at 327 N. Beverly Dr., Beverly Hills (☎ 310/274-8277) and several other locations throughout the city. To find the one nearest you, call ☎ 800/221-7282.

Emergencies

Call ☎ **911** to report a fire, call the police, or get an ambulance. This is toll free from any phone.

If you encounter traveler's problems, call the Los Angeles chapter of the **Traveler's Aid Society** (☎ 310/646-2270; www.travelersaid.org), a nationwide, nonprofit, social service organization that helps travelers in difficult situations.

Getting There

Most visitors fly into **Los Angeles International Airport** (☎ 310/646-5252; www.lawa.org/lax), better known as LAX, which is situated ocean side, between Marina del Rey and Manhattan Beach. LAX is a convenient place to land; it's located within minutes of Santa Monica and the beaches, and not more than a half-hour from downtown, Hollywood, and the Westside. **TRAVELING BY CAR FROM THE AIRPORT** To reach Santa Monica, head north on Sepulveda and following signs for Calif. 1; to reach Beverly Hills and Hollywood, head north on I-405 to Santa Monica Boulevard east; to reach Pasadena or downtown, head south on Sepulveda to I-105 east to I-110 north.

Typical cab fares from the airport are approximately $42 to downtown, $35 to Hollywood, $20 to Santa Monica, and these fares don't include the airport surcharge ($2.50), possible extra bag fees, or tip.

Shuttles are available and typically run $15 to $35 depending on your destination. Try SuperShuttle (☎ 800/258-3826; www.supershuttle.com).

Bus and rail options are cheaper, but can take a good chunk of time, possibly up to 2 hours. Check with **Los Angeles County Metropolitan Transit Authority** (MTA; ☎ 213/922-2000; www.mta.net) for schedules, fees, and routes.

For some travelers, one of the area's smaller airports might be more convenient than LAX. **Bob Hope Airport,** 2627 N. Hollywood Way, Burbank (☎ 818/840-8840; www.bobhopeairport.com), is especially easy to use and is accessible to the Valley, Hollywood, and downtown L.A. **BY CAR** Coming **from the east,** you'll be traveling on I-10, which passes through downtown and ends at the coast. Coming **from the north,** you may travel down I-5, (which continues on to downtown), or down the coastal route U.S. 101 (which continues into Hollywood then downtown). Coming **from the south,** you'll be traveling along I-5 (which continues to the east side of Hollywood and downtown), or along the I-405 (which continues to the Westside beach communities). **BY TRAIN Amtrak** (☎ 800/USA-RAIL (872-7245); www.amtrak.com) connects L.A. to 500 American cities. The Sunset Limited runs a transcontinental route to Florida and back, while the Coast Starlight runs the West Coast from Seattle to Los Angeles. The Pacific Surfliner (www.amtrakcalifornia.com) runs along the coast between San Diego and San Francisco with several stops. The L.A. train terminus is Union Station, located on the northern edge of downtown.

Getting Around

BY CAR L.A.'s urban sprawl is connected by an elaborate network of well-maintained freeways, so a car is the best way to get around. The system works well enough, although rush hour (roughly 6–9am and 3–7pm) traffic is often bumper-to-bumper, particularly on the congested I-405.

Renting a car here is a breeze. All the major car-rental agencies are represented at the airports. Rates are relatively cheap when compared to other major cities in the U.S. Do, however, reserve a car in advance—especially if you have visions of driving a specialty car like a convertible.

Also, keep in mind that what you drive, you must park. There are some frustrating parts of town where it's easiest to use valet parking. Restaurants and nightclubs usually charge anywhere between $3 and $20. Some areas, like Santa Monica and Beverly Hills, offer self-park lots and garages near the neighborhood action; costs range from $2 to $10. Also, have plenty of quarters for meters and read posted restrictions carefully. **BY PUBLIC TRANSPORTA-TION** L.A. is a car-crazy city that grew up around the automobile. Environmentally friendly as it may be, public transport is neither an efficient nor good way to get around the city. It might work for short hauls over a short period of time, but in the long run, all you'll get is stress and aggravation. To sum it up: Rent a car. If you choose not to heed this warning, the city's trains and buses are operated by the **Los Angeles County Metropolitan Transit Authority** (MTA; ☎ 213/922-2000; www.mta.net), and MTA brochures and schedules are available at every area visitor center. The **Metro Red Line** is a potentially handy, if limited, subway line that runs from downtown's Union Station to North Hollywood (in the Valley) and has stops at Hollywood and Vine, Hollywood & Highland, and Universal City. **BY TAXI** Typically, distances are long in Los Angeles, and cab fares can run high—even a short hop might cost $20. A ride costs $2.65 to begin, and then it's $2.45 per mile. It's possible to hail a cab when you're downtown, but everywhere else you'll need to order a taxi in advance from **Checker Cab** (☎ 323/654-8400), **L.A. Taxi** (☎ 213/627-7000), or **United Taxi** (☎ 213/483-7604). I reiterate: Rent a car.

Hospital

The centrally located **Cedars-Sinai Medical Center,** 8700 Beverly Blvd., Los Angeles (☎ 310/423-3277; www.csmc.edu), has a 24-hour emergency room staffed by some of the country's finest doctors.

Internet Access

Most hotels and many cafes have wireless access.

Groundworks Coffee (☎ 323/871-0107) provides 2 hours of free Wi-Fi and is conveniently located at 1501 Cahuenga Blvd. (at Sunset Blvd.), across the street from Amoeba Music.

In **West Hollywood,** Wi-Fi is provided for free on Santa Monica Boulevard, from La Brea to Fairfax. The signal works best outdoors, along Santa Monica Boulevard, in Plummer Park, and the Gateway Center.

Pharmacies

A **Rite Aid** pharmacy is located in Hollywood at 6726 W. Sunset Blvd., at Highland Avenue;

for the location of the store nearest you, call ☎ 800/RITE-AID (748-3243) or go to www.riteaid.com.

Police

In an emergency, dial ☎ **911.** For nonemergency police matters, call ☎ 877/ASK-LAPD (275-5273). In Beverly Hills, call ☎ 310/550-4951. In West Hollywood, call ☎ 310/855-8850. In Santa Monica, call ☎ 310/458-8491.

Post Offices

The main post office is located at 7101 S. Central Ave. (Mon–Fri 7am–7pm; Sat 7am–3:30pm). A centrally located post office is at Hollywood & Highland Center, 6801 Hollywood Blvd. (at Highland Ave.), Ste. 167 (Mon–Fri 10am–6pm).

Safety

Los Angeles is a relatively safe city, but like any big city, there are areas that are suspect. Some rundown blocks in East L.A., downtown, and even Hollywood, for example, should be approached with caution, especially at night.

Taxes

Sales tax in Los Angeles is 9.75%. Hotel tax is charged on the room tariff only (which is not subject to sales tax) and is set by the city, ranging from 12% to 17% around Southern California.

Toilets

Public toilets or "restrooms" are not readily available on the streets of L.A., but they can be found in hotel lobbies, bars, restaurants, museums, department stores, railway and bus stations, and service stations. Large hotels and fast-food restaurants are often the best bets for clean facilities. Restaurants and bars in heavily visited areas usually reserve their restrooms for paying customers.

Visitor Information

The **Los Angeles Convention and Visitors Bureau (L.A. INC.;** ☎ 800/228-2452 or 213/624-7300; www.discoverlosangeles.com) is the city's main source for information. The bureau also provides two **walk-in visitor centers:** downtown at 685 S. Figueroa St. (Mon–Fri 9am–5pm) and in Hollywood at the Hollywood & Highland Center, 6801 Hollywood Blvd. (at Highland Ave.) Ste. 237 (daily 10am–11pm).

11
Orange County

The Best of Orange County in 3 Days

Some neighbors (I'm talking to you, Los Angeles) dismiss Orange County as blandly consumerist, an asphalt jungle of shopping malls and homogeneous homes, but the O.C. is home to California's best-loved tourist destination, the Disneyland Resort, and some of the state's most beautiful beaches.

> PREVIOUS PAGE *Find the perfect setting at Corona del Mar along the Orange County coast.*
> THIS PAGE *Night and day, the magic of Disneyland still seduces and charms the masses.*

START Disneyland Resort, in Anaheim, is 28 miles south of Los Angeles. TRIP LENGTH 55 miles.

❶ ★★★ **Disneyland Resort.** This is the park that started Disney's empire, and the one truest to the vision of Uncle Walt himself, who sought to create a "magical park" where families could spend time together. The resort encompasses the original ★★★ **Disneyland Park,** a newer park called ★★ **Disney's California Adventure,** three hotels, and ★**Downtown Disney,** a promenade that links them all.

Classic attractions remain, such as **Sleeping Beauty Castle,** one of the park's original buildings, and the still-thrilling **Space Mountain** adventure, which debuted in 1977. One of

the newer favorites is a techno-wonder 3-D experience, **Toy Story Mania!**

A Park Hopper pass admits you to both parks, but with only a day to spend, you'll need to do some strategizing beforehand. Staying at or near the resort can maximize time, energy, and sanity. ⏲ 1 day. See p. 506.

On Day 2, take I-5 south for 15 miles, then take exit 95 for CA-133 south. Head south on CA-133 for 10 miles to Laguna Beach and check into your hotel.

❷ ★★★ **Laguna Beach.** With its woodsy canyons, coastal bluffs, and clean pocket beaches, Laguna Beach may be the prettiest town in Southern California.

1 Disneyland Resort
2 Laguna Beach
3 Huntington Beach

Founded in the 1910s by plein-air landscape artists, Laguna is a vibrant arts community that hosts the ★**Laguna Art Museum** (p. 518, ❶) and crowd-pleasing summer art festivals, including the ★**Pageant of the Masters** (p. 518), which transforms paintings into performance art.

Reserve the sunniest part of the day for the beach. ★★ **Main Beach** (p. 513), is the town's most active and accessible beach, but it's worth seeking out secluded gems like ★★★ **1000 Steps Beach** (p. 513). Go tidepooling at the beaches below the bluffs of **Heisler Park** (p. 518, ❹) or in the coves below the Montage Laguna Beach (p. 519). ⊕ 1 day.

A Not-So-Stellar Debut

Disneyland's opening day was disastrous—a major gas leak shut down Fantasyland, counterfeit tickets were prevalent while food and drink were not, and heels kept getting stuck in the soft ground of the too-freshly laid parking lot. The press predicted the park would close within the year. In true Disney style, however, a happy ending prevailed.

On Day 3, head north on Hwy. 1 (the Pacific Coast Hwy.) for 15 miles.

❸ ★★ **Huntington Beach.** Start your day early, as so many locals do, and hit the surf. This is Surf City, after all, with miles of flat, sandy shoreline and great waves. If you've never tried surfing, contact **Corky Carroll's Surf School** (p. 514, ❷) for lessons, which take place at Bolsa Chica State Beach.

Visit nearby **Bolsa Chica Ecological Reserve** for a self-guided tour through reclaimed wetlands, home to over 200 species of birds, and the site of a Native settlement more than 8,000 years ago.

With a renewed appreciation for the sport's difficulty, visit the **International Surfing Museum** (p. 514, ❸) downtown, then peruse the surf shops and **Surfing Walk of Fame** at the corner of Main Street and the PCH.

Stroll the iconic **Huntington Pier** (p. 514, ❹), the center of all the action. At **Duke's** (p. 515) enjoy a cocktail at sunset, then drift south down the Strand toward **Huntington State Beach** (p. 512), where you might relax around a beach bonfire. ⊕ 1 day.

The Best of Orange County in 1 Week

Take the first 2 days of your week to get your fill of theme parks (although for some Disney fanatics, no amount of time is enough). Then enjoy several days breezing through the Orange Coast (Huntington Beach, Newport Beach, Laguna Beach), adding a sojourn to unspoiled Catalina Island. Along the way, visit a world-class museum, a presidential library, and one of California's most popular historical sites.

> It's easy to dig the enticing sands of Huntington State Beach, one of the few allowing public bonfires.

START Disneyland Resort. Anaheim is 28 miles south of Los Angeles. TRIP LENGTH 94 miles.

① Disneyland Resort. Spend one day apiece at ★★★ Disneyland Park and ★★ Disney's California Adventure. If you're more interested in adrenaline than nostalgia, then you can swap in ★Knott's Berry Farm (p. 503) for Disneyland Park. ⊙ 2 days. See p. 506.

On Day 3, from Disneyland, head north to Ball Rd., then take a right. Take Ball Rd. 2 miles to CA-57 and head north. After 5 miles, take exit 8 for Yorba Linda Rd. and turn right. Go 4 miles to the

② ★ Nixon Presidential Library and Museum. Museum highlights include Richard Nixon's humble farmhouse birthplace; a World Leaders room with life-size statues of Nixon's contemporaries; and random keepsakes, such as

1. Disneyland Resort
2. Nixon Presidential Library and Museum
3. Bowers Museum of Cultural Art
4. Newport Beach
5. Santa Catalina Island
6. Huntington Beach
7. Laguna Beach
8. Mission San Juan Capistrano
9. Salt Creek Beach

a chunk of the Berlin Wall and a 3-billion-year-old moon rock. Unfortunately, the Watergate Gallery is currently closed (check website for updates). Stop by the gift shop for such must-haves as Christmas ornaments with the classic photo of Nixon shaking hands with Elvis. ⊕ At least 1 hr. 18001 Yorba Linda Blvd., Yorba Linda. ☎ 714/993-5075. www.nixonfoundation. com. $10 adults, $5 kids 7–11, free for kids 6 & under. Mon–Sat 10am–5pm, Sun 11am–5pm.

Return to CA-57 and head south for 8 miles until it merges with I-5 south. Continue for about 1 mile, and exit on Main St. heading south for ½ mile.

❸ ★ **Bowers Museum of Cultural Art.** Founded in 1936, this museum has a permanent collection of 130,000 pieces of art and is strongest in the Native American, Pacific Island, Asian, and pre-Columbian departments. Past exhibits have included First Californians, which displayed Native American art and artifacts, including intricate plant-fiber basketry, and an acclaimed exhibit on terra cotta warriors from China—a North American debut. ⊕ 1 hr. 2002 N. Main St., Santa Ana. ☎ 714/567-3600. www. bowers.org. $12 adults, $9 seniors and kids 6–17, free for kids under 6. Tues–Sun 10am–4pm.

> Take a spin on the charmingly simple rides at Balboa Fun Zone—no Mickey but still fun for the kids.

Return to I-5 and head south for 2.5 miles until exit 103, then merge onto CA-55 heading south to Newport Beach for 10½ miles.

4 Newport Beach. ★ **Newport Harbor** is one of the largest in the world for small yachts—an aquatic playground for the wealthy, including many celebrities such as the late John Wayne. Rent a boat at **Duffy Electric Boat Company** (p. 516, **2**) and join the fun, or stop for fresh seafood at the fun and casual **Crab Cooker** (p. 517) near the **Newport Pier.**

> Dive in to discover extraordinary underwater life in the protected waters surrounding Santa Catalina Island.

Head down Balboa Peninsula to ★ **Balboa Beach** (p. 512), a great beach for swimming. Think twice about taking on the infamous **Wedge** at the end of the jetty; local lore claims that a young John Wayne ruined his USC football career when he injured himself bodysurfing here.

Walk around the historic ★ **Balboa Pavilion & Balboa Fun Zone** (p. 516, **4**) where you can ride a Ferris Wheel, duck into the **Newport Harbor Nautical Museum** (p. 516), or take the **Balboa Island Ferry** to ★**Balboa Island** (p. 516, **5**) and sample the local treat, the **Balboa Bar.** ☺ At least 4 hr.

On Day 4, take the Catalina Ferry from Balboa Pavilion to Avalon, Catalina Island, for the day.

5 Santa Catalina Island. The ride to the island is part of the fun—keep your eyes peeled for

Knott's Berry Farm: America's First Theme Park

Surprisingly, it was another Walt who created the first theme park among the vast acres of farmland in Orange County. Farmer Walter Knott built Old West Ghost Town in 1940 as a way to entertain the folks waiting in line to buy his wife Cordelia's famous chicken dinners and boysenberry pies.

Today **Knott's Berry Farm,** 8039 Beach Blvd., Buena Park (☎ 714/220-5200; www. knotts.com) thrives in Disney's shadow by targeting a different crowd—teens and tweens who wouldn't be caught dead singing "It's a Small World." High-speed thrill rides like the suspended coaster ★ **Silver Bullet** and the ★**Supreme Scream** (with the tagline "30 stories up, 3 seconds down") are the park's main draws. ★★★ **Ghost Rider** is one of the world's longest and tallest wooden roller coasters, and a bona fide classic. The super-scary ★★ **Xcelerator** hits 82 mph in 2⅓ seconds before shooting 205 feet up in the air. More sedate parts of the park include the Peanuts-themed **Camp Snoopy** and **Ghost Town,** a tribute to the Wild West with stunt shows, panning for gold, and the Western Museum filled with historical artifacts. Next door to the original park is **Knott's Soak City Water Park.**

The park is open daily, though hours vary seasonally; check the website for current times. Admission is $54 for adults and kids 12 and older, $24 for kids 3 to 11 and seniors, and free for kids 2 and under.

whales and dolphins. On landing, make for the distinct round building that dominates the bay, the ★**Catalina Casino** (p. 520, ❶), an entertainment complex built in 1929. The tour takes you through the casino's past as a hopping Hollywood getaway in the '30s and '40s.

Enjoy snorkeling at the clear waters of ★★ **Lover's Cove Marine Preserve**, southeast of the harbor, whose clear, shallow waters make an ideal spot for observing the rich marine life—spotted calico bass; opaleye; and the not-shy, neon-orange garibaldi. **Catalina Snorkeling Adventures** (☎ 877/766-7535; www. catalinasnorkelscuba.com) can rent you all the gear necessary to explore the cove; they also conduct 1½-hour marine ecotours ($39 per person; reservations required). For relaxation, in the late spring and summer try the ★ **Descanso Beach Club** (☎ 310/510-7410; beach admission $2), located around the point from the casino; the nifty beach cove is a great place to enjoy a cocktail in the sun, especially if you spring for a private cabana ($125 per day). Stop by the activity center to sign up for the thrilling Zip Line Eco Tour ($92.50), which sends you on five adrenaline-filled "runs" (or "zips") through Descanso Canyon on a zip line 300 feet above the canyon floor.

If you have time, consider taking a tour into the wild interior of the island, where you can spot bald eagles and bison. If not, rent a golf cart and buzz around the harbor town of **Avalon** on your own. The ★ **Wrigley Memorial & Botanical Gardens** (p. 520, ❹) is a great place to see rare desert flora as well as pay homage to the former owner of the island, William Wrigley, Jr.

If you're seeking seclusion, head for the remote village of ★★ **Two Harbors** (p. 520, ❻), the island's northwest "neck" linking the oceanside Catalina Harbor with the channel-side Isthmus Cove. ☺1 day.

On Day 5, leave Newport Beach and head north on the Pacific Coast Highway for 5 miles.

❻ ★★ **Huntington Beach.** See p. 514.

On Day 6, head south on the Pacific Coast Highway for 15½ miles.

❼ ★★★ **Laguna Beach.** See p. 518.

> *The payoff for descending all those over 200 stairs at 1000 Steps Beach? The perfect marriage of sand, sea, and sky.*

On **Day 7**, from Laguna Beach take CA-133 north for 4 miles. Merge right onto CA-73, go 6½ miles, and merge with I-5 south. Continue 2½ miles, exit Ortega Highway (CA-74), and head west. Take the first right.

8 ★★★ **Mission San Juan Capistrano.** Founded in 1776, the seventh of the 21 California missions and the only one in Orange County, Mission San Juan Capistrano is called the "Jewel of the Missions." You can't miss the Acropolis-style ruins of the **Great Stone Church,** completed in 1806 and felled by an earthquake in 1812. The lovely **Serra Chapel,** with its ornate carved-wood and gold-leaf altar, remains intact—the only surviving chapel in any of the missions where Father Junípero Serra (1713–1784) performed services. Built in 1777, it's the oldest building still in use in California. Take the free audio tour, or simply relax in the flower-filled **courtyard.** Every March 19, crowds swarm the **Festival of the Swallows** to mark the return (in theory, at least) of the migrating **swallows** from Argentina. ⏰ At least

Getting Around by Bike

Renting **bicycles** is a great way to explore the beach towns in this chapter. In Huntington Beach, try **Dwight's Beach Concession,** 201 Pacific Coast Hwy., on the Strand (☎ 714/536-8083). In Newport Beach (pictured above), try **Balboa Bike and Beach Stuff,** 601 Balboa Blvd. (☎ 949/723-1516). In Laguna Beach, try **Laguna Cyclery,** 240 Thalia St. (☎ 949/494-1522; www.lagunabeachcyclery.com). Depending on the bike, rates can range from $10 per hour to $85 a day. Safety equipment is included.

> *Bringing Franciscan faith to Native Americans, Father Serra created 21 missions in California, including Mission San Juan Capistrano.*

2 hr. 31414 El Camino Real, San Juan Capistrano. ☎ 949/234-1300. www.missionsjc.com. Admission $9 adults, $8 seniors, $5 kids 4–11, free for kids 3 & under. Daily 8:30am–5pm.

Head south until Del Obispo Street, and take a right on Camino Del Avion. Take a left on Niguel Road and go 1 mile to Hwy. 1.

❾ ★ Salt Creek Beach. End your afternoon (and the week) in pure relaxation on this beautiful stretch of sandy beach. The mile-long public beach is visited by thousands of sun-seekers and surfers (you'll find some of the best swells on the California coast here) each year, but almost never feels crowded. ☺ At least 2 hr. See p. 513.

Long Beach

If you're traveling between Los Angeles and Orange County, consider stopping off en route at Long Beach to take in two major attractions.

The ★**Aquarium of the Pacific** at 100 Aquarium Way (☎ 562/590-3100; www.aquariumofpacific.org; $24 adults, $12 kids 3–11, free for kids under 3; daily 9am–6pm) is one of the largest aquariums in the world, home to 11,000 sea creatures representing 500 species. The aquarium is designed to celebrate the vastness and diversity of the Pacific, and three galleries represent three areas of that great ocean: the sunny Southern California and Baja regions, the cold Northern Pacific, and the colorful reefs of the Tropical Pacific. A 10,000-square-foot Shark Lagoon features 150 sharks, some of which you can touch.

Across the harbor is the **Queen Mary** at 1126 Queen's Hwy. (☎ 877/342-0738; www.queenmary.com; general admission $25 adults, $13 kids 5–11; daily 10am–5pm, with extended hours for restaurants and bars). The 81,237-ton luxury ocean liner, built in 1936, is one of the last survivors of its kind. Long retired from cruise duty, the ship is now a museum and hotel, and is home to several restaurants as well. To stroll the teakwood decks is to take a voyage back in time. Sip a cocktail in the Observation Bar, an immaculately detailed Art Deco lounge.

Dining Tip

For a standout dining experience while visiting San Juan Capistrano, stop by the **Ramos House Café,** built in 1881 in the Los Rios Historic District—the oldest residential street in California. This little place cooks up big Southern-inflected American cuisine: apple-cinnamon beignets, corn and buttermilk crab cakes, and a soju Bloody Mary with pickled beans and crab claws. 31752 Los Rios St. ☎ 949/443-1342. www.ramoshouse.com. Entrees $13–$17, brunch $35. Breakfast & lunch Tues–Fri, brunch Sat–Sun. AE, MC, V.

Disneyland Resort

In 1955 Walt Disney unveiled his whimsical amusement park, ★★★ **Disneyland,** featuring 18 attractions spread across 160 acres surrounded by orange groves. Today it's a Californian icon and a mandatory stop for fun-seeking families. **Disneyland Resort** encompasses the original park, called the "Happiest Place on Earth"; ★★ **Disney's California Adventure,** a thrill-driven theme park added in 2001 as a sanitized, scaled-down version of the Golden State; three Disney hotels; and **Downtown Disney,** a shopping, eating, and entertainment complex.

> Everybody's favorite mouse aims to deliver a magical day to everyone who steps inside his Magic Kingdom.

START Disneyland Resort. Anaheim is 28 miles south of Los Angeles.
TRIP LENGTH 2 days; if you have only 1 day, you might be best off sticking to one park.

① 🍽 **La Brea Bakery Café.** The lone outpost of Nancy Silverton's beloved L.A. bakery, this cafe produces artisan breads and pastries, breakfast sandwiches, and panini. 1556 Disneyland Dr., Downtown Disney. ☎ 714/490-0233. www.labrea bakery.com. Entrees $11–$22, pastries $4.50. Daily breakfast, lunch & dinner.

② ★ **Main Street USA.** An idealization of small-town America at the turn of the 20th century, Main Street takes you back to an innocent time of ice-cream parlors, barbershop quartets, horse-drawn trolleys, and shiny fire engines. Above the firehouse is the room where Walt often stayed during the park's construction; it remains fully furnished with a lamp in the front window that shines eternally as a tribute. Entrance, Disneyland.

③ ★ **Sleeping Beauty Castle.** Modeled after Bavaria's romantic Schloss Neuschwanstein,

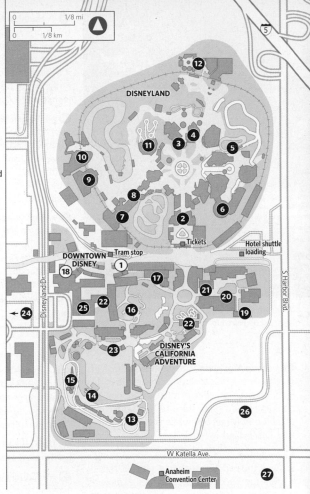

this turreted, 77-foot-tall castle appears even grander due to the forced perspective of its architecture. One of the spires is deliberately missing a small patch of gold leaf, per instructions from Walt, who never wanted to think of the park as complete. The castle is one of the park's original 17 attractions. **Entrance to Fantasyland, Disneyland.**

4 ★ Fantasyland. This storybook section of the park, catering primarily to kids and lovers of all things Disney, is loaded with rides featuring such classic characters as Dumbo, Snow White, the Mad Hatter, and Peter Pan. It's also home to the iconic "It's a Small World"—riding it is a must-do (and some would say a masochistic) Disney rite of passage. **North of Sleeping Beauty Castle, Disneyland.**

5 ★ Finding Nemo Submarine Voyage. Through the portal of a bright yellow submarine, you'll see Nemo and his pals swimming in the sea. You can also listen to the action with "sonar hydrophones." **Tomorrowland, Disneyland.**

> Get your "arg" on at Pirates of the Caribbean, now jazzed up with a Johnny Depp-style Captain Jack Sparrow.

6 ★ Space Mountain. The pitch-blackness of outer space denies the power of sight, but this roller coaster—the park's most adrenaline-pumping ride, around since 1977—is an assault on the rest of your senses. **Tomorrowland, Disneyland.**

7 ★★ Indiana Jones Adventure. Showcasing some of the park's best special effects, this rumble-tumble ride dodges arrows, explosions, snakes, and collapsing bridges, illustrating that archaeology is not the safest choice of professions. The tumbling boulder gets me every time. **Adventureland, Disneyland.**

8 ★★ Pirates of the Caribbean. After the success of the *Pirates of the Caribbean* movies, this elaborate boat ride was updated with special effects and an animated version of Johnny Depp's character, Captain Jack Sparrow. Thankfully, the off-putting display of lascivious pirates chasing "wenches" has been cut. The queue entrance is a tad jarring (you start in a New Orleans swamp and then suddenly end up in the Caribbean), but it's still one of Disney's best rides in the theme-detailing department. **New Orleans Square, Disneyland.**

9 ★ Haunted Mansion. This antebellum home of 999 Happy Haunts is more funny than scary, thanks to its old-school (but still quite attention-getting) special effects, but it's the thematic detailing that gives this oldie but goodie a devoted fan following. **New Orleans Square, Disneyland.**

10 ★★ Splash Mountain. If you need a quick cool down, you'll get an entertaining (and exhilarating) one at this flume ride, loosely based on Disney's *Song of the South*. It's a "Zip-A-Dee-Doo-Dah" experience that will definitely leave you soaking wet. **Critter Country, Disneyland.**

11 ★ Big Thunder Mountain Railroad. This "runaway train" roller coaster is a winner in that its Old West mining setting is just as good as the ride—and the atmosphere is actually better later in the day. It's tame by modern standards, but the rush is still there for many. **Frontierland, Disneyland.**

12 ★ Toontown. This part of the park—inspired by *Who Framed Roger Rabbit*—is meant to look as though you tripped into a cartoon: Everything is bright and poofy, and you can't find a straight line (or a straight face) anywhere. Little kids love meeting Mickey or Goofy and romping around the playground. *Tip:* Crowds thin out in the early evening. **Toontown, Disneyland.**

On Day 2, head out early to Disney's California Adventure.

13 ★★ California Screamin'. Paradise Pier evokes the great beachfront amusement parks of yesteryear, such as Santa Monica or Venice. This classic roller coaster, one of the fastest rides in either of Disney's parks, does a vertical loop along the outline of Mickey's head. **Paradise Pier, Disney's California Adventure.**

14 ★★ Toy Story Mania! Don your 3-D glasses, and ride through a virtual midway of booths with interactive *Toy Story* characters. Use the toy cannon on your vehicle to toss rings, throw pies, and shoot darts at your targets. **Paradise Pier, Disney's California Adventure.**

15 ★ Maliboomer. Mimicking those ring-a-bell, sledgehammer tests of strength found at carnivals, this ride slingshots you nearly 200 feet into the air in 4 seconds. For a brief moment, at 18 stories high, you'll experience zero gravity. Best to try this one before you eat lunch. **Paradise Pier, Disney's California Adventure.**

16 ★ **Grizzly River Run.** Every amusement park needs a ride to cool you down on a hot day, right? This white-water raft trip around Grizzly Peak—the bear-shaped mountain is the park's centerpiece—splashes through mine shafts and caves before dropping your raft down a geyser-filled gorge. **Grizzly Peak Recreation Area, Golden State, Disney's California Adventure.**

17 ★★★ **Soarin' Over California.** Rush over to this virtual ride, a state-of-the-art simulation of a hang-glider ride over the best parts of the state. Wheeee, there's Yosemite! And thanks to special olfactory effects, you'll smell those pines and oranges as you fly by. **Condor Flats, Golden State, Disney's California Adventure.**

> The little guys love Toontown, one of the best places to get autographs and hugs from favorite characters.

How to Conquer (& Enjoy) Disneyland

It's D-Day—are you ready? The parks can get extremely crowded, especially on holidays and summer weekends, so a little preparation may stave off a lot of frustration.

You'll save both time and money by purchasing tickets online prior to your visit (consider package deals, which can offer substantial discounts). If you have only 1 day and you're determined to see everything, opt for the Park Hopper pass; it costs a little more than the 1-Day 1-Park ticket, but it gets you into both parks. Other multiday, multipark combinations are available and offer even greater savings.

Here are a few essential strategies for maximizing your visit:

1. First, be aware of the FASTPASS—essential for handling the popular rides with long lines. At rides with the FASTPASS system, you'll find automated machines where you can receive a voucher with a later boarding time (say, an hour or two later) and return at that designated time, then bypass the long line (suckers!) and enter the FASTPASS gate for a much shorter wait (typically around 10 min.). **Note:** You can use only one FASTPASS voucher at a time, and because there's a limited number of FASTPASS vouchers on a given day, it's smart to arrive early.

2. Arrive a half-hour before the gates open.

3. Have a plan; know which attractions you (or more important, your kids) most want to see.

4. Go against the grain—take advantage during mealtimes or parades, when lines may be shorter.

5. Stay at the resort (or nearby), and follow the schedule perfected by wily veterans of the park—hit as much as possible as early as possible, retreat in the afternoon to recharge (nap, meal, dip in the pool), then return with renewed vigor for the evening festivities.

Oh, and remember: You're having fun! 1313 S. Harbor Blvd., Anaheim. ☎ 714/781-4565. www.disneyland.com. 1-Day 1-Park: $72 adults and kids 10 & up, $62 kids 3–9. 1-Day Park Hopper: $97 adults and kids 10 & up, $87 kids 3–9. Free for kids 2 & under.

> *Dazzling thrill-seekers with rides like California Screamin', Disney's California Adventure adds its own twists and adventures to the Disney mix.*

⑱ 🦞 Ralph Brennan's Jazz Kitchen Express. The tastiest snack option in Downtown Disney is this Big Easy–themed restaurant, where you can chow down on Cajun-style po' boys, crab cakes, fried catfish, jambalaya, and authentic New Orleans desserts like beignets and bread pudding. 1590 S. Disneyland Dr., Downtown Disney. ☎ 714/776-5200. www.rbjazzkitchen.com. Items $5–$10.

⑲ ★★ Twilight Zone Tower of Terror. So, does it sound like fun to plummet down an abandoned elevator shaft in the creepy Hollywood Tower Hotel, the tallest building in the entire resort? The *Twilight Zone* tidbits make the buildup to the heart-stopping climax excruciatingly tense. Hollywood Pictures Backlot, Disney's California Adventure.

⑳ ★ Disney Animation. This attraction is a hidden gem and rarely crowded. Galleries and interactive exhibits offer a lively behind-the-scenes look at how Disney animators create their magic. Kids (and adults) can learn how to draw a Disney character or add their voices to a cartoon. The biggest hit is *Turtle Talk with Crush*, a real-time animated conversation with the 152-year-old turtle from *Finding Nemo*. Hollywood Pictures Backlot, Disney's California Adventure.

㉑ ★ Muppet Vision 3D. Kermit, Miss Piggy, and the rest of the gang all come to life in this 3-D film with big laughs and big special effects. This one is equally popular with kids and nostalgic adults. Hollywood Pictures Backlot, Disney's California Adventure.

㉒ ★★ It's Tough to Be a Bug. The characters from *A Bug's Life* take you on a hilarious romp through the insect kingdom in this 3-D blitzkrieg of special effects. Some little kiddies may be overwhelmed by the spectacle, but most are shaken only by their own laughter. A Bug's Land, Disney's California Adventure.

㉓ ★★ World of Color. This nighttime extravaganza is a dazzling display of music, light, color, fire, animation, and water. Some 1,200 individually controlled fountains are coordinated to create spectacular flowing shapes, and sheets of mist form a multilayered movie screen for animated clips. Paradise Park, Disney's California Adventure.

Where to Stay & Dine

> *Patterned after Yosemite's grand Ahwahnee, Disney's Grand Californian Hotel & Spa ranks as the resort's premier lodging.*

★ kids **Candy Cane Inn** ANAHEIM
A great value not far from the main gate, this courtyard motel offers bright rooms, a heated pool, and a friendly attitude. 1747 S. Harbor Dr. ☎ 714/774-5284. www.candycaneinn.net. 172 units. Doubles $99–$189. Free parking and Disneyland shuttle. AE, DC, DISC, MC, V.

★★ kids **Disneyland Hotel** DISNEYLAND
The official hotel of the Magic Kingdom is a great choice for families with young kids. The comfortable rooms aren't anything special (though they're loaded with Disney-themed items), but there are a number of programs for children, the pool area is great, and it's connected by monorail to Downtown Disney. 1150 W. Magic Way. ☎ 714/956- 6425. www. disneyland.com. 990 units. Doubles $255–$355. AE, DC, DISC, MC, V.

★★★ kids **Disney's Grand Californian Hotel & Spa** DISNEYLAND The grand lobby will wow you with its massive stone hearth, soaring ceiling with skylights and exposed beams, and Arts and Crafts–style fixtures and furniture. Request a room (all are spacious and comfy) with a view of the Disney's California Adventure park. 1600 S. Disneyland Dr. ☎ 714/635-2300. www.disneyland.com. 745 units. Doubles $260–$390. AE, DC, DISC, MC, V.

kids **Goofy's Kitchen** DISNEYLAND *AMERICAN*
Think of the buffet as a "meet and greet"

rather than an "all you can eat." After a hug and a photo with one of the many Disney characters, everything—the PB&J pizza, the Mickey Mouse waffles—tastes a little better. 1150 Magic Way, Disneyland Hotel. ☎ 714/956-6755. www.disneyland.com. Reservations recommended. Buffets (child/adult): dinner $18–$40, breakfast/lunch $18–$32. AE, DC, DISC, MC, V.

★★★ **Napa Rose** DISNEYLAND *CALIFORNIAN*
Enjoy sophisticated wine country cuisine in a dazzling setting. The wine list is phenomenal, and dessert is a must. 1600 S. Disneyland Dr. (in Disney's Grand Californian Hotel). ☎ 714/300-7170. www.disneyland.com. Reservations recommended. Entrees $32–$40. AE, DC, DISC, MC, V. Lunch & dinner daily.

★★ kids **Portofino Inn & Suites** ANAHEIM
This family-friendly complex sports a cheery yellow exterior, a fab location within walking distance of Disney's California Adventure, and suites that work just as well for business travelers as they do for families. The latter should opt for one of the delightful Kids Suites, which sport separate bedrooms for kids (bunk beds!) and adults. 1831 S. Harbor Blvd. (at Katella Ave.). ☎ 800/398-3963 or 714/782-7600. www.portofinoinnanaheim.com. 190 units. Doubles $104–$169, suites $119–$229. AE, DC, DISC, MC, V.

Orange County's Best Beaches A to Z

★★ kids **Aliso Beach.** A popular choice for families, this sandy beach has easy waves, fine tidepooling along its rocky promontories, fire pits, picnic tables, playground equipment, and ample parking. It's Laguna's best spot to go skimboarding. **31131 S. Pacific Coast Hwy., Laguna Beach.** ☎ 949/923-2280. www.ocparks.com. **Daily 6am–10pm.**

★ kids **Balboa Beach.** This laid-back swimming beach runs from Balboa Pier to the infamous Wedge, an intense (and dangerous) shore break that draws intrepid bodysurfers. **Balboa Peninsula, Newport Beach.** ☎ 949/644-3044. **Daily 6am–10pm.**

★★★ kids **Crystal Cove State Park.** Gorgeous coves set against coastal bluffs make a wonderful rustic retreat, with easy access to tidepooling, snorkeling, and hiking into the hills of El Moro Canyon. Grab refreshments at The Beachcomber (p. 517) or the historic Shake Shack. **Pacific Coast Highway, btw. Corona del Mar & Laguna Beach.** ☎ 949/494-3539. www.

> Look but don't touch—only experienced body-surfers and boogey-boarders should attempt Balboa Beach's Wedge.

crystalcovestatepark.com. **Parking $15. Daily 6am–sunset.**

★★ **Huntington City Beach.** The pride of Surf City, the beach surrounding the pier is Huntington's main event beach, hosting the U.S. Open of Surfing and the AVP pro beach volleyball tournament. **400 Pacific Coast Hwy., Huntington Beach.** ☎ 714/536-5281. www.surfcityusa.com. **Daily 6am–10pm.**

★ **Huntington State Beach.** This flat, long, and wide beach is popular for swimming and surfing, and is a protected sanctuary for the least tern and the snowy plover. Beach bonfires in the concrete fire rings are a major draw. **Beach Boulevard at Pacific Coast Highway, Huntington Beach.** ☎ 714/536-1454. www.parks.ca.gov. **Parking $15. Daily 6am–10pm.**

Tidepooling Tip

Please do not disturb the sea life while tidepooling. Tread lightly, and resist the urge to collect rocks and shells or to dislodge creatures from their natural habitat.

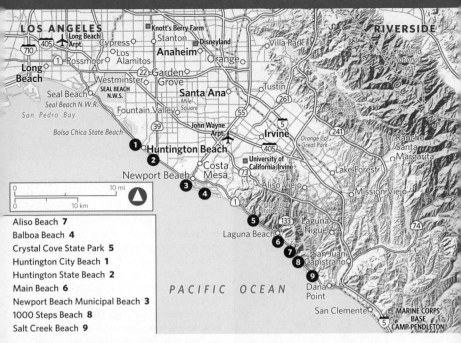

Aliso Beach **7**
Balboa Beach **4**
Crystal Cove State Park **5**
Huntington City Beach **1**
Huntington State Beach **2**
Main Beach **6**
Newport Beach Municipal Beach **3**
1000 Steps Beach **8**
Salt Creek Beach **9**

★★ **Main Beach.** Laguna's largest and most popular beach has it all—a historic lifeguard tower, basketball and volleyball facilities, restrooms and showers, access to coves and tide pools, and a waterfront perfect for a sunset stroll or people-watching. Broadway & Ocean avenues at Pacific Coast Highway, Laguna Beach. Daily 6am–10pm.

★ **Newport Beach Municipal Beach.** One of the cleanest in the country, this big, bustling beach was recently named Orange County's Best Beach by the *O.C. Weekly*. Early mornings, buy freshly caught fish at Dory Fishing Fleet (www.doryfleet.com) at the end of Newport Pier, a state landmark. Pacific Coast Highway & Balboa Avenue, Newport Beach. ☎ 949/644-3309. Metered parking. Daily 6am–10pm.

★★★ **1000 Steps Beach.** Descend 230 steep steps to reach this secluded gem of a beach, a locals' favorite for surfing, bodysurfing, and volleyball. At low tide, poke around in the hidden sea caves. Simple facilities include restroom and shower. Limited parking is available along the north side of the PCH. Ninth St. & Pacific Coast Highway, at South Laguna. Daily 6am–10pm.

★★ **Salt Creek Beach.** This beautiful fine-sand beach is family friendly and rarely crowded; offers great surfing and sunbathing; and has easy parking, concessions, lifeguards, and views of Catalina Island. 33333 S. Pacific Coast Hwy., Dana Point. ☎ 949/923-2280. www.ocparks.com. Daily 5am–midnight.

Skimboarding: Run, Drop & Slide

Skimboarding is a combination of skateboarding and surfing. *Run* along the shoreline as the waves retreat, *drop* your skimboard (a small, sleek, finless board) into the shallow water and hop on, and *slide* toward the breaking waves. The sport originated in Laguna Beach, which has many beaches with perfect skimming conditions, including Aliso Beach (see above), which hosts the World Championship of Skimboarding every June. Buy or rent a skimboard (a woodie or a foamie) at Victoria Skimboards, 2955 Laguna Canyon Rd., Ste. 1, Laguna Beach (☎ 949/494-0059; www.victoriaskimboards.com; $10–$20 per day).

Huntington Beach

Huntington Beach proudly rides the wave of its surfing history and culture, earning its nickname Surf City (after a gnarly legal battle with Santa Cruz; see p. 334). There's been an upswing in commercial development in recent years, but it's the long stretch of beaches that entices visitors.

> You'll find dozens of opportunities to hang ten in Huntington Beach—and all the boards and grown-up beach toys you'll need to hit the surf.

START Huntington Beach is 39 miles south of Los Angeles.

❶ ★ **Bolsa Chica Ecological Preserve.** Destroyed after a century of oil production and farming, these 1,350 acres of coastal wetlands and surrounding upland areas have been restored by 30 years of hard work by the Bolsa Chica Conservancy. In 2006, for the first time in 107 years, ocean water flowed back into the wetlands. Several interesting tours are available (one is free on the first Sat each month, others are $1 per person with a $25 minimum; call ☎ 714/840-1575); you might spot any of 200 species of birds that call the marsh home. ⏱ At least 1 hr. Warner Boulevard at Pacific Coast Highway, Huntington Beach. ☎ 714/846-1114. www.amigosdebolsachica.org. Free admission and parking. Daily dawn–dusk.

❷ ★ **Corky Carroll's Surf School.** The school provides boards, wet suits, and friendly instruction in the fundamentals of surfing. It's especially adept with younger students. ⏱ At least 1 hr. 17851 S. Pacific Coast Hwy., Huntington Beach. Lessons at Bolsa Chica State Beach. ☎ 714/969-3959. www.surfschool.net. Lessons: private $60 per hr.; semi-private $45.

❸ ★★ **International Surfing Museum.** Check out rad exhibits on the legendary Duke Kahanamoku (1890–1968), vintage wooden longboards, and surf music (including Dick Dale's guitar). If you're now sufficiently stoked, continue onto the Hollywoodesque Surfing Walk of Fame at the corner of Main Street & the Pacific Coast Highway. ⏱ 1 hr. 411 Olive Ave. ☎ 714/960-3483. www.surfingmuseum.org. Admission $2 adults, $1 students, free for kids 6 & under. Mon–Fri noon–5pm, Sat–Sun 11am–6pm.

❹ ★ **Huntington Beach Pier.** One of the largest piers on the West Coast, this is the hub of Huntington. You can fish, eat, or watch the brave wave riders all around the pier. It's the perfect place to watch the sun dip into the Pacific. ⏱ 1 hr. Daily 5am–midnight.

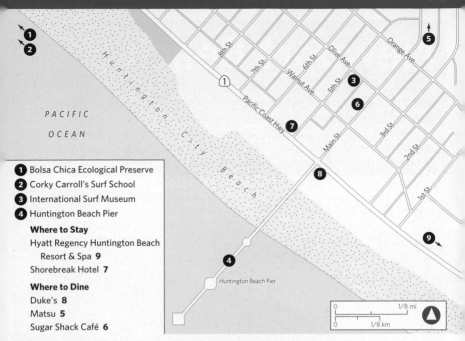

1. Bolsa Chica Ecological Preserve
2. Corky Carroll's Surf School
3. International Surf Museum
4. Huntington Beach Pier

Where to Stay
Hyatt Regency Huntington Beach
    Resort & Spa **9**
Shorebreak Hotel **7**

Where to Dine
Duke's **8**
Matsu **5**
Sugar Shack Café **6**

Where to Stay & Dine

★★ Duke's *SEAFOOD*

Cap a great day at the beach with a tropical cocktail and a Hawaiian-style seafood dish like crispy coconut shrimp or seasonal mahimahi with macadamia nut crust. 317 Pacific Coast Hwy. ☎ 714/374-6446. www.dukeshuntington. com. Entrees $9–$30. AE, DISC, MC, V. Dinner daily, lunch Tues–Sat, brunch Sun.

★★★ Hyatt Regency Huntington Beach Resort & Spa *WATERFRONT*

Just across the highway from Huntington State Beach, this Andalusian-style property has an appropriately beachy atmosphere; large guest rooms, many with ocean views; a first-rate spa; great service; and a plethora of resort amenities. 21500 Pacific Coast Hwy. [tel] 714/698-1234. www.hyatt regencyhuntingtonbeach.com. 574 units. Doubles $250–$400. AE, DC, DISC, MC, V.

★ Matsu *JAPANESE*

Tired of Huntington's throbbing "burgers on the beach" scene? Seek relief at this traditional Japanese restaurant, which presents fresh, high-quality sushi and sashimi in a sedate, dimly lit atmosphere. 18035 Beach Blvd. ☎ 714/848-4404. www.matsusogood. com. Sushi rolls $4–$9, entrees $12–$24. AE, DC, MC, V. Dinner daily, lunch Mon–Fri.

★★ Shorebreak Hotel *WATERFRONT*

Perfectly situated along the water near the pier and downtown, this new hotel features quiet rooms with modern decor and beachy accents, spacious bathrooms, and high-tech touches. A "beach butler" can arrange outdoor activities like bike riding, kite flying, and surf lessons. 500 Pacific Coast Hwy. ☎ 714/861-4470. www.shorebreakhotel.com. 157 units. Doubles $189–$279. AE, DC, DISC, MC, V.

★ Sugar Shack Café *BRUNCH*

Locals flock to this casual, family-owned favorite for its cheap and tasty breakfast fare: omelets, breakfast burritos, and pancakes. Sidewalk tables make for delicious people-watching, but expect a wait on weekends. 213½ Main St. ☎ 714/536-0355. www.hbsugar shack.com. Entrees $5–$8.50. AE, DISC, MC, V. Breakfast & lunch daily.

Newport Beach

Newport Beach is perhaps best defined by its huge harbor sprinkled with yachts and multimillion-dollar homes. Favorite local pastimes include shopping, golfing, and yachting. Still, it's a surprisingly down-to-earth place to visit, full of family-friendly beaches and such simple pleasures as strolling the boardwalk, fishing, renting a small boat, or enjoying a cold treat like the Balboa Bar.

> Explore sparkling tide pools trimming Crystal Cove State Park, an idyllic arc north of Laguna Beach.

START Newport Beach is 45 miles south of Los Angeles.

1 ★★★ kids **Crystal Cove State Park.** Start your day at this state park with beautiful coves and tidepools galore. ◷ At least 1 hr. See p. 512.

2 ★ **Newport Harbor.** The best way to see one of the world's largest small-craft harbors, home to eight small islands and 10,000 small boats, is to take to the water yourself. Duffy boats are great for small groups that feel like celebrating. Try Duffy's Electric Boat Company, 2001 W. Pacific Coast Hwy. (☎ 949/645-6812; www.duffyofnewport beach.com; $85–$99 per hr.). ◷ At least 1 hr.

3 ★★ **Lovell Beach House.** Take a moment to gaze upon Rudolph Schindler's (1887–1953) 1926 marvel of Modernist architecture. ◷ 10 min. 1242 W. Ocean Front St., Balboa Peninsula. Privately owned; please do not disturb.

4 ★ kids **Balboa Pavilion & Balboa Fun Zone.** The **Pavilion**, a historical landmark, was built in 1906 as a bathhouse; became a big-band dance hall (doing the "Balboa Hop") in the '30s and '40s; and today is the place to go for sport-fishing charters, harbor and whale-watching cruises, and service to Catalina Island. Nearby is the old-fashioned **Fun Zone** (☎ 949/673-0408; www.thebalboafunzone.com), where kids can hop on a Ferris Wheel ($3) or carousel ($2). Visit the **Newport Harbor Nautical Museum** (☎ 949/675-8915; www.nhnm.org; $5 suggest-ed donation) to meet sea creatures like prickly urchins, see model ships, and learn about the town's maritime heritage. ◷ 1 hr. 400 Main St., Newport Beach. ☎ 800/830-7744. www.bal boapavilion.com.

5 ★ **Balboa Island.** Take the **Balboa Island Ferry,** 410 S. Bayfront (☎ 949/673-1070; www. balboaislandferry.com; $1 per person, $2 per

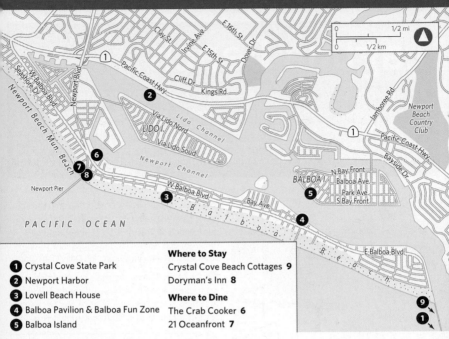

1 Crystal Cove State Park
2 Newport Harbor
3 Lovell Beach House
4 Balboa Pavilion & Balboa Fun Zone
5 Balboa Island

Where to Stay
Crystal Cove Beach Cottages 9
Doryman's Inn 8

Where to Dine
The Crab Cooker 6
21 Oceanfront 7

car), 800 feet to and from little cutesy Balboa Island. A sidewalk stroll—the best time is at night, when 1,400 small white bulbs light up the Balboa Pavilion across the water—leads you past quaint cottages on small parcels of land

that originally sold for $250. Be sure to swing by Marine Avenue to try Balboa Island's original creations— the Frozen Chocolate Banana or the Balboa Bar (vanilla ice cream dipped in warm chocolate and coated with nuts).

Where to Stay & Dine

★ The Crab Cooker SEAFOOD

This funky red shack has been one of Newport's favorite seafooders since 1951. You can't miss with the cracked crab or the Manhattan-style (tomato-based) clam chowder. 2200 Newport Blvd. ☎ 949/673-0100. www.crabcooker.com. No reservations. Entrees $11–$30. AE, MC, V. Lunch & dinner daily.

★★★ Crystal Cove Beach Cottages

For truly one-of-a-kind accommodations, book a rustic beach cottage in the Crystal Cove State Park and Historic District. It may be the toughest reservation to come by on the coast, but it's well worth the effort. Stop by the adjacent Beachcomber for a meal or drink right on the sand. 35 Crystal Cove. ☎ 800/444-7275. www.crystalcovebeachcottages.com. 13 units. Individual cottages $125–$356. AE, MC, V.

★ Doryman's Inn

On the bustling boardwalk, this vintage-style boutique hotel, once a fishermen's flophouse, offers romantic rooms outfitted with brass beds, marble sunken tubs, rich wood furniture, and Victorian wallpaper. 2102 W. Oceanfront Blvd. ☎ 949/675-7300. www.dorymansinn.com. 10 units. Doubles $199–$429. AE, DC, DISC, MC, V.

★★ 21 Oceanfront STEAKHOUSE

Tuck into a leather booth at this swanky restaurant with stellar ocean views for a "special occasion" dinner of filet mignon or lobster tail. 2102 W. Oceanfront Blvd. ☎ 949/673-2100. www.21oceanfront.com. Reservations recommended. Entrees $25–$49. AE, DISC, MC, V. Dinner daily.

Laguna Beach

Artsy, romantic, and warm—with 7 miles of dramatic coastline—Laguna Beach dazzles visitors, especially those who pony up for a stay at one of its high-end resorts and spas. Nature lovers will find plenty to explore in craggy coves and tide pools, while art lovers will enjoy learning about Laguna's long tradition of plein-air ("open air") landscape painting.

> Protected pockets and coves make Heisler Park an appealing destination; kids love the sea anemones and hermit crabs.

START Laguna Beach is 51 miles south of Los Angeles.

① ★ **Laguna Art Museum.** This museum focuses on Californian artists in its tidy collection; exhibits have included retrospectives on Wayne Thiebaud and Roger Kuntz. With roots going back to 1918, this local institution anchors a thriving arts community with more than 100 galleries. On the first Thursday of each month, the museum stays open late to support the **Laguna Beach Artwalk** (www.

firstthursdaysartwalk.com), a free spin through more than 40 galleries. ⏱ 1 hr. 307 Cliff Dr., Laguna Beach. ☎ 949/494-8971. www.lagunaart museum.org. Admission $12 adults, $10 students & seniors, free for kids under 12. Daily 11am–5pm.

② ★★ **Main Beach.** Laguna's coastline offers 30 tucked-away beaches and coves, but your first beach stop should be here, the best snapshot of locals at play. ⏱ At least 1 hr. See p. 513.

③ 🍨 ★ **Gelato Paradiso.** Deliciously creamy, authentically Italian gelato made in small batches from scratch daily. Try the *Stracciatella* (chocolate chip) or the *Dulce de Leche* (sweet crème and caramel). 448 S. Coast Hwy., Ste. A (enter on alley behind building). ☎ 949/464-9255. www.gelato paradiso.net. Gelato $3.50–$6.

④ ★ **Heisler Park.** Stroll along a landscaped path atop coastal bluffs that offer ocean views framed by swaying palm trees, then take the

Laguna's Art Festivals

If you're visiting during July and August, catch the **Festival of the Arts,** 650 Laguna Canyon Rd. (☎ 949/494-1145; www.foapom. com), a Laguna tradition since 1932. The biggest attraction is the "living art" display at the ★ **Pageant of the Masters,** a stage event that painstakingly recreates classic art pieces using actual people (dressed, made up, and posed as their two-dimensional counterparts)—sounds goofy, but the effect is slightly giddying. The **Sawdust Festival**, 935 Laguna Canyon Rd. (☎ 949/494-3030; www.sawdustartfestival.org), is an alternative, more free-spirited festival.

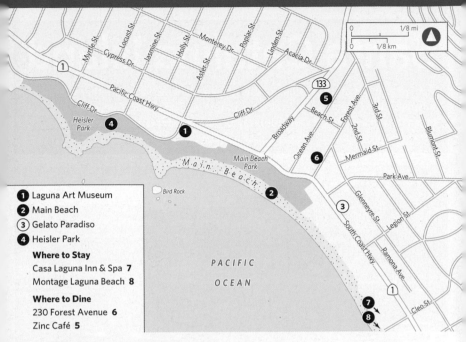

1 Laguna Art Museum
2 Main Beach
3 Gelato Paradiso
4 Heisler Park

Where to Stay
Casa Laguna Inn & Spa **7**
Montage Laguna Beach **8**

Where to Dine
230 Forest Avenue **6**
Zinc Café **5**

stairs down to the coves below. The park's beaches, **Picnic Beach** and **Rockpile Beach,** are marine protected areas, where you'll find terrific tide pools with sea anemones, red urchins, hermit crabs, and maybe a sea cucumber. Myrtle St. & Cliff Dr. ⊕ At least 1 hr.

Where to Stay & Dine

★★ Casa Laguna Inn & Spa

This Mission-style hillside hideaway is brightened by bougainvillea and Mexican tiles. Spring for a room with an ocean view, and do not miss the complimentary gourmet breakfast. 2510 S. Coast Hwy. ☎ 800/233-0449, 949/494-2996. www.casalaguna.com. 21 units. Doubles $139–$337, w/breakfast. AE, DISC, MC, V.

★★★ Montage Laguna Beach

Perched on an oceanfront bluff, this Craftsman-style beauty presents pure luxury at every turn—lush grounds, spacious rooms with ocean views, lavish amenities, and impeccable service. When you tire of the mosaic-tile infinity pool, dip down to the pristine pockets of white sandy beach below, or hit the world-class Spa Montage. 30801 S. Coast Hwy. ☎ 866/271-6953, ☎ 866/271-6953, 949/715-6000.

www.montagelagunabeach.com. 250 units. Doubles $450–$795. AE, DISC, MC, V.

★★ 230 Forest Avenue *AMERICAN*

The modern, arty dining space keeps the crowds happy with such well-executed dishes as pan-seared Chilean sea bass, short rib ravioli, and pistachio profiteroles. Or maybe it's the specialty martinis and mojitos. 230 Forest Ave. ☎ 949/494-2545. www.230forestavenue.com. Reservations recommended. Entrees $12–$34. Lunch & dinner daily. AE, MC, V.

★ Zinc Café *BRUNCH*

A popular outdoor spot to fuel up with tasty vegetarian eats like *huevos rancheros* with mango-papaya salsa and veggie burgers. 350 Ocean Blvd. ☎ 949/494-6302. www.zinccafe.com. Entrees $5–$9. Breakfast & lunch daily. AE, MC, V.

Santa Catalina Island

A mere 22 miles off the mainland, this rugged island feels like another world—unspoiled land, clean air, crystal-clear waters, and no traffic. Chewing-gum magnate William Wrigley, Jr. (1861–1932), purchased the island in 1919 as a getaway playground for the exploding population of Southern California.

> Drop anchor off picture-postcard-pretty Avalon, then head to shore for ecotours, shopping, dining, and water play.

START   **The island is 22 miles west of mainland Los Angeles. For details on transport to the island, see "Getting There" on p. 522.**

❶ ★ **Catalina Casino.** This Moorish-style palace was erected in 1929 as an entertainment destination (no, not gambling). Big-band legends such as Benny Goodman used to pack in crowds at the **Casino Ballroom** in the '30s and '40s. There's also a glamorous, Art Deco movie house, the **Avalon Theatre,** and the **Catalina Island Museum,** which illustrates 7,000 years of island history. The best way to experience the casino is a 50-minute tour (☎ 310/510-8687; 2pm daily; $17.50 adults, $15.75 seniors, $13.25 kids). ⏱ 1 hr. 1 Casino Way, Avalon.

❷ ★ **Descanso Beach Club.** ⏱ At least 1 hr. See p. 502, ❺.

❸ ★★ **Lover's Cove.** ⏱ 1 hr. See p. 502, ❺.

❹ ★ **Wrigley Memorial & Botanical Gardens.** Head up into Avalon Canyon to see the Romanesque Wrigley Memorial and a 37-acre garden of rare desert plants, many of which are endemic to Catalina. ⏱ 1 hr. 1400 Avalon Canyon Rd. ☎ 310/510-2288. Admission $5 adults, free for kids under 13. Daily 8am–5pm.

❺ ★★ **Jeep Eco-Tour.** In an open-air vehicle, rumble through Cape Canyon, where you may spot American bald eagles, American bison (descended from a herd imported for a film shoot in 1925), and Catalina Island foxes. ⏱ At least 2 hr. 125 Clarissa St. ☎ 310/510-2596, ext. 108. www.catalinaconservancy.org. Reservations required. Tours start at $65 for 2 hr. Daily 8:30am–4:30 pm.

❻ ★★ **Two Harbors.** Escape to this wild side of the island where you'll find fewer tourists and more rugged natural beauty that you can explore by camping, hiking, and other outdoor activities. ⏱ At least 2 hr. www.visittwoharbors.com.

1 Catalina Casino
2 Descanso Beach Club
3 Lover's Cove
4 Wrigley Memorial & Botanical Gardens
5 Jeep Eco-Tour
6 Two Harbors

Where to Stay
The Inn on Mt. Ada 9

Where to Dine
Catalina Country Club 8
Harbor Reef Restaurant and Saloon 7

Where to Stay & Dine

★★ **Catalina Country Club** *CALIFORNIAN*
The spring training clubhouse of the Chicago Cubs from 1921 to 1951, this elegant Mission-style building is now the island's best restaurant for fine dining. 1 Country Club Dr., Avalon. ☎ 310/510-7404. Reservations recommended. Entrees $10–$34 dinner. Lunch & dinner daily. AE, DISC, MC, V.

★ **Harbor Reef Restaurant and Saloon** *STEAK/ SEAFOOD* This beachside restaurant cooks hearty chow like prime rib and freshly caught swordfish. The saloon's house drink, the "buffalo milk," is a potent mix of vodka, crème

de cacao, banana liqueur, milk, and whipped cream. Catalina Isthmus. ☎ 310/510-4215. Reservations recommended. Entrees $22–$33. Dinner daily. AE, DISC, MC, V.

★★★ **The Inn on Mt. Ada**
Built in 1921 as Wrigley's summer mansion, this luxury B&B lets you play king of Catalina. The hilltop setting provides breathtaking views of sparkling Avalon Harbor. 398 Wrigley Rd., Avalon. ☎ 800/608-7669, 310/510-2030. www.innonmtada.com. 6 rooms. Doubles $375–$640, w/breakfast & lunch. AE, MC, V.

Fast Facts

American Express

The closest American Express Travel Services office is located at 650 Anton Blvd., Ste. A, Costa Mesa (☎ 714/540-3611; Mon–Fri 9am–5pm, Sat 10am–2pm).

Dentists & Doctors

For a dentist, call **1-800-DENTIST** (☎ 800/336-8422; www.1800dentist.com). For doctors, see "Emergencies," below.

Emergencies

Call ☎ **911** to report a fire, call the police, or get an ambulance. This is a toll-free call from any phone.

Near **Disneyland,** seek medical assistance at Western Medical Center, 1025 South Anaheim Blvd., Anaheim (☎ 714/533-6220; www.westernmedanaheim.com). In **northern Orange County,** seek medical assistance at Orange Coast Memorial Medical Center, 9920 Talbert Ave., Fountain Valley (☎ 714/378-7000; www.memorialcare.org). In **Newport Beach,** seek medical assistance at Hoag Memorial Hospital, 1 Hoag Dr., Newport Beach (☎ 949/764-4624; www.hoaghospital.org).

For nonemergency police matters, call the following numbers: in **Anaheim,** ☎ 714/765-4311; in **Huntington Beach,** ☎ 714/960-8811; in **Newport Beach,** ☎ 949/644-3717; in **Laguna Beach,** ☎ 949/497-0701; on **Santa Catalina Island,** ☎ 310/510-0174. The **Orange County Sheriff's Department** (www.ocsd.org) can be reached at ☎ 714/647-7000.

Getting There

BY PLANE The county's main airport is John Wayne Airport (SNA) (☎ 949/252-5200; www.ocair.com). It's located in Santa Ana at the intersection of I-405 and MacArthur Boulevard, about 15 miles from Disneyland. There are bus and shuttle services to Disneyland at the airport (expect to pay about $15 per person one way), and several major car-rental agencies have desks at the airport. Taxi fare to Disneyland from the airport will run about $30. **BY CAR** From Los Angeles, take I-5 (inland route) or I-405 (coastal route) heading south. The Pacific Coast Highway (aka the PCH, or Highway 1) winds directly along the coast, linking the Orange Coast communities from Seal Beach in the north to just south of Dana Point, where it merges with I-5. A toll road, Highway 73, runs 15 miles from Costa Mesa to San Juan Capistrano.

To reach the beach communities directly, take the following freeway exits: for **Seal Beach,** Seal Beach Boulevard from I-405; for **Huntington Beach,** Beach Boulevard/California 39 from either I-405 or I-5; for **Newport Beach,** California 55 from either I-405 or I-5; for **Laguna Beach**, California 133 from I-5; for **San Juan Capistrano,** Ortega Highway/California 74 from I-5; and for **Dana Point,** Pacific Coast Highway/California 1 from I-5.

Try to avoid freeways during rush hour: 6 to 9am and 3 to 7pm. Most freeways and highways have an express lane marked with diamonds or as car pool lanes. To use these lanes, there must be two or more passengers in your car. **BY FERRY** To get to Santa Catalina Island, you can take the Catalina Express ferry, a 1 to 1½-hour trip departing several times daily from Long Beach and once a day from Dana Point (☎ 800/481-3470; www.catalinaexpress.com; round-trip $66.50 adults, $60 seniors, $51 kids 2–11). From Newport Beach's Balboa Island, the Catalina Flyer ferry makes one round-trip a day (☎ 800/830-7744; www.catalinainfo.com; round-trip $68 adults, $63 seniors, $51 kids 2–11). Check the ferry websites for up-to-date departure schedules. **BY TRAIN** Amtrak's Pacific Surfliner, which runs from San Diego to San Luis Obispo, has several stops in Orange County, including Anaheim, and on the coast at the San Clemente Pier. Metrolink (☎ 800/371-5465; www.metrolinktrains.com) connects Los Angeles and Orange County.

Getting Around

Cars are the best mode of transportation within Orange County. That said, traffic on freeways, especially on the I-5 and the I-405, can get very congested with both weekday commuters and weekend beachgoers.

If you want to try public transportation, buses travel between the coastal towns; for specific routes, check out www.octa.net. The fare is $1.50; day passes are $4.

Laguna Beach is the only Orange County town with its own public transit system. A bus system offers three fixed routes and 75¢ fares. During the summer art festivals, the Summer Shuttle Service provides free rides on buses and trolleys between the most frequently visited areas. Check out www.lagunabeachcity. net for more information.

Catalina Island does not allow cars. To get around, order a cab at **Catalina Cab Company** (☎ 310/510-0025) or rent bikes at **Brown's Bikes,** 107 Pebbly Beach Rd. (☎ 310/510-0986; www.catalinabiking.com; $5–$10 per hour, $12–$25 per day). You can also rent a golf cart from **Cartopia Golf Cart Rentals** on Crescent Avenue at Pebbly Beach Road (☎ 310/510-2493) or **Island Rentals** (☎ 310/510-1456) at 125 Pebbly Beach Road; rates are approximately $45 an hour with deposit.

Hospitals
See "Emergencies," above.

Internet Access
Most hotels and many cafes in Orange County have wireless access. Check www.wiffreespot. com for a comprehensive list of Wi-Fi hotspots, which includes omnipresent chains like Starbucks, Kinko's, and McDonald's. In **Huntington Beach,** there's free Wi-Fi at the Huntington Beach Beer Company at 201 Main St., Ste. E (☎ 714/960-5343; www.hbbeerco. com).

Pharmacies
Near **Disneyland,** Rite Aid is located at 921 South Brookhurst St., Anaheim (☎ 714/772-0240). In **Huntington Beach,** Rite Aid is located at 21132 Beach Blvd. (☎ 714/536-8359). The major chains—**Rite Aid, CVS, Walgreens**—are well represented throughout Orange County, although none of them offer a 24-hour pharmacy.

Post Office
In **Anaheim,** the main post office is at 701 N. Loara St. (☎ 714/520-2639; Mon–Fri 8:30am–5pm, Sat 9am–3pm). In **Huntington Beach,** the main post office is at 316 Olive Ave.

(☎ 714/536-4973; Mon–Fri 9am–5pm). In **Newport Beach,** the main post office is at 191 Riverside Ave. (☎ 949/646-7812; Mon–Fri 8:30am–5:30pm). In **Laguna Beach,** the main post office is at 350 Forest Ave. (☎ 949/362-8306; Mon–Fri 9am–5pm). On **Catalina Island,** the main post office is at 118 Metropole St. (☎ 310/510-2850; Mon–Fri 8:30am–5pm, Sat 11am–1pm).

Safety
With planned communities and sunny and mild weather, Orange County is a relatively safe area. Its beaches are known for their beauty, but caution should be used if you're heading into the water to swim or surf. Strong undertow and large rocks can present hazards. The Wedge, for example, in Newport Beach is a powerful surf break that is especially dangerous for novices. Read all warning signs at the beaches, especially those without lifeguards.

Taxes
Sales tax in Orange County 8.75%. Hotel tax is charged on the room tariff only (which is not subject to sales tax) and ranges from 10% to 15%.

Visitor Information
In **Anaheim,** the visitor center is at 800 W. Katella Ave., inside the Anaheim Convention Center (☎ 714/765-8888; www.anaheimoc.org).

In **Huntington Beach,** the visitor center is at 301 Main St., Ste. 208 (☎ 800/729-6232 or 714/969-3492; www.surfcityusa.com)

In **Newport Beach,** the visitor center is at 110 Newport Center Dr., Ste. 120 (☎ 800/942-6278 or 949/719-6100; www.visit newportbeach.com)

In **Laguna Beach,** the visitor center is at 252 Broadway (☎ 800/877-1115 or 949/497-9229; www.lagunabeachinfo.org).

On **Catalina Island,** the visitor center is on the Green Pleasure Pier, Avalon (☎ 310/510-1520; www.catalinachamber.com); there's another center at the foot of Isthmus Pier in Two Harbors village (☎ 310/510-4205). Another useful website is www.visitcatalinaisland.com.

12

The Southern California Desert

The Best of the Southern California Desert in 3 Days

It would be a violation of Mother Nature to venture out to the sunny, sleepy desert, then rush around like mad. With 3 days at your disposal, do what harried Los Angelenos do on long weekends—book a few nights at a midcentury modernist hotel with a pool, and make day trips as your energy, or the heat, allows. Explore Joshua Tree National Park, known for its tormented-looking trees and jumbled boulders, its natural beauty both eerie and playful.

> PREVIOUS PAGE *Be dwarfed by the soaring sand dunes of Death Valley, particularly beautiful at dawn and dusk.* THIS PAGE *Don't be put off by the 20-minute detour; the panoramic Keys View overlook in Joshua Tree National Park is a stunner.*

START **Palm Springs is 120 miles east of Los Angeles and 135 miles northeast of San Diego.** TRIP LENGTH **Approximately 148 miles.**

❶ Palm Springs. At the edge of town, you'll see rows of 300-foot-high steel towers, their 60-foot arms spinning in the breeze. The ★ **San Gorgonio Pass Wind Farm,** in one of the windiest spots in the state, has 4,500 wind turbines—they're far too sophisticated to be called windmills—pumping out 650 megawatts of clean energy, enough to power 200,000 homes. A 90-minute Palm Springs

1 Palm Springs
2 Joshua Tree National Park
3 Pioneertown

Windmill Tour (☎ 760/320-1365; www. thebestofthebesttours.com; $30 adults, $27 seniors; daily 9am, 11am, 2pm) takes you close to the giants and blows you over with the facts about wind energy.

In 1935 an electrical engineer named Francis F. Crocker proposed a cable car to the top of Mount San Jacinto, an idea the local paper dubbed "Crocker's Folly." Work on the **Palm Springs Aerial Tramway** (p. 554, **2**) began in 1949 and finally ended in 1963. Still zipping along today, it's the perfect way to see the entire Coachella Valley. The alpine wilderness at the top runs 30 to 40 degrees cooler than the desert floor below (bring layers of clothes), and in the winter, a heavy blanket of snow wonderfully illustrates the contrast.

Across the street from the tramway is the sleek and stylish **Palm Springs Visitor Center** (p. 554, **1**) where you can pick up a raft of nifty guides. The Palm Springs Modern Committee sells a map for a self-guided tour of **midcentury modernist** architecture (p. 556, **5**)—an appreciation of these buildings is essential to understanding Palm Springs as a town.

Start your tour with Richard Neutra's recently restored 1946 masterpiece, the

Kaufman Desert House, characterized by its horizontal planes and sliding glass walls that merge indoor and outdoor spaces. John Lautner's imaginative **Elrod House** has a poured-concrete dome roof with wedges of skylights; it made a memorable appearance in the James Bond flick *Diamonds Are Forever.* Originally the home of Bob Alexander, developer of 2,000 modernist tract homes, Bill Krisel's **Elvis Honeymoon Hideaway** features four perfect circles on three tiers and was once known as "the House of Tomorrow." This is where Elvis and Priscilla honeymooned in 1967 and later lived; tours are available (☎ 760/322-1192; www.elvishoneymoon.com; $25–$35). Albert Frey designed a number of significant buildings in Palm Springs: **Palm Springs City Hall, Tramway Gas Station** (now the visitor center), **Tramway Valley Station, Loewy House,** and his own home, **Frey House II.** E. Stewart Williams designed **Twin Palms** (p. 529) for Frank Sinatra, **Tramway Mountain Station, Movie Colony Hotel,** and the **Palm Springs Art Museum** (see below). Donald Wexler is best known for his **Alexander Steel Houses,** and William Cody's **Del Marcos Hotel** and **Horizon Hotel** are fun places to stay.

Next head downtown to the **Palm Springs**

> *Visionary Richard Neutra was never more successful in bringing the outdoors in than with his breathtaking Kaufman Desert House.*

Art Museum (p. 556, **3**), where you can view desert-influenced contemporary art or learn more about architecture.

Finish the evening at Cary Grant's old property, now a charming restaurant called **Copley's** (p. 560), with intimately lit courtyard tables.

Start Day 2 early in Palm Desert at **the Living Desert** (p. 557, **8**), a zoo and gardens where you'll learn about the ecology of the low desert and see such animals as golden eagles, rattlesnakes, and bighorn sheep.

Shoppers may want to hit nearby **El Paseo,** which is promoted as the "Rodeo Drive of the Desert" and offers a bevy of high-end boutiques and galleries. For more shopping, head to **Palm Canyon Drive,** a hotbed for midcentury furniture, art, and design (p. 561) as well as vintage couture.

If it's not too hot for a hike, visit the historic land of the Agua Caliente tribe, **the Indian Canyons,** where you can make your way through **Palm Canyon,** home to a few thousand native California fan palms (*Washingtonia filifera*), one of the largest groves of its kind in the world.

Return to your hotel for an afternoon dip. Most places—like the Orbit Inn, the Viceroy, and the Parker (p. 559)—are happy to serve **cocktails by the pool,** which is a quintessential part of Palm Springs living. So is getting a **spa treatment**—the Palm Springs Yacht Club at Le Parker Meridien is delightful.

For evening entertainment, kick it old school and catch the **Fabulous Palm Springs Follies,** an extravagant song-and-dance show featuring senior citizens, which the Associated Press called "part shtick, part extravaganza, and part minor miracle." ⏱ 2 days. See p. 554 for more on Palm Springs.

On Day 3, head north on Indian Canyon Drive until it hits CA-62, and travel about 35 miles to the Oasis Visitor Center on the north side of

2 Joshua Tree National Park. Grab maps and get a sense of the park's wonders at the **Oasis Visitor Center,** then drive south to **Jumbo Rocks,** which is true to its name. See the much-photographed **Skull Rock,** a giant rock that appears to have eye sockets; it's the park's natural version of the statues at Easter Island.

On Park Boulevard, you'll see trail heads for the easy stroll to **Cap Rock,** the site of musician Gram Parsons' haphazard funeral pyre, and **Ryan Mountain,** a popular and invigorating 3-mile loop with great views of **Wonderland of Rocks** (p. 549, ❹) and Hidden Valley. If you're feeling adventurous, hop out and explore one or both of these trails.

Drive to the highest point reachable by car to check out one of the park's finest panoramas, the mile-high **Keys View** (p. 549, ❼). Then head for **Hidden Valley** (p. 537, ❻), an old hideout for cattle rustlers that's enclosed by a ring of massive boulders. Today, it's a premier destination for rock climbers and stargazers.

If you have four-wheel drive, take the rugged, 18-mile-long **Geology Tour Road** (p.549, ❽). Otherwise, visit the **Cholla Cactus Garden** (p. 550, ❿) in the park's lower desert, and walk the short trail through the funky cacti, whose fuzzy arms seem to radiate in the sun's afternoon light. The cuteness is a ruse—watch out for their "jumping" needles. ⏱ At least 4 hr.

Exit the park on Park Boulevard near the west entrance. Take a left on CA-62, aka Twentynine Palms Highway, and head west for 8 miles. Take a right on Pioneertown Road and go 4 miles to

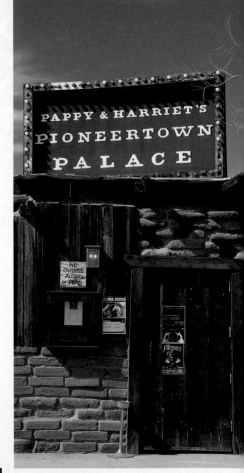

> *Rock out in the desert at Pappy & Harriet's Palace, an unexpected music outpost with surprisingly good gigs in Pioneertown.*

A Ring-a-ding-ding for Frank-o-philes

For a pretty penny, you can luxuriate at ★★★ **Twin Palms,** 1148 E. Alejo Rd., Palm Springs (☎ 760/320-1058; www.sinatra-house.com). Frank Sinatra's former four-bedroom, 4,500-square-foot estate has a piano-shaped pool. From 1947 to 1954, this is where Ol' Blue Eyes lived large, partied hard, and raged through a tumultuous love affair with wife Ava Gardner (there's still a crack in the bathroom sink where he smashed a liquor bottle during one of their infamous rows). The rate is $1,950 to $2,600 a night.

❸ ★ **Pioneertown.** Mosey on over to this village, built in the 1940s as a Western movie set (if you head here in summer, you might just see a mock gunfight break out). End your 3 days with a bang at **Pappy & Harriet's Palace** (p. 551), a musical outpost—sometimes raucous, but always memorable—boasting an eclectic lineup that has recently included indie sensation Vampire Weekend, rock 'n' roll legend Robert Plant, and Johnny Cash cover bands. ⏱ At least 1 hr. www.pioneertown. com/f-index.htm.

The Best of the Southern California Desert in 1 Week

Start your week off with 2 relaxing days in Palm Springs—
don't feel guilty, this town was built on golf courses and cocktails. Then try a
sampler platter of California's desert parks: Anza-Borrego, Joshua Tree, the
Mojave, and Death Valley. The physical conditions may be harsh, even brutal, but
the rewards are spectacular—which is not unlike the situation the mining industries
found themselves in when they tapped the area more than a century ago.

> Washes, canyons, mountains, outcroppings—see the drama of Anza-Borrego's Badlands from Font's Point.

START Palm Springs is 120 miles east of Los
Angeles and 135 miles northeast of San
Diego. A vehicle with four-wheel drive is
recommended for this tour. TRIP LENGTH
Approximately 710 miles.

❶ **Palm Springs.** ⏲ 2 days. See p. 554.

On Day 3, take CA-111 east to CA-86, then
head south to Salton City, then west on S22
into Borrego Springs.

❷ **Anza-Borrego Desert State Park.** To make
sense of California's largest state park, stop
first at the **Anza-Borrego Desert State Park
Visitor Center** (p. 552, ❶) for self-guided

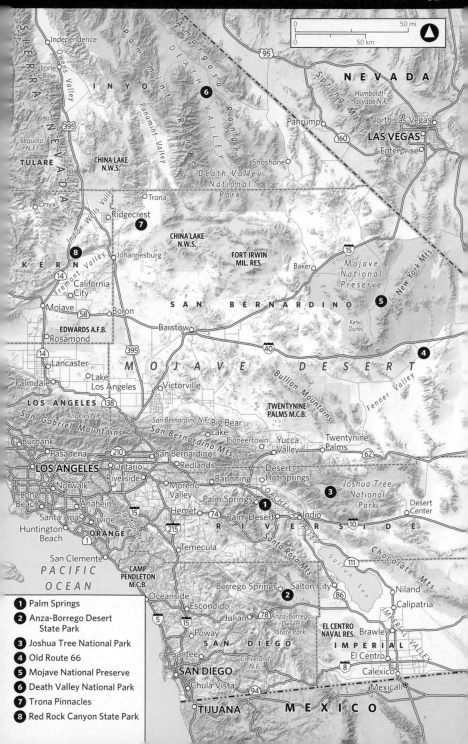

1 Palm Springs
2 Anza-Borrego Desert State Park
3 Joshua Tree National Park
4 Old Route 66
5 Mojave National Preserve
6 Death Valley National Park
7 Trona Pinnacles
8 Red Rock Canyon State Park

> *Limestone curtains trimmed with stalactites drip from the ceiling of Mitchell Caverns, where guides also point out archeological finds.*

maps that will immediately set you afoot. Nearby, you can access the park's most popular hike, the 3-mile loop **Borrego Palm Canyon Trail** (p. 552, ❷), which takes you through one of the largest palm oases in the state. You stand a good chance of spotting some bighorn sheep (or *borrego*), after whom the park is (partly) named.

You'll most likely need a four-wheel-drive vehicle to navigate the dirt roads leading to major geological highpoints: **Font's Point**, the best place to see the forbidding Borrego Badlands, rugged and rosy in the late-afternoon sun, and **the Slot,** a narrow passage of smooth, curved, water-carved canyon walls. ⏲1 day.

❸ **Joshua Tree National Park.** For Day 4, follow the itinerary on p. 548, ❶–❿.

On Day 5, get on the road to Mojave National Preserve. Head north on Utah Trail to Amboy Road. Follow Amboy west, then north, for a total of 45 miles until National Trails Highway, aka Old Route 66.

❹ ★★ **Old Route 66.** This desolate stretch, from Essex to Ludlow, of the fabled roadway seems forgotten, littered with dried-up little towns like Amboy, where you'll want to stop for a shot of an atomic-age landmark, the sign for **Roy's Motel & Café** (www.rt66roys.com). ⏲1 hr. trip time.

From National Trails Highway, head north on Essex Road for 22 miles.

❺ **Mojave National Preserve.** Arrange for a tour of the **Mitchell Caverns** (p. 541, ❻),

where you can see a mindboggling array of limestone rock formations in caves used by the Chemehuevi Indians for hundreds of years.

The **Kelso Dunes** (p. 540, ❷) comprise a magnificent 45-square-mile field of sand. These dunes, some of which top out at 600 feet, are known for their "booming" or "singing" qualities—a low rumbling sound that occurs when the sand shifts with your footsteps.

Swing by the historic **Kelso Depot,** now a restored visitor center with an art gallery, a screening room, and exhibits. Cool off with a milkshake at the lunch counter of **The Beanery** (p. 541).

Cinder Cone National Natural Monument (p. 540, ❸) is a tableau of 8 million years of volcanic history, with 32 red-and-black cinder cones rising over a bed of hardened basaltic lava. Many of the cinder cones are visible from the road, but you should head 5 miles down a dirt road to the point where you can descend into an intact lava tube.

Try to get on the road to Death Valley while you still have daylight. ⏲ At least 4 hr.

Head north on Cima Road to I-15, then head west for 26 miles. At Hwy. 127, head north for 83 miles. Turn left on Hwy. 190, and go 30 miles to Furnace Creek in

❻ **Death Valley National Park.** Before dawn on Day 6, arrive at **Zabriskie Point** (p. 543, ❷), and wait for the first rays of the sun to warm the eroded badlands of the Amargosa Range. This is one of Death Valley's most breathtaking moments. Hike down into **Gower Gulch** below.

At the **Furnace Creek Visitor Center & Museum** (p. 542, ❶), stock up on guidebooks and sign up for any ranger-led walks that may interest you.

One of the park's must-dos is a quick trip through **Badwater Basin** (p. 543, ❹), which, at 282 feet below sea level, is the lowest point in North America. Not a lot to do there and it can be blindingly hot, but it's fascinating nonetheless. Take a moment to roam the crusted salt flats that stretch out for miles.

From **Dante's View** (p. 543, ❸), with Badwater sparkling below you, you can see Mount Whitney in the distant Sierra Nevada range—a panorama that offers in a single, dazzling view the lowest and highest points in the contiguous 48 states.

> *A flurry of winter storms can turn already-dramatic Dante's View into a frosty desert dreamscape.*

One of the park's most popular attractions is the scenic 9-mile **Artist's Drive** (p. 544, ❻) through multicolored mudhills, stained by various mineral deposits. Stop at the vivid **Artist's Palette** for a closer look.

Kick off Day 7 with a tour of **Scotty's Castle** (p. 545, ❽), an extravagant castle built in the 1920s, and home to Death Valley Scotty, one of the most unusual personalities to traffic these parts. Take a stroll around half-mile-wide **Ubehebe Crater** (p. 545, ❾) and the surrounding field of "explosion pits"—smaller craters and cinder cones. The soil appears both burnt and rusted. ⏲ 1½ days.

From Panamint Springs, head south on Panamint Valley Road for 14 miles. Continue south on Trona Wildrose Road for 29 miles. Eight miles past Trona, take a left onto a dirt road.

❼ ★ **Trona Pinnacles.** This national natural landmark is an otherworldly landscape with more than 500 tufa spires—calcium carbonate deposits formed underwater—climbing up to 140 feet from an arid lakebed. No wonder it's popped up in so many sci-fi movies, such as *Star Trek V: The Final Frontier* and *Planet of the Apes* (2001). ⏲ 1 hr. Dirt road CA-178, 8 miles south of Trona. ☎ 760/384-5400. www.blm.gov.

Take CA-178 west for 30 miles. At CA-14, head south for 20 miles.

❽ ★ **Red Rock Canyon State Park.** This small but spectacular park boasts gigantic rock cliffs that, from a distance, look like melting layers of red, pink, white, gray, brown, and black. Another favorite backdrop for Hollywood movies, the unique landscape has been used in *Jurassic Park* as well as countless Westerns and sci-fi flicks. ⏲ 1 hr. Hwy. 14, 25 miles north of Mojave. ☎ 661/231-4389. www.parks.ca.gov. Visitor center open Fri–Sun; closed in winter. Park hours sunrise to sunset.

Desert Stargazing

The night desert skies sparkle with stars. The Andromeda Society (www.andromedasociety.org) hosts monthly star parties (check website for dates; usually before a new moon) at Hidden Valley in **Joshua Tree National Park.** It's free, and the amateur astronomers provide telescopes and information.

The International Dark-Sky Association (www.darksky.org), an advocacy group for dark-sky protection and stargazing, recently named **Borrego Springs** an International Dark-Sky Community, making it one of only two in the world, and *USA Today* called the town one of the 10 best stargazing spots in the country.

The Best Outdoor Adventures

The Southern California desert, by virtue of its extreme geology, makes a great playground for outdoor adventurers. Explore desert canyons, scale rocky summits, listen to "singing" sand dunes, and travel backcountry roads past forgotten towns. Just be sure to cool off at an oasis from time to time.

> *A crackup of gigantic proportions, the San Andreas Fault—where two tectonic plates collide—cleaves the desert at Carrizo Plain.*

START **Palm Springs is 120 miles east of Los Angeles and 135 miles northeast of San Diego. A vehicle with four-wheel drive is strongly recommended for this tour.** TRIP LENGTH **5 days. Total distance traveled is approximately 530 miles.**

1 ★★ **Palm Springs Aerial Tramway.** From mid-November to mid-April, the Adventure

Center is open to rent snowshoes and cross-country skis. There are also self-guided nature walks and 54 miles of hiking trails—the toughest is a 5.5-mile trek to the peak of San Jacinto, 10,834 feet above sea level. ⏱ At least 1 hr. See p. 554, **2**.

2 ★ **Indian Canyons.** The best hiking close to downtown Palm Springs is on the tribal land

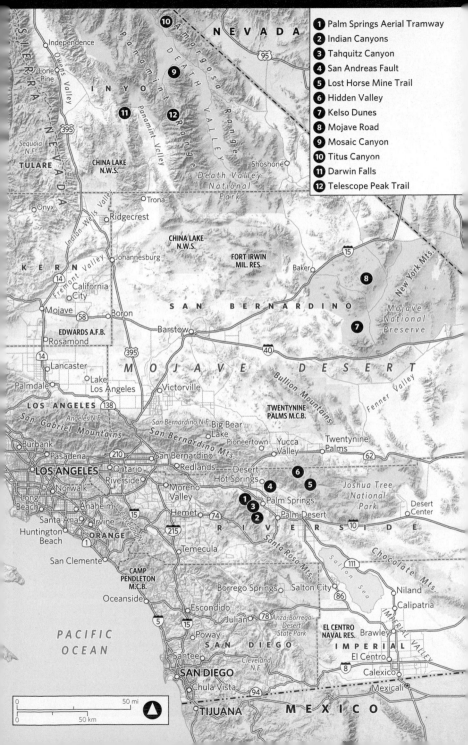

1. Palm Springs Aerial Tramway
2. Indian Canyons
3. Tahquitz Canyon
4. San Andreas Fault
5. Lost Horse Mine Trail
6. Hidden Valley
7. Kelso Dunes
8. Mojave Road
9. Mosaic Canyon
10. Titus Canyon
11. Darwin Falls
12. Telescope Peak Trail

> *An absolute desert must-do, Palm Springs Aerial Tram slowly spins as it rises nearly 6,000 feet above Coachella Valley.*

❸ ★★ **Tahquitz Canyon.** The star attraction is the lovely 60-foot **Tahquitz Falls** (seasonal, as it relies on snow melt from Tahquitz Peak), which can be reached by a 2-mile round-trip hike over rocky terrain. Either a trail guide from the excellent visitor center or a ranger can point out the highlights along the way. These include Sacred Rock, one of the Cahuillas' oldest village sites, with rock art and bedrock mortars; and Piled Boulders, where artifacts dating back 2,000 years have been found. ⊕ At least 2 hr. See p. 557, ❻.

❹ ★★ **San Andreas Fault.** An open-air jeep tour by **Desert Adventures** takes you to a private, 1,000-acre preserve where you can stand over the 1,000-mile-long San Andreas fault line, where the Pacific Plate grinds against the North American Plate. ⊕ 3 hr. Desert Adventures: ☎ 760/340-2345 www. red-jeep.com. $99–$125 per person.

On Day 2, from the Palm Springs area, take Indian Canyon Drive north for 13 miles. Take a right onto Hwy. 62 (aka Twentynine Palms Highway), and go 20 miles to Joshua Tree National Park's entrance at Park Boulevard.

of the Agua Caliente Cahuilla people. In **Palm Canyon** an easy trail follows along a shaded stream before rising into the drier desert hillside dotted with cacti. A 1-mile loop through **Andreas Canyon** passes through jutting rock formations around a burbling creek. For longer, more remote hiking, try **Murray Canyon,** where you're more likely to spot bighorn sheep than other tourists. Cool off at the small waterfall.

Some prefer to see the canyons on horseback; ★ **Smoke Tree Stables,** 2500 Toledo Ave (☎ 760/327-1372; www.smoketrees tables.com; $50–$90) offers several guided trail rides. ⊕ At least 2 hr. See p. 557, ❾.

Desert Wildflowers

Early spring paints the **Anza-Borrego** desert with wildflowers—yellow desert dandelions, pink sand verbena, purple phacelia, and white desert lilies. Depending on the amount of rain in winter and how quickly temperatures rise, the flowers may bloom as early as February and may stay until mid-April. Sometimes the most spectacular displays last only a couple of weeks, so check the wildflower hotline at ☎ 760/767-4684 for the latest information.

In the grasslands of the western Mojave, the **Antelope Valley California Poppy Reserve,** 15101 Lancaster Rd., Lancaster (☎ 661/724-1180; www.parks.ca.gov), springs to life between March and May each year with golden poppies, California's state flower. The cost is $8 per vehicle for the scenic drive through the bright-orange countryside, which hosts perhaps the greatest concentration of poppies in the state.

5 ★ **Lost Horse Mine Trail.** Hike up an old wagon road 2 miles to the ruins of Joshua Tree's most successful gold-mining operation, whose bounty was first discovered, so the legend goes, by a cowboy looking for his lost horse. Wander among the remains of stone buildings, peek down mine shafts, and check out the 10-stamp mill used to process the ore. ⏱ 2 hr. End of Lost Horse Mine Rd., off Keys View Rd.

6 ★ ★ **Hidden Valley.** Joshua Tree is one of the best rock-climbing destinations in the state, with thousands of climbs. Beginners can hop around the round boulders in the Wonderland of Rocks, but serious scalers look for major vertical formations such as Sports Challenge Rock and Hidden Tower. If you need help, get a foothold with **Joshua Tree Rock Climbing School** (☎ 760/366-4745; www. joshuatreerockclimbing.com), which offers one-on-one instruction ($295 per day) as well as group lessons ($125 per person). ⏱ At least 3 hr. Park Blvd., Hidden Valley (9 miles from the west entrance).

Early on Day 3, from Twentynine Palms Highway, head north on Utah Trail for 2 miles. Take a right at Amboy Road, and follow it for 45 miles. Take a right onto National Trails Highway, and go 6½ miles. Take a left at Kelbaker Road, and go north for 34 miles to the visitor center for Mojave National Preserve.

> Chill out in the desert at Tahquitz Canyon, a deeply spiritual site for the Agua Caliente tribe, which offers guided tours of the area.

Safety Tips

Before you set out, pack your car with an emergency kit: spare tire, maps, flares, water, extra food, first aid. It's a good idea to inform somebody if you plan on camping or taking a long hike.

Carefully consider the heat before exerting yourself. It's not unusual for parts of the desert to exceed 110°F in the summer. Wear loose clothing and a wide-brimmed hat, and use sunscreen. Always carry plenty of water, and stay hydrated!

Do not enter abandoned mine shafts, and do not approach wildlife, especially dangerous creatures such as rattlesnakes and scorpions.

7 ★ ★ **Kelso Dunes.** Don't just look at the dunes soaring against the blue sky; listen to them sing as well. Your footsteps will cause a "booming" noise as layers of golden rose quartz sand shift and vibrate against one another. The dunes are best experienced at sunrise or sunset, when the angled light rays bring the sand patterns and shapes into sharp relief. ⏱ At least 2 hr. See p. 540, **2**.

8 ★ **Mojave Road.** Take a trip back in time on this rugged road, which spans the entire preserve east to west for 138 miles; it looks nearly identical to the way it did centuries ago, when it was first blazed as an Indian trade route and later followed by Western settlers. Sometimes called the "Other Mother Road," it can be

> *Like bands of taffy that turned to stone, the polished, red-rock narrows of Mosaic Canyon twist and swirl in intricate patterns.*

dangerous and definitely requires a four-wheel-drive vehicle. Pick up the trail on the Kelso Cima Road across from the Cedar Canyon Road, and rumble along for a spell. ☺ 2 hr.

On Day 4, head north on Kelso Cima Road for 5 miles, then continue on Cima Road for 18 miles. At I-15, head west for 26 miles. Head north on Hwy. 127 for 84 miles. Take a left at Hwy. 90, and go 30 miles to the visitor center at Death Valley National Park.

❾ ★★ **Mosaic Canyon.** The intricate patterns of the water-polished canyon walls are breccias—angular rock fragments bound by a natural cementing process. A popular 3.5-mile hike curves through smooth narrows and opens up to crumbling, colorful rockfalls that test your rock-scrambling skills. ☺ At least 2 hr. Mosaic Canyon Road, off Hwy. 190, just south of Stovepipe Wells Village.

❿ ★★ **Titus Canyon.** One of Death Valley's most popular adventures, this 27-mile back-country road rolls over the rugged Grapevine Mountains and swoops down into deep, colorful canyons that culminate in winding narrows. A map from the visitor center points out the Leadfield ghost town, ancient Indian petroglyphs at Klare Springs, and geological highlights. Keep your eyes peeled for bighorn sheep. ☺ At least 2 hr. Titus Canyon Rd. Start at Hwy. 374, aka Daylight Pass Rd. (nearly 3 miles east of the park, and across the Nevada border), and head east to Scotty's Canyon Rd. High-clearance vehicles only, four-wheel drive recommended.

⓫ ★★ **Darwin Falls.** An easy mile-long hike through the shade of willows and cottonwoods takes you to the postcard-perfect lower falls. A 20-foot waterfall plunges onto a large boulder, splitting the water into two smaller

Desert Camping

Joshua Tree National Park has nine campgrounds with nearly 500 spots ($10–$15 per night). Black Rock and Indian Cove campgrounds accept reservations (☎ 877/444-6777; www.recreation.gov); all others are first-come, first-served. Water is available only in five places in the park: Oasis Visitor Center, Indian Cove Ranger Station, West Entrance (Joshua Tree), and the Black Rock and Cottonwood campgrounds.

Mojave National Preserve has two main campgrounds ($12 per night; first-come, first-served) with pit toilets, potable water, fire rings, and picnic tables; there are no utility hookups. Mid Hills, at 5,600 feet in elevation, is cooler in temperature than the lower elevation Hole-in-the-Wall, surrounded by yuccas and volcanic rock walls. Roadside vehicle camping is allowed with restrictions; see www.nps.gov/moja.

Death Valley National Park has nine campgrounds (free–$18) at various elevations and with various amenities, including flush toilets, water, and fire pits. Furnace Creek accepts reservations (☎ 877/444-6777; www.recreation.gov); all others are first-come, first-served. Backcountry camping is allowed with some restrictions; see www.nps.gov/deva.

For all camping and hiking, please remember to follow the rule of **Leave No Trace** (www.lnt.org).

> *Like a miracle in the desert, moss- and fern-trimmed Darwin Falls is well worth the occasional rock scrambles to get here.*

streams that splash into the shallow pool surrounded by ferns and moss-covered rocks. Most folks stop here, content to find such a green oasis within the harsh desert. But strong climbers should follow the trail to the left of the falls and scramble up the steep, rocky face. From an overlook, you can view an 80-foot waterfall cascading into a slot canyon. ⏲ 2½ hr. Darwin Canyon Rd., off Hwy. 190 (1 mile west of Panamint Springs).

Go back to your hotel and rest up for Day 5, which you'll spend on the

⓬ ★★★ **Telescope Peak Trail.** This taxing 14-mile round-trip scales the summit of the Panamint Range, Telescope Peak, which at 11,049 feet is the highest point in the park. Hopefully you're not huffing so hard at the 3,000-foot gain in elevation that you miss the scenery—juniper and pinyon pine trees, wildflower meadows, and (as you get higher) the gnarled limbs of ancient bristlecone pines. The peak rewards you with breathtaking 360-degree views of Death Valley, Panamint Valley, and the Sierra Nevadas. The hike takes around 8 hours and is best done in the fall or spring. ⏲ At least 7 hr. Mahogany Flat Campground, off Wildrose Canyon Rd., south of Charcoal Kilns.

Mojave National Preserve

Established in 1994 as part of the California Desert Protection Act, Mojave National Preserve is home to 1.6 million acres of tortured desert landscape filled with lots of wildlife and scenic vistas. It's as off-the-grid an experience as you're likely to find in California.

> Go retro inside the Kelso Depot train station, where The Beanery cafe serves up cups o' joe, ice cream, and PB&Js.

START The preserve's Kelso Depot Visitor Center is 235 miles east of Los Angeles (about a 3½-hr. drive).

1 ★ Kelso Depot Visitor Center. Built by the Union Pacific railroad in 1924 and closed in 1985, this historic train station has been recently restored to its Spanish-style grandeur and now acts as the preserve's main visitor center, with a bookstore, an art gallery highlighting local artists, and a theater screening a short film on the area's history. The ticket and telegraph office and the baggage room are frozen in time, decked out in genuine prewar artifacts. ⏱30 min. Kelbaker Rd., Kelso (35 miles south of Baker). ☎760/252-6108. www.nps.gov/moja. Free park admission.

2 ★★ Kelso Dunes. Rolling out from the base of the Providence Mountains, these 45 square miles of wind-sculpted sand are home to magnificent 600-foot high dunes, the third tallest on the continent. Unique acoustic conditions cause the dunes to emit a low-frequency "boom" when you walk on them. Ranger-led tours are free; they depart from the trail head every Saturday at 11am and last an hour. ⏱2 hr. Kelso Dunes Rd., 10 miles southwest of Kelso Depot. www.nps.gov/moja.

3 ★ Cinder Cone National Natural Monument. Visible from Kelbaker and Aiken Mine roads are these well-preserved reddish cinder cones and black basalt lava beds. For a small

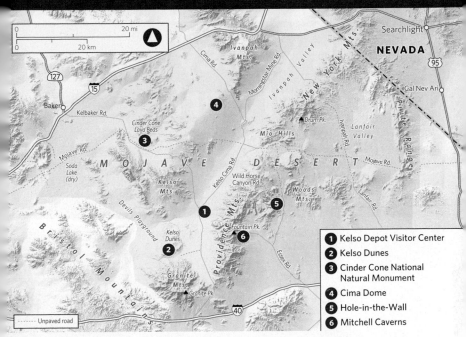

1	Kelso Depot Visitor Center
2	Kelso Dunes
3	Cinder Cone National Natural Monument
4	Cima Dome
5	Hole-in-the-Wall
6	Mitchell Caverns

adventure, hike the short **Lava Tube Trail** off Aiken Mine Road, which leads to an intact lava tube that you can explore after climbing down a ladder. ⏱ 1 hr. Aiken Mine Rd., off Kelbaker Rd.

4 ★ **Cima Dome.** Surrounded by one of the largest Joshua tree forests in the world, this smooth granite dome is 1,500 feet high, 75 square miles in size, and nearly symmetrical. The **Teutonia Peak Trail,** a 4-mile round-trip, provides an excellent up-close look, although the dome's gentle slope may be best appreciated from a distance (Mid Hills Campground offers a superb view). ⏱ 20 min. (without hike). Off Cima Rd.

5 ★ **Hole-in-the-Wall.** Named by a member of the Butch Cassidy gang, this pockmarked rock formation is the result of explosive volcanic activity nearly 20 million years ago. Take the Rings Trail, where metal rings anchored in rock help you descend 215 feet down into the striking **Banshee Canyon,** named for the high-pitched sound the wind makes as it blows through the volcanic walls' holes and hollows. Afterwards, take the scenic drive to Mid Hills along the lovely **Wild Horse Canyon Road,** the first in the nation to be designated as a "Back Country Byway." ⏱ 1 hr. Black Canyon Rd., 10

miles north of Mitchell Caverns, Mojave National Preserve. www.nps.gov/moja. Oct–Apr daily 9am–4pm; May–Sept Fri–Sun 9am–4pm.

6 ★★ **Mitchell Caverns.** Enthusiastic rangers lead informative tours through these limestone caves in which you'll see stalactites, stalagmites, and other cool formations with names like spaghetti, lily pads, and popcorn. You'll also learn about previous visitors, including a prehistoric ground sloth and the Chemehuevi Indians, who considered the site sacred. ⏱ 1½ hr. Essex Rd., Providence Mountain State Recreation Area. ☎ 760/928-2586. www.mitchell-caverns.com. Tours $6 adults, $3 kids under 16. Winter weekends 10am, 1:30pm, & 3pm; weekdays 1:30pm. Summer daily 1:30pm.

If You Get Hungry...

The preserve is largely undeveloped, so food and lodging are scarce. Your best dining bet is ★ **The Beanery** (☎ 760/252-6165), a simple U-shaped lunch counter in the Kelso Depot Visitor Center that evokes a bygone era. Grab simple salads and deli sandwiches ($8–$9), or beat the heat with a cold milkshake. It's open for lunch, Tuesday to Friday.

Death Valley National Park

At over 3.3 million acres, Death Valley National Park is the largest national park in the United States outside of Alaska. This is remote, pristine wilderness: a challenging place that rewards patience and persistence with such spectacular scenery as multihued canyons, majestic dunes, and rock formations carved by millions of years of wind and water.

> Keep your camera handy when snaking along the 9-mile loop into Artist's Palette, with wildly colored vistas around every bend.

START Furnace Creek Visitor Center is 290 miles northeast of Los Angeles and 110 miles northwest of Baker. From Baker, head north on Hwy. 127 for 83 miles. Turn left on Hwy. 190, and go 30 miles to Furnace Creek. To beat the heat, start each day as early in the morning as possible. **TRIP LENGTH** 2 days.

❶ ★ **Furnace Creek Visitor Center & Museum.** Get road and weather information here, as well as maps. The center has an excellent bookstore, sign-ups for ranger-led nature walks, and a slide show on the area's history and geology. Also check out the **Borax Museum** (one block south) chronicling the valley's chief industry in the late 1800s: the mining of borax (so-called white gold), still used to make detergents. A mile north up the road, you can peruse the rusted ruins of the old refinery at **Harmony Borax Works**. ⏱ 1 hr. Hwy. 190 (near Airport Rd.), Furnace Creek. ☎ 760/786-3200. www.nps.gov/deva. Park entrance fee $20 per car (good for 7 days). Summer daily 8am–6pm; winter daily 8am–5pm.

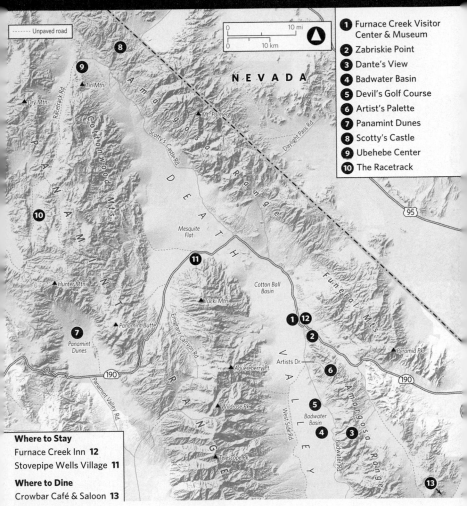

----- Unpaved road

0 ____ 10 mi
0 ____ 10 km

NEVADA

1 Furnace Creek Visitor Center & Museum
2 Zabriskie Point
3 Dante's View
4 Badwater Basin
5 Devil's Golf Course
6 Artist's Palette
7 Panamint Dunes
8 Scotty's Castle
9 Ubehebe Center
10 The Racetrack

Where to Stay
Furnace Creek Inn **12**
Stovepipe Wells Village **11**

Where to Dine
Crowbar Café & Saloon **13**

2 ★★ Zabriskie Point. This is a breathtaking vista that's not to be missed. Serious nature photographers lie in wait to capture dawn breaking over the dramatic landscape—ridges and furrows colored yellow, brown, and gold—but the late afternoon is no slouch either. Cineastes may enjoy seeing the location of Michelangelo Antonioni's 1970 film *Zabriskie Point,* revered for its sublime cinematography of these starkly beautiful badlands. ○ 20 min. Zabriskie Point Rd., off Hwy. 190.

3 ★★ Dante's View. From this glorious vantage point nearly 5,500 feet high in the Black Mountains, you can see across the entire valley—over the salt flats of Badwater Basin

to Telescope Peak in the Panamint Range. On clear days, it's possible to make out the lowest point in the contiguous 48 states, **Badwater,** as well as the highest, **Mount Whitney,** in the Sierra Nevadas 85 miles away. ○ 20 min. Dante's View Rd., 13 miles south of Hwy. 190.

4 ★★★ Badwater Basin. At 282 feet below sea level, this desiccated ancient lakebed is the lowest spot on the continent. For perspective, look up at the cliffs for the sign that indicates sea level. An observational boardwalk abuts spring-fed, salty, shallow pools, and out beyond are 200 square miles of shimmering salt flats. The evaporation cycle shapes the basin's surface into crusty, white, geometric

> *Desert snow job? Walter Scott claimed gold diggings paid for Scotty's Castle (the funds really came from a Chicago millionaire).*

patterns. If you're visiting during summer, you won't want to linger—this is one of the hottest places on the planet. ⏱ 30 min. Badwater Rd., 18 miles south of Furnace Creek.

5 ★ **Devil's Golf Course.** Only the devil could play golf on this truly bizarre-looking, jagged field of salt pinnacles. Sitting atop a salt bed hundreds of feet deep, crystals are constantly forming and reforming; in fact, sometimes you can hear them crackle as they expand and contract with fluctuations in temperature and moisture. ⏱ 20 min. Badwater Rd., 13 miles south of Furnace Creek.

6 ★ **Artist's Palette.** Take Artist's Drive, a one-way, 9-mile spin through gorgeous, pastel-colored hills—the result of the oxidation of various mineral deposits. The highpoint is the Artist's Palette, whose greens, pinks, reds, and purples pop against the desert's dusty beige, especially when viewed just before sunset. ⏱ 30 min. Artist's Dr., off Badwater Rd.

On Day 2, head for

7 ★★ **Panamint Dunes.** Dune lovers have plenty of options in Death Valley. The **Eureka Sand Dunes** crest at nearly 700 feet, making them the tallest in California, and the popular **Mesquite Flat Sand Dunes** near Stovepipe Wells are the easiest to access. But the most pristine dune field is in the Panamint Valley. It takes a 4-mile trek across a parched lakebed to reach these lovely, star-shaped dunes, some of

The Amargosa Opera House

Traveling through godforsaken Death Valley Junction in 1967, professional dancer Marta Beckett chanced upon a dilapidated building erected by the Pacific Borax Company in the 1920s, and envisioned her own private theater where she could perform dance and mime for the rest of her days. After taking 6 years to paint the theater's walls and ceiling with detailed murals—faces of Renaissance-era kings, queens, monks, and gypsies—Marta lived that dream. Though she recently hung up her ballet slippers, the show goes on with a former *Sesame Street* performer named Sandy Scheller, whose one-woman show brings Marta's murals to life. If it all seems a little David Lynchian to you, you're on to something—the director shot parts of his *Lost Highway* here. Hwy. 127, Death Valley Junction. ☎ 760/852-4441. www.amargosa-opera-house.com. Reservations required. Admission $15 adults, $12 kids 5–12. Check website for current show schedule.

which rise to 300 feet. ☉ 3–4 hr. Lake Hill Rd., off Hwy. 190 (5 miles east of Panamint Springs).

⑧ ★★ Scotty's Castle. Millionaire Albert Johnson hired fast-talking Walter Scott, aka Death Valley Scotty, to mine for gold in Death Valley. But the greatest discovery Scott made was that he could convince Johnson of anything, like the need to build an extravagant Moorish-style mansion in the desert. Construction began in 1924 and ate up 5 years and $2.5 million—time and money well spent, I suppose, if you simply must have a waterfall in the bedroom, 18 fireplaces, a clock tower, and a remote-controlled pipe-organ. Park rangers in 1930s-era costumes conduct daily 50-minute tours. ☉ 1½ hr. Scotty's Castle Rd., off Hwy. 190. ☎ 760/786-2392. www.nps.gov/deva. Reservations required. Tours $11 adults, $9 seniors, $6 kids 6–15, free for kids 5 & under. Daily 9am–5pm.

⑨ ★ Ubehebe Crater. A tremendous volcanic steam explosion, called a phreatic eruption, created this half-mile-wide, 600-foot-deep crater around 3,000 years ago, making it a youngster by Death Valley geologic standards. A loop around the singed-looking rim is about 1.5 miles long and leads past several cinder cones and smaller craters such as Little Hebe. In spring, tiny yellow, pink, and purple wildflowers cheer up the gray-black volcanic soil. ☉ 1 hr. Ubehebe Crater Rd., off Scotty Canyon Rd. (33 miles north of Hwy. 190).

> *Play desert solitaire at Zabriskie Point, one of the finest overlooks of Death Valley's wildly eroded badlands.*

⑩ ★★ The Racetrack. No matter when you arrive, you've always just missed the race. Strewn across the landscape are a few heavy rocks, each at the end of a long dirt track, indicating the path of an unseen journey. Scientists theorize that the clay surface becomes slick with moisture and ice, allowing powerful gusts of wind to scoot these "sailing stones," but I like to think of it as the desert's great parlor trick. *Warning:* The 28-mile road from Ubehebe Crater is of the rough, gravel variety, best suited for four-wheel drive. ☉ 30 min. Ubehebe Crater Rd.

Where to Stay & Dine

★ Crowbar Café & Saloon SHOSHONE AMERICAN/MEXICAN If you're passing through the old mining village of Shoshone, this scruffy restaurant makes a great pit stop for burgers, beers, and a slice of Americana. Hwy. 127. ☎ 760/852-4123. Entrees $6–$16. AE, MC, V. Breakfast & lunch daily.

★★★ Furnace Creek Inn DEATH VALLEY Retreat from the dry desert heat at this 1927-built stone lodge with full resort amenities: spring-fed swimming pools, lush landscaping, tennis courts, horse stables, Jeep rentals, and a golf course that's billed as the world's lowest—214 feet below sea level. Cheaper accommodations can be found at its sister site, the **★ Furnace Creek Ranch,** which has 224 modest rooms. Hwy. 190. ☎ 760/786-2345. www.furnacecreekresort.com. Inn open mid-Oct to mid-May; Ranch open year-round. 66 units. Inn doubles $230–$420; Ranch doubles $102–$252. AE, DISC, MC, V.

★ Stovepipe Wells Village STOVEPIPE WELLS An Old West theme perks up this basic motel complex, which also has a restaurant, saloon, general store, and great location at the foothills of the Panamint Mountain range. Hwy. 190 (23 miles northwest of Furnace Creek). ☎ 760/786-2387. www.stovepipewells.com. 83 units. Doubles $80–$120. AE, DC, DISC, MC, V.

A TALE OF TWO DESERTS

BY MEGAN MCFARLAND

OVER THE PAST CENTURY CALIFORNIA'S DESERTS have played host to a panoply of competing interests, from miners in the Mojave to farmers near the Mexican border to the rich and famous in Palm Springs. Californians refer to the "high desert" and "low desert," corresponding respectively to the cooler, higher area northeast of Los Angeles and the arid, more populated deserts southeast of Orange County. Today, both face serious environmental challenges: As Southern California's population swelled in the 1980s, development pushed farther east, with housing tracts, golf courses, and agribusiness continuing to swallow up large swaths of the once-pristine desert and competing for ever-precious water.

The High Desert:

THE MOJAVE

Where: Between Los Angeles and Las Vegas. Includes Death Valley National Park, Mojave Desert National Preserve

Elevation: Varies from below sea level to over 11,000 feet

Fact: Badwater, in Death Valley, is the lowest point in the Western Hemisphere at 282 feet below sea level.

Features: Badlands, lava beds, sand dunes, cinder cones

The Low Desert:

THE COLORADO AND SONORAN

Where: Southern California, east of Orange County and San Diego County. Includes Palm Springs, part of Joshua Tree National Park, and Anza-Borrego Desert State Park

Elevation: Below 3,000 feet. Most of the Colorado desert lies below sea level.

Fact: About 10,000 acres within Palm Springs' city limits is part of the reservation of the Agua Caliente band of Cahuilla Indians.

Features: Creosote bush, palo verde, cholla cactus, palm oases

Sample Species Under Threat

DESERT PUPFISH
HABITAT: Pools, streams, and marshes, concentrated near the Salton Sea **FACT:** Can live in water 2½ times saltier than seawater.

DESERT TORTOISE
HABITAT: Mojave and Sonoran deserts **FACT:** Spends up to 95% of its lifetime underground and can store up to a liter of water in its bladder.

PENINSULAR BIGHORN SHEEP
HABITAT: Low desert, San Jacinto mountains south to Baja California **FACT:** It's

estimated that only about 800 remain in the wild.

Conservation Efforts

Congress designated the California Desert Conservation Area in 1976, placing 25 million acres under protection. In 1994, Death Valley and Joshua Tree were designated as national parks; Mojave, as a national preserve.

ENERGY: A federal Electric Transmission Corridor in southern California and Arizona would allow large electric transmission towers and lines on protected lands. Wind farms in the Mojave Desert are also being considered.

AGRICULTURE: Agricultural runoff from the vast farmlands of Imperial County, near the Mexican border, pollutes streams, seeps, and the Salton Sea.

WASTE DISPOSAL: A 20-year battle rages over the world's largest proposed landfill, ¾ mile from Joshua Tree.

Joshua Tree National Park

On land first set aside in 1936 by Franklin Roosevelt, the Joshua Tree National Park was formally designated in 1994 and encompasses nearly 800,000 acres where the low desert (the Colorado) meets the high desert (the Mojave). A million visitors a year enjoy the park's striking, nearly surreal scenery—an arid landscape broken up by cholla cacti and spiky ocotillos, desert palm oases, granite monoliths, jumbled boulders, abandoned mine shafts, and of course, the twisted-limbed trees that lend the park its name.

> *Fred Flintstone would feel right at home in the big-blob boulders of Hidden Valley, once a hangout for cattle rustlers.*

START The park is 40 miles northeast of Palm Springs and 135 miles east of Los Angeles. **TRIP LENGTH** 2 days.

1 ★ Oasis Visitor Center. Load up on maps and guides, and get the latest information on trail and weather conditions. If you have time, take the short, self-guided nature trail through the Oasis of Mara, home to the native Serrano tribe centuries ago. ⏱ 20 min. 74485 National Park Dr. (at Utah Trail), Twentynine Palms. www.nps.gov/jotr. Visitor center 8am–5pm. Vehicle permit $15 (good for 7 days).

2 ★★ Fortynine Palms Oasis. One of the park's most popular trails, this demanding 3-mile hike takes you through a rocky gorge to a grove of desert palms huddled around a natural oasis. Desert birds and bighorn sheep are drawn to the lush vegetation. ⏱ 2 hr. End of Canyon Rd., off Hwy. 62.

3 ★ Hidden Valley. Cattle rustlers used to hide out in this spot encased by massive boulders. From the parking area, an easy mile-long trail makes a fascinating trip through striking rock formations, many of which have earned

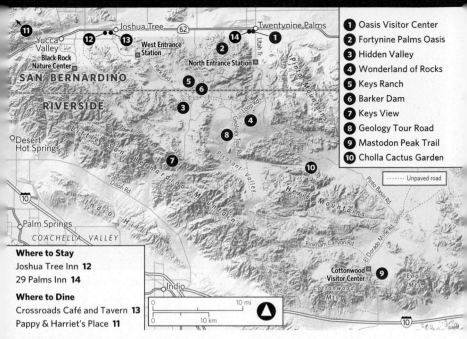

1. Oasis Visitor Center
2. Fortynine Palms Oasis
3. Hidden Valley
4. Wonderland of Rocks
5. Keys Ranch
6. Barker Dam
7. Keys View
8. Geology Tour Road
9. Mastodon Peak Trail
10. Cholla Cactus Garden

------- Unpaved road

Where to Stay
Joshua Tree Inn **12**
29 Palms Inn **14**

Where to Dine
Crossroads Café and Tavern **13**
Pappy & Harriet's Place **11**

playful nicknames—the Giant Burrito, the Trojan—for their seemingly purposeful design. ⏱1 hr. **Across from Hidden Valley Campground.**

4 ★★ **Wonderland of Rocks.** These 12 square miles of jigsaw rock piles, narrow canyons, and rounded boulders are a mecca for serious rock climbers. Novice climbers and children can enjoy the playground quality of the more gently sloped formations. You might spot bighorn sheep seeking replenishment at such seasonal waterholes as **Willow Hole.** ⏱1½ hr. **Off Park Blvd., south of the west entrance.**

5 ★ **Keys Ranch.** Eccentric Bill Keys (1879–1969), one of the area's earliest homesteaders, scraped together a living with his family on this 150-acre ramshackle ranch still littered with rusted machinery. A ranger-led tour provides a fascinating view of early settler life, especially that of Keys, who was at various times one of Teddy's Roosevelt's Rough Riders, a gold miner, a convicted (and later pardoned) manslaughterer, and a Disney actor. ⏱1½ hr. 2 miles north of Barker Dam Rd. ☎ 760/367-5555. Reservations required. Guided tours $5 adults, $2.50 kids. Oct–May Mon–Fri 10am & 1pm.

6 ★ **Barker Dam.** Constructed in a natural rock basin by ranchers around 1900 as a way to hold water for thirsty cattle, the rain-fed pool ringed by the Wonderland of Rocks draws plenty of desert wildlife, especially birds. Along the **Barker Dam Trail,** look for petroglyphs carved into a rocky overhang; sadly, these remnants of Native American culture got a full-blown Hollywood "makeover" when a movie was shot here 50 years ago. ⏱1 hr. **Trail head begins at Barker Dam parking area.**

On Day 2, head for

7 ★★ **Keys View.** From the observation area near the parking lot, take in the stunning panorama that on clear days includes the San Bernardino Mountain Range, the Coachella Valley, the Salton Sea, the San Andreas Fault, Palm Springs, the San Gorgonio Mountain, and more. On spectacularly clear days, it's even possible to see Signal Hill in Mexico. ⏱30 min. **End of Keys View Rd.**

8 ★★ **Geology Tour Road .** This 18-mile dirt road through some of the park's major geological sites, the results of a few billion years of erosion and seismic upheaval, is best

> Sit a spell at Keys View, where a wait for sunset rewards with a colorful play of light and shadow.

navigated in a car with four-wheel drive. At the visitor center or in a metal box at the start of the trail, pick up an informative brochure that explains each of the 16 highlights, well marked with signposts along the way. You'll pass by desert valleys, dry lake beds, alluvial fans, volcanic peaks, scenic vistas, old mining sites with abandoned tunnels and rusted vats, and fascinating monzogranite rock "sculptures," carved and rounded by wind and water. ⏱ At least 1 hr. Start in Queen Valley, 2 miles west of Jumbo Rocks Campground.

⑨ ★ Mastodon Peak Trail. This strenuous, well-marked, 3-mile hike runs through the remnants of the Winona mill site and the Mastodon Mine (an old gold mine) en route to a rocky summit with outstanding views of the Coachella Valley and the Salton Sea. On the return trail, you can access Cottonwood Spring Oasis or head a few miles out to the Lost Palms Oasis. ⏱ 2 hr. Start at Cottonwood Spring parking lot, near the Cottonwood Visitor Center.

⑩ ★★ Cholla Cactus Garden. In the Pinto Basin at the center of the park, where the Mojave gives way to the Colorado Desert, you'll come across this funny batch of fuzzy-looking cacti, also called "teddy bear" cholla (for their seemingly cuddly appearance) or "jumping" cholla (for the way their barbed spines attach onto passersby). Take the short but sweet nature trail through the garden. Experienced photographers know to visit in the late afternoon, when the golden light sets the cactus bulbs aglow. ⏱ 30 min. Off Pinto Basin Rd.

The Joshua Tree

The park's namesake is a not a cactus but a variety of large yucca that thrives in the Mojave Desert (the western half of the park). The tree's contorted appearance took a lot of heat from early explorers—Captain John Charles Frémont called it "the most repulsive tree in the vegetable kingdom." To Mormon pioneers in search of the promised land, however, the tree's upraised limbs evoked an image of the Old Testament prophet Joshua in prayer. The Mormons kept going, but the name stayed.

Where to Stay & Dine

> Order a steak, sit back, and take in the hangout scene—bikers, desert rats, and musicians—at raucous Pappy & Harriet's Palace.

★ **Crossroads Café and Tavern** TWENTYNINE PALMS *AMERICAN* Fuel up for your Joshua Tree excursions with home-style soups, salads, and sandwiches at this restaurant with an artsy, coffeehouse vibe, or just kick back with a hot cup of coffee, a fruit smoothie, or a cold beer. 61715 Twentynine Palms Hwy. ☎ 760/366-5414. www.crossroadscafeandtavern.com. Entrees $6–$11. AE, MC, V. Breakfast, lunch & dinner Thurs–Tues.

★★ **Joshua Tree Inn** JOSHUA TREE This funky courtyard motel boasts a rich rock-'n'-roll history, having hosted the Rolling Stones, the Eagles, the Byrds, and most infamously, Gram Parsons, who died of an overdose in room no. 8. 61259 Twentynine Palms Hwy. ☎ 760/366-1188. www.joshuatreeinn.com. 10 units. Doubles $85–$155. AE, DISC, MC, V.

★★ **Pappy & Harriet's Palace** PIONEERTOWN *TEX-MEX/BBQ* Steaks, chili, big ol' burgers, and Santa Maria–style barbecue—this is straight-up cowboy chow for bikers, rock climbers, and hardcore honky-tonkers. This saloon-type restaurant and music venue is the real deal, even though it started life as part of a Western movie set (p. 529, ❸). 53688 Pioneertown Rd. ☎ 760/366-5956. www.pappy andharriets.com. Reservation recommended on weekends. Entrees $7–$10. AE, DISC, MC, V. Lunch & dinner Thurs–Mon, dinner Mon.

★ **29 Palms Inn** TWENTYNINE PALMS These adobe bungalows and wood-frame cabins, many dating back the 1920s, may not be fancy, but for guests craving peace and solitude, they hit the spot. The two-room suites make an economical choice for families. Folks flock to the restaurant here for the garden-fresh ingredients and fresh-baked bread. 73950 Inn Ave. ☎ 760/367-3505. www.29palmsinn.com. 23 units. Doubles $85–$163. AE, DISC, MC, V.

Anza-Borrego Desert State Park

California's largest state park, encompassing more than 600,000 acres of the low Colorado Desert, Anza-Borrego derives it name from Spanish explorer Juan Bautista de Anza (1736–1788), who navigated this territory in 1774, and the Spanish word for bighorn sheep, which still roam these desert mountainsides.

> Casting deep shadows in the desert, native fan palms like these in Palm Canyon are surprisingly cool and alive with birds.

START **The park is 90 miles northeast of San Diego.**

❶ ★ **Anza-Borrego Desert State Park Visitor Center.** The 7,000-square-foot center is set into the ground beneath the garden, so it stays cool in the blistering summer heat. Exhibits include a geology video, a model of a slot canyon, wildlife displays, and prehistoric fossils. Volunteers are happy to provide essential maps and brochures. ⊕ 30 min. 200 Palm Canyon Dr., Borrego Springs. ☎ 760/767-5311. www.parks.ca.gov. Free park admission. Oct–May Thurs–Mon 9am–5pm; June–Sept Sat–Sun 9am–5pm.

❷ ★★ **Borrego Palm Canyon Trail.** Near the visitor center (pick up a self-guided tour brochure), access one of the park's most popular hikes: a 1.5-mile trek through a boulder-strewn desert wash to a grove of California fan palms congregating beside a small stream. Be on the lookout for bighorn sheep, which clamber down the rocky slopes to find a sip of water. ⊕ 2 hr. Trail head begins 1 mile west of visitor center. Admission $8 per vehicle. Dawn to dusk.

❸ ★ **Galleta Meadows Estate.** This privately owned meadow extends an open invitation to view its "free standing art"—life-size steel sculptures of prehistoric creatures (such as saber-toothed tigers, raptors, and giant sloths) that roamed the area 3 million years ago. ⊕ 30 min. Borrego Springs Rd. (btw. Big Horn & Henderson rds.), Borrego Springs. www.galleta meadows.com.

❹ ★★ **The Slot.** This is the park's most popular slot canyon—a narrow chasm formed by water flowing through rock. Descend into the sandstone ravine with 50-foot high walls, then follow the desert wash path as it twists and turns "downstream." In a couple of spots, a large adult will need to maneuver sideways to pass through. ⊕ 1½ hr. Buttes Pass (a dirt road off Hwy. 78).

❺ ★ **Split Mountain.** A geologist's jackpot, this narrow gorge that "splits" the Fish Creek Mountains and the Vallecito Mountains has 600-foot walls that showcase a patchwork of rock layers formed by millions of years of earthquakes and water erosion. Follow the trail to the **Wind Caves,** sandstone formations carved by wind. ⊕ 1½ hr. Split Mountain Road, 9 miles south of Hwy. 78.

❻ ★★ **Font's Point.** Time your visit to this spectacular vantage point of the **Borrego Badlands** with the setting sun, which accentuates every knot and wrinkle of this lifeless and forbidding landscape. ⊕ 30 min. Follow sign on dirt road (off S22, 13 miles east of Borrego Springs).

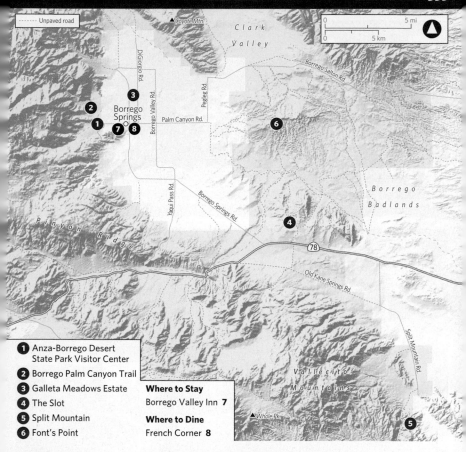

----- Unpaved road

0   5 mi
0   5 km

1. Anza-Borrego Desert
   State Park Visitor Center
2. Borrego Palm Canyon Trail
3. Galleta Meadows Estate
4. The Slot
5. Split Mountain
6. Font's Point

Where to Stay
Borrego Valley Inn **7**

Where to Dine
French Corner **8**

Where to Stay & Dine

★ **Borrego Valley Inn** BORREGO SPRINGS
Situated on 10 acres of desert gardens, this
luxurious Santa Fe-style inn strives for serenity. The pueblo-style rooms have Southwestern decor, Mexican-tiled floors, and private
patios. Two pools with hot tubs are available;
one is secluded and clothing optional. 405
Palm Canyon Dr. ☎ 760/767-0311. www.bor-
regovalleyinn.com. 16 units. Doubles $180–$260
w/breakfast. Two-night minimum. AE, DISC,
MC, V. No kids under 14.

★★ **French Corner** BORREGO SPRINGS *FRENCH*
Sure, the menu is limited and a mite overpriced, but this charming spot is easily the
best restaurant in town. Dig into French comfort food like coq au vin and beef bourguignon,
with a glass of good French wine, and enjoy
crepes or profiteroles for dessert. 721 Avenida
Sureste. ☎ 760/767-5713. www.thefrench
corner.biz. Reservations recommended. Entrees
$10–$28. AE, DISC, MC, V. Oct–May lunch &
dinner Wed–Sun; closed June–Sept.

Travel Tip

You'll need a car with four-wheel drive to
handle some of the dirt roads that lead to
many of the park's most interesting sights.
Be sure to bring water and stay hydrated,
especially on your hikes. And don't forget a
hat and sunscreen when tackling the park's
trails.

Greater Palm Springs

Palm Springs first kicked up dust as a Hollywood getaway
in the 1920s, and by the '50s and '60s, serious money—the kind that builds golf courses and architecturally significant second homes—began pouring in. Today this sunny resort town is popular with golf- and tennis-playing retirees, gays and lesbians, and hipsters looking for a throwback to the Rat Pack era.

> Dive into the midcentury-mod world of king of the Rat Pack, Frank Sinatra, on a tour of his and other celebrity desert pads.

START **Palm Springs is 120 miles east of Los Angeles; 135 miles northeast of San Diego.** TRIP LENGTH **2 days.**

❶ ★ **Palm Springs Visitor Center.** Originally designed as a gas station in 1965 by Albert Frey (1903–98), this Palm Springs landmark is known for its soaring rooflines, which the historic marker refers to as "hyperbolic paraboloid." Maps and brochures are readily available, including a nifty guide to modernist architecture (see ❺). ⏱ 20 min. 2901 N. Palm Canyon Dr., Palm Springs. ☎ 800/347-7746 or 760/778-8418. www.visitpalmsprings.com. Daily 9am–5pm.

❷ ★★ **Palm Springs Aerial Tramway.** Get the lay of the Coachella Valley by hopping aboard the world's largest tram cars on a steep vertical cable ride that climbs 2½ miles through Chino Canyon in 10 minutes, taking you from the dusty desert floor to the alpine forest of Mount San Jacinto. At the Mountain Station, you can take in views (all the way

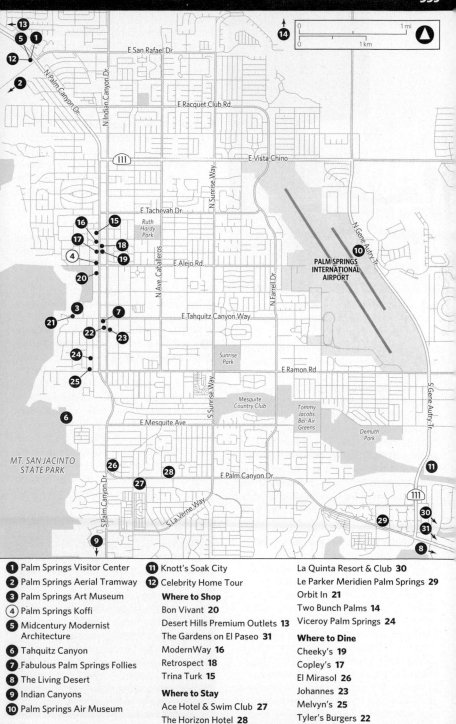

E San Rafael Dr.
E Racquet Club Rd.
E Vista Chino
N Palm Canyon Dr.
N Indian Canyon Dr.
E Tachevah Dr.
Ruth Hardy Park
N Sunrise Way
E Alejo Rd.
N Ave. Caballeros
N Gene Autry Tr.
PALM SPRINGS INTERNATIONAL AIRPORT
N Farrell Dr.
E Tahquitz Canyon Way
Sunrise Park
E Ramon Rd.
Mesquite Country Club
S Sunrise Way
Tommy Jacobs Bel-Air Greens
Demuth Park
S Gene Autry Tr.
MT. SAN JACINTO STATE PARK
E Mesquite Ave.
E Palm Canyon Dr.
S Palm Canyon Dr.
S La Verne Way

1 mi
1 km

1. Palm Springs Visitor Center
2. Palm Springs Aerial Tramway
3. Palm Springs Art Museum
4. Palm Springs Koffi
5. Midcentury Modernist Architecture
6. Tahquitz Canyon
7. Fabulous Palm Springs Follies
8. The Living Desert
9. Indian Canyons
10. Palm Springs Air Museum

11. Knott's Soak City
12. Celebrity Home Tour

Where to Shop
Bon Vivant **20**
Desert Hills Premium Outlets **13**
The Gardens on El Paseo **31**
ModernWay **16**
Retrospect **18**
Trina Turk **15**

Where to Stay
Ace Hotel & Swim Club **27**
The Horizon Hotel **28**

La Quinta Resort & Club **30**
Le Parker Meridien Palm Springs **29**
Orbit In **21**
Two Bunch Palms **14**
Viceroy Palm Springs **24**

Where to Dine
Cheeky's **19**
Copley's **17**
El Mirasol **26**
Johannes **23**
Melvyn's **25**
Tyler's Burgers **22**

> *Bunny hops by the pool are part of the stellar sculpture collection at the Palm Springs Art Museum.*

to the Salton Sea) at the observation deck, picnic, eat or grab a drink at either of two restaurants, shop at the gift shop, or watch a short film about the tramway. The tramway stations themselves are noteworthy, as they represent the work of renowned midcentury architects Albert Frey and E. Stewart Williams (1909–2005). ⏲ At least 1 hr. 1 Tram Way, off Hwy. 111, Palm Springs. ☎ 888/515-TRAM, 760/322-4800. www.pstramway.com. Admission $23 adults, $21 seniors, $16 kids 3–12, free for kids 2 & under. Mon–Fri 10am–8pm, Sat–Sun 8am–8pm. Tram runs every 30 min., last tram down at 9:45pm.

❸ ★★ **Palm Springs Art Museum.** Bolstered by private donations from such generous locals as Frank Sinatra and William Holden, this museum showcases contemporary art, including American photography and sculpture, as well as artwork related to the desert or the American West. It also features a fascinating collection of art, basketry, and relics from Native Americans, especially the Cahuilla tribe. Architecture lovers will be pleased by the museum's modern design (by E. Stewart Williams) and to find the archives of Williams and Albert Frey, as well as a drawings collection with work by Richard Neutra

and Frank Gehry. ⏲ 1 hr. 101 Museum Dr., Palm Springs. ☎ 760/325-7186. www.psmuseum.org. Admission $13 adults, $11 seniors, $5 kids, free for kids 5 & under; free admission for all Thurs 4–8pm. Tues–Wed & Fri–Sun 10am–5pm, Thurs noon–8pm.

❹ ☕ ★ **Palm Springs Koffi.** Get a caffeine fix at this sleek coffeehouse, a favorite among locals for the quality java, friendly service, free Wi-Fi, dog-friendly courtyard, and warm social scene. 515 N. Palm Canyon Dr., Palm Springs. ☎ 760/416-2244. www.kofficoffee.com. Cup of coffee $2.

❺ ★★★ **Midcentury Modernist Architecture.** For midcentury modernist architecture and design, there's no place hotter than Palm Springs, which blossomed like a desert flower in the '40s, '50s, and '60s, with the influx of the rich and famous (and stylish).

The easiest way to see prime examples of midcentury modernist architecture is to swing by Albert Frey's **Palm Springs Visitor Center** (❶), buy a map created by the **Palm Springs Modern Committee** (www.psmodcom.com), and drive around at your leisure. But if you want to dig beneath the surface, and I highly recommend that you do, consider the 2½-hour tour run by Robert Imber of **PS Modern Tours** (☎ 760/318-6118; psmoderntours@aol. com; reservations recommended; $75 per person, no credit cards). A van takes you by the iconic buildings while Robert enthusiastically explains the finer points of the structures, the architects, and the historical context. ⏲ 2½ hr.

The Coachella Valley's Great Date

From a handful of trees transplanted from the Middle East nearly a century ago, the date palm groves of the Coachella Valley now produce 95 percent of the world's date supply. In Indio, the Date Knight sign (off Hwy. 111) points you to the ★★ **Shields Date Garden,** 80225 Hwy. 111 (☎ 760/347-7768; www.shieldsdates.com; daily 9am–5pm), a roadside attraction since 1924. Cool off with their famous date crystal shake ($3.75)— cold, creamy, and delicious—and check out the 15-minute video called "The Romance and Sex Life of a Date."

❻ ★★ Tahquitz Canyon. The Cahuilla people believe the canyon possesses a raw spiritual power, and named it after Tahquitz, the guardian spirit of all shamans. ⏱ At least 1 hr. 500 W. Mesquite (west of Palm Canyon Dr.), Palm Springs. ☎ 760/416-7044. www.tahquitz canyon.com. Admission $13 adults, $6 kids 6–12. Self-guided hiking 7:30am–3:30pm; 2½-hr. ranger-led hikes 8am, 10am, noon, 2pm.

❼ ★ Fabulous Palm Springs Follies. Combining two great Palm Springs traditions—show business and aging gracefully—this musical stage act at the historic Plaza Theatre pays homage to the feel-good song-and-dance shows of the '40s, '50s, and '60s using a "mature" cast of retired singers, dancers, and comics ranging from 56 to 86 years young. 128 S. Palm Canyon Dr., Palm Springs. ☎ 760/327-0225. www.psfollies.com. Tickets $50–$92. Nov–May.

Start Day 2 at

❽ ★★ kids The Living Desert. Learn about the desert's unique flora and fauna in their natural habitat on 1,200 preserved acres in the Colorado Desert. The zoo and gardens' scenic trails snake through different sections representing specific desert ecologies such as the

> It's never boring at The Living Desert, where kids can scramble on sculptures of animals and hang out with live ones too.

Colorado, Sonoran, Mojave, and Chihuahuan deserts.

Observe golden eagles, bighorn sheep, mountain lions, rattlesnakes, and hummingbirds. The zoo also includes wildlife from the African deserts, such as cheetahs, dromedary camels, aardwolves, and reticulated giraffes. Village WaTuTu, a re-creation of a northeastern African village, features mud huts and the Petting Kraal, where kids can meet African goats and donkeys. ⏱ At least 1 hr. 47900 Portola Ave., Palm Desert. ☎ 760/36-5694. www.livingdesert.org. Admission (varies according to season) $10–$13 adults, $10–$11 seniors, $5–$8 kids 3–12. Oct–May daily 9am–5pm; June–Sept daily 8am–1:30pm.

❾ ★ Indian Canyons. Several centuries ago the Agua Caliente Cahuilla people settled in the Palm, Murray, and Andreas canyons. Today the remnants of their culture can be seen in the canyons' rock art, irrigation systems, and grinding mortars for food preparation. ⏱ At least 1 hr. End of S. Palm Canyon Dr., Palm Springs. ☎ 760/323-6018. www.indian-canyons.com. Admission $8 adults, $6 students and seniors, $4 kids 6–12. Oct–June daily 8am–5pm; July–Sept weekends 8am–5pm.

❿ ★ kids Palm Springs Air Museum. A shiny hangar is home to one of the world's largest collections of World War II aircraft—30 in all—including a Grumman F-14 Tomcat, a

A Gay Oasis

Palm Springs is one of the gay-friendliest cities in the country. Pick up a **Palm Springs Official Gay Guide** at the visitor center, or the **Bottom Line** (www.psbottomline.com), a free biweekly paper for the gay reader, available at newsstands around town. There are about 30 exclusively gay hotels in the area, most along Warm Sands Drive south of Ramon.

The **Dinah Shore Week** (www.thedinah.com), every year in March or April, is fast becoming one of the biggest lesbian gatherings in the world. Also in April, usually on Easter weekend, the monstrously popular **White Party** (www.jeffreysanker.com) rolls like a 3-day gay Mardi Gras, if you substitute DJs for floats. During the first weekend in November, the **Greater Palm Spring Pride** (☎ 760/416-8711; www.pspride.org) takes place with a colorful parade and 2 days of events.

> *Four stories of surf-dude fun, Kahuna's Beach House at Knott's Soak City includes four water slides.*

Curtiss P-40 Warhawk, and the famous Boeing B-17 Flying Fortress, most of which are still flyable. This nonprofit institution has detailed models of warships, flight simulators, and a volunteer crew of proud veterans. ⊙ 1 hr. 745 N. Gene Autry Trail, Palm Springs. ☎ 760/778-6262. www.palmspringsairmuseum.org. Admission $12 adults, $10 seniors and teens 13–17, $5 kids 6–12, free for kids 5 & under. Daily 10am–5pm.

11 **kids** **Knott's Soak City.** Hotel pool not cutting it? Make a splash at this water park with 13 waterslides, a river for tubing, and an 800,000-gallon wave pool for surfing and boogie boarding. ⊙ At least 2 hr. 1500 S. Gene Autry Trail, Palm Springs. ☎ 760/327-0499. www.knotts.com. Admission $26 adults and kids over 11, $20 seniors and kids 3–11. Memorial Day–Labor Day, daily 10am–6pm; rest of year, Sat–Sun 11am–5pm.

12 ★ **Celebrity Home Tour.** Pick up a map of celebrity homes at the visitor center (**1**) and take a spin through Palm Springs' history as a Hollywood getaway. Navigating the town's most glamorous neighborhoods, such as Movie Colony and Las Palmas, you'll see the former pads of Greta Garbo, Bob Hope, Elvis Presley, Dean Martin, and Frank Sinatra, as well as plenty of architecturally significant residences. ⊙ 1 hr.

Palm Springs Villagefest

The weekend in Palm Springs unofficially kicks off on Thursday evenings with ★ **Villagefest**, a street fair that takes over several blocks of the town's commercial hub. There's live entertainment, street performers, a farmers market, and more than 200 vendors offering antiques, hot food, and handcrafted art and jewelry. The action takes place on North Palm Canyon Drive (btw. Baristo and Amado roads) on Thursday nights from 6 to 10pm October to May, and from 7 to 10pm June to September. For information, call ☎ 760/320-3781 or go online to www.villagefest.org.

Where to Stay

> *Hipsters dip into the Ace Hotel pool, a cool retreat that offers a good deal with plenty of style.*

★ **Ace Hotel & Swim Club** PALM SPRINGS
Young hipsters dig the cheeky desert camp aesthetic, lively pool scene, and fair rates. The hotel's restaurant, King's Highway, and bar, the Amigo Room, warrant a stop. 701 E. Palm Canyon Dr. ☎ 760/325-9900. www.acehotel.com/palmsprings. 180 units. Doubles $150–$240. AE, DC, DISC, MC, V.

★★ **The Horizon Hotel** PALM SPRINGS
This low-slung, sharply-angled modernist gem—designed by influential modern architect William Cody (1918–80)—once drew the likes of Marilyn Monroe and Betty Grable. It features chic, minimalist decor, a poolside bar, and luxurious rooms with al fresco showers. 1050 E. Palm Canyon Dr. ☎ 800/377-7855. 22 units. www.thehorizonhotel.com. Doubles $160–$250. AE, MC, V.

★★★ **La Quinta Resort & Club** LA QUINTA
Built as a Hollywood hideaway in 1926 with 20 Spanish-style casitas—Frank Capra called it his "Shangri-La for scriptwriting"—this luxe complex now includes five golf courses, tennis courts, dozens of pools, a huge spa, and bougainvillea-draped grounds. 49499 Eisenhower Dr. ☎ 800/598-3828, 760/564-4111. www.laquintaresort.com. 796 units. Doubles $280–$550. AE, MC, V.

★★★ **Le Parker Meridien Palm Springs** PALM SPRINGS Perhaps the hippest digs in town, this 13-acre property boasts a cheeky aesthetic by designer Jonathan Adler, relaxing grounds, a fabulous spa, two top-notch restaurants, two lively pool areas, and sumptuous rooms with balconies. 4200 E. Palm Canyon Dr. ☎ 760/770-5000. www.theparkerpalmsprings.com. 144 units. Doubles $255–$595. AE, DC, DISC, MC, V.

★★ **Orbit Inn** PALM SPRINGS
Go retro at this 1957-built hotel, which maintains a groovy, midcentury mind-set with stylized rooms (Atomic Paradise, Rat Pack Suite, Leopard Lounge) decked out in vintage pieces (an Eames chair, a Nelson clock). Sip your complimentary "Orbitini" by the pool. 562 W. Arenas Rd. ☎ 760/323-3585. www.orbitin.com. 9 units. Doubles $139–$259. AE, DISC, MC, V.

★★ **Two Bunch Palms** DESERT HOT SPRINGS
Once a hideout for Al Capone, this legendary property prides itself on its air of privacy, natural hot springs, and superb spa treatments. 67-425 Two Bunch Palms Trail. ☎ 760/329 8791. www.twobunchpalms.com. 50 units. Doubles $190–$270. AE, DC, DISC, MC, V.

★★ **Viceroy Palm Springs** PALM SPRINGS
With an eye-popping black, white, and yellow color scheme (designer Kelly Wearstler's over-the-top take on Hollywood Regency), this hotel appeals to the fashionable and the fabulous. 415 S. Belardo Rd. ☎ 800/670-6184, 760/320-4117. www.viceroypalmsprings.com. 68 units. Doubles $190–$270. AE, DC, MC, V.

Where to Dine

> *Cary Grant would approve of the sophisticated elegance of Copley's, housed in his former Spanish hacienda.*

★ **Cheeky's** PALM SPRINGS *BRUNCH*
This bright and friendly brunch spot offers flights of bacon (five different flavors, including jalapeno and dark chocolate), freshly squeezed juices, homemade sausages and pastries, and an ever-changing menu emphasizing local, sustainable ingredients. 622 N. Palm Canyon Dr. ☎ 760/327-7595. www.cheekysps.com. Entrees $8–$14. AE, MC, V. Breakfast & lunch Wed–Mon.

★★ **Copley's** PALM SPRINGS *AMERICAN*
In a Spanish-style hacienda once owned by Cary Grant, this popular restaurant offers courtyard dining and such sophisticated but unstuffy fare as roasted pumpkin ravioli with goat cheese, lobster pot pie, and basil-infused homemade ice cream. 621 N. Palm Canyon Dr. ☎ 760/327-9555. www.copleyspalmsprings. Reservations recommended. Entrees $27–$37. AE, MC, V. Dinner daily Jan–Apr; Tues–Sun May–Dec.

El Mirasol PALM SPRINGS *MEXICAN*
For authentic Mexican food, locals rush to this friendly restaurant with lip-smacking margaritas and such tasty dishes as crab enchiladas, chicken mole, and crispy pork rinds in tomatillo sauce. 140 E. Palm Canyon Dr. ☎ 760/323-0721. Entrees $11–$16. AE, MC, V. Lunch & dinner daily.

★★ **Johannes** PALM SPRINGS *MODERN EUROPEAN* Austrian-born chef Johannes Bacher deftly mixes European classics, Pan-Asian influences, and fresh California ingredients. Standouts include the traditional Wiener schnitzel, rack of lamb, and endive salad. 196 S. Indian Canyon Dr. ☎ 760/778-0017. www.johannes-restaurant.com. Reservations recommended. Entrees $22–$26. AE, MC, V. Lunch & dinner Tues–Sun.

★ **Melvyn's** PALM SPRINGS *AMERICAN*
This restaurant and bar, an old Sinatra staple, is the very definition of old school, and its elegant service makes it the perfect place for a steak and a martini. No hipper-than-thou design makeover here—the faded decor and mirrored walls evoke a feeling of *Dynasty* in the desert. The piano bar, the Casablanca Room, entertains nightly. 200 W. Ramon Rd. ☎ 760/325-2323. www.inglesideinn.com. Entrees $24–$34. AE, DC, DISC, MC, V. Dinner daily, lunch Mon–Fri, brunch Sat–Sun.

★ **Tyler's Burgers** PALM SPRINGS *BURGERS*
Lines are long, and the patio gets packed at this locals' favorite for big, fat, juicy burgers. Round out your meal with creamy potato salad, tangy coleslaw, and cold lemonade or a thick milkshake. 149 S. Indian Canyon Dr. ☎ 760/325-2990. Burgers and sandwiches $7–$9. Cash only. Lunch Mon–Sat.

Where to Shop

> *A reflection of the region's wealth, The Gardens on El Paseo is touted as the "Rodeo Drive of the Desert."*

★ **Bon Vivant** PALM SPRINGS
A fave of designers Jonathan Adler and Trina
Turk, this friendly shop offers a wide range
of vintage decorative accessories, including
midcentury sculptures, '60s-era pottery, and
modernist glass, as well as costume and
estate jewelry. 457 N. Palm Canyon Dr., Ste. 3.
☎ 760/534-3197. www.gmcb.com. AE, MC, V.

★ **Desert Hills Premium Outlets** CABAZON
A popular pit stop for Los Angelenos on the way
to Palm Springs, this huge outlet mall offers savings at 130 stores on merchandise sporting such
names as Prada, Lacoste, Dolce & Gabbana,
Tumi, and Bose. 48400 Seminole Dr. ☎ 951/849-
6641. www.premiumoutlets.com. AE, MC, V.

★ **The Gardens on El Paseo** PALM DESERT
Anchored by Saks Fifth Avenue and Tiffany &
Co., this tasteful outdoor mall and surround-
ing shopping district calls itself the "Rodeo
Drive of the Desert," and although that may be
overselling it, there are plenty of upscale stores
(Williams-Sonoma, Cole Haan, Gucci) to tug at
your wallet. 73-545 El Paseo, Ste. 2500 (within El
Paseo Shopping District). ☎ 760/862-1990.
www.thegardensonelpaseo.com. AE, MC, V.

★★ **ModernWay** PALM SPRINGS
Find groovy midcentury modernist furniture
like Eames lounge chairs, pieces made of
molded Lucite, and conversation-starting
lamps. 745 N. Palm Canyon Dr. ☎ 760/320-5455.
www.psmodernway.com. AE, MC, V.

★ **Retrospect** PALM SPRINGS
This is the go-to place for finely restored
vintage furniture and for Knoll couches and
chairs. 666 N. Palm Canyon Dr., Palm Springs.
☎ 760/416-1766. AE, MC, V.

★ **Trina Turk** PALM SPRINGS
Two Trina Turk shops occupy a 1960s Albert
Frey building. One presents Turk's "California
chic" line of clothing (fun, flowing, brightly patterned resort wear); the other applies her bold
print style to pillows, upholstery, and other
home accessories. 891, 895 N. Palm Canyon Dr.
☎ 760/416-2856. www.trinaturk.com. AE, MC, V.

Ghost Towns

Across Death Valley and the Mojave Desert
there are scores of ghost towns, places
where a community sprang up quickly
around a mining operation (silver, gold,
borax, quicksilver), then just as quickly
collapsed. **Calico Ghost Town** (☎ 760/254-
2122; www.calicotown.com; $6 adults, $3
children) is the most commercialized of the
lot, with its billboards blanketing the roadside from Los Angeles to Las Vegas, but kids
love it. For a more "authentic" representa-
tion of the Old West a century or more ago,
scope out nuggets like **Cerro Gordo, Darwin,
Leadfield,** and **Ballarat.**

Fast Facts

American Express

In **Palm Springs**, obtain American Express travel services at Anderson Travel Service, 1801 E. Tahquitz Canyon Way, Ste. 100 (☎ 760/325-2001; www.travelanderson.com; Mon–Fri 9am–5pm).

Dentists & Doctors

For a dental recommendation, call **1-800-DENTIST** (☎ 800/336-8422; www.1800dentist.com). For medical treatment, see "Emergencies," below.

Emergencies

Call ☎ **911** toll-free from any phone to report a fire, call the police, or get an ambulance. Be aware that cellphones do not always work according to plan in the remote desert. If you plan on long excursions into these areas, talk to your provider about coverage, or consider using a satellite phone.

For nonemergency police matters, in **Palm Springs**, call ☎ 760/323-8116; in **Twentynine Palms**, call 760/367-9546; in the **Coachella Valley**, call ☎ 951/955-2400; and in **Death Valley**, call ☎ 760/786-2238.

In the **greater Palm Springs area**, seek medical assistance at the Desert Region Medical Center, 1150 N. Indian Canyon Dr., Palm Springs (☎ 760/323-6511; www.desertmedctr.com).

In **Twentynine Palms** and the **north Joshua Tree** area, seek medical assistance at Hi-Desert Medical Center, 6601 White Feather Rd., Joshua Tree (☎ 760/366-3711; www.hdmc.org).

In **Death Valley**, seek medical assistance at the Death Valley Health Clinic, Hwy. 127, Shoshone (☎ 760/852-4383).

Getting There

BY PLANE The closest airport is **Palm Springs International Airport,** 3400 E. Tahquitz Canyon Way (tel. 760/323-8161), just 2 miles east of downtown Palm Springs. Car rentals are readily available at the airport. Some visitors to Mojave and Death Valley opt to fly into Las Vegas, Nevada, and drive in from there. BY CAR To get to **Palm Springs** from Los Angeles, take I-10 east to the Hwy. 111 turnoff to Palm Springs; it's nearly 2 hours, depending on traffic. From San Diego, take I-15 north to I-215 and pick up I-10 east; it takes a bit more than 2 hours.

To get to **Joshua Tree** from Los Angeles, it's roughly a 2½-hour journey. Take I-10 to Hwy. 62, and head northeast to the park entrances near Joshua Tree and Twentynine Palms. You can also enter the park's southern entrance off I-20 at Cottonwood Springs, 25 miles east of Indio. Admission to the park is $15 per car (good for 7 days).

If you're headed for **Mojave National Preserve**, I-15, the well-traveled highway from Los Angeles to Las Vegas, runs along the northern boundary of the preserve, while I-40 runs along the southern boundary. Amboy Road runs north to the preserve from Joshua Tree.

A scenic drive into **Death Valley** is via Hwy. 190, east of Hwy. 178 from Ridgecrest. Another scenic drive is via Hwy. 127 and Hwy. 190 from Baker. The $15-per-car entrance fee is valid for 7 days.

To get to **Anza-Borrego Desert State Park** and the Coachella Valley, go south on Hwy. 86 to Salton City, then west on Hwy. S22 into Borrego Springs.

Getting Around

Cars are the best way to get around in the desert. Public transportation is practically nonexistent.

The downtown **Palm Springs** area runs along North Palm Canyon Drive for a half-mile or so, between Alejo and Ramon streets. Palm Canyon splits into South Palm Canyon, which runs toward Indian Canyons, and East Palm Canyon, which becomes Hwy. 111 and travels past the towns of Palm Desert and La Quinta. To reach Desert Hot Springs from Palm Springs, head north up Gene Autry Trail.

In the desert parks, four-wheel-drive vehicles are a big help, allowing you to access some of the rougher and more interesting roads.

Hospital

See "Emergencies," above.

Internet Access

Most hotels and resorts in the greater Palm Springs area have Wi-Fi, often free of charge.

Wireless access in the desert parks, however, is extremely difficult to find.

Pharmacies

A centrally located pharmacy in **Palm Springs** is **Rite Aid**, 366 South Palm Canyon Rd. (☎ 760/325-2326; Mon–Fri 9am–9pm, Sat 9am–6pm, Sun 10am–6pm).

Post Office

In **Palm Springs**, a post office is at 333 E. Amado Rd. (☎ 760/322-4111; Mon–Fri 8am–5pm, Sat 9am–3pm). For more information, including other post offices in the area, go to www.usps.com.

Safety

It bears repeating: Do not underestimate the raw power of the sun in the desert. Daytime temperatures can top 120°F in the summer. Protect yourself with loose clothing, hats, and sunscreen, and remember to stay hydrated. Hiking and other physical activities are best done in the morning, when temperatures are markedly cooler than later in the day. Yet winter nights can drop below freezing and can be dangerous for unprepared campers.

If you plan on driving off-road, make sure your vehicle is up to the task—you'll need four-wheel drive in many places. Be sure to pack a spare tire and maps.

The desert encourages a sense of adventure, but do not enter abandoned mine shafts or approach wildlife, especially rattlesnakes and scorpions.

If you do plan on camping or making an excursion into a remote area, travel with a partner, or at least inform someone (preferably a ranger) of your plans.

Taxes

Sales tax in San Bernardino, Riverside, and Inyo counties is 8.75%. Hotel tax is charged on the room tariff only (which is not subject to sales tax) and ranges from 11.5% to 13.5% in the Palm Springs area.

Visitor Information

The excellent **Palm Springs Visitors Information Center**, 2901 N. Palm Canyon Dr., Palm Springs (☎ 800/347-7746; www.visitpalm springs.com), offers maps, brochures, advice, and souvenirs. It's open Monday through Saturday from 9am to 5pm, and Sunday 8am to 4pm.

Joshua Tree National Park has three visitor centers: the Oasis Visitor Center (☎ 760/367-5500) at the Twentynine Palms entrance, Cottonwood Visitor Center at the south entrance, and the privately owned Park Center near the west entrance. The Oasis Visitor Center is open daily (except Dec. 25) from 8am to 5pm, and offers maps and schedules of ranger-guided walks. For information before you go, visit www.nps.gov/jotr.

In **Mojave National Preserve**, go to the Kelso Depot Visitor Center (☎ 760/252-6108), which is open daily 9am to 5pm. You can also go to the Hole-in-the-Wall Visitor Center (☎ 760/928-2572), open 9am to 4pm Wednesday to Sunday for most of the year, Friday to Sunday in summer. You can visit the preserve online at www.nps.gov/moja.

The Furnace Creek Visitor Center & Museum (☎ 760/786-3200) is located 15 miles inside the eastern park boundary of **Death Valley National Park** on CA-190. The center is open daily from 8am to 6pm in summer (to 5pm in winter). For camping and road information before you go, visit www.nps.gov/deva.

The **Anza-Borrego Desert State Park Visitor Center** (☎ 760/767-4205; www.parks. ca.gov) is just west of the town of Borrego Springs, at 200 Palm Canyon Drive. It offers information and maps, plus a great selection of guidebooks for sale. It's open October through May daily from 9am to 5pm, June through September weekends from 9am to 5pm. For information before you go, visit www.parks.ca.gov.

13
San Diego

Our Favorite San Diego Moments

If you think San Diego is just about wiggling your toes in the sand or cooing over cuddly panda bears, think again. Combining big-city style with small-town heart, this seaside destination offers an embarrassment of riches: stunning natural beauty, high-octane nightlife, world-class cultural organizations, family-friendly attractions, and sophisticated dining. Oh, did I mention it has the country's best weather as well? San Diego is also perched on the world's busiest international border, with the sights, sounds, and tastes of Mexico just a Chihuahua's length away.

> PREVIOUS PAGE *Mission Bay's Fiesta Island is a popular place for staging outdoor events, including cool bonfires.* THIS PAGE *Making a point, Cabrillo National Monument recounts San Diego's rich history.*

❶ Escaping to Torrey Pines State Reserve. Dramatically set atop 300-foot cliffs overlooking the Pacific, this reserve is home to the rarest pine tree in North America. Short trails crisscross the delicate landscape, which also incorporates one of San Diego's best beaches. See p. 626, ❶.

❷ Taking in the city's best panorama. Cabrillo National Monument not only offers a whirlwind history tour, beginning with San Diego's European discovery in 1542, but it also provides unsurpassed 360-degree views of downtown and beyond. From its location at the tip of Point Loma—and at 422 feet above sea level—it's also a great vantage point from which to watch migrating Pacific gray whales in the winter. See p. 574, ❶.

❸ Communing with seals and sea lions. The Children's Pool, a picturesque cove in La Jolla, was named for the toddlers who could safely frolic behind its protective, man-made seawall. A colony of pinnipeds came to like it equally, and now the beach is shared—sometimes a little uneasily—between humans and seals. See p. 595, ❸.

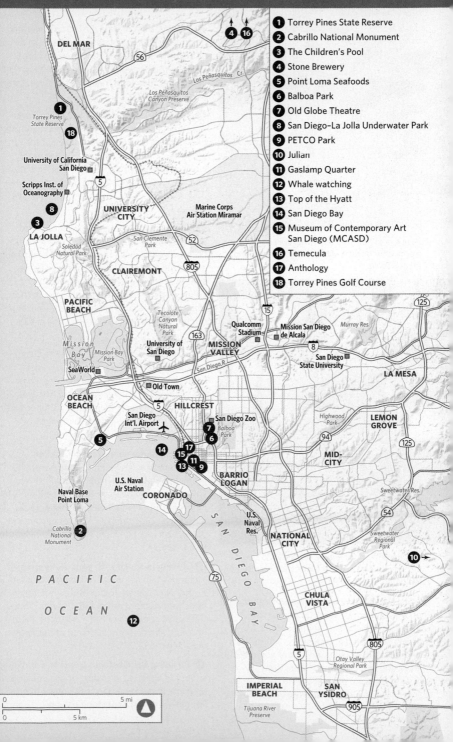

1 Torrey Pines State Reserve
2 Cabrillo National Monument
3 The Children's Pool
4 Stone Brewery
5 Point Loma Seafoods
6 Balboa Park
7 Old Globe Theatre
8 San Diego–La Jolla Underwater Park
9 PETCO Park
10 Julian
11 Gaslamp Quarter
12 Whale watching
13 Top of the Hyatt
14 San Diego Bay
15 Museum of Contemporary Art San Diego (MCASD)
16 Temecula
17 Anthology
18 Torrey Pines Golf Course

> *People aren't the only ones who love La Jolla's warm, clear waters—look for seals, whales, and other wildlife.*

> *Buzzing with young energy, the Gaslamp Quarter has over 40 bars and nightclubs, many in restored Victorians.*

4 Quaffing locally brewed beer. With more than 30 local breweries producing a myriad of fabulous suds, it's no wonder *Men's Journal* has proclaimed San Diego as America's number-one beer city. And no brewer in the county does it better than Stone Brewery, whose stylish and elegant World Bistro and Gardens is San Diego's ultimate beer-drinking destination. See p. 623.

5 Tasting a bit of Baja. Fish tacos migrated north from the fishing towns of Baja California to become San Diego's signature fast food. Drop by the dockside seafood emporium Point Loma Seafoods for a fresh-off-the-boat, tangy treat. See p. 613.

6 Spending an idyllic day in Balboa Park. This is one of the world's great urban cultural parks, home to more than a dozen of the city's top museums. There are dazzling gardens, glorious Spanish colonial revival architecture, and the world-famous San Diego Zoo as well. Balboa Park is San Diego's crown jewel. See p. 582.

7 Being a groundling. You won't have to stand like they did in William Shakespeare's day, but you can see the Bard's works alfresco at the Old Globe Theatre's summer Shakespeare Festival. The Tony Award–winning Old Globe performs Shakespeare's work in true repertory style, alternating three different productions at its open-air theater. See p. 625.

8 Paddling with the fishes. The calm surfaces and clear waters of the San Diego–La Jolla Underwater Park are the ultimate local spot for some kayaking or snorkeling. This ecological reserve features sea caves and vibrant marine life, including California's state marine fish, the electric-orange garibaldi. See p. 596.

9 Buying some peanuts and Cracker Jacks. San Diego's Major League Baseball team, the Padres, plays at PETCO Park, a state-of-the-art ballpark that opened in 2004. Incorporating seven buildings that date as far back as 1909, PETCO's clever design and downtown location have made it a fan favorite. See p. 624.

10 Getting in touch with your pioneer spirit. The mountain hamlet of Julian was founded as a gold-mining town in the 1860s, but it gained fame for another mother lode: apples. Today, this rustic community has a distinctly Victorian, Old West charm, redolent of hot apple pies. See p. 632.

11 Strolling the Gaslamp Quarter. For dining, shopping, dancing, drinking, or just soaking up some local flavor, this is the place to be. People-watching opportunities abound—if you can manage to take your eyes off the exquisitely restored Victorian commercial buildings in this 16½-block district. See p. 590.

12 Scouting for whales. Every year, from December through March, Pacific gray whales pass through San Diego waters, making their way to and from breeding lagoons in Mexico. There are ample opportunities to observe these gentle giants from both land and sea as they undertake one of the longest migrations of any mammal. See p. 600.

13 Watching for the green flash. There's no better place to watch for the storied "green flash"—which occurs when the sun sinks beneath the horizon—than the Top of the Hyatt. This luxe lounge is located 40 stories above the Embarcadero in the West Coast's tallest waterfront building. See p. 624.

14 Cruising the bay. Whether it's a weekend-brunch sightseeing tour, a chartered sailboat excursion, or just a water-taxi ride to Coronado, don't miss an opportunity to spend some time on San Diego Bay. Spanish conquistador Sebastián Vizcaíno described it in 1602 as "a port which must be the best to be found in all the South Sea." Discover it for yourself. See p. 637.

15 Challenging your perception. The city's most important museum is the Museum of Contemporary Art San Diego (MCASD). With a flagship space in La Jolla and two downtown annexes, this internationally prominent museum offers ongoing exhibitions of cutting-edge art, as well as a roster of special events. A visit to any of MCASD's facilities is guaranteed to be a thought-provoking experience. See p. 594, **2**.

> *Introducing new ideas throughout its galleries, Museum of Contemporary Art San Diego aims to challenge conventions.*

16 Toasting the good life. Just across the county line in Temecula, about 60 miles north of downtown San Diego, are some two-dozen wineries. They range from mom-and-pop operations with minimal amenities to slick commercial ventures with fancy tasting rooms, retail boutiques, and restaurants. Cheers. See p. 631.

17 Eating to the beat. Architecturally smashing, culinarily superb, and musically sophisticated, Anthology is a fine-dining restaurant masquerading as an acoustically excellent concert venue. Or is it the other way around? Anthology hosts top-name jazz, world music, blues, and rock artists, and you don't have to eat dinner to see the show (but you'd miss out on half the fun). See p. 609.

18 Swinging by the sea. Torrey Pines Golf Course is one of the country's most scenic links. Featuring lots of sea-facing play, it's home to the annual PGA Tour's Farmers Insurance Open and was the setting for a memorable U.S. Open in 2008. Come play with the legends. See p. 581.

The Best of San Diego in 1 Day

If you have only 24 hours in San Diego, you may be tempted to spend the whole day on the beach or at the zoo. While it's hard to argue with that approach, it would deprive you of experiencing San Diego's colorful cultural heritage as the birthplace of California, with deep ties to Spain, Mexico, and Wild West history. Besides, you'll still get plenty of sun as you tour through Old Town, and you just might hear the animals squawk and roar from the zoo as you explore Balboa Park next door.

> *Look up in Balboa Park, and you're bound to see Spanish colonial revival–style buildings that are the park's signature.*

START Blue or Green Line trolley to Old Town Transit Center.

SITE GUIDE PAGE 572

❶ ★ Old Town State Historic Park. Dedicated to re-creating the early life of the city from 1821 to 1872, this is where San Diego's frontier heritage is best celebrated. It's California's most-visited state park, featuring 20 structures (some original, some reconstructed), restaurants, shops, and reenactments of life in the 1800s by costumed volunteers.

❷ ★★★ kids Balboa Park. New York has Central Park, San Francisco has Golden Gate Park—San Diego's crown jewel is Balboa Park, a 1,174-acre city-owned playground and the largest urban cultural park in the nation. The park's most distinctive features are its mature landscaping, the architectural beauty of the Spanish colonial revival–style buildings lining the pedestrian thoroughfare (byproducts of expositions in 1915 and 1935), and its 15 engaging and diverse museums. You'll also find eight different gardens, walkways, 4½ miles of hiking trails in Florida Canyon, an ornate pavilion with the world's largest outdoor organ, an old-fashioned carousel,

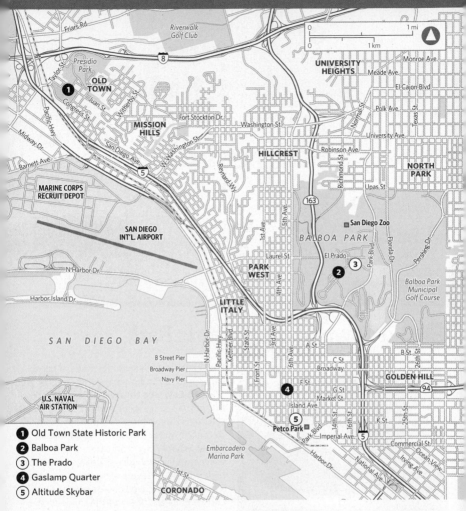

1 Old Town State Historic Park
2 Balboa Park
3 The Prado
4 Gaslamp Quarter
5 Altitude Skybar

an IMAX domed theater, the acclaimed Old Globe Theatre, and the San Diego Zoo. ⏱ At least 3 hr. Primary entrances are at Sixth Ave. and Laurel St. on the west side and Park Blvd. and Presidents Way on the east side. ☎ 619/239-0512. www.balboapark.org. Museum prices vary; several are free on Tues (check the website for the schedule). Free organ concerts Sun 2pm and Mon–Thurs 7:30pm in summer. Free and for a fee self-guided tours are available from the Visitor Center daily 9:30am–4:30pm (extended hours in summer). Attraction hours vary, but many are 10am–5pm. Bus: 1, 3, 7, or 120; a free tram operates within the park daily 8:30am–6pm (extended hours in summer).

③ 🍴 **The Prado.** Balboa Park's sophisticated but casual Prado restaurant is a great place to catch your breath and set a spell. This sprawling restaurant complex located in the baroque House of Hospitality has lovely patio dining and a lounge where you can often find live entertainment in the evening. 1549 El Prado. ☎ 619/ 557-9441. www.cohn restaurants.com. Entrees $11–$30.

❹ ★★ **Gaslamp Quarter.** Where others had seen only dismal mudflats melting into a shallow bay, businessman Alonzo Horton (1813–1909) saw untapped potential. In 1867 he undertook an audacious plan to lure citizens

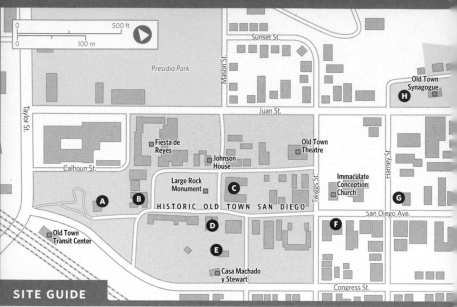

Sunset St.

Presidio Park

Mason St.

Old Town Synagogue

Juan St.

Taylor St.

Fiesta de Reyes

Johnson House

Old Town Theatre

Harney St.

Twiggs St.

Calhoun St.

Large Rock Monument

Immaculate Conception Church

 HISTORIC OLD TOWN SAN DIEGO

San Diego Ave.

Old Town Transit Center

Casa Machado y Stewart

Congress St.

SITE GUIDE

❶ Old Town State Historic Park

The park's interpretive center is in the **ⓐ McCoy House,** a historically accurate reproduction of the home of James McCoy, a larger-than-life lawman/legislator who lived on this site until the devastating fire of 1872, and is also the starting point for free daily guided walking tours of the park (time: 1 hr.). An original adobe building from 1827, **ⓑ Robinson-Rose House** has a large model of Old Town the way it looked prior to 1872 and is also the starting point for free daily guided walking tours of the park (time: 1 hr.). **ⓒ La Casa de Estudillo,** was the home of a wealthy family and is representative of upper-class living of

the era; the patio covering is made of corraza cane, from seeds brought by Father Serra in 1769. **ⓓ Colorado House** was San Diego's original two-story hotel and is now home to the Wells Fargo Museum with exhibits on the overland express business. The **ⓔ Mason Street School** was commissioned by San Diego's first mayor, Joshua Bean, in 1865 and built from the leftovers of house construction (note the mismatched boards inside). Grab a cup of coffee and enjoy a little shade on the patio of the **ⓕ Living Room Cafe & Bistro** before exploring the **ⓖ Whaley House,** the first two-story brick structure in Southern California—it's furnished with lovely period furniture and is said to be haunted by multiple spirits. Finally, don't miss **ⓗ Heritage Park;** there are seven buildings of varying Victorian architectural styles in this grassy canyon, moved here from other parts of the city. They now function as a B&B, stores, offices, and a teahouse. ⏱ 1½ hr. The park is bordered by Juan, Congress, Twiggs & Wallace sts. ☎ 619/220-5422. www. parks.ca.gov. Free admission to state park sites; Whaley House $6 adults, $4 ages 3–12. Museums daily 10am–5pm; most restaurants till 9pm. Trolley: Blue or Green Line to Old Town.

> *Nighttime is the right time at the Gaslamp Quarter; it's especially lively after games at nearby Petco Park.*

away from Old Town with the founding of "New Town," several miles to the south. New Town is now known as the Gaslamp Quarter, and it has become more successful than anything Alonzo could have ever hoped for. It comprises 16½ blocks of restored historic buildings housing dozens of restaurants, bars, clubs, and boutiques—this is where you'll find San Diego's most vigorous nightlife, fabulous Victorian and Edwardian architecture, and excellent people-watching. PETCO Park, the San Diego Padres' state-of-the-art stadium, also cozies up to the Gaslamp Quarter and features seven historic structures melded into the design. You can begin your tour of the area at Horton Plaza shopping mall, where you can not only shop and dine, but also catch a play or a movie. ⏰ At least 1½ hr. The district is bordered by Broadway on the north, L St. and the waterfront to the south, Fourth Ave. to the west, and Sixth Ave. to the east. Gaslamp Quarter Association ☎ 619/233-5227. www.gaslamp.org. Mall stores Mon–Fri generally 10am–9pm, Sat 10am–8pm, Sun 11am–7pm; independent stores generally Mon–Thurs 11am–7 or 8pm, Fri–Sat 10am–8 or 9pm, Sun 11am–6 or

7pm. Restaurants usually Sun–Thurs till 10pm, longer hours Fri–Sat. Bars generally till 2am daily; most clubs till 2am Thurs–Sat. Crowds are thick Thurs–Sat and whenever there's a large convention in town or a baseball game at PETCO Park. Parking structures are available (for a fee) at Horton Plaza, Market St. & Sixth Ave., and Sixth Ave. & K St. Trolley: Orange Line. Bus: Any downtown route.

⑤　🍸 **Altitude Skybar.** Finish off your day by rising above it all for a nightcap at this open-air bar 22 floors above the Gaslamp commotion. This long, narrow space is located in the Gaslamp Quarter Marriott and looks down on PETCO Park and the Convention Center. It offers fire pits, lounges, and DJ-spun grooves, as well as appetizers from the first-floor restaurant. As with many Gaslamp Quarter venues, lines begin forming around 10pm on weekends (or whenever the Padres are playing). 660 K St. (btw. Sixth & Seventh Aves.). ☎ 619/696-0234. www.altitudeskybar.com.

The Best of San Diego in 2 Days

You don't have to venture far to find stunning natural settings in San Diego, which means it's easy to season your outdoor recreation with a little history, great food, and even some shopping. You'll really need your sunscreen on your second day in town—this itinerary showcases the extremes of So Cal coastal living, from rollicking Pacific Beach to refined La Jolla. A car is in order too. While it is possible to tackle this itinerary via public transportation, it's much more practical to have your own set of wheels.

> Pinch yourself—it really is that perfect at La Jolla Cove, where photo-op sunsets are as common as waves.

START Bus route 84 to Cabrillo National Monument.

1 ★★★ kids **Cabrillo National Monument.** Breathtaking views mingle with the early history of San Diego, specifically the arrival of Juan Rodríguez Cabrillo (1499–1543), a Portuguese conquistador in the employ of Spain, who sailed into San Diego Bay in 1542. His statue is prominently featured here, along with a historic lighthouse built in 1855, a small museum, the remnants of World War II artillery batteries, a visitor center with lots of books and souvenirs for sale, and a theater screening short videos about local natural history and the age of exploration.

The park's setting 422 feet above sea level at the tip of Point Loma makes it a great vantage point for watching migrating Pacific gray

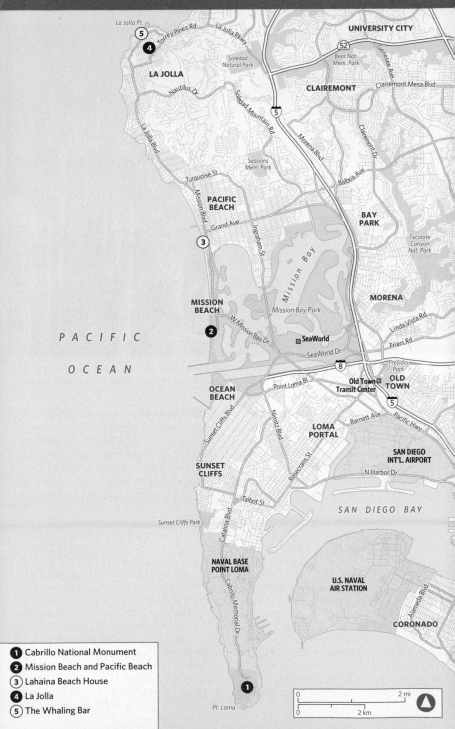

UNIVERSITY CITY

LA JOLLA

CLAIREMONT

Soledad
Natural Park

Bear Nat.
Mem. Park

La Jolla Pt.
5
4
Torrey Pines Rd.
La Jolla Pkwy.
52
Genesee Ave.

Nautilus Dr.
Clairemont Mesa Blvd.

La Jolla Blvd.
Soledad Mountain Rd.
5
Clairemont Dr.

BAY
PARK

Turquoise St.
*Sessions
Mem. Park*
Morena Blvd.
Balboa Ave.

PACIFIC
BEACH

Grand Ave.
Ingraham St.

Mission Blvd.
3

*Tecolote
Canyon
Nat. Park*

Mission Bay

MORENA

MISSION
BEACH

Mission Bay Park
2
W. Mission Bay Dr.
Linda Vista Rd.

PACIFIC

OCEAN

SeaWorld
SeaWorld Dr.
Friars Rd.

8
*Presidio
Park*
OCEAN
BEACH
Point Loma Bl.
Old Town
Transit Center
OLD
TOWN
5

Sunset Cliffs Blvd.
Nimitz Blvd.
LOMA
PORTAL
Barnett Ave.
Pacific Hwy.

SUNSET
CLIFFS
Rosecrans St.
SAN DIEGO
INT'L. AIRPORT

Catalina Blvd.
Talbot St.
N. Harbor Dr.

Sunset Cliffs Park
SAN DIEGO BAY

NAVAL BASE
POINT LOMA

U.S. NAVAL
AIR STATION
Alameda Blvd.

Cabrillo Memorial Dr.
CORONADO

1
Pt. Loma

1 Cabrillo National Monument
2 Mission Beach and Pacific Beach
3 Lahaina Beach House
4 La Jolla
5 The Whaling Bar

0   2 mi
0   2 km

> *Etching a noble profile against the sky, Juan Cabrillo's statue stands at the very mouth of San Diego Bay.*

> *Shake, rattle, and roll—and maybe scream a little—on the 1925 classic wooden roller coaster at Belmont Park.*

whales December through March. National Park Service rangers also lead walks at the monument, and there are tide pools to explore at the base of the peninsula. The Bayside Trail is an easy hike (3.2 miles round-trip) along an interpreted walkway that leads to a lookout over the bay. There are great places for picnicking here, but no food facilities, so pack a lunch.

At Fort Rosecrans National Cemetery, located just before you reach the park entrance, you can pay your respects to those who served. Remains interred here date back to 1846, and with its row upon row of gleaming white headstones and sweeping ocean vistas, this is a very moving and inspirational place. ⏱ 2 hr. 1800 Cabrillo Memorial Dr. ☎ 619/557-5450. www.nps.gov/cabr. Admission $5 per vehicle (valid for 7 days). Daily 9am–5pm. Fort Rosecrans National Cemetery ☎ 619/553-2084. www.cem.va.gov. Mon–Fri 8am–4:30pm; Sat–Sun 9:30am–5pm. Bus: Route 28 from Old Town Transit Center, transfer to Route 84 at Shelter Island.

❷ kids **Mission Beach and Pacific Beach.** This is it—ground zero for the party hearty, free-wheeling Southern California beach lifestyle. These two beaches form a 3-mile stretch of sand paralleled by a cement boardwalk that hosts a nonstop parade of surfers, skaters, bikers, joggers, and plain old beach lovers. South Mission Beach is where you'll find serious beach volleyball and a seaside basketball court.

Farther north is **Belmont Park,** an amusement park whose star attraction is a 1925 wooden roller coaster; the park also includes Wave House, a self-described "royal palace of youth culture" that features wave machines for surfers of all levels; bars; DJs; and live music. Another 1925 holdover is **Crystal Pier** at the foot of Garnet Avenue in Pacific Beach (or P.B. as it's known). This 400-foot-long wooden pier now supports rental cottages, but is open daily to the public, offering great views of local surfers.

The street-side action in these beach zones takes place primarily on Mission Boulevard

> Take the sun, surf, and sand in stride along the car-free paths of Mission Beach Park.

(heading north from Belmont Park) and Garnet Avenue (running east from Mission Blvd.), which are both overflowing with restaurants, clubs, and retailers. Rent a bike and join the parade. ⏱ At least 3 hr. Discover Pacific Beach, ☎ 858/273-3303. www.pacificbeach.org. Beaches daily 24 hr. (overnight sleeping not permitted). Belmont Park, 3190 Mission Blvd. ☎ 858/488-1549. www.giantdipper.com. Unlimited rides $23; wave rides start at $25. Hours vary seasonally, usually daily 11am–8pm. Cheap Rentals, 3689 Mission Blvd. ☎ 800/941-7761 or 858/488-9070. www.cheap-rentals.com. Bike rentals start at $7 per hour. Bus: Route 8 from Old Town Transit Center.

③ 🍺 **Lahaina Beach House.** This old beach bungalow transformed into a simple, unpretentious, utterly rocking dive bar and eatery, has been a Pacific Beach institution for a generation. Its weathered wooden deck, just inches from the boardwalk, is standing room only on sunny weekends, and provides a sensory overload of sights and sounds. The food is basic—omelets, burgers, fish tacos; the atmosphere is pure beach party. Cash only. 710 Oliver Ave. (along the boardwalk btw. Reed Ave. & Pacific Beach Dr.). ☎ 858/270-3888. Entrees $7–$11.

④ ★★★ **La Jolla.** About the only thing La Jolla **shares** in common with the beach communities to the south is the Pacific Ocean. Locals refer to La Jolla's principal shopping and dining district as "the Village," and it's one of the classiest villages you could imagine. High-end boutiques, antiques stores, art galleries, and fine restaurants line the streets; while just steps away, a dramatic coastline of sandstone cliffs and picturesque coves with tropical-blue waters awaits. And this beauty has brains, too—La Jolla is a center for local arts and culture, providing a home for the University of California, San Diego (where you'll find the Tony Award–winning La Jolla Playhouse, p.625; and the Stuart Collection of site-specific art); the flagship space for the Museum of Contemporary Art San Diego (p. 594, ❷); and the Athenaeum Music and Arts Library (p. 597, ❾), which presents concerts and art exhibits. ⏱ At least 3 hr. www.lajollabythesea.com. ☎ 858/454-5718. Bus: Route 30 from Mission Blvd. and Grand Ave. in P.B.

⑤ 🍺 ★ **The Whaling Bar.** La Valencia Hotel is the grande dame of La Jolla. The Pink Lady originally opened in 1926, and its Mediterranean style and killer location made it a favorite of Hollywood golden age celebs like Greta Garbo and Charlie Chaplin. The hotel's clubby watering hole, the Whaling Bar, became something of a West Coast Algonquin for literary types, as well as a popular spot for a second generation of movie stars brought in by La Jolla native Gregory Peck, who also cofounded the La Jolla Playhouse. Stop in for a drink and listen closely—you just might hear those walls talking. In La Valencia Hotel, 1132 Prospect St. (at Herschel Ave.). ☎ 800/451-0772 or 858/454-0771. www.lavalencia.com.

The Best of San Diego in 3 Days

Now that you have an overview of the city—from its Spanish-colonial and Mexican-American frontier roots to its high-octane nightlife and lively, lovely beach communities—it's time to go where the wild things are. Put on a pair of comfortable shoes on Day 3 and head out to San Diego's best-known attraction, the San Diego Zoo. Then cap your day with a stroll along the scenic waterfront and a visit to the area's most iconic structure, the Hotel del Coronado.

> *The small but nimble Klipspringer antelope, native to Africa, is just one of many exotic species that call the San Diego Zoo home.*

START Bus 7 to the San Diego Zoo.

❶ ★★★ kids **San Diego Zoo.** "World famous" often precedes any mention of the San Diego Zoo, and for good reason. Established in 1916, the zoo was a pioneer in developing naturalistic, humane enclosures; it's also a global leader in endangered species preservation thanks to its breeding programs. The zoo's most recent addition is Elephant Odyssey, featuring a herd of Asian elephants, as well as life-size replicas of prehistoric animals that roamed the San Diego region. Other highlights include adorable giant pandas (this is one of only four zoos in the country with pandas in residence); Monkey Trails and Forest Tales, which re-creates a wooded forest filled with a variety of rare creatures; the renovated Polar Bear Plunge, home to a family of polar bears, and Gorilla Tropics, housing two troops of

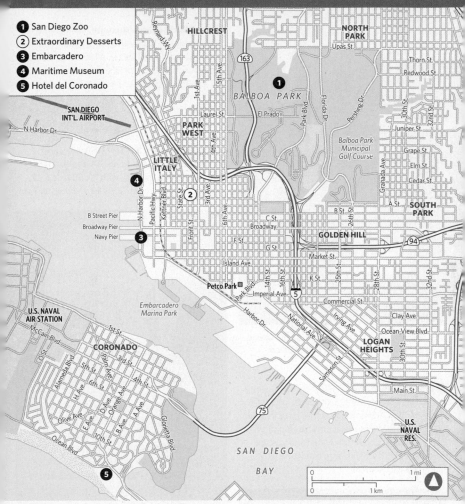

1. San Diego Zoo
2. Extraordinary Desserts
3. Embarcadero
4. Maritime Museum
5. Hotel del Coronado

lowland gorillas. Also notable are Ituri Forest, which simulates an African rainforest (complete with hippos underwater viewed via a wall of glass), and the ever-popular Children's Zoo, featuring lots of pettable animals. ⏲ At least 3 hr. 2920 Zoo Dr. ☎ 619/234-3153 (recorded info) or 619/231-1515. www.sandiegozoo.org. Admission $29 adults, $19 children 3–11, free for children 2 & under and active military (U.S. and foreign). Best Value package (admission, 35-min. guided bus tour, round-trip Skyfari aerial tram) $35 adults, $31 seniors, $26 children. Sept to mid-June daily 9am–4pm (grounds close at 5 or 6pm); mid-June to Aug daily 9am–8pm (grounds close at 9pm). Bus: 7.

2 🍽 ★★★ **Extraordinary Desserts.** After all the walking you've done, even the most demanding diet plan will surely allow for a sinful creation from this local standout. Set in an architecturally striking space, Extraordinary Desserts also serves panini, salads, and artisan cheeses, as well as wine and beer. Chef/proprietor Karen Krasne sells her own line of jams, confections, and syrups, too, if you want to take a taste of San Diego home. 1430 Union St. ☎ 619/294-7001. www.extraordinarydesserts.com. Entrees $2–$15. See p. 610.

> *Go down under at the Maritime Museum, where you can roam around inside a Cold War–era submarine.*

❸ Embarcadero. Take a leisurely stroll along San Diego's waterfront. Sights include the Art Deco County Administration building, fronted by the beautiful granite sculpture *Guardian of Water,* and the collection of historic vessels that make up the San Diego Maritime Museum (**❹**). ⏱ 30 min.

Taking the Ferry to Coronado Island

Ferries to Coronado Island depart from the Broadway Pier, 1050 N. Harbor Dr., at the intersection of Broadway (☎ 800/442-7847 or 619/234-4111; www.sdhe.com). Ferries run Sunday to Thursday on the hour from 9am to 9pm; Friday and Saturday until 10pm. They return from the Ferry Landing in Coronado to the Broadway Pier Sunday to Thursday every hour on the half-hour 9:30am–9:30pm; Friday and Saturday until 10:30pm. The ride takes 15 minutes and the fare is $3.50 each way. Buy tickets at the Harbor Excursion kiosk on Broadway Pier or at the Ferry Landing in Coronado. Ferries do not accommodate cars.

❹ ★★ kids Maritime Museum. This flotilla of classic ships is led by the full-rigged merchant vessel *Star of India* (1863), a National Historic Landmark and the world's oldest ship that still goes to sea. Other vessels include the HMS *Surprise,* which played a supporting role to Russell Crowe in the film *Master and Commander,* and a Cold War–era Soviet submarine. You can board and tour each vessel. ⏱ 1 hr. 1492 N. Harbor Dr. ☎ 619/234-9153. www.sdmaritime.org. Admission $14 adults; $11 seniors and active military with ID; $8 kids 6–17; free for kids 5 & under. Daily 9am–8pm (till 9pm

San Diego Missions

If you have some extra time in the city, take in the **Mission Basilica San Diego de Alcala.** The first link in a chain of 21 California missions, it was founded by Spanish priest Junípero Serra in 1769. It was moved from Presidio Hill above Old Town to its present Mission Valley site in 1774, and it remains an active Catholic parish. The mission is at 10818 San Diego Mission Rd. (☎ 619/281-8449. www.missionsandiego.com). Admission is $3 for adults, $2 for seniors and students, $1 for kids 11 and under; admission is free Sunday and for daily masses. It's open daily 9am to 4:45pm.

In the North County, Oceanside's **Mission San Luis Rey de Francia** (above) reigns as the "King of the Missions." Founded in 1798, it's California's largest mission; in its cemetery you'll find the names of some of the state's most important early families. The mission is at 4050 Mission Ave. (☎ 760/757-3651. www.sanluisrey.org). Admission is $6 adults, $5 seniors and military, $4 for ages 6–18, and free for kids 5 and under. It's open daily 10am to 4pm.

> *The grande dame of California coastal lodgings, the 1888 Hotel del Coronado borders an impeccable beach.*

in summer). Bus: 2, 210, 810, 820, 850, 860, 923, or 992. Trolley: County Center/Little Italy.

5 ★★★ **Hotel del Coronado.** This is the last of California's stately old seaside hotels. In continuous operation since 1888, the Hotel Del is a monument to Victorian grandeur, boasting cupolas, turrets, and gingerbread trim, making it San Diego's most recognizable property.

There is plenty here to engage a nonguest, including a gallery devoted to the hotel's history, a shopping arcade, and several wonderful options for drinks or dining—not to mention the fact the hotel sits on one of San Diego's best beaches. ⏱ 1 hr. 1500 Orange Ave., Coronado. ☎ 800/468-3533 or 619/435-6611. www.hoteldel.com. Bus: 904 from the Ferry Landing.

Tee Time

If you're more interested in birdies and eagles than pandas and elephants, a morning on one of the country's most beautiful golf courses might be the perfect option for you. **Torrey Pines Golf Course,** perched on the coastal cliffs between La Jolla and Del Mar, is the home of the PGA Tour's Farmers Insurance Open every January or February and is second only to Pebble Beach as the state's top golf destination. This municipal course features two 18-hole championship links (the South Course is considered more challenging), and tee times can be reserved 8 to 90 days in advance (☎ 877/581-7171; $39 booking fee). For reservations up to 7 days advance call ☎ 619/570-1234. Greens fees on the South Course are $160 weekdays and $200 weekends; the North Course is $90 weekdays and $113 weekends. For information about club rentals or lessons (which

guarantee you a spot on the course) call ☎ 800/985-4653 or log onto www.torrey pinesgolfcourse.com.

If you're looking for a golf outing closer to downtown, there are several great options. **Coronado Municipal Golf Course** (☎ 619/435-3121; www.golfcoronado.com) offers distractingly nice views of San Diego Bay and the downtown skyline; **Riverwalk Golf Club** (☎ 619/296-4563; www.riverwalkgc.com) meanders along the floor of Mission Valley, located just minutes from the beaches and downtown; and humble **Balboa Par Municipal Golf Course** (☎ 619/570-1234; www.sandiego.gov/golf) is convenient and affordable. You can also check in with San Diego Golf Reservations (☎ 866/701-4653 or 858/964-5980; www.sandiegogolf.com). It can arrange tee times for you at San Diego's premier courses for free (except Torrey Pines; $25 per person).

Balboa Park

Established in 1868, Balboa Park is the second-oldest city park in the United States. Much of its striking architecture, which houses a variety of museums, was the product of the 1915–16 Panama-California Exposition and the 1935–36 California Pacific International Exposition. What makes Balboa Park unique is its extensive and mature botanical collection, owing largely to the efforts of Kate Sessions (1857–1940), a horticulturist who devoted her life to transforming the desolate mesas and scrub-filled canyons into the oases they are today.

> One of San Diego's best-known buildings, the Botanical Building shelters over 2,000 orchids, ferns, and other plants.

START Bus 1, 3, 7, or 120 to Balboa Park.

❶ ★ Marston House. This elegant Craftsman home was built for a local businessman in 1905 by noted architects Irving Gill and William Hebbard. The house, listed on the National Register of Historic Places, features classic furnishings and art pottery, and is open for tours on weekends. ⏱ 45 min. ☎ 619/297-9327 or 619/298-3142. www.sohosandiego.org. Admission $8 adults; $6 seniors; $4 kids 6–12; free for kids 5 & under. Fri–Sun 10am–5pm.

❷ ★ kids San Diego Museum of Man. This anthropological museum has an emphasis on the peoples of North and South America; there are also Egyptian mummies and relics, and a museum store with great folk art. ⏱ 1 hr. ☎ 619/239-2001. www.museumofman.org. Admission $10 adults; $7.50 seniors, students, and active military; $5 kids 3–12; free for kids 1 & under. Daily 10am–4:30pm.

NAVAL HOSPITAL
COMPLEX

SAN DIEGO ZOO

Miniature
Railroad

Spreckels
Organ Pavilion

Plaza de
Panama

Balboa Park
Club

Cabrillo
Bridge

El Prado

163

Park Blvd

Park Blvd.

Zoo Dr

Village Pl.

Old Globe Wy.

Pan American Rd. W.

Pan American Rd. E.

Presidents Wy.

Balboa Dr.

8th Dr.

1 Marston House
2 San Diego Museum of Man
3 Old Globe Theatre
4 Alcazar Garden
5 Mingei International Museum
6 SDAI Museum of the Living Artist
7 San Diego Museum of Art
8 Timken Museum of Art
9 Visitors Center
10 Japanese Friendship Garden Tea Pavilion
11 Palm Canyon
12 House of Pacific Relations International Cottages
13 San Diego Automotive Museum
14 San Diego Air & Space Museum
15 San Diego Hall of Champions Sports Museum
16 Botanical Building and Lily Pond
17 Museum of Photographic Arts
18 Museum of San Diego History
19 San Diego Model Railroad Museum
20 Reuben H. Fleet Science Center
21 San Diego Natural History Museum
22 Spanish Village Art Center
23 Balboa Park Miniature Railroad and Carousel
24 Gardens

1/4 mi
1/4 km

> *Unwind at the San Diego Museum of Art, where even the seating has creative flair.*

❸ ★★★ Old Globe Theatre. This Tony Award–winning theater complex, built for 1935's California Pacific International Exposition, is patterned after Shakespeare's original. It succumbed to arson twice (in 1978 and 1984), but always manages to rise from the ashes; in 2010 the theater completed a massive renovation just in time for its 75th anniversary. ⏲10 min. Backstage tours some Sat–Sun 10:30am. $5 adults, $2 seniors and students. For reservations call ☎ 619/231-1941, ext. 2142. See p. 625.

❹ Alcazar Garden. Patterned after the gardens surrounding the Alcazar castle in Sevilla, Spain, this colorful floral display is formally laid out and trimmed with hedges; two star-shaped tile fountains add to the overall sense of tranquillity. ⏲10 min. www.balboapark.org. Free admission. Open daily 24 hr., but caution should be exercised after dark.

❺ ★★ Mingei International Museum. The Mingei stages exhibitions that celebrate folk art, including textiles, costumes, jewelry, toys, pottery, paintings, and sculpture. The gift shop alone is worth a visit. ⏲ At least 30 min. ☎ 619/239-0003. www.mingei.org. Admission $7 adults; $5 seniors; $4 kids 6–17, students, and active military; free for kids 5 & under. Tues–Sun 10am–4pm.

❻ SDAI Museum of the Living Artist. The San Diego Art Institute runs this municipal gallery where local artists get their due. A variety of mediums and styles are presented, and young artists from area schools are also exhibited. ⏲30 min. ☎ 619/236-0011. www.sandiego-art.org. Admission $3 adults; $2 seniors, students, and military; free for kids 12 & under. Tues–Sat 10am–4pm; Sun noon–4pm.

❼ ★ San Diego Museum of Art. Here you'll find San Diego's most extensive collection of fine art, housed in a building marked by an exquisite Spanish facade. Major touring exhibitions are also presented, and there's an ongoing schedule of concerts, films, and lectures. The museum's free sculpture garden is a lovely spot with works by Joan Miró, Henry Moore, and others. ⏲ At least 1 hr. ☎ 619/232-7931. www.sdmart.org. Admission $10 adults, $8 seniors and military, $7 students, $4.50 kids 6–17, free for kids 5 & under. Admission to special exhibits varies. Free admission to the Sculpture Garden. Tues–Sat 10am–5pm; Sun noon–5pm.

❽ ★ Timken Museum of Art. It's small, but the always-free Timken features a worthy collection of 19th-century American paintings, Russian icons, and works by European old masters (including San Diego's only Rembrandt, *Saint Bartholomew*). ⏱ 20 min. ☎ 619/239-5548. www.timkenmuseum.org. Free admission. Tues–Sat 10am–4:30pm; Sun 1:30–4:30pm.

⑨ Visitors Center. Pick up maps, souvenirs, and discount tickets to the museums; guided and self-guided tours begin here, too. If you plan to visit more than three of the park's museums, buy the Passport to Balboa Park ($39 adults, $21 ages 3–12)—it allows entrance to 13 museums and is valid for a week. The Deluxe Passport ($65 adults, $36 children) includes entrance to the zoo. ☎ 619/239-0512. www.balboapark.org. Daily 9:30am–4:30pm (extended hours in summer).

⑩ ☕ ★ Japanese Friendship Garden Tea Pavilion. This tranquil spot serves fresh sushi, noodle soups, and Asian salads—it also carries quirky imported Japanese candies and beverages in addition to familiar American snacks. ☎ 619/231-0048. www.cohnrestaurants.com. Items $3–$8.

⑪ ★ Palm Canyon. Fifty species of palm, plus magnolia trees and a Moreton Bay fig tree, provide a tropical canopy, making for a great respite on a hot day. *Note*: The walkway dead-ends, so you have to exit from where you entered. Also, this is a very secluded area and it's not recommended you venture here after dark. ⏱ 15 min. www.balboapark.org. Free admission. Daily 24 hr.

⑫ House of Pacific Relations International Cottages. This cluster of 17 charming one- and two-room cottages disseminates information about the culture, traditions, and history of more than 30 countries. Light refreshments are served, and outdoor lawn programs are presented by one of the nations every Sunday, 2 to 3pm, March through October. ⏱ At least 15 min. ☎ 619/234-0739. www.sdhpr.org. Free admission (donations welcome). Sun noon–4pm; 4th Tues of each month 11am–3pm.

⑬ ★ San Diego Automotive Museum. Whether you're a gear head into muscle cars or someone who appreciates the sculptural beauty of fine design, this collection of fabulous wheels has something for everyone. ⏱ 45

> *Front and center in Balboa Park is the elaborately embellished Museum of Man, sporting impressive Spanish styling.*

min. ☎ 619/231-2886. www.sdautomuseum.org. Admission $8 adults, $6 seniors and military, $5 students, $4 kids 6–15, free for kids 5 & under. Daily 10am–5pm (last admission 4:30pm).

⑭ ★★ kids San Diego Air & Space Museum. This kid pleaser has more than 60 aircraft on display, providing an overview of aeronautical history from the days of hot-air balloons to space travel. ⏱ 1 hr. ☎ 619/234-8291. www.sandiegoairandspace.org. Admission $15 adults; $12 seniors, students, and retired military; $6 kids 3–11; free for kids 2 & under and active military. Sept–May daily 10am–4:30pm; June–Aug daily 10am–5:30pm.

⑮ San Diego Hall of Champions Sports Museum. From baseball great Ted Williams to skateboard icon Tony Hawk, this slick museum celebrates San Diego's best-ever athletes and the sports they played. ⏱ 1 hr.

> *So Cal life in miniature charms adults and kids alike at the expansive San Diego Model Railroad Museum.*

☎ 619/234-2544. www.sdhoc.com/museum. Admission $8 adults; $6 seniors, students, and military; $4 children 7–17; free for kids 6 & under. Daily 10am–4:30pm.

16 ★ **Botanical Building and Lily Pond.** Ferns, orchids, impatiens, begonias, and other plants (2,100 in total) are sheltered in a graceful 250-foot-long lath building, part of the 1915 Panama-California Exposition and one of the largest of its kind in the world. ⊕ 15 min. ☎ 619/235-1100. Free admission. Fri–Wed 10am–4pm; closed Thurs and major holidays.

17 ★★ **Museum of Photographic Arts.** This is one of the few museums in the United States devoted exclusively to the photographic arts. There's also a plush cinema that screens classic films and a great bookstore. ⊕ At least 30 min. ☎ 619/238-7559. www.mopa.org. Admission $6 adults; $4 seniors, students, and retired military; free for kids 11 & under and active military. Tues–Sun 10am–5pm.

18 **Museum of San Diego History.** Operated by the San Diego Historical Society, this museum offers permanent and changing exhibits on topics related to the history of the region.

Past shows have examined subjects ranging from San Diego's role as a Hollywood film location to the city's architectural heritage. Books and other items about San Diego history are available in the gift shop. ⊕ 30 min. ☎ 619/232-6203. www.sandiegohistory.org. Admission $5 adults; $4 students, seniors, and military with ID; $2 kids 6–17; free for kids 5 & under. Tues–Sun 10am–5pm.

19 ★ kids **San Diego Model Railroad Museum.** Four permanent, scale-model railroads depict Southern California's transportation history and terrain with astounding attention to miniature details. The exhibits occupy a 27,000-square-foot space, making it the world's largest indoor model railroad display. ⊕ 20 min. 619/696-0199. www.sdmrm.org. Admission $7 adults; $6 seniors; $3 students; $2.50 military; free for kids 14 & under. Tues–Fri 11am–4pm; Sat–Sun 11am–5pm.

20 ★★ kids **Reuben H. Fleet Science Center.** A must see for kids, this tantalizing collection of interactive exhibits and virtual rides is designed to stimulate the imagination and teach scientific principles. This center is also

> Take a spin on the 1910 Balboa Park Carousel, with original animals, hand-painted murals, and oom-pah-pah music.

home to the world's first domed IMAX theater, as well as a planetarium simulator; check the website for show schedules. ⏱ At least 1 hr. ☎ 619/238-1233. www.rhfleet.org. Exhibits $10 adults, $8.75 seniors and kids 3–12. Exhibits and one IMAX show $15 adults, $12 seniors and kids 3–12. Planetarium (1st Wed of month 7pm & 8pm) $10.50 adults, $9 seniors and kids 3–12. Daily 9:30am–5pm (hours may vary).

㉑ kids San Diego Natural History Museum. Founded in 1874, this is one of the West's oldest scientific institutions, focusing on the flora, fauna, and mineralogy of the San Diego region. The museum also has a 3-D movie theater. ⏱ At least 1 hr. ☎ 619/232-3821. www.sdnhm.org. Admission $16 adults; $14 seniors; $11 kids 13–17, students, and active military; $10 kids 3–12; free for kids 2 & under. Two films are included with admission. Daily 10am–5pm.

㉒ ★ Spanish Village Art Center. This collection of 37 picture-perfect casitas is home to more than 250 artists, specializing in everything from glass blowing to woodcarving. Many of the artists work on-site, allowing you to watch the art-making process. ⏱ 20 min.

☎ 619/233-9050. www.spanishvillageart.com. Free admission. Daily 11am–4pm.

㉓ kids Balboa Park Miniature Railroad and Carousel. The open-air railroad takes a 3-minute journey through a grove of eucalyptus trees, while the charming carousel, built in 1910, is one of the last in the world to still offer a ring grab (free ride if you seize the brass one). ⏱ 20 min. Railroad: ☎ 619/231-1515. www.sandiegozoo.org. Admission $2 per person (free for kids 11 months & under). Summer daily 11am–6:30pm; Sept–May weekends & holidays only 11am–4:30pm. Carousel: ☎ 619/239-0512. www.balboapark.org. Admission $2 per person (free for kids 11 months & under). Summer daily 11am–5pm; Sept–May weekends & holidays only 11am–5pm.

㉔ ★★ Gardens. Cross Park Boulevard via a pedestrian overpass and you'll find, to your left, a Desert Garden; and to your right, the Inez Grant Parker Memorial Rose Garden, home to 2,400 roses. ⏱ 30 min. www.balboapark.org. Free admission. Open 24 hr., but not recommended after dark.

CALIFORNIA'S CHICANO MURALS

BY MEGAN MCFARLAND

CALIFORNIA'S BIG THREE CITIES—Los Angeles, San Francisco, and San Diego—are a virtual open-air museum of murals, with a large concentration of them found in the cities' Mexican-American, or Chicano, barrios. Colorful portraits, graffiti-like collages, and traditional Mexican symbols enliven the outside walls of stores, schools, community centers, and even concrete flood-control channels.

Mural painting in California dates to the early 1930s and follows in the tradition of the Mexican muralists of the post-Revolution era, among them David Alfaro Siqueiros (1896–1974) and Diego Rivera (1886–1957). In the 1970s, inspired by the Civil Rights and Black Power movements as well as the work of César Chavez and the United Farm Workers, young Mexican-Americans began to campaign for greater socio-economic power, better education, and workers' rights. Murals were a visual expression of that social protest, as well as emblems of cultural pride. Today, as then, a broad range of painting styles express political views and cultural pride, and honor civil rights leaders as well as everyday people important to the barrio or city.

CARNAVAL
Joshua Sarantitis, Emmanuel Montoya, Carlos Loarca, and others, 1994
Harrison at 19th Street. This mural depicts the Caribbean and Latin American celebration of the pre-Lenten carnival.

Los Angeles: East L.A. and Boyle Heights

Los Angeles is known as the mural capital of the world: there are reportedly more than 3,000 murals throughout the county. East Los Angeles is the heart of the Chicano mural district. In the early 1970s, Judith Baca, a painter and art professor, began working on murals with local teenagers and gang members. In 1976 she cofounded SPARC (Social and Public Art Resource Center), a nonprofit arts organization that continues to produce and promote public art in L.A.

THE GREAT WALL OF LOS ANGELES
SPARC, 1976–83
Tujunga Flood Control Channel, North Hollywood/San Fernando Valley. This is the longest mural in the world at nearly 1/2 mile. The 13-foot-high wall presents a multiethnic history of Los Angeles from prehistoric times to the 1950s.

San Diego: Chicano Park

Tucked into a corner between the I-5 freeway and the Coronado Bay Bridge entrance is Chicano Park, a treasure-trove of Chicano culture and home to about 30 murals painted on the bridge's concrete supports. The area, known as Barrio Logan, had long been a Mexican-American neighborhood, but in the 1960s residents were slowly displaced by construction of the new Interstate and the bridge. On April 22, 1970, when bulldozers arrived to begin building a California Highway Patrol station on the land, barrio residents were outraged. They formed a human chain to block the construction, and eventually the land was dedicated as a community park. Mural-painting began in 1973 and continued through the decade.

QUETZALCOÁTL
1973; renovated 1987
The first mural in Chicano Park, it depicts the mythical feathered serpent of pre-Colombian Mexico and includes ancient symbols of transformation such as the Chinese Yin-Yang and a swastika, and traditional Mexican symbols such as an eagle, *nopal* (prickly pear cactus), and Catholic rose.

San Francisco: The Mission District

Mural-making in San Francisco also has Mexican connections: Diego Rivera completed four murals in the Bay Area from 1931 to 1940. In the 1970s, Latinos began settling the Mission District, and in 1971 spontaneous mural creation began on a narrow street named Balmey Alley. Some of the early murals were done by Mujeres Muralistas, a women's art collective. The nonprofit Precita Eyes Mural Arts Association, established in 1977, is responsible for more than 80 murals in the Mission. Themes range from a tribute to Monseñor Oscar Romero, the assassinated Archbishop of San Salvador, to a lighthearted cheer for the San Francisco Giants, *Vamos Gigantes* (Go Giants).

Gaslamp Quarter

A National Historic District covering 16½ city blocks, the Gaslamp Quarter features many Victorian-style commercial buildings built between the Civil War and World War I. The father of modern San Diego, Alonzo Horton, purchased 1,000 acres of muddy, bay-front land for $260 in 1867 and ignited a real estate boom. His "New Town" is today's Gaslamp Quarter, and with its proliferation of restaurants, shops, clubs, and hotels the district is a mirror image of its 1880s heyday. The Gaslamp Quarter—bound by Fourth Avenue to the west, Sixth Avenue to the east, Broadway to the north, and L Street and the waterfront to the south—is easily covered, and best experienced, on foot.

> Everything old is new again in the Gaslamp Quarter, where renovated Victorians house shops, restaurants, and clubs.

START Any downtown bus to Horton Plaza, Blue or Orange Line trolley to Civic Center.

❶ ★ Horton Plaza. A colorful conglomeration of shops, eateries, and entertainment options, Horton Plaza spearheaded the revitalization of downtown when it opened in 1985. Bordered by Broadway, First & Fourth aves., and G St. ☎ 619/239-8180. www.westfield.com/hortonplaza.

❷ ★★ Balboa Theatre. Built in 1924, this Spanish renaissance–style building presented plays and vaudeville shows in its early days. After years of sitting dormant and decrepit, the Balboa is once again hosting live performances. 868 Fourth Ave. (southwest corner of Fourth Ave. & E St.). ☎ 619/570-1100. www.sdbalboa.org.

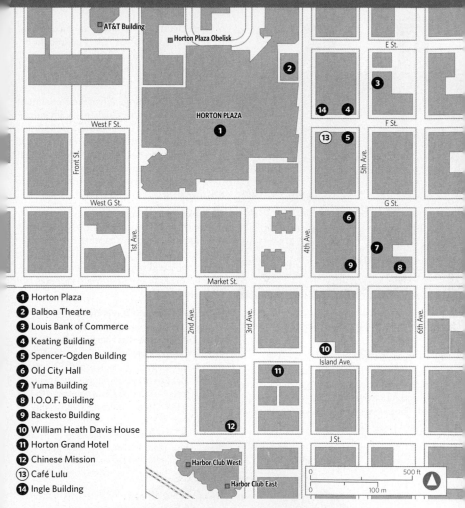

1 Horton Plaza
2 Balboa Theatre
3 Louis Bank of Commerce
4 Keating Building
5 Spencer-Ogden Building
6 Old City Hall
7 Yuma Building
8 I.O.O.F. Building
9 Backesto Building
10 William Heath Davis House
11 Horton Grand Hotel
12 Chinese Mission
13 Café Lulu
14 Ingle Building

3 ★★ **Louis Bank of Commerce.** Built in 1888, this granite building once housed an oyster bar frequented by Wyatt Earp (of O.K. Corral shootout fame); upstairs was the Golden Poppy Hotel, a brothel run by a fortuneteller named Madame Coara. 835 Fifth Ave.

4 ★ **Keating Building.** A San Diego landmark dating from 1890, this structure was once heralded as one of the city's most prestigious office buildings, with such extravagances as steam heat and a wire-cage elevator. A sleek boutique hotel, the Keating, is now ensconced here. 432 F St. (northwest corner of Fifth Ave. & F St.).

5 ★ **Spencer-Ogden Building.** Built in 1874, this is one of the oldest buildings in the Gaslamp Quarter—and it's lucky to still be standing. It escaped major damage after an explosion in 1887 caused by a druggist who was making fireworks. 770 Fifth Ave.

6 ★ **Old City Hall.** Also dating from 1874, this Florentine Italianate building features 16-foot ceilings, 12-foot windows framed with brick arches, antique columns, and a wrought-iron cage elevator. Notice the windows on each floor are different—the top two stories were added in 1887, when it became the city's public library. 664 Fifth Ave. (southwest corner of Fifth Ave. & G St.).

> Look way up to see iron eagles topping the 1888 Louis Bank of Commerce, San Diego's first granite building.

7 ★★ **Yuma Building.** The brothel at the Yuma (built in 1888) was the first to be closed during the infamous 1912 cleanup of the area. In the end, 138 women (and no men) were arrested. They were given a choice: join the Door of Hope charity and reform or take a one-way train ride to Los Angeles. One hundred thirty-six went to L.A.; one woman was pronounced insane; and the last became San Diego's first telephone operator. 631 Fifth Ave.

8 ★ **I.O.O.F. Building.** When the cornerstone was finally laid for this building (a joint lodge for the Masons and Odd Fellows) in 1882, a parade was held with King Kalakaua of Hawaii as the grand marshal. Gaslamp lore has it that, sitting on the balcony, he caught a cold and died soon after of pneumonia in San Francisco. 526 Market St.

9 **Backesto Building.** When this classical revival structure was built in 1873, this part of the Gaslamp was known as the Stingaree, the city's notorious red-light district. Gambling, opium dens, and wild saloons were all part of the mix. 617 Fifth Ave. (northwest corner of Fifth Ave. & Market St.).

10 ★ **William Heath Davis House.** Downtown's oldest surviving structure, this prefabricated lumber home was shipped to San Diego around Cape Horn from New England in 1850. Alonzo Horton lived in the house in 1867, at its original location at the corner of Market and State streets. Around 1873 it was moved to 11th Avenue and K Street, where it served as the

> Topped off with the name of the building's developer, the Keating Building now houses a boutique hotel.

county hospital. It was relocated to this site in 1984 and completely refurbished. The house, now a museum and educational gift shop, and the small park adjoining it are open to the public. The Gaslamp Quarter Historical Foundation is also headquartered here. ⏱30 min. 410 Island Ave. (at Fourth Ave.). ☎ 619/233-4692. www.gaslampquarter.org. Admission $5 per person, $4 seniors. Tues–Sat 10am–6pm; Sun 9am–3pm. Walking tours Sat 11am. $10 per person; $8 seniors, students, and military.

⓫ ★ **Horton Grand Hotel.** Two 1886 hotels were moved here from other sites, and then renovated and connected by an atrium; the original Grand Horton is to your left, the Brooklyn Hotel to your right. Now it's all one: the Horton Grand Hotel (p. 616). Wyatt Earp lived upstairs at the Brooklyn for most of his 7 years in San Diego. 311 Island Ave. (southwest corner of Island & Fourth aves.).

⓬ **Chinese Mission.** Originally located on First Avenue, this charming brick building built in 1927 was a place where Chinese immigrants (primarily men) could learn English and find employment. The building was rescued from demolition and moved to its present location, where it now houses the San Diego Chinese Historical Museum. There's also a gift shop

> The curtain rises once again at the 1924 Balboa Theatre, shuttered for years but once again presenting shows and performances.

and a small garden. ⏱30 min. 404 Third Ave. (at J St.). ☎ 619/338-9888. www.sdchm.org. Admission $2 adults, free for kids 11 & under. Tues–Sat 10:30am–4pm; Sun noon–4pm. Walking tours of the remains of San Diego's Chinatown leave from here the second Sat of the month at 11am; $2.

⓭ 🍴 **Café Lulu.** It aims for a hip, bohemian ambience, but if you're a straight-arrow conservative, don't be put off—it's an inclusive place. The sidewalk tables are perfect for people-watching while you enjoy your espresso and sweets. 419 F St. (near Fourth Ave.). ☎ 619/238-0114. Cash only. Items $3–$9.

⓮ ★ **Ingle Building.** It dates from 1906 and is now home to the Hard Rock Cafe. The mural on the F Street side of the building depicts a group of deceased rock stars (Jimi Hendrix, John Lennon, Janis Joplin, and Elvis) lounging at sidewalk tables. Inside, the restaurant's stained-glass ceiling was taken from an Elks Club. 801 Fourth Ave. (northeast corner of Fourth Ave. & F St.).

Downtown Museums

Amid the boutiques, restaurants, and clubs of the Gaslamp Quarter, downtown San Diego also makes room for art, culture, and education with several unique museums. The ★★★ **Museum of Contemporary Art San Diego,** 1100 and 1001 Kettner Blvd. (☎ 858/454-3541; www.mcasd.org), is home-based in La Jolla (p. 594, ❷), but has two downtown annexes featuring cutting-edge work and exciting arts programs. The **New Children's Museum,** 200 W. Island Ave. (☎ 619/233-8792; www.thinkplaycreate.org), is an ultramodern facility that offers everything from pillow fights to photography workshops. Along the waterfront are two floating museums: the ★★ **Maritime Museum** (p. 580, ❹) and the **USS Midway Museum,** 910 Harbor Dr. (☎ 619/544-9600; www.midway.org). Guests can tour these ships to get a real taste of maritime history.

La Jolla

La Jolla is a Southern California Riviera. It features a gorgeous coastline, outstanding restaurants, a slew of upscale boutiques and galleries, and an inordinate number of wealthy residents. The heart of La Jolla is referred to as the Village, and it's a pedestrian-friendly area, roughly delineated by Pearl Street to the south, Prospect Street to the north, Torrey Pines Road to the east, and the rugged coast to the west. It's unknown whether "La Jolla" (pronounced la-*hoy*-ya) is misspelled Spanish for "the jewel" or an indigenous people's word for "cave," but once you see it, you'll likely go with the first definition.

> *Sink into the striking, edgy artwork displayed inside—and outside—the thrilling Museum of Contemporary Art San Diego.*

START Bus route 30 to Silverado St. and Girard Ave.

❶ ★ Mary, Star of the Sea. Above the entrance to this beautiful little church, dedicated in 1937, is a striking mosaic that re-creates the original fresco painted there by Mexican artist Alfredo Ramos Martínez (1871–1946). An influential art instructor in Mexico, Martínez' students included Rufino Tamayo and David Alfaro Siqueiros. Inside the church, the unique mural above the altar was painted by

accomplished Polish artist John De Rosen (1891–1982). It depicts the Virgin Mary on a crescent moon, presiding over a storm-tossed sea. ⏱ 15 min. 7669 Girard Ave. ☎ 858/454-2631. www.marystarlajolla.org. Mon–Fri 6am-noon and daily services.

❷ ★★★ Museum of Contemporary Art San Diego (MCASD). Focusing on work produced since 1950, this museum's holdings include noteworthy examples of minimalism, light and space work, conceptualism, installation, and

1	Mary, Star of the Sea
2	Museum of Contemporary Art San Diego (MCASD)
3	Children's Pool
4	Ellen Browning Scripps Park
5	La Jolla Cove
6	Sunny Jim Cave
7	Coast Walk
8	La Valencia Hotel
9	Athenaeum Music and Arts Library
10	Girard Gourmet

site-specific art. MCASD also offers lectures, cutting-edge films, and special events on an ongoing basis; the bookstore is a great place for contemporary gifts, and the cafe is a pleasant stop before or after your visit. The museum is on a cliff overlooking the Pacific Ocean and the views from the galleries are gorgeous. ⏱ 1½ hr. 700 Prospect St. ☎ 858/454-3541. www.mcasd.org. Admission $10 per person; $5 seniors, students 26 and over, and military; free for students 25 & under; free 3rd Thurs of the month 5–7pm. Admission good for 7

days here and at downtown location. Thurs–Tues 11am–5pm; 3rd Thurs of the month 11am–7pm; closed Wed.

3 ★★ **kids Children's Pool.** A seawall protects this pocket of sand—originally intended as a calm swimming bay for children, it is now a sanctuary for a colony of harbor seals. While it is usually possible to go in the water here, keep in mind those are federally protected *wild* animals, and it is illegal to approach them or harass them in any way. The water here can also have a high level of bacteria from seal waste, so content yourself with viewing the animals from a safe distance. Also note that volunteers keep an eye on things and will report anyone who bothers the colony. **Coast Blvd. at Jenner St.**

4 ★★ **Ellen Browning Scripps Park.** This park and the bluff-side walkway that courses through it afford some of California's finest coastal scenery. A series of rustic wooden shelters—popular with seagulls, pigeons, and pedestrians—overlooks La Jolla's shapely curves. The La Jolla Cove Bridge Club—dating back to 1939—might be one of the world's most view-enhanced card rooms.

Visiting with the Fishes

The beautiful ★★ **Birch Aquarium at Scripps,** 2300 Expedition Way (☎ 858/534-3474; www.aquarium.ucsd.edu), is both an aquarium and a museum, operated by the world-renowned Scripps Institution of Oceanography. It features more than 60 marine-life tanks affording close-up views of the underwater inhabitants of the Pacific Northwest, the California coast, Mexico's Sea of Cortés, and the tropical seas. It also offers smashing views of the La Jolla coast.

> *Posh it up at La Valencia Hotel, where you can sip a cocktail and take in to-die-for views.*

⑤ ★★★ kids La Jolla Cove. These protected calm waters, celebrated as the clearest along the coast, attract snorkelers, scuba divers, and families (and, subsequently, can get crowded in summer). The unique underwater park stretches from here to the northern end of Torrey Pines State Reserve and incorporates kelp forests, artificial reefs, two deep canyons, and tidal pools.

⑥ kids Sunny Jim Cave. The only one of La Jolla's seven sea caves accessible by land, the Sunny Jim Cave is reached by a narrow, often slippery, staircase in the Cave Store. This cliff-top shop is equal parts art gallery and antiques store and also rents snorkel equipment. The passageway was dug through the rock in 1902–03 and has 145 steps. ⏱ 20 min. 1325 Cave St. (just off Prospect St.). ☎ 858/459-0746. www.cavestore.com. Admission $4 adults, $3 kids 3–16, free for kids 2 & under. Daily 9am–5pm.

Kayaking the Cove

The placid waters of La Jolla Cove and nearby La Jolla Shores are San Diego's top spots for kayaking. As you glide over this ecological reserve, where boating and fishing have been banned since 1929, the clear water will allow you to spot electric-orange garibaldis, California's state marine fish; endangered giant black sea bass; and frolicking seals. There are sea caves to explore, as well.

In summer, leopard sharks come to breed in the shallow waters here—but don't worry; they can reach lengths of up to 6 feet, but are completely harmless. In winter, migrating Pacific gray whales are the main attraction. Check in with **Hike Bike Kayak,** 2246 Avenida de la Playa (☎ 866/425-2925 or 858/551-9510; www.hikebikekayak.com). Those who want to get to even closer to the action in this 533-acre ecological reserve will find it's the perfect place for snorkeling and scuba diving. **OEX Dive & Kayak Center,** 2158 Avenida de la Playa (☎ 858/454-6195; www.oexcalifornia.com), can get you geared up.

⑦ ★★ Coast Walk. As you face the ocean, continue past the Cave Store. You'll find two paths; one leads to a fabulous wood-platform overlook, the other continues along the bluffs. It's a cool little trail, affording expansive views

> *Catch polished performances, hear lectures, and see art in the elegant 1899 Athenaeum in La Jolla.*

of the coast. You can exit at a stairway that leads back to Prospect Street (before you come to the white wooden bridge) and circle back into town. If you continue along the trail, it will put you on Torrey Pines Road, an extra 10- to 15-minute walk back to La Jolla.

⑧ ★★★ La Valencia Hotel. This bluff-top hotel, which looks much like a Mediterranean villa, has been the centerpiece of La Jolla since opening in 1926. Within its bougainvillea-draped walls and wrought-iron garden gates, this bastion of gentility resurrects the golden age, when celebrities like Greta Garbo and Charlie Chaplin vacationed here. There are several lounges and restaurants, some with incredible vistas, which can be enjoyed by nonguests; the Whaling Bar (p. 577, ⑤) is a classic, old-school haunt. ⏱ 15 min. 1132 Prospect St. (at Herschel Ave.). ☎ 800/451-0772 or 858/454-0771. www.lavalencia.com.

⑨ ★★ Athenaeum Music and Arts Library. Founded in 1899, the Athenaeum hosts art

exhibits, jazz and classical concerts, lectures, and special events open to the general public. Visitors can browse through the vast collection of books, music, and more, but only members can check items out. ⏱ 30 min. 1008 Wall St. (at Girard Ave.). ☎ 858/454-5872. www.ljathenaeum.org. Free admission to gallery exhibits. Tues and Thurs–Sat 10am–5:30pm; Wed 10am–8:30pm. Free tours 3rd Sat of the month 11am.

⑩ ☕ ★ Girard Gourmet. This small bakery and restaurant always draws a crowd with its cookies, quiches, soups, salads, and deli sandwiches. The Belgian proprietor also whips up heartier fare such as lamb stew and duck *à l'orange*. It's the perfect place to gather goods for a picnic. 7837 Girard Ave. ☎ 858/454-3325. www.girard gourmet.com. Entrees $2–$22.

Mission Bay Park

Originally known as False Bay, this swampy marshland was transformed in the 1940s into Mission Bay Park. A vast outdoor playground, it encompasses more than 4,200 acres—about half of it water, half of it land—with 27 miles of shoreline, 19 sandy beaches, grassy parks, wildlife preserves, boat docks and launches (with rental facilities), basketball courts, and an extensive system of pathways. Locals and visitors alike flock to Mission Bay for everything from kite flying to power boating.

> Set sail across the turquoise waters of Mission Bay, where you can rent just about anything that floats.

START Bus 8/9 to Santa Clara Place.

1 ★★ kids **Santa Clara Point.** Recreation centers don't get any cooler than this. Surrounded by the bay waters, there are tennis courts, a softball field, lighted basketball courts, a playground, and weight room. Also located on the point is Mission Bay Sportcenter, where you can rent sailboats, catamarans, pedal boats, sailboards, kayaks, WaveRunners, motorboats, or surfboards. ⏱ At least 15 min. Recreation Center, 1008 Santa Clara Place. ☎ 858/581-9928. www.sandiego.gov. Mon, Wed, & Fri noon–7pm; Tues & Thurs noon–7:30pm; Sat 10am–2pm; closed Sun. Mission Bay Sportcenter, 1010 Santa Clara Place. ☎ 858/488-1004. www.missionbaysportcenter.com. Daily 9am–7pm. Bus: 8/9.

② 🍽 ★ **The Mission.** The menu features all-day breakfasts, from traditional pancakes to nouvelle egg dishes to burritos and quesadillas. At lunch, the menu expands with sandwiches, salads, and a few Chino-Latino items like ginger-sesame chicken tacos. 3795 Mission Blvd. (at San Jose Place). ☎ 858/488-9060. www.the mission1.signonsandiego.com. Items $7–$11.

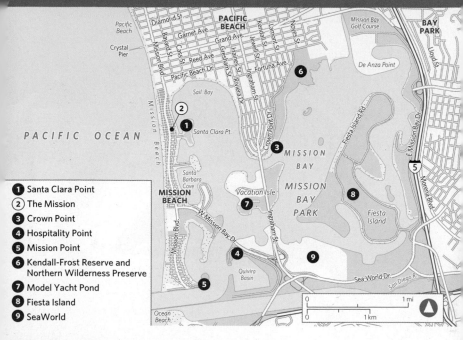

1. Santa Clara Point
2. The Mission
3. Crown Point
4. Hospitality Point
5. Mission Point
6. Kendall-Frost Reserve and Northern Wilderness Preserve
7. Model Yacht Pond
8. Fiesta Island
9. SeaWorld

3 ★ kids Crown Point. You'll find everything you need for a day of recreation: large grassy expanses, a white-sand beach, picnic tables, fire rings, barbecue grills, basketball courts, and a boat launch. There are also restrooms and showers here. Crown Point Dr. www.sandiego. gov. Daily 4am–2am. Smoking, alcohol, & glass containers prohibited. Free parking available in lots until 10pm. Bus: 8/9.

4 ★ Hospitality Point. This popular spot lacks a beach but draws visitors with its ocean, bay, and channel views. The walking and bike path will take you alongside the Flood Control Channel, which doubles as the Southern Wildlife Preserve, part of the Pacific Flyway for migratory birds. South end of Quivira Rd. www.sandiego.gov. Smoking, alcohol & glass containers prohibited. Free parking available in lots. Bus: 8/9 to Dana Landing at W. Mission Bay Dr., then it's a little less than a mile on Quivira Rd. to the point.

5 ★ kids Mission Point. This grass-and-sand recreation area is just a short walk from the Mission Beach jetty and the Pacific. Mission Point has fire rings, picnic tables, a children's playground, and restrooms with showers. Bayside Lane. www.sandiego.gov. Daily 4am–10pm.

Smoking, alcohol & glass containers prohibited. Free parking available in lots until 10pm. Bus 8/9 to Mission Blvd. at W. Mission Bay Dr., then about a mile south.

6 ★★★ Kendall-Frost Reserve and Northern Wilderness Preserve. Due to its fragile nature, most of this 30-acre area is off-limits to the public. You can get close to it, though, via the pathway that extends north from Crown Point (3) or by kayak. This saltwater marsh provides sanctuary to a wide variety of birds: avocets to vireos, coots to loons.

7 ★ kids Model Yacht Pond. Just about any weekend you can find hobbyists with their sophisticated, radio-controlled craft competing or just having fun. Some of the models are incredibly detailed. Bus: 8/9 to W. Vacation Rd.

8 Fiesta Island. A rather barren island at the eastern edge of the bay, it's often used for events such as the Annual World Championship Over-the-Line Tournament (a type of softball) in July and cycling time trials and races. There is a 4-mile road that loops around the island, and fire rings are situated throughout. Picnics are not permitted; there are no restrooms. Daily 6am–10pm. Bus: 105 to SeaWorld Dr.

> *Splashy shows at SeaWorld include Shamu and friends (sit in the front rows to get soaked to the bone).*

9 ★★ kids **SeaWorld.** Mission Bay's most famous attraction is this marine-life theme park where crowd-pleasing shows and rides are made politically correct with a nominally informative atmosphere. The 20-minute shows—starring orcas, otters, dolphins, household pets, and (in summer) human acrobats—run several times throughout the day. A number of 4-ton killer whales function as the park's mascot, Shamu, who performs in a 7-million-gallon pool with see-through walls. SeaWorld's real strengths, though, are its simulated marine environments, including Wild Arctic (with beluga whales, walruses, and polar bears), Manatee Rescue, the Shark Encounter, and the ever-popular Penguin Encounter. ☺ At least 4 hr. 500 SeaWorld Dr. ☎ 800/257-4268 or 619/226-3901. www.seaworld.com. Admission $65 adults, $55 kids 3–9, free for kids 2 & under. In summer daily 9am–11pm; rest of year daily 10am–5pm . (Hours vary; check the website or call ahead.) Parking $12. Bus: 8 or 9.

Thar She Blows

Whale-watching is an eagerly anticipated wintertime activity in San Diego, as Pacific gray whales pass close by on their annual trek to and from their breeding lagoons in Baja California. From mid-December to mid-March you can watch this incredible migration from a number of vantage points. Landlubbers can head to **Cabrillo National Monument** (p. 574, **1**), which features a glassed-in observatory and educational exhibits; better yet you can put to sea aboard various guided tours. **Hornblower Cruises,** 1066 N. Harbor Dr. (☎ 888/467-6256 or 619/686-8715; www.hornblower.com), and **San Diego Harbor Excursion,** 1050 N. Harbor Dr. (☎ 800/442-7847 or 619/234-4111; www.sdhe.com), both feature large, comfortable ships.

Best Beaches

Looking for the best surf and sand combo? Here's a brief rundown of the city's top choices, from north to south. And remember to put on your sunscreen, even when San Diego's notorious May Gray and June Gloom obscure the sun.

Torrey Pines State Beach. This fabulous, underused strand of sand is located at the foot of Torrey Pines State Reserve (p. 626, ❶). While here take a hike through the reserve for the quintessential outdoor San Diego experience.

Black's Beach. The somewhat difficult access—a trail located next to the Torrey Pines Gliderport (2800 Torrey Pines Scenic Dr., La Jolla)—helps keep this San Diego's unofficial nude beach, though technically nude sunbathing is illegal. The sight of hang gliders soaring off the cliffs above and surfers out shredding waves makes this an unforgettable spot.

La Jolla Shores. The gentle wave action at this family-friendly beach (Camino del Oro, just north of Avenida de la Playa, La Jolla) keeps it popular with divers, kayakers, and novice surfers. You can also trek north to Black's Beach from here.

La Jolla Cove. This small but oh-so-beautiful spot is San Diego at its most picture-perfect. See p. 596, ❺.

Windansea. Legendary among California's surfing elite, this (above) is one of San Diego's prettiest beaches (Bonair St. at Neptune Place, La Jolla). It's not recommended for swimming or novice surfers, though.

Pacific Beach & Mission Beach. Three miles of sand, boardwalk, restaurants, clubs, shops—even a roller coaster. See p. 576, ❷.

Coronado Beach & Silver Strand. The Hotel del Coronado provides the elegant backdrop for the huge, sandy Coronado Beach. Head south and you'll find the lovely, and often deserted, Silver Strand. See p. 617.

San Diego Shopping Best Bets

Best Jewelry That Doubles as Artwork
★★★ **Taboo Studio,** 1615½ W. Lewis St. (p. 607)

Best Urban-Fabulous Sneakers
★★ **Mint,** 525 University Ave., (p. 604)

Best Vintage Clothing
★★★ **Wear It Again Sam,** 3823 Fifth Ave.
(p. 604)

Best Gallery
★★★ **Quint Contemporary Art,** 7739 Fay Ave.
(p. 603)

Best Place to Find Your Bearings
★★★ **Ruderman Antique Maps,** 7463 Girard
Ave., Ste. 2C (p. 603)

Best Shopping/Entertainment Combo
★★ **Horton Plaza,** 324 Horton Plaza (p. 607)

Best Place for Midcentury Modernists
★★★ **Boomerang for Modern,** 2475 Kettner
Blvd. (p.606)

Best Shopping with a View
★ **Seaport Village,** 849 W. Harbor Dr. (p. 607)

Best Breakables
★★ **Kita Ceramics & Glassware,** 517 Fourth
Ave. (p. 606)

Best Pop Culture Gifts
★ **Babette Schwartz,** 421 University Ave.
(p. 606)

Best Place to Find Local Artisans
★★ **Spanish Village Art Center,** 1770 Village
Place (p. 603)

Best Stuff from Out of Africa
★★ **Africa and Beyond,** 1250 Prospect St.
(p. 603)

Best Toy Store
★★ **Apple Box,** 837 W. Harbor Dr., Ste. C.
(p.604)

Best Trip Down Memory Lane
★ **Antiques on Kettner,** 2400 Kettner Blvd.,
Ste. 106. (p. 603)

Best Place for the Surfing Set
★★ **Quiksilver/Roxy,** 1111 Prospect St. (p. 604)

Best Shopping Center for Fashionistas
★★ **Fashion Valley Center,** 7007 Friars Rd.
(p. 607)

> *Showcasing what it calls "vintage modern," Boomerang for Modern offers furniture finds for midcentury fans.*

San Diego Shopping A to Z

Antiques & Collectibles

★ **Antiques on Kettner** LITTLE ITALY
Nearly 30 individual dealers share this huge space jampacked with a wide selection of quality antiques and collectibles. 2400 Kettner Blvd., Ste. 106 (at W. Kalmia St.). ☎ 619/234-3332. www.antiquesonkettner.com. MC, V. Bus: 83. Map p. 605.

★★ **D.G. Wills Books** LA JOLLA
This charmingly musty bookstore has tomes stacked to its wood rafters. If you're looking for something out of print, offbeat, or esoteric, this place is a browser's delight. 7461 Girard Ave. (at Pearl St.). ☎ 858/456-1800. www. dgwillsbooks.com. AE, DISC, MC, V. Bus: 30. Map p. 604.

★★★ **Ruderman Antique Maps** LA JOLLA
History buffs won't want to miss this place—it sells maps, atlases, and books that date from the 15th through the 19th centuries. 7463 Girard Ave., Ste. 2C (at Ivanhoe Ave.). ☎ 858/551-8500. www.raremaps.com. AE, DISC, MC, V. Bus: 30. Map p. 604.

Art

★★ **Africa and Beyond** LA JOLLA
A collection of contemporary and traditional African sculpture, textiles, jewelry, and furnishings. 1250 Prospect St. (east of Ivanhoe Ave.). ☎ 858/454-9983. www.africaandbeyond. com. AE, DISC, MC, V. Bus: 30. Map p. 604.

★★ **Morrison Hotel Gallery** LA JOLLA
I know, it's only rock'n'roll photography, but I like it. 1230 Prospect St. (east of Ivanhoe Ave.). ☎ 858/551-0835. www.morrisonhotelgallery. com. AE, DISC, MC, V. Bus: 30. Map p. 604.

★★★ **Quint Contemporary Art** LA JOLLA
A bit off the beaten tourist path, this gallery is worth seeking out for its roster of compelling artists. 7739 Fay Ave. (entrance on Drury Lane, btw. Silverado & Kline sts.). ☎ 858/454-3409. www.quintgallery.com. AE, MC, V. Bus: 30. Map p. 604.

★★ **Spanish Village Art Center** BALBOA PARK
A collection of 37 charming casitas set around a colorful courtyard, hosting more than 250 artists working in a vast array of media. 1770 Village Place (at Park Blvd.). ☎ 619/233-9050. www.spanishvillageart.com. AE, MC, V at most galleries. Bus: 7. Map p. 605.

> *Step into the artistic vision of more than 250 artists with studios in the Spanish Village Art Center.*

0 1/4 mi
0 1/4 km

La Jolla Pt
La Jolla Cove
Scripps Park
Spindrift Dr.

PACIFIC OCEAN

Children's Pool

Coast Blvd.
Coast Blvd. S.
Cave St.
Prospect Pl.
Amalfi St.

Wall St.
Ivanhoe Ave.
Park Row
Olivet St.
Soledad Ave.
Crespo Dr.

Silverado St.
Girard Ave.
Kline St.
Torrey Pines Rd.
Virginia Wy.

La Jolla Comm. Park

La Jolla Natural Park

Coast Blvd. Park
Prospect St.
Coast Blvd. S.
Draper Ave.
Herschel Ave.
High Ave.
Cabrillo Ave.
Country Club

Pearl St.
La Jolla Blvd.
Eads Ave.
Fay Ave.

Olivetas Ave.
Marine St.
Sea Ln.
Genter St.
Rushville St.

La Jolla Country Club

La Jolla Shopping

Africa and Beyond **1**
Blondstone **4**
D.G. Wills Books **9**
Laura Gambucci **7**
Morrison Hotel Gallery **2**
My Own Space **5**
Quiksilver/Roxy **3**
Quint Contemporary Art **6**
Ruderman Antique Maps **8**

Children: Fashion & Toys

★★ kids Apple Box EMBARCADERO

This shop specializes in wooden toys. You'll find everything from puzzles and pull toys to rocking horses and toy chests. In Seaport Village, 837 W. Harbor Dr., Ste. C (at Kettner Blvd.). ☎ 800/676-7529. www.appleboxtoys.com. AE, DISC, MC, V. Trolley: Orange Line to Seaport Village. Map p. 605.

★★ kids Quiksilver/Roxy LA JOLLA

Teens and 'tweens will love the surf and skate gear at this conjoined boys/girls shop in the heart of La Jolla. 1111 Prospect St. (at Herschel Ave.). ☎ 858/459-1267. www.quiksilver.com. AE, DISC, MC, V. Bus: 30. Map p. 604.

Fashion

★★★ Carol Gardyne LITTLE ITALY

One-of-a-kind and limited-edition silk scarves and wall hangings, hand painted at this studio/boutique. 1840 Columbia St. (at Fir St.). ☎ 619/233-8066. www.carolgardyne.com. AE, DISC, MC, V. Bus: 83. Map p. 605.

★★ G-Star GASLAMP QUARTER

This international chain has a cool San Diego boutique, selling Euro-style denim. 470 Fifth Ave. (btw. Island Ave. & J St.). ☎ 619/238-7088. www.g-star.com. AE, DISC, MC, V. Bus: 992. Trolley: Orange Line to Gaslamp Quarter. Map p. 605.

★★★ Laura Gambucci LA JOLLA

Bucking the conservative La Jolla trend, this women's boutique features unique, contemporary styles and sexy shoes and handbags. 7629 Girard Ave., Ste. C3 (btw. Kline St. & Torrey Pines Rd.). ☎ 858/551-0214. AE, DISC, MC, V. Bus: 30. Map p. 604.

★★ Mint HILLCREST

An excellent selection of urban sneakers and casual footwear for him and her. 525 University Ave. (btw. 5th & 6th aves.). ☎ 619/291-6468. AE, MC, V. Bus: 1, 3, 10, 11, or 120. Map p. 605.

★★★ Wear It Again Sam HILLCREST

This classy vintage clothing store sells high-quality goods from the 1920s through the 1950s. 3823 Fifth Ave. (btw. University & Robinson aves.). ☎ 619/299-0185. www.wearitagainsamvintage.com. AE, MC, V. Bus: 1, 3, 10, 11, or 120. Map p. 605.

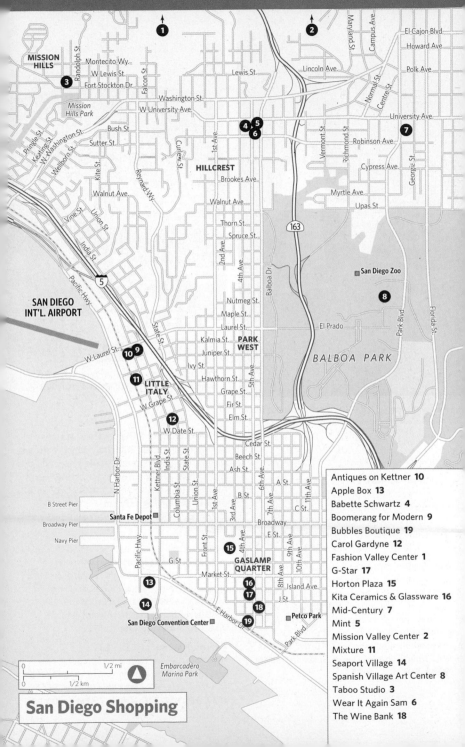

Montecito Wy.
W Lewis St.
Fort Stockton Dr.
Randolph St.
Falcon St.
Washington St.
W University Ave.
Lewis St.
Lincoln Ave.
El Cajon Blvd.
Howard Ave.
Polk Ave.
Maryland St.
Campus Ave.

Mission Hills Park

Pringle St.
Keating St.
W. Washington St.
Wellborn St.
Kite St.
Bush St.
Sutter St.
Reynard Wy.
1st Ave.
HILLCREST
Brookes Ave.
Walnut Ave.
Normal St.
Centre St.
Vermont St.
Richmond St.
University Ave.
Robinson Ave.
Cypress Ave.
Georgia St.

Walnut Ave.
Vine St.
Union St.
India St.
Thorn St.
Spruce St.
2nd Ave.
4th Ave.
Balboa Dr.
Myrtle Ave.
Upas St.

163

SAN DIEGO INT'L. AIRPORT

State St.

Nutmeg St.
Maple St.
Laurel St.
Kalmia St.
Juniper St.
Ivy St.
Hawthorn St.
Grape St.
Fir St.
Elm St.

PARK WEST
5th Ave.

San Diego Zoo

BALBOA PARK

El Prado

Park Blvd.
Florida St.

Spanish Village Art Center

W. Laurel St.
LITTLE ITALY
W. Grape St.
W. Date St.

Kettner Blvd.
India St.
State St.
Union St.
Columbia St.
1st Ave.
3rd Ave.
4th Ave.
6th Ave.
7th Ave.
8th Ave.
9th Ave.
10th Ave.
11th Ave.

Cedar St.
Beech St.
Ash St.
A St.
B St.
C St.
Broadway
E St.

Santa Fe Depot

B Street Pier
Broadway Pier
Navy Pier

N. Harbor Dr.
Pacific Hwy.
Front St.

G St.
GASLAMP QUARTER
Market St.
Island Ave.
J St.

Horton Plaza

Petco Park

San Diego Convention Center
E. Harbor Dr.
Park Blvd.

Embarcadero Marina Park

0   1/2 mi
0   1/2 km

San Diego Shopping

Antiques on Kettner **10**
Apple Box **13**
Babette Schwartz **4**
Boomerang for Modern **9**
Bubbles Boutique **19**
Carol Gardyne **12**
Fashion Valley Center **1**
G-Star **17**
Horton Plaza **15**
Kita Ceramics & Glassware **16**
Mid-Century **7**
Mint **5**
Mission Valley Center **2**
Mixture **11**
Seaport Village **14**
Spanish Village Art Center **8**
Taboo Studio **3**
Wear It Again Sam **6**
The Wine Bank **18**

> *Bangles, baubles, and bling go ultra-class at Taboo Studio, selling one-of-a-kind, art-piece jewelry.*

Gifts

★ **Babette Schwartz** HILLCREST

Camp meets kitsch at this fun-loving gift store stocked with novelties, cards, and T-shirts. 421 University Ave. (btw. 4th & 5th aves.). ☎ 619/220-7048. www.babette.com. MC, V. Bus: 1, 3, 10, 11, or 120. Map p. 605.

Bubbles Boutique GASLAMP QUARTER

An assortment of cute gifts, fashions, and accessories for women, but the main selling point here is the array of handcrafted soaps and bath items; try the banana shake–flavored bath bombs. 226 Fifth Ave. ☎ 619/236-9003. www.bubblesboutique.com. AE, MC, V. Bus: 992. Trolley: Orange Line to Gaslamp Quarter. Map p. 605.

> *Mod design reigns at Horton Plaza, ironically named after one of San Diego's visionary 19th-century developers.*

★★ **Kita Ceramics & Glassware** GASLAMP QUARTER

Objets d'art from Italy, Japan, and San Diego, including Murano glass jewelry and lighting, pottery, and home accessories. 517 Fourth Ave., Ste. 101 (at Island Ave.). ☎ 619/239-2600. www.kitaceramicsglass.com. AE, MC, V. Bus: 992. Trolley: Orange Line to Convention Center. Map p. 605.

Home Decor

★★★ **Boomerang for Modern** LITTLE ITALY

Sleek vintage modern furniture and accessories by Herman Miller, Vitra, Eames, and Noguchi. 2475 Kettner Blvd. (at Laurel St.). ☎ 619/239-2040. www.boomerangformodern.com. AE, DISC, MC, V. Bus: 83. Map p. 605.

★★★ **Mid-Century** HILLCREST

Way-cool pottery, light fixtures, cocktail accessories, furniture, and more from the 1940s, '50s, and '60s. 3795 Park Blvd. ☎ 619/295-4832. AE, DISC, MC, V. Bus: 7. Map p. 605.

★★ **Mixture** LITTLE ITALY
This old brick warehouse has been beautifully transformed into a repository of modern design and decor. 2210 Kettner Blvd. (at Ivy St.). ☎ 619/239-4788. www.mixturedesigns.com. AE, MC, V. Bus: 83. Map p. 605.

★★ kids **My Own Space** LA JOLLA
Hello Kitty meets midcentury modernism at this whimsical furniture and accessories boutique. 7840 Girard Ave. (btw. Silverado & Wall sts.). ☎ 858/459-0099. www.mosmyownspace.com. MC, V. Bus: 30. Map p.604.

Jewelry
★★ **Blondstone** LA JOLLA
Creative jewelry designs, including one-of-a-kind rings, pendants, earrings, and bracelets incorporating seashells and tumbled sea-glass "mermaid tears." 925 Prospect St. (at Drury Lane). ☎ 858/456.1994. www.blondstone.com. AE, MC, V. Bus: 30. Map p. 604.

★★★ **Taboo Studio** MISSION HILLS
The jewelry here is more than just simple ornamentation; these pieces are works of art created by nationally and internationally known jewelry artists. 1615½ W. Lewis St. (btw. Stephens St. & Palmetto Way). ☎ 619/692-0099. www.taboo studio.com. AE, DISC, MC, V. Bus: 83. Map p. 605.

Shopping Centers
★★ **Fashion Valley Center** MISSION VALLEY
This upscale shopping center features Nordstrom and Neiman Marcus department stores, as well as more than 200 specialty shops and an 18-screen movie theater. 7007 Friars Rd. (btw. Hwy. 163 & Fashion Valley Rd.). ☎ 619/688-9113. www.simon.com. Bus: 6, 14, 20, 25, 41, 120, or 928. Trolley: Blue or Green Line to Fashion Valley. Map p. 605.

★★ **Horton Plaza** GASLAMP QUARTER
This colorful shopping center has more than 130 specialty shops, two performing arts venues, a 14-screen cinema, two major department stores, and a variety of restaurants and short-order eateries. 324 Horton Plaza (bordered by Broadway, 1st & 4th aves., and G St.). ☎ 619/239-8180. www.westfield.com/ hortonplaza. Bus: 2, 3, 5, 7, 11, 15, 20, 30, 50, 120, 150, 210, 901, 923, 929, or 992. Trolley: Blue or Orange Line to Civic Center. Map p. 605.

> *Cape Cod meets San Diego at Seaport Village, a bayfront complex of shops, restaurants, and a popular carousel.*

Mission Valley Center MISSION VALLEY
This old-fashioned outdoor mall has budget-minded offerings such as Nordstrom Rack outlet store and Target; there's also a 20-screen movie theater and 150 other stores and places to eat. 1640 Camino del Rio N. (alongside I-8 at Mission Center Rd.). ☎ 619/296-6375. www. westfield.com/missionvalley. Bus: 6 or 14. Trolley: Blue or Green Line to Mission Valley Center. Map p. 605.

★ kids **Seaport Village** EMBARCADERO
This 14-acre bayfront outdoor mall provides an idyllic setting that visitors love. Many of the more than 50 shops are of the Southern California cutesy variety, but the atmosphere is pleasant, and there are a few gems. 849 W. Harbor Dr. (at Kettner Blvd.). ☎ 619/235-4014. www.seaportvillage.com. Trolley: Orange Line to Seaport Village. Map p. 605.

Wine
★★★ **The Wine Bank** GASLAMP QUARTER
This treasure trove of wine, spirits, and liqueurs sells vintages (including some rare ones) from all over the globe. And there are weekend tastings, too. 363 Fifth Ave. (at J St.). ☎ 619/234-7487. www.sdwinebank.com. AE, MC, V. Trolley: Orange Line to Gaslamp Quarter. Map p. 605.

San Diego Restaurant Best Bets

Best Mexican
Candelas, 416 Third Ave. and 1201 First St. (p. 610)

Best Mexican in Old Town
El Agave Tequileria, 2304 San Diego Ave. (p. 610)

Best Breakfast with a View
Brockton Villa, 1235 Coast Blvd. (p. 610)

Best Lunch with a View
George's Ocean Terrace at George's at the Cove, 1250 Prospect St. (p. 612)

Best Dinner with a View
Bertrand at Mister A's, 2550 Fifth Ave. (p. 609)

Best Place to Put Yourself at the Mercy of the Chef
Nine-Ten, 910 Prospect St. (p. 612)

Best Hipster Italian
Cucina Urbana, 505 Laurel St. (p. 610)

Best Steak
Cowboy Star, 640 10th Ave. (p. 610)

Best Seafood
The Oceanaire Seafood Room, 400 J St. (p. 613)

Best Seafood with a View
Island Prime, 880 Harbor Island Dr. (p. 612)

Best Pan-Asian
Red Pearl Kitchen, 440 J St. (p. 613)

Best Pizza
Bronx Pizza, 111 Washington St. (p. 609)

Best Desserts
Extraordinary Desserts, 2929 Fifth Ave. (p. 610)

Best Bistro
Cafe Chloe, 721 Ninth Ave. (p. 609)

Best Supper Club
Anthology, 1337 India St. (p. 609)

Best Picnic Fare
Bread & Cie, 350 University Ave. (p. 609)

Most Romantic
The Marine Room, 2000 Spindrift Dr. (p. 612)

Best Sushi
Zenbu, 7660 Fay Ave. (p. 613)

Best for Hipster Foodies
Cucina Urbana, 505 Laurel St. (p. 610)

> *Window seats never had it better than in the Marine Room (if you can't nab a table, try for a spot at the bar).*

San Diego Restaurants A to Z

★★★ **Anthology** LITTLE ITALY *AMERICAN*
It's hard to say what deserves more attention—the new American cuisine or the eclectic lineup of musical talent on stage. 1337 India St. ☎ 619/595-0300. www.anthologysd.com. Entrees $19–$28. AE, DISC, MC, V. Dinner Tues–Sun. Bus: 83. Map. p. 611.

★★★ **Bertrand at Mister A's** BALBOA PARK *AMERICAN/MEDITERRANEAN* This special occasion favorite of locals serves a seasonal menu in sophisticated surroundings. A bar/patio menu gives diners on a budget access to the million-dollar vistas. 2550 Fifth Ave. ☎ 619/239-1377. www.bertrandatmisteras.com. Entrees $13–$50. AE, DC, MC, V. Lunch Mon–Fri; dinner daily. Bus: 3 or 120. Map. p. 611.

★★ **Bread & Cie** HILLCREST *LIGHT FARE/MEDITERRANEAN* The traditions of European artisan bread making are proudly carried on here. You can get a light breakfast or a great sandwich, as well as loaves of specialty breads. 350 University Ave. ☎ 619/683-9322. www.breadand cie.com. Sandwiches and light meals $4–$9. DISC, MC, V. Breakfast, lunch, & dinner daily. Bus: 1, 3, 10, 11, or 120. Map. p. 611.

★ **Brockton Villa** LA JOLLA *CALIFORNIAN*
A restored 1894 beach bungalow, this charming cafe occupies a breathtaking perch overlooking La Jolla Cove. 1235 Coast Blvd. ☎ 858/454-7393. www.brocktonvilla.com. Entrees $7–$30. AE, DISC, MC, V. Breakfast & lunch daily; dinner Thurs–Sun. Bus: 30. Map p. 610.

★★ **Bronx Pizza** HILLCREST *ITALIAN*
This tiny pizzeria serves up arguably San Diego's best pies—other than calzones, that's all it makes. There's usually a line out the door. 111 Washington St. ☎ 619/291-3341. www.bronx pizza.com. Pies $13–$19; by the slice $2.50. Cash only. Lunch & dinner daily. Phone orders accepted for full pies. Bus: 3, 10, or 83. Map. p. 611.

★★ **Cafe Chloe** EAST VILLAGE *FRENCH*
The conviviality of this bistro—combined with a short but sweet French-inspired menu—makes for a winning dining experience. 721 Ninth Ave. ☎ 619/232-3242. www.cafechloe. com. Entrees $8–$23. AE, MC, V. Breakfast, lunch & dinner daily. Bus: 3, 5, 11, 901, or 929. Map. p. 611.

★★ **Caffé Bella Italia** PACIFIC BEACH *ITALIAN*
The location might be less than inspiring,

> *Try a side of whale-watching with your breakfast at stunning Brockton Villa, with the ocean nearly at your feet.*

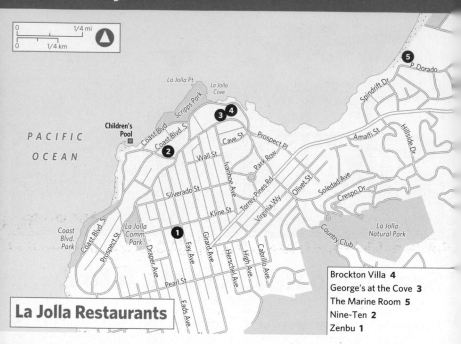

La Jolla Restaurants

Brockton Villa	**4**
George's at the Cove	**3**
The Marine Room	**5**
Nine-Ten	**2**
Zenbu	**1**

but the fresh, homemade Italian cuisine and the warm staff here are definitely not. The shellfish and pasta dishes are divine and you won't find better wood-fired pizza in the city. 1525 Garnet Ave. (btw. Ingraham & Haines sts.). ☎ 858/273-1224. www.caffebellaitalia.com. Entrees $13–$27. Dinner daily. Bus: 8, 9, or 27. Map. p 611.

★★ **Candelas** GASLAMP QUARTER/CORONADO MEXICAN If you're looking for tacos and burritos, go somewhere else—if you're in the mood for a sophisticated, romantic fine dining experience, look no further. The Coronado location has stellar bay views. Gaslamp Quarter: 416 Third Ave. ☎ 619/702-4455. www.candelas-sd. com. Entrees $22–$53. AE, DC, DISC, MC, V. Dinner daily. Bus: 11 or 120. Trolley: Convention Center. Coronado: 1201 First St. ☎ 619/435-4900. Entrees $9–$53. Breakfast Sat–Sun; lunch & dinner daily. Bus: 904. Coronado Ferry. Map. p. 611.

★★ **Cowboy Star** EAST VILLAGE AMERICAN This restaurant and butcher shop is an unabashed homage to classic Hollywood Westerns, specializing in dry-aged meats and game fowl. 640 10th Ave. ☎ 619/450-5880. www. thecowboystar.com. Entrees $10–$82. AE, DISC, MC, V. Lunch Tues–Fri; dinner Tues–Sun. Bus:

3, 5, 11, 901, or 929. Trolley: Park & Market. Map. p. 611.

★★★ **Cucina Urbana** BALBOA PARK ITALIAN A hip, happening spot serving artisanal pizza, antipasti, and cocktails. 505 Laurel St. ☎ 619/239-2222. www.sdurbankitchen.com. Entrees $10–$20. AE, DC, DISC, MC, V. Dinner Tues–Sun. Bus: 3 or 120. Map. p. 611.

★ **Dobson's Bar & Restaurant** GASLAMP QUARTER CALIFORNIAN By day it buzzes with the energy of movers and shakers; in the evening it segues from happy-hour watering hole to sophisticated pre- and post-theater American bistro. 956 Broadway Circle (at Broadway). ☎ 619/231-6771. www.dobsonsrestaurant.com. Entrees $10–$39. Lunch Mon–Fri; dinner Mon–Sat. Bus: 7, 929, or 992. Map. p. 611.

★★ **El Agave Tequileria** OLD TOWN MEXICAN The regional Mexican cuisine and rustic elegance here leave the touristy joints of Old Town far behind. It also boasts more than 850 tequilas and mescals and some of the best margaritas in town. 2304 San Diego Ave. ☎ 619/220-0692. www.elagave.com. Entrees $8–$32. AE, MC, V. Lunch & dinner daily. Bus: 8, 9, 10, 14, 28, or 30. Trolley: Old Town. Map. p. 611.

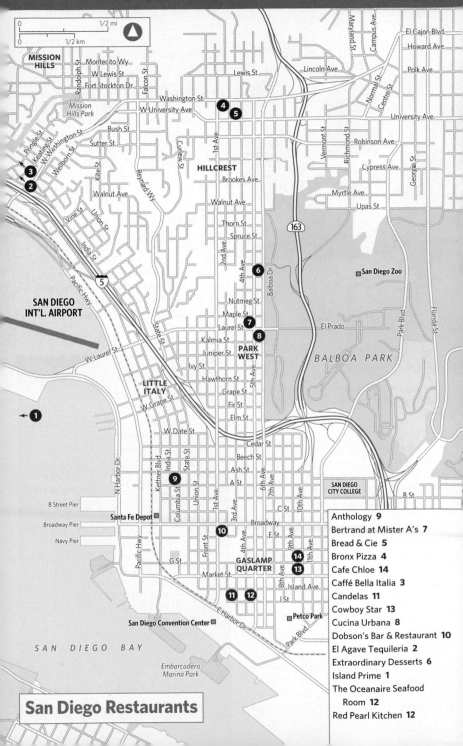

San Diego Restaurants

Anthology **9**
Bertrand at Mister A's **7**
Bread & Cie **5**
Bronx Pizza **4**
Cafe Chloe **14**
Caffé Bella Italia **3**
Candelas **11**
Cowboy Star **13**
Cucina Urbana **8**
Dobson's Bar & Restaurant **10**
El Agave Tequileria **2**
Extraordinary Desserts **6**
Island Prime **1**
The Oceanaire Seafood
　　Room **12**
Red Pearl Kitchen **12**

> Ditch the diet and indulge in the delectable (and gorgeous) creations at aptly named Extraordinary Desserts.

★★★ **Extraordinary Desserts** HILLCREST DESSERTS/LIGHT FARE Some of the dozens of divine creations are available here are garnished with edible gold, and they are all worth every calorie. An exclusive line of jams, syrups, spices, and confections is also for sale. See p. 579, ❷ for info on the Little Italy branch. 2929 Fifth Ave. ☎ 619/294-2132. www.extraordinarydesserts.com. Entrees $6–$20; desserts $2–$9. AE, MC, V. Breakfast, lunch, & dinner daily. Map. p. 611

★★★ **George's at the Cove** LA JOLLA CALIFORNIAN Two restaurants, one location. George's California Modern has it all: stunning ocean views, style, impeccable service, and above all, a world-class chef. Those seeking fine food and incomparable views at more modest prices can head upstairs to George's Ocean Terrace for lunch or dinner on the roof. 1250 Prospect St. 858/454-4244. www. george

satthecove.com. California Modern: entrees $28–$90. Dinner daily. Ocean Terrace: entrees $10–$25. Lunch & dinner daily. AE, DC, DISC, MC, V. Bus: 30. Map. p. 610.

★★ **Island Prime** EMBARCADERO SEAFOOD With its spectacular bay and skyline vistas, it would be easy to understand if Island Prime didn't even bother to make its food interesting—but the views actually have some competition here. 880 Harbor Island Dr. ☎ 619/298-6802. www.cohnrestaurants.com. Entrees $11–$49. AE, DC, DISC, MC, V. Lunch & dinner daily. Bus: 923 or 992. Map. p. 611.

★★★ **The Marine Room** LA JOLLA FRENCH/CALIFORNIAN Open since 1941, this shorefront institution is San Diego's most celebrated dining room. Executive chef Bernard Guillas sees to it that the food lives up to its room with a view. 2000 Spindrift Dr. ☎ 866/644-2351. www.marineroom.com. Entrees $27–$48. AE, DC, DISC, MC, V. Dinner daily. Bus: 30. Map. p. 610.

A Better Burger

The humble burger has seen a resurgence of popularity in San Diego, and it's no longer so humble. Upscale hamburger spots have been springing up all over town, and they are not generic fast-food joints. Think grass-fed organic beef mixed with snazzy beer and wine menus.

It's not fancy, but the don't-miss spot for burger lovers is ★ **Tioli's Crazee Burger,** 4201 30th St., North Park (☎ 619/282-6044), which has turned the burger into truly fine dining. There are more than 30 versions on the menu, featuring such exotic ingredients as ostrich and alligator.

For a big, messy burger in a classic beach environment, **Hodad's,** 5010 Newport Ave., Ocean Beach (☎ 619/224-4623; www.hodadies.com) is the place to go—many locals claim it's the best in town.

For a gourmet burger in a great setting (check out the skyline mural) stop by ★ **Neighborhood,** 777 G. St., downtown (☎ 619/446-0002; www.neighborhoodsd.com), which also has 27 beers on tap and a sophisticated wine list.

> *Dine in elegant surroundings at Candelas, serving sophisticated Mexican fare—think la langosta (lobster), not taco.*

★★★ Nine-Ten LA JOLLA *CALIFORNIAN*

The seasonal menu at this stylish spot is best enjoyed via small-plate grazing; better yet, turn yourself over to the "Mercy of the Chef," a five-course tasting menu. 910 Prospect St. ☎ 858/964-5400. www.nine-ten.com. Entrees $6–$40. AE, DC, DISC, MC, V. Breakfast, lunch & dinner daily. Bus: 30. Map p. 610.

★★ The Oceanaire Seafood Room GASLAMP

QUARTER *SEAFOOD* Featuring top local products as well as fish brought in daily from around the globe, the menu incorporates elements of Pacific Rim, Italian, classic French, and Asian cuisine. 400 J St. ☎ 619/858-2277. www.theoceanaire.com. Entrees $15–$50. AE, DISC, MC, V. Dinner daily. Bus: 3, 11, or 120. Trolley: Convention Center. Map. p. 611.

★★ Red Pearl Kitchen GASLAMP QUARTER

CHINESE/ASIAN FUSION This sexy restaurant and bar specializes in dim sum dishes with a contemporary, Pan-Asian flair. 440 J St. ☎ 619/231-1100. www.redpearlkitchen.com/ sandiego. Entrees $8–$20. AE, MC, V. Dinner daily. Bus: 3, 11, or 120. Trolley: Convention Center or Gaslamp Quarter. Map p. 611.

★★ Zenbu LA JOLLA *SUSHI/SEAFOOD*

You can order something from the sushi bar or maybe an entree like steak of locally harpooned swordfish. 7660 Fay Ave. ☎ 858/454-

Baja Fish Tacos

Migrating north from the fishing towns of Baja California, fish tacos are a San Diego staple, favored by everyone from surfers to CEOs. **Rubio's Fresh Mexican Grill** (www.rubios.com), now a sizable chain with outlets all over town, popularized fish tacos here in the early 1980s. Rubio's is still a good option when you're on the go, but better yet, drop into a fish market such as **Point Loma Seafoods**, 2805 Emerson St., Point Loma (☎ 619/223-1109; www.point lomaseafoods.com), for a tangy, messy fish taco.

4540. www.zenbusushi.com. Entrees $22–$30. AE, DC, DISC, MC, V. Dinner daily. Bus: 30. Map. p. 610.

San Diego Hotel Best Bets

Best Historic Hotel
Hotel del Coronado, 1500 Orange Ave. (p. 617)

Best Place to Stay and Play for Families
Paradise Point Resort & Spa, 1404 Vacation Rd. (p. 619)

Best Place to Stay and Play for Adults
Andaz Hotel, 650 F St. (p. 615)

Best Green Hotel
Hotel Indigo, 509 Ninth Ave. (p. 617)

Best for Business and Pleasure
Hilton San Diego Gaslamp Quarter, 401 K St. (p.616)

Best Moderately Priced Hotel
Horton Grand Hotel, 311 Island Ave. (p. 616)

Best Budget Hotel
La Pensione Hotel, 606 W. Date St. (p. 617)

Best Bed & Breakfast
Britt Scripps Inn, 406 Maple St. (p. 615)

Best Boutique Inn
Hotel Parisi, 1111 Prospect St. (p. 617)

Best Place to Stay on the Beach
Tower 23, 723 Felspar St. (p. 619)

Best Place to Stay Over the Beach
Crystal Pier Hotel, 4500 Ocean Blvd. (p. 615)

Best Place to Feel Like a Rock Star
Hard Rock Hotel San Diego, 207 Fifth Ave. (p. 616)

Best for Traditionalists
The US Grant, 326 Broadway (p. 619)

Best Trysting by the Pool
Sè San Diego, 1047 Fifth Ave. (p. 619)

Best Place to Pretend You're in the French Riviera
La Valencia Hotel, 1132 Prospect St. (p. 617)

Best Place to Pretend You're in the South Seas
Catamaran Resort Hotel, 3999 Mission Blvd. (p. 615)

> *Feel like Fergie at Hard Rock Hotel, 12 stories of hip, modern vibe soaring above the Gaslamp Quarter.*

San Diego Hotels A to Z

★★★ **Andaz Hotel** GASLAMP QUARTER
A dowdy old hotel magically transformed into a world-class, high-style luxury destination. Formerly known as the Ivy Hotel, it features a four-level nightclub and rooftop pool/entertainment area. 650 F St. ☎ 877/489-4489 or 619/814-1000. www.andaz.com. 159 units. Doubles $349–$449. AE, DC, DISC, MC, V. Bus: 3 or 120. Map p. 618.

The Beach Cottages PACIFIC BEACH
This family-owned operation has been around since 1948 and offers a variety of guest quarters, including cottages just steps from the sand. 4255 Ocean Blvd. ☎ 858/483-7440. www.beachcottages.com. 61 units. Doubles from $140; cottages from $285. AE, DC, DISC, MC, V. Bus: 8 or 9. Map p. 617.

★★★ **Britt Scripps Inn** BANKERS HILL
A glorious Victorian house lovingly converted into an intimate "estate hotel"—part B&B, part luxury hotel. 406 Maple St. ☎ 888/881-1991 or 619/230-1991. www.brittscripps.com. 9 units. Doubles $375–$525 w/breakfast and afternoon wine & hors d'oeuvres. AE, DC, MC, V. Bus: 3 or 120. Map p. 618.

★★ kids **Catamaran Resort Hotel** PACIFIC BEACH Right on Mission Bay, this Polynesian-themed resort has its own beach, complete with watersports facilities. 3999 Mission Blvd. ☎ 800/422-8386 or 858/488-1081. www.catamaranresort.com. 311 units. Doubles $249–$409. AE, DC, DISC, MC, V. Bus: 8 or 9. Map p. 617.

★★ kids **Crystal Pier Hotel** PACIFIC BEACH
This unique cluster of cottages literally sits over the surf on the vintage Crystal Pier. 4500 Ocean Blvd. ☎ 800/748-5894 or 858/483-6983. www.crystalpier.com. 29 units. Doubles $300–$375. DISC, MC, V. Bus: 8, 9, 27, or 30. Map p. 617.

★★★ **Estancia La Jolla Hotel and Spa** LA JOLLA This 9½-acre California rancho-style property opened in 2004 on the remains of a horse farm. The tastefully decorated, hacienda-style rooms and top-notch spa give it an even more romantic atmosphere. 9700 N. Torrey Pines Rd. (north of Almahurst Row). ☎ 877/437-8262. www.estancialajolla.com. 210 units. Doubles from $229. AE, DC, DISC, MC, V. Bus: 101. Map p. 616.

> *Double-decker beds might not be for everyone, but they fit the style at über-cool Andaz Hotel.*

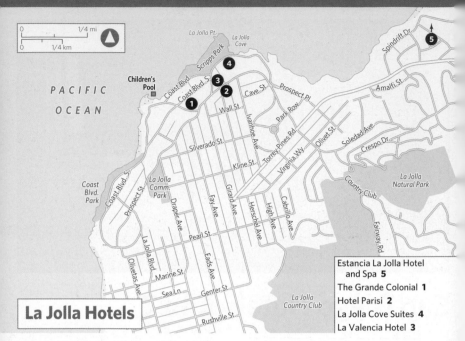

La Jolla Hotels

Estancia La Jolla Hotel
and Spa **5**
The Grande Colonial **1**
Hotel Parisi **2**
La Jolla Cove Suites **4**
La Valencia Hotel **3**

★★ **Glorietta Bay Inn** CORONADO
This pretty hotel consists of the charmingly historic John D. Spreckels mansion (1908) and several younger, motel-style buildings. 1630 Glorietta Blvd., Coronado. ☎ 800/283-9383 or 619/435-3101. www.gloriettabayinn.com. 100 units. Doubles from $185 w/breakfast. AE, DC, DISC, MC, V. Bus: 901 or 904. Map p. 618.

★★★ **The Grande Colonial** LA JOLLA
This refined hotel possesses an old-world European flair that's more London or Georgetown than seaside La Jolla. 910 Prospect St. ☎ 888/530-5766 or 858/454-2181. www. thegrandecolonial.com. 93 units. Doubles from $295. AE, DC, MC, V. Bus: 30. Map p. 616.

★★ **Hard Rock Hotel San Diego** GASLAMP QUARTER This 12-story condo-hotel has a sweet location, a celebrity-chef restaurant, and an outdoor concert space. The Black Eyed Peas designed one of the "Rock Star" suites. 207 Fifth Ave. ☎ 866/751-7625 or 619/702-3000. www.hardrockhotelsd.com. 420 units. Doubles $250–$500. AE, DC, DISC, MC, V. Trolley: Gaslamp Quarter. Map p.618.

★★★ **Hilton San Diego Gaslamp Quarter**
GASLAMP QUARTER This handsome hotel incorporates elements of a historic building. It's also a great place for guests who want to be in the heart of the Gaslamp action. 401 K St. ☎ 800/445-8667 or 619/231-4040. www. hilton. com. 282 units. Doubles $389. AE, DC, DISC, MC, V. Trolley: Gaslamp Quarter or Convention Center. Map p. 618.

★★ kids **Holiday Inn on the Bay** EMBARCADERO
This three-building high-rise complex has a scenic location across from the harbor; easy access to the airport and public transport; and basic rooms that are clean, comfy, and thoughtfully decked out. 1355 N. Harbor Dr. ☎ 800/972-2802 or 619/232-3861. www. holiday-inn.com/san-onthebay. 600 units. Doubles from $180. AE, DC, DISC, MC, V. Bus: 2, 210, 810, 820, 850, 860, 923, or 992. Trolley: America Plaza. Map p. 618.

★ **Horton Grand Hotel** GASLAMP QUARTER
This charming property combines two hotels built 1886. Both were saved from demolition and moved to this spot. 311 Island Ave. ☎ 800/542-1886 or 619/544-1886. www.hortongrand. com. 132 units. Doubles from $179. AE, DC, MC, V. Bus: 3, 11, or 120. Trolley: Convention Center. Map p. 618.

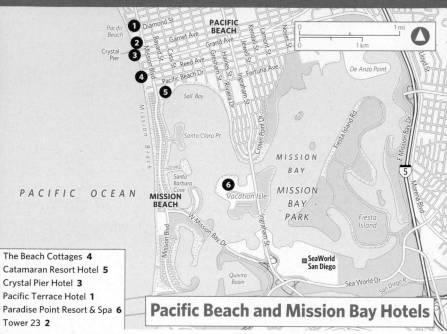

The Beach Cottages **4**
Catamaran Resort Hotel **5**
Crystal Pier Hotel **3**
Pacific Terrace Hotel **1**
Paradise Point Resort & Spa **6**
Tower 23 **2**

Pacific Beach and Mission Bay Hotels

★★★ Hotel del Coronado CORONADO
Opened in 1888 and designated a National Historic Landmark in 1977, the Hotel Del is the last of California's stately seaside hotels and a monument to Victorian grandeur. 1500 Orange Ave., Coronado. ☎ 800/468-3533 or 619/435-6611. www.hoteldel.com. 757 units. Doubles from $340. AE, DC, DISC, MC, V. Bus: 901 or 904. Map p. 618.

★★ Hotel Indigo EAST VILLAGE
Green is the primary color at this new boutique property—it's San Diego's first LEED-certified hotel. The state-of-the-art rooms don't scrimp on comfort—high tech or otherwise. 509 Ninth Ave. ☎ 877/846-3446 or 619/727-4000. www.hotelindigo.com/sandiego. 210 units. Doubles $225–$319. AE, DC, DISC, MC, V. Bus: 3, 11, 901, or 929. Trolley: Park & Market. Map p. 618.

★ Hotel Occidental BANKERS HILL
Just a block from Balboa Park, this attractive Mission-style building has been restored to its 1923 glory. 410 Elm St. ☎ 800/205-9897 or 619/232-1336. www.hoteloccidental-sandiego.com. 54 units. Doubles from $69 w/breakfast. AE, MC, V. Bus: 3 or 120. Map p. 618.

★★★ Hotel Parisi LA JOLLA
Feng shui principles hold sway at this boutique hotel; the Italy-meets-Zen composition is modern yet comfy. 1111 Prospect St. ☎ 877/472-7474 or 858/454-1511. www.hotelparisi.com. 28 units. Doubles from $295 w/breakfast. AE, DC, DISC, MC, V. Bus: 30. Map p. 616.

La Jolla Cove Suites LA JOLLA
Sitting across from Ellen Browning Scripps Park, this family-run 1950s-era hotel has to-die-for ocean views and is steps away from the cove. 1155 Coast Blvd. ☎ 888/525-6552 or 858/459-2621. www.lajollacove.com. 90 units. Doubles from $242 w/breakfast. AE, DC, DISC, MC, V. Bus: 30. Map p. 616.

★ La Pensione Hotel LITTLE ITALY
Pluses at this budget property include modern amenities, remarkable value, a convenient location, a friendly staff, and free parking. 606 W. Date St. ☎ 800/232-4683 or 619/236-8000. www.lapensionehotel.com. 75 units. Doubles $90. AE, DC, DISC, MC, V. Bus: 83. Trolley: County Center/Little Italy. Map p. 618.

★★★ La Valencia Hotel LA JOLLA
This bluff-top hotel, which looks like a Mediterranean vjlla, has been the centerpiece of

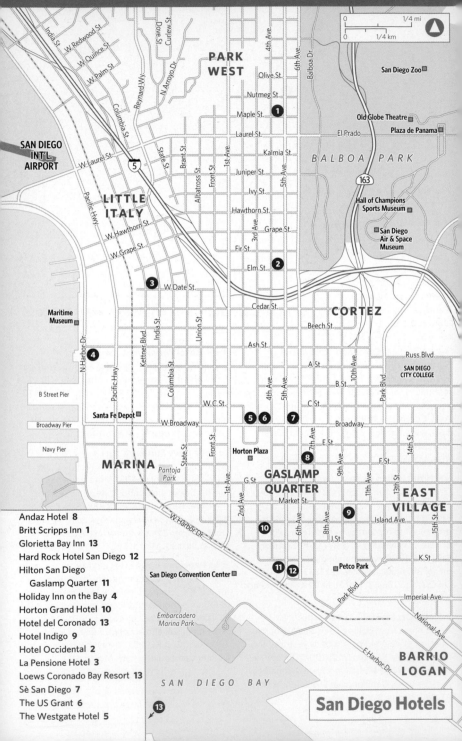

San Diego Hotels

> *A beach beauty beyond compare, the still-exquisite Hotel del Coronado has catered to presidents, princes, and Marilyn Monroe.*

La Jolla since opening in 1926. La V's clubby Whaling Bar is a classic. 1132 Prospect St. ☎ 800/451-0772 or 858/454-0771. www.lavalencia.com. 113 units. Doubles from $295. AE, DC, DISC, MC, V. Bus: 30. Map p. 616.

★★ **kids Loews Coronado Bay Resort** CORONADO Located on its own private peninsula 4 miles south of downtown Coronado, this isolated resort destination has a plethora of water-related activities, supervised children's programs, and private beach access. 4000 Coronado Bay Rd. (off Silver Strand Blvd.), Coronado. ☎ 800/235-6397. www.loewshotels/sandiego.com. 438 units. Doubles from $240. AE, DC, DISC, MC, V. Bus: 901. Map p. 618.

★ **Pacific Terrace Hotel** PACIFIC BEACH More upscale than most of the casual places nearby, this boardwalk hotel features a South Seas–meets–Spanish colonial ambience. 610 Diamond St. ☎ 800/344-3370 or 858/581-3500. www.pacificterrace.com. 73 units. Doubles from $359 w/breakfast. AE, DC, DISC, MC, V. Bus: 30. Map p. 617.

★★ **kids Paradise Point Resort & Spa** MISSION BAY Smack-dab in the middle of Mission Bay Park, this hotel complex is almost as much a theme park as its closest neighbor, SeaWorld (a 3-min. drive). 1404 Vacation Rd. ☎ 800/344-2626 or 858/274-4630. www.paradisepoint.com. 462 units. Doubles from $329. AE, DC, DISC, MC, V. Bus: 8 or 9. Map p. 617.

★★ **Sè San Diego** DOWNTOWN This sexy hotel features a Zen-chic vibe and a happening pool lounge where the beautiful people come to party. 1047 Fifth Ave. ☎ 619/515-3000. www.sesandiego.com. 184 units. Doubles $259–$359. AE, DISC, MC, V. Bus: 2, 3, 7, 120, or 923. Trolley: Fifth Ave. Map p. 618.

★★ **Tower 23** PACIFIC BEACH This modernist beach resort sits right alongside the boardwalk in Pacific Beach. 723 Felspar St. ☎ 866/869-3723. www.t23hotel.com. 44 units. Doubles from $309. AE, DC, DISC, MC, V. Bus: 8, 9, 27, or 30. Map p. 617.

★★★ **The US Grant** DOWNTOWN Built in 1910, this 11-story property is one of San Diego's most plush and historic hotels. 326 Broadway. ☎ 800/237-5029 or 866/837-4270. www.usgrant.net. 270 units. Doubles from $341. AE, DC, DISC, MC, V. Bus: 2, 3, 7, 20, 120, 923, or 992. Trolley: Civic Center. Map p. 618.

★★ **The Westgate Hotel** DOWNTOWN With its regal and lavish interior decor, this is about as "Old World" as San Diego gets. It's a hub of cultural and culinary activities, as well. 1055 Second Ave. (btw. Broadway & C St.). ☎ 800/522-1564. www.westgatehotel.com. 223 units. Doubles from $245. AE, DC, DISC, MC, V. Bus: 2, 7, 923, or 929. Trolley: Blue or Orange Line to Civic Center. Map p. 618.

San Diego Nightlife & Entertainment Best Bets

Best Bar with a View
Top of the Hyatt, 1 Market Place (p. 624)

Best Rock-'n'-Roll Club
The Casbah, 2501 Kettner Blvd. (p. 621)

Best Megaclub
Stingaree, 454 Sixth Ave. (p. 624)

Best Place for Jazz
Dizzy's, 200 Harbor Dr. (p. 623)

Best Supper Club
Anthology, 1337 India St. (p. 621)

Best 2-for-1 Experience
The Onyx Room/Thin, 852 Fifth Ave. (p. 623)

Best Outsider Art Collection
House of Blues, 1055 Fifth Ave. (p. 623)

Best Spot for Latin Music
Sevilla, 555 Fourth Ave. (p. 623)

Best Place for Horsing Around
Del Mar Fairgrounds, 2260 Jimmy Durante Blvd. (p. 624)

Best Sports Venue
PETCO Park, 100 Park Blvd. (p. 624)

Best Classical Music Festival
La Jolla Music Society SummerFest, various locations (p. 621)

Best Place for Culture in a Mall
San Diego Repertory Theatre, Horton Plaza (p. 625)

Best Use of Strings and Pyrotechnics
San Diego Symphony Summer Pops, Embarcadero Marina Park South (p. 621)

Best Place for Tragic Heroines
San Diego Opera, 1200 Third Ave. (p. 621)

Best Broadway-Bound Fare
La Jolla Playhouse, 2910 La Jolla Village Dr. (p. 625)

Best Place to Be a Groundling
The Old Globe Theatre, Balboa Park (p. 625)

> *Making music along the Embarcadero, sight of the exceptional San Diego Summer Pops series.*

San Diego Nightlife & Entertainment A to Z

Classical Music/Opera

★★ **La Jolla Music Society** VARIOUS LOCATIONS This well-respected organization has been bringing marquee names to town since 1968; the acclaimed SummerFest in August features concerts, lectures, and workshops. Box office, 7946 Ivanhoe Ave., La Jolla. ☎ 858/459-3728. www.ljms.org. Tickets $25–$95. Bus: 30. Map p. 622.

★★★ **San Diego Opera** DOWNTOWN A season of both well-trod warhorses and edgier works runs from late January to mid-May, performed at the Civic Theatre by local singers and talent from around the world. 1200 Third Ave. ☎ 619/533-7000 (box office) or 619/232-7636 (admin). www.sdopera.com. Tickets $35–$200. Bus: 30, 50, 150, 923, or 992. Trolley: Civic Center. Map p. 622.

★ **San Diego Symphony** DOWNTOWN/EMBARCADERO Top talent performs at Copley Symphony Hall, then transfers to the waterfront for open-air summer pops concerts with fireworks. Symphony Hall, 750 B St. ☎ 619/235-0804. www.sandiegosymphony.com. Tickets $20–$100. Bus: 3 or 120. Trolley for downtown: Fifth Ave. Trolley for Embarcadero: Gaslamp Quarter. Map p. 622.

Bars/Clubs

★★★ **Anthology** LITTLE ITALY You don't have to eat at this fine-dining establishment in order to enjoy the show at this top-notch music venue, where a host of marquee-name jazz, blues, and world-music artists take care of the entertainment. See p. 609.

★ **The Bitter End** GASLAMP QUARTER This trilevel hot spot manages to be a sophisticated martini bar, dance club, music venue, and relaxing cocktail lounge all in one. 770 Fifth Ave. ☎ 619/338-9300. www.thebitterend.com. Cover Fri–Sat $10 after 9pm. Bus: 3, 120, or 992. Trolley: Fifth Ave. Map p. 622.

★ **The Casbah** LITTLE ITALY This rockin' dive has a well-earned rep for showcasing alternative and punk bands that either are, were, or will be famous; live music can be counted on at least 6 nights a week. 2501 Kettner Blvd. ☎ 619/232-4355. www.thecasbah.com. Cover usually under $15. Bus: 83. Map p. 622.

> *Class acts take to the stage at La Jolla Playhouse, one of the country's leading regional theaters.*

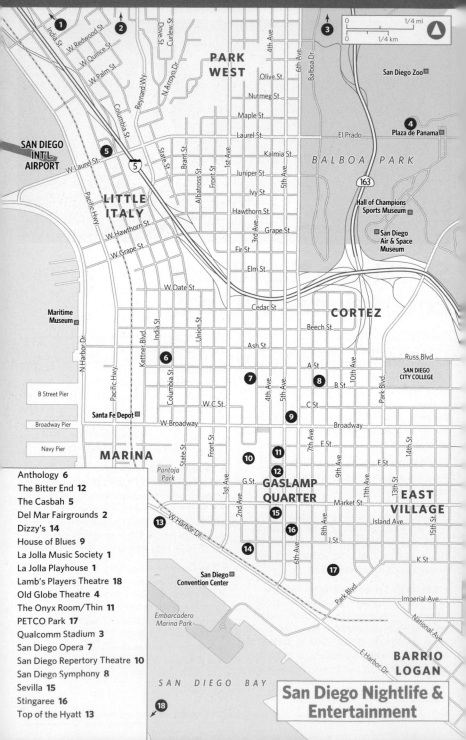

0   1/4 mi

0   1/4 km

PARK WEST

San Diego Zoo

Olive St.

Nutmeg St.

Maple St.

Laurel St.

El Prado

Plaza de Panama

BALBOA PARK

SAN DIEGO INT'L. AIRPORT

Kalmia St.

Juniper St.

Ivy St.

Hall of Champions Sports Museum

LITTLE ITALY

Hawthorn St.

Grape St.

San Diego Air & Space Museum

W. Hawthorn St.

Fir St.

W. Grape St.

Elm St.

W. Date St.

CORTEZ

Cedar St.

Maritime Museum

Beech St.

Ash St.

A St.

Russ Blvd.

SAN DIEGO CITY COLLEGE

B St.

B Street Pier

W. C St.

C St.

Broadway

Santa Fe Depot

Broadway Pier

W. Broadway

Navy Pier

MARINA

E St.

F St.

Pantoja Park

G St.

GASLAMP QUARTER

EAST VILLAGE

Market St.

Island Ave.

W. Harbor Dr.

J St.

K St.

San Diego Convention Center

Embarcadero Marina Park

Imperial Ave.

National Ave.

BARRIO LOGAN

E. Harbor Dr.

SAN DIEGO BAY

San Diego Nightlife & Entertainment

★ **Dizzy's** GASLAMP QUARTER
This all-ages venue, located in the San Diego Wine & Culinary Center, is centrally located and serves up uncompromising jazz. 200 Harbor Dr. ☎ 858/270-7467. www.dizzyssandiego. com. Tickets $10–$20, available at the door (cash only). Bus: 992. Trolley: Convention Center. Map p. 622.

★★ **House of Blues** DOWNTOWN
A visual feast of outsider art, there's also an 1,100-person concert space and a restaurant serving Southern-inspired cuisine (open for lunch daily and Sun gospel brunch). 1055 Fifth Ave. ☎ 619/299-2583. www.hob.com/sandiego. Ticket prices vary. Bus: 3, 120, or numerous Broadway routes. Trolley: Fifth Ave. Map p. 622.

★★★ **The Onyx Room/Thin** GASLAMP QUARTER
This twofer is hard to beat. At subterranean Onyx the atmosphere is lounge, the music is chill. At street level is hypermodern Thin, run by the same crew. 852 Fifth Ave. ☎ 619/235-6699. www.onyxroom.com. Cover Thurs–Fri $10, Sat $15 (includes both bars). Bus: 3, 120, 992, or numerous Broadway routes. Trolley: Fifth Ave. Map p. 622

★★ **Sevilla** GASLAMP QUARTER
This Latin-themed club is the spot for salsa dancing (and lessons); there's also a tapas bar and dining room. Live flamenco and Gypsy music dinner shows are staged Friday and Saturday. 555 Fourth Ave. ☎ 619/233-5979. www. sevillanightclub.com. Cover $5–$15. Bus: 3, 11, or 120. Trolley: Convention Center. Map p. 622.

Brewpubs & Wine Bars

Over the last decade, San Diego has been making a name for itself in the beer world, with local brewers earning props at the World Beer Cup and Great American Beer Festival. While San Diego's regional wineries haven't earned the same respect, whether you are a beer drinker or a wine sipper, there are plenty of great places to quaff local (and international) libations. If you'd like someone else to do the driving, check out the beer tours run by **Brew Hop** (☎ **858/361-8457;** www.brewhop.com) and **Brewery Tours of San Diego** (☎ **619/961-7999;** www.brewery toursofsandiego.com).

San Diego's most acclaimed brewery, **Stone Brewery World Bistro and Gardens,** 1999 Citracado Pkwy., Escondido (☎ **760/471-4999;** www.stonebrew.com), is the maker of Arrogant Bastard Ale. Both lunch and dinner are served at this elegant, beautifully landscaped indoor/outdoor eatery.

Pizza Port Brewing Company (www. pizzaport.com), located at 135 N. Hwy. 101, Solana Beach (☎ **858/481-7332**) and 571 Carlsbad Village Dr., Carlsbad (☎ **760/720-7007**), has creative pizzas and giant pretzels to go along with award-winning beers, including the signature Sharkbite Red ale. Kids can enjoy the house-made root beer.

Pacific Beach AleHouse, 721 Grand Ave. (☎ **858/581-2337;** www.pbalehouse.

com), has a rooftop deck where you can sip a Pacific Sunset IPA while you actually watch a Pacific sunset. With its multitude of flatscreen TVs, it's a great place to catch a sporting event, too.

Wine and beer drinkers can find common ground at the **Vine,** 1851 Bacon St., Ocean Beach (☎ **619/222-8463;** www.theobvine. com), which serves quality wines by the glass and by the flight and offers an excellent selection of beer. It also has an eclectic menu of tapas.

Hillcrest's **Wine Steals,** 1243 University Ave. (☎ **619/295-1188;** www.winestealssd. com), has a casual, neighborhood feel and includes a wine-shop component And don't let the nondescript strip-mall setting dissuade you from checking out the **Wine Encounter,** 690 University Ave. (☎ **619/543-9463;** www.thewineencounter.com), where you'll find probably the city's largest by-the-glass selection, with more than 150 wines available, along with nearly 30 flights.

Downtown, ultracool **Vin de Syrah,** 901 Fifth Ave. (☎ 619/234-4166; www.syrah wineparlor.com), uncorks on the weekends and becomes a jamming club. The **Cask Room,** 550 Park Blvd., East Village (☎ **619/ 822-1606;** www.caskroom.com), offers free Wi-Fi, a selection of cheeses and appetizers, and plenty of beer selections.

> *Pony up your wagers at Del Mar Race Track, where horse-racing fans root for their favorite steed in summer.*

★★ Stingaree GASLAMP QUARTER
This trilevel club has more than 22,000 square feet of space, a fine-dining component, a handful of bars and private nooks, and a rooftop deck with cabanas and a fire pit. 454 Sixth Ave. ☎ 619/544-9500. www.stingsandiego.com. Cover $20. Trolley: Gaslamp Quarter. Map p. 622.

★★★ Top of the Hyatt EMBARCADERO
Perched on the 40th floor of the West Coast's tallest waterfront building, this is San Diego's ultimate bar with a view. 1 Market Place. ☎ 619/232-1234. www.manchestergrand.hyatt.com. Trolley: Seaport Village. Map p. 622.

Spectator Sports
★★★ Del Mar Fairgrounds DEL MAR
Thoroughbred racing takes place at the Del Mar Race Track from mid-July to early September. Post-time is usually 2pm; there's no racing on Tuesday. Concerts and other special events are often part of the season, as well.

There's also year-round satellite wagering here at the Surfside Race Place (☎ 858/755-1167; www.surfsideraceplace.com). The Del Mar National Horse Show is held at the fairgrounds mid-April to early May. 2260 Jimmy Durante Blvd., Del Mar. ☎ 858/793-5555 or 858/755-1141. www.sdfair.com or www.delmarracing.com. Admission $5–$15. Bus: 101. Map p. 622.

★★ PETCO Park EAST VILLAGE
Opened in downtown in 2004, this architecturally striking facility holds more than 44,000 spectators. This "pitcher's park" is the home of the San Diego Padres Major League Baseball team; it might be short on long balls, but the views of the bay and downtown are great. Baseball season runs April to September. 100 Park Blvd. ☎ 877/374-2784 or 619/795-5000. www.petcoparkevents.com or www.padres.com. Padres tickets $5–$69. Trolley: Gaslamp Quarter, 12th & Imperial Transit Center, or Park & Market. Map p. 622.

Qualcomm Stadium MISSION VALLEY
Also known as "The Q," this 71,000-seat facility was once the home of the San Diego Padres, but now plays host to the city's football teams, the NFL San Diego Chargers (who actually played the first game held here back in 1967) and the San Diego State University Aztecs. Football season runs from August to December. 9449 Friars Rd. ☎ 619/220-8497 or 877/242-7437. www.sandiego.gov/qualcomm or www.chargers.com. Charger tickets $54–$98. Trolley: Qualcomm Stadium. Map p. 622.

Theater

★★★ La Jolla Playhouse LA JOLLA
This Tony Award–winning playhouse is known for its contemporary take on classics and its commitment to commedia dell'arte style, as well as for producing Broadway-bound blockbusters. 2910 La Jolla Village Dr. ☎ 858/550-1010. www.lajollaplayhouse.org. Tickets $25–$75. Bus: 30, 41, 48, 49, 101, 150, or 921. Map p. 622.

★★ Lamb's Players Theatre CORONADO
A resident professional company presents premieres and classics at its home theater in the heart of Coronado. The drama tends to be of the safe, noncontroversial variety. 1142 Orange Ave., Coronado. ☎ 619/437-0600. www.lambsplayers.org. Tickets $22–$58. Bus: 901 or 904. Map p. 622.

★★★ The Old Globe Theatre BALBOA PARK
Originally built in 1935, this Tony Award–winning, three-theater complex attracts big-name playwrights and performers, and has spawned a number of Broadway hits. The summer Shakespeare Festival features three works by the Bard in nightly rotation. In Balboa Park, 1363 Old Globe Way. ☎ 619/234-5623. www.theoldglobe.org. Tickets $29–$89. Bus: 3, 7, or 120. Map p. 622.

★★ San Diego Repertory Theatre GASLAMP
QUARTER The Rep, founded in 1975, mounts plays and musicals with a strong multicultural bent; they perform at the two-stage Lyceum Theatre at Horton Plaza. In Horton Plaza, 79 Broadway Circle. ☎ 619/544-1000. www.sdrep.org. Tickets $25–$53. Bus: all Broadway routes. Trolley: Civic Center. Map p. 622.

> *All the world's a stage at the Old Globe Theatre, presenting works by both the Bard and modern playwrights.*

What a Deal

Half-price tickets to theater, music, and dance events are available at the ARTS TIX booth in Horton Plaza Park, at Broadway and Third Avenue. The kiosk is open Tuesday to Thursday 11am to 6pm, Friday and Saturday 10am to 6pm, and Sunday 10am to 5pm. Half-price tickets are available only for same-day shows, except for Monday performances, which are sold on Sunday. For a daily listing of offerings, call ☎ 619/497-5000 or check www.sandiego performs.com. Full-price advance tickets are also available—the booth doubles as a Ticketmaster outlet.

North County

Don't be fooled by the laid-back, surf-dude ethic that prevails among the string of picturesque coastal communities north of La Jolla. For decades, the area's slower pace and stunning physical beauty have attracted artists, writers, celebrities, spiritualists, and others who could afford a piece of coastal solitude. The result is a casual sophistication and territorial pride that distinguishes this region from San Diego.

> *Even if you only have time for a quick drive by, don't miss the saturated colors of the Carlsbad Ranch flower fields.*

START You will need a vehicle to effectively tour North County. From downtown San Diego take I-5 north and exit Carmel Valley Rd. west. Turn left at Hwy. 101 to Torrey Pines State Reserve. **TRIP LENGTH** 2 days, about 50 miles.

① ★★★ **Torrey Pines State Reserve** SAN DIEGO One of San Diego's most breathtaking locations, featuring hiking trails, dramatic 300-foot sandstone cliffs, and an excellent beach. It's also home to the gnarled tree that is North America's rarest indigenous pine. ⏱ At least 1 hr. Hwy. 101 at Carmel Valley Rd.

☎ 858/755-2063. www.parks.ca.gov or www. torreypine.org. Admission $10 per car, $9 seniors. Daily 8am–sunset. Bus: 101.

② ★★★ **Cedros Design District** SOLANA BEACH More than two-dozen chic and eclectic shops and galleries highlight this vivacious neighborhood. You'll also find one of the county's best concert venues, the Belly Up Tavern (☎ 858/481-9022; www.bellyup.com). ⏱ At least 1 hr. Primarily the 100 and 200 blocks of S. Cedros Ave., Solana Beach. www.cedros designdistrict.net. Bus: 101. Train: Solana Beach.

1 Torrey Pines State Reserve
2 Cedros Design District
3 Self-Realization Fellowship Hermitage and Meditation Gardens
4 Swami's Cafe
5 Lux Art Institute
6 The Flower Fields at Carlsbad Ranch
7 California Surf Museum
8 San Diego Zoo Safari Park

Where to Stay
Beach Terrace Inn **9**
L'Auberge Del Mar
    Resort & Spa **13**
The Lodge at Torrey Pines **14**

Where to Dine
Blanca **12**
Market Restaurant + Bar **11**
Q'ero **10**

3 ★★ Self-Realization Fellowship Hermitage and Meditation Gardens ENCINITAS
Paramahansa Yogananda, a guru born and educated in India, opened this retreat with exotic lotus domes in 1937, and the site still serves as a spiritual sanctuary for his followers and a retreat for holistic healers. The serene meditation gardens (check out the beautiful koi ponds and seasonal flower displays) offer spectacular ocean views—and disciples won't give you a sales pitch. ⏱ 45 min. 215 W. K St. (off S. Coast Hwy. 101), Encinitas. ☎ 760/753-2888. www.yogananda-srf.org. Free admission. Tues–Sat 9am–5pm; Sun 11am–5pm. Hermitage Sun 2–5pm. Bus: 101.

4 ☕ ★ Swami's Cafe. Locals crowd into this casual spot for tasty, health-conscious breakfasts and lunch. It gets its name from the legendary surf spot across the highway, which in turn was named for the yogi's retreat on the clifftop. 1163 S. Coast Hwy. 101 (at W. K St.). ☎ 760/944-0612. www.swamis.signonsandiego.com. Daily 7am–4pm. Entrees $5–$9.

5 ★★ Lux Art Institute ENCINITAS
This unique facility allows visitors to watch as an artist in residence paints, sculpts, or draws in a studio environment. The building itself is a work of art. ⏱ 45 min. 1550 S. El Camino Real,

> Flowers are not the only items that bloom in North County; you'll find several varieties of cacti in the mountains as well.

6 ★ The Flower Fields at Carlsbad Ranch
CARLSBAD A sea of ranunculus blossoms every March to mid-May, creating a blanket of color covering some 50 acres. Visitors are welcome to tour the grounds and enjoy a number of special floral installations. This is a working retail nursery the rest of the year. ☉ 1 hr. 5704 Paseo del Norte, Carlsbad. ☎ 760/431-0352. www.theflowerfields.com. Admission $10 adults, $9 seniors, $5 kids 3–10. Free parking. Mar to mid-May daily 9am–6pm.

7 ★ California Surf Museum OCEANSIDE
This slick, oceanfront facility opened in 2009 and features an extensive collection documenting the early days of surfing. There's also a gift shop selling surf-themed goods. ☉ 45 min. 312 Pier View Way, Oceanside. ☎ 760/721-6876. www.surfmuseum.org. Admission $3 adults, $1 seniors and students, free for kids 11 & under. Fri-Wed 10am–4pm; Thurs 10am–8pm.

Check into a North County hotel or drive back to San Diego for the night. On Day 2, from San Diego, take I-15 north to Exit 27 (Via Rancho Pkwy.), then head east and follow the signs to the San Diego Zoo Safari Park. Trip time is about an hour from San Diego.

8 ★★★ San Diego Zoo Safari Park ESCONDIDO Originally a breeding facility for the San Diego Zoo, the 1,800-acre Zoo Safari Park now holds 3,500 animals representing some 430 different species. Many of the animals roam freely in vast enclosures, allowing giraffes to

Encinitas. ☎ 760/436-6611. www.luxartinstitute. com. Admission $10 adults (good for 2 visits), free for ages 20 & under. Thurs–Fri 1–5pm; Sat 11am–5pm.

Flower Power

San Diego's North County is a noted flower-growing region. If you're horticulturally minded, in addition to checking out the Flower Fields at Carlsbad Ranch, you might also visit the tranquil San Diego Botanic Garden, 230 Quail Gardens Dr., Encinitas (☎ 760/436-3036; www.sdbgarden.org), which boasts the country's largest bamboo collection, an interactive children's garden, plus some 35 acres of native and exotic flora.

Special Programs at the Park

The San Diego Zoo Safari Park runs a number of special programs for visitors, ranging from sleepovers inside the park (from $29, plus park admission) to zip line rides over the park ($70, plus park admission) to Segway tours ($80, plus park admission); check the website for the most current rundown of offerings. If you're a shutterbug, for a real treat, make a reservation for a Photo Caravan (from $90), a safari truck ride out into the middle of an enclosure for an up-close and personal interaction with the animals (I got to feed a giraffe, cozied up to a rhino and exotic birds, and snagged a nifty shot of an hour-old eland hidden in a field by its mom).

> The beautiful natural surroundings of the Self-Realization Fellowship Hermitage and Meditation Gardens are a great place to meditate, relax, or catch some truly stunning ocean views.

interact with antelopes, much as they would in Africa (nothing like seeing an entire herd of antelope come to attention when the cheetahs in the habitat across the way wake up from their afternoon siesta and start eyeing their neighbors). An open-air tram ride included with the admission price allows guests to get pretty close to the animal action, though lines can build (arrive early to avoid them—as an added bonus, the animals are more active earlier in the morning). Notable finds here include the largest crash of rhinos at any zoological facility in the world, a cheetah breeding program, a petting zoo with more than just the usual goats, and some rare California condors. Although the San Diego Zoo may be "world famous," it's the Safari Park (formerly know as Wild Animal Park) that many visitors celebrate as their favorite and it's a must for animal lovers, conservationists, and families. ☉ At least 5 hr. 15500 San Pasqual Valley Rd. ☎ 760/747-8702. www.sandiegozoo. org. Admission $37 adults, $27 kids 3–11, free for kids under 3 and active-duty military (U.S. and foreign). Daily 9am–4pm (grounds close at 5pm); extended hours during summer and Festival of Lights (2 weekends in Dec). Parking $9.

> The fastest cats on earth, cheetahs are a star attraction at the amazing San Diego Zoo Safari Park.

Family Fun

Adults traveling with children should also consider making a stop at ★ **LEGOLAND California,** 1 Legoland Dr., Carlsbad (☎ 877/534-6526 or 760/918-5346; www.legoland.com; $67 adults, $57 kids). This theme park in Carlsbad, 40 minutes north of downtown San Diego, offers a full day of entertainment for families. There are more than 50 rides, shows, and attractions, including hands-on interactive displays, scale models of international landmarks (the Eiffel Tower, etc.) constructed of LEGO bricks, and a water park with slides and pools. LEGOLAND is geared toward children ages 2 to 12, with just enough of a thrill-ride component that preteens will be amused, but most teenagers will find this place a bit of a snooze. A sister attraction, the **SEA LIFE Aquarium** (www.sealifeus.com; $19 adults, $12 kids), is located next door, displaying live fish in giant tanks. The **LEGOLAND Water Park**, with its water slides, wading pools, and play areas where you can get a good soaking, opened in 2010. It's located within LEGOLAND and requires an upgraded park ticket ($10 per person). Visit www.legolandwaterpark.com for more information.

Where to Stay & Dine

> *Settle down into a Stickley rocker on the deck of the Lodge at Torrey Pines, a Craftsman-style beauty along the coast.*

★ **Beach Terrace Inn** CARLSBAD
Carlsbad's only beachside hotel, where almost every room has an ocean view. 2775 Ocean St. ☎ 800/433-5415 or 760/729-5951. www.beachterraceinn.com. 49 units. Doubles $185–$265 w/ breakfast. AE, DC, DISC, MC, V.

★★★ **Blanca** SOLANA BEACH *CALIFORNIAN/ FRENCH* This cosmopolitan space is one of the best restaurants in the region, serving creative prix-fixe tasting menus. 437 S. Coast Highway 101. ☎ 858/792-0072. Tasting menus $46–$66. AE, DC, DISC, MC, V. Dinner Tues–Sun. Bus: 101.

★★★ **L'Auberge Del Mar Resort & Spa** DEL MAR An excellent spa and a fine restaurant highlight this elegant hotel, near Del Mar's shopping and dining scene. 1540 Camino del Mar. ☎ 800/245-9757 or 858/259-1515. www.laubergedelmar.com. 120 units. Doubles from $350. AE, DC, MC, V. Bus: 101.

★★★ **The Lodge at Torrey Pines** LA JOLLA
This Craftsman-style fantasy resort has clinker-brick masonry and Stickley furniture. 11480 N. Torrey Pines Rd. ☎ 800/656-0087 or 858/453-4420. www.lodgetorreypines.com. 171 units. Doubles from $325. AE, DC, DISC, MC, V. Bus: 101.

★★★ **Market Restaurant + Bar** DEL MAR *CALIFORNIAN* This comfortably elegant restaurant showcases the best ingredients from the area's top farms, ranches, and seafood providers. 3702 Via de la Valle. ☎ 858/523-0007. www.marketdelmar.com. Entrees $24–$35; sushi $4–$22. AE, MC, V. Dinner daily. Bus: 308.

★★ **Q'ero** ENCINITAS *LATIN AMERICAN*
This tiny Peruvian restaurant serves familiar Latin American fare as well as exotic dishes that will keep adventurous diners happy. 564 S. Coast Highway 101. ☎ 760/753-9050. www.qerorestaurant.com. Entrees $9–$28. AE, DISC, MC, V. Lunch & dinner Tues–Sat. Bus: 101.

Grape Escape

In Riverside County, 60 miles north of San Diego via I-15, is the wine country of Temecula (pronounced "ta-*meck*-you-la"). There are 20-plus wineries in the region where year-round you can tour, taste, and stock up. For more information contact the Temecula Valley Winegrowers Association (☎ 800/801-9463 or 951/699-6586; www.temeculawines.org). Grapeline (☎ 888/894-6379 or 951/693-5755; www.gogrape.com) can shuttle you from your San Diego hotel to wine country; prices start at $42 per person.

Julian

A trip to Julian is a trip back in time to the Old West.

Prospectors first ventured into these fertile hills (elevation 4,225 ft.) in search of gold in the late 1860s, and within 10 years, 18 mines were operating, producing up to an estimated $13 million worth of gold. After the rush played out, this quaint Victorian town (pop. 3,000) found fame thanks to another mother lode: apples. Weekend crowds can be heavy, especially during the fall apple harvest season. (**Note:** fall temperatures are brisk; snow is possible in winter.)

> Climb into another era at Pioneer Cemetery, a remarkable chronicle of this quaint town's history.

START You will need a vehicle for this trip. From downtown San Diego take I-15 north to Hwy. 78 east to Julian or take I-15 north to I-8 east to Hwy. 79 to Julian. Take one route going and the other on the way back—Hwy. 79 winds through Cuyamaca Rancho State Park, while Hwy. 78 traverses open country and farmland. TRIP LENGTH about 1½ hr., about 60 miles.

❶ **Julian Chamber of Commerce.** Chamber staffers, located in the foyer of the creaky old Town Hall (built in 1913), always have enthusiastic suggestions for local activities. Be sure to duck into the auditorium itself to check out the photos of Julian's bygone days. ⏱ 15 min. 2129 Main St. ☎ 760/765-1857. www.julianca.com. Daily 10am–4pm.

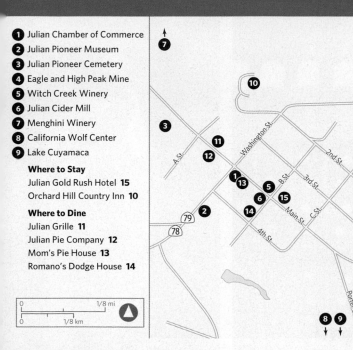

1. Julian Chamber of Commerce
2. Julian Pioneer Museum
3. Julian Pioneer Cemetery
4. Eagle and High Peak Mine
5. Witch Creek Winery
6. Julian Cider Mill
7. Menghini Winery
8. California Wolf Center
9. Lake Cuyamaca

Where to Stay
Julian Gold Rush Hotel **15**
Orchard Hill Country Inn **10**

Where to Dine
Julian Grille **11**
Julian Pie Company **12**
Mom's Pie House **13**
Romano's Dodge House **14**

2 **Julian Pioneer Museum.** This small museum is dedicated to illuminating the life and times of Julian's townspeople from 1869 to 1913. It displays clothing, tools, gold-mining equipment, household and military items, and a fine collection of lace doilies, quilts, and scarves. Look out back to see the Julian Transportation Garage museum's vintage machinery and vehicles. ⏱ 30 min. 2811 Washington St. ☎ 760/765-0227. $3 donation requested. Apr-Nov, Wed-Sun, 10am-4pm; Dec-Mar Sat-Sun 10am-4pm.

3 ★ **Julian Pioneer Cemetery.** This small, hillside graveyard is straight out of *Our Town*. Julian's citizenry have been laid to rest here since 1870, when the only way to deliver caskets to the gravesite was to carry them up the long, stone staircase in front. If you don't want to huff and puff up the stairs (just imagine carrying a casket), there's now a parking lot behind the cemetery that provides easy access. ⏱ 20 min. A St. (at Farmer Rd).

4 ★ kids **Eagle and High Peak Mine.** Although seemingly a tourist trap, this mine, which dates from around 1870, offers an interesting and educational look at the town's one-time economic mainstay. Tours take you underground to the 1,000-foot hard-rock tunnel to experience the mining and milling process. ⏱ 1 hr. End of C St. ☎ 760/765-0036. Tours $10 adults, $5 kids 6-16, $1 for kids 5 & under. 1 hr. tours start at 10am (hours vary so call ahead).

5 **Witch Creek Winery.** There are a handful of wineries in the Julian area, but this is the only wine-tasting operation right in town, best known for its full-bodied red and white varietals (obtainable only through the winery itself). What it lacks in ambience, it makes up for in convenience and friendliness. ⏱ 30 min. 2100 Main St. ☎ 760/765-2023. www. witchcreekwinery.com. Daily 11am-5pm.

6 ★★ **Julian Cider Mill.** You can see cider presses at work here October through March. It offers free tastes of the fresh nectar and jugs to take home. Throughout the year, the mill also carries the area's widest selection of food products, from apple butters and jams to berry preserves, several varieties of local honey, candies, and other goodies. ⏱ 20 min. 2103 Main St. ☎ 760/765-1430. Mon-Thurs 9:30am-5pm; Fri-Sun 9:30am-5:30pm.

> *Sample local wines and picnic among grape vines and apple orchards at rustic Menghini Winery.*

> *Meet the leader of the pack at California Wolf Center; tours teach about wolf conservation efforts, while you observe resident wolves.*

7 ★★ **Menghini Winery.** The rustic facilities and rolling picnic grounds of this winery make it a popular spot not only for wine tasting but also for special events like the annual Grape Stomp Festa and the Julian Art and Music Festival in September, and the Apple Days Festival in October. It's located about 3 miles out of town. ⊙ 45 min. 1150 Julian Orchards Dr. (at Wynola Rd.). ☎ 760/765-2072. www. menghini winery.com. Mon–Fri 10am–4pm; Sat–Sun 10am–5pm.

8 ★ kids **California Wolf Center.** At this education and conservation center, located about 4 miles from town, you can learn about wolves on one of several guided tours and visit with the resident wolf pack. Families and animal lovers will find it a very worthwhile stop. ⊙ 1½ hr. 18457 Hwy. 79 (at KQ Ranch Campground, look for Wolf Center sign). ☎ 760/765-0030 or

619/234-9653. www.californiawolfcenter.org. Reservations required. Group tours $10–$20 per person. Sat–Sun 10am and 2pm. Private tours $25 per person. Tues–Fri.

9 ★ kids **Lake Cuyamaca.** Eight miles south of Julian, this 110-acre lake offers boating, fishing, and camping. Anglers try for bass, catfish, crappie, bluegill, and trout (stocked year-round). There's also a general store and restaurant at the lake's edge. ⊙ At least 1 hr. 15027 Hwy. 79 (btw. Milk Ranch & Wolahi rds.). ☎ 877/581-9904 or 760/765-0515. www.lakecuyamaca.org. Fishing $6 per day adults, $3.50 per day kids 8–15, free for kids 7 & under. A California fishing license required for ages 16 & over. One-day license $13 per person. Rowboats $15 per day, motorboats $45 per day ($35 after 1pm), canoes and paddle boats (summer only) $15 per hour. Daily 6am–sunset (weather permitting).

Where to Stay & Dine

> *Dig into perfect pie in Julian, known golden-crusted, apple-filled beauties made from locally grown fruit.*

★ **Julian Gold Rush Hotel**
Built in 1897 by a freed slave, this frontier-style hotel is a living monument to the area's boom-town days and is one of the oldest continuously operating hotels in Southern California. It's not secluded or plush, but it's a wonderful time warp. 2032 Main St. ☎ 800/734-5854 or 760/765-0201. www.julianhotel.com. 16 units. Doubles $135–$165 w/breakfast. AE, MC, V.

★ **Julian Grille** *AMERICAN*
Set in a cozy cottage, the fare here is pretty straightforward—soups and sandwiches for lunch, seafood and prime rib for dinner—but it is the nicest eatery in town. If it's a sunny day, lunch on the shady terrace is a treat. 2224 Main St. ☎ 760/765-0173. Entrees $8–$28. AE, DISC, MC, V. Lunch daily; dinner Tues–Sun.

★★ **Julian Pie Company** *DESSERT/LIGHT FARE*
This blue and white cottage boasts outdoor seating where overhanging apples are literally up for grabs. Among its specialties are no-sugar-added pies and cider donuts; light lunches of soup and sandwiches are offered weekdays (11am–2pm). 2225 Main St. ☎ 760/765-2449. www.julianpie.com. Entrees $5–$16. AE, DISC, MC, V. Breakfast & lunch daily.

★★ **Mom's Pie House** *DESSERT/LIGHT FARE*
Through the front windows you can observe the mom on duty rolling crust, filling pies, and crimping edges. The shop routinely bakes several varieties of apple pie as well as seasonal specialties such as pecan and pumpkin. Lunch is served weekdays (11am–3pm) and some weekends. 2119 Main St. ☎ 760/765-2472. www.momspiesjulian.com. Entrees $5–$16. AE, DISC, MC, V. Mon–Fri 8am–5pm. Breakfast & lunch daily.

★★ **Orchard Hill Country Inn**
This inn is the most upscale lodging in Julian— a surprisingly posh, two-story Craftsman lodge (with a massive stone fireplace) and a dozen romantic, luxurious cottages on a hill overlooking town. 2502 Washington St. ☎ 800/716-7242 or 760/765-1700. www.orchardhill.com. 22 units. Doubles $195–$250; cottages from $295. Rates include breakfast & afternoon hors d'oeuvres. AE, MC, V.

★ **Romano's Dodge House** *ITALIAN*
This home-style Italian spot in a historic home just off Main Street is proud to be the only restaurant in town not serving apple pie. The small lounge in back sometimes stays open late. 2718 B St. ☎ 760/765-1003. www.romanosjulian.com. Entrees $8–$19. DISC, MC, V. Lunch & dinner Wed–Mon.

Fast Facts

Emergencies

Call ☎ **911.** For nonurgent issues, call the **San Diego Police Department,** 1401 Broadway (☎ 619/531-2000; www.sandiego.gov/police).

UCSD Medical Center-Hillcrest, 200 W. Arbor Dr. (☎ 619/543-6222; www.health. ucsd.edu) has the city's most convenient emergency room.

Getting There

BY PLANE **San Diego International Airport** (☎ 619/231-2100; www.san.org), also known as Lindbergh Field (airport code SAN), is 3 miles northwest of downtown San Diego.

Bus route 992 provides service between the airport and downtown San Diego ($2.25), running along Broadway. The ride takes about 15 minutes. Private shuttles, including **SuperShuttle** (☎ 800/974-8885; www.supershuttle. com), serve the entire county. Fares are about $8 per person to downtown hotels; $31 ($9 for each additional person) to La Jolla. A taxi to downtown costs a little over $10, to Coronado it's $25, and to La Jolla it's about $35. **BY TRAIN** **Amtrak** trains (☎ 800/872-7245; www.amtrak. com) run between L.A. and downtown San Diego about 11 times daily each way, arriving at Santa Fe Depot on Broadway at Kettner Boulevard (☎ 619/239-9021). Travel time from Los Angeles to San Diego is about 2 hours and 45 minutes (driving time can be as little as 2 hr., or as much as 4 hr. during rush hour). A one-way ticket costs $29 to $43. **BY CAR** I-5 is the primary route from San Francisco, central California, and Los Angeles; it runs along the coast straight through downtown to the U.S.-Mexico border. I-8 cuts across California from points east like Phoenix, terminating just west of I-5 at Mission Bay. I-15 runs north–south from Riverside County through the North County to southeast San Diego where it meets I-5; Hwy. 163 runs north–south through Balboa Park and ends in the downtown area.

Getting Around

BY BUS The **Metropolitan Transit System** (☎ 619/233-3004 or 619/685-4900 for 24-hr. automated info; www.transit.511sd. com) operates the MTS Transit store, 102 Broadway (at First Ave.; ☎ 619/234-1060; Mon–Fri 9am–5pm), where you can pick up passes, timetables, and so forth. Most bus fares are $2.25. If you need to make a transfer to another bus or the trolley, purchase a $5 day pass from the driver, trolley station vending machine, online, or at the MTS Store. It gives you unlimited use of most bus and trolley routes for the rest of the service day. **BY TROLLEY** The Blue Line travels from the U.S.-Mexico border (San Ysidro) north through downtown and Old Town, with some trolleys continuing into Mission Valley. The Orange Line runs from downtown east through the cities of Lemon Grove and El Cajon. The Green Line runs from Old Town through Mission Valley to Qualcomm Stadium, San Diego State University, and on to the city of Santee. The trip to the border takes 40 minutes from downtown; from downtown to Old Town takes 10 to 15 minutes. Riders buy tickets from machines in stations before boarding; it's $2.50 for travel between any two stations. A $5 day pass is also available, good for all trolley trips and most bus routes. The trolley generally operates daily from 5am to about midnight. **BY CAR** For up-to-the-minute traffic info, dial ☎ 511. A few things to note: San Diego gas prices are often among the highest in the country; the main beach arteries (Grand Ave., Garnet Ave., and Mission Blvd.) sometimes have random checkpoints set up to catch drunk drivers; finding parking can be tricky, especially in downtown.

All major car-rental firms have an office at the airport and several have them in larger hotels. **BY TAXI** Other than in the Gaslamp Quarter after dark, taxis don't cruise the streets; call ahead for quick pickup. Local companies include **Orange Cab** (☎ 619/291-3333) and **San Diego Cab** (☎ 619/226-8294); **Coronado Cab Company** (☎ 619/435-6211) serves the city of Coronado (Coronado Island). Rates are $2.50 for the first 1/9 mile and 30¢ for each additional 1/9 mile. **BY TRAIN** The **Coaster** travels between downtown and the city of Oceanside, with stops at Old Town, Sorrento Valley, and the cities of Solana Beach, Encinitas, and Carlsbad. Fares range from $5 to $6.50 each way, and can be paid by credit card at vending machines at each station. Eligible seniors and riders with disabilities pay $2.50 to $3.25. The scenic trip between downtown San Diego and Oceanside takes 1 hour. Trains run Monday through Friday, from about 6:30am to 7pm, with four trains in each direction on Saturday. Call ☎ 800/262-7837 or log on to www.transit.511sd.com for more info. BY FERRY & WATER TAXI There's regularly scheduled ferry service (☎ 800/442-7847 or 619/234-4111; www.sdhe.com) between San Diego and Coronado. Ferries leave from the Broadway Pier (1050 N. Harbor Dr., at Broadway) and the Fifth Avenue Landing behind the Convention Center. Hours are roughly 9am to 9pm, with extended hours on weekends. The ride takes 15 minutes; the fare is $3.50 each way. Water taxis (☎ 619/235-8294; www.sdhe.com) will pick you up from any dock around San Diego Bay. They operate Friday to Sunday from 3 to 10pm, with extended hours in summer. It costs $7 per person to most locations; reservations advised.

Internet Access

For those without a computer, **Lestat's Coffee House,** 3343 Adams Ave. (☎ 619/291-4043; www.lestats.com) is open 24 hours. Libraries are another good option, including the main branch at 820 E St. (☎ 619/236-5800; www.sandiego.gov). Wi-Fi is readily available at hotels and cafes throughout the city.

Pharmacies

Rite Aid and **CVS** drugstores are found around the city. CVS has a 24-hour location in La Jolla at 8831 Villa La Jolla Dr. (☎ 858/457-4390); Rite-Aid has one in Hillcrest at 535 Robinson Ave. (☎ 619/291-3703).

Post Offices

There are downtown post offices in Horton Plaza, next to the Westin Hotel, and at 815 E St. For other locations call ☎ 800/275-8777 or go to www.usps.com.

Safety

San Diego is a safe destination, by big-city standards. Caution should be exercised in remote portions of Balboa Park and in parts of downtown east of PETCO Park.

At beaches, beware of rip currents and territorial surfers. And always wear sunscreen, even on an overcast day.

Smoking

San Diego has banned smoking at all city beaches and parks, which includes Mission Bay Park and Balboa Park, as well as piers and boardwalks.

Taxes

San Diego sales tax in restaurants and shops is 8.75%; hotel tax is 10.5%, or 12.5% for locations with more than 70 rooms.

Toilets

Hotels, fast-food restaurants, and department stores are reliable choices; other possibilities include shopping centers, Balboa Park (though caution should be exercised after dark), and service stations. Some restaurants and bars reserve restrooms for patrons only.

Tours

Old Town Trolley Tours (☎ 619/298-8687; www.historictours.com) and **Vizit Tours** (☎ 619/ 727-4007; www.vizitsandiegotours. com) are narrated tours, offering on-and-off privileges at various locations throughout the city.

Visitor Information

The **San Diego Convention & Visitors Bureau (ConVis)** operates the International Visitor Information Center on the Embarcadero, 1040⅓ W. Broadway, at Harbor Drive (☎ 619/236-1212; www.sandiego.org). Daily summer hours are 9am to 5pm (till 4pm the rest of the year). In La Jolla, ConVis operates a walk-up facility at 7966 Herschel Ave., near the corner of Prospect Street. It's open daily in summer 11am to 7pm (Sun 10am–6pm); it's open daily with more limited hours the rest of the year.

For information on San Diego's North County, check in with the **San Diego North Convention & Visitors Bureau** (☎ 800/848-3336 or 760/745-4741; www.sandiegonorth.com).

For beach and surf information in San Diego, call ☎ 619/221-8824 or go to www.sandiego.gov/lifeguards/beaches.

14
California's History, Culture, Art & Architecture

California's 10 Greatest Cultural Hits

> *Mice and apples took on a whole new meaning when a couple of Steves started fiddling in a Cupertino garage.*

> PREVIOUS PAGE *Painting an idyllic scene, this 1871 lithograph puts a cheerful face on the demanding life of early gold miners.* THIS PAGE *Even plaid shirts became cool when worn by the Beach Boys.*

❶ Marilyn Monroe. Norma Jeane Baker (1926–62) was born in the charity ward of the Los Angeles County Hospital and grew up in suburban foster homes while dreaming of becoming the next Jean Harlow. She did even better, becoming Marilyn Monroe, one of the silver screen's most enduring sex goddesses. No other blond bombshell, before or after, stacks up to her legend.

❷ The Fender Stratocaster. With its contoured body, double-cutaway design, distinct "dogleg" headstock, three single-coil pick-ups, and tremolo bar, the Stratocaster has been called the Stradivarius of electric guitars. Created by Leo Fender's company in Fullerton, California, in 1954, the "Strat" quickly became a rock-music staple and achieved legendary status over the years, first at the hands of Buddy Holly,

then Jimi Hendrix, Eric Clapton, Stevie Ray Vaughn, and countless others.

❸ The Beach Boys. With sunny surf-rock ditties such as "Surfin' Safari," "I Get Around," and "Good Vibrations," the Beach Boys perfectly captured the idea of California as the promised land—at least for teenage boys—of surfing, hot-rodding, and pretty girls. They had 36 singles crack the Top 40, more than any other American band, and their *Pet Sounds* is regarded as one of the greatest and most influential albums in pop history.

❹ McDonald's. The world's biggest name in hamburgers was opened by the McDonald brothers in San Berrnadino in 1940 and now has over 30,000 locations in 125 countries, including France, Russia, and China. The McDonalds— neither named Ronald by the

way—applied Henry Ford's assembly-line techniques to making burgers, french fries, and milkshakes at their drive-in restaurant, creating the model for modern-day fast food.

❺ The Blockbuster. Sure, anyone anywhere can make a feature film, but nobody creates the kind of spectacles that thrill global audiences like Hollywood, which specializes in big-budget, high-concept, and (typically) special-effects-driven movies, including such global megahits as *Star Wars*, *Jurassic Park*, and *Titanic*.

❻ Apple Inc. Started in the mid-seventies by a couple of college dropouts toiling away in a Cupertino garage, Apple first revolutionized the world of personal computers, then decades later changed the way we listen to music with the introduction of the iPod. Blending cutting edge technology with gorgeous, "gotta have it" industrial design, their

> The original happy place, the world's first McDonald's in San Bernardino featured a 15-cent burger.

> The Force is definitely with Hollywood when it comes to producing blockbuster films like Star Wars.

products, such as the iPhone and iPad, continue to change the way we work and play.

7 The Sierra Club. Blessed with such an abundance of natural beauty, it's no wonder that California sports such a strong streak of environmentalism. The Sierra Club, whose mission is "to explore, enjoy, and protect the wild places of the earth," was founded in 1892 in San Francisco by John Muir (1838–1914), the famously devout conservationist who was also instrumental in the creation of the National Park Service.

8 Flower Power. An extension of the Beatniks, the hippie counterculture, rejecting the conformity and consumerism of the '50s and the war in Vietnam, descended in droves upon Haight-Ashbury during the Summer of Love in 1967 to frolic in a psychedelic swirl of flowers, long hair, rainbow garb, marijuana smoke, no-strings sex, and groovy tunes, and to espouse fuzzy concepts like peace, love, and understanding, man.

9 Case Study Houses. In 1945, *Arts & Architecture* challenged the best architects of midcentury modernism—Richard Neutra, Charles and Ray Eames, and Eero Saarinen—to create cheap and efficient residential designs to meet the surging postwar demand for housing. The innovative homes—almost all in the Los Angeles area—are immortalized in Julius Shulman's (1910–2009) striking black-and-white photographs. His iconic photograph of Koenig's Case Study House No. 22 depicts a luminous glass and steel structure virtually levitating over a twinkling metropolis.

10 John Steinbeck. The quintessential California writer, Steinbeck (1902–68) was a man rooted in the land of Monterey County, his socially conscious novels documenting the struggles of the little guys: farmhands, migrant workers, cannery workers. He won the Pulitzer Prize for Fiction in 1940 for *The Grapes of Wrath,* and the Nobel Prize for Literature in 1962 for a body of work that included *Of Mice and Men, East of Eden,* and *Cannery Row.*

A Timeline of California History

1500–1800

1542 Portuguese explorer Juan Rodriquez Cabrillo lands at San Diego Bay, "discovering" California for the Spanish Crown. An estimated 300,000 Native Americans already live there.

1579 English explorer Sir Francis Drake (pictured left), ordered by Queen Elizabeth I to plunder Spanish ships and settlements, lands near Point Reyes.

1602 Spanish explorer Sebastian Vizcaino maps the California coast from San Diego to Mendocino.

1769 In San Diego, Spain establishes the first of 21 missions in an effort to colonize Alta California and convert the Native Americans to Christianity. The missions span 650 miles along the El Camino Real.

1800–1850

1821 Mexico wins independence from Spain, making Alta California a Mexican state.

1846 The United States declares war on Mexico (pictured left).

1848 The Treaty of Hidalgo, the result of the Mexican-American War, transfers half of Mexican land, including California, to the United States. James Marshall discovers gold at Sutter's sawmill along the American River.

1849 A convention at Colton Hall in Monterey drafts a constitution. The Gold Rush begins, with 300,000 fortune-seekers streaming into California.

1850–1900

1850 California is admitted as the 31st state in the Union.

1854 Sacramento becomes the state capital.

1869 The transcontinental railroad is completed, connecting California to the rest of the country.

1870 Oranges are planted in Riverside County. Within a few years Southern California is producing most of the nation's oranges and almost all of its lemons.

1892 Edward Doheny discovers oil near present-day Dodger Stadium. Within two decades the greater Los Angeles area is one of the world's largest producers of oil (pictured left).

1900-WWII

1906 A massive earthquake rattles San Francisco, and ensuing fires ravage the city.

1911 The Nestor Company opens the first movie studio in Hollywood. Within a decade Hollywood becomes the center of the American motion picture industry (pictured left).

1930s Dust storms in the Midwest drives thousands of agricultural workers to the Central Valley and the Central Coast looking for work.

1940 The Arroyo Seco Parkway, the first of many California freeways, opens, connecting Pasadena to Downtown.

1942 Japanese Americans are ordered to an internment camp at Manzanar.

POST WWII

1958 The New York Giants and Brooklyn Dodgers baseball teams move to San Francisco and Los Angeles respectively.

1966 Actor Ronald Reagan is elected Governor.

1967 The Summer of Love (pictured left) takes place in Haight-Ashbury.

1976 At the Judgment of Paris, Napa Valley wines best French wines in a blind tasting, rocking the wine world.

1996 Two doctoral students at Stanford University, Larry Page and Sergey Brin, create a search engine that they later name "Google."

21ST CENTURY

2000-01 A state electricity crisis, the result of energy deregulation legislation, causes major blackouts that affect millions of customers and bankrupts the Pacific Gas and Electric Company.

2003 Actor Arnold Schwarzenegger (pictured left) is elected Governor during a special recall election of incumbent Gray Davis.

2008 The California Marriage Protection Act (Proposition 8) passes, effectively banning same-sex marriage.

2009 Facing a budget shortfall of $26.3 billion, Governor Schwarzenegger furloughs state workers, raises the sales tax, raises tuition at state universities, writes IOUs to contractors, and threatens to close state parks.

A Brief History of California

> *No man is an island, but apparently California was one in this (thankfully erroneous) 17th-century map of North America.*

California has always been an artful blend of fantasy and reality. Spanish explorers were partly driven by the myth of an Island of California, a paradise filled with nothing but gold and beautiful women, a notion based on a Spanish novel from the early 1500s called *The Adventures of Esplandian*. So what did **Juan Rodriquez Cabrillo** (1499–1543), the first European explorer of California's coastline, get for his troubles? He broke his leg on the rocky shores of the Channel Islands, contracted gangrene, and died on San Miguel Island.

Dust Bowl refugees poured into California in the 1930s under the illusion that oranges, lemons, and plentiful jobs were falling off trees—years earlier, the citrus industry had spread the motto "Oranges for health, California for wealth"—only to find shantytowns of fellow migrant workers. Every day young actors/writers/

musicians/artists journey to California, especially Los Angeles, to become a star, and while they don't all end up like Peg Entwhistle, a disillusioned actress who jumped to her death from the top of the HOLLYWOOD Sign, they're also not all "discovered" like Lana Turner, sipping a milkshake at a soda shop. Not every start-up in a garage in Silicon Valley will turn into a Hewlett-Packard, an Apple, or a Google, but don't you want in on the IPO if it does? California fosters a feeling among its residents that they're *thiiis* close to something big, something new, something better than before. The Golden State is a land that nurtures dreams and has been doing so for centuries. That's the reality.

The Native Americans

Archaeologists estimate that sometime around 16,500 B.C. human beings crossed over from Asia into North America on the icy Bering land bridge.

Nomadic hunters followed the herds of bison and mammoths, eventually migrating down the West Coast. On the Channel Islands, human bones and fire pits have been found that date back to approximately 13,000 B.C. Tribes first settled along the coastal regions but later branched out into other geographical areas—the deserts and mountains—where they developed in relative isolation from one another, creating distinct languages and cultural traditions. The **Chumash** people created spectacular rock art, immaculately woven basketry, and plank boats that allowed them to fish and trade along the coast. By the time European settlers reached the area in the 16th century, an estimated 300,000 Native Americans were living peacefully off the abundance of the land.

European Explorers

Juan Rodriquez Cabrillo, a Portuguese explorer sailing for the Spanish crown, became the first European to "discover" California when his ship arrived in San Diego Bay in 1542. Over the next 200 years, dozens of European explorers mapped the California coastline. Englishman **Sir Francis Drake** (1540–96), sent by Queen Elizabeth I to hunt for Spanish booty, landed near Point Reyes in 1579 and claimed the land for England, calling it Nova Albion. In 1602, Spanish explorer **Sebastian Vizcaino**

(1548–1624) traveled the coastline looking for safe harbors for Spain's trading galleons that sailed between Manila, Philippines and Acapulco, New Spain (today's Mexico). Many place names used today in California—San Diego, Santa Barbara, Point Lobos, Carmel, Monterey—trace back to Vizcaino.

The Missions & Ranchos

For over a century and a half, Spain was more concerned with the Manila-Mexican spice trade than the land it called **Alta California**, until competition emerged when Russian and English explorers began looking for inroads into the continent. Spain answered with the Sacred Expedition, a series of missions to settle and lay claim to the land, as well as to "save" the indigenous "savages" by converting them to Christianity and turning them into productive subjects of the Spanish empire. In 1769, a Franciscan priest named **Junipero Serra** (1713–84) established the first mission and *presidio* (fort) in San Diego. By 1823 a total of 21 missions—most still remain and are open to the public for tours—stretched from San Diego to San Francisco along a dirt trail called **El Camino Real** (The Royal Road), each mission a day's journey by horseback to the next. Father Serra, they say, walked the 650-mile road barefoot.

Each mission was laid out in a large, orderly quadrangle, which contained

CALIFORNIA REPUBLIC

Bear Flag Republic

Before news of the Mexican-American War reached California in June of 1846, American settlers in Sonoma Valley raised the "Bear Flag" over what they christened the "California Republic." While the folly only lasted a few weeks, the bear design still graces the state flag as do the words "California Republic."

A few days before the Treaty of Guadalupe Hidalgo formally handed over California to U.S. rule, carpenter James Marshall discovered a nugget of gold while working at a sawmill on the American River in the foothills of the Sierra Nevada. California would never be the same. In 1849, the non-Native American population of California was 14,000. Over the next five years, nearly 300,000 men and women—later they'd be called "forty-niners"—poured into California looking to make their fortunes, one of the largest and fastest migrations in human history. In two years San Francisco was transformed from a small sleepy settlement of 600 into a rambunctious seaport of 25,000 people. Along the present-day Highway 49, hundreds of towns sprung up with names like Gouge Eye, Hangtown, and Rough and Ready; 15 years later when the gold ran out, many turned into ghost towns. Many merchants and entrepreneurs who came to "mine the miners" had a lasting impact on business: for example, Levi Strauss sold the miners denim work pants, and a new company called Wells Fargo offered them mail and banking services.

The increase in population made California's push toward statehood all the faster. Settlers convened at Colton Hall in Monterey in 1849 and drew up a state constitution that prohibited slavery and, in a progressive move, recognized the separate property of married women (a move designed to attract potential brides to the area). In 1850, California was admitted as the 31st state in the union.

> *The Mexican War (1846-48) led to 525,000 square miles of former Mexican territory—including California—becoming part of the U.S.*

a self-sustaining village with workshops (tannery, blacksmith, weaving) and dormitories. In the surrounding fields, the missionaries introduced European irrigation techniques, livestock and agriculture—this marked the beginning of California's love affair with the grape. Missionaries baptized thousands of Native Americans who were then forced to work, pray, and stay at the missions; they were not allowed to return to their former lives. The Native Americans suffered under the barbaric treatment by their "saviors," and many died from diseases for which they lacked immunity. It's estimated that the Native population from San Diego to San Francisco dropped 75% during the period of the first European settlements. There was resistance by some Native tribes; they repeatedly attacked many missions and small towns called **pueblos**, particularly with fire, resulting in the missions adopting their iconic—and fireproof—red-tile roofs.

In 1821, Mexico won its independence from Spain, whose resources were drained by the Napoleonic Wars. The Mexican governors of the Alta California lacked the religious zeal of the Spanish, and by 1834, the missions were officially secularized. The Mexican method for taming the remote territory was to grant large swaths of land, 16,000-acre ranchos, to ambitious Mexican settlers. These **rancheros**, or **Californios**, operated huge cattle ranches and quickly became the financial, cultural, and political elite of California. Essentially, a feudal system emerged with the Native Americans again supplying cheap labor for the wealthy landowners. The missions, meanwhile, were neglected, and in 1845, the properties and crumbling churches were auctioned off.

American Expansion

Encouraged by Manifest Destiny, the fervently held belief that America should stretch from coast to coast, settlers from the United States pushed ever westward in the late 1820s. Sea-otter hunters from America worked along the California coastline, and many settled in Monterey. Traders, trappers, and other explorers followed and found eager trading partners with the cattle-raising *rancheros*. In 1826, beaver-trapper **Jedediah Smith** (1799–1831) became the first American to enter California overland, and a year later, the first white man to traverse the Sierra Nevada. In 1841, the first covered wagon made its way across the Truckee Pass north of Lake Tahoe, though

Railroad Barons

The overwhelming success, at least in terms of development, of the railroads in the late 19th century heaped enormous wealth and power on its owners—Charles Crocker, Leland Stanford, Collis Huntington, and Mark Hopkins were known colloquially as the "Big Four"—all of whom erected ostentatious mansions atop San Francisco's Nob Hill. Not everybody was enamored of the railroad system, sometimes referred to as "The Octopus" (also the title of Frank Norris' 1902 muckraking novel on the topic) for its stranglehold on the state's economy and politics. Perhaps to deflect some of the accusations of corruption, the Big Four became some of California's first philanthropists. Leland Stanford, for example, established Stanford University in 1891.

> *Charlie Chaplin films, such as the 1915 classic,* City Lights, *helped make Hollywood the center of America's film industry*

Aside for a single skirmish in San Pasquale, California was untouched by the war, but it landed in new hands in 1848 when, per the **Treaty of Guadalupe Hidalgo**, Mexico ceded half of their land including California, Arizona, and New Mexico to the ever-expanding United States.

The Growth of Industry

Despite its population growth, the state remained hard to reach until the transcontinental railroad was completed in 1869, finally making California accessible to the rest of the United States. A 2-month-long journey became a 5-day train ride. Los Angeles was finally connected in 1876 via San Francisco on the Southern Pacific

the path was hardly easy. In 1847, the tragedy of the infamous Donner Party became a cautionary tale regarding the hardship of westward expansion: A wagon train of settlers ended up snowbound and without sufficient supplies in the Sierra Nevada. Dying of starvation, some of the party resorted to cannibalizing those who had already died, and only about half the original group made it to California.

The U.S. was in negotiations to purchase California from Mexico in the early 19th century, but any possibility of a deal went south in 1845 after the United States annexed Texas, which had seceded from Mexico in 1836. Mexico, which still claimed Texas as a territory, took the annexation as an act of aggression, and war broke out in 1846.

The Great San Francisco Earthquake

On April 18, 1906 a catastrophic earthquake measuring 7.8 on the Richter scale decimated San Francisco, California's biggest city. The quake and ensuing fires that engulfed the city for 3 days killed 3,000 people, leveled 28,000 buildings, and left 250,000 people—half of the city's population—homeless. But Mother Nature couldn't keep a good city down for long. San Francisco bounced back and 9 years later showcased its amazing recovery by hosting the Panama-Pacific International Exposition.

> *Sunny images and lush graphics adorned early produce boxes shipped all over the U.S. from the Golden State.*

line. When the Sante Fe transcontinental line to L.A. was completed in the mid-1880s, competition slashed fares, attracting hundred of thousands of people to Southern California, which, prior to the railroads, had a population of 10,000, split between San Diego and Los Angeles.

Two industries in particular boomed with the railroads: agriculture, because perishable farm products could now reach the East Coast markets, and real estate, to handle the large number of new Californians. Another beneficiary was the image of California, which came to be viewed by the rest of the country as a near mythical paradise of fertile land and year-round sunshine.

Another major industry that took off during the early 20th century and established Los Angeles as a major city—and the U.S. movie capital—was the motion picture industry, which arrived in 1910. Director **D.W. Griffith** (1875-1948), a director from Biograph Company, traveled from the East Coast to L.A. to shoot a few scenes on location for his movie *Ramona*. Griffith figured that Southern California—specifically a sleepy, citrus-filled neighborhood called **Hollywood**—with its abundant sunlight, varied geography, and mild climate, would make the perfect location for a permanent movie studio. Others soon followed, especially smaller producers looking to escape the watchful eye of the litigious Edison Trust, a group of film companies that had a monopolized the industry on the East Coast. By 1915, the majority of American films were shot in Southern California, and by 1920, Hollywood emerged as the undisputed center of American cinema. Its films, especially those of Charlie Chaplin, became a global commodity, a trend that continues to this day, albeit on productions of a much grander scale such as *Avatar*.

Early Hollywood films—which, unlike today's, were shot virtually exclusively in Southern California—perpetuated a glamorous, idealized image of the Golden State. This romanticization played a part in drawing Dust Bowl refugees across the country during the Great Depression. John Steinbeck's 1939 novel *The Grapes of Wrath* captured the plight of the migrant workers, and a year later Hollywood adapted the book into a celebrated film starring Henry Fonda. Hollywood is so slick that it's able to sell both the myth and the wrecking of the myth at the same time.

Post World War II

World War II brought major manufacturing to California—the production of ships, airplanes, and munitions. After the war, many industries segued into what was later termed the military-industrial complex, and the population continued to boom as many

Red State vs. Blue State

California is popularly perceived as a liberal state. Indeed, it has tipped Democrat in the last five presidential elections, and the Speaker of the House is San Francisco's own Nancy Pelosi. But it's not all blue. Orange County and San Diego are well-established Republican strongholds, and the state's vast agricultural areas trend towards the conservative. And don't forget the legacy of President Ronald Reagan (1911-2004), a two-term Governor of California; and President Richard Nixon (1913-94), who was born in California and served as a Congressman and Senator.

servicemen and factory workers remained. In the 1950s, freeways were built, giving rise to suburbs, like those that sprang up in the San Fernando Valley and Orange County.

The 1960s saw a backlash to the conformity and mass consumerism of the previous decade. San Francisco's Haight-Ashbury became the center of the **counterculture movement** and attracted free-loving (and drug-loving) flower children from all over. But the decade had a dark side as well: the Berkeley student riots, the Watts riots in 1965, Robert Kennedy's assassination in Los Angeles in 1968, and the Manson family murders in 1969.

In the 1970s, the counterculture of the '60s gave way to **New Age philosophy**, but the major revolution in the state was happening in **Silicon Valley**, where technology's brightest minds at companies such as Intel and Apple were developing the world's fastest semiconductors and most innovative computers and software.

As California's tech industry continued to grow, the 1980s and 1990s were marked by several boom-and-bust economic cycles, the rise of AIDS, bouts of increased racial tension (exemplified by L.A.'s Rodney King riots in 1992), and significant growth in environmental awareness. The turn of the century brought with it the bursting of the dot-com bubble, a number of illegal immigration conflicts, and serious energy problems after the state engaged in a deregulation scheme that backfired.

> *Topping off the '60s was the free-loving, drug-loving (and sometimes oddly adorned) Flower Power generation.*

California Today

The image of California as a land of opportunity is why so many people—from laborers to political refugees to tech entrepreneurs—have flocked to California over the years, creating a rich diversity of skills and cultures within its population. California welcomes the largest number of immigrants in America each year, and only very recently, owing perhaps to a contracting job market and larger trends in foreign immigration, have native-born Californians regained a majority status. With 36.8 million inhabitants, California is America's most populous state, boosted by the presence of two megalopolises—the San Francisco's Bay Area in the north and the greater Los Angeles basin in the south.

It is also the state with the largest economy, with a gross state product of $1.85 trillion dollars in 2008, roughly 13% of the U.S. gross domestic product. If California were a sovereign nation, its economy would rank the eighth largest in the world. Gold, silver, and oil have all had their heydays here, as well as manufacturing, especially in the aviation and defense industries, but today's economy is driven by technology, entertainment, and a reliable staple—agriculture.

But not all is golden in these parts. California, like the entire country, was hit hard by the 2008 subprime mortgage crisis when the real estate bubble burst, taking down the financial industry and the stock market with it. The resulting shortfall in California's income has wreaked havoc on the state budget with massive deficits in the tens of billions of dollars in 2008, 2009, and 2010. In 2009, Governor Schwarzenegger spoke frankly: "Our wallet is empty, our bank is closed, and our credit is dried up." The impact: forced furloughs for some state employees, raised tuition for state universities, and a drastic reduction in services—if you're heading for a state park, check ahead for the latest fees and available services.

Lay of the Land

> A toppled giant helps visitors sense the scale of aptly named giant sequoias, which are known to grow only in the Sierra Nevada.

Geographical Diversity

The word California immediately brings to mind sunshine and golden sand beaches, but there's so much more to the 160,000 square miles of land in the state. In fact, no state in America boasts a greater diversity of landscape than California where—it's often said, but so rarely acted upon—you can surf the Pacific Ocean in the morning and snow ski in the afternoon.

A layman can tell Northern California (redwood trees) from Southern California (palm trees) at a glance, but scientists break the state down into many distinct geomorphic zones, each with its own climate and ecosystem. These include the Sierra Nevada, the Coast Ranges, the Cascade Range, the Central Valley, the Los Angeles Basin, the Mojave Desert and the Colorado Desert, and the Channel Islands.

The state is a study in contrasts. The deserts of the southeastern region are surrounded by high mountains that block moisture from reaching the lowest elevations, resulting in a zone that's both desolate and breathtaking; the northern forests get enough rain to support trees that soar towards the heavens; and the state's Central Valley is amazingly fertile and home to many of its famous wineries and farms. The coastline stretches an amazing 1,100 miles. Southern California beaches are typically sandy with great weather—warm and clear—while further up the coast the landscape tends to be foggier, cooler, and more heavily wooded.

California also contains the highest point in the contiguous United States, Mount Whitney (p. 288, ⑤) in the Sierra Nevada, as well as the lowest point—Badwater Basin (p. 543, ④) in Death Valley.

Native Flora

The state is home to nearly 5,900 different natives species of plants—almost as many as all of those found in the rest of the United States combined. Notable among the native flora are several superlative species of trees. **Coast redwoods** (*Sequoia sempervirens*) are the tallest trees on earth and can be found along the northern coast between Big Sur and southern Oregon. They can reach up to 370 feet and live more than 2,000 years. Two good locations for viewing these trees are **Redwood National and State Parks** (p. 231, **9**) and **Humboldt Redwoods State Park** (p. 221, **6**).

Giant sequoias (*Sequoia-dendron giganteum*) are the biggest trees in the world in terms of volume and can only be found on the Western slopes of the Sierra Nevada.

They grow to be up to 280 feet high and up to 24 feet wide, and can live for 3,500 years. The best place to see these mammoth trees is inside **Sequoia and Kings Canyon National Parks** (p. 286). **Bristlecone pines** (*Pinus longaeva*are) are the oldest trees in the world and are found in the White Mountains near Bishop, California. One specimen inside the **Ancient Bristlecone Pine Forest** (p. 275, **20**), the Methuselah, is 4,700 years old.

Native Fauna
California's diverse ecosystems are populated with an equal variety of wildlife.

There are over 630 species of bird that call the state home, ranging from swallows and owls to woodpeckers and warblers. It'll be tough to get a look in the wild at the famed (but rare) **California Condor**, whose wingspan can reach 9 feet, making it the largest land bird in North America; you can spot them without too much trouble, however, at the San Diego Zoo Safari Park (p.628, **8**). San Diego's also a great spot for birders to seek out **hummingbirds**—at least 14 species of these fascinating birds go nectar hunting in various locations in Southern California. The **California Quail**, the official state bird, is appropriately found throughout California, especially in woodland areas, such as Yosemite National Park (p. 276). Though all of California's national and state parks are great locations for bird-watching, the best spot for birders in the state is arguably **Mono Lake Tufa State Natural Reserve** (p. 269, **13**); it's a crucial habitat for migrating bird species and a great place to spot **California Gulls** and other shorebirds.

Numerous mammals also call the state home, from jackrabbits and beavers to porcupines and skunks. It should come as no surprise to find majestic **bighorn sheep** in Anza-Borrego Desert State Park (p. 552), when you

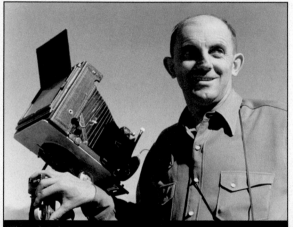

Ansel Adams

Born in San Francisco, photographer and environmentalist Ansel Adams (1902–84) fell in love with Yosemite National Park as a teen and became a proud member if the Sierra Club in 1917. It was only years later that he gave any real thought to photography, not publishing his first efforts until 1921, but eventually grew to become one of history's most renowned photographers. A proponent of realism, he sought to inspire viewers of his work with the beauty of nature. His classic photographs of Yosemite are a double delight: first, there's the subject, say, a snow-dusted Half Dome reflected in the still Merced River; then there's his Zone System, a technique that renders full-tonal gradation in his black-and-white photographs.

> *Sipping sweet nectar from native wildflowers, 14 species of jewel-like hummingbirds thrive in Southern California.*

consider that the park's name is partially derived from the Spanish word for sheep. In the predatory department, both **bobcats** (actually a form of lynx) and **mountain lions** (North America's largest big cat) can be found in several locations in California, including Lassen Volcanic National Park (p. 224, ❺), Sequoia and Kings Canyon National Parks (p. 286), and McArthur-Burney Falls Memorial State Park (p. 235, ❻). **Coyotes** are found all over the state, though a good place to spot them (or at least hear them) is Yosemite National Park (p 276).

With such a long coast, it's unsurprising to discover that California plays host to a lot of water-loving species. Two great places to spot **California Sea Lion** couldn't be more different: they like to hang out in the wilderness of the Lost Coast (p. 231, ❽), where you'll also find **harbor seals**,

and can also be found sunning themselves right off of San Francisco's Fisherman's Wharf (p. 56, ❹). Head to Crystal Cove State Park (p. 512) from December to February and you might glimpse the **California gray whale** from the beach.

Do note that though the **Grizzly Bear** appears on the state's flag and is, in fact, the official state animal, the species can no longer be found in California (ironically, its official designation came over 30 years after the bears had been exterminated from the region in 1922). The **American black bear** (the inspiration behind the legendary Teddy Bear), however, can be spotted primarily in the northeastern sections of the state; one good spot for viewing is Emerald Bay State Park (p. 273, ❽).

Reptiles make their home primarily in the California desert regions. Joshua Tree

National Park (p. 548), Anza-Borrego Desert State Park (p. 552), and Death Valley National Park all play host to a number of snakes and lizards, including several species of **rattlesnake** and the official state reptile, the **desert tortoise**.

Environmentalism
Sure, the presence of so many natural wonders—Big Sur's rugged coast, the granite monoliths of Yosemite Valley, the stark desert landscape of Death Valley—contributes to a certain elevated awareness of the environment and conservation, but California isn't necessarily green for altruistic reasons. In many ways, it's self-preservation. For example, within the U.S., auto-emission standards are toughest in California precisely because the state has the most registered vehicles in the country, and public transportation options are few and far between.

California may have a tree-hugging image, but the reality of sustaining a population this large is a far more complicated picture. This is the land that launched the Sierra Club, but it's also the state ruled by the car.

For information on water issues in California, see p. 290.

Natural Disasters

California is home to many fault lines (fractures in the earth's crust), making it very vulnerable to earthquakes. The most feared of all of its faults is the world-famous (or maybe that should be notorious) San Andreas Fault, the sliding boundary of the Pacific Plate and the North American Plate. The fault runs 650 miles from the Mexican border to the Mendocino coast, and is accessible in many places where you can identify each of the tectonic plates by the juxtaposition of different rock formations.

The result of this geological upheaval has been a number of significant **earthquakes** throughout the state's history. Earthquakes wreaked havoc in San Francisco in 1906, Santa Barbara in 1925, the Bay Area again in 1989 (rather famously captured live on national TV, when it began during the start of the third game of the 1989 World Series between the Oakland Athletics and the San Francisco Giants), and Northridge (just north of Los Angeles) in 1994. Residents tend to be blasé about the occasional small tremor, but the fact is the San Andreas Fault is historically overdue for a major rupture—the longer the wait,

the bigger the quake. Scientists fear that the "Big One" would be utterly devastating, but contrary to some misperceptions, California would not simply crack and fall into the ocean.

Earthquakes, however, are not the only natural disaster that has plagued California. Thanks to the Santa Ana winds (extremely dry winds that usually sweep up from Mexico and through Southern California and are noted for bringing increased temperatures), **wildfires** are prevalent in the arid regions of Southern California, especially in places such as Malibu, Santa Barbara, and the areas north of San Diego. Wildfire season usually runs from June to October, and a brutal one

can result in the destruction of hundreds of thousands of acres of land (in 2009, almost 350,000 acres were destroyed by numerous fires during the season).

And when rain finally does fall, previously arid conditions can lead to dangerous **mudslides**. In 2010, Southern California suffered a string of mudslides after Pacific storms overwhelmed parched soil in the region.

Oh, and California does, in fact, have active volcanoes, though they rank lower on the "natural worries" totem pole. Lassen Peak (p. 224, **5**) hasn't erupted in close to 100 years, though when it last blew its top, it did plenty of damage and the threat remains.

> *Fire is a natural part of California's ecosystem, but that doesn't make it any better when houses lie in an inferno's path.*

EXTREME
SKATEBOARDING

A childhood toy goes radical **BY HARRIOT MANLEY**

TEARING IT UP IN HALF-PIPES AND RAMPS, extreme skateboarders catch big air on a daily basis. Skate parks dot the globe, and amateur and pro events draw huge crowds. This new skating craze and culture can be traced to Southern California in the '70s, when surfers from a scruffy area around Venice Beach capitalized on the region's drought and applied their wave-carving skills to drained swimming pools. Using flexible boards and polyurethane wheels, they performed gravity-defying stunts and blew the lid off the sport. The story of these skateboarding legends was captured in *Dogtown and Z-Boys*, a 2001 documentary narrated by another infamous So Cal bad boy, Sean Penn. Amongst those early Z-Boys? A 12-year-old phenom named Tony Hawk.

Hall of Fame

TONY HAWK This "rail-thin geek" from San Diego went pro at age 14, and when the skateboarding craze skidded in the early '90s, he made the sport cool again.

MARK GONZALES The pioneer of modern street skating uses stairs, rails, and structures as his playground. He's also the author of several poetry books.

CHRISTIAN HOSOI "Christ" was the sport's big-air rock star in the '80s but was sidelined by a drug conviction in 2000. He's now skating pro again.

PAUL RODRIGUEZ Über-hot on today's pro-skating scene, "P-Rod" (named for his famous comedian dad) is known for his flawless, almost robotic execution.

CARA BETH (CB) BURNSIDE The first breakthrough woman in modern skateboarding. Also a competitive snowboarder, she was on the 1994 U.S. Olympic Team and won gold at the X Games.

Skating Hot Spots

SKATELAB SKATEPARK (SIMI VALLEY). The adjacent museum and Skateboarding Hall of Fame welcome 50,000 visitors annually.

POTRERO DEL SOL (SAN FRANCISCO). In the heart of the Mission District, a long-standing hotbed of skateboarding culture.

CUNNINGHAM SKATEPARK (SAN JOSE). At 68,000 square feet, the largest park in California.

VENICE SKATEPARK (VENICE BEACH). Dogtown has come a long way with this $2.4 million park, opened in 2009 right on the beach.

VANS AT THE BLOCK (ORANGE). Designers of the first skate shoe, Vans built this indoor/outdoor playground complete with 12-foot-deep (empty) pools.

MAGDALENA ECKE FAMILY YMCA (ENCINITAS). Don't let the name fool you—this Y's skate scene rocks, with hometown boys including Tony Hawk.

The Lingo

AIR: getting all four wheels off the ground.

FAKIE: skating backwards while facing forward in a normal stance.

GRIND: scraping one or both axles on a curb, railing, or other surface.

HALF-PIPE: a U-shaped ramp of any size, usually with a flat section in the middle.

MCTWIST: a 540-degree turn performed on a ramp, named after Mike McGill.

OLLIE: a jump performed by tapping the tail of the board on the ground; basis of most tricks.

STREET: skating the urban landscape, including curbs, stairs, benches, and handrails.

California Literature

> *Samuel Clemens (aka Mark Twain) first hit literary gold when he wrote about the jumping frogs of Calaveras County.*

A number of vaunted American writers were either born or spent time honing their craft in California. Their work provides insight into the lives and issues of their times.

Lauded by William Faulkner as the father of American Literature, Samuel Clemens (1835–1910)—better known by his nom de plume, **Mark Twain**—arrived in California with so many other pioneers in the mid-19th century. The humorist and novelist rose to national attention in 1865 when he published "The Celebrated Jumping Frog of Calaveras County," a story about a jumping frog contest in Gold Rush-era Angels Camp (p. 174, ❾), California.

Another literary transplant was **Helen Hunt Jackson** (1830–85), an activist who used literature to showcase the plight of Native Americans in the United States. Her seminal work, *Ramona* (1884), was a sentimental but hugely popular novel about a half-Native American girl growing up in Southern California after the Mexican-American War.

Social critic **Ambrose Bierce** (1842–1914) moved to San Francisco in 1866 and proceeded to achieve fame for his reporting and commentary in various city papers and magazines. "Bitter Bierce" nevertheless wrote in many genres and was noted for his realistic and judicious style.

Muckraking journalist **Upton Sinclair** (1878–1968) first moved to California after World War II but wrote a considerable number of his 90-plus books while residing in the Golden State. Most notable of his California works is *Oil!* (1927), which constitutes thinly veiled fiction about the bribery, scandal, and corruption at the heart of the oil industry in Southern California.

Like Sinclair, California native **John Steinbeck** (1902–68) was passionately concerned with issues of social justice. The author of 27 books, his greatest work is arguably his 1939 Pulitzer Prize-winner, *The Grapes of Wrath*. Set during the Great Depression, a family of migrant workers, the Joads, head west on Route 66 to the Promised Land of California only to discover more hardship. For more on Steinbeck, see p. 641.

One of the country's first professional writers, **Jack**

Writers of the Bay

For more information on writers native to Northern California, see p. 226.

> *A self-described shy, bookish child, author Joan Didion grew into a literary star thanks to books like* Slouching Towards Bethlehem.

London (1876–1916), too, was a California native, born in San Francisco. An avowed socialist thanks mostly to his working-class upbringing, the largely self-educated author drew upon his political beliefs and personal experiences while penning such classics as *The Call of the Wild* (1903) and *White Fang* (1906).

Not all California authors were concerned with direct or indirect social commentary. Some sought to revolutionize or outright create entire genres. **Samuel Dashiell Hammett** (1894–1961) was proclaimed by no less than the *New York Times*, "the dean of the hard-boiled school of detective fiction." His *Red Harvest* (1929) is considered an American classic, but his best-known work may be *The Maltese Falcon* (1930), set in 1920s San Francisco, in which Hammett introduced the world to the quintessential American private eye, Sam

Spade. **Raymond Chandler** (1888–1959) moved to Los Angeles from his native Chicago in 1913 and was inspired by Hammett to take his own crack at the genre, giving it a lyrical style that had been previously lacking. His tour de force *The Big Sleep* (1939) features wisecracking detective Philip Marlowe and scratches the dark underbelly of sunny Los Angeles. The novel inspired many writers the world over (Ian Fleming, the creator of James Bond, was a huge fan).

Another literary pioneer, albeit in a very different fashion, was **Henry Miller** (1891–1980), who moved to Big Sur in 1940 and was famous for defining literary convention and pushing the boundaries of the novel form. Though better known for his earlier controversial works, such as *Tropic of Cancer* (1939), Miller was also a master of the memoir: *Big Sur*

and the Oranges of Hieronymus Bosch (1957) waxes rhapsodic on the natural beauty of his adopted home.

Miller was also a huge influence on the writers of the Beatnik (or Beat) movement, which took off in San Francisco in 1955 thanks to **Allen Ginsberg's** (1926–97) *Howl*. The movement challenged the idea of limits on free expression, extolled nonconformity, and resulted in writing with a decidedly visceral style. Perhaps the greatest writer of the Beat movement was **Jack Kerouac** (1922–69), who actually coined the phrase "Beat Generation" in 1948 and inspired many subsequent writers, including Hunter Thompson and Ken Kesey. Kerouac's seminal work, *On the Road*, was published in 1957 after serious difficulties in finding a publisher for a work that was labeled by many as immoral; his best California-specific title was *Big Sur* (1962), in which a writer and his alter ego descend into alcoholism and madness in a remote cabin in the Big Sur wilderness.

Sacramento native **Joan Didion's** (b. 1934) novels and essays have much to say about the anxieties of modern life. *The White Album* (1970) is a collection of personal essays on the warped lifestyle and paranoid atmosphere of Los Angeles in the 1960s, with appearances by the Black Panthers, Charles Manson, drugs, and The Doors.

California Music

> *Taking center stage during the drug-laced late-'60s, The Doors, with lead singer Jim Morrison, heated up rock 'n' roll.*

California's earliest music was influenced in large part by the various ethnic groups—Spanish, Chinese, Russian, etc.—that settled the state, but didn't truly coalesce into a music scene it could truly call its own until the mid-1950s.

It was during that decade that the Bakersfield Sound genre was launched by **Buck Owens** (1929–2006) in the honky-tonk bars of Bakersfield, California. This type of gritty country music was a response to the more slick Nashville sound and was popularized by artists like **Merle Haggard** (b. 1937), who would go on to influence many of today's country stars.

The 1960s would see the launch of several major musical genres in California, the first of which would be forever associated with the state: surf rock. Guitarist **Dick Dale** (b. 1937) is largely credited with launching surf rock in 1961, and he did shape the instrumental form, but the genre found its zenith in the surf vocal-pop form pioneered by the **Beach Boys**. Founder Brian Wilson's meticulous production and harmony-drenched compositions on the legendary *Pet Sounds* (1966) raised the bar for the artistry of pop music, and was lauded by fellow musicians like the Beatles, Bob Dylan, and Elton John.

The late 1960s (and the growing use of mind-altering substances during that era) served as the launching pad for psychedelic music (aka acid rock) in L.A. and San Francisco. Standout albums from the era include *The Doors* (1967), in which **The Doors'** lead singer Jim Morrison's druggy poeticism and roadhouse swagger elevate a hard-rocking band that honed their chops on the Sunset Strip; and *Forever Change* (1967) by **Love**, a combination of garage rock and sunny psychedelia that *Rolling Stone* ranked as number 40 of the greatest 500 albums of all time.

Perhaps the best known (and longest lasting) practitioners of psychedelic rock were the **Grateful Dead**; though best known for their live performances, the Dead's *American Beauty* (1970) is a rare studio gem, featuring such classics as "Sugar Magnolia" and "Truckin'."

San Francisco's "Summer of Love" scene did more than just launch psychedelic trips. Funk bands, featuring music with extended vamps on a single chord, would also originate there. **Sly & the Family Stone** were the funkiest band to come out of the era and their *Stand!* (1969) blended social commentary with effervescent grooves.

Rock fused with country in California in the early 1970s, and the country-rock genre reached the height of its power in one the best-selling records of all time: *Hotel California* (1976) by the L.A.-based **Eagles** (though admittedly, it's more rock than country). In the late 1970s, the music scene (especially in Southern California) shifted more to hard-edged punk rock. A classic album of the genre is *Los Angeles* (1980) by **X**; the debut album of these L.A. punk rockers (discovered by The Doors' Ray Manzarek) combines punk's energy with rockabilly riffs and vocal harmonies. Though punk would decline for a time in California, it would eventually be revitalized in the 1990s by a band out of Berkeley (p. 126). **Green Day** re-energized the pop-punk scene with *Dookie* (1994), which sold over 10 million copies and spawned five top-10 singles, and took the evolution of punk rock to even greater heights with 2004's *American Idiot*, essentially an entire punk-rock opera.

The origins of glam metal (aka hair metal) may have started in the 1970s (**Van Halen** is often credited with getting things started), but the genre really kicked off in the 1980s, and L.A. was its acknowledged center. Though

> *Hip-hop lost a star when red-hot Tupac Shakur, based in Oakland, was murdered in Las Vegas in 1996.*

often derided as more style than substance, the genre combined the style of '70s glam rock with the power chords of heavy metal. Standout bands included Mötley Crüe, Poison, Quiet Riot, and **Guns N' Roses**—the latter's *Appetite for Destruction* demonstrating the beginning of the shift towards rock over glam towards the end of the '80s.

The 1980s were also a banner decade for hip-hop and rap in California, particularly in the ghettos of Los Angeles, where West Coast hip-hop (which made major use of sampling and spawned gangsta rap) grew. 1988's *Straight Outta Compton* by **N.W.A** moved the power center for rap from New York (where it originated) to California. Other famous West Coast artists included Ice T, Tupac Shakur, and **Snoop Doggy Dogg**, whose *Doggstyle* (1993) is a West Coast

hip-hop classic with an infectious funky flow. The mid-1990s collapse, due to legal troubles, of West Coast hip-hop's biggest label, Death Row Records, toppled it from its hip-hop throne, and the East Coast and South subsequently moved to the forefront of hip-hop and rap.

California also lost its position atop the American rock music scene in the 1990s with the rise of grunge (and Seattle) but still remained a force in alternative rock. The most notable band to play during the era was **The Red Hot Chili Peppers**, formed by three buds from Fairfax High in Hollywood. Their *Blood Sugar Sex Magic* (1991) shows off a perfected punk-funk-rock style and features the memorable "Under a Bridge," an addict's elegy to the City of Angels.

For more on California music, see p. 326.

Great California Movies

> *Leaving audiences (and Jimmy Stewart) reeling, Hitchcock's* Vertigo *put a creepy spotlight on San Francisco landmarks.*

> *Sticking his nose into a buddy's business, Paul Giamatti leads a wine-soaked road trip in* Sideways.

Perhaps unsurprisingly, the movie capital of the world has aimed its lens at California on more than one occasion...to good (and sometimes pretty great) effect. Here are some classics and hidden gems that get our thumbs up.

American Graffiti (1972). George Lucas' look at the early '60s cruising culture in small-town California with teenagers, cool cars, drive-ins, and rock-'n'-roll (the soundtrack is a masterpiece!).

Big Lebowkski (1998). A profane cult classic, with an iconic performance by Jeff Bridges as the ultimate L.A. stoner...err, dude.

Bottle Shock (2008). The rise of California's wine industry is explored in this movie, which depicts the events that led up to the 1976 Judgment at Paris

competition in which California wines unexpectedly triumphed over French vintages.

Boyz n the Hood (1991). John Singleton directed this film, one of the first fully dimensional looks into the gangridden, poverty-stricken South Central, a predominantly African-American neighborhood in Los Angeles.

Bullitt (1968). The car chase sequence through the streets of San Francisco in this Steve McQueen classic is regarded by many as the most influential of its kind in film history.

Chinatown (1974). This Oscar nominee, directed by Roman Polanski, was inspired by the story of William Mulholland finagling the water from the Owens River Valley and routing it to thirsty Los Angeles, leaving the farmers

high and dry.

Citizen Kane (1941). This Orson Welles classic, a huge controversy on its release, paints an unflattering portrait of Charles Foster Kane—a character based on one of the most powerful men in California, William Randolph Hearst—and depicts his castle at San Simeon to be a vast, dark, and empty shell. See p. 356.

East of Eden (1955). Elia Kazan's Oscar-nominated take on John Steinbeck's classic novel features a debut performance by James Dean and some great shots of Mendocino (which was standing in for Monterey in the film).

It's a Mad, Mad, Mad, Mad World (1963). Though the much-sought-after Santa Rosita in this Stanley Kramer comedy doesn't exist, the movie does show off many locations in Southern California (from the Pacific Coast Highway to San Diego) as they looked before development took over.

L.A. Confidential (1997). 1950s L.A. is the real star of this neo-noir Oscar winner, based on James Ellroy's acclaimed novel about police corruption and celebrity.

L.A. Story (1991). Steve Martin's spot-on satire of the superficiality of the Los Angeles lifestyle in the early 1990s, with riffs on freeway shootouts, high colonics, plastic surgery, and the fine art of ordering a coffee drink.

Monterey Pop (1968). This documentary perfectly captures the Summer of Love spirit with concert footage of Jefferson Airplane, the Mamas and the Papas, and Janis Joplin.

The Player (1992). Robert Altman skewers the Hollywood studio system—as well as its narrative conventions—in a movie featuring cameos by celebrity and trendy industry spots such as the mud baths at Two Bunch Palms (p. 559).

Play Misty for Me (1971). Clint Eastwood made his directorial debut with this psychological thriller that shows off locations in Carmel, Monterey, and Big Sur. He obviously became fond of the area—he was elected mayor of Carmel in 1986.

> *Painting a larger-than-life portrait of a California megalomaniac, Orson Wells showed his cinematic genius in* Citizen Kane.

Point Break (1991). Watch this action-packed cult film more for its looks than brains, but its look at California's surfing scene is impressive—*Entertainment Weekly* ranked one of its surfing scenes among the 10 best ever in film.

Sideways (2004). This critically acclaimed comedy follows a road trip through Santa Barbara's wine country and singlehandedly upped pinot noir's coolness quotient.

Some Like it Hot (1959). The American Film Institute named this Bill Wilder film, which features screwball antics by Marilyn Monroe, Tony Curtis, and Jack Lemmon at the Hotel del Coronado (p. 617), the greatest comedy of all time.

Valley Girl (1983). Martha Coolidge directed this bitchin' story of a boy and girl bridging the cultural gap in early eighties L.A.—the gritty Hollywood punk scene versus the bubblegum mall culture of bland suburbia.

Vertigo (1958). Routinely listed among the best films ever made, this Hitchcock classic practically gives you a tour of the Bay Area thanks to extensive footage of such landmarks as the Golden Gate Bridge, Coit Tower, Palace of Fine Arts, and Mission San Juan Bautista.

Who Framed Roger Rabbit (1988). A combination of live action and animation, this Robert Zemeckis film touched off a major revitalization of classic animation even as it skewered Hollywood, film noir, and California's obsession with freeways.

Zabriskie Point (1970). A bizarre meditation on the California counterculture, it was a critical and commercial bomb but has been rediscovered for its gorgeous cinematography, particularly the scenes in Death Valley.

15 The Best Special Interest Trips

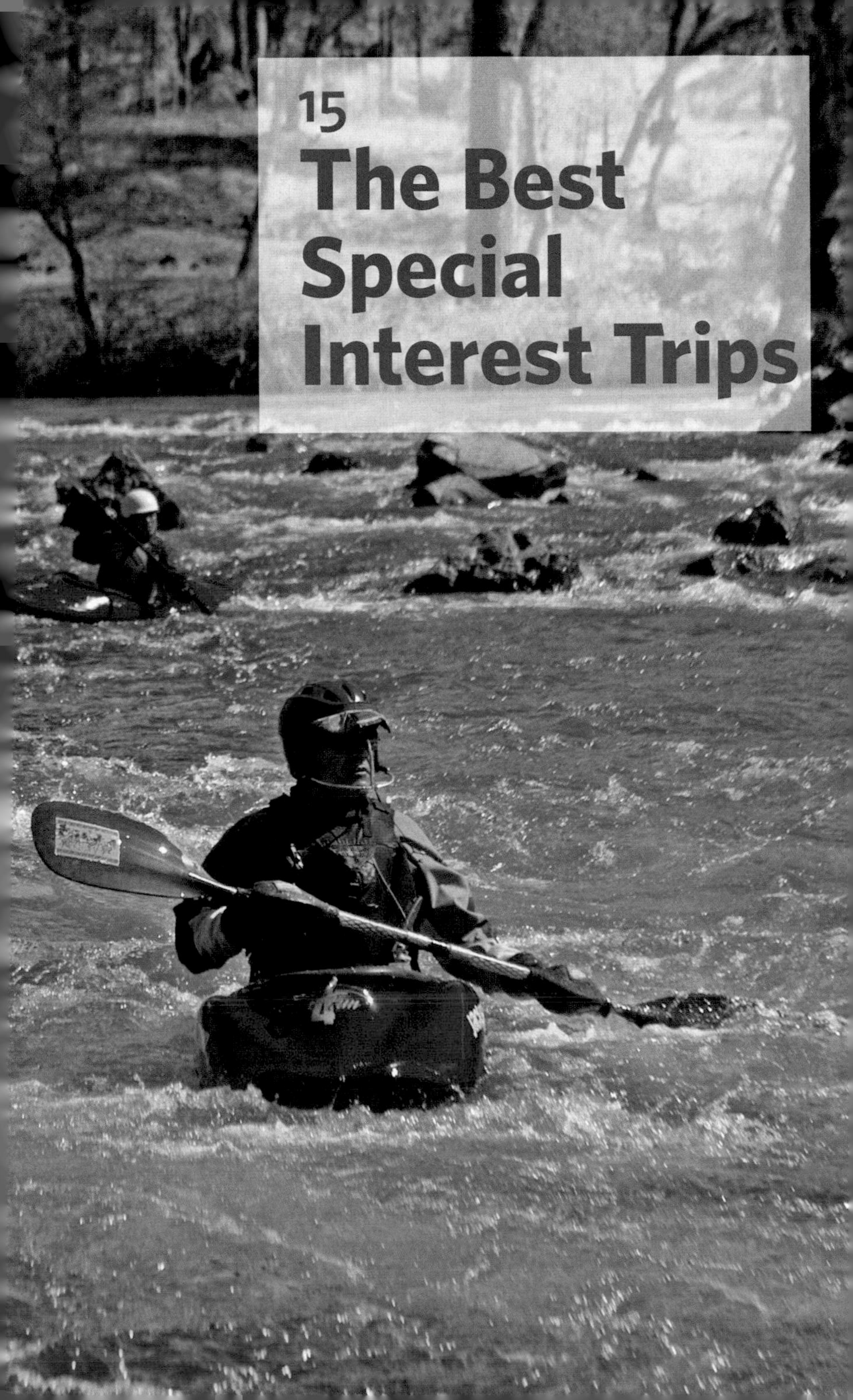

> **PREVIOUS PAGE** *The American River, a prime destination for white-water rafting and kayaking.* **THIS PAGE** *Pedal perfect in the lush Wine Country north of San Francisco.*

Multi-Activity Outfitters

Formerly known as Elderhostel, **Road Scholar** is a not-for-profit group that offers dozens of organized California trips—focusing on anything from birding to painting to cooking to skiing. There are no age restrictions, but participants are generally over 50. **11 Avenue de Lafayette, Boston, MA 02111.** ☎ 800/454-5768. www.roadscholar.org.

Specializing in trips for the 18-to-35 set, **Contiki Tours** has a number of California itineraries that primarily appeal to young professionals. Some focus on cities only (L.A. and San Francisco), but others take in the coast and national parks as well. **c/o Vacations To Go 5851 San Felipe, Ste. 500, Houston, TX 77057.** ☎ 800/680-2858 or 713/974-2121. www.contikivacations.com.

Collette Tours has a variety of escorted California tours, including trips to Pasadena's Tournament of Roses Parade and Northern California's Napa Valley and Sonoma Valley wine country. **162 Middle St., Pawtucket, RI 02860.** ☎ 800/340-5158. www.collettevacations.com.

Globus is a veteran travel company with more than 80 years of experience, offering escorted tours that hit the state's highlights from San Francisco to San Diego. It also offers packages that visit the Wine Country and several national parks. **5301 S. Federal Circle,** Littleton, CO 80123. ☎ 866/755-8581. www.globusjourneys.com.

From the Hollywood Walk of Fame to Napa Valley Wine Country; or from Carmel-by-the-Sea to Yosemite, **California Tours** has a variety of itineraries that cover the Golden State's highlights. You can pick up tours from either San Francisco or Los Angeles, and even work in a theme park or two. **500 Sutter St., San Francisco, CA 94102.** ☎ 877/338-3883 or 415/393-4211. www.california-tour.com.

Outdoor Activities A to Z

Biking

Cycle your way through Napa Valley and Sonoma Valley Wine Country with **Getaway Adventures** on 3- to 6-day guided tours (van supported) that include wine tastings, picnic lunches, and free time for shopping or a spa treatment. Multisport tours incorporate hiking and kayaking along the Russian River, as well. **2228 Northpoint Pkwy., Santa Rosa, CA 95407.** ☎ 800/499-2453 or 707/568-3040. www.getawayadventures.com.

Undiscovered Country has a slew of California road bike tours, heading to more locations than any other company. You'll find everything from long weekend outings in Gold Country to a spectacular 12-day jaunt along the central coast from Monterey to Santa Barbara. **2625 Middlefield Rd., PMB 562, Palo Alto, CA 94306.** ☎ 877/322-1667 or 650/494-1635. www.udctours.com.

Bird-Watching

Field Guides will lead you into some of the state's most distinctive birding environments—from old-growth redwood forests to the surreal landscape of Mono Lake—for bird-watching expeditions where you'll spot everything from marbled murrelets to sooty shearwaters. **9433 Bee Cave Rd., #1-150, Austin, TX 78733.** ☎ 800/728-4953 or 512/263-7295. www.fieldguides.com.

Camping

Backroads, the highly regarded active-travel company, has a number of California itineraries—including Napa Valley Wine Country and Death Valley biking—as well as a deluxe 5-day family camping trip to Redwood National Park and Humboldt Redwoods State Park.

> *Wave riders splash through the surf along the Mendocino coast on a guided adventure out of Ricochet Ridge Ranch.*

Kayaking, mountain biking, and hiking are all part of the adventure. 801 Cedar St., Berkeley, CA 94710. ☎ 800/462-2848 or 510/527-1555. www.backroads.com.

California Overland features 2-hour to 2-day trips into Anza-Borrego Desert State Park. You'll visit spectacular canyons, caves, ancient Native American sites, and more aboard military-style vehicles. 1233 Palm Canyon Dr., Borrego Springs, CA 92004. ☎ 866/639-7567 or 760/767-1232. www.california overland.com.

Enjoy a 3-day family getaway with **Point Reyes Outdoors** that includes kayaking, swimming, and hiking in and around the Bay Area's spectacular Point Reyes National Seashore. This outfitter also offers guided kayak, hiking, and biking tours. 11401 State Route 1, Point Reyes Station, CA 94956. ☎ 415/663-8192. www.pointreyesoutdoors.com.

Diving

Truth Aquatics runs multiday live-aboard dive trips to the kelp forests of the Channel Islands National Marine Sanctuary; some outings cater to nondivers and include kayaking and hiking. Half-day dives are also available. 301 W. Cabrillo Blvd., Santa Barbara, CA 93101. ☎ 805/962-1127. www.truthaquatics.com.

Hiking/Backpacking/Mountaineering

Leading tours since 1978, **Call of the Wild** runs adventure travel tours for women—all ages and all levels of experience—to some of the state's most pristine and dramatic wilderness. Look for backpacking trips to Northern California's Lost Coast, trekking through Death Valley, or scaling Mount Whitney. A major plus: It's famous for

its gourmet camp food. PO Box 1412, Mountain View, CA 94042. ☎ 888/378-1978 or 650/265-1662. www.callwild.com.

Outdoor recreation megastore REI can not only outfit you with the latest gear, but it also has some pretty cool trips. **REI Adventures** offers a variety of trips including a 6-day Death Valley hike, rock climbing in Joshua Tree National Park, and a hike to the summit of Mount Whitney. There's also a family outing to Lake Tahoe, where REI has its own private campground. PO Box 1938, Sumner, WA 98390. ☎ 800/622-2236 or 253/437-1100. www.rei.com.

Challenging Mount Shasta can be summitted by novices and **Shasta Mountain Guides** can get you there. This company also offers women-only trips and mountaineering and rock climbing classes. PO Box 1543, Mount Shasta, CA 96067. ☎ 530/926-3117. www. shastaguides.com.

Acclaimed outfitter **Southern Yosemite Mountain Guides** offers California hiking, mountaineering, fly-fishing, and rock climbing trips—everything from backpacking weekends to an extreme 26-day, 195-mile Kings Canyon to Yosemite trek. 621 Highland Ave., Santa Cruz, CA 95060. ☎ 800/231-4575. www.symg.com.

Tahoe Trips & Trails runs hiking and multisport (kayaking, biking, horseback riding) tours to various California destinations. There are 3- and 5-day guided trips to Lake Tahoe, the North Coast, Yosemite, the Wine Country, and Death Valley. PO Box 6952, Tahoe City, CA 96145. ☎ 800/581-4453 or 530/583-4506. www.tahoetrips.com.

Since 1969, **Yosemite Mountaineering School and Guide Service** (YMS) has been

> *Sample Peking duck, dim sum, and other traditional dishes on a Wok Wiz walking tour of Chinatown.*

teaching folks how to "go climb a rock," as well as leading experienced climbers on multiday ascents of formidable El Capitan. YMS also offers women-only classes and backpacking outings. PO Box 578, Yosemite National Park, CA 95389. ☎ 209/372-8344. www.yosemitepark.com.

Horseback Riding

For a true taste of the West, take a multiday wilderness horseback vacation into the High Sierra with **Mammoth Lakes Pack Outfit,** a family-run company that has been operating since 1915. Other special trips include a 4-day ride to the ghost town of Bodie. 100 Lake Manor Place, Mammoth Lakes, CA 93546. ☎ 888/ 475-8747 or 760/934-2434. www. mammothpack.com.

Ricochet Ridge Ranch offers weeklong horseback riding vacations along the incredible Mendocino coast; you'll journey along deserted beaches and through redwood forests, and spend your evenings at charming B&Bs. Daily and custom rides are also available. 24201 N. Hwy. 1, Fort Bragg, CA 95437. ☎ 888/873-5777 or 707/964-7669. www.horse-vacation.com.

Kayaking/Rafting

Join **Aquasports** for multiday guided kayaking/camping trips to the Channel Islands off the coast of Santa Barbara. Sea caves, crystal clear water, deserted beaches, and abundant wildlife make for a memorable experience; day trips are available as well. 111 Verona Ave., Goleta, CA 93117. ☎ 800/773-2309 or 805/968-7231. www.islandkayaking.com.

Proclaimed the "best river and sea outfitter on earth" by *National Geographic Adventure* magazine, **O.A.R.S.** offers a range of white-water rafting excursions on nine different Northern California rivers. There's an outing for all skill levels, and family trips—including a 4-day adventure camp that also features hiking, kayaking, and sightseeing—are a specialty. PO Box 67, Angels Camp, CA 95222. ☎ 800/346-6277 or 209/736-4677. www.oars.com.

Zephyr Whitewater Expeditions features half-day to 5-day white-water rafting journeys in the Yosemite, Sequoia, and Kings Canyon national park areas. Trips run from April to September, and first timers, families, and seasoned veterans will all find something to suit them. PO Box 510, Columbia, CA 95310. ☎ 800/431-3636 or 209/532-6249. www.zrafting.com.

Sports

Explore the state's fields of dreams with **Roadtrips'** California Classic Tour. From San Diego's PETCO Park to AT&T Park in San Francisco, you'll catch a game at California's four Major League Baseball parks. In L.A., you'll also get a behind-the-scenes tour of Dodger Stadium. 800-191 Lombard Ave., Winnipeg, MB, R3B 0X1, Canada. ☎ 800/465-1765 or 204/947-5690. www.roadtrips.com.

Food & Wine Trips

Cooking enthusiasts can indulge themselves at Napa Valley's **Culinary Institute of America at Greystone.** This renowned culinary college has

One-Stop Shopping

Looking for more things to do in California? An excellent overall resource is **Shaw-Guides,** an online resource to learning vacations, cooking schools, art and photography workshops, and much more. Browse through the offerings at www.shawguides.com.

an assortment of offerings: There are 2-day "sophisticated palate" experiences that combine cooking classes with off-campus excursions to local restaurants and vineyards; 2- to 5-day "boot camps"; and multiday career discovery programs for those considering a career in cooking. 2555 Main St. (Hwy. 29), St. Helena, CA 94574. ☎ 707/967-2328. www.ciachef.org.

Classic Journeys, one of *Travel + Leisure* magazine's "world's best tour operators," offers a culinary trip through the Napa Valley and Sonoma Valley Wine Country. This tasteful adventure includes wine tastings, cooking classes, visits to local farms, and meals in world-class restaurants. You'll also spend some time in San Francisco. 7855 Ivanhoe Ave., Ste. 220, La Jolla, CA 92037. ☎ 800/200-3887 or 858/454-5004. www.classicjourneys.com.

Wok Wiz Chinatown has daily San Francisco Chinatown walking tours, with or without dim sum lunch, but it's the epic **I Can't Believe I Ate My Way Through Chinatown** tour that adventurous diners will want to try. 250 King St., Ste. 268, San Francisco, CA 94107. ☎ 650/355-9657.www.wokwiz.com.

Learning Trips

Art Excursions, Inc. is owned and operated by a husband-and-wife team of art historian university professors who lead small tours for travelers interested in architecture, art, and gardens. California tours might include a visit to Frank Gehry's Walt Disney Concert Hall, a concert by the L.A. Philharmonic, or a guided exploration of the Getty Center. PO Box 92, Riverside, IL 60546. ☎ 630/671-9745. www.artexcursions.com.

Promising to "make girls out of women," **Manifesta** schedules a variety of active and engaging tours for women only. The offerings include "creative safaris" ; art-making vacations in Carmel-by-the-Sea punctuated with wine breaks; hiking, biking, and kayaking excursions; and golf programs for players of all levels. PO Box 4669, Carmel-by-the-Sea, CA 93921. ☎ 831/625-5748. www.manifestasafaris.com.

Nurture your inner Ansel Adams with a photo tour led by **Y explore Yosemite Adventures.** Year-round there are a variety of workshops offered (all require a certain amount of hiking), ranging from beginner to professional level. *National Geographic* photographer Phil

Schermeister leads the teaching staff. PO Box 4951, Sonora, CA 95370. ☎ 800/886-8009. www.yexplore.com.

Image Quest leads casual, low-cost photo safaris throughout California; locations might include Route 66 through the Mojave Desert, Yosemite in winter, or California's central coast. Outings are led by lensman Dave Wyman, who has been organizing photo tours since 1982. 1164 Alvira St., Los Angeles, CA 90035. ☎ 323/377-7565. www.davewyman.net.

Volunteer Trips

The **Sierra Club** donates some 27,000 hours of labor annually to state and federal land agencies, doing everything from building and maintaining trails to helping with archaeological digs. You don't have to be a member to join in, but plumb assignments at places like Yosemite National Park do fill up. The Sierra Club's 13 California chapters also offer a wide variety of outings ranging from backpacking trips along the Lost Coast to day hikes in San Diego's Cuyamaca Mountains. Sierra Club Outings Department, 85 Second St., 2nd Floor, San Francisco, CA 94105. ☎ 415/977-5522. www.sierraclub.org.

Wellness Trips

Founded by holistic guru Deepak Chopra, the **Chopra Center for Wellbeing** offers yoga and meditation classes, spa treatments, and multiday healing programs and workshops designed to restore physical and emotional health. It's located in Carlsbad at the La Costa Resort and Spa, which offers a special rate for Chopra guests. 2013 Costa del Mar Rd., Carlsbad, CA 92009. ☎ 888/424-6772 or 760/494-1600. www.chopra.com.

Combine outdoors adventure with spiritual rejuvenation on trips with **HeroQuest.** Utilizing the structure of author Joseph Campbell's *The Hero's Journey,* these tours combine whitewater canoeing on the Eel and Trinity rivers with exercises designed to raise consciousness and awareness of issues that may be holding you back. Navigate the rivers as you navigate your psyche. 1001 Bridgeway, Ste. 455, Sausalito, CA 94965. ☎ 800/990-4376. www.innerquest.com.

> Historic trolleys once used in
the city of brotherly love now
roll in the city by the bay.

Before You Go

Tourist Offices

For information on the state as a whole, log on to the **California Travel & Tourism Commission** website at www.visitcalifornia.com. U.S. and Canadian residents can receive free travel planning information via mail by calling ☎ 877/225-4367. Most cities and towns also have a tourist bureau or chamber of commerce that distributes information on the area. These are listed in the preceding chapters, organized geographically.

To learn more about California's national parks, contact the **Pacific West Region Information Center,** Fort Mason, Bldg. 201, San Francisco, CA 94123 (☎ 415/561-4700; www. nps.gov).

For information on state parks, contact the **Department of Parks and Recreation,** P.O. Box 942896, Sacramento, CA 94296-0001 (☎ 800/777-0369; www.parks.ca.gov).

For information on fishing and hunting licenses, contact the **California Department of Fish and Game** at ☎ 916/445-0411, or log on to their website at www.dfg.ca.gov.

Best Times to Go

California enjoys ideal weather nearly year-round, but the time between Memorial Day and Labor Day (late May to early Sept) is high tourist season everywhere except for desert areas such as Palm Springs and Death Valley, where scorching temperatures discourage all but the hardiest bargain hunters. Naturally, prices are highest at this time, and they can drop dramatically before and after that period. (Exceptions to this rule include the aforementioned deserts and winter ski resorts.) *Insider tip:* Many Californians think the best time to travel the state is autumn. From late September to early December, crowds drop off, shoulder-season rates kick in, and winter rains have yet to start looming.

Festivals & Special Events

Please note that, as with any schedule of upcoming events, the following information is subject to change; always confirm details before you plan your trip around an event. For an exhaustive list of events beyond those mentioned here, check http://events.frommers. com, where you'll find a searchable, up-to-the-minute roster of what's happening in cities all over California.

JANUARY

Tournament of Roses, Pasadena. A spectacular parade marches down Colorado Boulevard, with lavish floats, music, and extraordinary equestrian entries, followed by the Rose Bowl football game and a nightlong party along the boulevard. For details, call ☎ 626/449-4100, or see www.tournamentofroses.com. January 1.

Santa Barbara International Film Festival. For 10 days, Santa Barbara does its best impression of Cannes. There's a flurry of foreign and independent film premieres, appearances by actors and directors, and symposia on cinematic topics. For a rundown of events, call ☎ 805/963-0023, or see www.sbiff.org. Late January to early February.

FEBRUARY

Chinese New Year and Golden Dragon Parade, Los Angeles. Dragon dancers and martial arts masters parade through the streets of downtown's Chinatown. Chinese opera and other events are scheduled. For this year's schedule, contact the Chinese Chamber of Commerce at ☎ 213/617-0396, or visit www. lachinesechamber.org. Late January or early February.

AT&T Pebble Beach National Pro-Am, Pebble Beach. For this PGA-sponsored tour, pros team up with celebrities to compete on three famous golf courses. Call ☎ 800/541-9091 or 831/649-1533, or visit www.attpbgolf.com. Early February.

National Date Festival, Indio. Crowds gather to celebrate the Coachella Valley desert's most beloved cash crop, with events such as camel and ostrich races, the Blessing of the Date Garden, and Arabian Nights pageants. Plenty of date-sampling booths are set up, along with rides, food vendors, and other county-fair trappings. Call ☎ 800/811-3247 or 760/863-8247, or visit www.datefest.org. Two weeks in mid-February.

Mustard Festival, Napa Valley. Celebrating the blossom of yellow-petaled mustard flowers, which coat the valley during February and March, this event was conceived to drum up visitors during this once-slow season. The festival has evolved into 6 weeks of events, including a gourmet gala, a wine auction, recipe and photography competitions, and plenty of food and wine. For a schedule, call ☎ 707/944-1133, or visit www.mustardfestival.com. February and March.

MARCH

Festival of Whales, Dana Point. The Dana Point community celebrates the return of gray whales migrating off the coast with an annual street fair, food, games, entertainment, and a "Majestic Migration" parade. It's great for families. Call ☎ 949/496-5794, ext. 7, or go to www.festivalofwhales.com for details. Early March.

Return of the Swallows, San Juan Capistrano. Each St. Joseph's Day, visitors flock to this village for the arrival of the loyal flock of swallows that nest in the mission and remain until October. The celebration includes a parade, dances, and special programs. Call ☎ 949/234-1300, or visit www.missionsjc.com for details. March 19.

Kraft Nabisco Championship, Rancho Mirage. This 33-year-old LPGA golf tournament takes place near Palm Springs. After the celebrity Pro-Am early in the week, the best female pros get down to business. For further information, call ☎ 760/324-4546, or visit www.nabiscochampionship.com. Other special-interest events for women usually take place around the tournament, including the Dinah Shore Weekend (www.thedinahshore.com), the country's largest annual lesbian gathering. Last week of March/first week of April.

Redwood Coast Dixieland Jazz Festival, Eureka. Four days of jazz featuring some of the best Dixieland, blues, and zydeco bands in the world. Call ☎ 707/445-3378, or see www.redwoodcoastmusicfestivals.org. Late March.

Flower Fields in Bloom at Carlsbad Ranch. One of the most spectacular sights in San Diego's North County are the ranunculus blossoms that create a striped, floral blanket. This is a working ranch, but visitors are welcome to tour the fields. For information, call ☎ 760/431-0352, or see www.theflowerfields.com. March and April.

APRIL

San Francisco International Film Festival. This is one of the nation's oldest film festivals, featuring more than 100 films and videos from 30-plus countries. Tickets are inexpensive, and screenings are open to the general public. Call ☎ 415/561-5000, or visit www.sffs.org. Mid-April to early May.

Toyota Grand Prix, Long Beach. An exciting weekend of Indy-class auto racing and entertainment in downtown Long Beach draws world-class drivers from the United States and Europe, plus many celebrity contestants and spectators. Contact the Grand Prix Association at ☎ 888/82-SPEED or www.longbeachgp.com. Mid-April.

Coachella Music Festival, Indio. This multistage festival draws tens of thousands of scantily-clad hipsters to the desert with legendary lineups that blend some of the biggest names in music like Radiohead and Madonna with the hottest upstarts in indie rock, electronica and hip-hop. For the latest information, check out **www.coachella.com**. Mid to late April.

ArtWalk, San Diego. This free, 2-day festival in stylish Little Italy is the largest art event in the San Diego/Tijuana region, attracting some 70,000 people each year. It features visual and performing arts—painting, sculpture, photography, music, and dance—in outdoor venues, galleries, artist's studios, and businesses. The event also offers hands-on art experiences for kids. Call ☎ 619/615-1090, or visit www.missionfederalartwalk.org. Late April.

MAY

Doo Dah Parade, Pasadena. This outrageous spoof of the Rose Parade features such participants as the Briefcase Precision Drill Team and a kazoo-playing marching band. Call ☎ 626/590-1134, or visit www.pasadenadoodahparade.info. May 1.

Cinco de Mayo. A weeklong celebration of one of Mexico's most jubilant holidays takes place throughout **Los Angeles** near May 5. Large crowds, live music, dances, and food create a carnival-like atmosphere. The main festivities are held in El Pueblo de Los Angeles State Historic Park. Call ☎ 213/485-6855 for information.

The Cinco de Mayo celebration in **Old Town San Diego** features folkloric music, dance, food, and historical reenactments. Call ☎ 619/260-1700 for more information. Early May.

Calaveras County Fair and Jumping Frog Jubilee, Angels Camp. Inspired by Mark Twain's "The Celebrated Jumping Frog of Calaveras County," this race draws frog contestants and their guardians from all over. Call ☎ 209/736-2561, or see www.frogtown.org. Third weekend in May.

Paso Robles Wine Festival. What began as a small, neighborly gathering has grown into the largest outdoor wine tasting in California. The 3-day event features winery open houses and tastings, a golf tournament, a 5K run and 10K bike ride, and concerts, plus a festival in downtown's City Park. For a schedule, call ☎ 805/239-8463, or visit www.pasowine.com. Third weekend in May.

Bay to Breakers Foot Race, San Francisco. One of the city's most popular annual events. Thousands of entrants show up dressed—or undressed—in their best costumes for the 7.5-mile run. Call ☎ 415/359-2800, or log on to www.baytobreakers.com. Third Sunday in May.

Carnaval, San Francisco. The Mission District's largest annual event is a 2-day series of festivities culminating with a parade on Mission Street. Half a million spectators line the route, and samba musicians and dancers continue playing on 14th Street, near Harrison, after the march. Call ☎ 415/920-0125, or visit www.carnavalsf.com. Memorial Day weekend.

JUNE

Ojai Music Festival. This event has been drawing world-class classical and jazz personalities to the open-air Libbey Bowl since 1947. Past events have featured Igor Stravinsky, Aaron Copland, and the Juilliard String Quartet. Seats (and local lodgings) fill up quickly. Call ☎ 805/646-2094 for more information, or log on to www.ojaifestival.org. Early June.

San Diego County Fair. Referred to by locals as the Del Mar Fair, this is the other big happening (besides horse racing) at the Del Mar Fairgrounds. The entire county turns out for the 3-week event, with livestock competitions, rides, flower and garden shows, food and craft booths, carnival games, and home-arts exhibits. There are also grandstand concerts by big-name performers. Call ☎ 858/793-5555, or check www.sdfair.com. Mid-June through early July.

Mariachi USA Festival, Los Angeles. For this 2-day, family-oriented celebration of Mexican culture at the Hollywood Bowl, festivalgoers pack their picnic baskets and enjoy music, folkloric ballet, and related performances by top groups. The all-day, all-night event is one of the largest mariachi festivals in the world. For tickets, call ☎ 800-MARIACHI or 323/850-2000 (the Hollywood Bowl), or log on to www.mariachiusa.com. Late June.

Los Angeles Film Festival. With an attendance of 60,000-plus, the festival showcases more than 175 American and international indies, short films, and music videos during a 10-day event. Call ☎ 866/345-6337, or log on to www.lafilmfest.com. Late June.

San Francisco Lesbian, Gay, Bisexual, Transgender Pride Parade. Gay pride is celebrated over various weekends throughout the state in June and July, but San Francisco's party draws up to half a million participants. The parade heads west along Market Street from Beale Street to Eighth Street, where hundreds of food, art, and information booths are set up around several stages. Call ☎ 415/864-0831, or visit www.sfpride.org for info. Late June.

JULY

Mammoth Lakes Jazz Jubilee. This 4-day festival features 20 bands on 10 different stages, plus food, drinks, and dancing—all under the pine trees and stars. Call ☎ 760/934-2478, or see www.mammothjazz.org. Second weekend in July.

World Championship Over-the-Line Tournament, San Diego. This beach softball event, dating from 1953, is renowned for boisterous, beer-soaked, anything-goes behavior. More than 1,000 three-person teams compete, and upward of 50,000 people attend. It's a heap of fun for the open-minded but a bit much for small kids. It takes place on Fiesta Island in Mission Bay; admission is free. For more details, call ☎ 619/688-0817, or visit www.ombac.org. Mid-July.

Gilroy Garlic Festival. At this gourmet food fair, more than 85 booths serve garlicky food from almost every ethnic background, plus close to 100 arts, crafts, and entertainment booths. Call ☎ 408/842-1625, or visit www.gilroygarlic festival.com. Last full weekend in July.

Thoroughbred Racing Season, Del Mar. "Turf meets surf" during the thoroughbred racing season at the Del Mar Race Track. Post time is 2pm most days; the track is dark on Tuesdays. Special events are held throughout the season, including Friday afternoon concerts by top bands. For this year's schedule, call ☎ 858/755-1141, or visit www.dmtc.com. Mid-July to mid-September.

Festival of Arts & Pageant of the Masters, Laguna Beach. A 60-plus-year tradition in artsy Laguna, this festival centers on a fantastic performance-art production in which actors recreate famous Old Masters paintings. Other festivities include live music, crafts sales, art demonstrations and workshops, and the grassroots Sawdust Festival across the street. Call ☎ 800/487-FEST or 949/494-1145; there's online info at www.foapom.com. July through August.

Comic-Con International, San Diego. Some 140,000 people attend America's largest comic-book convention each year when it lands at the San Diego Convention Center for a weekend of auctions, dealers, autographs, and seminars focusing on graphic novels and fantasy/sci-fi movies and television shows. Past special guests include Hugh Jackman, Matt Groening, Halle Berry, Stan Lee, Angelina Jolie, and Quentin Tarantino. For details, call ☎ 619/491-2475, or check www.comic-con. org. Late July.

U.S. Open Sandcastle Competition, Imperial Beach. This is the quintessential beach event: a parade and children's castle-building contest on Saturday, followed by the adult event on Sunday. Astounding creations are plundered after the awards ceremony. For details, call ☎ 619/424-6663, or visit www.usopen sandcastle.com. Late July.

U.S. Open of Surfing, Huntington Beach. Hundreds of thousands of tanned bodies line the beach to catch gutsy performances by the world's best surfers. There are also rowdy exhibitions of skateboarding, motocross, and BMX biking, as well as less extreme activities like beach limbo, live music, and people-watching. For more information, call ☎ 424/653-1900, or log onto www.usopenofsurfing. com.Late July to early August.

AUGUST

Old Spanish Days Fiesta, Santa Barbara. The city's biggest annual event, this 5-day festival features a parade with horse-drawn carriages, music and dance performances, marketplaces, and a rodeo. Call ☎ 805/962-8101, or visit www.oldspanishdays-fiesta.org. Early August.

La Jolla SummerFest, San Diego. This is perhaps San Diego's most prestigious annual music event. It features a range of classical and contemporary music, from tango to Tchaikovsky, with guest composers and musicians ranging from Chick Corea to Yo-Yo Ma. SummerFest also offers master classes, open rehearsals, and workshops. Contact the La Jolla Music Society at ☎ 858/459-3728, or visit www.ljms.org. Early to mid-August.

Nisei Week Japanese Festival, Los Angeles. This weeklong celebration of Japanese culture and heritage is held in the Japanese American Cultural and Community Center Plaza in Little Tokyo. Festivities include parades, food, music, arts, and crafts. Call ☎ 213/687-7193, or see www.niseiweek.org. Mid-August.

SEPTEMBER

Los Angeles County Fair, Pomona. Horse racing, arts, agricultural displays, celebrity entertainment, and carnival rides are among the attractions at one of the largest county fairs in the world, held at the Los Angeles County Fair and Exposition Center. Call ☎ 909/623-3111, or visit www.fairplex.com for information. Throughout September.

Monterey Jazz Festival. One of the oldest annual jazz festivals in the world features top names in traditional and modern jazz. Call ☎ 831/373-3366, or see www.monterey jazzfest.com for more info. Mid-September.

Danish Days, Solvang. Since 1936, this 3-day event has been celebrating old-world customs and pageantry with a parade, gymnastics exhibitions by local schoolchildren, demonstrations of Danish arts and crafts, and plenty of *aebleskivers* (Danish fritters) and *medisterpolse* (Danish sausage). Call ☎ 800/468-6765 for more information, or see www.solvangusa.com. Mid-September.

Long Beach Blues Festival. Great performances by such blues legends as Etta James, Dr. John, the Allman Brothers, and Ike Turner make this an event you won't want to miss. In Rainbow Lagoon Park, the festival also offers cold beer, wine, and food. Call ☎ 562/985-2999, or log on to www.kkjz.org. Labor Day weekend.

Sausalito Art Festival, Sausalito. This juried exhibit of more than 180 artists is accompanied by music provided by Bay Area jazz, rock, and blues performers and international cuisine enhanced by wines from some 50 Napa and Sonoma producers. Call ☎ 415/331-3757, or log on to www.sausalitoartfestival.org for information. Labor Day weekend.

Simon Rodia Watts Towers Jazz Festival, Los Angeles. This event pays tribute to the roots of jazz in gospel and blues, as well as celebrating the avant-garde and Latin jazz scene. It's also a great opportunity to visit the Watts Towers. Call ☎ 213/847-4646, or log on to www.try watts.com. Late September.

OCTOBER

The Half Moon Bay Art & Pumpkin Festival, Half Moon Bay. The festival features a Great Pumpkin Parade, pie-eating contests, a pumpkin-carving competition, arts and crafts, and all manner of squash-based cuisine. The highlight of the event is the World Championship Pumpkin Weigh-Off. For exact date and details, call the hot line at ☎ 650/726-9652 or check www.miramarevents.com.

Fleet Week, San Diego. The name is a bit of a misnomer; the nation's largest military appreciation event actually lasts a full month. It features Navy ship tours, a college football game, an auto race of classic speedsters, the renowned Miramar air show, and more. For more info call ☎ 800/FLEET-WEEK, or log on to www.fleetweeksandiego.org. Mid-September to mid-October.

Catalina Island Jazz Trax Festival, Catalina Island. Contemporary jazz artists travel to the island to play in the legendary Catalina Casino Ballroom in Avalon. The festival is held over two consecutive 3-day weekends. Call ☎ 866/872-9849, or visit www.jazztrax.com for advance ticket sales and a schedule of performers. Early October.

Sonoma County Harvest Fair. A 3-day celebration of the harvest with exhibitions, art shows, and judging of local wines. Contact ☎ 707/545-4200 or www.harvestfair.org. Dates vary.

Hollywood Film Festival, Los Angeles. More than 50 films from the U.S. and abroad are screened, amid celebrities galore. Actors and filmmakers will find a variety of workshops and marketplaces. Call ☎ 310/288-1882, or visit www.hollywoodawards.com for info and tickets. Mid-October.

West Hollywood Halloween Costume Carnaval, Los Angeles. This is one of the world's largest Halloween parties. More than 400,000 people, many dressed in outlandish drag couture, party all night along Santa Monica Boulevard. Call ☎ 310/289-2525, or see www.visitwesthollywood.com for info. October 31.

NOVEMBER

Catalina Island Triathlon. This is one of the top triathlons in the world. Participants run on unpaved roads, swim in the cleanest bay on the West Coast, and bike on challenging trails. There's also a "kid's tri." Call Pacific Sports at ☎ 714/978-1528, or visit www.PacificSports LLC.com. Early November.

Hollywood Christmas Parade, Los Angeles. This spectacular, star-studded parade marches through the heart of Hollywood. For information, call ☎ 323/469-2337 or visit www.thehollywoodchristmasparade.com. Sunday after Thanksgiving.

DECEMBER

Balboa Park December Nights, San Diego. The city's urban park is decked out in holiday splendor for a weekend of evening events, including a candlelight procession, caroling and baroque music, craft displays, ethnic food, and hot cider. The event and the park's 13 museums are free these evenings. For more information, call ☎ 619/239-0512, or visit www.balboapark.org. First weekend in December.

Christmas Boat Parade of Lights. Following longstanding tradition, sailors decorate their crafts with colorful lights. Several Southern

California harbors hold nighttime parades to showcase the creations, which range from tiny dinghies draped with a single strand of lights to showy yachts with entire Nativity scenes twinkling on deck. Contact the following for schedules and information: **Ventura Harbor** (☎ 805/382-3001), **Long Beach** (☎ 562/435-4093), **Huntington Harbor** (☎ 714/840-7542), and **San Diego Bay** (www.sdparadeoflights.org). December.

Whale-Watching Season, San Diego. From mid-December to mid-March, more than 25,000 California gray whales make the trek from chilly Alaskan seas to the warm-water breeding lagoons of Baja California. Cabrillo National Monument, on the panoramic Point Loma peninsula, offers a glassed-in observatory from which to spot the whales, examine whale exhibits, and listen to taped narration describing these popular mammals. Many boating excursion companies offer whale-watching tours throughout the season. For more information, visit www.sandiego.org. Mid-December through mid-March.

College Bowl Games, San Diego. The city hosts two college football bowl games. The **Holiday Bowl** features top teams from the Pac 10 and Big 12 Conferences, while the **Poinsettia Bowl** pits a team from the Mountain West Conference against an at-large opponent. The fledgling Poinsettia Bowl (☎ 619/285-5061; www.poinsettiabowl.net) was inaugurated in 2005, while the Holiday Bowl (☎ 619/283-5808; www.holidaybowl.com) has been played since 1978, augmented by several special events, including the nation's biggest parade of giant inflatable characters. Late December.

New Year's Eve Torchlight Parade, Big Bear Lake. Watch dozens of nighttime skiers follow a serpentine path down Snow Summit's ski slopes bearing glowing torches—it's one of the state's loveliest traditions. Afterward, the party continues indoors with live bands, food, and drink. Call ☎ 909/866-5766, or log on to www.bigbearmountainresorts.com. December 31.

Weather

California's climate is so varied that it's impossible to generalize about the state.

San Francisco's temperate marine climate means relatively mild weather year-round. In summer, temperatures rarely top 70°F (21°C; pack sweaters, even in August), and the city's famous fog rolls in most mornings and evenings. In winter, the temperature seldom dips below freezing, and snow is extremely rare. Because of the fog, summer rarely sees more than a few hot days in a row. Head a few miles inland, though, and it's likely to be clear and hot.

The **Central Coast** shares San Francisco's climate, although it gets warmer as you get farther south. Seasonal changes are less pronounced south of San Luis Obispo, where temperatures remain relatively stable year-round. The **Northern Coast** is rainier and foggier; winters tend to be mild but wet.

Summers are cool around **Lake Tahoe** and in the **Shasta Cascades.** The climate is ideal for hiking, camping, and other outdoor activities, making these regions popular with residents of the state's sweltering deserts and valleys. From late November to early April, skiers also flock to this area for terrific snowfall.

Southern California—including **Los Angeles** and **San Diego**—is usually much warmer than the Bay Area, and it gets significantly more sun. Even in winter, daytime temperatures regularly reach into the 60s (15°C–20°C) and warmer. Summers can be very hot inland, but Southern California's coastal communities are comfortable. The area's limited rainfall is generally seen between December and mid-April, but it's rarely intense enough to be more than a slight inconvenience. Sunbathing is possible throughout the year, but the ocean is quite cold in the winter, strictly for extremists and wet-suited surfers. The water is warmest in summer and fall, but even then, the Pacific is too chilly for many.

The **deserts,** including **Palm Springs** and the desert national parks, are sizzling hot in summer; temperatures regularly top 100°F (38°C). Winter is the time to visit the desert resorts (and remember, it gets surprisingly cold at night in the desert).

Cellphones

Just because your cellphone works at home doesn't mean it'll work everywhere in California. Take a look at your wireless company's coverage map on its website before heading out; T-Mobile, Sprint, and Nextel are particularly weak in rural areas. If you need to stay in touch at a destination where you know your

CALIFORNIA'S AVERAGE DAILY TEMPERATURE

	JAN	FEB	MAR	APR	MAY	JUNE	JULY	AUG	SEPT	OCT	NOV	DEC
SAN FRANCISCO												
HIGH °F	56	59	60	61	63	64	64	65	69	68	63	57
HIGH °C	13	15	16	16	17	18	18	18	21	20	17	14
LOW °F	46	48	49	49	51	53	53	54	56	55	52	47
LOW °C	8	9	9	9	11	12	12	12	13	13	11	8
LOS ANGELES												
HIGH °F	65	66	67	69	72	75	81	81	81	77	73	69
HIGH °C	18	19	19	21	22	24	27	27	27	25	23	21
LOW °F	46	48	49	52	54	57	60	60	59	55	51	49
LOW °C	8	9	9	11	12	14	16	16	15	13	11	9
SAN DIEGO												
HIGH °F	65	66	66	68	70	71	75	77	76	74	70	66
HIGH °C	18	19	19	20	21	22	24	25	24	23	21	19
LOW °F	46	47	50	54	57	60	64	66	63	58	52	47
LOW °C	8	8	10	12	14	16	18	19	17	14	11	8

phone won't work, rent a phone that does from **InTouch USA** (☎ 800/872-7626; www.intouchglobal.com) or a rental car location, but beware that you'll pay $1 a minute or more for airtime.

Even so, cellphone coverage in remote areas can be somewhat more unpredictable than in major cities and can vary according to provider. Yosemite National Park, for example, has decent coverage, while the coverage in Death Valley National Park is not good. Many of the park websites have notes on cellphone coverage, but it behooves you to contact your provider as well. If you have any doubts and plan on heading deep into the wilderness, you may wish to consider the use of a **satellite phone.**

If you're not from the U.S., you'll be appalled at the poor reach of the **GSM (Global System for Mobile Communications) wireless network,** which is used by much of the rest of the world. Your phone will probably work in most major California cities; it definitely won't work in many rural areas. To see where GSM phones work in California, check out www.t-mobile.com/coverage. And you may or may not be able to send SMS (text messaging) home.

For visitors arriving via LAX, a phone rental company called **Triptel** has a rental kiosk located on the arrival level of the international terminal. Triptel also has a San Francisco rental location at 1525 Van Ness Ave. The daily rental fee is $3, and nationwide coverage is 95¢ per minute. At the end of your stay, the phone can be dropped off at the airport or shipped back via Federal Express for an additional fee. For more information, call ☎ 877/TRIPTEL, or log on to www.triptel.com.

Strategies For Seeing California

Let's face it: Having fun sometimes takes a bit of work. While the bulk of this guide is dedicated to illuminating *what* the high points of this dynamic and versatile destination are, here's a quick list of *how* to go about seeing them. Hopefully, these strategies will lift any roadblocks you encounter on your travels. If not, perhaps try a dose of that laid-back attitude that Californians are known to cultivate.

Tip #1: Grab the wheel. While Amtrak does a fine job connecting a limited number of California cities, the fact is that most of the state is best accessed by car, and you'll make your trip much easier if you're prepared to do a little (and sometimes a lot more than a little) driving yourself. In fact, some of California's quintessential experiences belong to the roads, like cruising scenic Highway 1 through Big Sur, or rambling through forgotten stretches of Route 66. Keep in mind that it's sometimes cheaper to book a car for a week rather than a day or two here and there. There are exceptions to the "car as king" rule of course; the Bay Area, for example, has a very effective public transportation system. You can enjoy San Francisco without a car, although you'll likely need one if you're planning on taking day trips (Napa, Point Reyes).

Tip #2: Check the calendar. High tourist season in most of California runs between Memorial Day and Labor Day, but the multidimensional state can delight visitors during all seasons. So it's up to you: Do you want to see the golden poppies blooming in spring? Watch as Napa's grapes are harvested in the fall? Enjoy snow skiing at Lake Tahoe? Escape the reach of winter in Death Valley? Or lay in the summer sun on Malibu's golden beaches? Even better, look to time your visit to coincide with special events such as Coachella Music Festival in April or the Sonoma County Harvest Fair in October.

Tip #3: Don't sweat it—you're not going to see everything. With nearly unlimited funds and time, yes, you can do it all. But for most of us, California is simply too vast and too diverse to expect to see in a single trip. Don't feel bad about that—rare is even the native Californian who's seen the entire state. It's far easier for San Diegans, for example, to visit another country—just a skip across the border to Mexico—than it is to make the 800-mile trek to the Redwood National and State Parks in the state's northeast corner. So slow down and enjoy as much as you can, and in the back of your mind, begin compiling a must-see list for your next visit. If you try to see everything at once, you'll only end up seeing more of the road than you do of the attractions.

Tip #4: Decide which California you want to visit. By "which California," I don't mean the most bandied about dichotomies of California—Northern or Southern, urban or agricultural, Red State or Blue. Do you want to prioritize for the "postcard" version of California, confirming a vision with which you're already

familiar, or do you want to see the "real" California? In other words, do you want to chase down the perfect photo of the HOLLYWOOD Sign, or would you rather catch an unknown band at a dive in Silver Lake? Both are valid ways to travel, but with limited time to explore, they may pull you in different directions in the Golden State, a place that has always been complicit in its own mythology.

Tip #5: Make a plan. Be prepared to throw the plan away. Booking ahead for popular hotels or sought-after restaurants is the smart move, especially when traveling during high season. But things happen: It rains on your beach day, or a road closes. Take these downers as opportunities, and keep moving. Maybe that rain will lead you to perfect afternoon at a museum. Even though you've done all the legwork, allow for the possibility of discovery.

Tip #6: Zig where they zag. Know where the crowds are going, and try to head the other way. California is a popular (and heavily populated) place, and crowds and traffic can present challenges for the visitor. Find out the peak seasons and peak times for major attractions, and plan around them. Locals know that navigating Disneyland, for example, is far easier on weekdays and non-holidays. If you don't have flexibility in terms of days or seasons, you can at least get a jump by starting as early in the morning as possible. And keep in mind that even though *you're* on vacation, rush hour still exists, especially on major freeways on Friday afternoons.

Tip #7: Remember that people-watching is free. Californians—the state's big-city dwellers, anyway—like to think of themselves as a step ahead of the curve in trends of fashion, music, and culture. Grab a seat at a cafe in San Francisco's North Beach or stroll the boardwalk at Venice Beach, and take in the rainbow of colorful characters. When you can, listen to the locals, too, and find out what's on their minds—drought, the state budget, the box office, gay marriage, gas prices, the Dodgers, etc.

Tip #8: Balance your meal budget. California cuisine should be experienced and savored, but not every meal needs to be fine dining. Offset the occasional splurge by taking advantage of the year-round farmers markets to load up on fresh and cheap produce. Pack a picnic when visiting the many state and national parks. Another option that's easy on the wallet and big on taste is the beloved taco or burrito. From roaming food trucks or mom-and-pop taco stands, these Mexican treats are staples of the California culinary scene, and the quickest way to start an argument is by declaring your favorite as the best in the state.

Tip #9: Make the Internet your friend. This is the Information Age, and experienced travelers know to leverage the vast amount of data at their fingertips. Almost all hotels, museums, restaurants, entertainment venues, and major tourist destinations in this guide have an online presence. Learn more about a museum's collection, or a see the full dinner menu of a restaurant you're considering. The Internet is especially handy in updating situations in flux, such as the operating hours of California parks while the state tends to its budget woes. Even if you're not carrying your own access point, you can usually get on a public computer that most hotels make available for guests, or try an Internet cafe (the FedEx Kinko's chain may be your easiest bet).

Tip #10: Book in blocks. Consider staying multiple days in one place, not simply for time and simplicity's sake, but for financial reasons. While most hotels balk at lowering their daily rates (even during a slower economy), many run promotions that provide discounts for longer stays. One place it really pays to go for the multiday discount is Disneyland, where you can also save money by booking hotel and travel in addition to park tickets.

Sustainable Tourism

California, a state that faces many environmental challenges, has more cars on the road than any other state in the country and suffers greatly from air pollution. Los Angeles is rated America's smoggiest city. As a result, the state is very conscious of the environment and offers numerous ways to be an eco-friendly visitor. One of the biggest favors you can do for the environment is keep your driving to a minimum, and in California there are numerous car-free adventures to choose from. Here are a few examples:

• Instead of driving though the Wine Country, consider a self-guided but fully supported 3-day biking tour with **Wine Country Bikes** (☎ 866/922-4537; www.winecountrybikes. com).

• **Santa Barbara** (p. 380) has a "Car Free" program (www.santabarbaracarfree.org) that nets travelers discounts for helping lower auto-related pollution.

• From San Francisco, you can take a bus to **Yosemite National Park** (p. 276) and join one of the numerous hiking, biking, and horseback-riding trips that explore Yosemite Valley.

• Tour the state via **Amtrak** (www.amtrak california.com). Some of the most beautiful train routes in the U.S. wend along the California coast, stopping in such coastal cities as San Lois Obispo, Los Angeles, San Juan Capistrano, and San Diego. (At some train stops, such as the one in Santa Barbara, you can literally walk to your hotel from the station.)

If you can't completely rid yourself of the use of a car, you can still try to minimize your impact:

• If you must rent a car, make it a hybrid vehicle or another fuel-efficient car.

• When possible on your adventures, employ green tour guides like **Holme Grown Brand** (www.holmegrownbrand.com), which whisks you through Napa's organic wineries in a biodiesel-powered Mercedes.

• Neutralize your emissions from driving a car (or taking a plane flight) through "carbon offsetting"—paying someone to invest your money in programs that reduce your greenhouse gas emissions by the same amount you've added. Reliable carbon offset companies include **Carbonfund** (www.carbonfund.org), **TerraPass** (www.terrapass.org), and **Carbon Neutral** (www.carbonneutral.org).

• Choose a hotel with green credentials. To determine the green credentials of a property, ask about trash disposal and recycling, water conservation, energy use, and the use of sustainable materials in constructing the property. The website **www.greenhotels.com** recommends green-rated member hotels around the world that fulfill stringent environmental requirements. Consult **www.environmentally friendlyhotels.com** for more green ratings.

At your hotel, request that your sheets and towels not be changed daily (many hotels already have programs like this in place). Any energy conserved is a good thing, but water in California is especially precious. Droughts are not uncommon and can have an enormous impact on agricultural production. Also, turn off the lights and air conditioner (or heater) when you leave your room.

Eat at locally owned and operated restaurants that use produce grown in the area, which (thankfully) is easy to do in California. This contributes to the local economy and cuts down on greenhouse gas emissions by supporting restaurants where the food is not flown or trucked in across long distances. Also try to patronize organic wineries; almost 20% of vineyards in Mendocino (p. 244; www.true-mendocinowine.com), for example, are eco-friendly. Visit **Sustain Lane** (www.sustainlane.com) **and Eat Well Guide** (www.eatwellguide.org) to find sustainable eating and drinking choices around California.

In San Francisco, ranked one of the U.S.'s greenest cities, there are numerous restaurants that purchase only organically grown foods (since processing foods and manufacturing fertilizers and pesticides take significant amounts of energy). The city's $25 million **Orchard Garden Hotel** (p. 114) is one of several hotels that meet the nationally accepted standards for green buildings developed by the U.S. Green Building Council. San Francisco's extensive public transportation system also makes it easy to get around without a car (in fact, we recommend not driving in that city).

For more information on ecologically responsible travel, visit **California Vagabond** (www.californiavagabond.com), where you'll find tips on environmentally friendly accommodations, car rentals, and more.

Getting There

By Plane
Most visitors will fly into one of California's major airports: San Francisco (SFO), Sacramento (SMF), San Jose (SJC), Los Angeles (LAX), John Wayne (SNA, in Orange County), or San Diego (SAN). There are also several smaller, regional airports that service some of the smaller or harder-to-reach destinations. And, if you're going to Lake Tahoe (p. ###), you might choose to fly into Reno, Nevada. For information on specific airports that service the region you want to tour, see the "Fast Facts" listed at the end of each destination chapter in this book.

U.S. and international airlines that service the state include **Air Canada** (☎ 888/247-2262; www.aircanada.com), **American** (☎ 800/433-7300; www.aa.com), **British Airways** (☎ 800/247-9297; www.britishair ways.com), **Continental** (☎ 800/523-3273; www.continental.com), **Delta** (☎ 800/221-1212; www.delta.com), **JetBlue** (☎ 800/538-2583; www.jetblue.com), **Northwest** (☎ 800/225-2525; www.nwa.com), **Qantas** (☎ 800/227-4500, www.qantas.com), **Southwest** (☎ 800/435-9792; www.south west.com), **United** (☎ 800/241-6522; www.united.com), **US Airways** (☎ 800/428-4322; www.usairways.com), and **Virgin America** (☎ 877/359-8474; www.virginamerica.com).

Flying time from New York or Boston to L.A. is about 6 hours; from Chicago it's about 4 hours; from London it's about 11 hours; and from Sydney it's about 14 hours.

International travelers should also see "Passports & Visas" (p. 688) for information on overseas flights into California. For details on air travel within California, see "Getting Around," below.

By Car
If you live close to California, then driving in is probably a good way to go (and will save you the cost of a rental car that you'd need to have in order to tour some of the regions in the state).

Major interstates leading into California include **I-5** (which runs from the northern border with Oregon all the way down to San Diego), **I-80** (which heads from Reno, Nevada, west to San Francisco), **I-15** (which runs from Las Vegas to just east of Los Angeles), **I-40** (which runs west all the way from Texas to just north of L.A.), **I-10** (which starts in New Orleans and runs through several states on the way to Southern California), and **I-8** (which links Tucson, Arizona, with San Diego).

It's 270 miles from Las Vegas to Los Angeles (drive time: about 5 hr.); 636 miles from

Portland, Oregon, to San Francisco (drive time: 10¼ hr.); and 407 miles from Tucson, Arizona, to San Diego (drive time: 6½ hr.).

If you're planning on a long road trip to get to California, it's a good idea to join **Automobile Association of America (AAA).** Members (who carry their cards with them) receive free roadside assistance and have access to a wealth of free travel information, including detailed maps. Also, many hotels and attractions throughout California offer discounts to AAA members—always ask. Call ☎ 800/222-4357, or visit www.aaa.com for membership details.

By Train

Amtrak (☎ 800/USA-RAIL; www.amtrak. com) connects California with about 500 American cities. The **Sunset Limited** is Amtrak's regularly scheduled transcontinental service, originating in Florida and making 52 stops along the way as it passes through Alabama, Mississippi, Louisiana, Texas, New Mexico, and Arizona, before arriving in Los Angeles 2 days later. The train, which runs three times a week, features reclining seats, a sightseeing car with large windows, and a full-service dining car. Round-trip coach fares begin at around $350; several varieties of sleeping compartments are also available for an extra charge. Unless you have a lot of time on your hands or you're a train buff, however, this is not the most efficient way to get to California, especially when you consider that you'll pay roughly the same amount to fly in.

Getting Around

By Car

The car is king in California. Unless you plan to spend the bulk of your vacation in a city (such as San Francisco) where walking is the best way to get around and parking is both hard to get and expensive, the most efficient and cost-effective way to travel is by car. That's not to say that it will be an especially cheap way to get around, however, as distances (especially in the far northern regions) can be long and gas prices are among the highest in the United States.

Traffic is also a consideration. Rush-hour traffic is to be avoided in the major cities, especially in Los Angeles, where gridlock on the freeways is a way of life. (Be very wary of the I-405 freeway, which connects the west side of the city with the beach communities to the south.) On the weekends when the weather is warm, coastal routes like Hwy. 101 and Hwy. 1 can get very congested.

All the major rental agencies have outlets in California, including **Alamo** (☎ 800/327-9633; www.alamo.com), **Avis** (☎ 800/331-1212; www. avis.com), **Budget** (☎ 800/527-0700; www. budget.com), **Dollar** (☎ 800/800-4000; www. dollar.com), **Hertz** (☎ 800/654-3131; www. hertz.com), **National** (☎ 800/227-7368; www. nationalcar.com), and **Thrifty** (☎ 800/367-2277; www.thrifty.com).

In addition to the regular agencies, check out **Breezenet.com,** which offers domestic car-rental discounts with some of the most competitive rates around. Also worth visiting are **Orbitz, Hotwire.com, Travelocity,** and **Priceline.com.** *Tip:* Southern California rentals tend to be cheaper than those in the north; if you plan on doing a long trip that covers both regions, look into flying into the south, getting a one-way rental, and then ending your trip in the north—you might get a better deal.

Note: Foreign driver's licenses are usually recognized in the U.S., but you should get an international one if your home license is not printed in English.

California's freeway signs often indicate direction by naming a town rather than a point on the compass. The best state road guide is the comprehensive ***Thomas Guide California Road Atlas,*** a 300-plus-page book of maps with schematics of towns and cities statewide. It costs about $15 and is a good investment if you plan to do a lot of exploring. Smaller, accordion-style maps are handy for the entire state or for individual cities and regions.

If you're heading into the Sierra or the Shasta Cascades region for a winter ski trip, stock up on antifreeze and carry snow chains for your tires. (Chains are mandatory in certain areas, including Lake Tahoe.) Also note that though interstates generally hold up pretty well in bad weather, the same can't be said about California's local roads, especially in the High Sierra—they'll close during the winter and when heavy storms arrive. You can check highway road conditions throughout the state online at www.dot.ca.gov/roadsandtraffic. html or by calling ☎ 800/427-7623.

Driving Rules

California law requires both drivers and passengers to wear seat belts, and a safety seat must be used for children under the age of 6 or weighing less than 60 pounds. Motorcyclists must wear helmets at all times. Auto insurance is mandatory; the car's registration and proof of insurance must stay in the car.

You can turn right at a red light, unless otherwise indicated—but be sure to come to a complete stop first.

Many California freeways have designated car-pool lanes, also known as high-occupancy vehicle (HOV) or "diamond" lanes. Some require two passengers, others three. Most on-ramps are metered during even light congestion to regulate the flow of traffic onto the freeway; cars in HOV lanes can pass the signal without stopping, while all other drivers are required to observe the stoplights—fines begin at $381.

By Plane

In addition to the major carriers listed earlier in this section, several airlines provide service within the state, including **Alaska Airlines/ Horizon Air** (☎ 800/252-7522), **American Eagle** (☎ 800/433-7300), **JetBlue** (☎ 800/ 538-2583), **Southwest** (☎ 800/435-9792), **United Express** (☎ 800/241-6522), **US Airways Express** (☎ 800/428-4322), and **Virgin America** (☎ 877/359-8474). The round-trip fare between Los Angeles and San Francisco ranges from $100 to $300, and the flight takes about 1 hour and 20 minutes.

By Train

Amtrak (☎ 800/USA-RAIL; www.amtrak. com) operates up and down the California coast, connecting San Diego, Los Angeles, San Francisco, and points in between. Multiple trains depart each day, and rates fluctuate according to season and special promotions. One-way fares for the most popular segments include $16 (L.A.-Santa Barbara), $29 (L.A.-San Diego), and from $50 to $78 (San Francisco–L.A.).

International visitors can buy a **USA Rail Pass,** good for 15 or 30 days of unlimited travel on Amtrak. The pass is available online or through many overseas travel agents. See Amtrak's website for the cost of travel within the western, eastern, or northwestern United States. Reservations are generally required and should be made as early as possible. Regional rail passes are also available.

By Bus

Bus travel is the cheapest form of public transit between California destinations. Buses are usually clean and reliable, but they're not necessarily the most enjoyable way to travel, nor are they the most efficient (particularly when the far more comfortable Amtrak offers similar rates for similar California routes). **Greyhound** (☎ 800/231-2222; www.greyhound. com) is the sole statewide bus line. International visitors can obtain information about the **Greyhound North American Discovery Pass** for unlimited travel and stopovers in the U.S. and Canada. The pass can be obtained from foreign travel agents or through www. discoverypass.com.

Tips on Accommodations

Accommodations, as in the rest of the United States, vary across the state—you'll find everything from budget motels to world-class resorts. Usually, all properties meet a pretty high standard. Typically, no matter what class of accommodations you opt for, you'll get a room with private bathroom (we note in this book where this is not the case), a double bed at the very least, air-conditioning, cable TV, telephone, and some form of Internet access (for which you may have to pay extra). A number of places also throw in a light breakfast as part your rate.

Booking in Advance

Smart travelers should always reserve rooms in advance in California, but during high season (which varies, depending on what region you're visiting; see "Best Times to Go," on p. 670) it's especially important. When making a reservation, always find out what the cancellation policy is so you can maintain some flexibility. The listings in this guide should help you zero in on the hotel you want. Also check with hotels directly for any specials. If you feel comfortable prepaying, you can book with various websites—for example, Expedia, Travelocity, and Orbitz.

Types of Accommodations

Hotels and **motels** (or "motor hotels") are

the two main types of accommodations in the state, but the quality and cost can run the gamut. California has no shortage of luxury hotels with impeccably appointed rooms and attentive service. Motels are typically more modest than hotels and designed for simple access to parking; many do, however, have pools. Chain hotels and motels are prevalent in California, especially when you get outside of the major cities. Middle-of-the-road chains are usually both reliable and predictable, which sometimes is just what a weary traveler needs.

Be advised that a number of hotels in California (even those that don't qualify as true resorts) charge a "resort fee" that is not included in your rate. It's an unfortunate part of a larger trend in nickel-and-diming guests for what they used to get for free; these fees can add up to $35 a day to your hotel rate. To avoid an unwelcome surprise at checkout, always call a hotel you're considering to find out if it charges a resort fee and what that cost will get you (in some, it might yield free local calls and a newspaper; in others, Wi-Fi access and parking).

Villa, Farmhouse & Apartment Rentals

To find one-of-a-kind accommodations in private houses and apartments in California, check out **www.vrbo.com** or **www.craigslist.org.** It may be difficult to verify a property without seeing it first, but if you're thorough, you can find some real gems this way.

Alternative Accommodations

Bed-and-Breakfasts These homey arrangements are quite popular in California, and many are recommended in this guide. Guests are given a room within a house, a bathroom (which may be private or shared), and a home-cooked breakfast in the morning. Some proprietors also offer snacks and wine in the afternoon as well. Some B&Bs might well qualify as luxe, but most don't have the breadth of options offered at a hotel. What B&Bs lack in amenities, however, they often make up for in charm and atmosphere. Do note that some B&Bs have restrictions on bringing children, and several require minimum stays during high season.

There are a number of reservation services that let you book rooms at B&Bs in California. One good one is the **California Association of Bed & Breakfast Inns** (☎ 800/373-9251; www.cabbi.com), which has 300 members spread all over the state.

Inns Similar to but often slightly larger than B&Bs, these unique accommodations equal their smaller brethren in the charm department, and usually are set in historic or atmospheric locations. They, too, don't usually have the breadth of amenities that larger hotels and motels have, but they often serve up breakfast and afternoon tea (or host wine tastings).

House-Swaps House-swapping is becoming a more popular and viable means of travel: you stay in their place, they stay in yours, and you both get an authentic and personal view of the area—the opposite of the escapist retreat that many hotels offer. Try **HomeLink International** (www.homelink.org), the largest home-swapping organization, founded in 1953, with more than 11,000 listings worldwide ($115 for a yearly membership). **HomeExchange.com** ($120 a year) and **InterVac.com** ($100 for more than 10,000 listings) are also reliable. Many travelers find great housing swaps on **Craigslist.org,** too, though the offerings cannot be vetted or vouched for. Swap at your own risk.

Youth Hostels These dirt-cheap accommodations, typically less than $30 per person, are a favorite among backpacking young people. A little like urban camping, a hostel usually offers shared rooms and bathrooms, and no-frills accommodations. For more information, check out www.hiusa.org or www.hostels.com.

Camping

In the state park system, thousands of campsites can be booked in advance by calling **ReserveAmerica** at ☎ 800/444-7275 or logging onto their website at www.reserveamerica.com. Make reservations at national park campsites—including Yosemite—via www.recreation.gov, or call ☎ 877/444-6777 within the U.S. (for international calls, dial ☎ 001-518-885-3639).

Fast Facts

Apartment/Condo Rentals

See "Tips on Accommodations" above.

ATMs/Cashpoints

In California, as elsewhere in the United States, the easiest and best way to get cash while away from home is from an ATM (automated teller machine), sometimes referred to as a "cash machine" or "cashpoint." The **Cirrus** (☎ 800/424-7787; www.mastercard.com) and **PLUS** (☎ 800/843-7587; www.visa.com) networks span the state; you can find them even in remote regions. Be sure you know your daily withdrawal limit before you depart.

Note: Many banks impose a fee every time you use your card at another bank's ATM, and the bank from which you withdraw cash may charge its own fee. Visitors from outside the U.S. should also find out whether their bank assesses a 1% to 3% fee on charges incurred abroad.

Tip: Avoid these fees by asking for cash back at grocery, drug, and convenience stores (and most post offices) that accept ATM cards for purchases.

Banking Hours

Banks are open weekdays from 9am to 3pm or later and sometimes Saturday mornings.

Bike Rentals

Bikes can be rented in larger towns and cities. Beaches and scenic areas (such as the Wine Country) are also popular places to rent a bike for an afternoon. In the summer, ski resorts like Lake Tahoe and Mammoth Mountain become mountain biking meccas.

The rates for bike rentals throughout the state vary from roughly $7 to $16 hourly, $20 to $30 daily, and $90 to $180 a week.

Business Hours

Offices are usually open weekdays from 9am to 5pm. Stores typically open between 9 and 10am and close between 5 and 6pm Monday through Saturday. Stores in shopping complexes or malls tend to stay open late (until about 9pm on weekdays and weekends); many malls and department stores are open on Sundays.

Car Rentals

See "Getting Around" on p 680.

Customs

Unless you or your baggage look suspicious, it's relatively quick and painless to clear customs after landing in a Californian airport. Every visitor over 21 years of age may bring in, free of duty, the following: (1) 1 liter of wine or hard liquor; (2) 200 cigarettes, 100 cigars (but not from Cuba), or 3 pounds of smoking tobacco; and (3) $100 worth of gifts. These exemptions are offered to travelers who spend at least 72 hours in the United States and who have not claimed them within the preceding 6 months. It is forbidden to bring into the country almost any meat products (including canned, fresh, and dried meat products such as bouillon, soup mixes, and so on). Because it must protect its agricultural industry from disease, California does not allow most food items such as fresh produce. Generally, condiments including vinegars, oils, spices, coffee, tea, and some cheeses and baked goods are permitted. Avoid rice products, as rice can often harbor insects.

International visitors may carry (in or out) up to $10,000 in U.S. or foreign currency, with no formalities; larger sums must be declared to U.S. Customs on entering or leaving, which includes filing form CM 4790. For details regarding U.S. Customs and Border Protection, consult your nearest U.S. embassy or consulate, or **U.S. Customs** (www.customs.gov).

For information on what you're allowed to bring home, contact one of the following agencies:

Canadian Citizens: Canada Border Services Agency (☎ 800/461-9999 in Canada, or 204/983-3500; www.cbsa-asfc.gc.ca).

U.K. Citizens: HM Customs & Excise at ☎ 0845/010-9000 (from outside the U.K., 020/8929-0152), or consult their website at www.hmce.gov.uk.

Australian Citizens: Australian Customs Service at ☎ 1300/363-263, or log on to www.customs.gov.au.

New Zealand Citizens: New Zealand Customs at ☎ 04/473-6099 or 0800/428-786; or consult their website at www.customs.govt.nz.

Dining

There is no shortage of chain restaurants like Denny's or fast-food joints like McDonald's in California, but the state is better known for its California cuisine, which focuses on the sophisticated preparation of fresh ingredients. With such a thriving agricultural industry, California has plenty of access to fresh food. San Francisco is a major foodie destination and is home to many of the country's best restaurants. Los Angeles runs a close second within the state. California is a famously casual culture, and even the best restaurants rarely call for a stuffy dress code.

Another attribute of the California culinary scene, owing to its diverse population, is the presence of so many different types of cuisines: Chinese, Japanese, Indian, Vietnamese, and Thai restaurants are commonplace and typically quite authentic. Mexican food is a staple in California—cheap, tasty, and easy to find.

An emerging trend in dining in the major cities is the presence of food trucks, often gourmet ones, that can be tracked via Twitter or websites. Farmers markets continue to be popular and offer a cheap way to obtain fresh produce.

Drinking Laws

The legal age for purchase and consumption of alcoholic beverages is 21; proof of age is required and often requested at bars, nightclubs, and restaurants, so it's always a good idea to bring ID when you go out. Supermarkets and convenience stores in California sell beer, wine, and liquor.

Most restaurants serve alcohol, but some serve only beer and wine (no liquor). By law, all bars, clubs, restaurants, and stores cannot sell or serve alcohol after 2am, and "last call" tends to start at 1:30am. Do not carry open containers of alcohol in your car or any public area that isn't zoned for alcohol consumption. The police can fine you on the spot, and nothing will ruin your trip faster than getting a citation for DUI (driving under the influence).

Electricity

Like Canada, the United States uses 110 to 120 volts AC (60 cycles), compared to 220 to 240 volts AC (50 cycles) in most of Europe, Australia, and New Zealand. Downward converters that change 220 to 240 volts to 110 to 120 volts are difficult to find in the United States, so bring one with you.

Embassies & Consulates

In case of an emergency, embassies have a 24-hour referral service.

All embassies are located in the nation's capital, Washington, D.C. Some consulates are located in major U.S. cities, and most nations have a mission to the United Nations in New York City. If your country isn't listed below, call for directory information in Washington, D.C. (☎ 202/555-1212), or check www.embassy.org/embassies.

The embassy of **Australia** is at 1601 Massachusetts Ave. NW, Washington, DC 20036 (☎ 202/797-3000; www.usa.embassy.gov.au). There are consulates in Los Angeles and San Francisco.

The embassy of **Canada** is at 501 Pennsylvania Ave. NW, Washington, DC 20001 (☎ 202/682-1740; www.canadianembassy.org). A Canadian consulate is located in Los Angeles.

The embassy of **Ireland** is at 2234 Massachusetts Ave. NW, Washington, DC 20008 (☎ 202/462-3939; www.embassyofirland.org). There is an Irish consulate in San Francisco.

The embassy of **New Zealand** is at 37 Observatory Circle NW, Washington, DC 20008 (☎ 202/328-4800; www.nzembassy.com/usa). New Zealand has consulates in Los Angeles and San Francisco.

The embassy of the **United Kingdom** is at 3100 Massachusetts Ave. NW, Washington, DC 20008 (☎ 202/588-7800; www.ukinusa.com). Other British consulates are in Los Angeles and San Francisco.

Emergencies

Call ☎ **911** to report a fire, call the police, or get an ambulance anywhere in California. This is a toll-free call. (No coins are required at public telephones.)

If you find yourself stranded or disconnected from your support system and are having difficulties, call the Los Angeles chapter of the **Traveler's Aid Society** (☎ 310/646-2270; www.travelersaid.org), a nationwide, nonprofit, social service organization.

Events Listings

California's official tourism website (**www.visitcalifornia.com**) does an excellent job keeping track of events in the state. You can even download a guide or have one sent to you. Also check out **www.beachcalifornia.com**, which has a comprehensive and detailed Events Calendar.

Family Travel

With its beaches and natural scenery, California has a lot to offer families, and its major cities—San Francisco, Los Angeles, San Diego—are full of amusement parks, zoos, museums, and other kid-friendly attractions. To make things easier for family vacationing, be sure to watch for the "Kids" icon throughout this guide. You should also check out the Family Fun section of California's official tourism website (**www.visitcalifornia.com**), or the Home & Family section of California's official government website (**www.ca.gov**).

General family travel websites with specific information on California include **Family Travel Forum** (www.familytravelforum.com), a comprehensive site that offers customized trip planning; **Family Travel Network** (www.familytravelnetwork.com), an online magazine providing travel tips; and **TravelWith YourKids.com,** a comprehensive site written by parents for parents, offering sound advice for travel with children.

Gay & Lesbian Travelers

California is one of the country's most progressive states when it comes to antidiscrimination legislation and workplace benefits for domestic partners. The gay and lesbian community spreads well beyond the famed enclaves of San Francisco, West Hollywood, and San Diego's Hillcrest. Gay travelers (especially men) will find a number of gay-owned inns in Palm Springs and the Russian River, north of the Bay Area.

San Francisco's gay community center is the **Charles M. Holmes Campus at the Center** (☎ 415/865-5555; www.sfcenter.org). Its publications, all of which are readily available for free in the Castro district, are the biweekly **San Francisco Bay Times** (☎ 415/626-0260; www.sfbaytimes.com), the weekly **Bay Area Reporter** (☎ 415/861-5019; www.ebar.com), and **Gloss Magazine** (☎ 510/451-2090; www.glossmagazine.net), with information on nightlife and entertainment.

The visitor bureau of West Hollywood runs the comprehensive website www.gogaywesthollywood.com, which features information on where to stay, eat, and party. The **L.A. Gay and Lesbian Community Center** (☎ 323/993-7400; http://laglc.convio.net) offers a variety of legal and medical services.

Local gay publications include **Frontiers** (www.frontierspublishing.com) for men and the **Lesbian News** (www.thelnmag.com) for women.

In Palm Springs, gay travelers can find the **Palm Springs Official Gay Guide** at the visitor center, or consult the **Bottom Line** (www.psbottomline.com), a free biweekly paper at newsstands around town. The **Desert Gay Tourism Guild** (☎ 760/322-7993; www.dgtg.org) is an organization of gay- and lesbian-owned businesses. For more information on the area's gay and lesbian life, visit www.palmspringsusa.com/LGBT.

The **International Gay & Lesbian Travel Association** (IGLTA; ☎ 954/630-1637; www.iglta.org) is the trade association for the gay and lesbian travel industry, and offers an online directory of gay- and lesbian-friendly travel businesses and tour operators.

Many agencies offer tours and travel itineraries specifically for gay and lesbian travelers. San Francisco–based **Now, Voyager** (☎ 800/255-6951; www.nowvoyager.com) offers worldwide trips and cruises. **Olivia** (☎ 800/631-6277; www.olivia.com) offers lesbian cruises and resort vacations.

OutTraveler (☎ 212/242-8100; www.outtraveler.com) is an excellent online magazine. It provides regularly updated information about gay-owned, gay-oriented, and gay-friendly lodging, dining, sightseeing, nightlife, and shopping establishments in every important destination worldwide.

Health

California is considered a "safe" destination. Food is safe and plentiful, and the water in cities and towns is potable. It is easy to find quality medical treatment and to get a prescription filled in California. Inoculations and vaccinations are not required for entry unless you're arriving from an area known to be suffering from an epidemic (particularly cholera or yellow fever).

If you suffer from a chronic illness, consult your doctor before your departure. Pack **prescription medications** in your carry-on luggage, and carry them in their original containers, with pharmacy labels—otherwise they won't make it through airport security. Carry the generic name of prescription medicines, in case a local pharmacist is unfamiliar with the brand name. If you have a medical condition that requires **syringe-administered medications,** carry a valid signed prescription from your physician; syringes in carry-on baggage will be inspected. Insulin in any form should have the proper pharmaceutical documentation. If you have a disease that requires treatment with **narcotics,** you should also carry documented proof with you—smuggling narcotics aboard a plane carries severe penalties in the U.S.

For **HIV-positive visitors,** requirements for entering the United States and California are somewhat vague and change frequently. For up-to-the-minute information, contact **AIDSinfo** (☎ 800/448-0440, or 301/519-6616 outside the U.S.; www.aidsinfo.nih.gov) or the **Gay Men's Health Crisis** (☎ 212/367-1000; www.gmhc.org).

The following government websites offer up-to-date, health-related travel advice.

Australia: www.dfat.gov.au/travel

Canada: www.hc-sc.gc.ca/index_e.html

U.K.: www.dh.gov.uk/en/index.htm

U.S.: www.cdc.gov/travel

For tips on travel and health concerns, and for lists of local doctors in California, contact the **International Association for Medical Assistance to Travelers** (IAMAT; ☎ 716/754-4883, or 416/652-0137 in Canada; www.iamat.org). The United States **Centers for Disease Control and Prevention** (☎ 800/232-4636; www.cdc.gov) provides up-to-date information on health hazards and offers tips on food safety. The website **www.tripprep.com** may also offer helpful advice on traveling. You can find listings of reliable clinics at the **International Society of Travel Medicine** (www.istm.org).

Holidays

Banks, government offices, post offices, and many stores, restaurants, and museums are closed on the following legal national holidays: January 1 (New Year's Day), the third Monday in January (Martin Luther King, Jr., Day), the third Monday in February (Presidents' Day), the last Monday in May (Memorial Day), July 4 (Independence Day), the first Monday in September (Labor Day), the second Monday in October (Columbus Day), November 11 (Veterans' Day/Armistice Day), the fourth Thursday in November (Thanksgiving Day), and December 25 (Christmas). The Tuesday after the first Monday in November is Election Day, a federal government holiday in presidential-election years (held every 4 years, and next in 2012).

Insurance

The cost of **travel insurance** varies widely, depending on the destination, the cost and length of your trip, your age and health, and the type of trip you're taking. Insist on seeing any policy and reading the fine print before buying. You can get estimates from various providers through **InsureMyTrip.com.** Enter your trip cost and dates, your age, and other information for prices from more than a dozen companies, or call ☎ 800/487-4722. You can also purchase travel insurance from the **Automobile Association of America** (http://travel.aaa.com) if you're a member of a local AAA club, or if you arrange your travel plans through AAA. In the United Kingdom, try **Columbus Direct** (☎ 0870/033-9988; www.columbusdirect.net).

Comprehensive policies typically include **trip-cancellation insurance,** which will help retrieve your money if you have to back out of a trip or depart early, or if your travel supplier goes bankrupt. Trip cancellation traditionally covers such events as sickness and natural disasters. The latest news in trip-cancellation insurance is the availability of "any reason" cancellation coverage—which costs more but covers cancellations made for any reason. **TravelSafe** (☎ 888/885-7233; www.travelsafe.com) offers both types of coverage. **Expedia** also offers any-reason cancellation coverage for its air-hotel packages.

These policies can also include **medical insurance** and insurance for **emergency evacuation** and **lost luggage.** U.S. citizens with health insurance who are traveling domestically should check their current policy to determine whether additional medical insurance for a trip is necessary. Medical insurance does not typically cover emergency evacuation, the transportation cost of getting to a person to the proper treatment facility. In dire circumstances, this can mean the use of a medically equipped helicopter or jet, and can be very expensive. **MedjetAssist** (☎ 800/5-ASSIST; www.medjetassist.com) offers this type of insurance.

For lost luggage on international flights (including the U.S. portion of an international trip), coverage is limited to approximately $9.07 per pound, up to approximately $635 per checked bag. For domestic coverage, the maximum liability coverage for baggage is $3,300 a person. If you plan to check high-value items, see if your homeowner's policy covers your valuables; if not, purchase baggage insurance as part of your comprehensive travel-insurance package. If your luggage is lost, immediately file a lost-luggage claim at the airport, detailing the luggage contents. Most airlines require that you report delayed, damaged, or lost baggage within 4 hours of arrival. The airlines are required to deliver luggage, once found, directly to your house or destination free of charge.

Internet Access

Most hotels offer wireless access (though you may have to pay for it), as do omnipresent national chains such as McDonald's and Starbucks, as well as the regional chain the Coffee Bean & Tea Leaf. To find public Wi-Fi hotspots at your destination, go to **www.jiwire.com** (its Wi-Fi Finder holds the world's largest directory of public wireless hotspots).

If you're not traveling with your own computer, stop by FedEx Kinko's to rent computers and Internet access. To find cybercafes in your destination, check **www.cybercaptive.com** and **www.cybercafe.com.**

Most major airports, including LAX and SFO, offer Wi-Fi as well as **Internet kiosks** that provide basic Web access for a per-minute fee that's usually higher than cybercafe prices.

It's even possible to stay connected while visiting many state and national parks in California. Yosemite National Park, for example, offers Wi-Fi in some places as well as access to an Internet kiosk. Check the website of parks you're interested in visiting.

Legal Aid

If you are "pulled over" for a minor infraction (such as speeding), never attempt to pay the fine directly to a police officer; this could be construed as attempted bribery. Pay fines

by mail or directly into the hands of the clerk of the court. If accused of a more serious offense, say and do nothing before consulting a lawyer. In California the burden is on the state to prove a person's guilt beyond a reasonable doubt, and everyone has the right to remain silent, whether he or she is suspected of a crime or actually arrested. Once arrested, a person can make one telephone call to a party of his or her choice. International visitors should call your embassy or consulate.

Penalties in California for drunk driving are among the nation's toughest. The legal limit is .08% blood alcohol level. In some areas, freeway speed limits are aggressively enforced after dark as a pretext for nabbing drivers who might have imbibed. If you choose to drink, don't get behind the wheel, or have a designated driver.

Lost Property

Alert your credit card companies the minute you discover that your wallet has been lost or stolen, and file a report at the nearest police precinct. Your credit card company or insurer may require a police report number or record of the loss. Most credit card companies have an emergency toll-free number to call if your card is lost or stolen: **Visa** (☎ 800/847-2911), **MasterCard** (☎ 800/627-8372), and **American Express** (☎ 800/528-4800). Companies may agree to wire you a cash advance immediately or deliver an emergency credit card in a day or two.

If you lose your passport, immediately report the loss to your consulate or embassy (see "Embassies & Consulates," above).

Mail & Postage

At press time, domestic postage rates are 28¢ for a postcard and 44¢ for a letter. For international mail, a first-class letter of up to 1 ounce costs 90¢ (75¢ to Canada and Mexico); a first-class postcard costs the same as a letter. For more information, go to **www.usps.com** and click on "Calculate Postage." You can also find and locate post offices throughout California on the same website.

Always include zip codes when mailing items in the U.S. If you don't know your zip code, visit www.usps.com/zip4.

Money

The most common bills are the $1 (a "buck"),

$5, $10, and $20 denominations. Coins come in seven denominations: 1¢ (1 cent, or a penny); 5¢ (5 cents, or a nickel); 10¢ (10 cents, or a dime); 25¢ (25 cents, or a quarter); 50¢ (50 cents, or a half-dollar); and the gold-colored Sacagawea coin, worth $1. For obtaining cash, see "ATMs/Cashpoints" above. It's always good to have cash on hand for parking, tips, and businesses that don't take credit cards (such as farmers markets).

Credit cards are the most widely used form of payment in California: **Visa** (Barclaycard in Britain), **MasterCard** (Eurocard in Europe, Access in Britain, Chargex in Canada), **American Express, Diners Club,** and **Discover.** They also provide a convenient record of all your expenses and offer relatively good exchange rates. You can withdraw cash advances from your credit cards at banks or ATMs, but high fees make credit card cash advances a pricey way to get cash.

It's highly recommended that you travel with at least one major credit card. You must have a credit card to rent a car, and hotels and airlines usually require one as a deposit against expenses.

ATM cards with major credit card backing, known as "debit cards," are now a commonly acceptable form of payment in almost all stores and restaurants in California.

Though credit cards and debit cards are more often used, traveler's checks are still widely accepted in California. Foreign visitors should make sure that traveler's checks are denominated in U.S. dollars; foreign-currency checks are often difficult to exchange.

The most popular traveler's checks are offered by **American Express** (☎ 800/807-6233; ☎ 800/221-7282 for cardholders—this number accepts collect calls, offers service in several foreign languages, and exempts Amex gold and platinum cardholders from the 1% fee); **Visa** (☎ 800/732-1322—AAA members can obtain Visa checks for a $9.95 fee (for checks up to $1,500] at most AAA offices or by calling ☎ 866/339-3378); and **MasterCard** (☎ 800/223-9920).

Passports & Visas

New regulations issued by the Department of Homeland Security now require virtually every air traveler entering the U.S. to show a passport. As of January 23, 2007, all persons, including U.S. citizens, traveling by air between the United States and Canada, Mexico, Central and South America, the Caribbean, and Bermuda are required to present a valid passport. As of January 31, 2008, U.S. and Canadian citizens entering the U.S. at land and sea ports of entry from within the Western Hemisphere will need to present government-issued proof of citizenship, such as a birth certificate, along with a government-issued photo ID, such as a driver's license. A passport is not required for U.S. or Canadian citizens entering by land or sea, but carrying one is strongly encouraged.

The websites listed provide downloadable passport applications as well as the current fees for processing those applications. For an up-to-date, country-by-country listing of passport requirements around the world, go to the "International Travel" tab of the U.S. Department of State website at http://travel.state.gov. International visitors to the U.S. can obtain a visa application at the same website. *Note:* Allow plenty of time before your trip to apply for a passport; processing normally takes 4 to 6 weeks (3 weeks for expedited service) but can take longer during busy periods (especially spring). And keep in mind that if you need a passport in a hurry, you'll pay a higher processing fee.

FOR RESIDENTS OF AUSTRALIA You can pick up an application from your local post office or any branch of **Passports Australia,** but you must schedule an interview at the passport office to present your application materials. Call the **Australian Passport Information Service** at ☎ 131-232, or visit the government website at www.passports.gov.au.

FOR RESIDENTS OF CANADA Passport applications are available at travel agencies throughout Canada or from the central **Passport Office,** Department of Foreign Affairs and International Trade, Ottawa, ON K1A 0G3 (☎ 800/567-6868; www.ppt.gc.ca). *Note:* Canadian children who travel must have their own passport. However, if you hold a valid Canadian passport issued before December 11, 2001 that bears the name of your child, the passport remains valid for you and your child until it expires.

FOR RESIDENTS OF IRELAND You can apply for a 10-year passport at the **Passport Office,**

Setanta Centre, Molesworth Street, Dublin 2 (☎ 01/671-1633; www.irlgov.ie/iveagh). Those under age 18 and over 65 must apply for a 3-year passport. You can also apply at 1A South Mall, Cork (☎ 21/494-4700) or at most main post offices.

FOR RESIDENTS OF NEW ZEALAND You can pick up a passport application at any New Zealand Passports Office, or download it from their website. Contact the **Passports Office** at ☎ 0800/225-050 in New Zealand or 04/474-8100, or log on to www.passports.govt.nz.

FOR RESIDENTS OF THE UNITED KINGDOM To pick up an application for a standard 10-year passport (5-year passport for children 15 and under), visit your nearest passport office, major post office, or travel agency, or contact the **United Kingdom Passport Service** at ☎ 0870/521-0410 or search its website at www.ukpa.gov.uk.

For an up-to-date, country-by-country listing of passport requirements around the world, go to the International Travel Information Web page of the U.S. Department of State website at http://travel.state.gov. International visitors can obtain a visa application at the same website. *Note:* Children are required to present a passport when entering the United States at airports. More information on obtaining a passport for a minor can be found at http://travel.state.gov.

For information about U.S. visas, go to http://travel.state.gov and click on "Visas."

Pet Travel

If you're thinking of taking your pet along with you to romp on a California beach, make sure you do a little research; dogs are restricted from most public beaches in the L.A. area. To find out where you can check in with man's best friend, **Pets Welcome** (www.pets welcome.com) lists accommodations that allow pets. The site also lists pet-related publications, medical travel tips, and links to other pet-related websites.

A good book to carry along is *The Dog Lover's Companion to California: The Insider's Scoop on Where to Take Your Dog* (Avalon Travel Publishing), a source for complete statewide listings of fenced dog parks, dog-friendly beaches, and other indispensable information.

California has strict leash laws (and stiff penalties for failing to pick up waste), prompting the formation of a dog owner/supporter group called **Freeplay** (☎ 310/379-1207; www.freeplay.org). Contact them for the latest on dog-related issues, including information on off-leash parks around the state.

Pharmacies

The major national chains—**Rite Aid, CVS, Walgreens**—are well represented throughout the state, although only a small percentage of them offer a 24-hour pharmacy, usually in the larger cities. To find the closest location and hours, visit www.riteaid.com, www.cvs.com, or www.walgreens.com.

Safety

The biggest issue on the minds of would-be visitors to California is **earthquakes,** but the incidence of earthquakes is far surpassed by the paranoia. Major quakes are rare, and they're localized enough that it is highly unlikely you will ever feel one.

In the rare event of an earthquake, *don't panic*. If you're in a tall building, don't run outside; instead, move away from windows and toward the building's center. Crouch under a desk or table, or stand against a wall or under a doorway. If you're in bed, get under the bed, stand in a doorway, or crouch under a sturdy piece of furniture. When exiting the building, use stairwells, *not* elevators. If you're in your car, pull over to the side of the road and stop, but wait until you're away from bridges or overpasses, as well as telephone or power poles and lines. Stay in your car. If you're outside, stay away from trees, power lines, and the sides of buildings.

Driving perils in California include winter driving on mountain roads. Chains may be required in the Sierra Nevada range during icy weather at elevations above 3,000 feet. The **California Department of Transportation** provides 24-hour info at ☎ 916/654-5266.

Conversely, driving in desert areas carries its own hazards: Always be aware of the distance to the next gas station. In some areas, they may be 50 miles apart, and summer temperatures well above 100°F (38°C) can turn a scenic drive into a disaster.

California's cities are relatively safe, but as with any American city, they aren't immune to crime. At night you should use caution when traveling alone on foot. Areas that are economically depressed, darkly lit, and sparsely populated should raise red flags. Touristy areas generally are known to be quite safe.

Senior Travelers

Members of **AARP,** 601 E St. NW, Washington, DC 20049 (☎ 888/687-2277; www.aarp.org), get discounts on hotels, airfares, and car rentals. AARP offers members a wide range of benefits, including *AARP The Magazine* and a monthly newsletter. Anyone over age 50 can join.

The U.S. National Park Service offers an **America the Beautiful—National Park and Federal Recreational Lands Pass—Senior Pass** (formerly the **Golden Age Passport**), which gives seniors 62 years or older lifetime entrance to all properties administered by the National Park Service—national parks, monuments, historic sites, recreation areas, and national wildlife refuges—for a one-time processing fee of $10. The pass must be purchased in person at any NPS facility that charges an entrance fee. Besides free entry, the America the Beautiful Senior Pass also offers a 50% discount on some federal-use fees charged for such facilities as camping, swimming, parking, boat launching, and tours. For more information, go to www.nps.gov/fees_passes.htm, or call the United States Geological Survey (USGS), which issues the passes, at ☎ 888/275-8747.

To seniors 62 or older with limited income, California State Parks offers a **Golden Bear Pass,** which provides free use of state park facilities. Apply for the $5 annual pass in person at most units of the California State Park System. For more details, see www.parks.ca.gov.

Smoking

Smoking in California is illegal in public buildings, sports arenas, elevators, theaters, banks, lobbies, restaurants, offices, stores, bed-and-breakfasts, most small hotels, and bars. That's right: You can't even smoke in California bars unless drinks are served solely by the owner (though you will find that many neighborhood bars turn a blind eye and pass you an ashtray).

Spectator Sports

Sports fans in California have a lot to cheer about.

The **National Football League** (www.nfl.com) has three teams in California: the Oakland Raiders, the San Diego Chargers, and the San Francisco 49ers. The season runs from September through January. College football also generates a lot of enthusiasm across the state, no place more than Los Angeles, which, although no longer home to an NFL team, has a heated rivalry between the UCLA Bruins and the USC Trojans. The Rose Bowl is held in Pasadena each New Year's Day.

The **National Basketball Association** (www.nba.com) has four California teams: the celebrated Los Angeles Lakers, the Los Angeles Clippers, the Sacramento Kings, and the Golden State Warriors (based in Oakland). Its regular season runs from November to April, with playoffs extending into June.

Major League Baseball (www.mlb.com) fields four Californian teams: the Los Angeles Angels of Anaheim, the Los Angeles Dodgers, the San Diego Padres, and the San Francisco Giants. Its season runs from April through September, with playoffs in October.

The **National Hockey League** (www.nhl.com) has three teams: the Anaheim Mighty Ducks, the Los Angeles Kings, and the San Jose Sharks. Its regular season runs from October through April, followed by several weeks of playoffs.

As far the world's most popular sport, soccer, California fields three **Major League Soccer** (www.mlssoccer.com) squads: the Los Angeles–based Chivas USA, the San Jose Earthquakes, and the Los Angeles Galaxy. The MLS season runs from late March through November.

Taxes

The United States has no value-added tax (VAT) or other indirect tax at the national level. Every state, county, and city may levy its own local tax on all purchases, including hotel and restaurant checks and airline tickets. These taxes will not appear on price tags. Sales tax in California is generally around 8%. Hotel tax is charged on the room tariff only (which is not subject to sales tax) and is set by the city, ranging from 12% to 17% throughout California.

Telephones

Generally, hotel surcharges on long-distance and local calls are astronomical, so you're better off using your **cellphone**. You can also use **public payphones,** which are still available in Californian cities and at roadside stops, although they're not as prevalent as they once were. Many convenience grocery stores and shipping services sell **prepaid calling cards** in denominations up to $50; for international visitors, these can be the least expensive way to call home. Many public pay phones at airports now accept American Express, MasterCard, and Visa credit cards. **Local calls** made from pay phones in most locales cost 35¢ (no pennies).

Most long-distance and international calls can be dialed directly from any phone. **For calls within the United States and to Canada,** dial 1 followed by the area code and the seven-digit number. **For other international calls,** dial 011 followed by the country code, the city code, and the number you are calling.

Calls to area codes **800, 888, 877,** and **866** are toll-free. However, calls to area codes **700** and **900** (chat lines, bulletin boards, "dating" services, and so on) can be very expensive—usually a charge of between 95¢ and $3 or more per minute, and they sometimes have minimum charges that can run as high as $15 or more.

For **reversed-charge or collect calls,** and for **person-to-person calls,** dial the number 0, then the area code and number; an operator will come on the line, and you should specify whether you are calling collect, person to person, or both. If your operator-assisted call is international, ask for the overseas operator.

For **local directory assistance** ("information"), dial 411; for long-distance information, dial 1, then the appropriate area code, plus 555-1212.

If you have Web access while traveling, you might consider a broadband-based telephone service (in technical terms, **Voice over Internet Protocol,** or **VoIP**), such as Skype (www.skype.com) or Vonage (www.vonage.com), which allows you to make free international calls if you use their services from your laptop or in a cybercafe. The people you're calling must also use the service for it to work; check the sites for details.

Time Zone

California is on Pacific Standard Time (PST). The continental United States is divided into **four time zones:** Eastern Standard Time (EST), Central Standard Time (CST), Mountain Standard Time (MST), and Pacific Standard Time (PST). Alaska and Hawaii have their own zones. For example, when it's 9am in Los Angeles (PST), it's 7am in Honolulu (HST), 10am in Denver (MST), 11am in Chicago (CST), noon in New York City (EST), 5pm in London (GMT), and 2am the next day in Sydney.

Daylight saving time takes effect at 2am the second Sunday in March and lasts until 2am the first Sunday in November, except in Arizona, Hawaii, the U.S. Virgin Islands, and Puerto Rico. Daylight saving moves the clock 1 hour ahead of standard time.

Tipping

Tips are a very important part of many workers' incomes, and gratuities are the standard way of showing appreciation for good service. In hotels, tip **bellhops** at least $1 per bag ($2–$3 if you have a lot of luggage) and tip the **chamber staff** $1 to $2 per day (more if you've left a disaster area for him or her to clean up). Tip the **doorman** or **concierge** only if he or she has provided you with some specific service (for example, calling a cab for you or obtaining difficult-to-get theater tickets). Tip the **valet-parking attendant** $1 every time you get your car.

In restaurants, bars, and nightclubs, tip **service staff** 15% to 20% of the check, tip **bartenders** 10% to 15%, tip **checkroom attendants** $1 per garment, and tip **valet-parking attendants** $1 per vehicle.

As for other service personnel, tip **cab drivers** 15% of the fare, and tip **skycaps** at airports at least $1 per bag ($2–$3 if you have a lot of luggage).

Toilets

You won't find public toilets or "restrooms" on the streets in most California cities (except San Francisco), but they can be found in hotel lobbies, bars, restaurants, museums, department stores, railway and bus stations, and service stations. Large hotels and fast-food restaurants are often the best bet for clean facilities. If possible, avoid the toilets at parks and beaches, which tend to be dirty; some may even be unsafe. Restaurants and bars in heavily visited areas may reserve their restrooms for paying customers.

Tourist Traps

Any place as rich in natural and cultural attractions as California is bound to have a few tourist traps seeking to siphon off dollars from eager-beaver sightseers. These tourist traps are rarely criminal enterprises; they're usually quick-buck artists preying on the undiscerning visitor. If someone's giving you the hard sell, ask yourself why.

Hollywood, for example, is rife with tacky trinket shops and halfhearted "museums" like Ripley's Believe It or Not or the Hollywood Wax Museum (try Madame Tussauds down the street instead). The costumed characters in front of Grauman's Chinese Theatre look like fun folks, but police have been known to clamp down on instances of overly aggressive panhandling. Resist taking a picture with them if you don't feel like tipping.

Other areas to approach with a healthy degree of skepticism are Cannery Row in Monterey and Fisherman's Wharf in San Francisco, places whose authentic histories are nearly obscured by a glossy veneer of touristy shops.

Travelers with Disabilities

California is a welcoming place for travelers with disabilities. Almost all public establishments (including hotels, restaurants, museums, and so on, but not including certain National Historic Landmarks) and at least some modes of public transportation provide accessible entrances and other facilities for those with disabilities.

The **America the Beautiful—National Park and Federal Recreational Lands Pass— Access Pass** (formerly the **Golden Access Passport**) gives visually impaired persons or those with permanent disabilities (regardless of age) free lifetime entrance to federal recreation sites administered by the National Park Service, including the Fish and Wildlife Service, the Forest Service, the Bureau of Land Management, and the Bureau of Reclamation. This may include national parks, monuments, historic sites, recreation areas, and national wildlife refuges. It does not cover California state parks.

The America the Beautiful Access Pass can be obtained only in person, at any NPS facility that charges an entrance fee. You need to show proof of a medically determined disability. Besides free entry, the pass also offers a 50% discount on some federal-use fees charged for such facilities as camping, swimming, parking, boat launching, and tours. For more information, go to www.nps.gov/fees_passes.htm, or call the United States Geological Survey (USGS), which issues the passes, at ☎ 888/275-8747.

Both California State Parks and the National Park Service strive to make facilities and information accessible to all people with disabilities. For information on specific features at state or national parks, see http://access.parks.ca.gov and www.nps.gov/access. For more on organizations that offer resources to travelers with disabilities, go to **Frommers.com.**

Index